almost American Girl

AN ILLUSTRATED MEMOIR

ROBIN HA

almost American Girl

BALZER + BRAY

IMPRINTS OF HARPERCOLLINS*PUBLISHERS*

HARPER alley

All the art featured in the background of the chapter
openers comes from comics I created as a teen.

Disclaimer

This book is a memoir and a work of creative nonfiction. Some names
and identifying details have been changed to protect the privacy of
the individuals involved. I have compressed some events and made
two or more people into one. I did my best to re-create the events
depicted in this book as faithfully as I could, by digging deep into
my memories, diaries, letters, photos, and various artifacts I've saved
from the past. The events that I didn't personally witness have been
fictionalized based on what I've been told by the people involved in
them. *Queen's Quest* (depicted in this memoir as my favorite Korean
comic book) is a made-up series, combining existing Korean comics
that I used to love as a kid.

Balzer + Bray is an imprint of HarperCollins Publishers.
HarperAlley is an imprint of HarperCollins Publishers.

Almost American Girl: An Illustrated Memoir
Copyright © 2020 by Robin Ha
All rights reserved. Manufactured in China. No part of this book may be used or
reproduced in any manner whatsoever without written permission except in the case
of brief quotations embodied in critical articles and reviews. For information address
HarperCollins Children's Books, a division of HarperCollins Publishers, 195 Broadway,
New York, NY 10007.
www.epicreads.com
ISBN 978-0-06-268510-0 — ISBN 978-0-06-268509-4 (paperback)
Typography by Robin Ha and Dana Fritts
Hand lettering by Alison Carmichael
19 20 21 22 23 SCP 10 9 8 7 6 5 4 3 2 1

First Edition

TO MY MOTHER,
WHOSE TENACITY HAS TAUGHT ME
NEVER TO GIVE UP

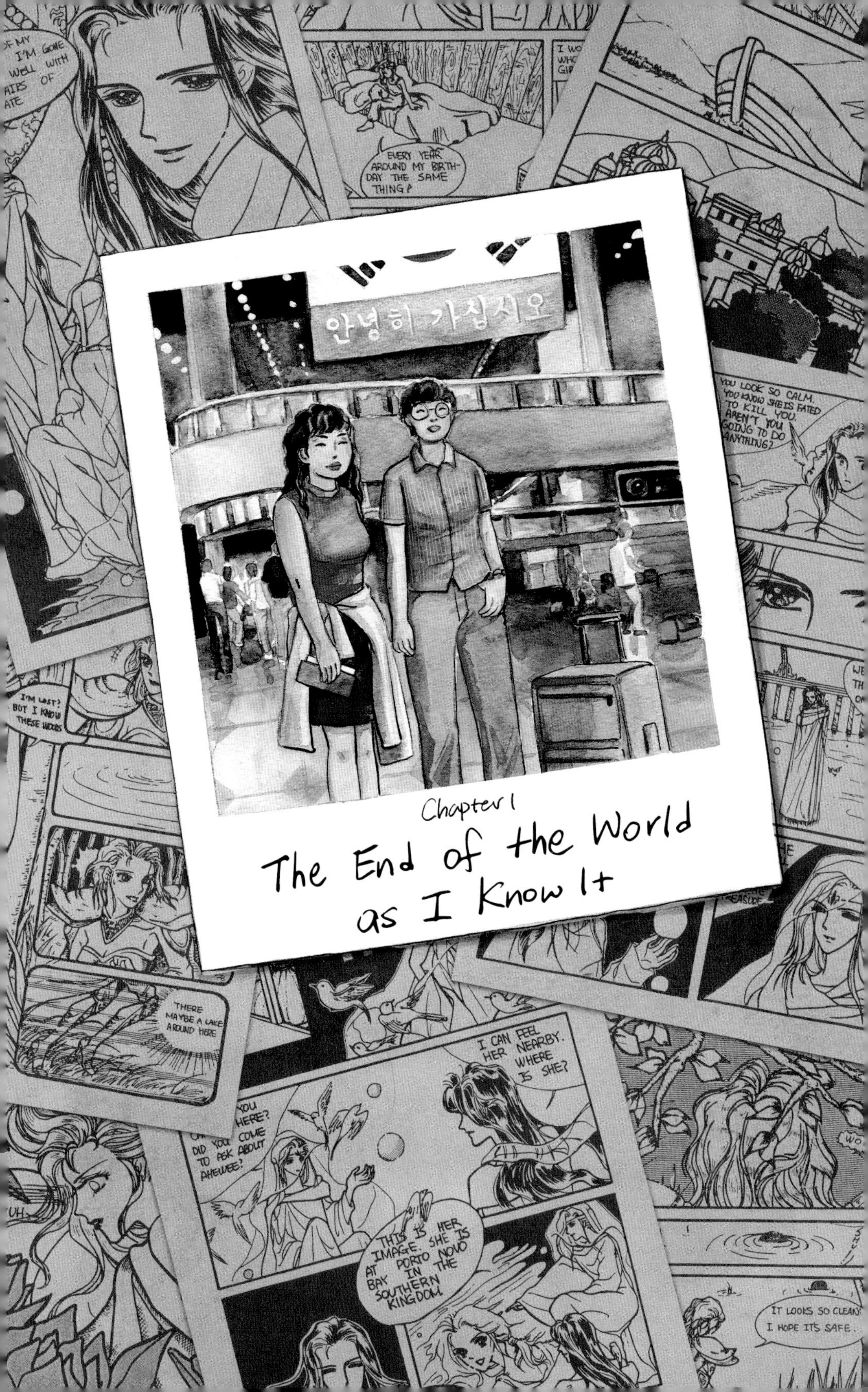
EVERY YEAR AROUND MY BIRTHDAY THE SAME THING?
안녕히 가십시오
YOU LOOK SO CALM. YOU KNOW SHE IS FATED TO KILL YOU. AREN'T YOU GOING TO DO ANYTHING?
I'M LOST? BUT I KNOW THESE WOODS
THERE MAYBE A LAKE AROUND HERE
I CAN FEEL HER NEARBY. WHERE IS SHE?
DID YOU COME TO ASK ABOUT AHEWEE?
THIS IS HER IMAGE. SHE IS AT PORTO NOVO BAY IN THE SOUTHERN KINGDOM.
IT LOOKS SO CLEAN. I HOPE IT'S SAFE.

Chapter 1

The End of the World as I Know It

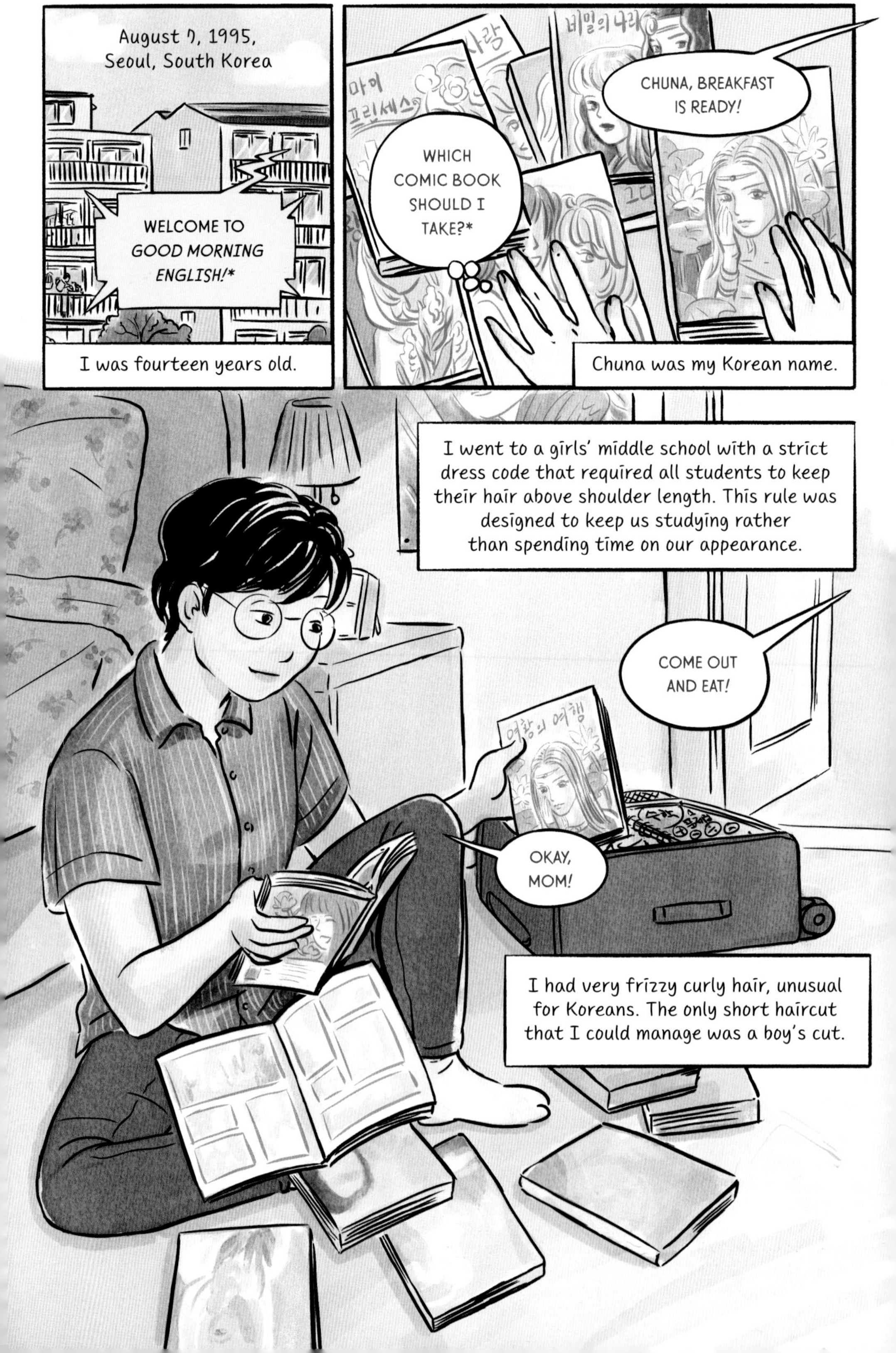
August 7, 1995,
Seoul, South Korea
WELCOME TO *GOOD MORNING ENGLISH!**
I was fourteen years old.
마이 프린세스
사랑
비밀의 나라
CHUNA, BREAKFAST IS READY!
WHICH COMIC BOOK SHOULD I TAKE?*
Chuna was my Korean name.
I went to a girls' middle school with a strict dress code that required all students to keep their hair above shoulder length. This rule was designed to keep us studying rather than spending time on our appearance.
COME OUT AND EAT!
여황의 여행
OKAY, MOM!
I had very frizzy curly hair, unusual for Koreans. The only short haircut that I could manage was a boy's cut.

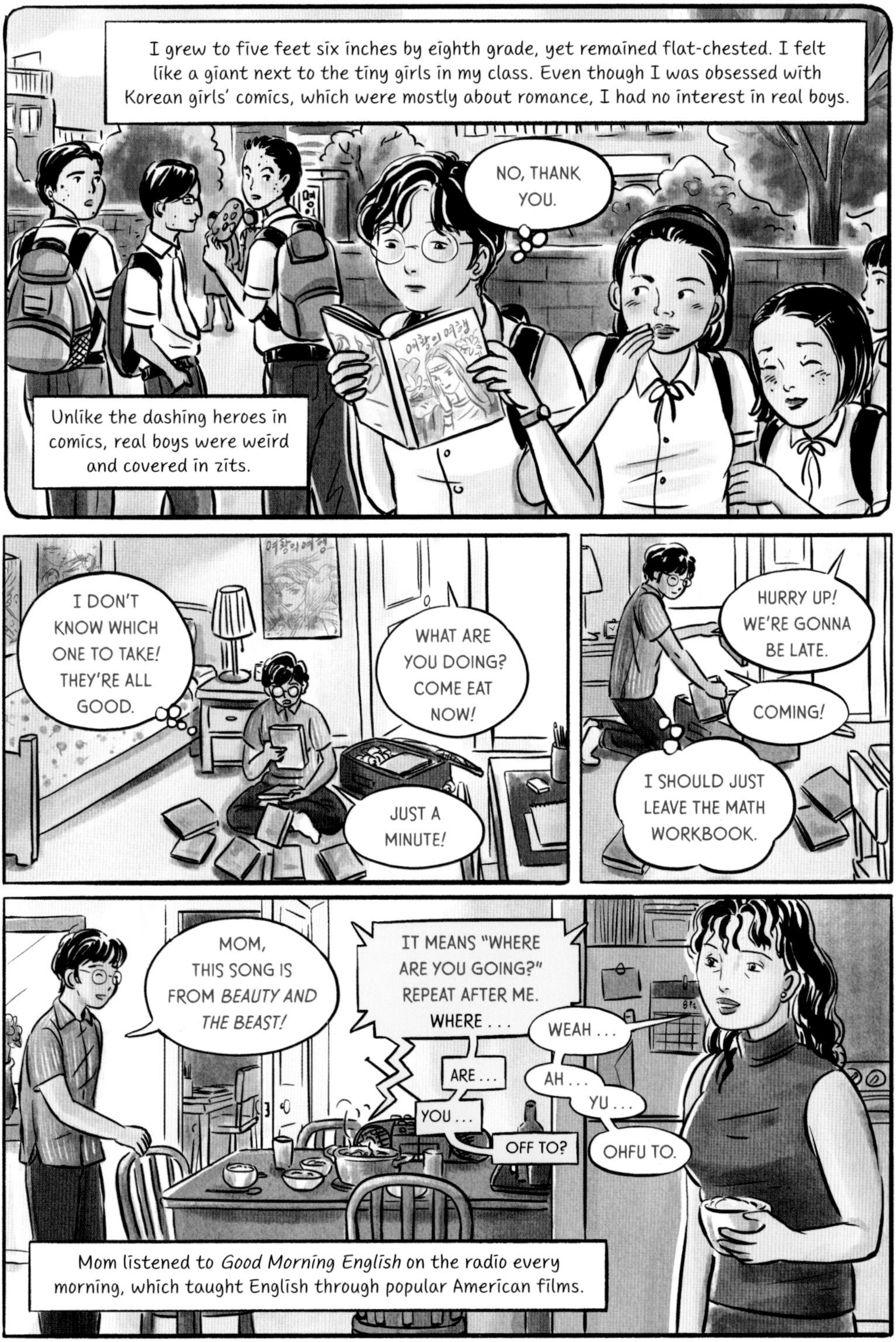
I grew to five feet six inches by eighth grade, yet remained flat-chested. I felt like a giant next to the tiny girls in my class. Even though I was obsessed with Korean girls' comics, which were mostly about romance, I had no interest in real boys.
NO, THANK YOU.
Unlike the dashing heroes in comics, real boys were weird and covered in zits.
I DON'T KNOW WHICH ONE TO TAKE! THEY'RE ALL GOOD.
WHAT ARE YOU DOING? COME EAT NOW!
JUST A MINUTE!
HURRY UP! WE'RE GONNA BE LATE.
COMING!
I SHOULD JUST LEAVE THE MATH WORKBOOK.
MOM, THIS SONG IS FROM *BEAUTY AND THE BEAST!*
IT MEANS "WHERE ARE YOU GOING?" REPEAT AFTER ME. WHERE . . .
WEAH . . .
ARE . . .
AH . . .
YU . . .
YOU . . .
OFF TO?
OHFU TO.
Mom listened to *Good Morning English* on the radio every morning, which taught English through popular American films.

*Speaking in KOREAN. *Speaking in ENGLISH.

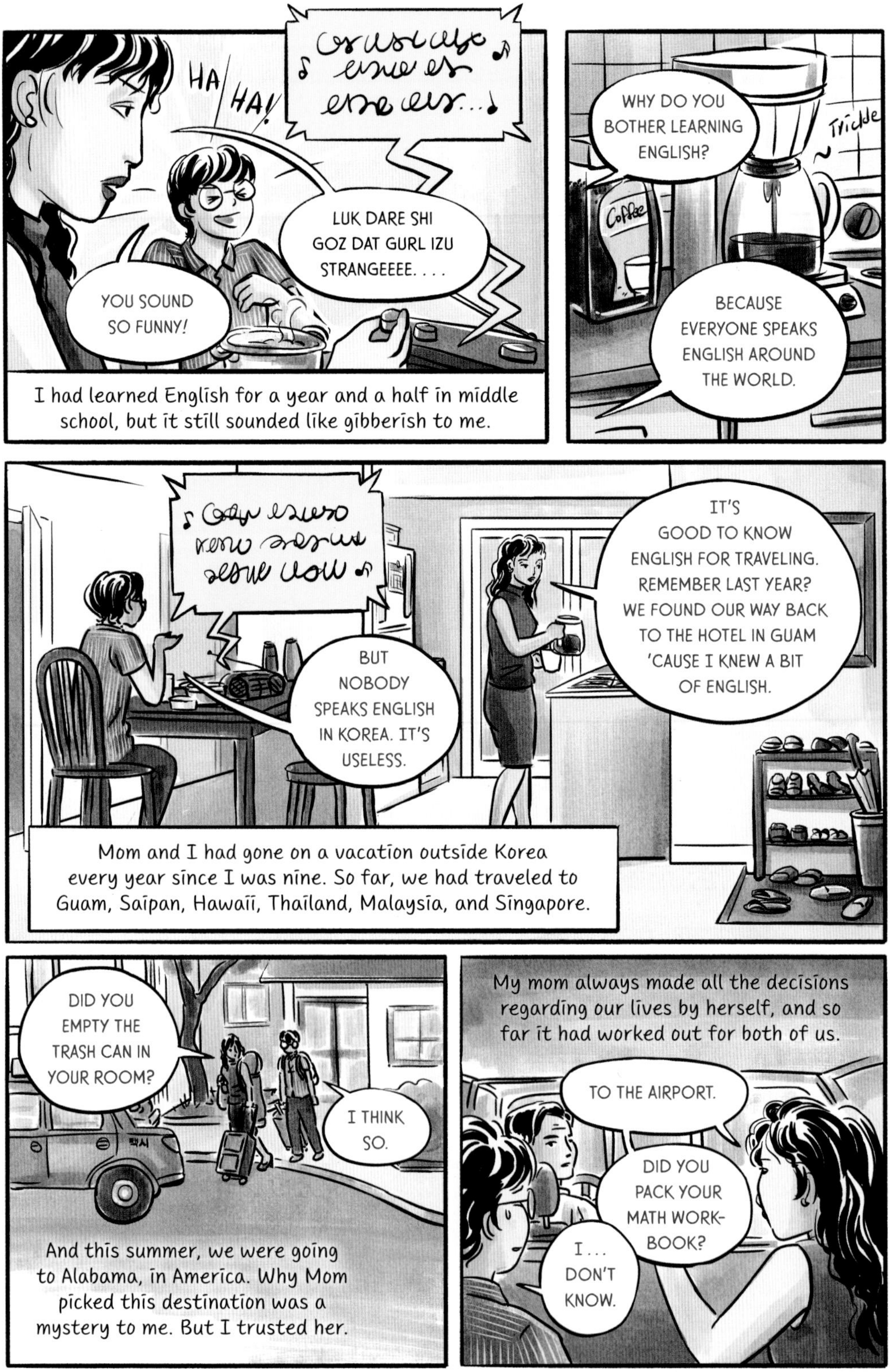

HA HA!
LUK DARE SHI GOZ DAT GURL IZU STRANGEEEE. . . .
YOU SOUND SO FUNNY!
I had learned English for a year and a half in middle school, but it still sounded like gibberish to me.
WHY DO YOU BOTHER LEARNING ENGLISH?
Trickle
BECAUSE EVERYONE SPEAKS ENGLISH AROUND THE WORLD.
BUT NOBODY SPEAKS ENGLISH IN KOREA. IT'S USELESS.
IT'S GOOD TO KNOW ENGLISH FOR TRAVELING. REMEMBER LAST YEAR? WE FOUND OUR WAY BACK TO THE HOTEL IN GUAM 'CAUSE I KNEW A BIT OF ENGLISH.
Mom and I had gone on a vacation outside Korea every year since I was nine. So far, we had traveled to Guam, Saipan, Hawaii, Thailand, Malaysia, and Singapore.
DID YOU EMPTY THE TRASH CAN IN YOUR ROOM?
I THINK SO.
And this summer, we were going to Alabama, in America. Why Mom picked this destination was a mystery to me. But I trusted her.
My mom always made all the decisions regarding our lives by herself, and so far it had worked out for both of us.
TO THE AIRPORT.
DID YOU PACK YOUR MATH WORK-BOOK?
I . . . DON'T KNOW.

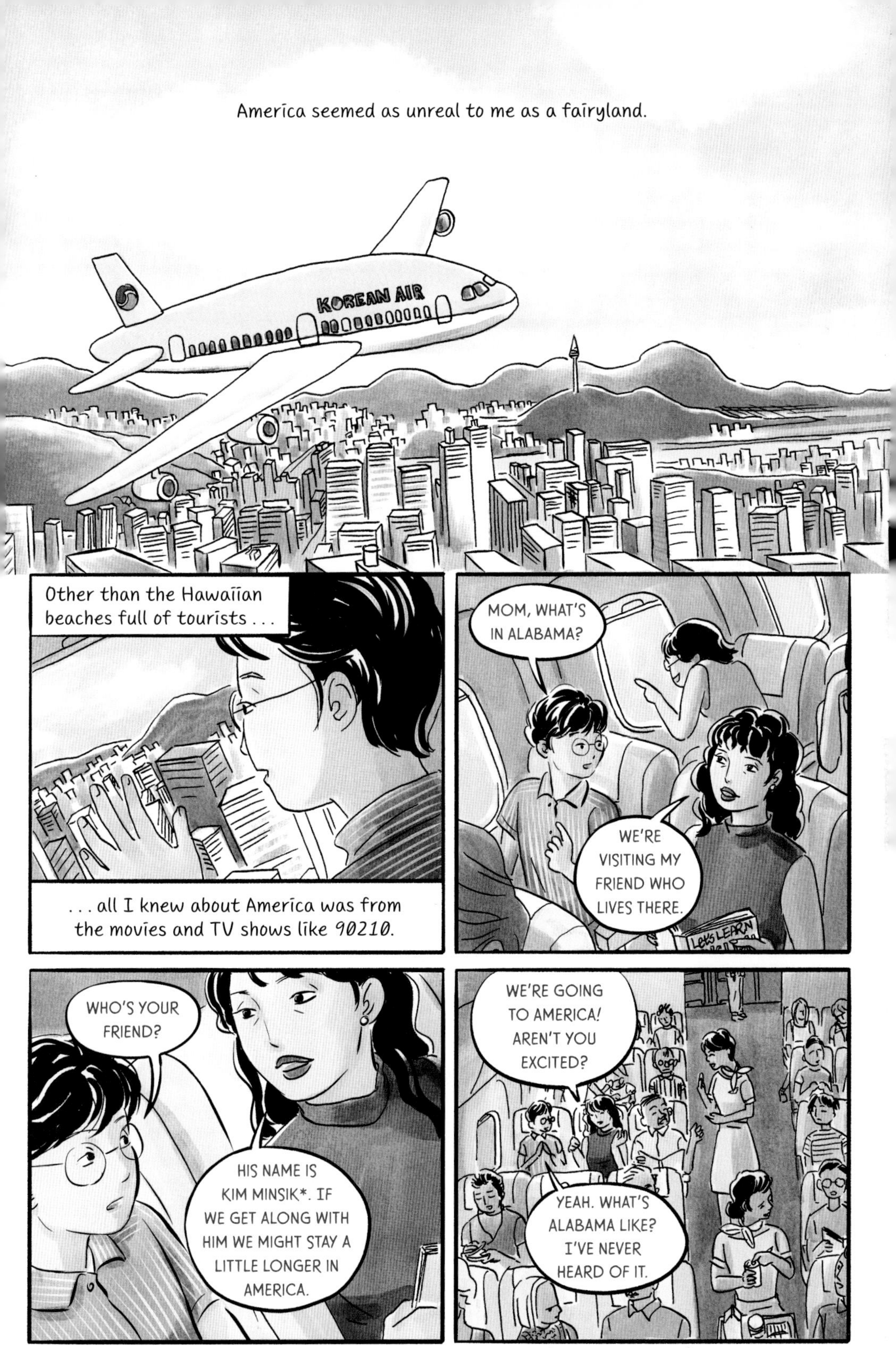
America seemed as unreal to me as a fairyland.
KOREAN AIR
Other than the Hawaiian beaches full of tourists . . .
. . . all I knew about America was from the movies and TV shows like 90210.
MOM, WHAT'S IN ALABAMA?
WE'RE VISITING MY FRIEND WHO LIVES THERE.
Let's LEARN
WHO'S YOUR FRIEND?
HIS NAME IS KIM MINSIK*. IF WE GET ALONG WITH HIM WE MIGHT STAY A LITTLE LONGER IN AMERICA.
WE'RE GOING TO AMERICA! AREN'T YOU EXCITED?
YEAH. WHAT'S ALABAMA LIKE? I'VE NEVER HEARD OF IT.

* Korean names are in reverse order of American names. The family name (last name in English) comes before the given name (first name in English). So instead of Minsik (given name) Kim (family name), Kim Minsik is the correct order for a Korean name.

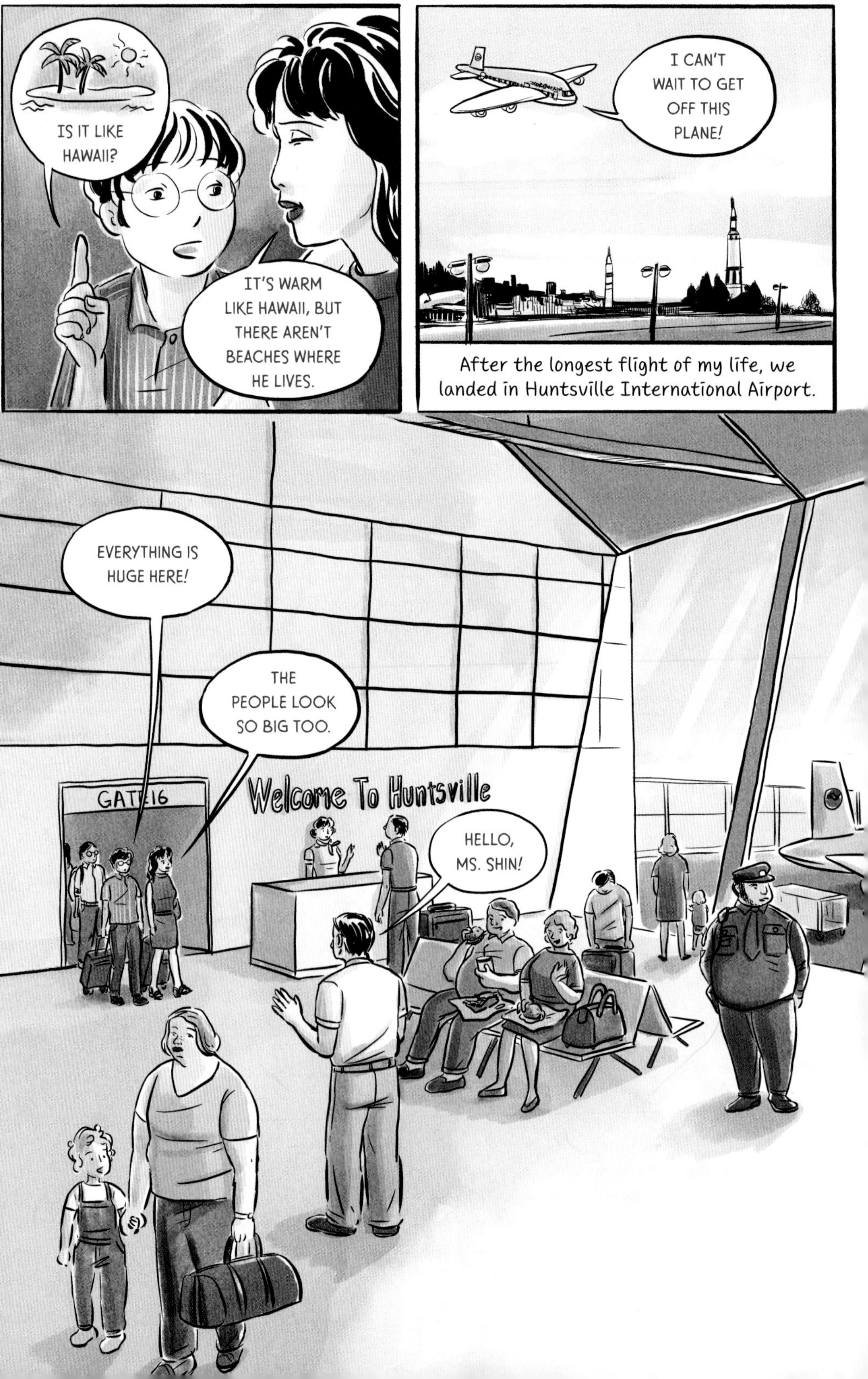
IS IT LIKE HAWAII?
IT'S WARM LIKE HAWAII, BUT THERE AREN'T BEACHES WHERE HE LIVES.
I CAN'T WAIT TO GET OFF THIS PLANE!
After the longest flight of my life, we landed in Huntsville International Airport.
EVERYTHING IS HUGE HERE!
THE PEOPLE LOOK SO BIG TOO.
GATE 16
Welcome To Huntsville
HELLO, MS. SHIN!

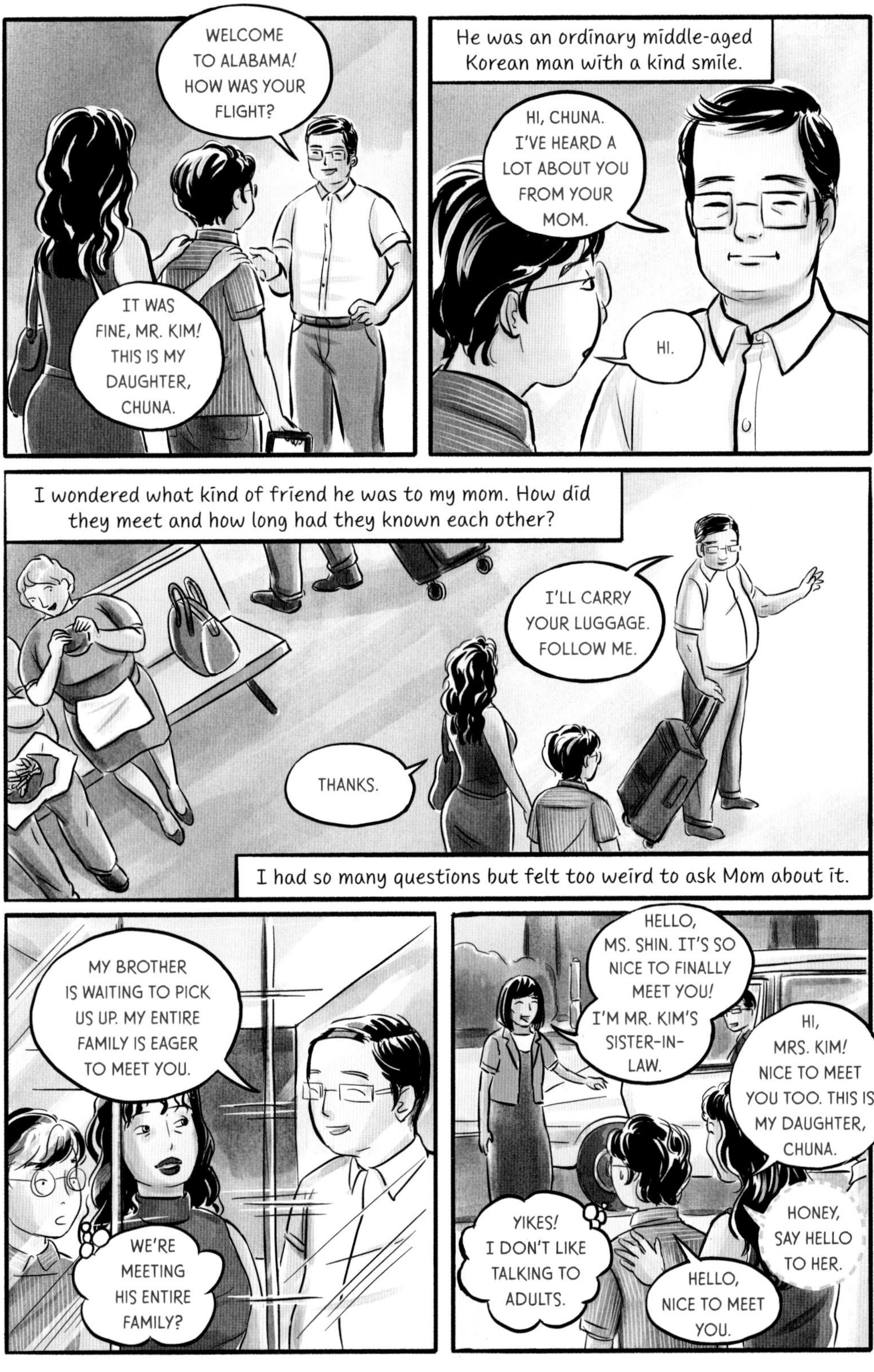
WELCOME TO ALABAMA! HOW WAS YOUR FLIGHT?
IT WAS FINE, MR. KIM! THIS IS MY DAUGHTER, CHUNA.
He was an ordinary middle-aged Korean man with a kind smile.
HI, CHUNA. I'VE HEARD A LOT ABOUT YOU FROM YOUR MOM.
HI.
I wondered what kind of friend he was to my mom. How did they meet and how long had they known each other?
I'LL CARRY YOUR LUGGAGE. FOLLOW ME.
THANKS.
I had so many questions but felt too weird to ask Mom about it.
MY BROTHER IS WAITING TO PICK US UP. MY ENTIRE FAMILY IS EAGER TO MEET YOU.
WE'RE MEETING HIS ENTIRE FAMILY?
HELLO, MS. SHIN. IT'S SO NICE TO FINALLY MEET YOU!
I'M MR. KIM'S SISTER-IN-LAW.
HI, MRS. KIM! NICE TO MEET YOU TOO. THIS IS MY DAUGHTER, CHUNA.
YIKES! I DON'T LIKE TALKING TO ADULTS.
HONEY, SAY HELLO TO HER.
HELLO, NICE TO MEET YOU.

Mr. Kim, his brother, and his sister-in-law were not that different from any other adults that I had met in Korea. They always asked the same questions.

MY KIDS ARE SO EXCITED TO ASK YOU ABOUT KOREA. THEY WERE ALL BORN HERE. HOW OLD ARE YOU?

MY OLDEST DAUGHTER IS ALSO FOUR-TEEN.

DO YOU GO TO CHURCH?

NO.

I'LL TAKE YOU GUYS TO MY CHURCH. YOU WILL LOVE IT!

UH . . . OKAY.

HOW ARE YOUR GRADES?

I'M FOURTEEN.

SHE'S AT THE TOP OF HER CLASS!

WOW, THAT'S IMPRESSIVE!

MOM, STOP.

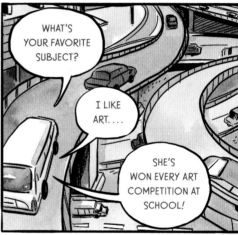

WHAT'S YOUR FAVORITE SUBJECT?

I LIKE ART. . . .

SHE'S WON EVERY ART COMPETITION AT SCHOOL!

HER TEACHERS THINK SHE HAS REAL TALENT.

I'D LOVE TO SEE HER ARTWORK.

MOM, PLEASE STOP!

Modesty was not one of my mom's virtues.

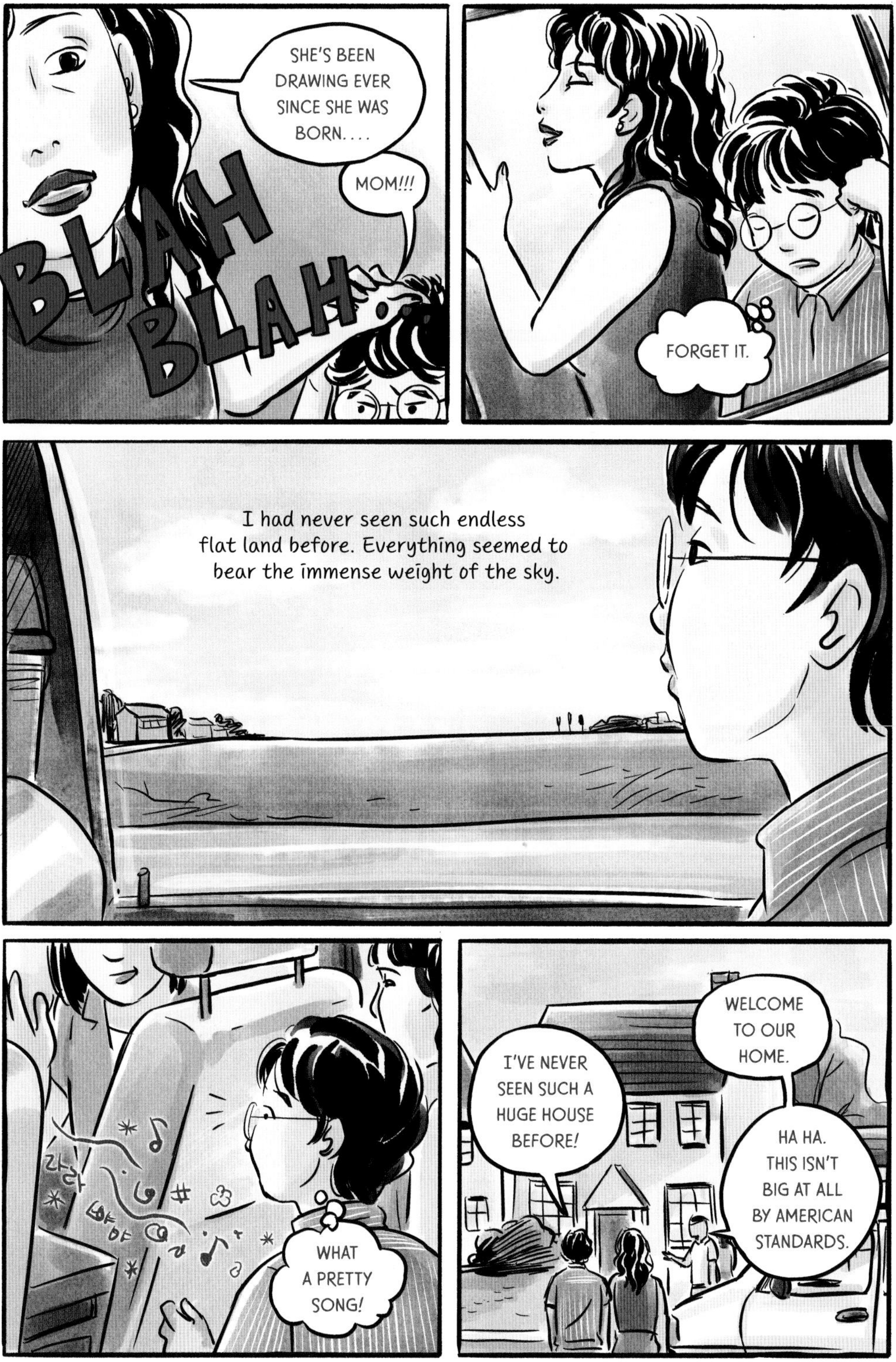
SHE'S BEEN DRAWING EVER SINCE SHE WAS BORN. . . .
BLAH BLAH
MOM!!!
FORGET IT.
I had never seen such endless flat land before. Everything seemed to bear the immense weight of the sky.
WHAT A PRETTY SONG!
WELCOME TO OUR HOME.
I'VE NEVER SEEN SUCH A HUGE HOUSE BEFORE!
HA HA. THIS ISN'T BIG AT ALL BY AMERICAN STANDARDS.

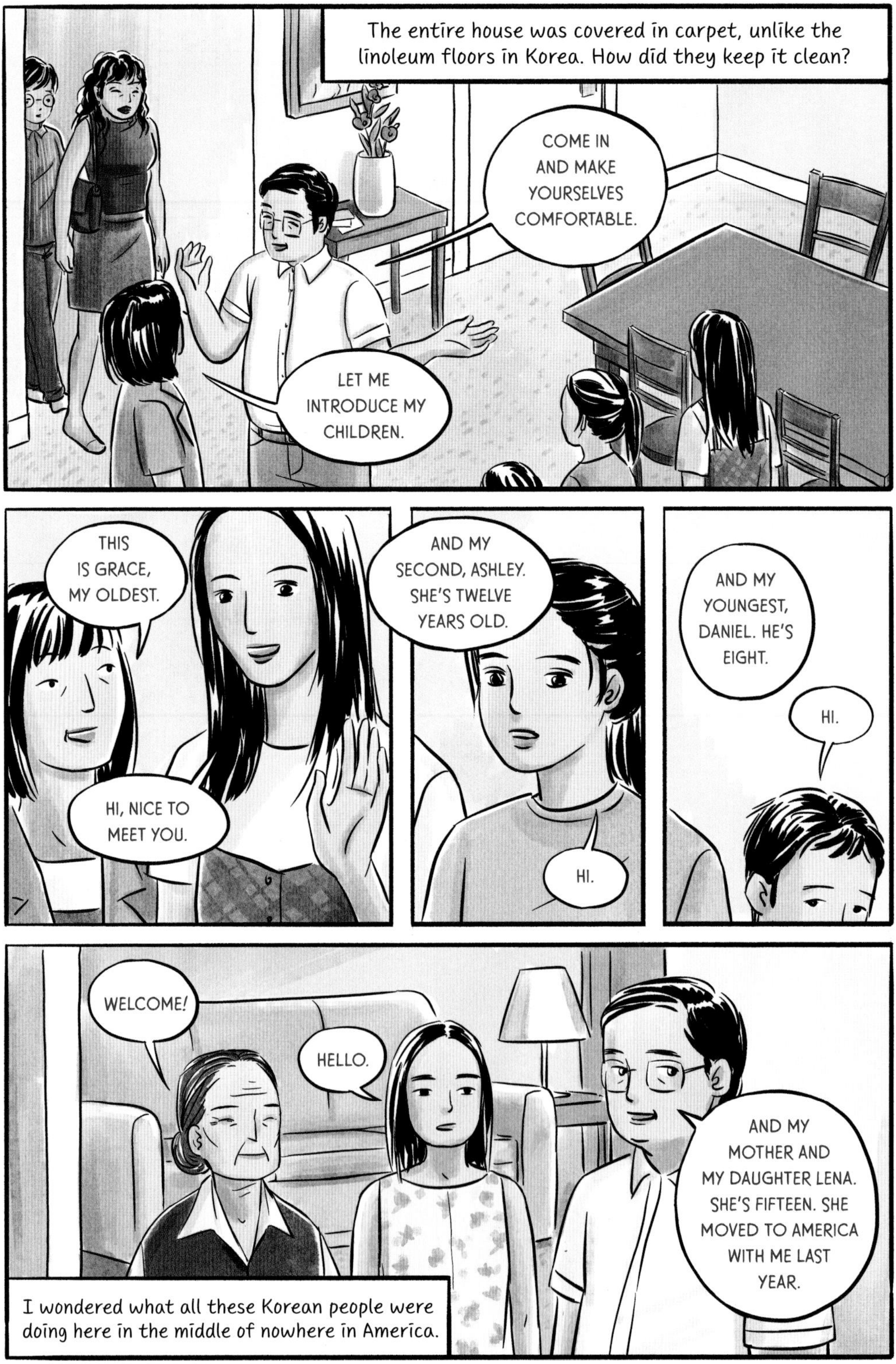
The entire house was covered in carpet, unlike the linoleum floors in Korea. How did they keep it clean?
COME IN AND MAKE YOURSELVES COMFORTABLE.
LET ME INTRODUCE MY CHILDREN.
THIS IS GRACE, MY OLDEST.
HI, NICE TO MEET YOU.
AND MY SECOND, ASHLEY. SHE'S TWELVE YEARS OLD.
HI.
AND MY YOUNGEST, DANIEL. HE'S EIGHT.
HI.
WELCOME!
HELLO.
AND MY MOTHER AND MY DAUGHTER LENA. SHE'S FIFTEEN. SHE MOVED TO AMERICA WITH ME LAST YEAR.
I wondered what all these Korean people were doing here in the middle of nowhere in America.

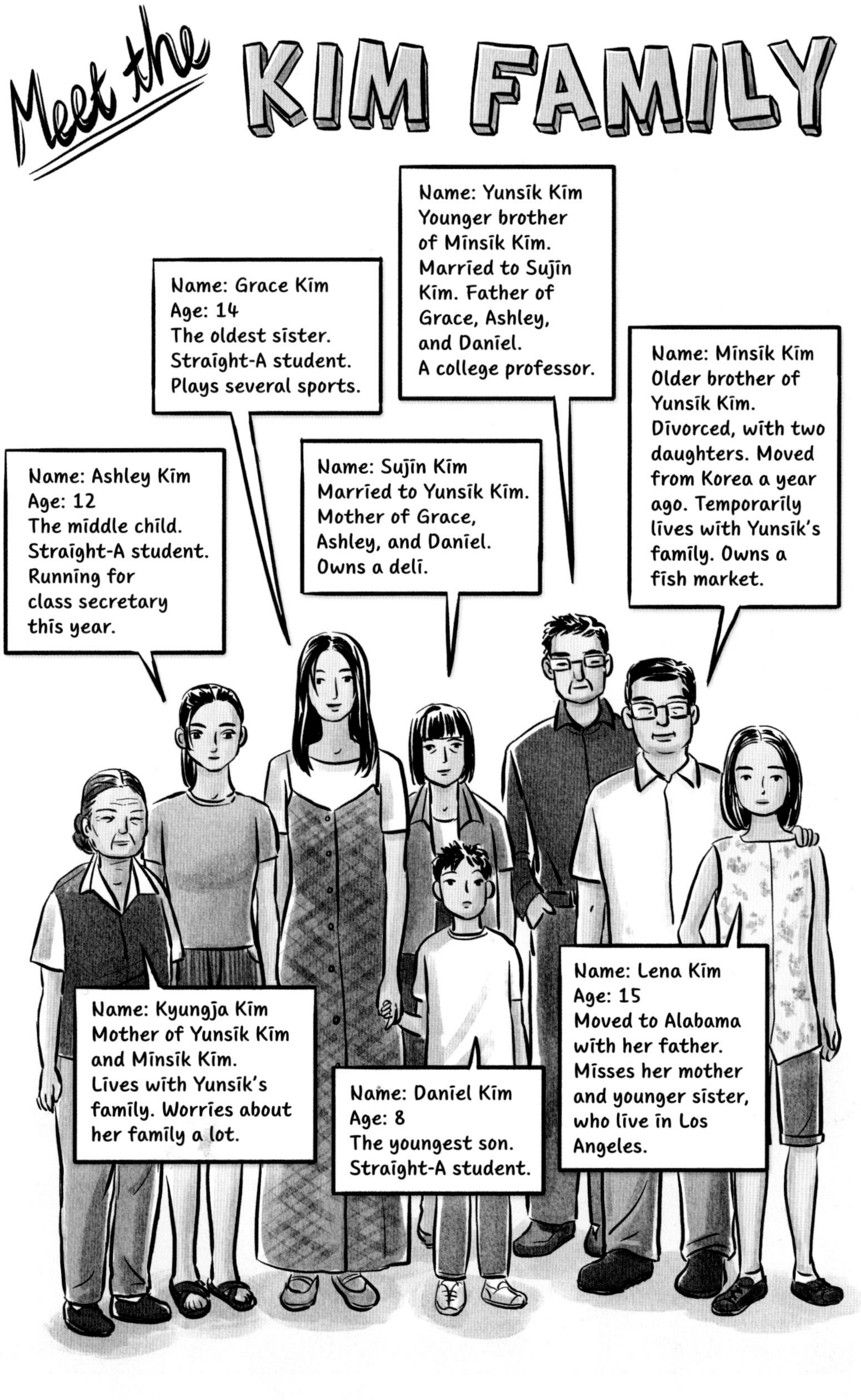
Meet the
KIM FAMILY
Name: Ashley Kim Age: 12 The middle child. Straight-A student. Running for class secretary this year.
Name: Grace Kim Age: 14 The oldest sister. Straight-A student. Plays several sports.
Name: Sujin Kim Married to Yunsik Kim. Mother of Grace, Ashley, and Daniel. Owns a deli.
Name: Yunsik Kim Younger brother of Minsik Kim. Married to Sujin Kim. Father of Grace, Ashley, and Daniel. A college professor.
Name: Minsik Kim Older brother of Yunsik Kim. Divorced, with two daughters. Moved from Korea a year ago. Temporarily lives with Yunsik's family. Owns a fish market.
Name: Kyungja Kim Mother of Yunsik Kim and Minsik Kim. Lives with Yunsik's family. Worries about her family a lot.
Name: Daniel Kim Age: 8 The youngest son. Straight-A student.
Name: Lena Kim Age: 15 Moved to Alabama with her father. Misses her mother and younger sister, who live in Los Angeles.

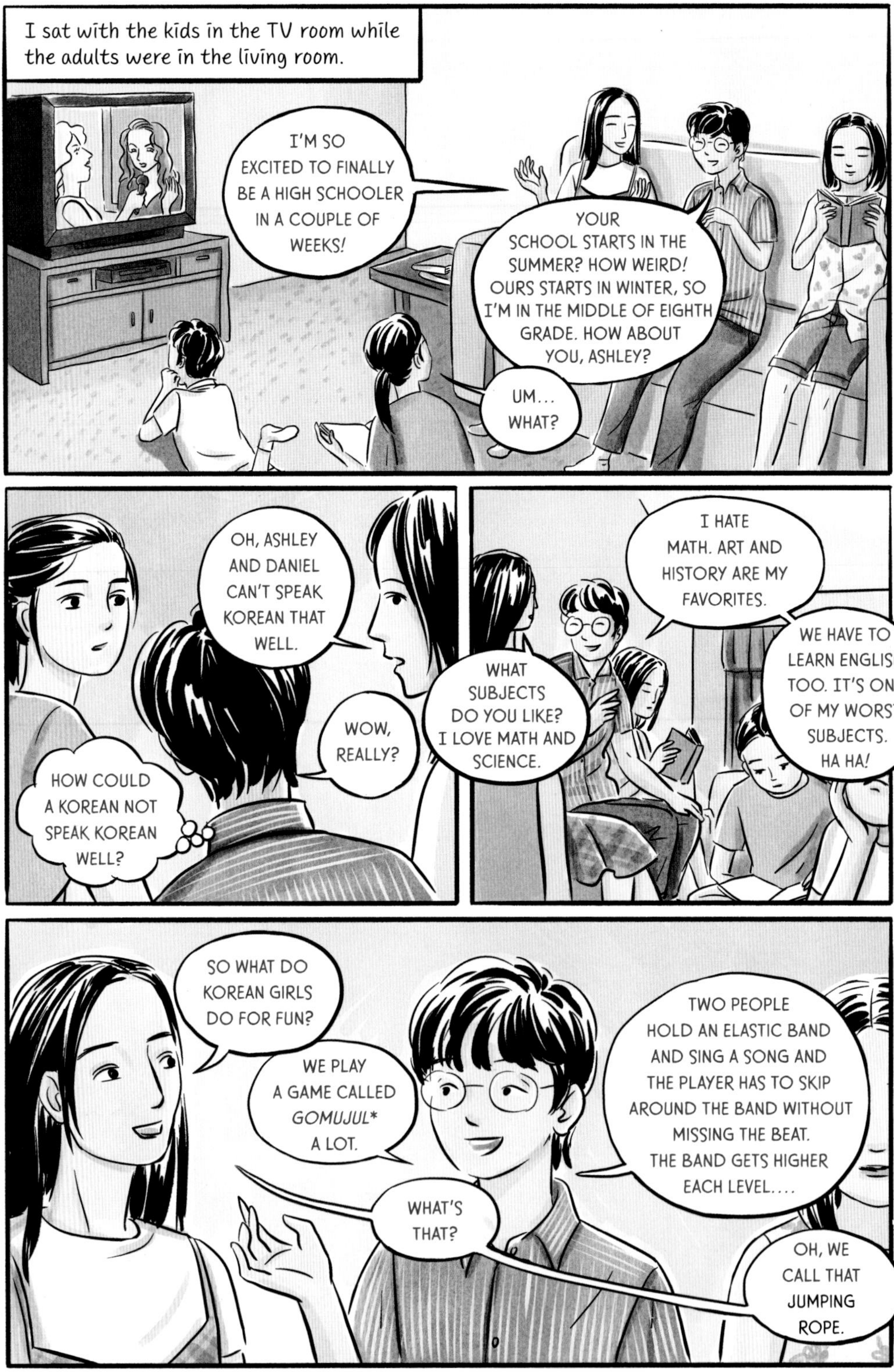
I sat with the kids in the TV room while the adults were in the living room.
I'M SO EXCITED TO FINALLY BE A HIGH SCHOOLER IN A COUPLE OF WEEKS!
YOUR SCHOOL STARTS IN THE SUMMER? HOW WEIRD! OURS STARTS IN WINTER, SO I'M IN THE MIDDLE OF EIGHTH GRADE. HOW ABOUT YOU, ASHLEY?
UM... WHAT?
OH, ASHLEY AND DANIEL CAN'T SPEAK KOREAN THAT WELL.
WOW, REALLY?
HOW COULD A KOREAN NOT SPEAK KOREAN WELL?
I HATE MATH. ART AND HISTORY ARE MY FAVORITES.
WHAT SUBJECTS DO YOU LIKE? I LOVE MATH AND SCIENCE.
WE HAVE TO LEARN ENGLISH TOO. IT'S ONE OF MY WORST SUBJECTS. HA HA!
SO WHAT DO KOREAN GIRLS DO FOR FUN?
WE PLAY A GAME CALLED *GOMUJUL** A LOT.
WHAT'S THAT?
TWO PEOPLE HOLD AN ELASTIC BAND AND SING A SONG AND THE PLAYER HAS TO SKIP AROUND THE BAND WITHOUT MISSING THE BEAT. THE BAND GETS HIGHER EACH LEVEL....
OH, WE CALL THAT JUMPING ROPE.

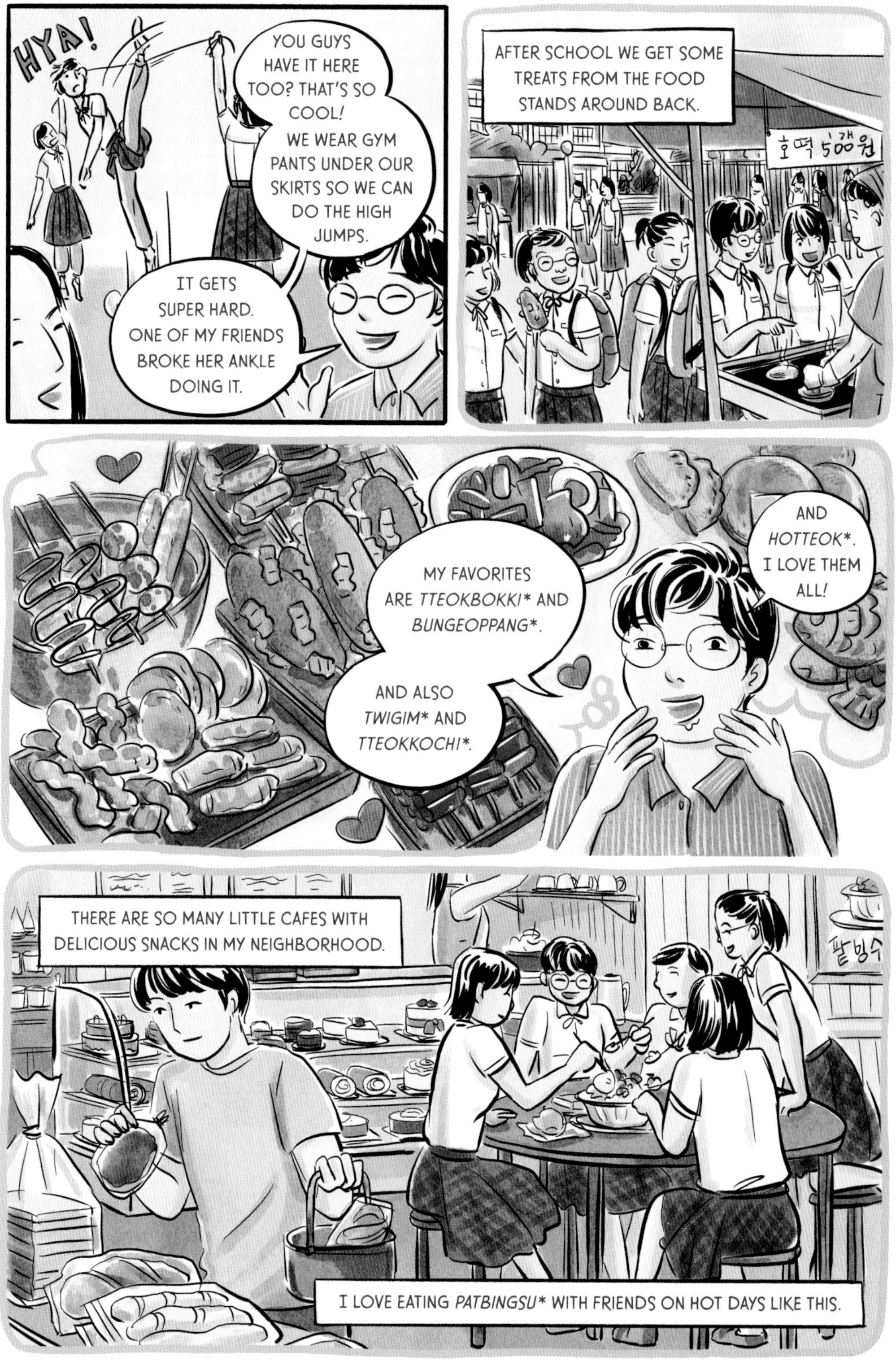
HYA!
YOU GUYS HAVE IT HERE TOO? THAT'S SO COOL!
WE WEAR GYM PANTS UNDER OUR SKIRTS SO WE CAN DO THE HIGH JUMPS.
IT GETS SUPER HARD. ONE OF MY FRIENDS BROKE HER ANKLE DOING IT.
AFTER SCHOOL WE GET SOME TREATS FROM THE FOOD STANDS AROUND BACK.
호떡 500원
MY FAVORITES ARE *TTEOKBOKKI** AND *BUNGEOPPANG**.
AND ALSO *TWIGIM** AND *TTEOKKOCHI**.
AND *HOTTEOK**. I LOVE THEM ALL!
THERE ARE SO MANY LITTLE CAFES WITH DELICIOUS SNACKS IN MY NEIGHBORHOOD.
팥빙수
I LOVE EATING *PATBINGSU** WITH FRIENDS ON HOT DAYS LIKE THIS.

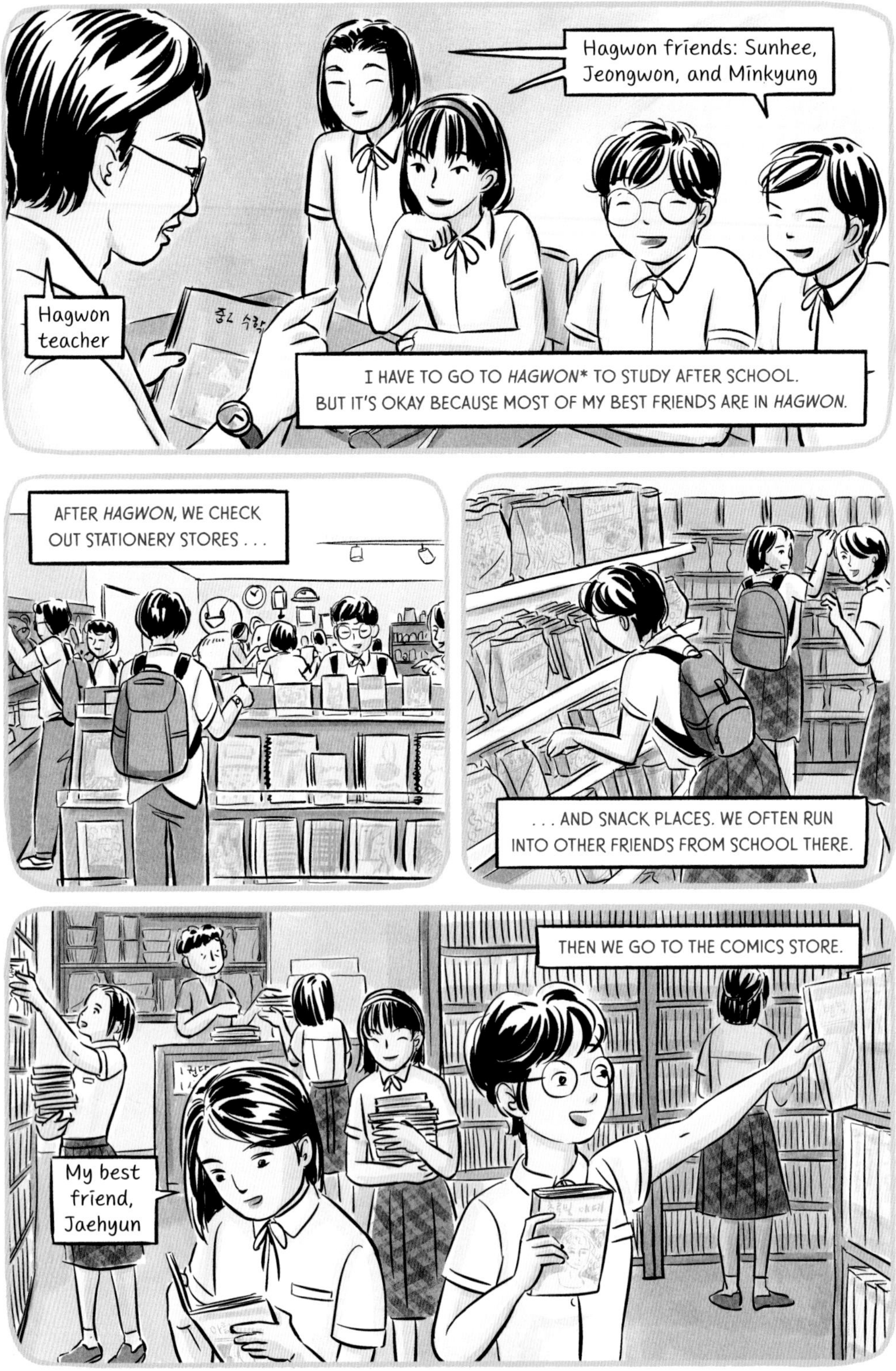
Hagwon friends: Sunhee, Jeongwon, and Minkyung
Hagwon teacher
I HAVE TO GO TO *HAGWON** TO STUDY AFTER SCHOOL. BUT IT'S OKAY BECAUSE MOST OF MY BEST FRIENDS ARE IN *HAGWON*.
AFTER *HAGWON*, WE CHECK OUT STATIONERY STORES . . .
. . . AND SNACK PLACES. WE OFTEN RUN INTO OTHER FRIENDS FROM SCHOOL THERE.
THEN WE GO TO THE COMICS STORE.
My best friend, Jaehyun

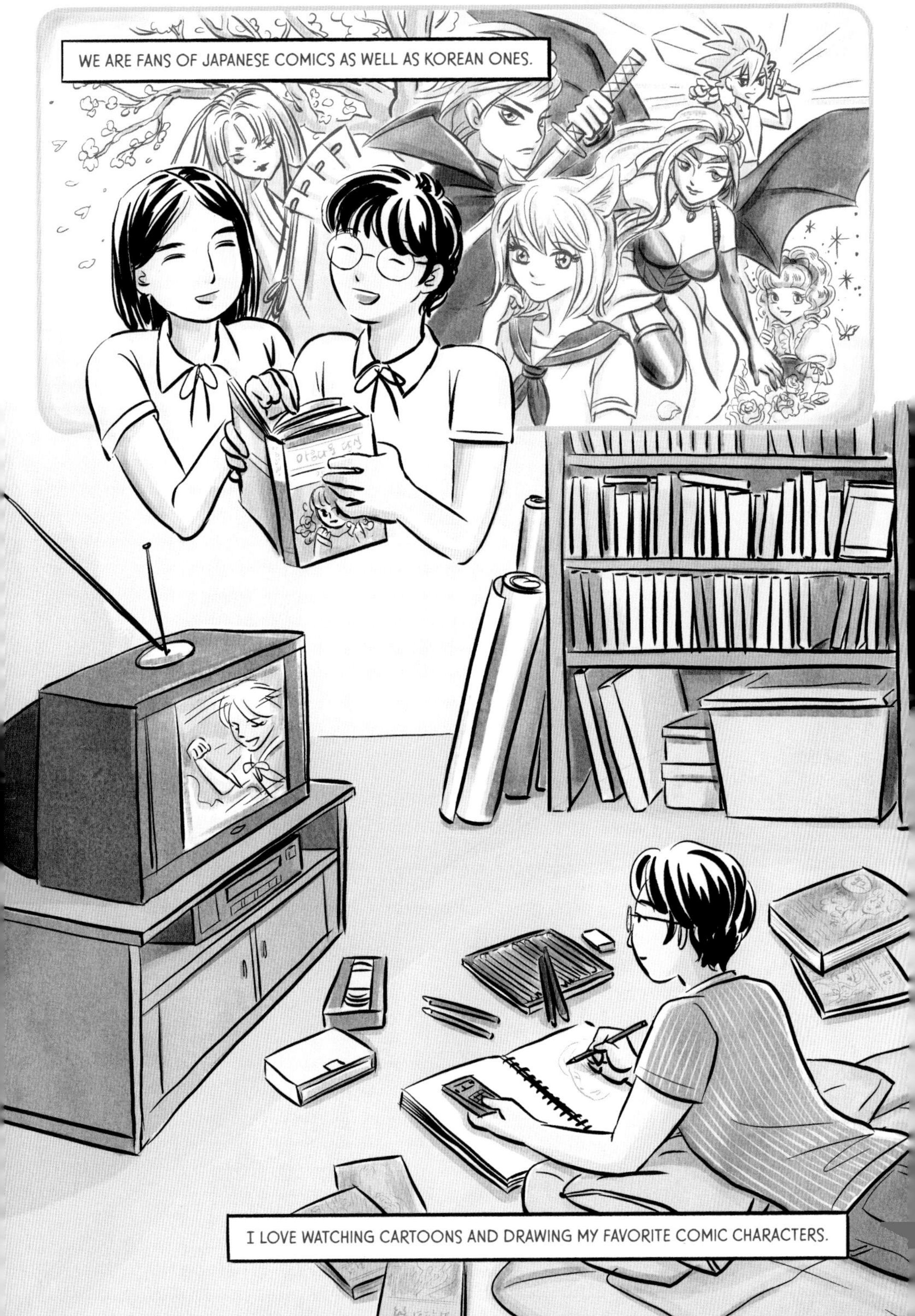
WE ARE FANS OF JAPANESE COMICS AS WELL AS KOREAN ONES.
I LOVE WATCHING CARTOONS AND DRAWING MY FAVORITE COMIC CHARACTERS.

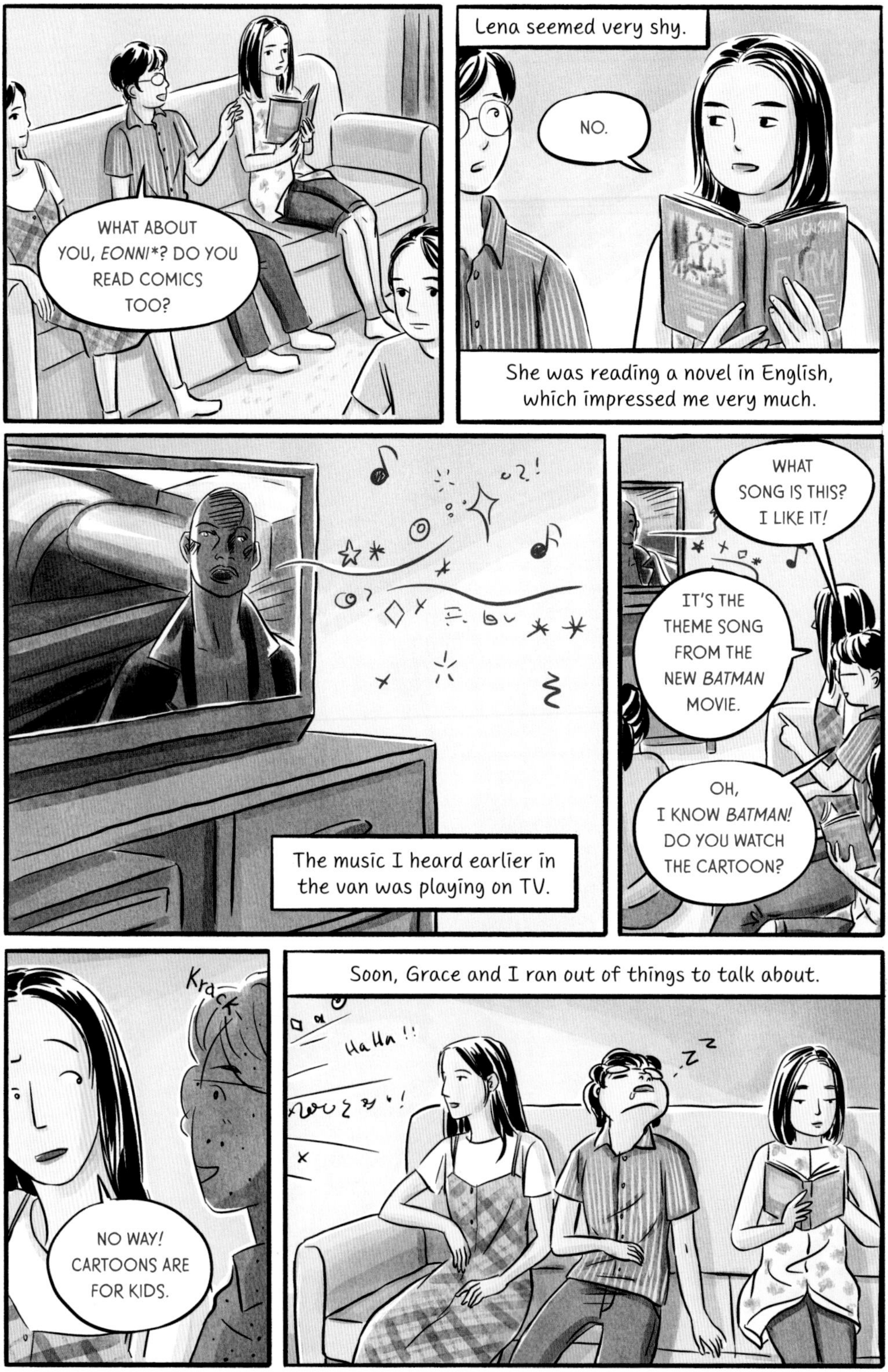
WHAT ABOUT YOU, *EONNI**? DO YOU READ COMICS TOO?
Lena seemed very shy.
NO.
She was reading a novel in English, which impressed me very much.
The music I heard earlier in the van was playing on TV.
WHAT SONG IS THIS? I LIKE IT!
IT'S THE THEME SONG FROM THE NEW *BATMAN* MOVIE.
OH, I KNOW *BATMAN!* DO YOU WATCH THE CARTOON?
Krack
NO WAY! CARTOONS ARE FOR KIDS.
Soon, Grace and I ran out of things to talk about.
Ha Ha !!

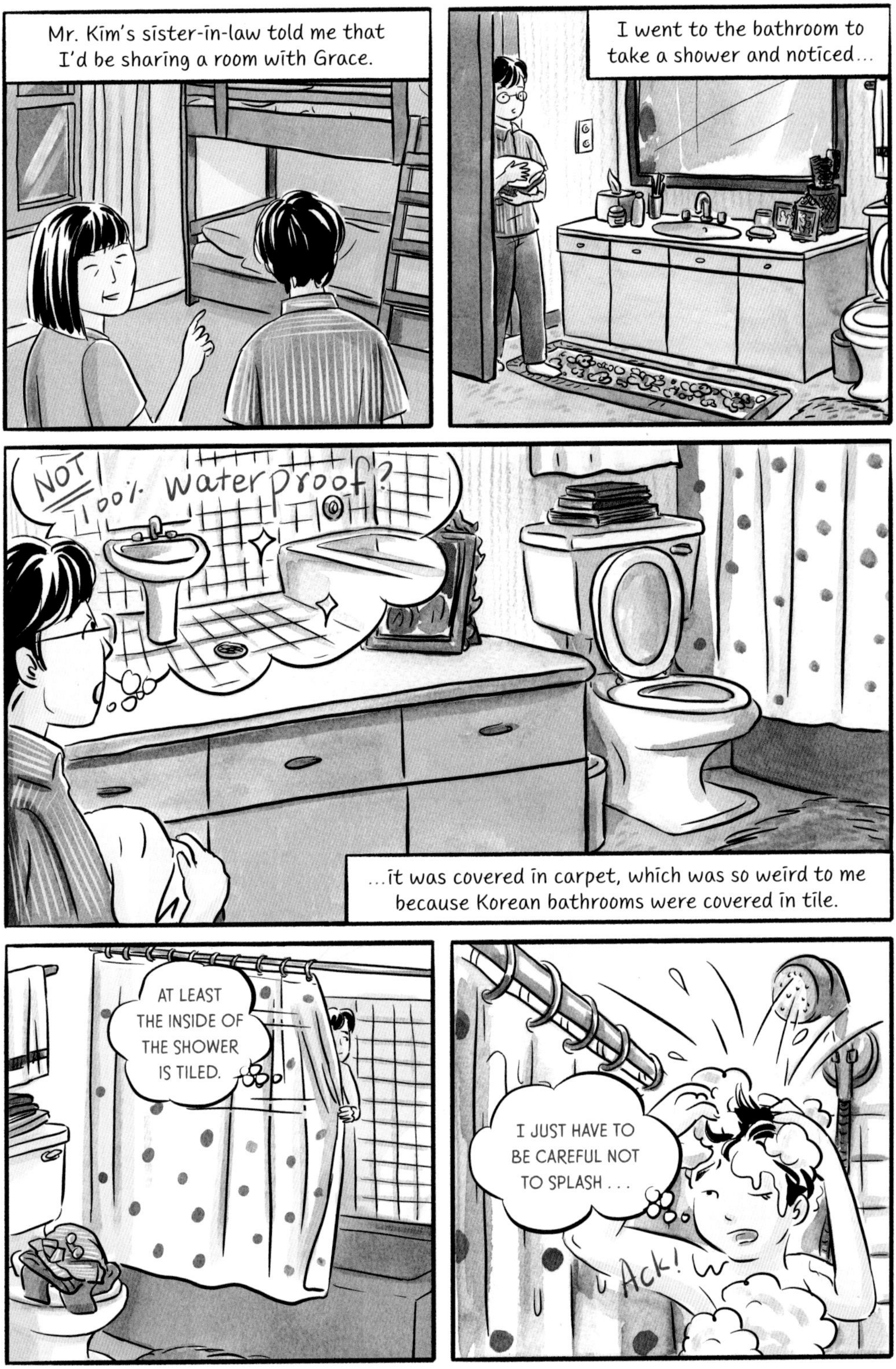
Mr. Kim's sister-in-law told me that I'd be sharing a room with Grace.
I went to the bathroom to take a shower and noticed...
NOT 100% waterproof?
...it was covered in carpet, which was so weird to me because Korean bathrooms were covered in tile.
AT LEAST THE INSIDE OF THE SHOWER IS TILED.
I JUST HAVE TO BE CAREFUL NOT TO SPLASH . . .
Ack!

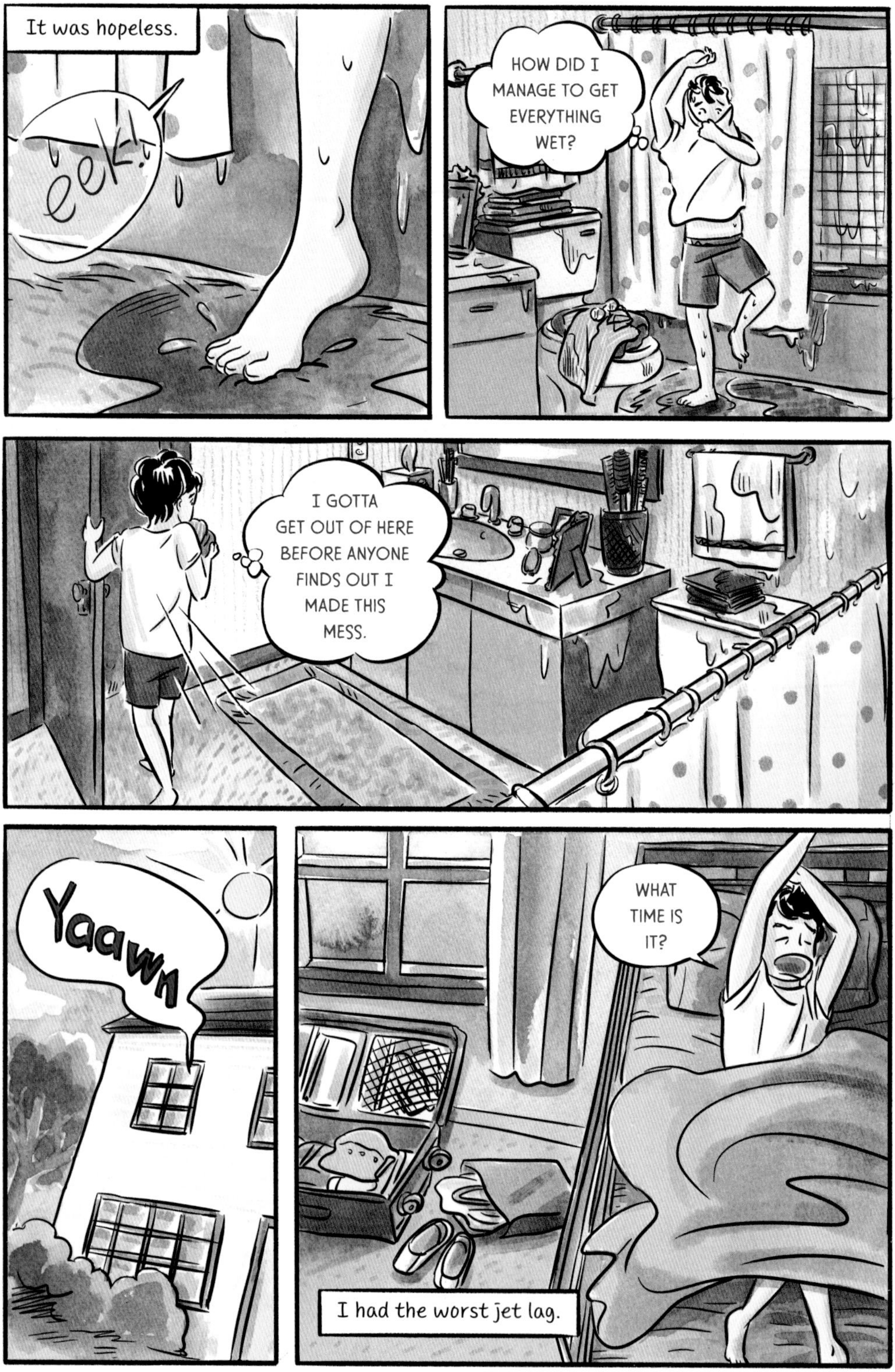
It was hopeless.
eek!
HOW DID I MANAGE TO GET EVERYTHING WET?
I GOTTA GET OUT OF HERE BEFORE ANYONE FINDS OUT I MADE THIS MESS.
Yaawn
WHAT TIME IS IT?
I had the worst jet lag.

WHAT DAY IS IT TODAY? IT'S BEEN A WEEK SINCE I GOT HERE. IT FELT LIKE A LOT LONGER THAN THAT.

MONDAY	TUESDAY	WEDNESDAY	THURSDAY	FRIDAY	SATURDAY	YESTERDAY
I ARRIVED.	NASA Space Center	NOTHING.	NOTHING.	...WENT SHOPPING. Bruno's	NOTHING.	WE WENT TO CHURCH.

IT'S SO QUIET.

MOM?

HELLO, ANYONE HOME?

Grace was always busy going to practice.

SEE YOU TONIGHT.

Ashley and Daniel were a lot younger than me.

MOM!

Lena kept to herself.

SHE THINKS SHE'S TOO COOL TO HANG OUT WITH ME.

19

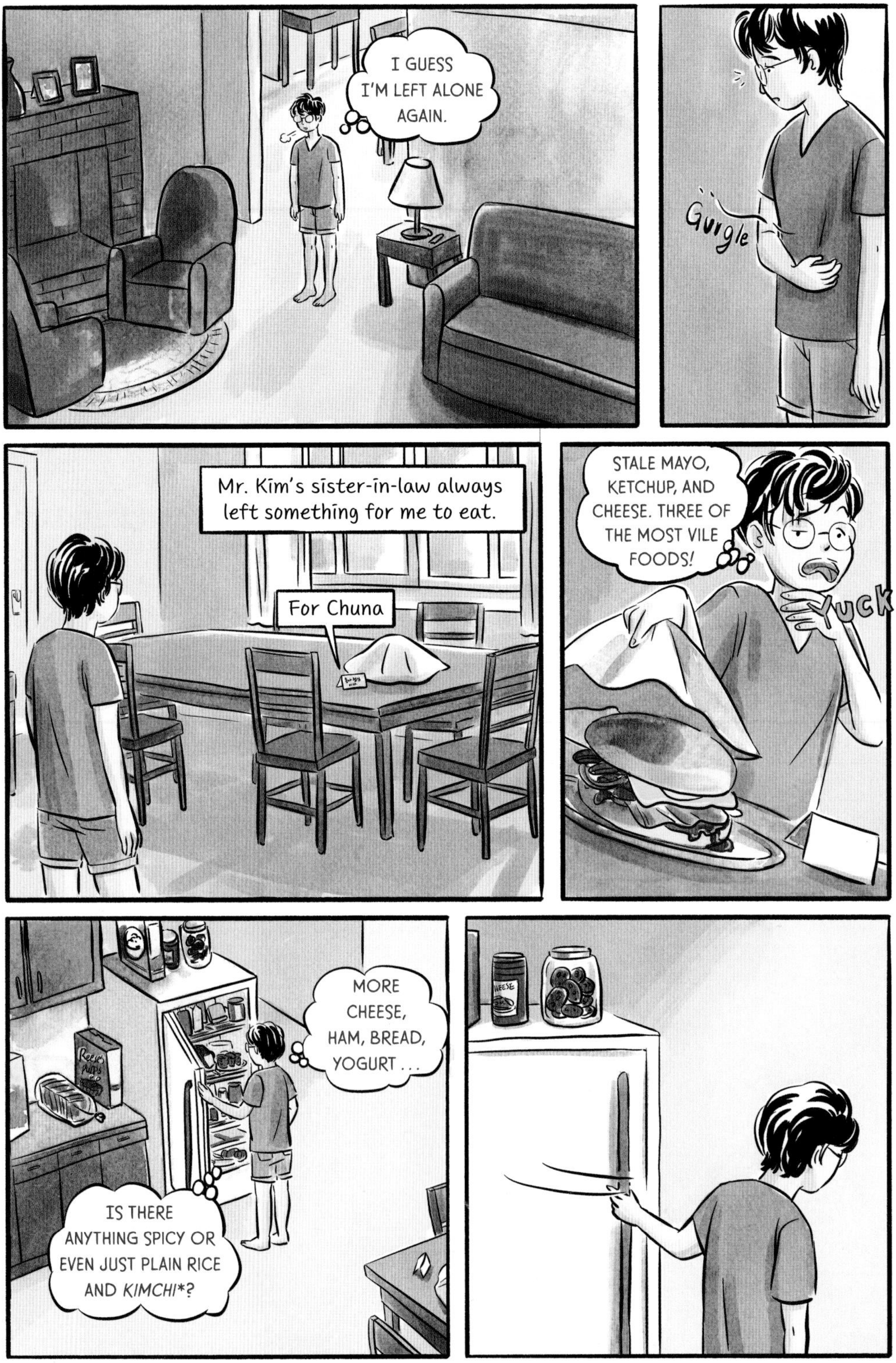
I GUESS I'M LEFT ALONE AGAIN.
Gurgle
Mr. Kim's sister-in-law always left something for me to eat.
For Chuna
STALE MAYO, KETCHUP, AND CHEESE. THREE OF THE MOST VILE FOODS!
YUCK!
MORE CHEESE, HAM, BREAD, YOGURT . . .
IS THERE ANYTHING SPICY OR EVEN JUST PLAIN RICE AND *KIMCHI**?

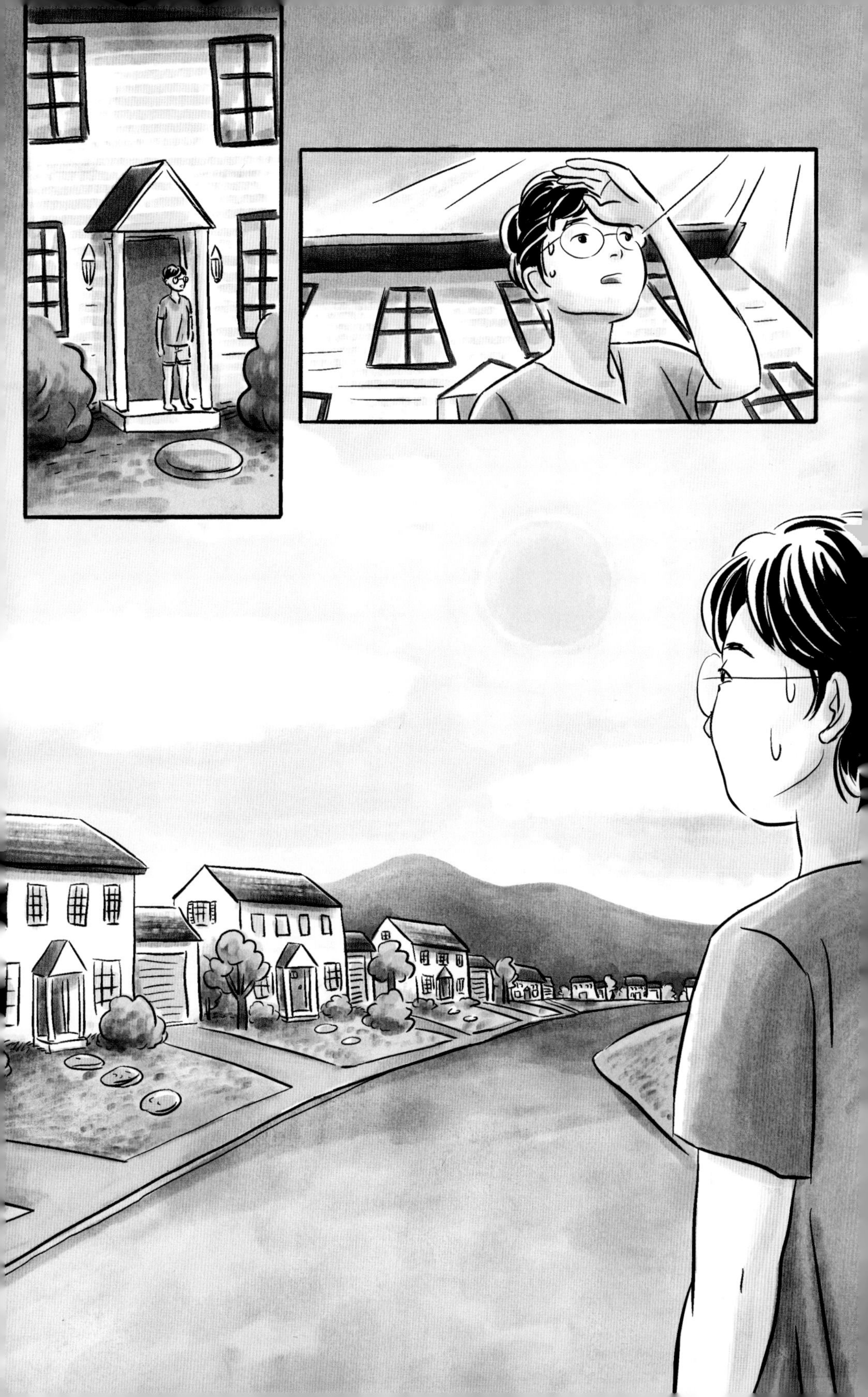

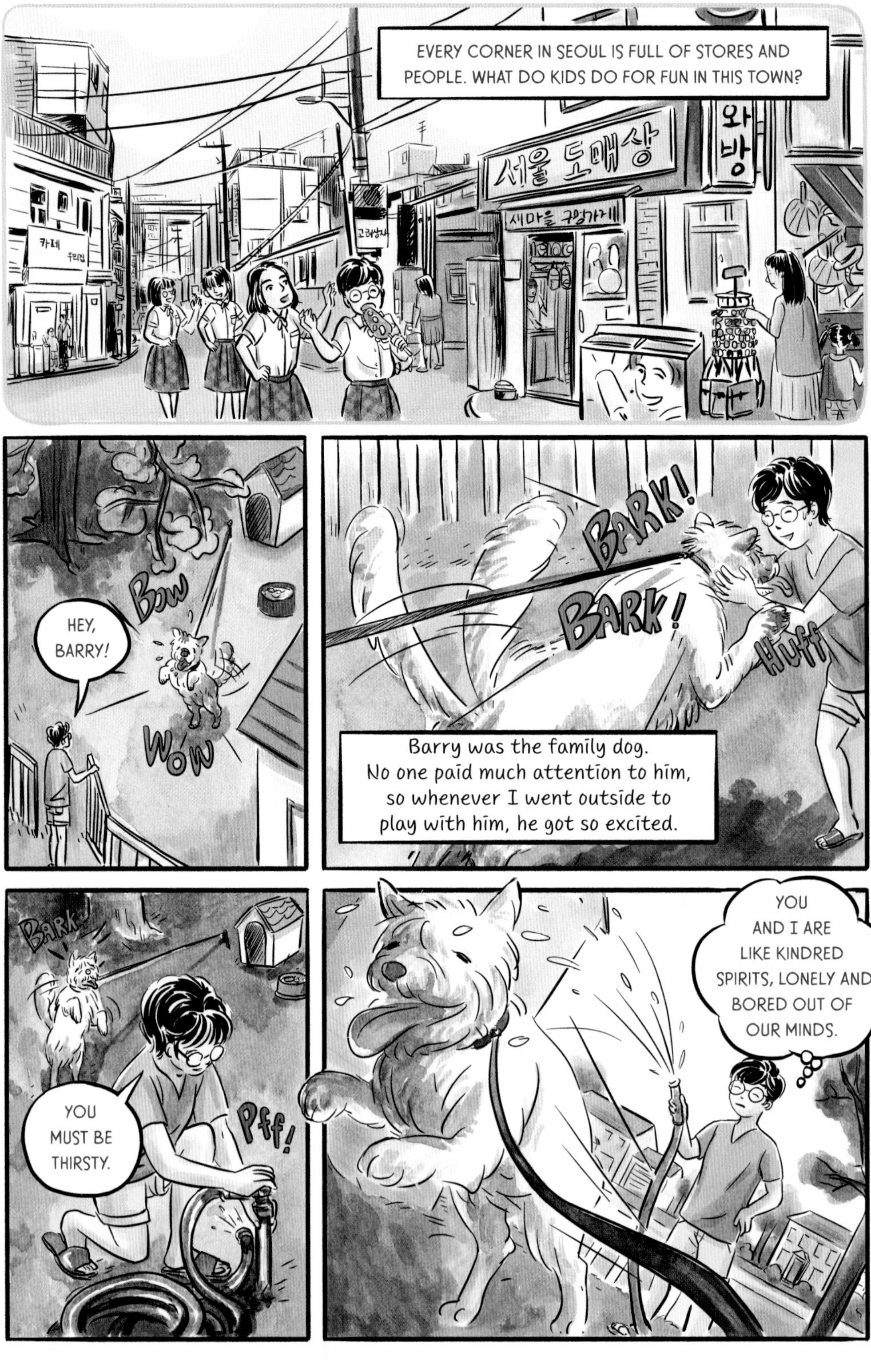
EVERY CORNER IN SEOUL IS FULL OF STORES AND PEOPLE. WHAT DO KIDS DO FOR FUN IN THIS TOWN?
서울 도매상
와 방
새마을 구멍가게
카페
HEY, BARRY!
Bow
Wow
BARK!
BARK!
Huff
Barry was the family dog. No one paid much attention to him, so whenever I went outside to play with him, he got so excited.
BARK
YOU MUST BE THIRSTY.
Pff!
YOU AND I ARE LIKE KINDRED SPIRITS, LONELY AND BORED OUT OF OUR MINDS.

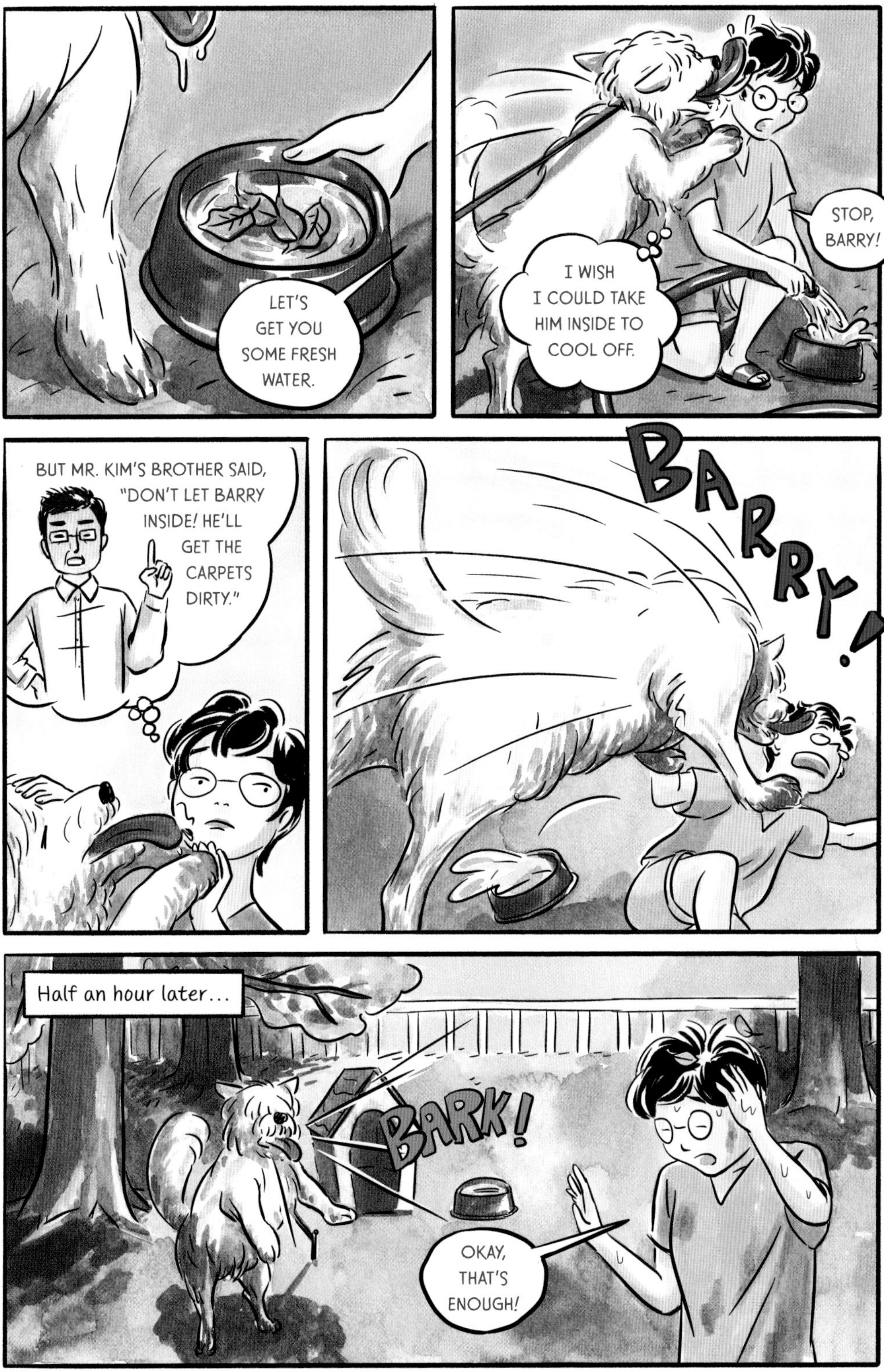
LET'S GET YOU SOME FRESH WATER.
STOP, BARRY!
I WISH I COULD TAKE HIM INSIDE TO COOL OFF.
BUT MR. KIM'S BROTHER SAID, "DON'T LET BARRY INSIDE! HE'LL GET THE CARPETS DIRTY."
BARRY!
Half an hour later...
BARK!
OKAY, THAT'S ENOUGH!

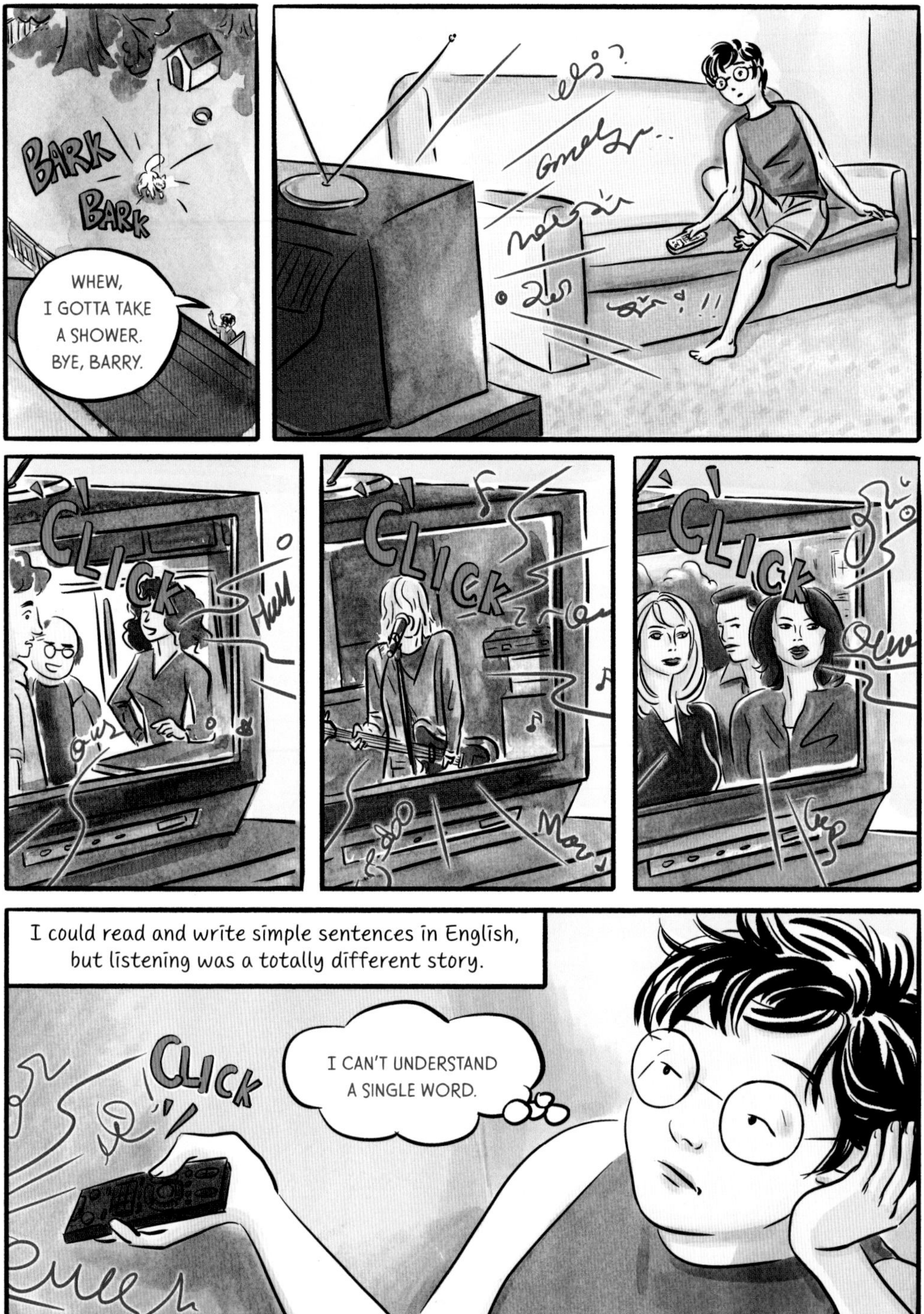
BARK
BARK
WHEW, I GOTTA TAKE A SHOWER. BYE, BARRY.
CLICK
CLICK
CLICK
I could read and write simple sentences in English, but listening was a totally different story.
CLICK
I CAN'T UNDERSTAND A SINGLE WORD.
Even so, I watched TV for hours because there was nothing else to do.

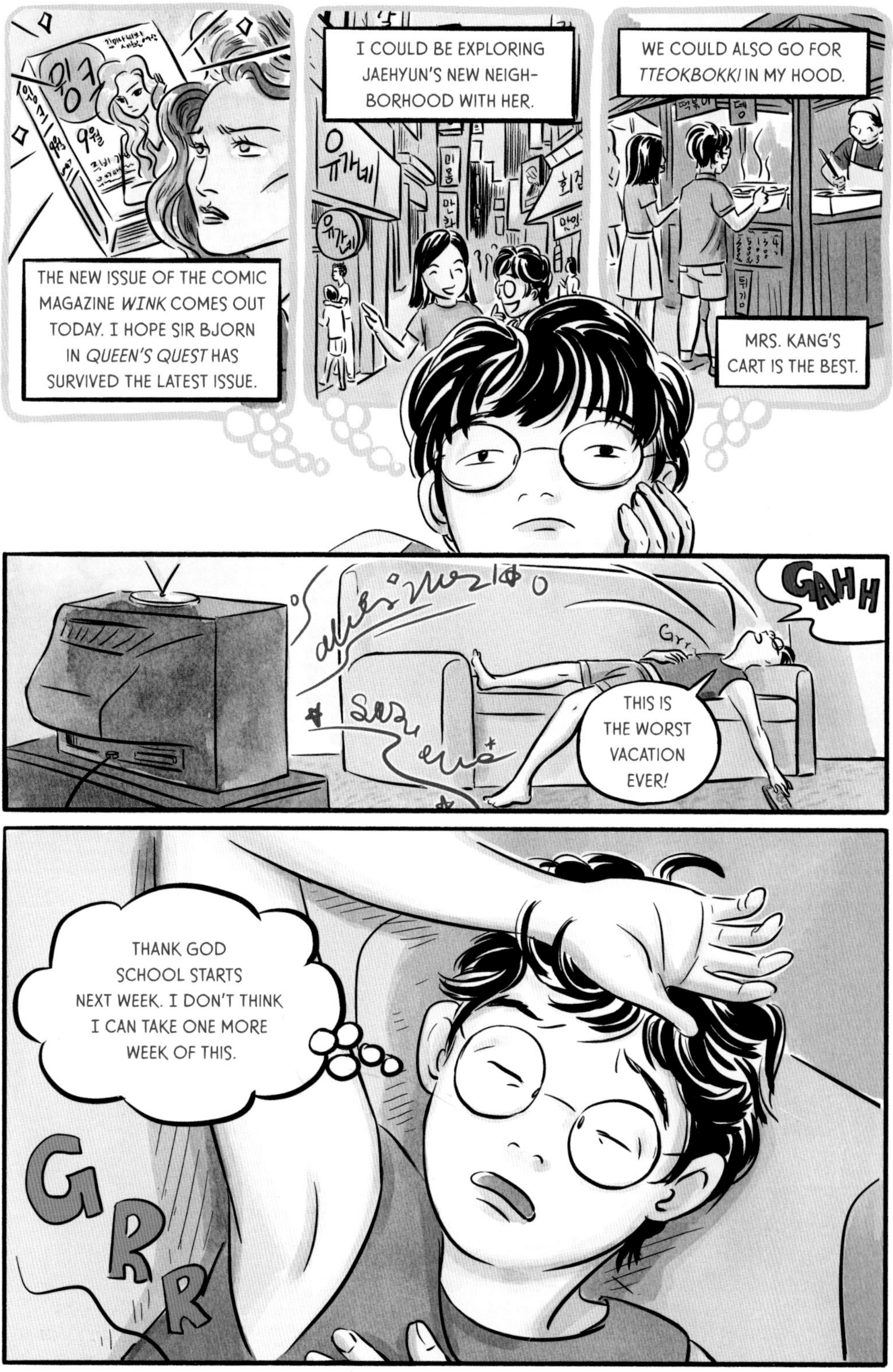
THE NEW ISSUE OF THE COMIC MAGAZINE *WINK* COMES OUT TODAY. I HOPE SIR BJORN IN *QUEEN'S QUEST* HAS SURVIVED THE LATEST ISSUE.
I COULD BE EXPLORING JAEHYUN'S NEW NEIGHBORHOOD WITH HER.
WE COULD ALSO GO FOR *TTEOKBOKKI* IN MY HOOD.
MRS. KANG'S CART IS THE BEST.
GAHH
Grr
THIS IS THE WORST VACATION EVER!
THANK GOD SCHOOL STARTS NEXT WEEK. I DON'T THINK I CAN TAKE ONE MORE WEEK OF THIS.
GRR

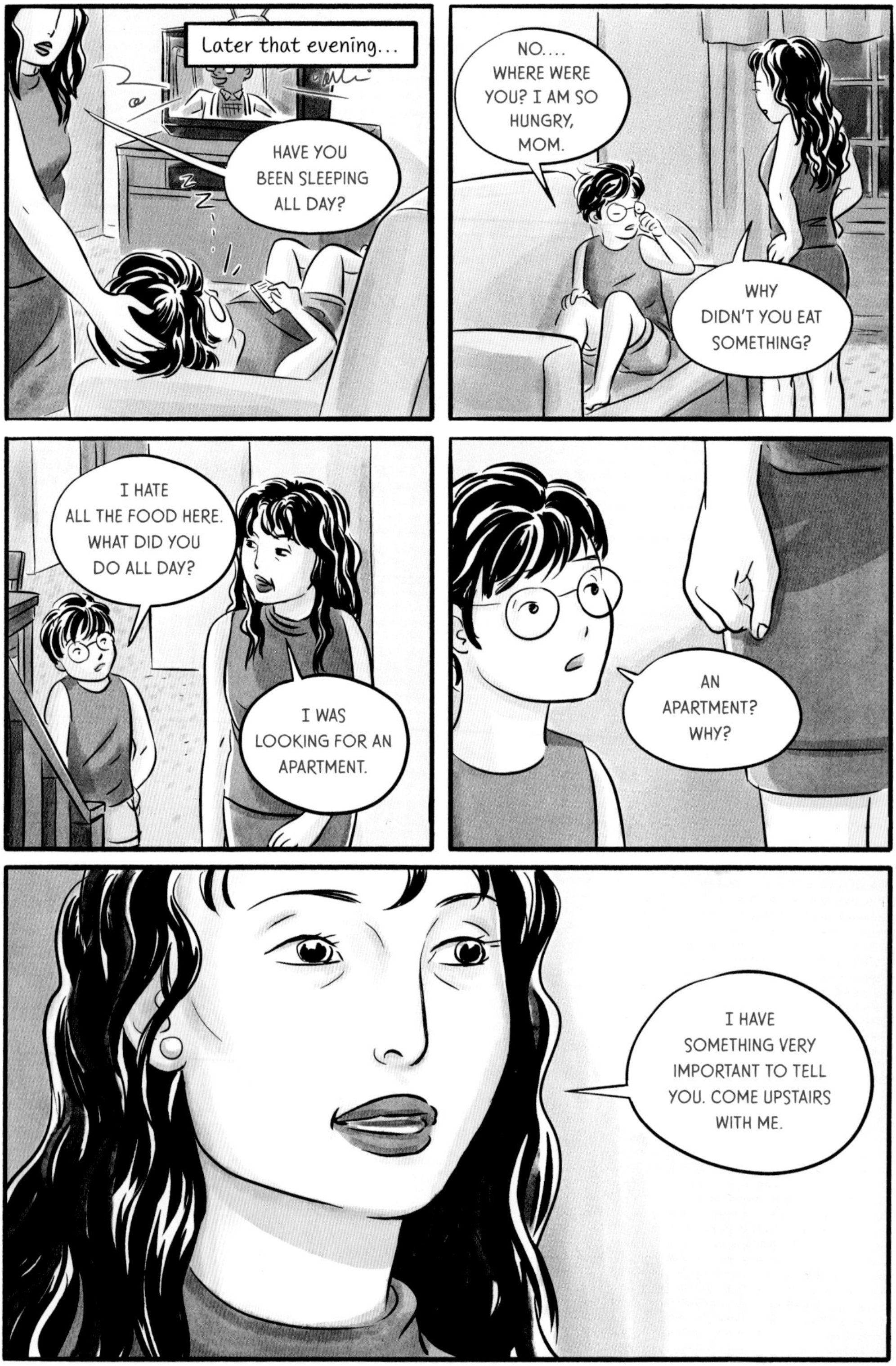
Later that evening...
HAVE YOU BEEN SLEEPING ALL DAY?
NO.... WHERE WERE YOU? I AM SO HUNGRY, MOM.
WHY DIDN'T YOU EAT SOMETHING?
I HATE ALL THE FOOD HERE. WHAT DID YOU DO ALL DAY?
I WAS LOOKING FOR AN APARTMENT.
AN APARTMENT? WHY?
I HAVE SOMETHING VERY IMPORTANT TO TELL YOU. COME UPSTAIRS WITH ME.

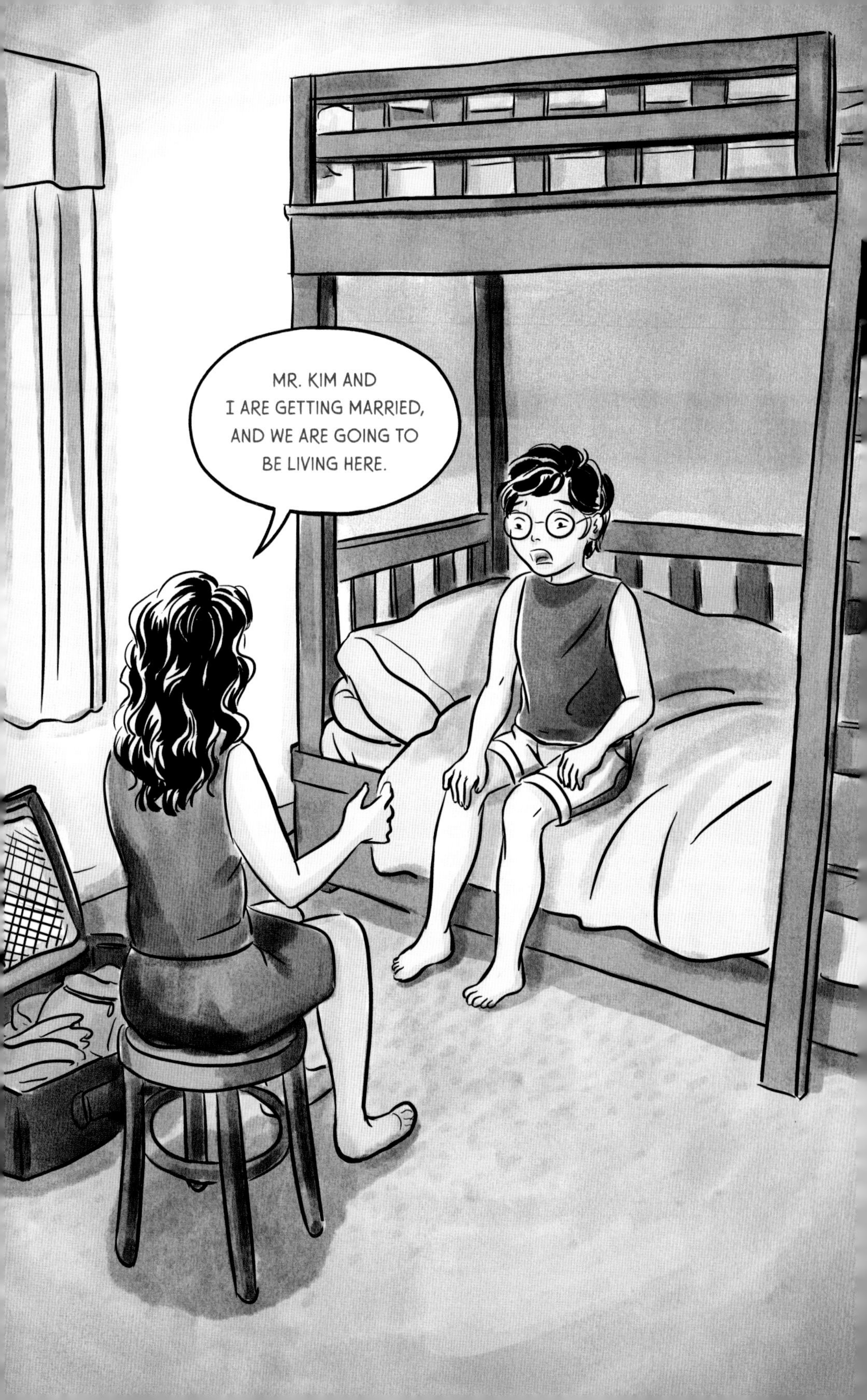
MR. KIM AND I ARE GETTING MARRIED, AND WE ARE GOING TO BE LIVING HERE.

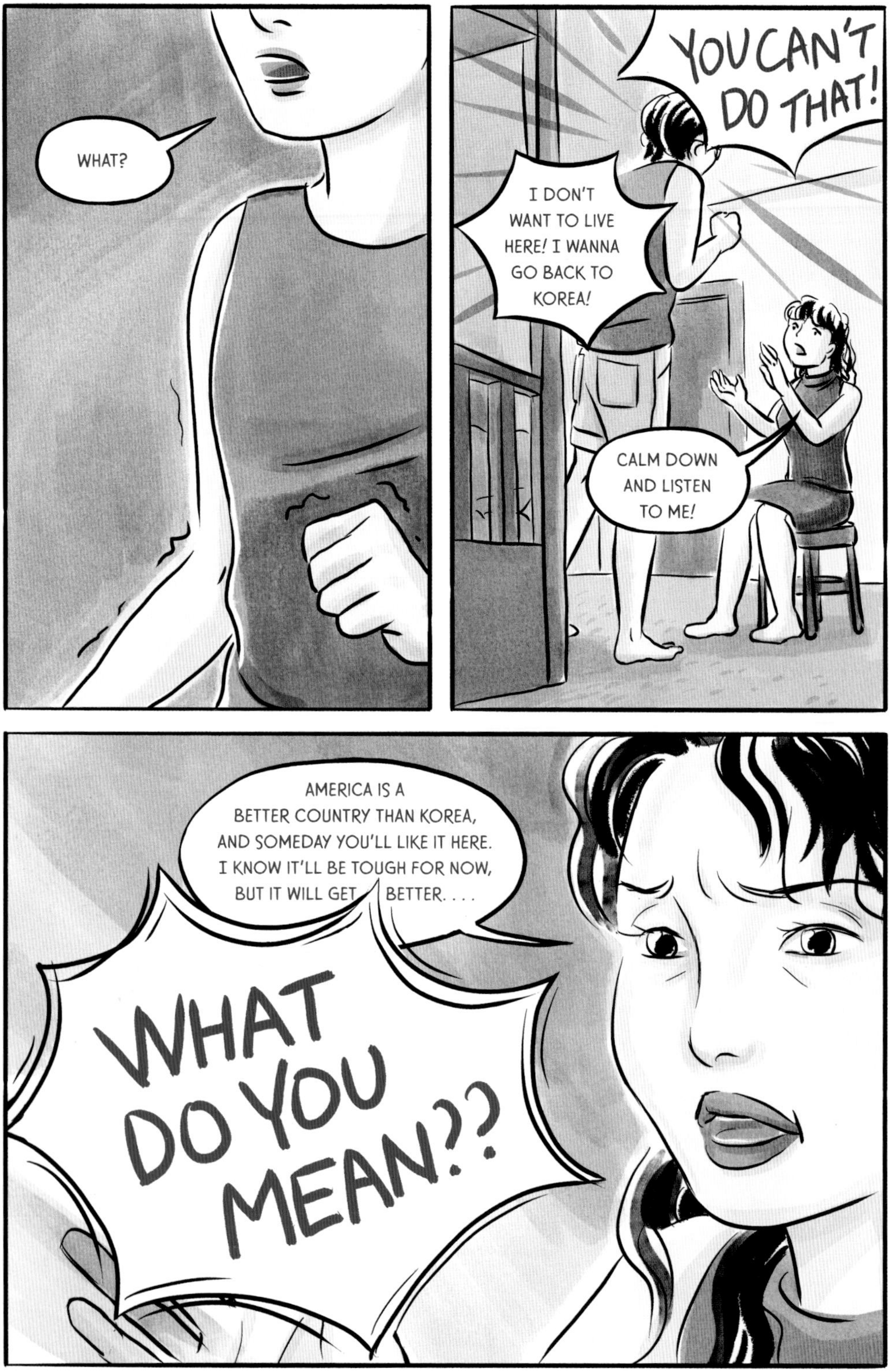
WHAT?
YOU CAN'T DO THAT!
I DON'T WANT TO LIVE HERE! I WANNA GO BACK TO KOREA!
CALM DOWN AND LISTEN TO ME!
AMERICA IS A BETTER COUNTRY THAN KOREA, AND SOMEDAY YOU'LL LIKE IT HERE. I KNOW IT'LL BE TOUGH FOR NOW, BUT IT WILL GET BETTER. . . .
WHAT DO YOU MEAN??

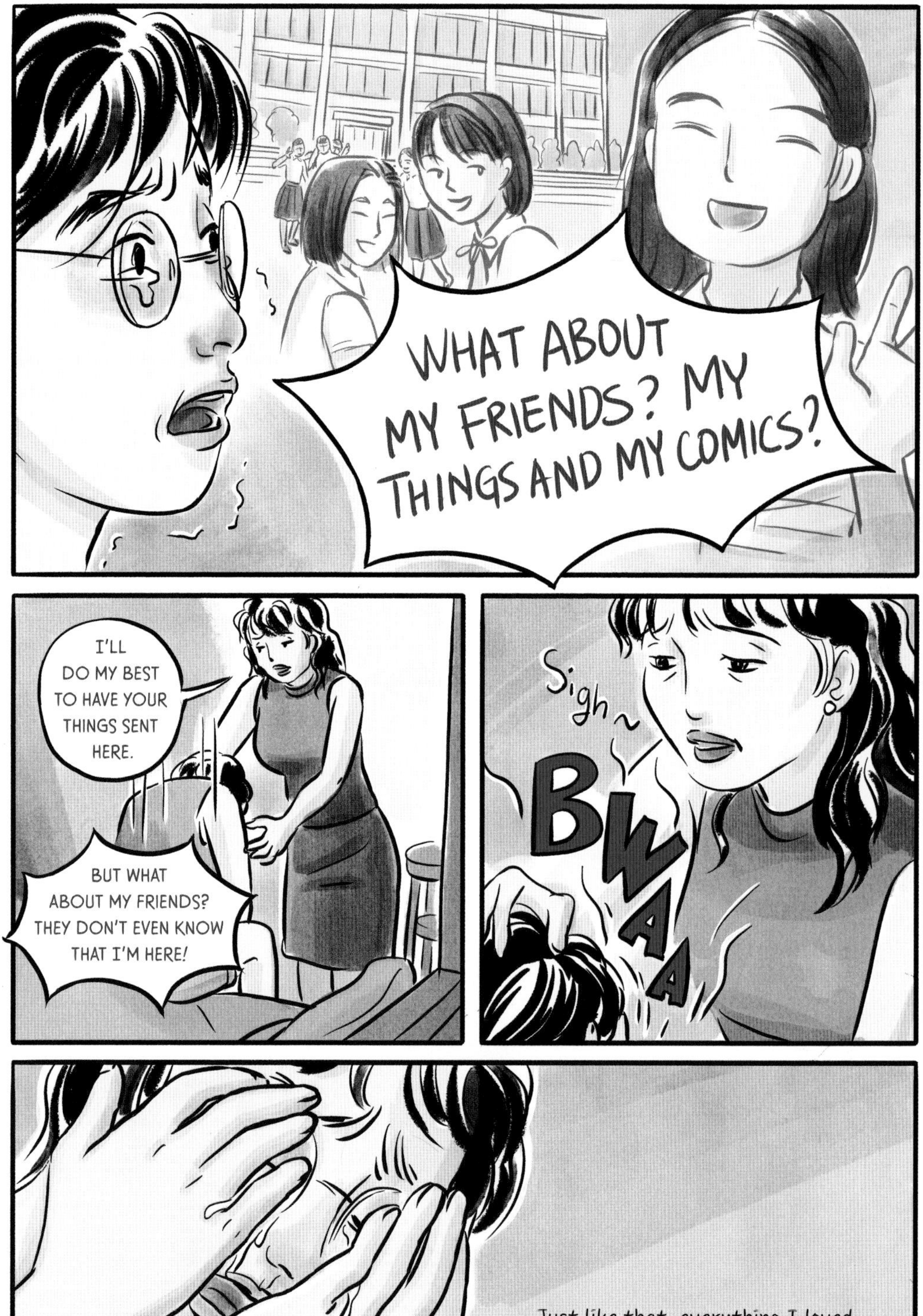
WHAT ABOUT MY FRIENDS? MY THINGS AND MY COMICS?
I'LL DO MY BEST TO HAVE YOUR THINGS SENT HERE.
BUT WHAT ABOUT MY FRIENDS? THEY DON'T EVEN KNOW THAT I'M HERE!
Sigh~
BWAAA
Just like that, everything I loved was suddenly snatched away from me.

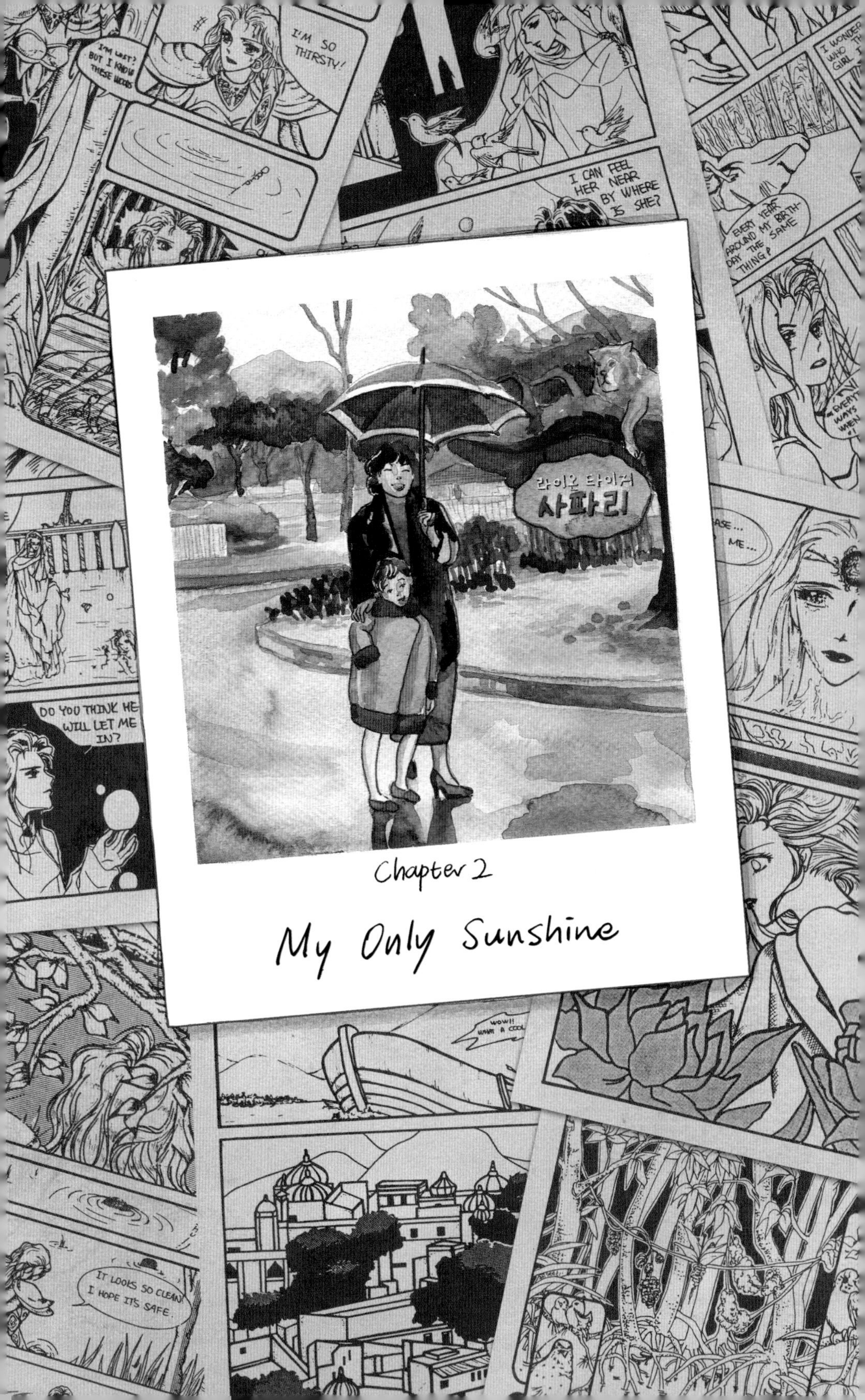
I'M LOST? BUT I KNOW THESE WOODS
I'M SO THIRSTY!
I CAN FEEL HER NEAR BY WHERE IS SHE?
EVERY YEAR AROUND MY BIRTHDAY THE SAME THING?
라이온 타이거
사파리
DO YOU THINK HE WILL LET ME IN?
WOW!! WHAT A COOL
IT LOOKS SO CLEAN I HOPE IT'S SAFE.

Chapter 2

My Only Sunshine

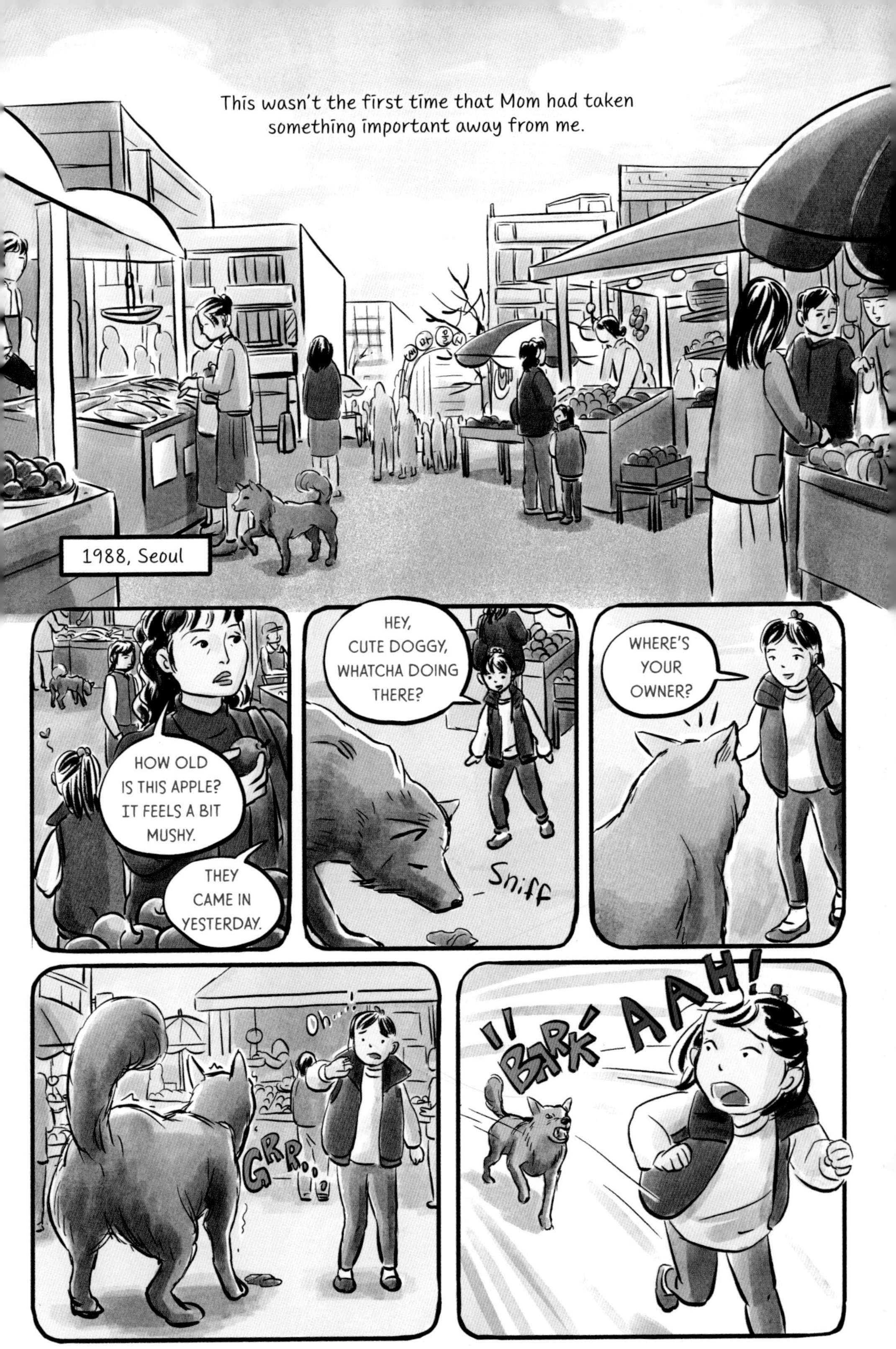
This wasn't the first time that Mom had taken something important away from me.
1988, Seoul
HOW OLD IS THIS APPLE? IT FEELS A BIT MUSHY.
THEY CAME IN YESTERDAY.
HEY, CUTE DOGGY, WHATCHA DOING THERE?
Sniff
WHERE'S YOUR OWNER?
Oh...!
GRR...
BARK
AAH!

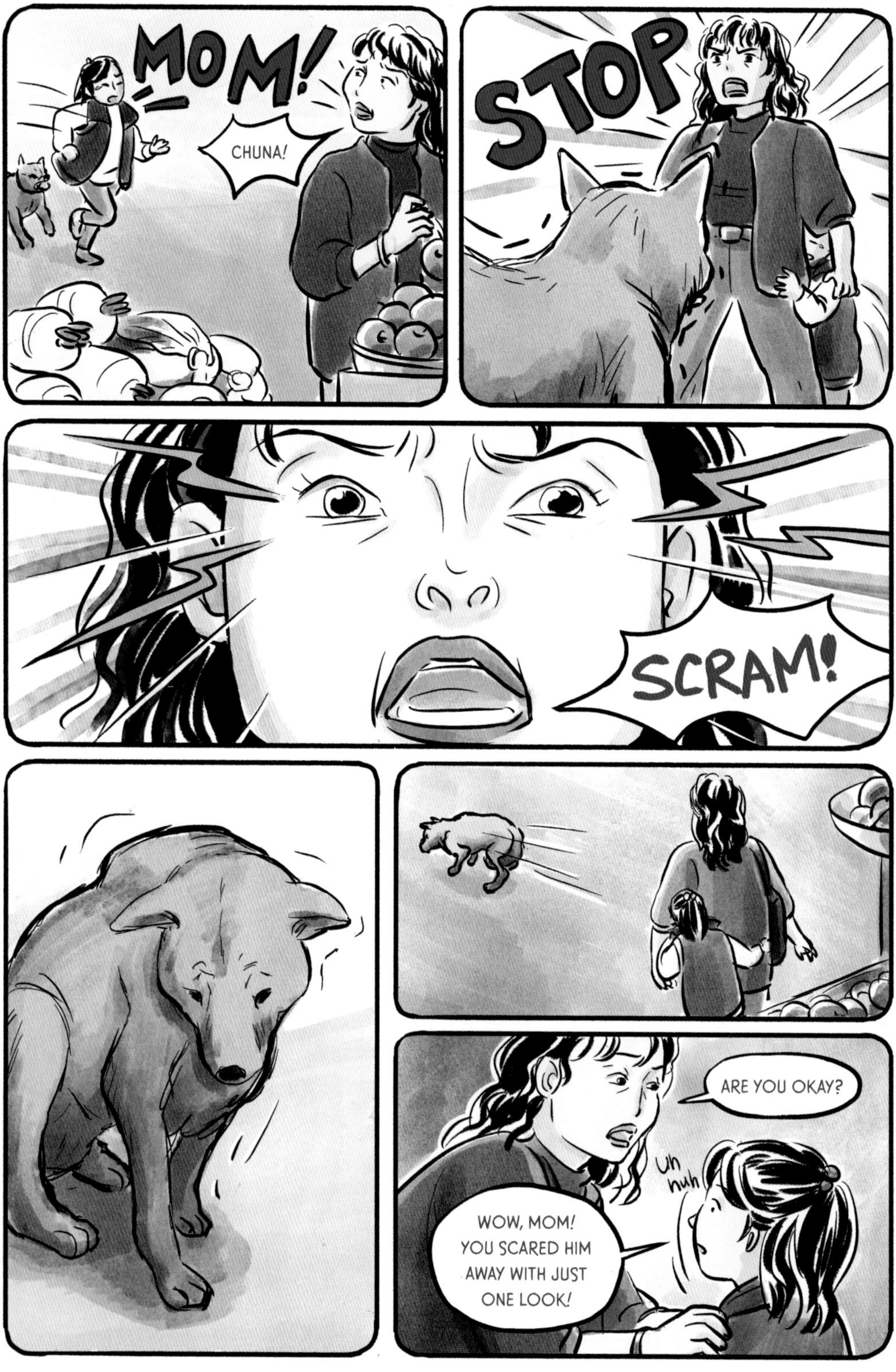
MOM!
CHUNA!
STOP
SCRAM!
ARE YOU OKAY?
Uh huh
WOW, MOM! YOU SCARED HIM AWAY WITH JUST ONE LOOK!

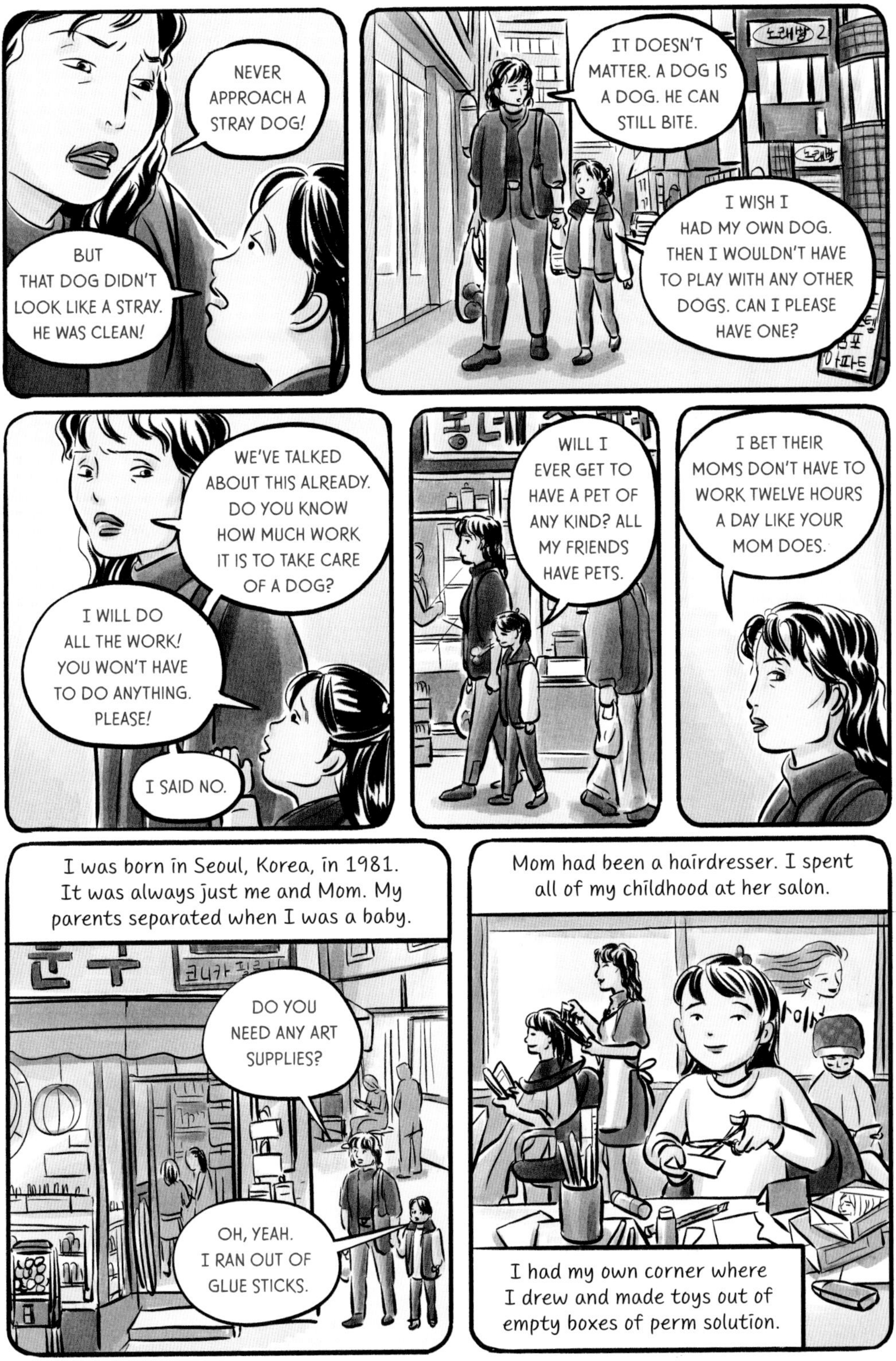
NEVER APPROACH A STRAY DOG!
BUT THAT DOG DIDN'T LOOK LIKE A STRAY. HE WAS CLEAN!
노래방 2
IT DOESN'T MATTER. A DOG IS A DOG. HE CAN STILL BITE.
노래방
I WISH I HAD MY OWN DOG. THEN I WOULDN'T HAVE TO PLAY WITH ANY OTHER DOGS. CAN I PLEASE HAVE ONE?
WE'VE TALKED ABOUT THIS ALREADY. DO YOU KNOW HOW MUCH WORK IT IS TO TAKE CARE OF A DOG?
I WILL DO ALL THE WORK! YOU WON'T HAVE TO DO ANYTHING. PLEASE!
I SAID NO.
WILL I EVER GET TO HAVE A PET OF ANY KIND? ALL MY FRIENDS HAVE PETS.
I BET THEIR MOMS DON'T HAVE TO WORK TWELVE HOURS A DAY LIKE YOUR MOM DOES.
I was born in Seoul, Korea, in 1981. It was always just me and Mom. My parents separated when I was a baby.
DO YOU NEED ANY ART SUPPLIES?
OH, YEAH. I RAN OUT OF GLUE STICKS.
Mom had been a hairdresser. I spent all of my childhood at her salon.
I had my own corner where I drew and made toys out of empty boxes of perm solution.

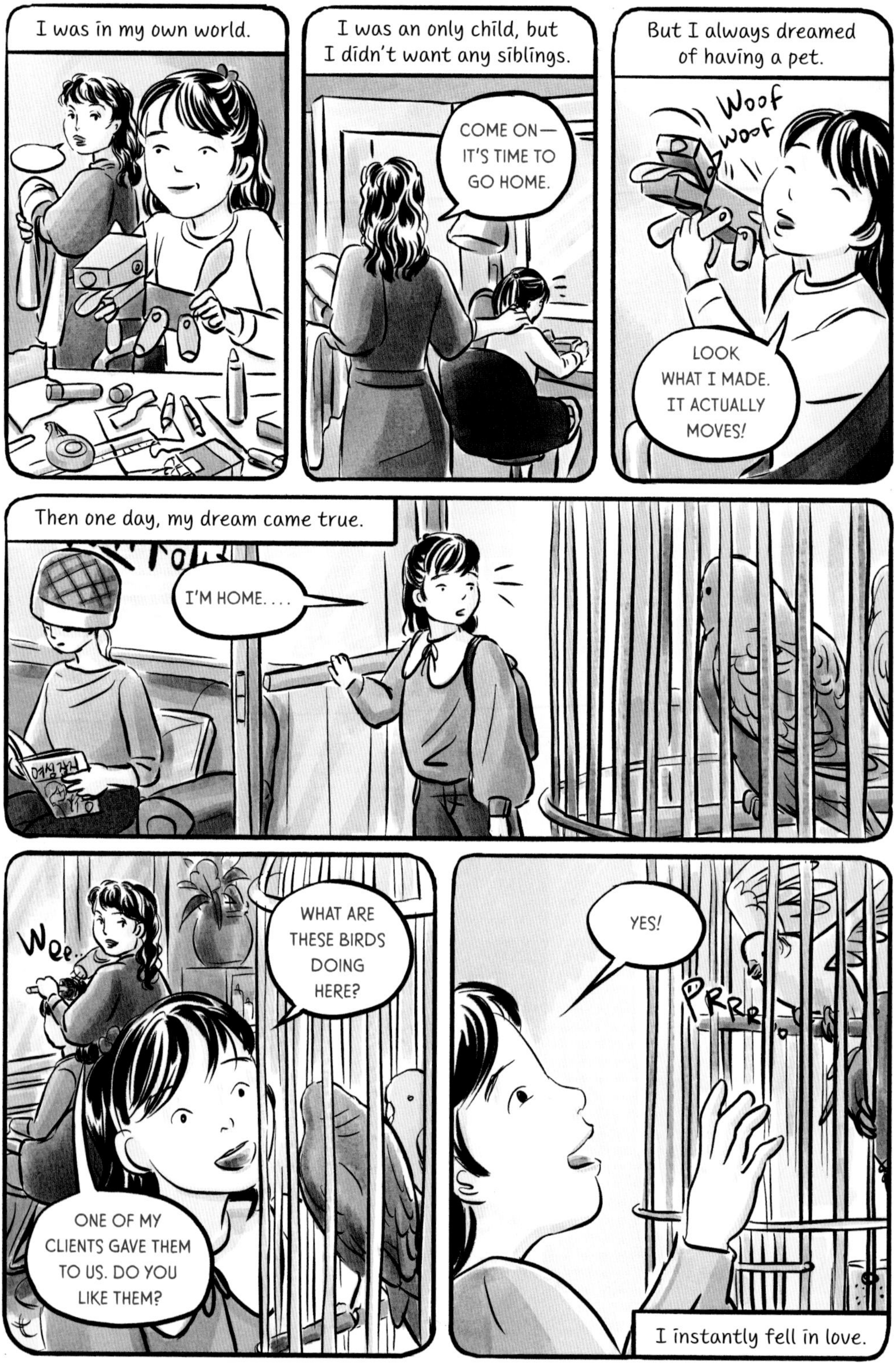
I was in my own world.
I was an only child, but I didn't want any siblings.
COME ON— IT'S TIME TO GO HOME.
But I always dreamed of having a pet.
Woof woof
LOOK WHAT I MADE. IT ACTUALLY MOVES!
Then one day, my dream came true.
I'M HOME. . . .
Wee...
WHAT ARE THESE BIRDS DOING HERE?
ONE OF MY CLIENTS GAVE THEM TO US. DO YOU LIKE THEM?
YES!
PRRR
I instantly fell in love.

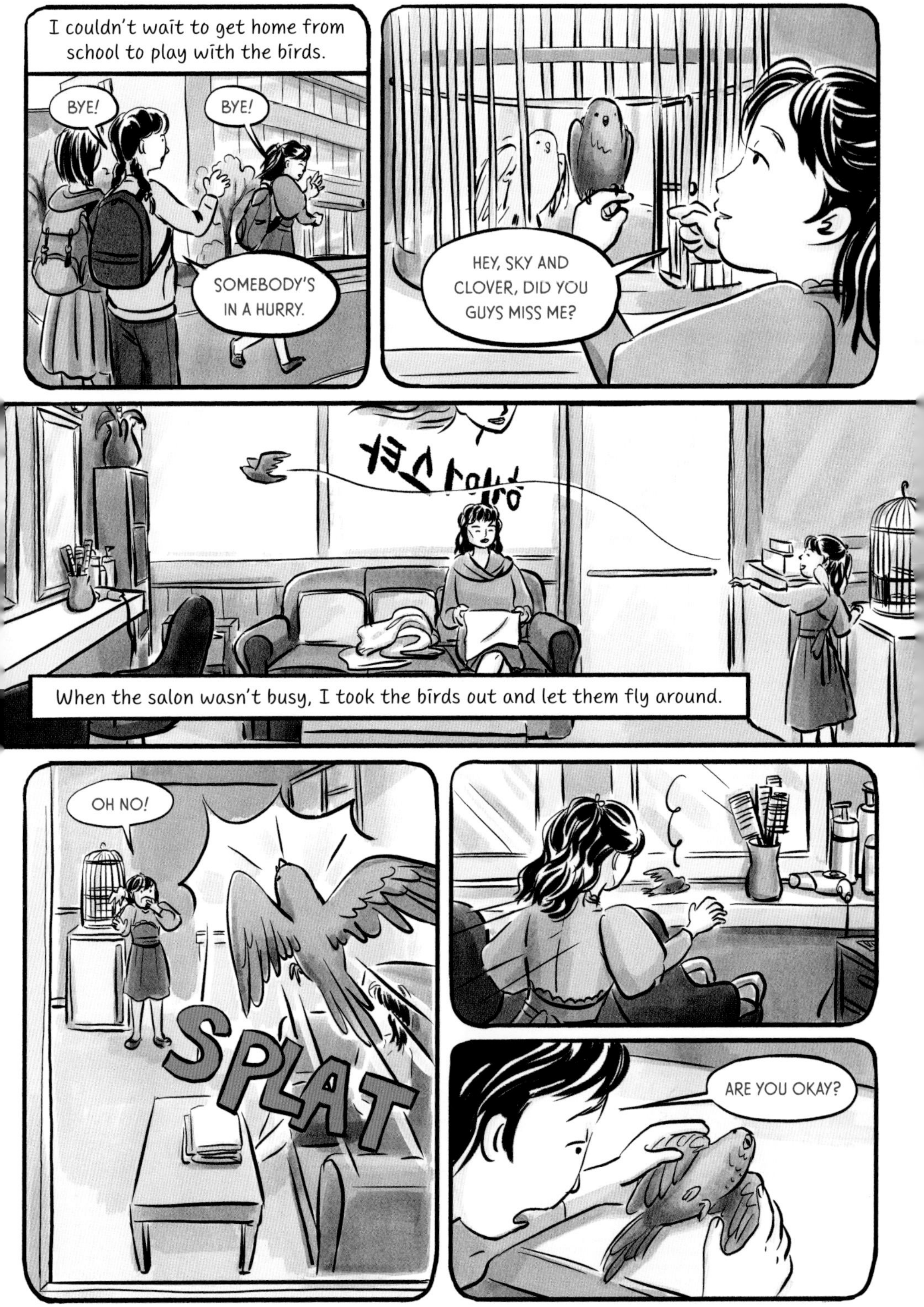
I couldn't wait to get home from school to play with the birds.
BYE!
BYE!
SOMEBODY'S IN A HURRY.
HEY, SKY AND CLOVER, DID YOU GUYS MISS ME?
When the salon wasn't busy, I took the birds out and let them fly around.
OH NO!
SPLAT
ARE YOU OKAY?

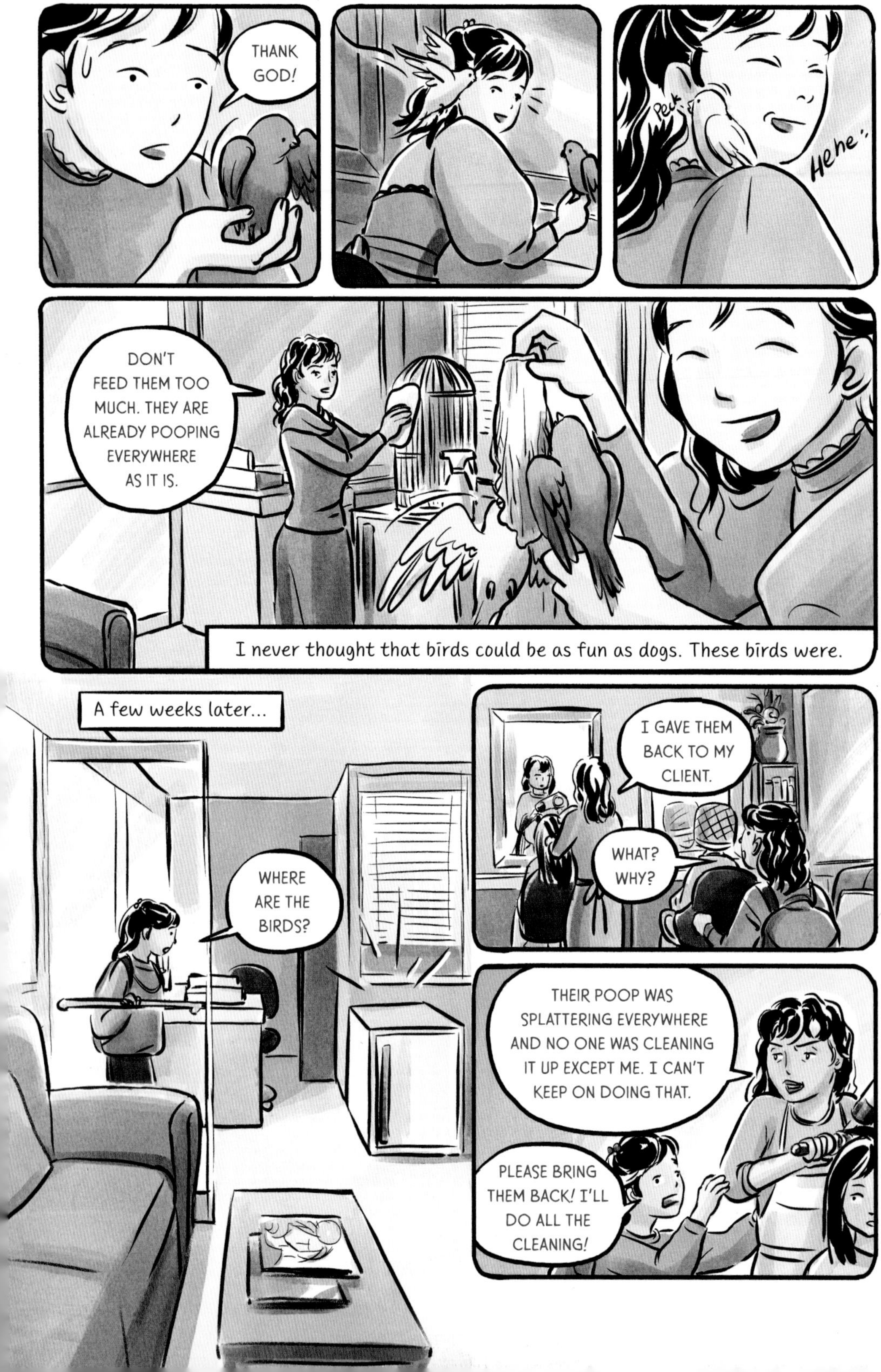
THANK GOD!
Peck
Hehe..
DON'T FEED THEM TOO MUCH. THEY ARE ALREADY POOPING EVERYWHERE AS IT IS.
I never thought that birds could be as fun as dogs. These birds were.
A few weeks later...
WHERE ARE THE BIRDS?
I GAVE THEM BACK TO MY CLIENT.
WHAT? WHY?
THEIR POOP WAS SPLATTERING EVERYWHERE AND NO ONE WAS CLEANING IT UP EXCEPT ME. I CAN'T KEEP ON DOING THAT.
PLEASE BRING THEM BACK! I'LL DO ALL THE CLEANING!

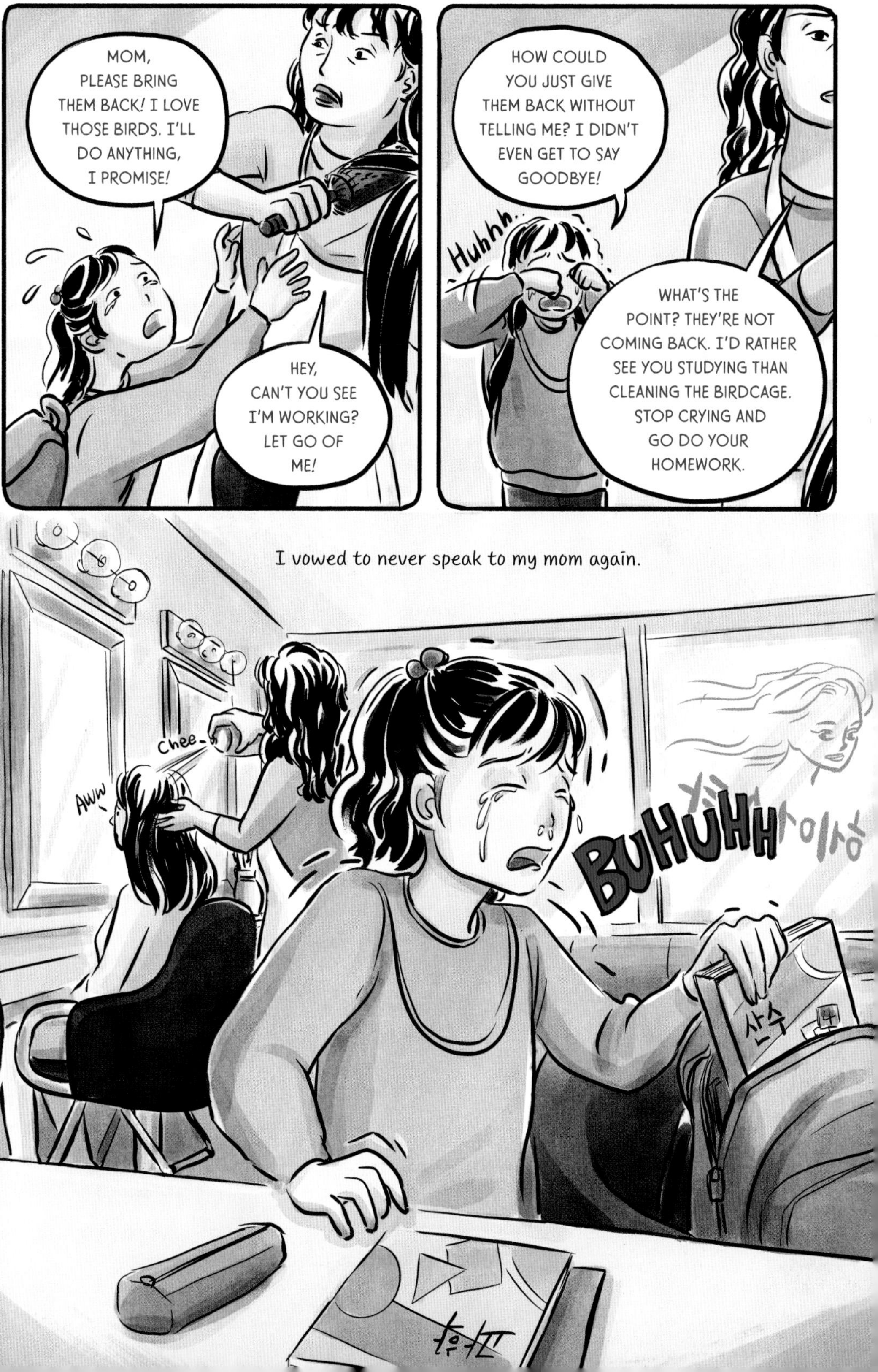
MOM, PLEASE BRING THEM BACK! I LOVE THOSE BIRDS. I'LL DO ANYTHING, I PROMISE!
HEY, CAN'T YOU SEE I'M WORKING? LET GO OF ME!
HOW COULD YOU JUST GIVE THEM BACK WITHOUT TELLING ME? I DIDN'T EVEN GET TO SAY GOODBYE!
Huhhh...
WHAT'S THE POINT? THEY'RE NOT COMING BACK. I'D RATHER SEE YOU STUDYING THAN CLEANING THE BIRDCAGE. STOP CRYING AND GO DO YOUR HOMEWORK.
I vowed to never speak to my mom again.
Chee-
AWW
BUHUHH
산수

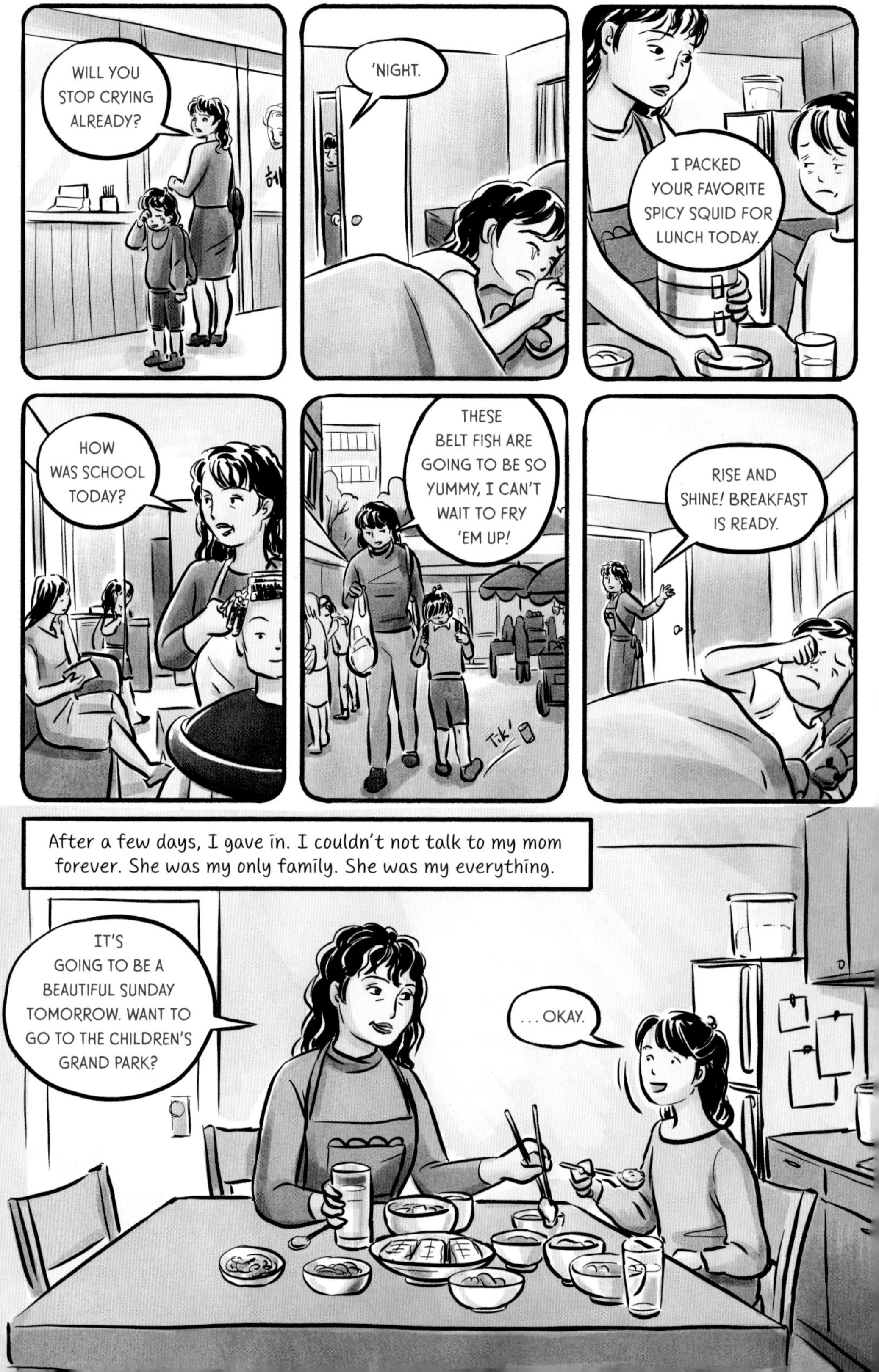
WILL YOU STOP CRYING ALREADY?
'NIGHT.
I PACKED YOUR FAVORITE SPICY SQUID FOR LUNCH TODAY.
HOW WAS SCHOOL TODAY?
THESE BELT FISH ARE GOING TO BE SO YUMMY, I CAN'T WAIT TO FRY 'EM UP!
Tik!
RISE AND SHINE! BREAKFAST IS READY.
After a few days, I gave in. I couldn't not talk to my mom forever. She was my only family. She was my everything.
IT'S GOING TO BE A BEAUTIFUL SUNDAY TOMORROW. WANT TO GO TO THE CHILDREN'S GRAND PARK?
...OKAY.

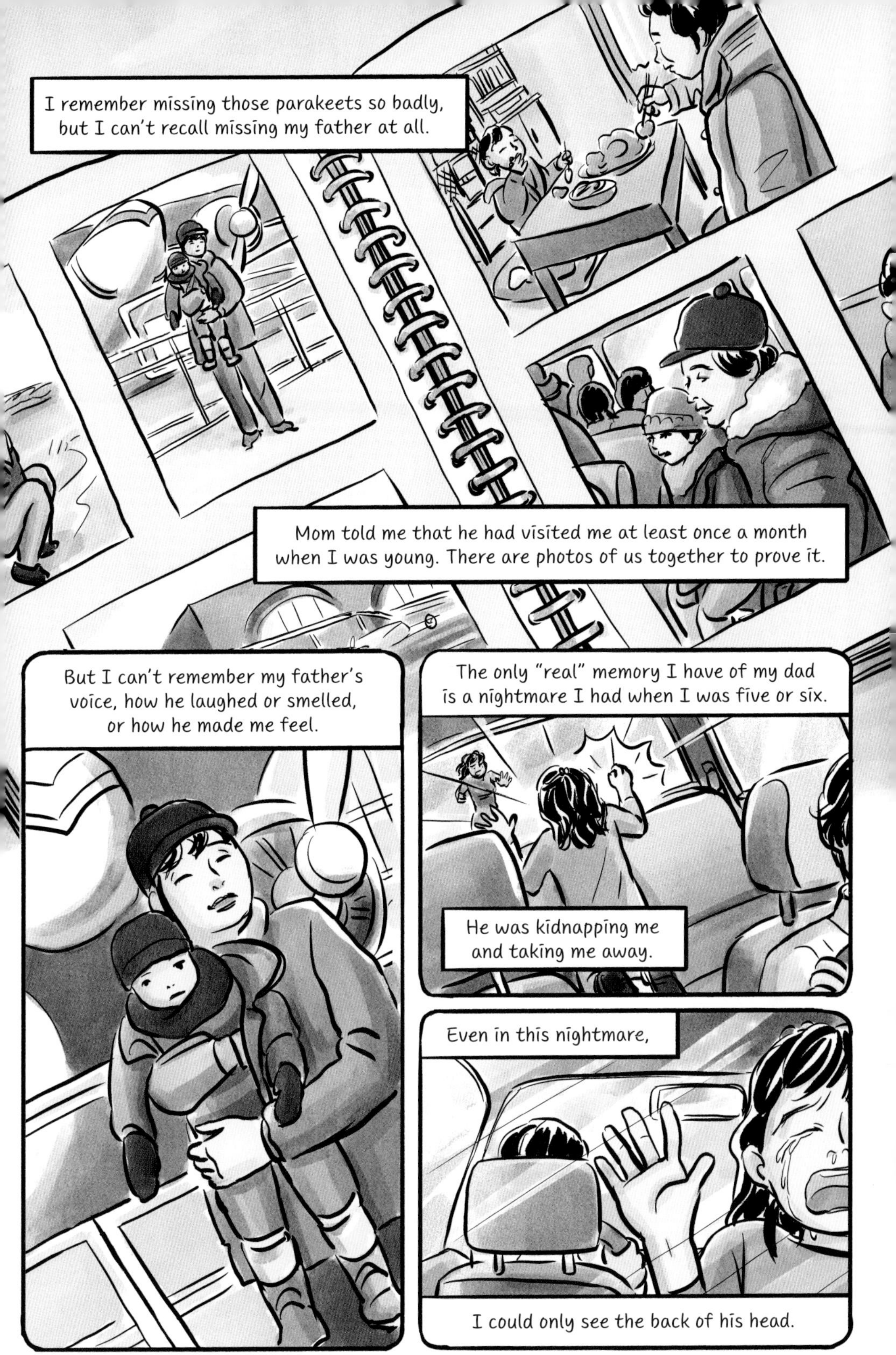
I remember missing those parakeets so badly, but I can't recall missing my father at all.
Mom told me that he had visited me at least once a month when I was young. There are photos of us together to prove it.
But I can't remember my father's voice, how he laughed or smelled, or how he made me feel.
The only "real" memory I have of my dad is a nightmare I had when I was five or six.
He was kidnapping me and taking me away.
Even in this nightmare,
I could only see the back of his head.

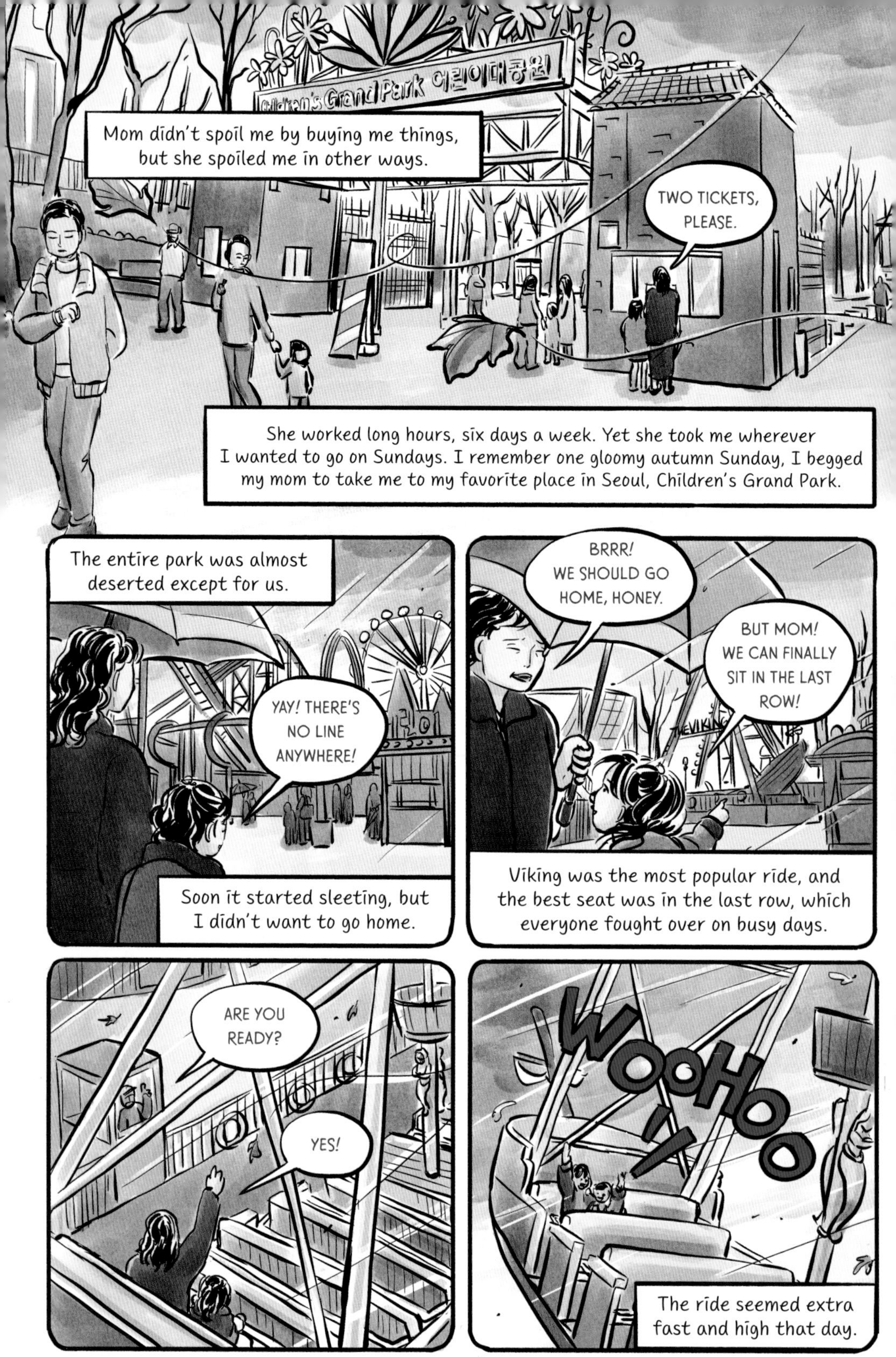
Children's Grand Park 어린이대공원
Mom didn't spoil me by buying me things, but she spoiled me in other ways.
TWO TICKETS, PLEASE.
She worked long hours, six days a week. Yet she took me wherever I wanted to go on Sundays. I remember one gloomy autumn Sunday, I begged my mom to take me to my favorite place in Seoul, Children's Grand Park.
The entire park was almost deserted except for us.
YAY! THERE'S NO LINE ANYWHERE!
Soon it started sleeting, but I didn't want to go home.
BRRR! WE SHOULD GO HOME, HONEY.
BUT MOM! WE CAN FINALLY SIT IN THE LAST ROW!
Viking was the most popular ride, and the best seat was in the last row, which everyone fought over on busy days.
ARE YOU READY?
YES!
WOOHOO!
The ride seemed extra fast and high that day.

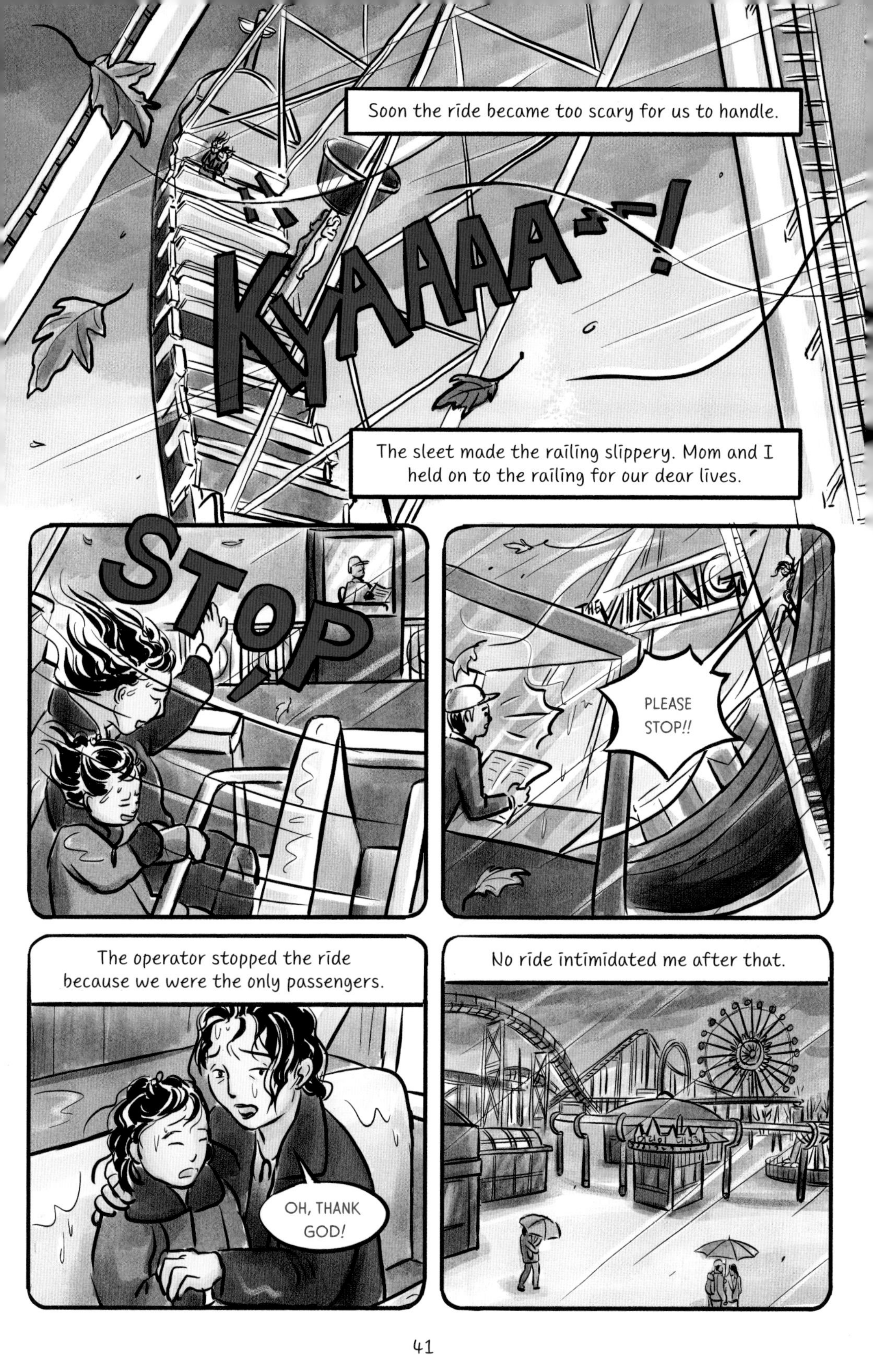
Soon the ride became too scary for us to handle.
KYAAAA!
The sleet made the railing slippery. Mom and I held on to the railing for our dear lives.
STOP
THE VIKING
PLEASE STOP!!
The operator stopped the ride because we were the only passengers.
OH, THANK GOD!
No ride intimidated me after that.

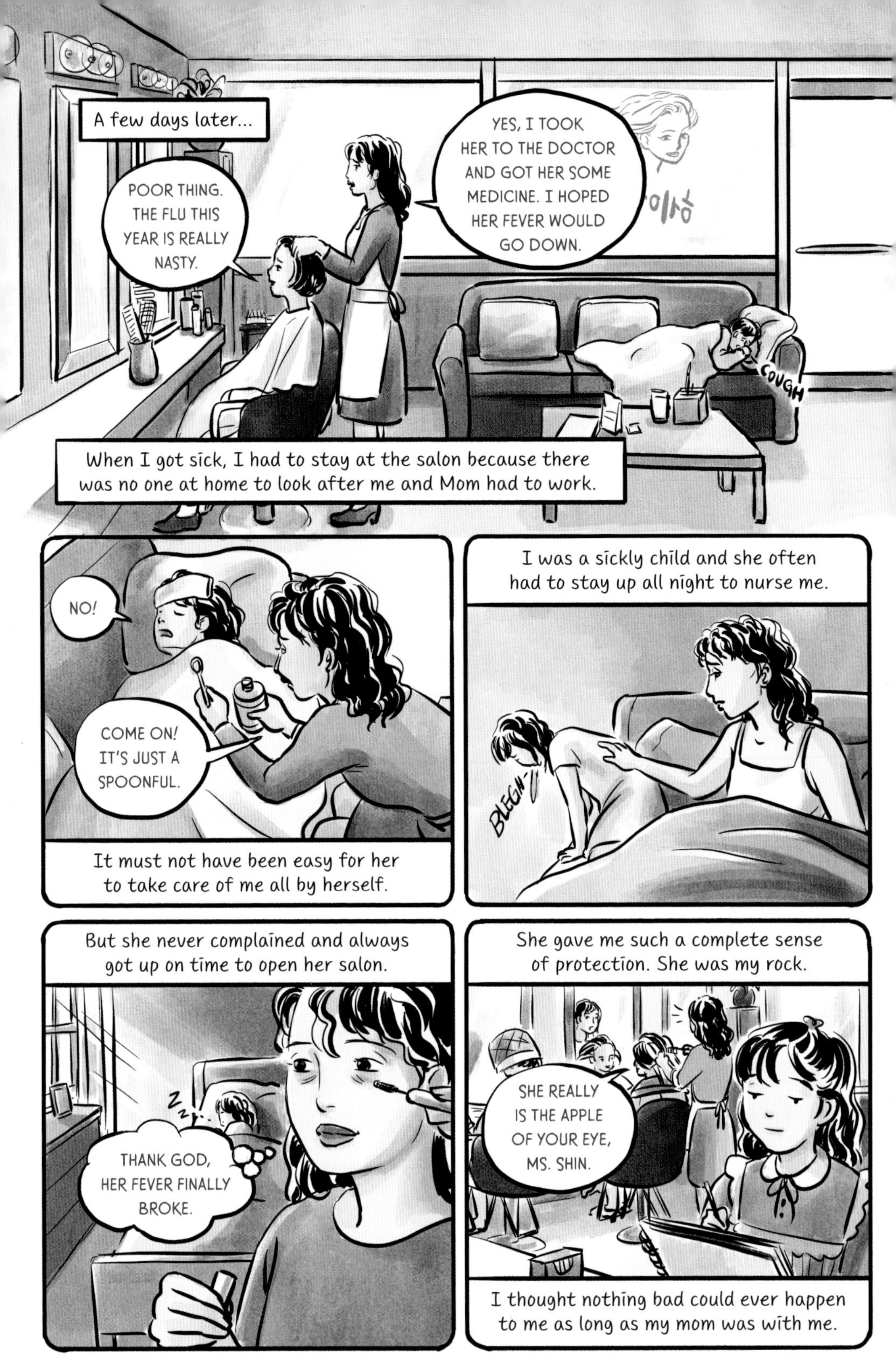
A few days later...
POOR THING. THE FLU THIS YEAR IS REALLY NASTY.
YES, I TOOK HER TO THE DOCTOR AND GOT HER SOME MEDICINE. I HOPED HER FEVER WOULD GO DOWN.
COUGH
When I got sick, I had to stay at the salon because there was no one at home to look after me and Mom had to work.
NO!
COME ON! IT'S JUST A SPOONFUL.
It must not have been easy for her to take care of me all by herself.
I was a sickly child and she often had to stay up all night to nurse me.
BLEGH-
But she never complained and always got up on time to open her salon.
Z Z Z
THANK GOD, HER FEVER FINALLY BROKE.
She gave me such a complete sense of protection. She was my rock.
SHE REALLY IS THE APPLE OF YOUR EYE, MS. SHIN.
I thought nothing bad could ever happen to me as long as my mom was with me.

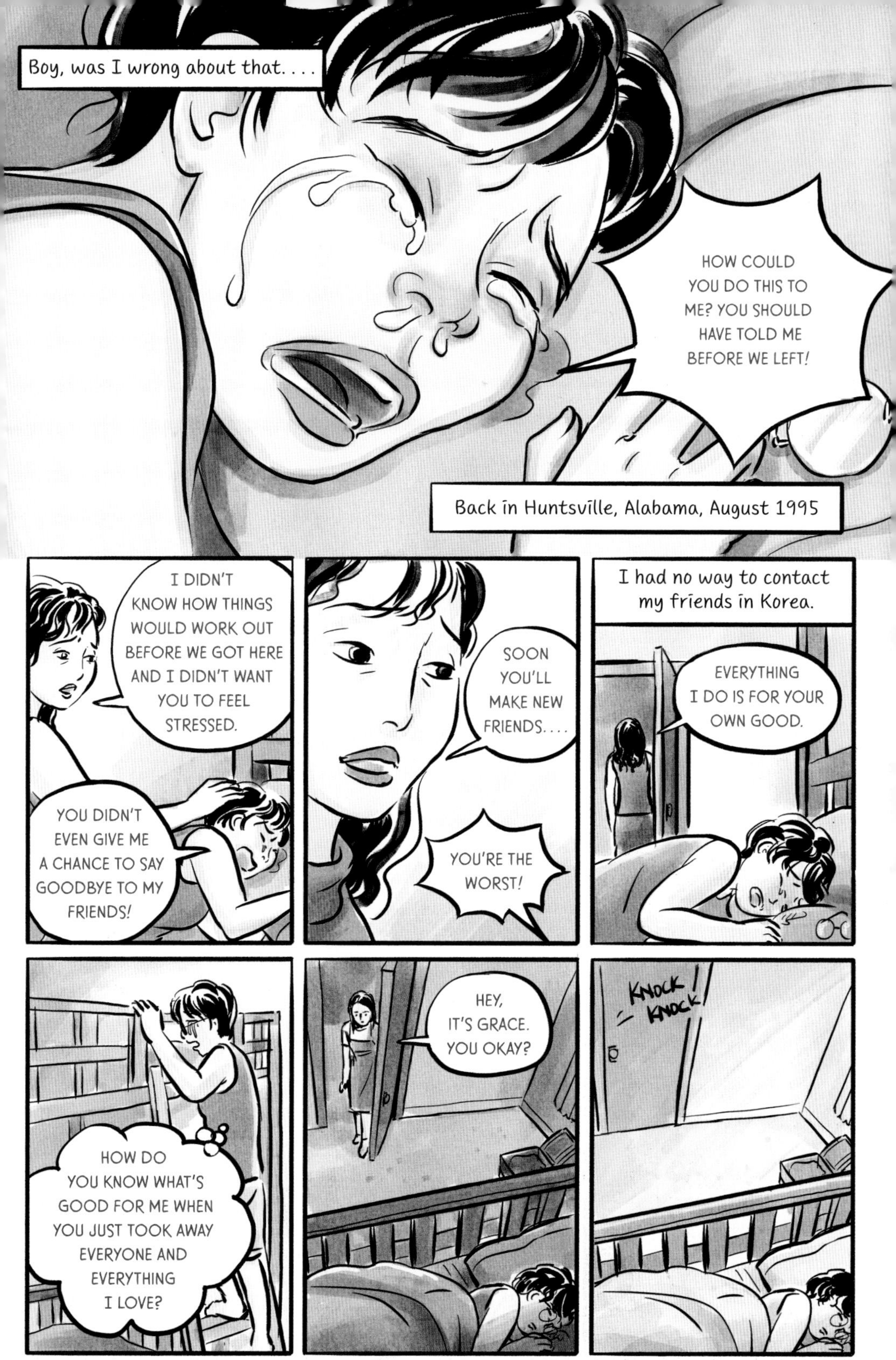

Boy, was I wrong about that. . . .
HOW COULD YOU DO THIS TO ME? YOU SHOULD HAVE TOLD ME BEFORE WE LEFT!
Back in Huntsville, Alabama, August 1995
I DIDN'T KNOW HOW THINGS WOULD WORK OUT BEFORE WE GOT HERE AND I DIDN'T WANT YOU TO FEEL STRESSED.
YOU DIDN'T EVEN GIVE ME A CHANCE TO SAY GOODBYE TO MY FRIENDS!
SOON YOU'LL MAKE NEW FRIENDS. . . .
YOU'RE THE WORST!
I had no way to contact my friends in Korea.
EVERYTHING I DO IS FOR YOUR OWN GOOD.
HOW DO YOU KNOW WHAT'S GOOD FOR ME WHEN YOU JUST TOOK AWAY EVERYONE AND EVERYTHING I LOVE?
HEY, IT'S GRACE. YOU OKAY?
KNOCK KNOCK

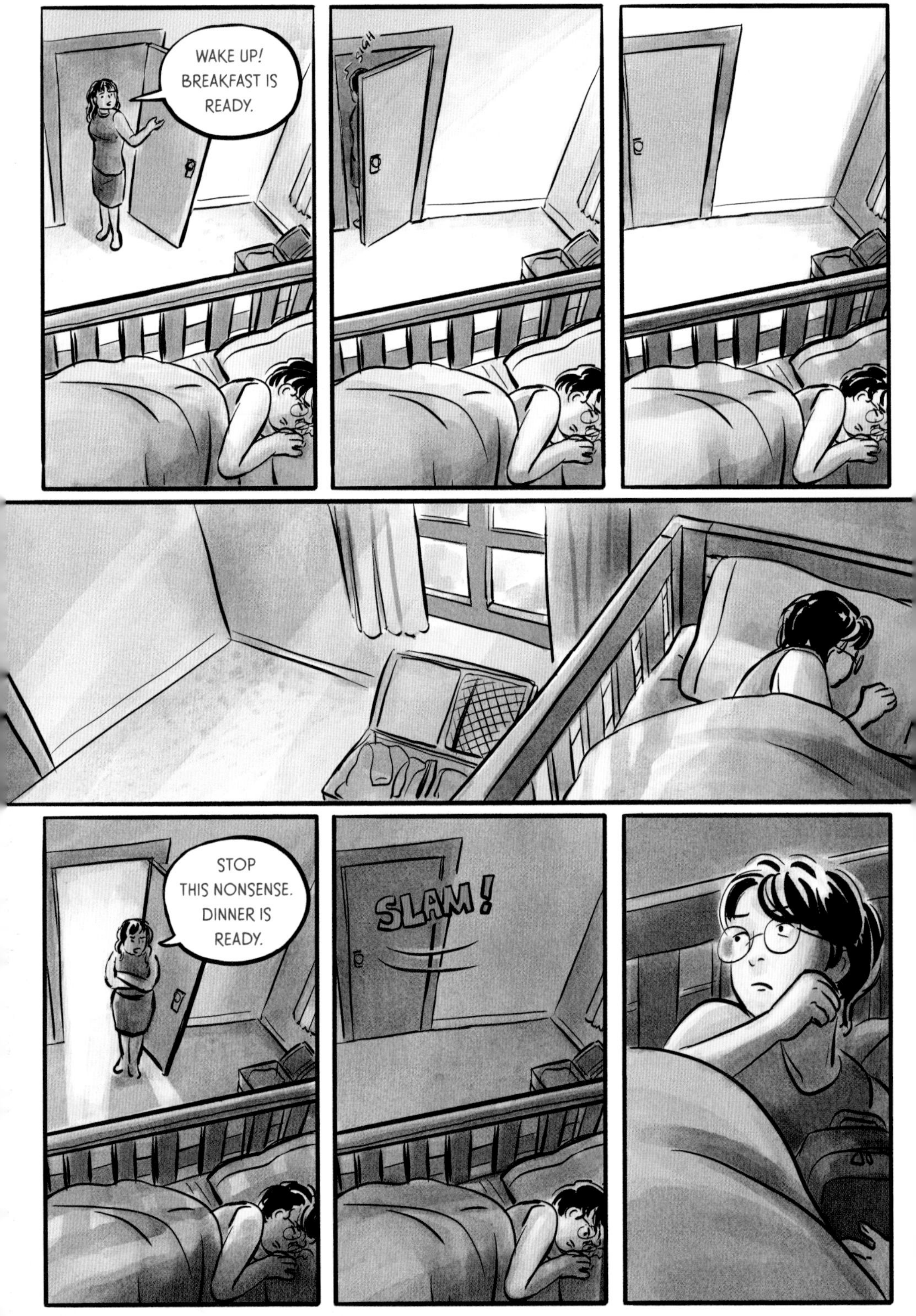
WAKE UP! BREAKFAST IS READY.
S-SIGH
STOP THIS NONSENSE. DINNER IS READY.
SLAM!

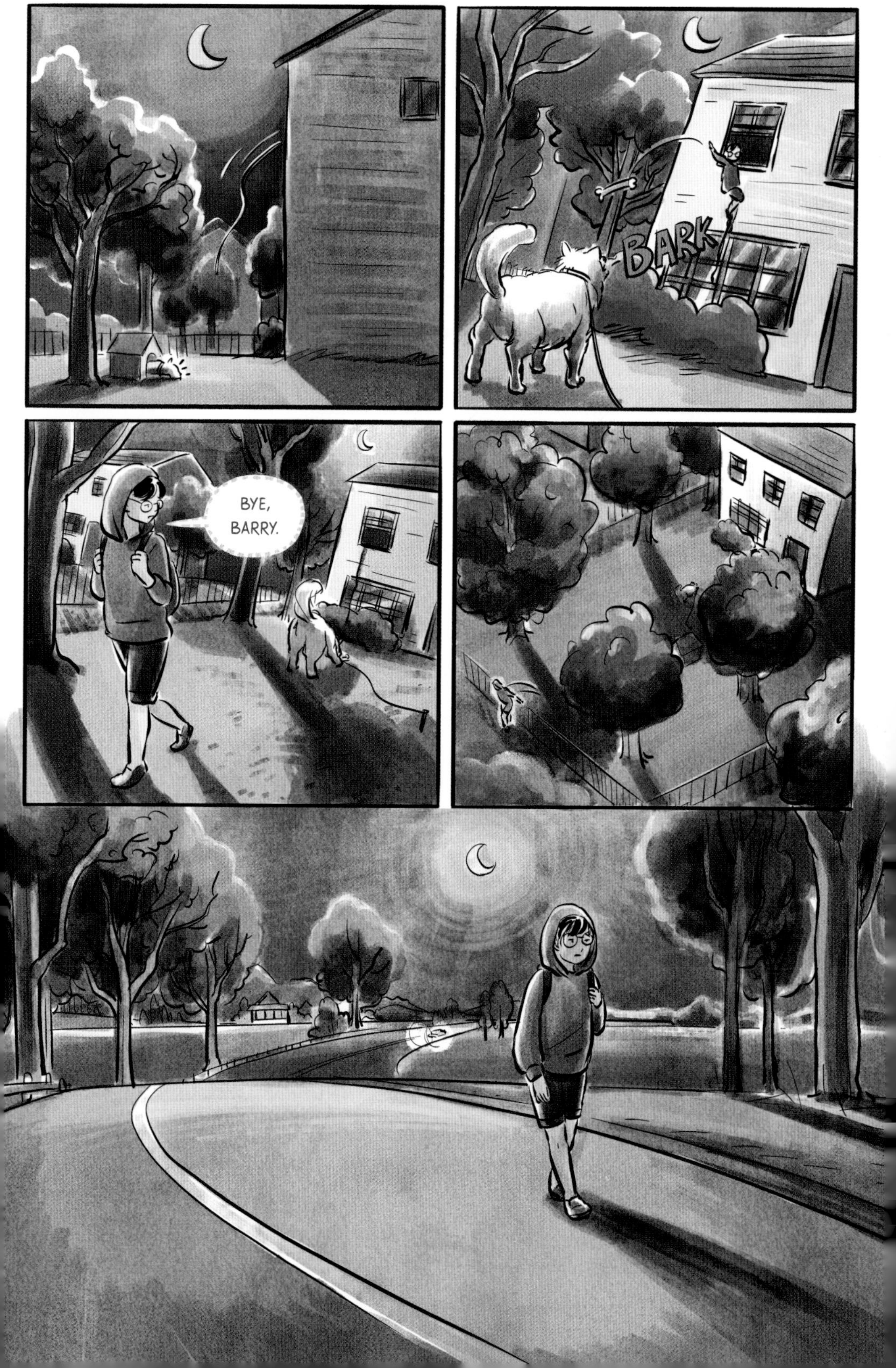
BARK
BYE, BARRY.

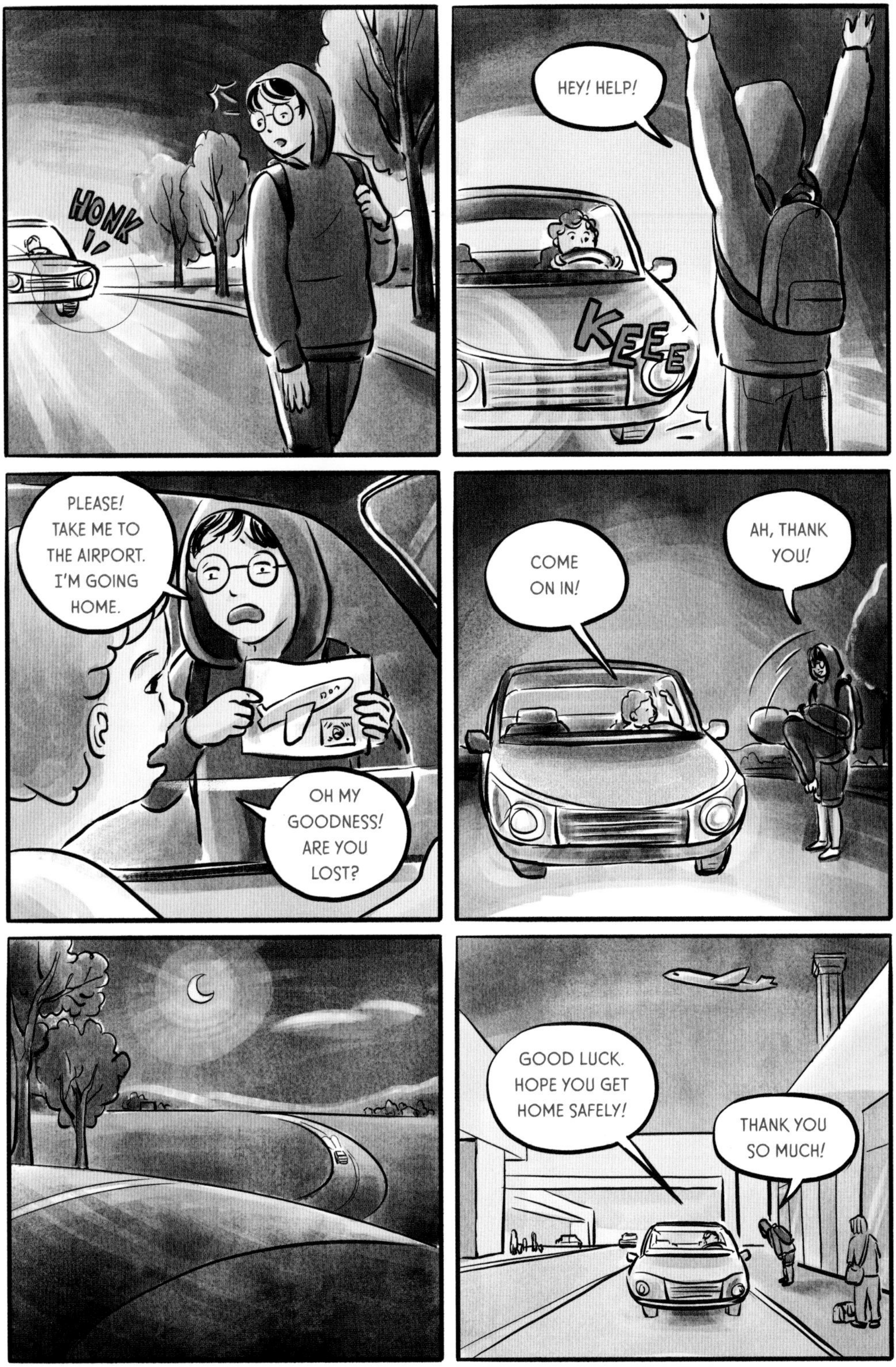
HONK
HEY! HELP!
KEEE
PLEASE! TAKE ME TO THE AIRPORT. I'M GOING HOME.
OH MY GOODNESS! ARE YOU LOST?
COME ON IN!
AH, THANK YOU!
GOOD LUCK. HOPE YOU GET HOME SAFELY!
THANK YOU SO MUCH!

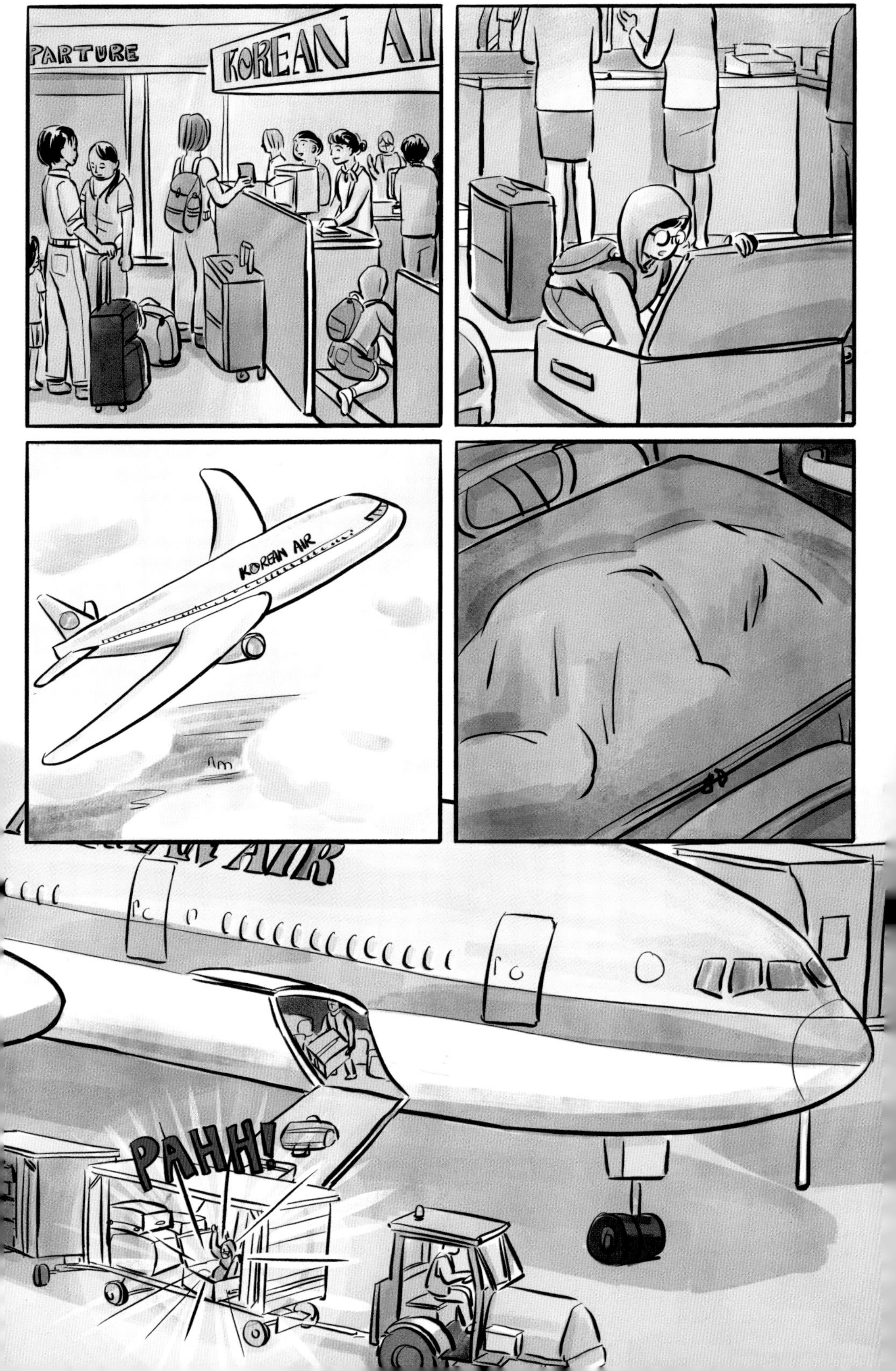
PARTURE
KOREAN AI
KOREAN AIR
PAHH!

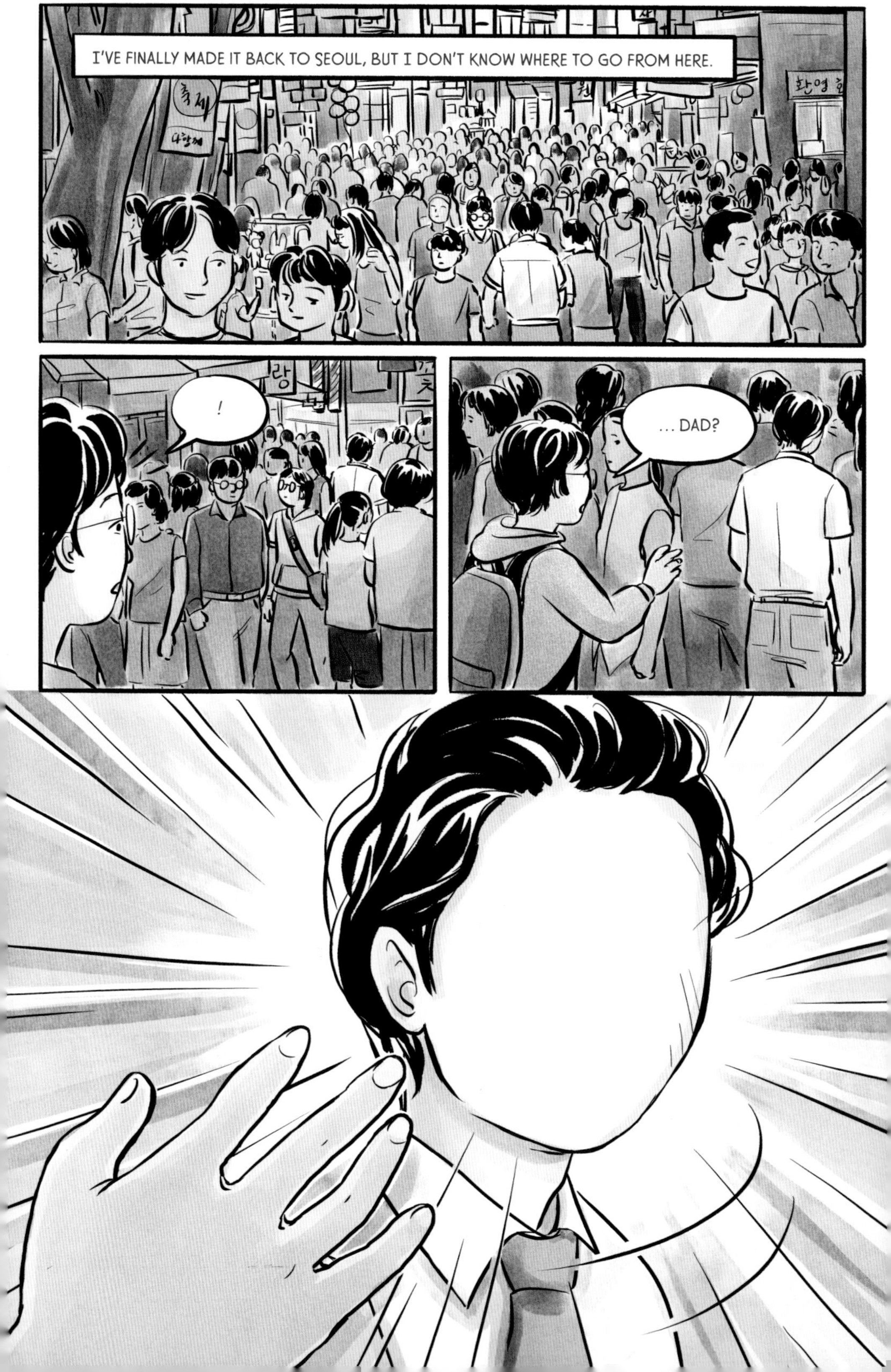
I'VE FINALLY MADE IT BACK TO SEOUL, BUT I DON'T KNOW WHERE TO GO FROM HERE.
!
... DAD?

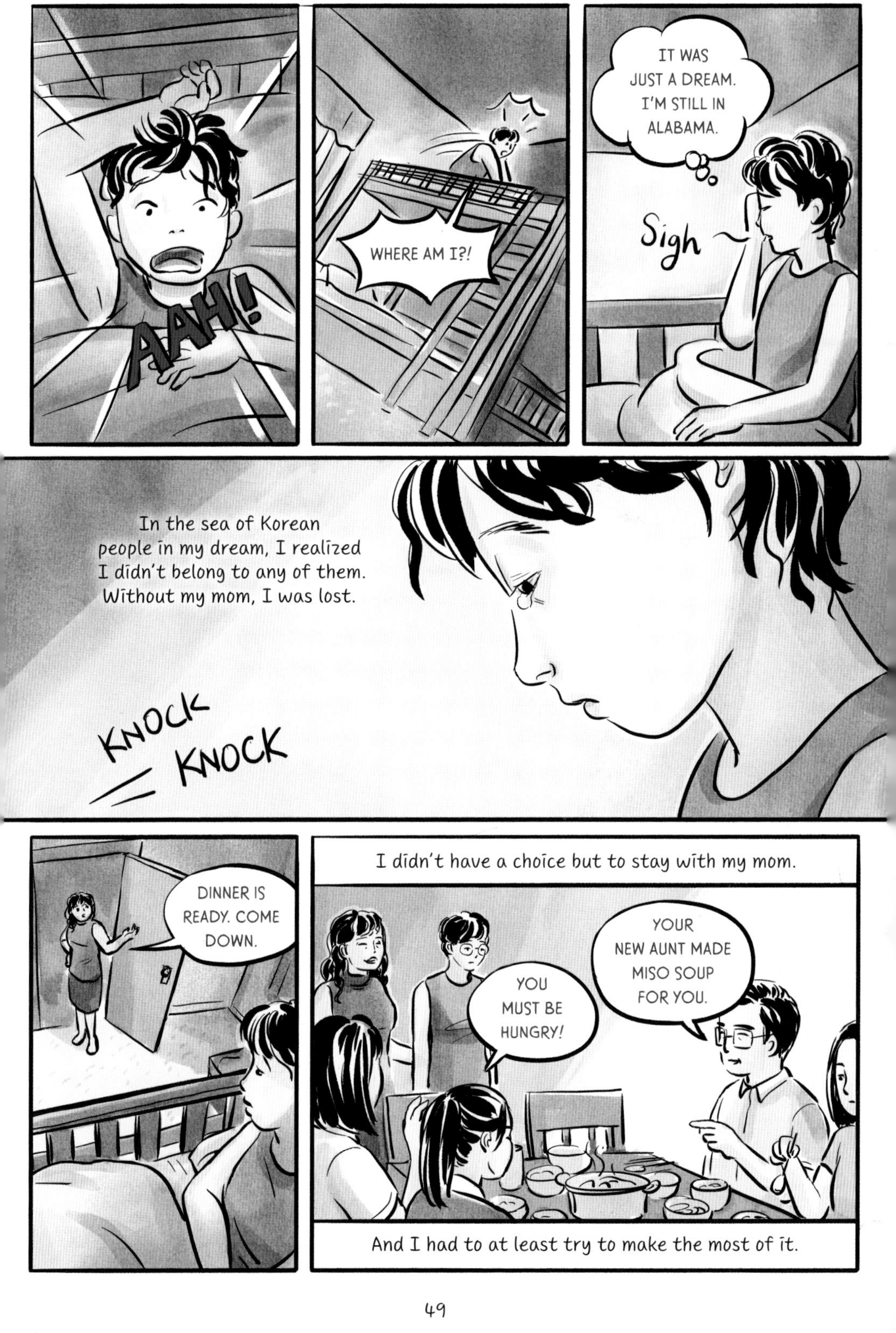
AAH!
WHERE AM I?!
IT WAS JUST A DREAM. I'M STILL IN ALABAMA.
Sigh
In the sea of Korean people in my dream, I realized I didn't belong to any of them. Without my mom, I was lost.
KNOCK KNOCK
DINNER IS READY. COME DOWN.
I didn't have a choice but to stay with my mom.
YOU MUST BE HUNGRY!
YOUR NEW AUNT MADE MISO SOUP FOR YOU.
And I had to at least try to make the most of it.

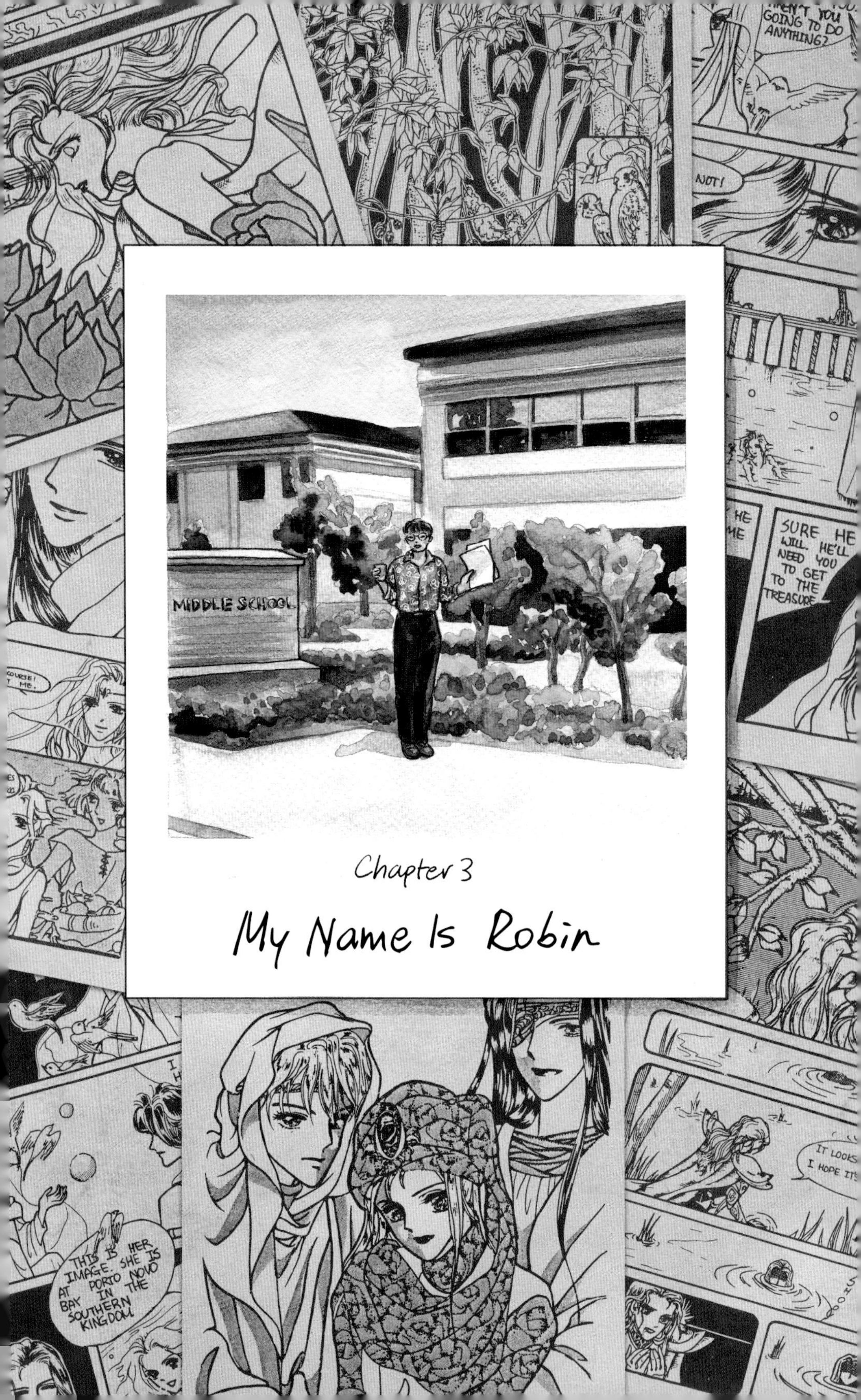
GOING TO DO ANYTHING?
NOT!
SURE HE WILL. HE'LL NEED YOU TO GET TO THE TREASURE
MIDDLE SCHOOL
THIS IS HER IMAGE. SHE IS AT PORTO NOVO BAY IN THE SOUTHERN KINGDOM
IT LOOKS

Chapter 3

My Name Is Robin

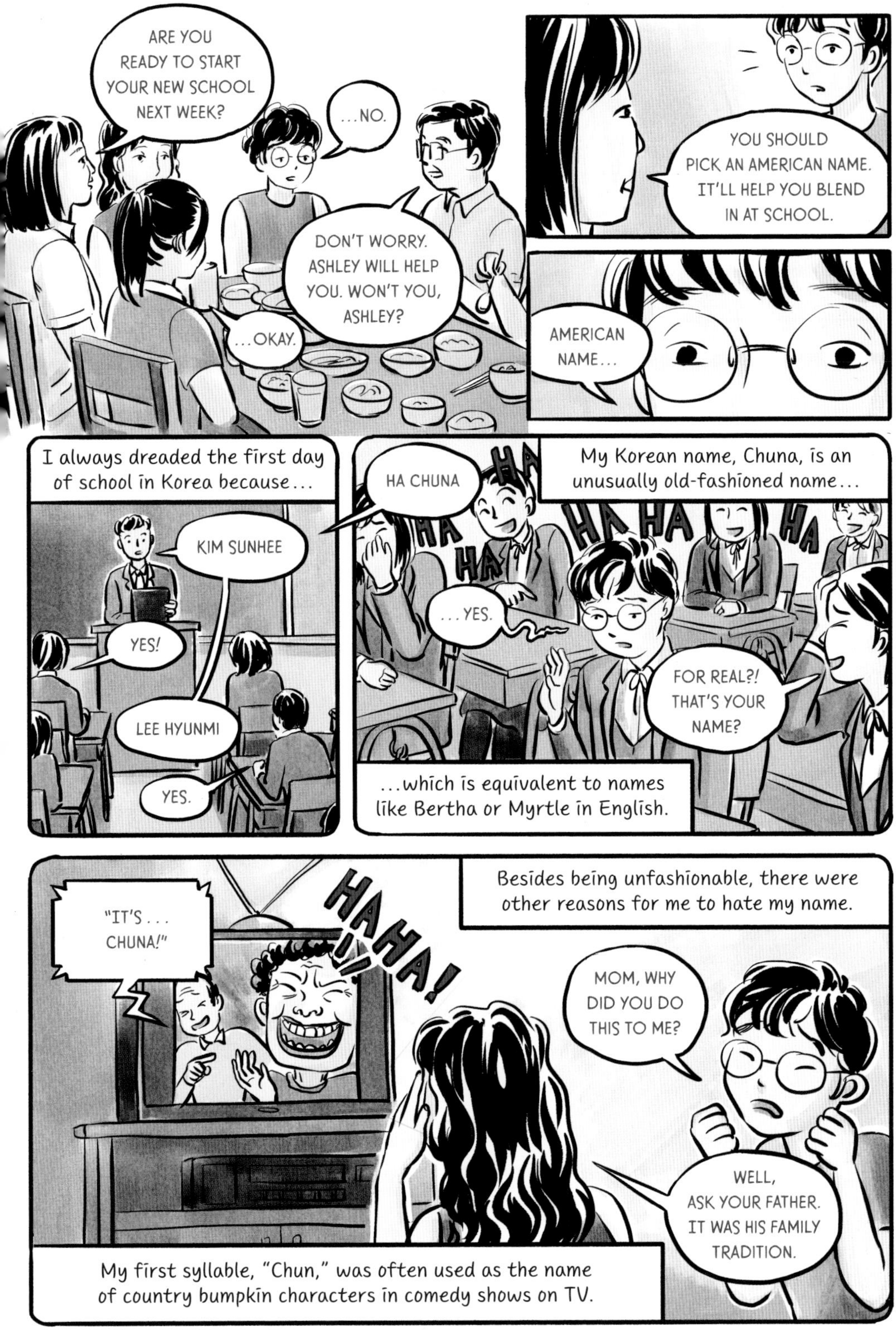
ARE YOU READY TO START YOUR NEW SCHOOL NEXT WEEK?
...NO.
DON'T WORRY. ASHLEY WILL HELP YOU. WON'T YOU, ASHLEY?
...OKAY.
YOU SHOULD PICK AN AMERICAN NAME. IT'LL HELP YOU BLEND IN AT SCHOOL.
AMERICAN NAME...
I always dreaded the first day of school in Korea because...
KIM SUNHEE
YES!
LEE HYUNMI
YES.
HA CHUNA
My Korean name, Chuna, is an unusually old-fashioned name...
HA
HA HA HA
HA
HA
HA
...YES.
FOR REAL?! THAT'S YOUR NAME?
...which is equivalent to names like Bertha or Myrtle in English.
Besides being unfashionable, there were other reasons for me to hate my name.
"IT'S . . . CHUNA!"
HAHAHA!
MOM, WHY DID YOU DO THIS TO ME?
WELL, ASK YOUR FATHER. IT WAS HIS FAMILY TRADITION.
My first syllable, "Chun," was often used as the name of country bumpkin characters in comedy shows on TV.

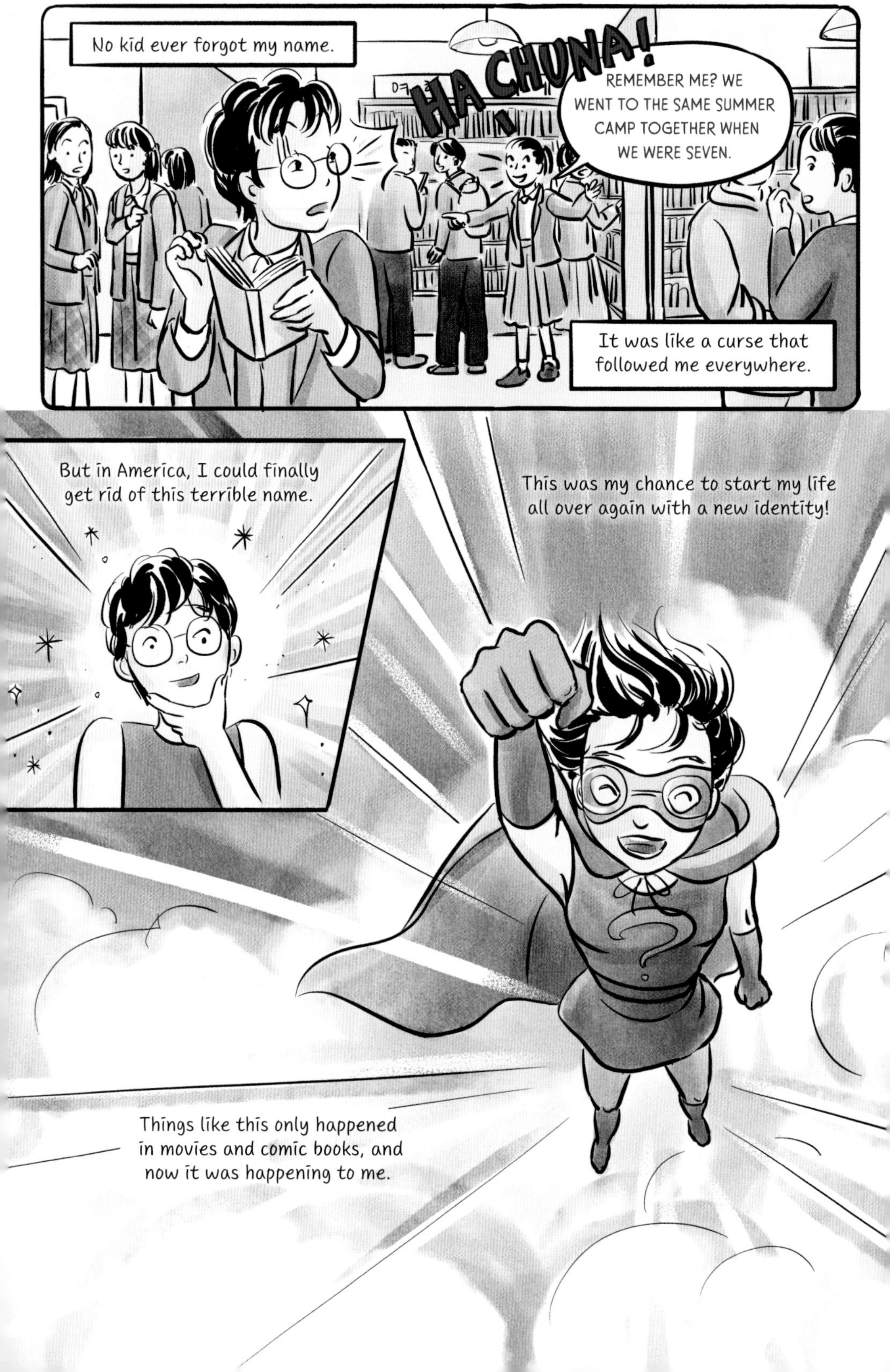
No kid ever forgot my name.
HA CHUNA!
REMEMBER ME? WE WENT TO THE SAME SUMMER CAMP TOGETHER WHEN WE WERE SEVEN.
It was like a curse that followed me everywhere.
But in America, I could finally get rid of this terrible name.
This was my chance to start my life all over again with a new identity!
Things like this only happened in movies and comic books, and now it was happening to me.

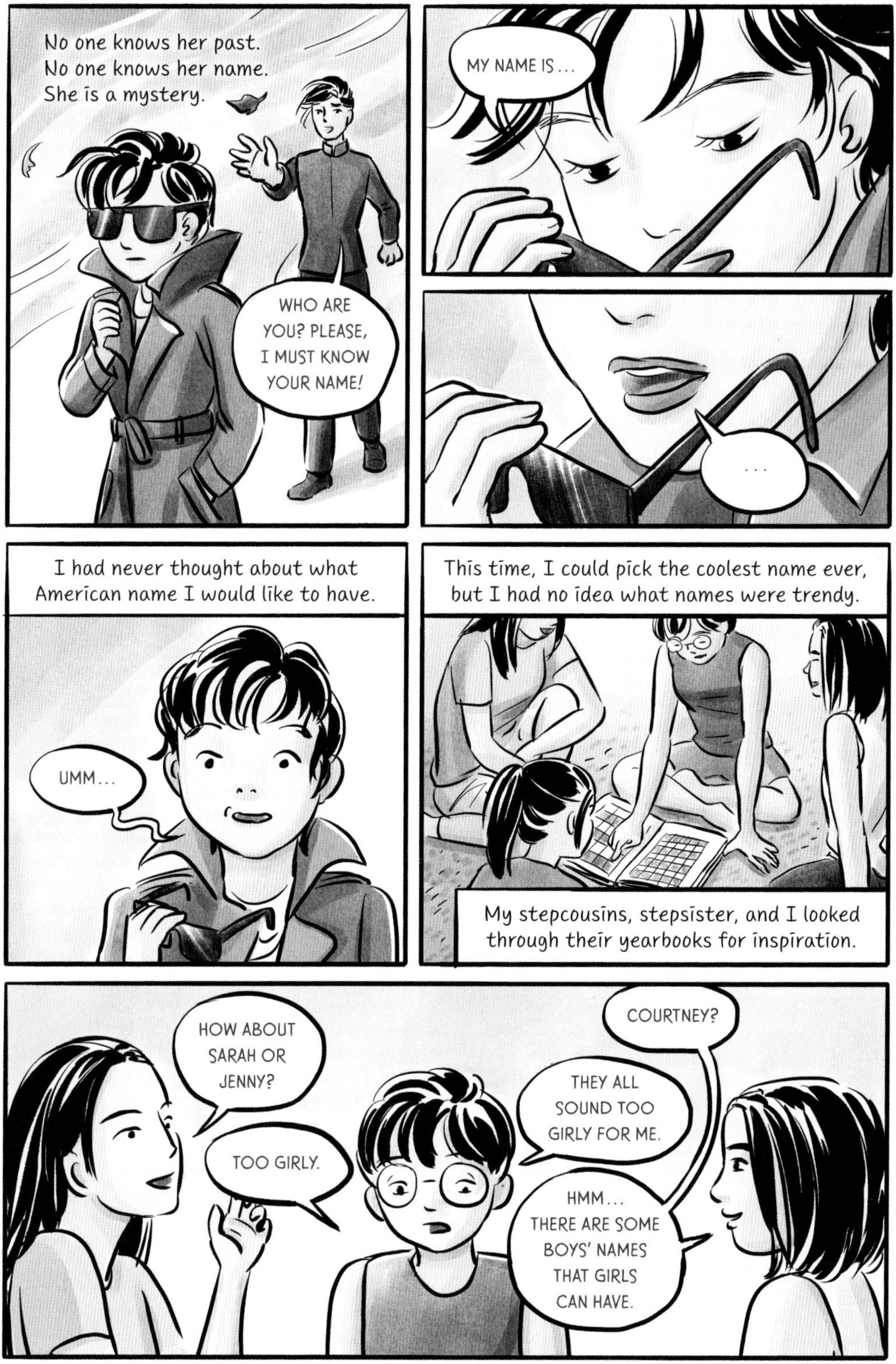
No one knows her past. No one knows her name. She is a mystery.
WHO ARE YOU? PLEASE, I MUST KNOW YOUR NAME!
MY NAME IS . . .
. . .
I had never thought about what American name I would like to have.
UMM . . .
This time, I could pick the coolest name ever, but I had no idea what names were trendy.
My stepcousins, stepsister, and I looked through their yearbooks for inspiration.
HOW ABOUT SARAH OR JENNY?
TOO GIRLY.
COURTNEY?
THEY ALL SOUND TOO GIRLY FOR ME.
HMM . . . THERE ARE SOME BOYS' NAMES THAT GIRLS CAN HAVE.

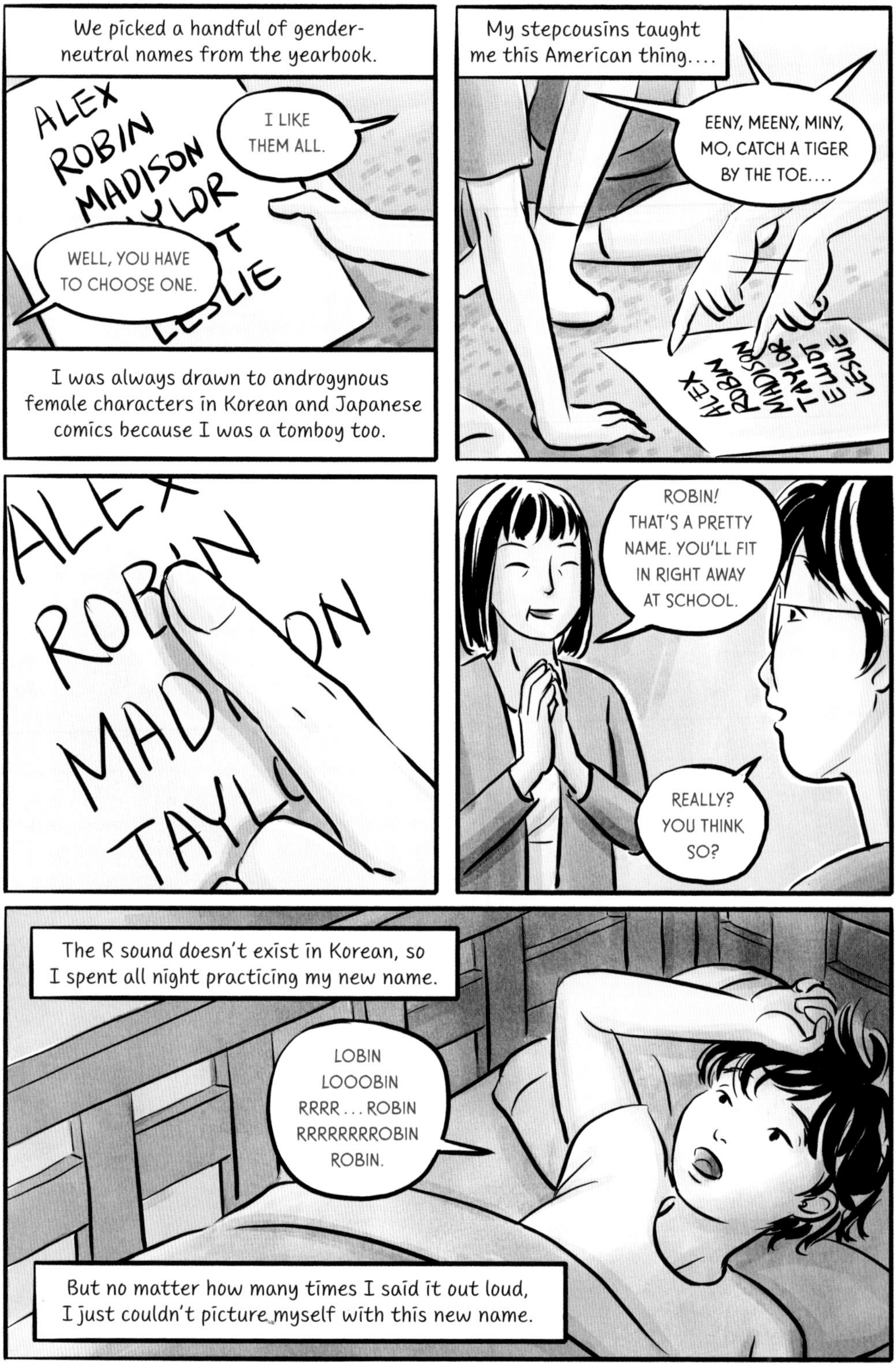
We picked a handful of gender-neutral names from the yearbook.
I LIKE THEM ALL.
WELL, YOU HAVE TO CHOOSE ONE.
I was always drawn to androgynous female characters in Korean and Japanese comics because I was a tomboy too.
My stepcousins taught me this American thing....
EENY, MEENY, MINY, MO, CATCH A TIGER BY THE TOE....
ROBIN! THAT'S A PRETTY NAME. YOU'LL FIT IN RIGHT AWAY AT SCHOOL.
REALLY? YOU THINK SO?
The R sound doesn't exist in Korean, so I spent all night practicing my new name.
LOBIN
LOOOBIN
RRRR... ROBIN
RRRRRRRROBIN
ROBIN.
But no matter how many times I said it out loud, I just couldn't picture myself with this new name.

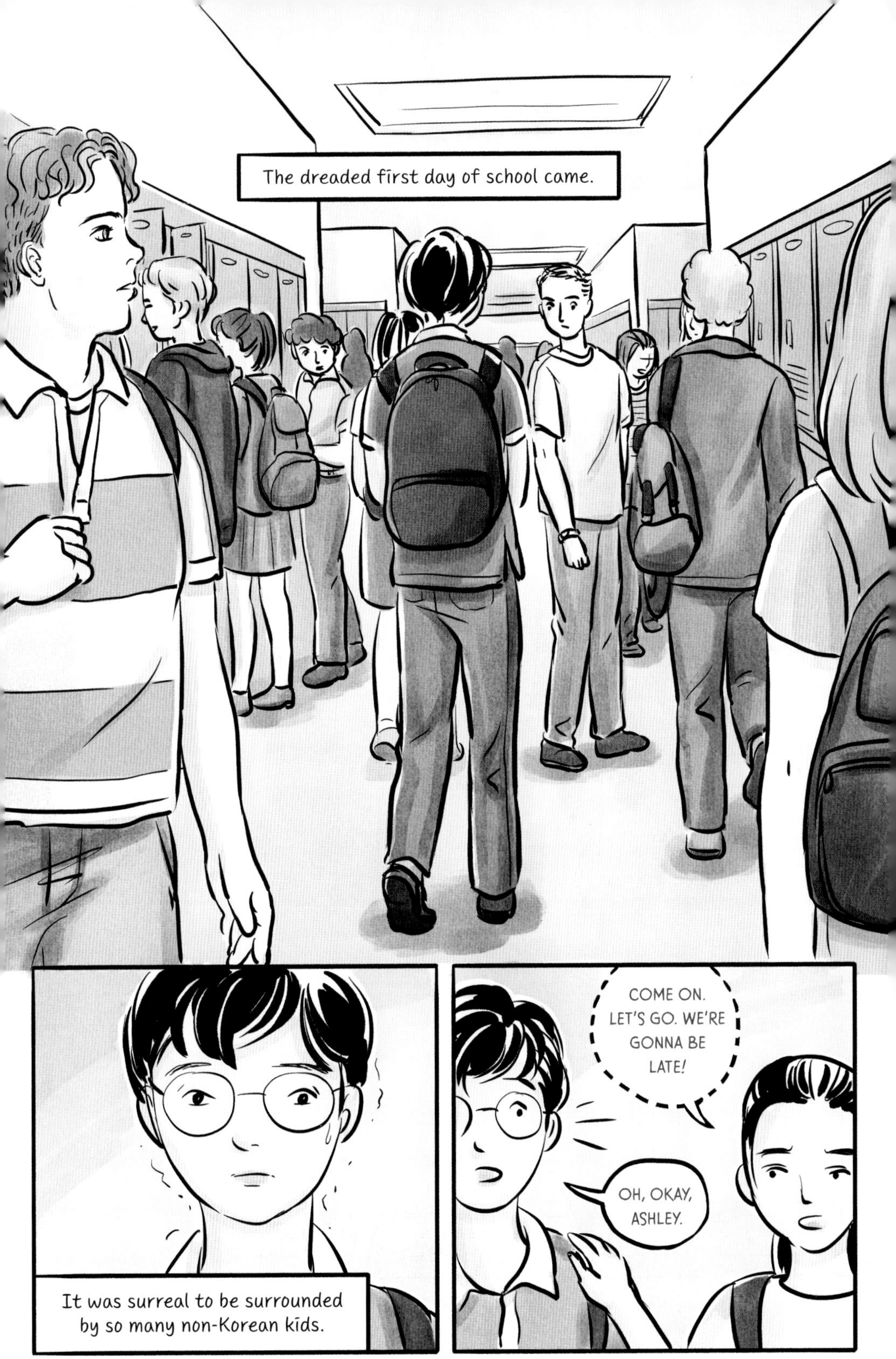
The dreaded first day of school came.
It was surreal to be surrounded by so many non-Korean kids.
COME ON. LET'S GO. WE'RE GONNA BE LATE!
OH, OKAY, ASHLEY.

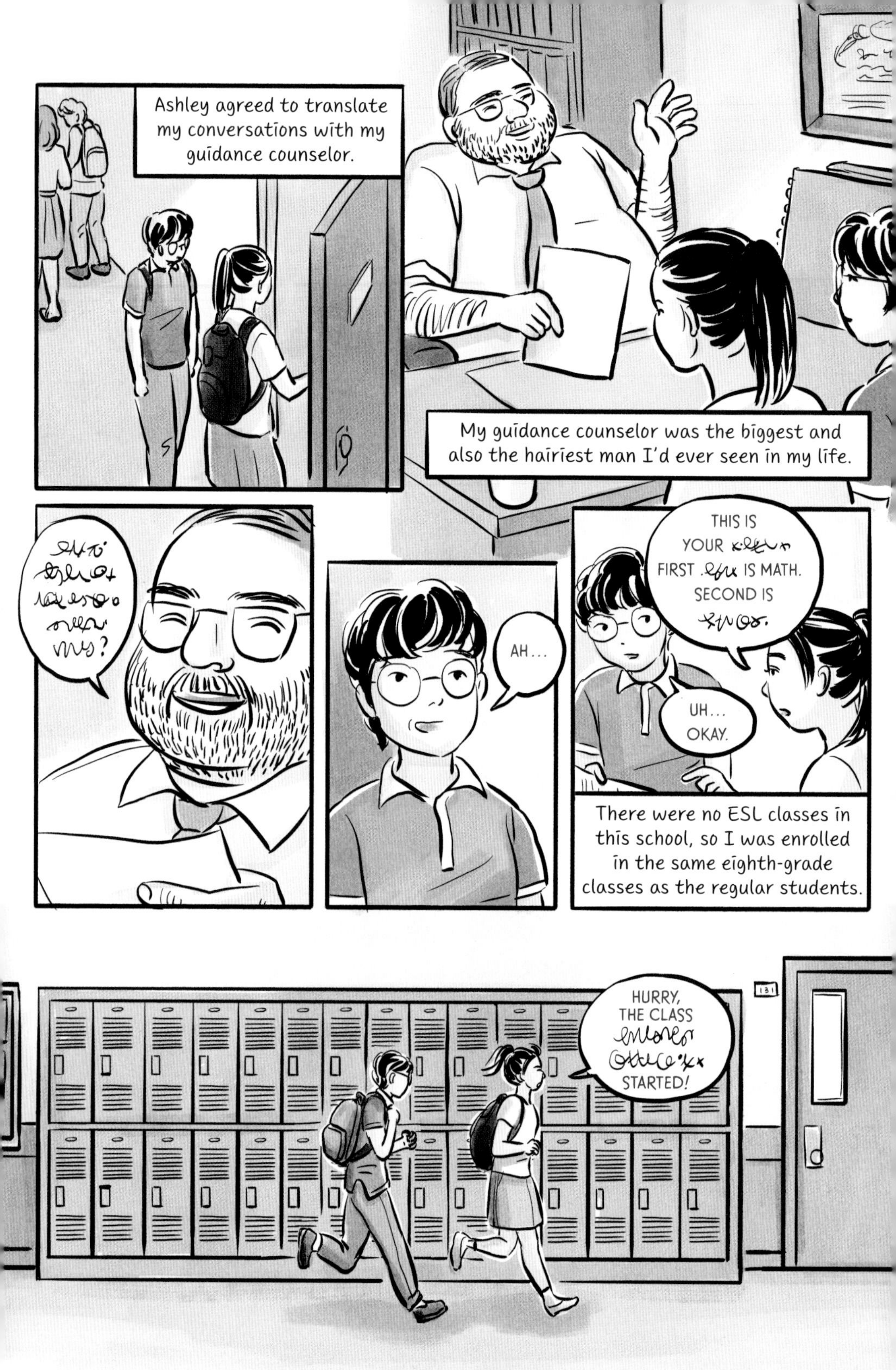

Ashley agreed to translate my conversations with my guidance counselor.
My guidance counselor was the biggest and also the hairiest man I'd ever seen in my life.
AH...
THIS IS YOUR
FIRST
IS MATH.
SECOND IS
UH... OKAY.
There were no ESL classes in this school, so I was enrolled in the same eighth-grade classes as the regular students.
HURRY, THE CLASS
STARTED!

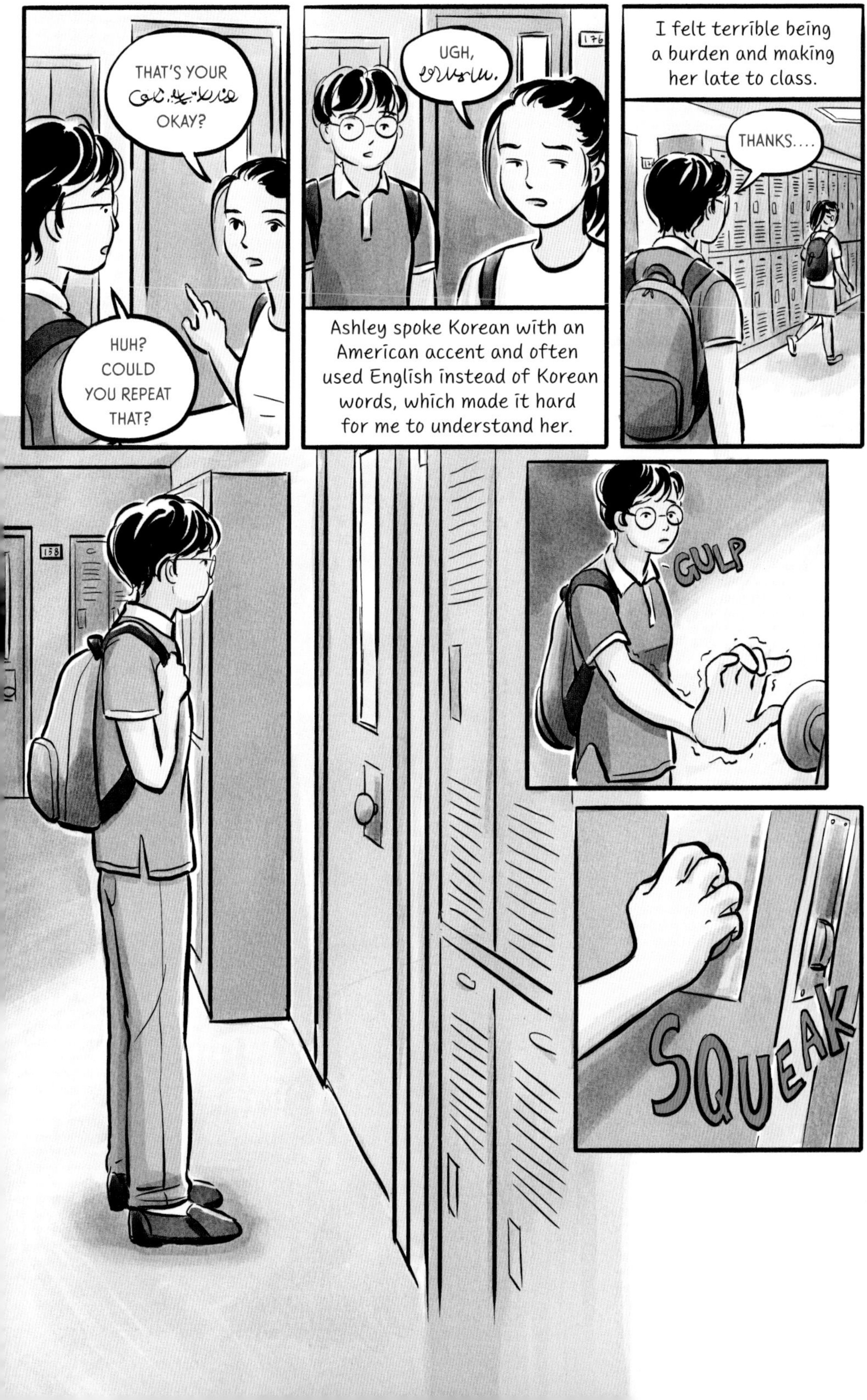
THAT'S YOUR
OKAY?
HUH? COULD YOU REPEAT THAT?
UGH,
Ashley spoke Korean with an American accent and often used English instead of Korean words, which made it hard for me to understand her.
I felt terrible being a burden and making her late to class.
THANKS....
GULP
SQUEAK

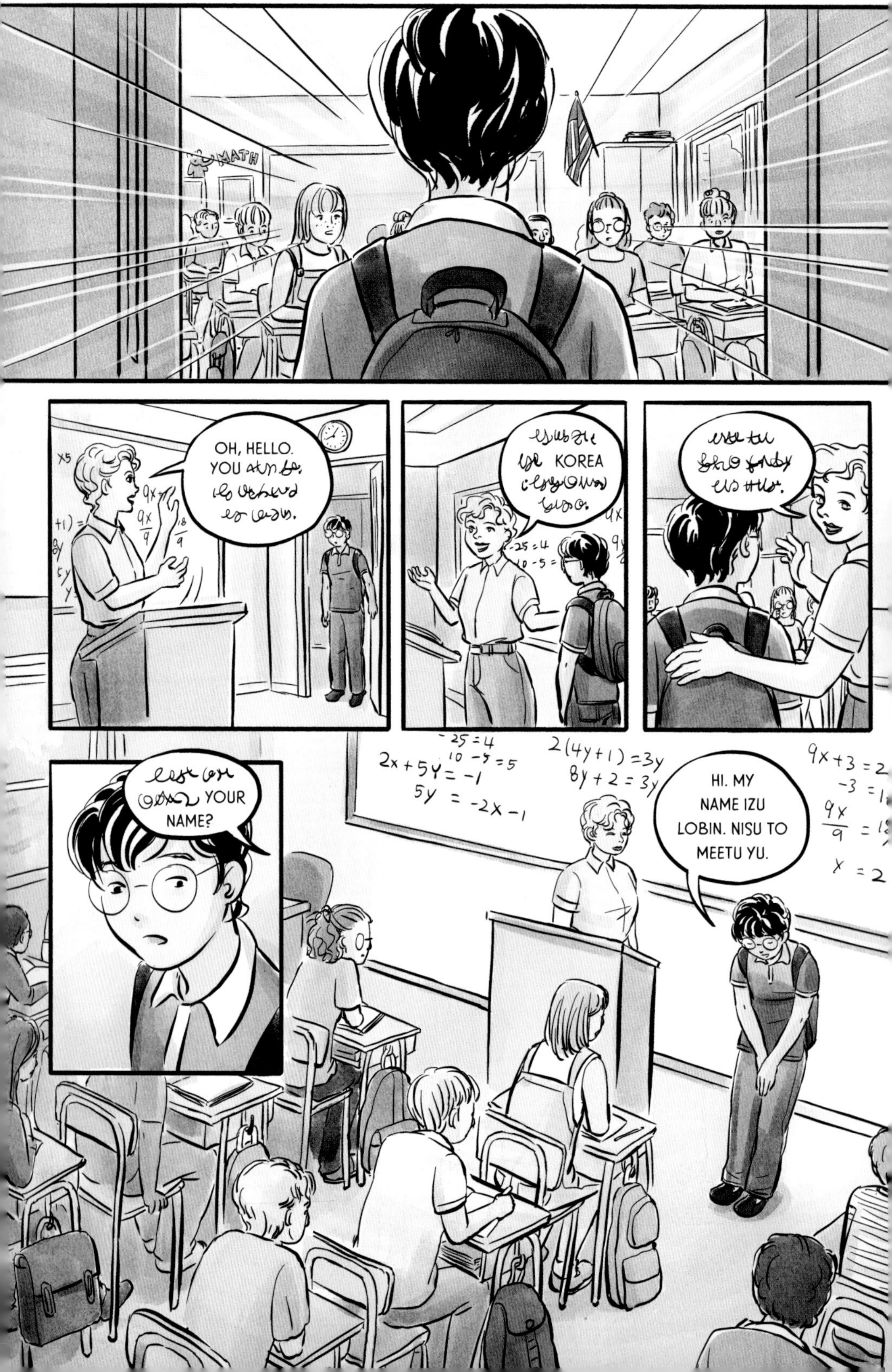
MATH
OH, HELLO. YOU
KOREA
YOUR NAME?
2x + 5y = -1
5y = -2x -1
2(4y+1) = 3y
8y + 2 = 3y
HI. MY NAME IZU LOBIN. NISU TO MEETU YU.

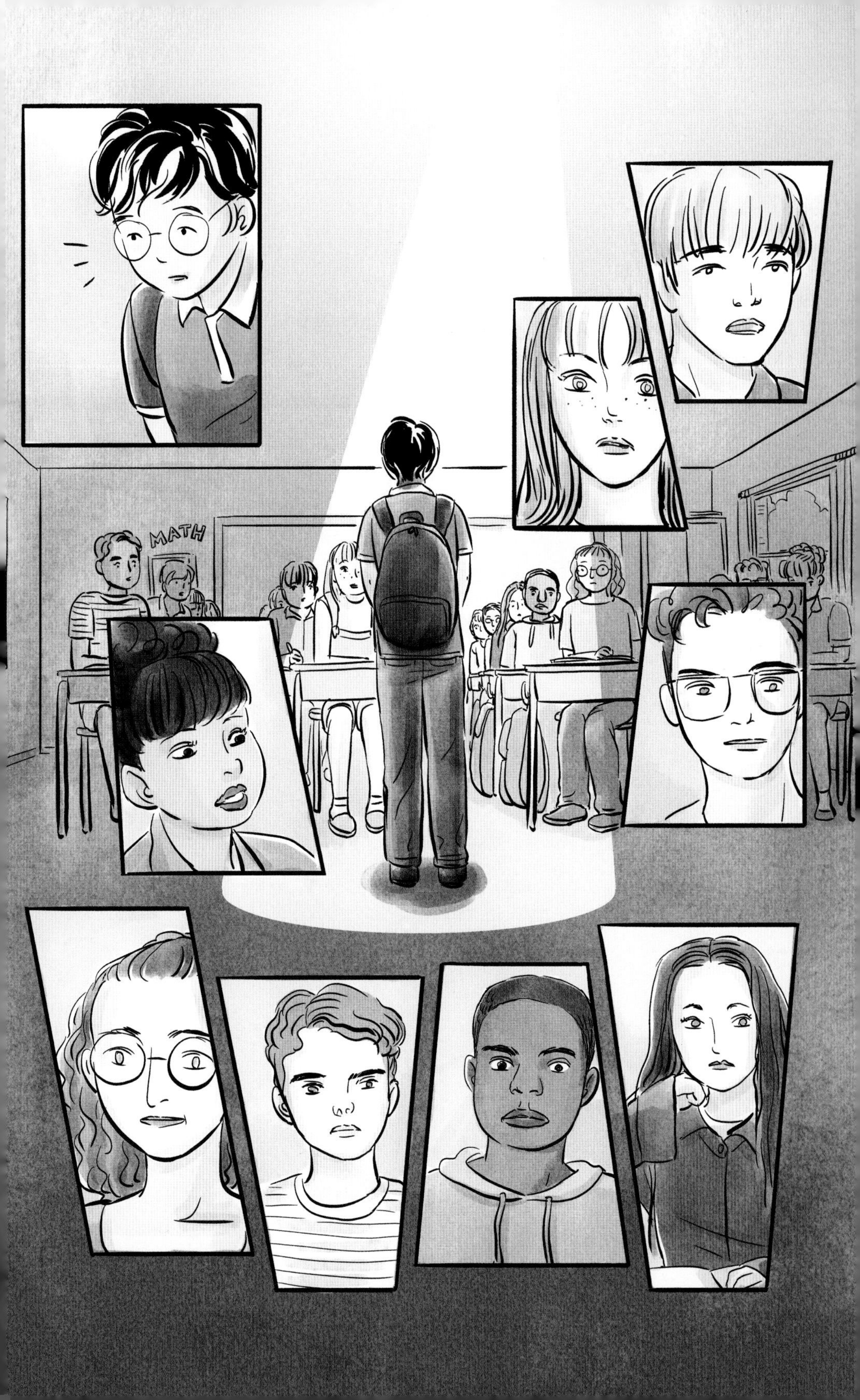
MATH

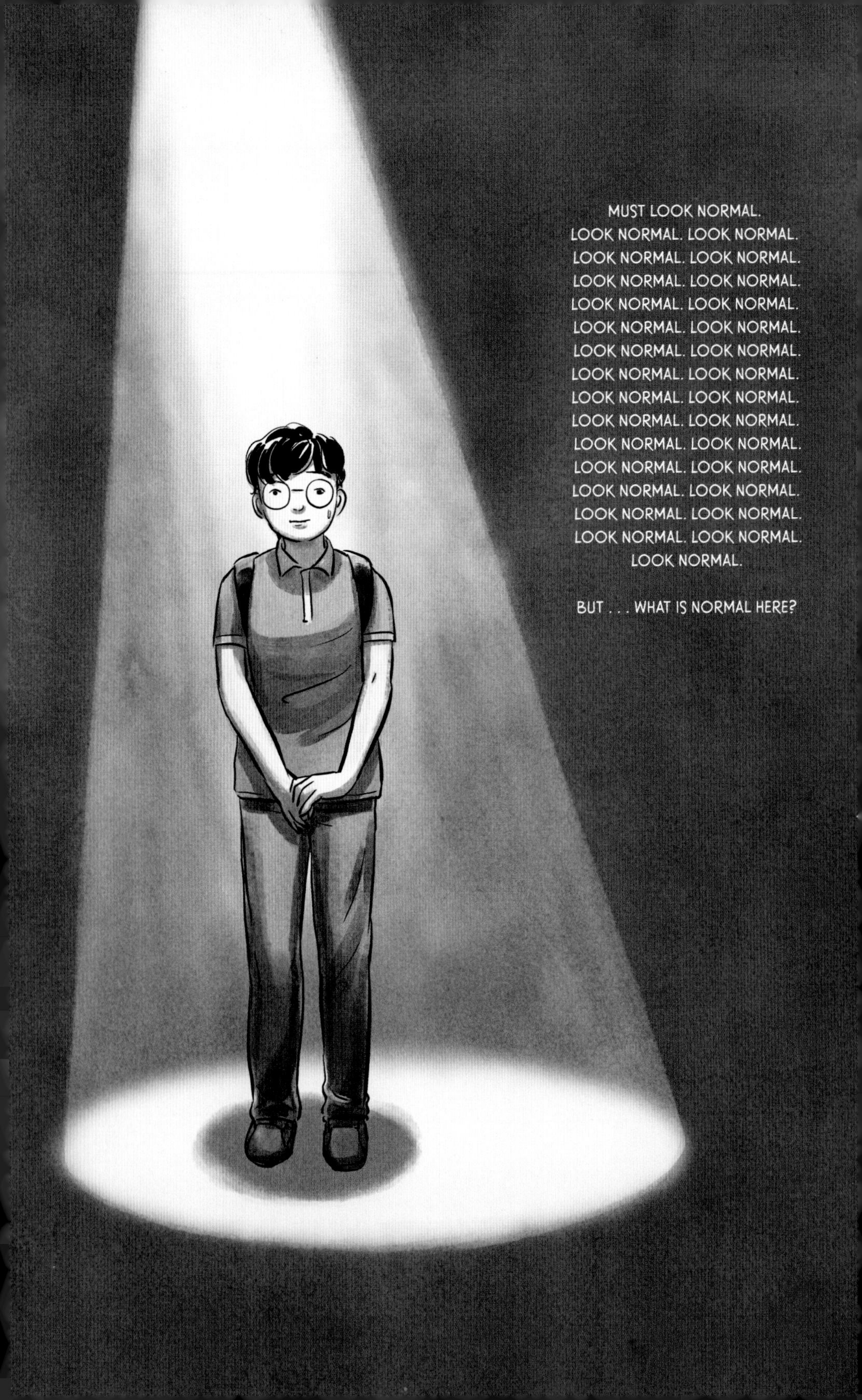
MUST LOOK NORMAL.
LOOK NORMAL. LOOK NORMAL.
LOOK NORMAL. LOOK NORMAL.
LOOK NORMAL. LOOK NORMAL.
LOOK NORMAL. LOOK NORMAL.
LOOK NORMAL. LOOK NORMAL.
LOOK NORMAL. LOOK NORMAL.
LOOK NORMAL. LOOK NORMAL.
LOOK NORMAL. LOOK NORMAL.
LOOK NORMAL. LOOK NORMAL.
LOOK NORMAL. LOOK NORMAL.
LOOK NORMAL. LOOK NORMAL.
LOOK NORMAL. LOOK NORMAL.
LOOK NORMAL. LOOK NORMAL.
LOOK NORMAL. LOOK NORMAL.
LOOK NORMAL.
BUT . . . WHAT IS NORMAL HERE?

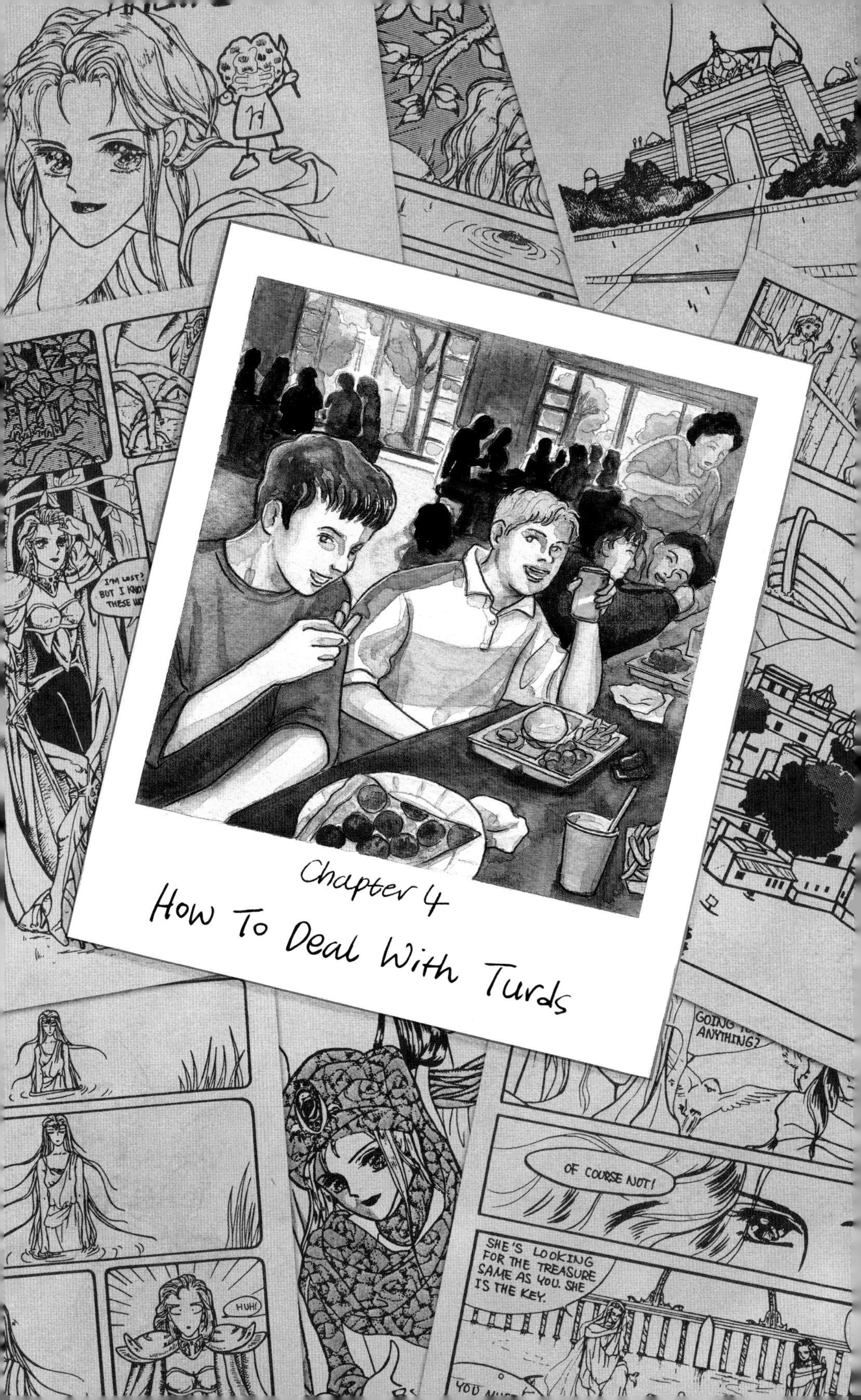
OF COURSE NOT!
SHE'S LOOKING FOR THE TREASURE SAME AS YOU. SHE IS THE KEY.
HUH!

Chapter 4

How To Deal With Turds

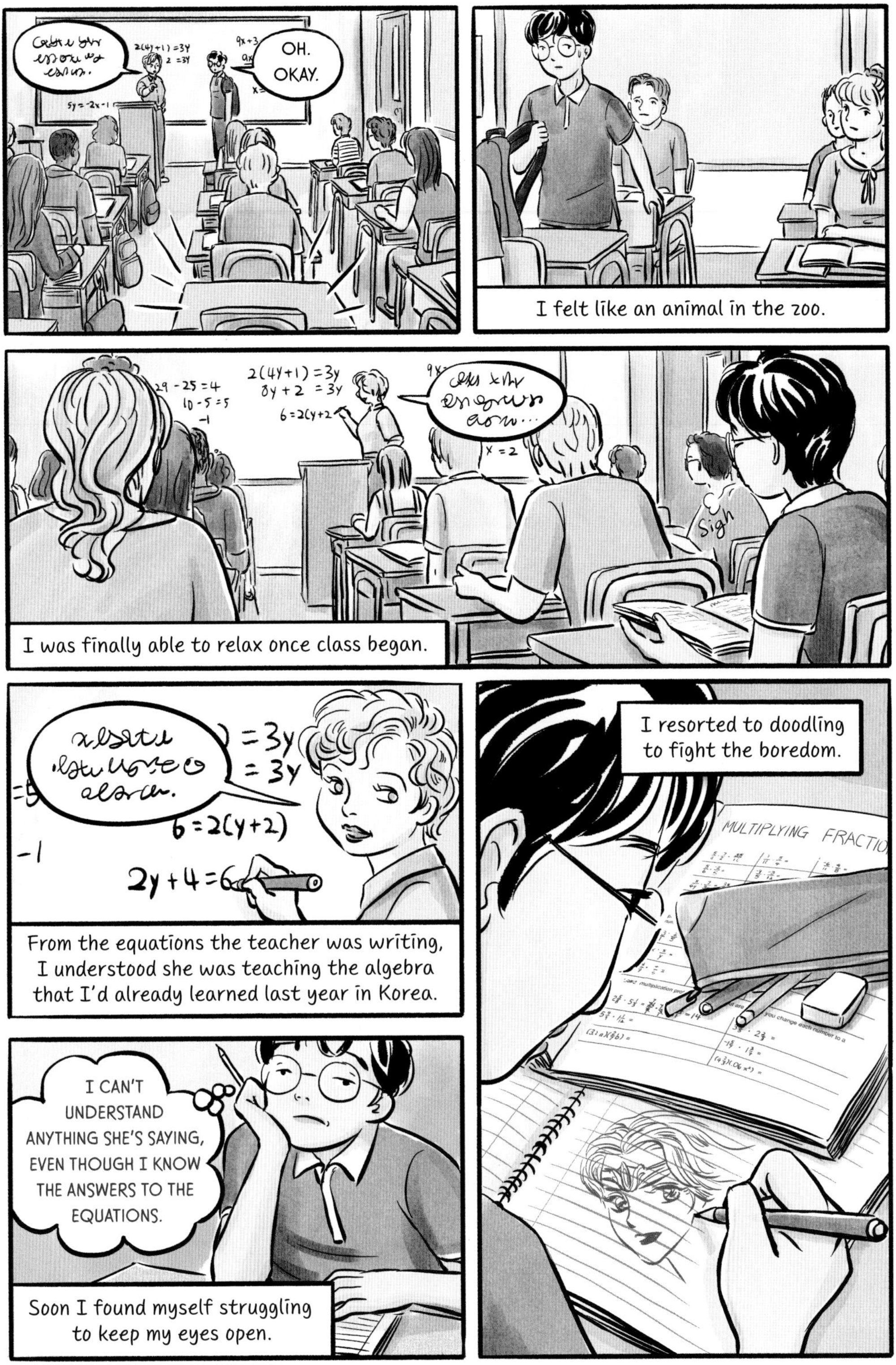
OH. OKAY.
I felt like an animal in the zoo.
I was finally able to relax once class began.
Sigh
From the equations the teacher was writing, I understood she was teaching the algebra that I'd already learned last year in Korea.
I CAN'T UNDERSTAND ANYTHING SHE'S SAYING, EVEN THOUGH I KNOW THE ANSWERS TO THE EQUATIONS.
Soon I found myself struggling to keep my eyes open.
I resorted to doodling to fight the boredom.
MULTIPLYING FRACTI

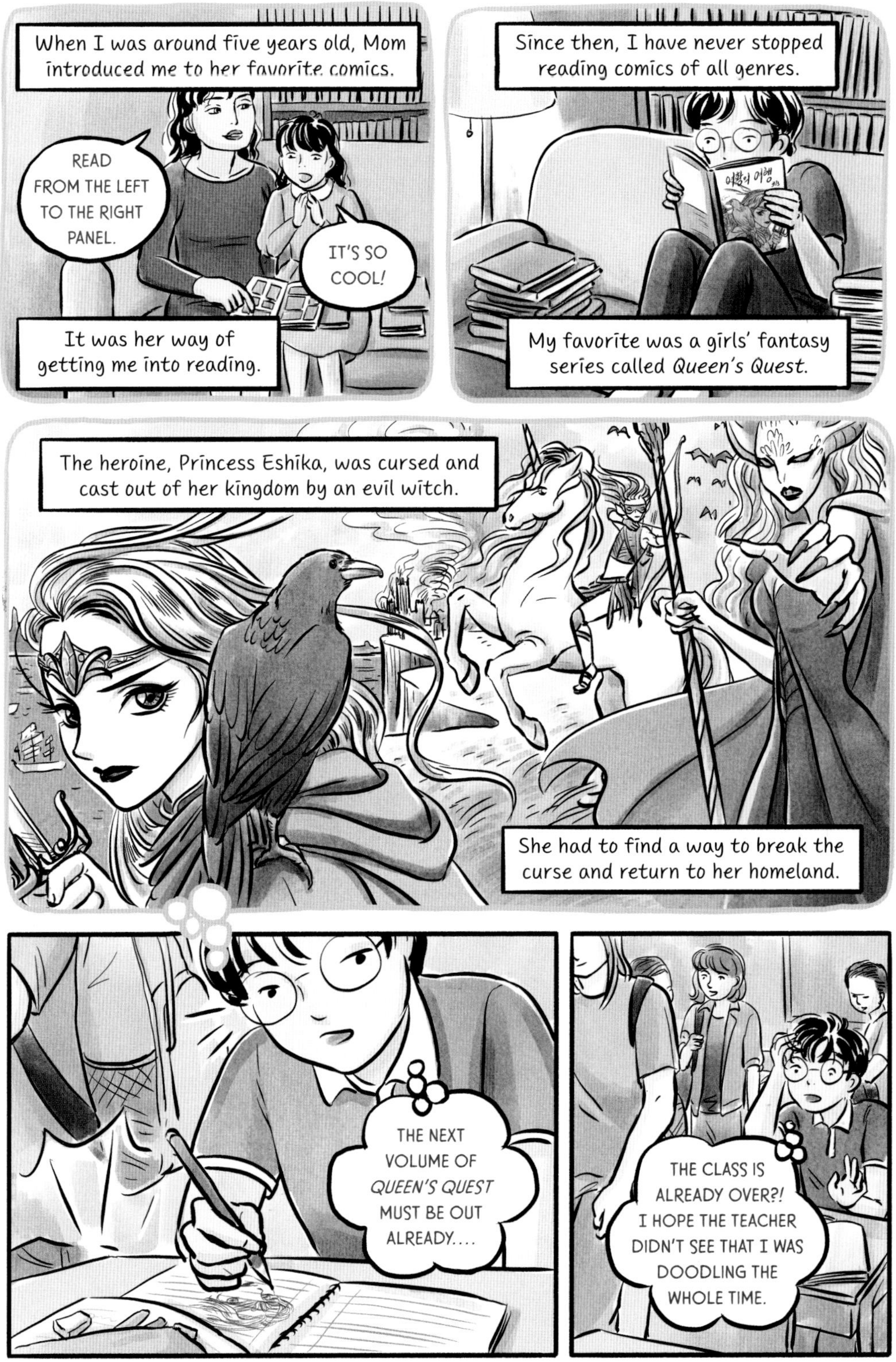
When I was around five years old, Mom introduced me to her favorite comics.
READ FROM THE LEFT TO THE RIGHT PANEL.
IT'S SO COOL!
It was her way of getting me into reading.
Since then, I have never stopped reading comics of all genres.
My favorite was a girls' fantasy series called *Queen's Quest*.
The heroine, Princess Eshika, was cursed and cast out of her kingdom by an evil witch.
She had to find a way to break the curse and return to her homeland.
THE NEXT VOLUME OF *QUEEN'S QUEST* MUST BE OUT ALREADY....
THE CLASS IS ALREADY OVER?! I HOPE THE TEACHER DIDN'T SEE THAT I WAS DOODLING THE WHOLE TIME.

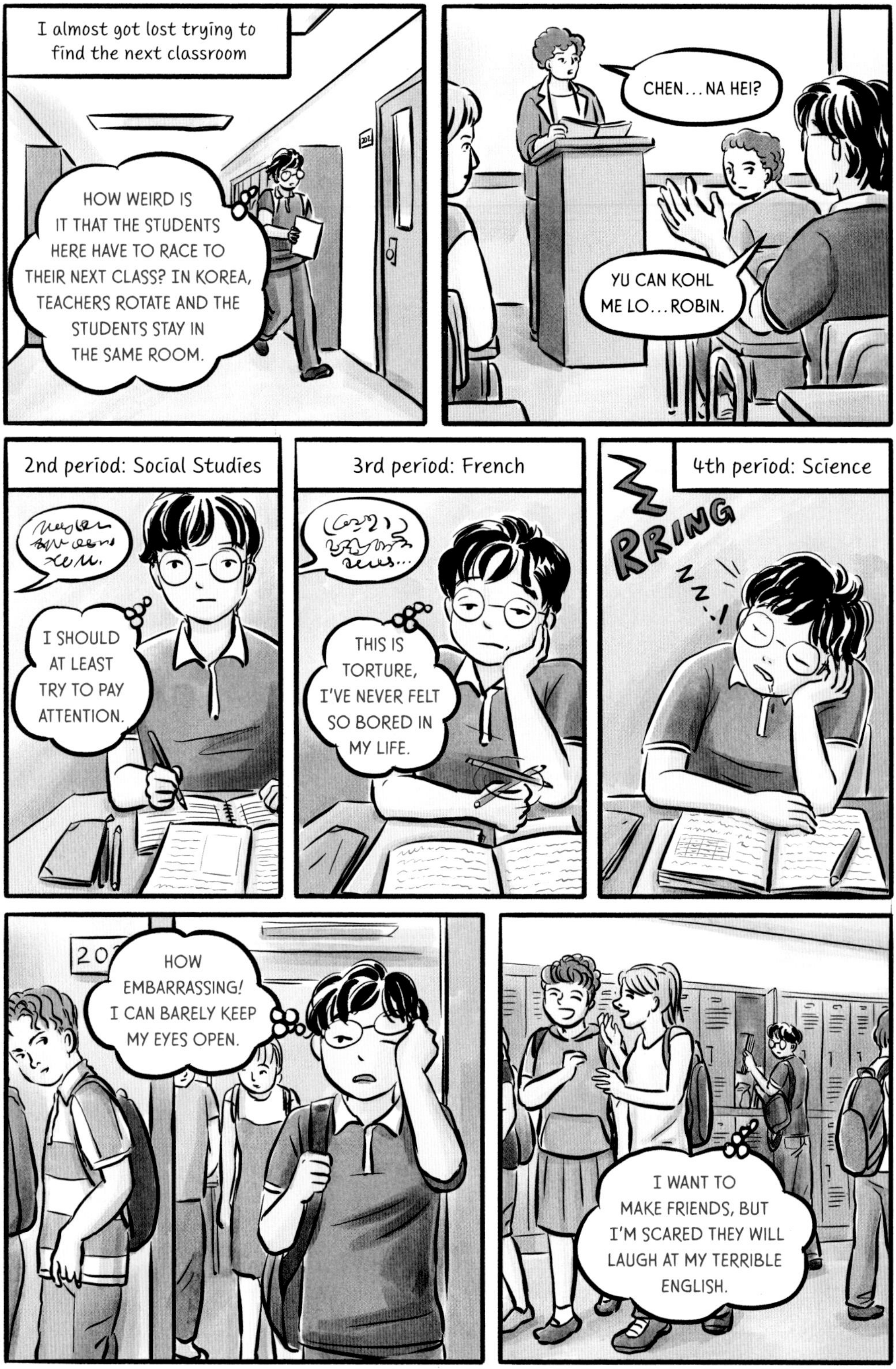
I almost got lost trying to find the next classroom
HOW WEIRD IS IT THAT THE STUDENTS HERE HAVE TO RACE TO THEIR NEXT CLASS? IN KOREA, TEACHERS ROTATE AND THE STUDENTS STAY IN THE SAME ROOM.
CHEN... NA HEI?
YU CAN KOHL ME LO... ROBIN.
2nd period: Social Studies
I SHOULD AT LEAST TRY TO PAY ATTENTION.
3rd period: French
THIS IS TORTURE, I'VE NEVER FELT SO BORED IN MY LIFE.
4th period: Science
RRING
Z Z Z..!
HOW EMBARRASSING! I CAN BARELY KEEP MY EYES OPEN.
I WANT TO MAKE FRIENDS, BUT I'M SCARED THEY WILL LAUGH AT MY TERRIBLE ENGLISH.

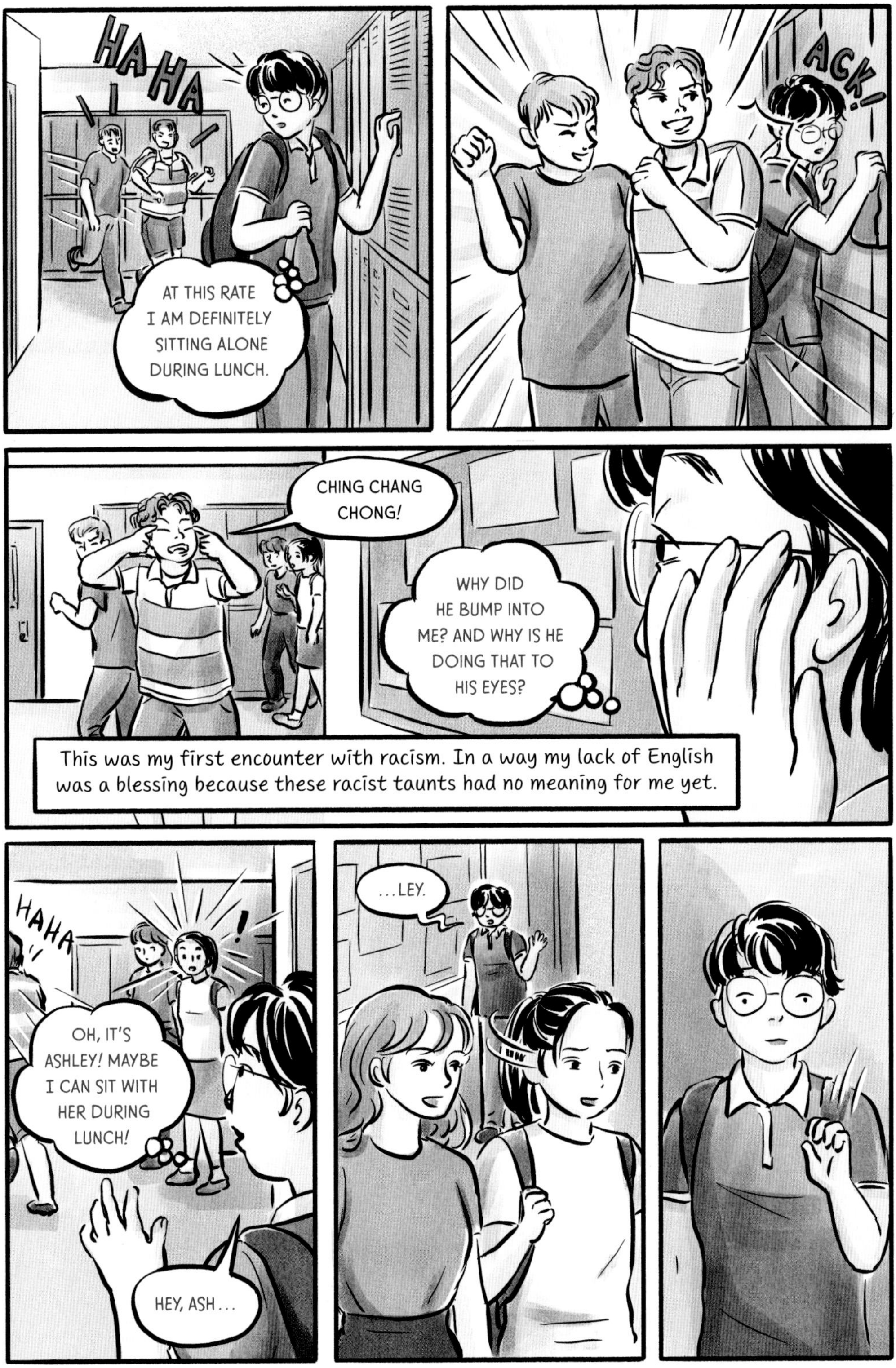
HAHA
AT THIS RATE I AM DEFINITELY SITTING ALONE DURING LUNCH.
ACK!
CHING CHANG CHONG!
WHY DID HE BUMP INTO ME? AND WHY IS HE DOING THAT TO HIS EYES?
This was my first encounter with racism. In a way my lack of English was a blessing because these racist taunts had no meaning for me yet.
HAHA
OH, IT'S ASHLEY! MAYBE I CAN SIT WITH HER DURING LUNCH!
HEY, ASH...
...LEY.

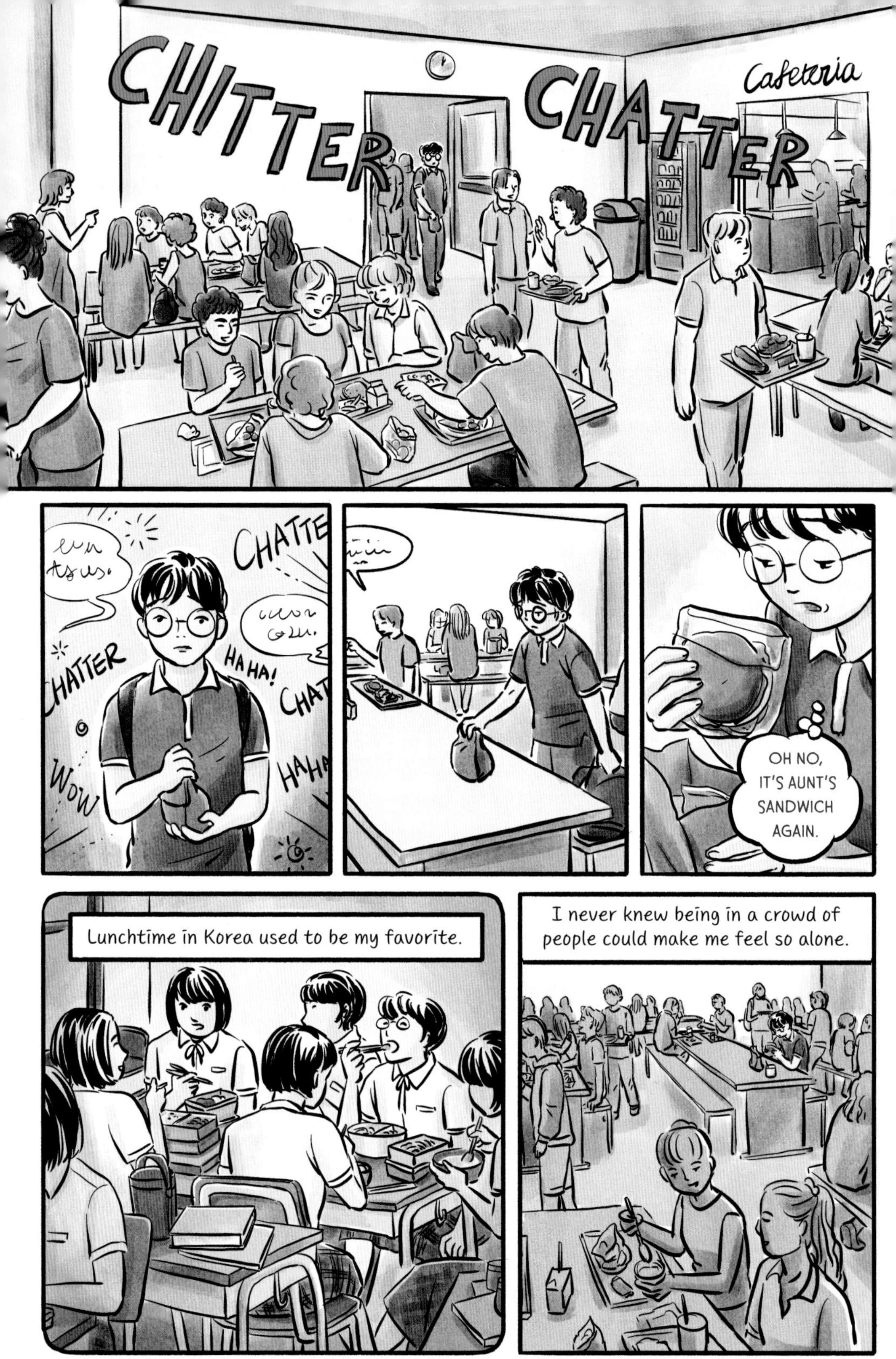
CHITTER CHATTER
Cafeteria
CHATTE
CHATTER
HA HA!
CHAT
WOW
HAHA
OH NO, IT'S AUNT'S SANDWICH AGAIN.
Lunchtime in Korea used to be my favorite.
I never knew being in a crowd of people could make me feel so alone.

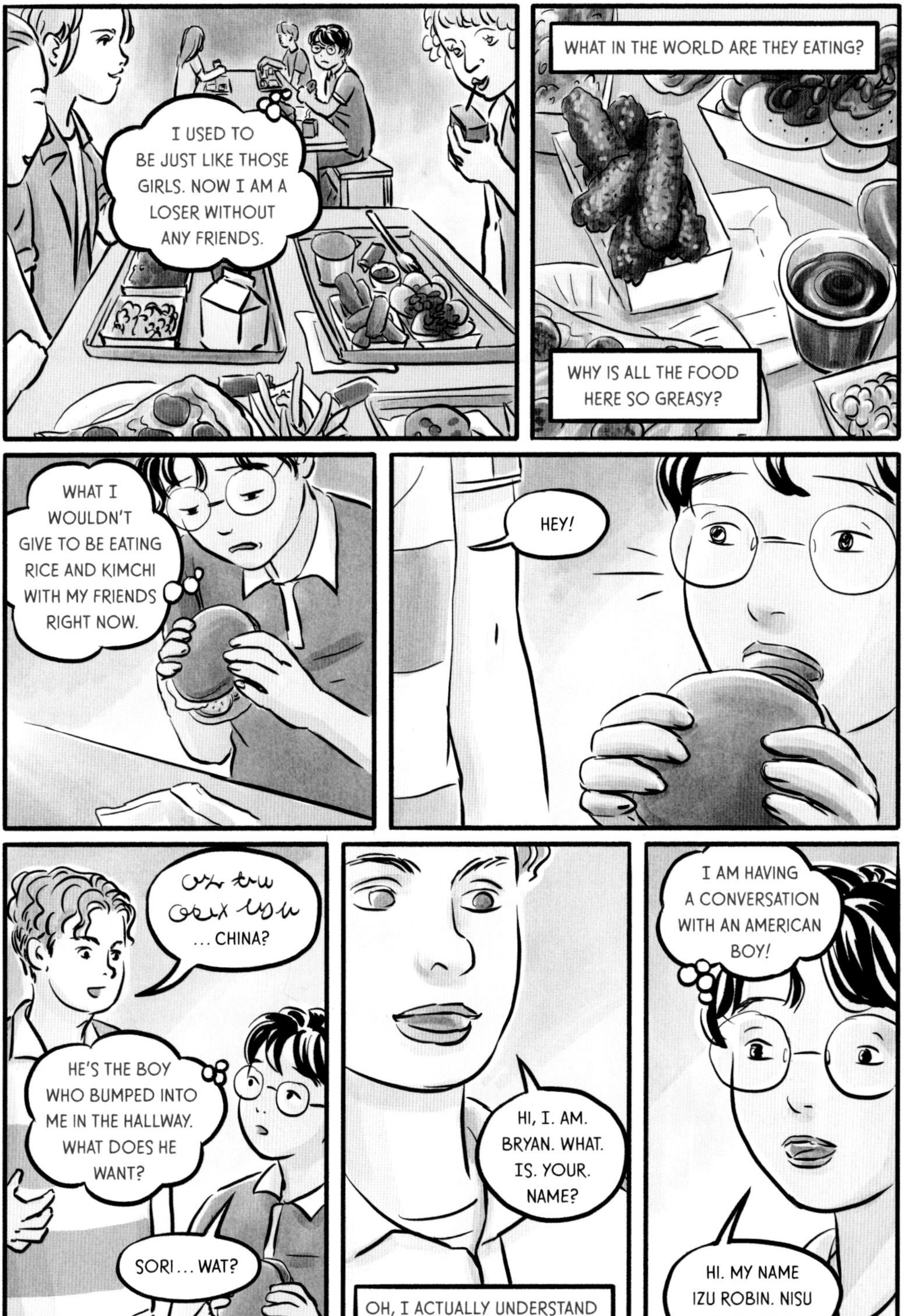
I USED TO BE JUST LIKE THOSE GIRLS. NOW I AM A LOSER WITHOUT ANY FRIENDS.
WHAT IN THE WORLD ARE THEY EATING?
WHY IS ALL THE FOOD HERE SO GREASY?
WHAT I WOULDN'T GIVE TO BE EATING RICE AND KIMCHI WITH MY FRIENDS RIGHT NOW.
HEY!
... CHINA?
HE'S THE BOY WHO BUMPED INTO ME IN THE HALLWAY. WHAT DOES HE WANT?
SORI... WAT?
HI, I. AM. BRYAN. WHAT. IS. YOUR. NAME?
OH, I ACTUALLY UNDERSTAND WHAT HE IS SAYING!
I AM HAVING A CONVERSATION WITH AN AMERICAN BOY!
HI. MY NAME IZU ROBIN. NISU TO MEET YU.

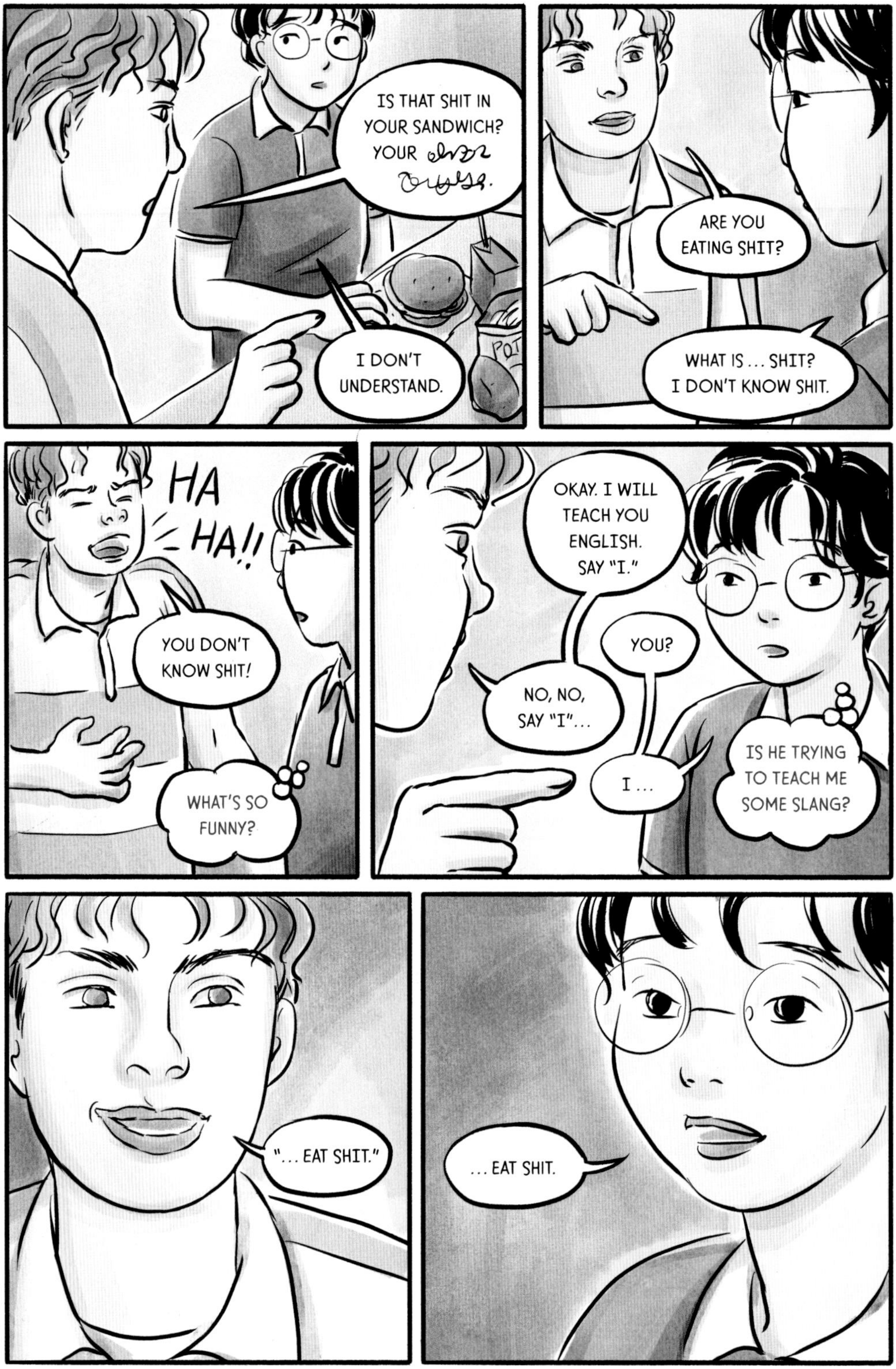
IS THAT SHIT IN YOUR SANDWICH? YOUR
I DON'T UNDERSTAND.
ARE YOU EATING SHIT?
WHAT IS ... SHIT? I DON'T KNOW SHIT.
HA HA!!
YOU DON'T KNOW SHIT!
WHAT'S SO FUNNY?
OKAY. I WILL TEACH YOU ENGLISH. SAY "I."
YOU?
NO, NO, SAY "I"...
I...
IS HE TRYING TO TEACH ME SOME SLANG?
"... EAT SHIT."
... EAT SHIT.

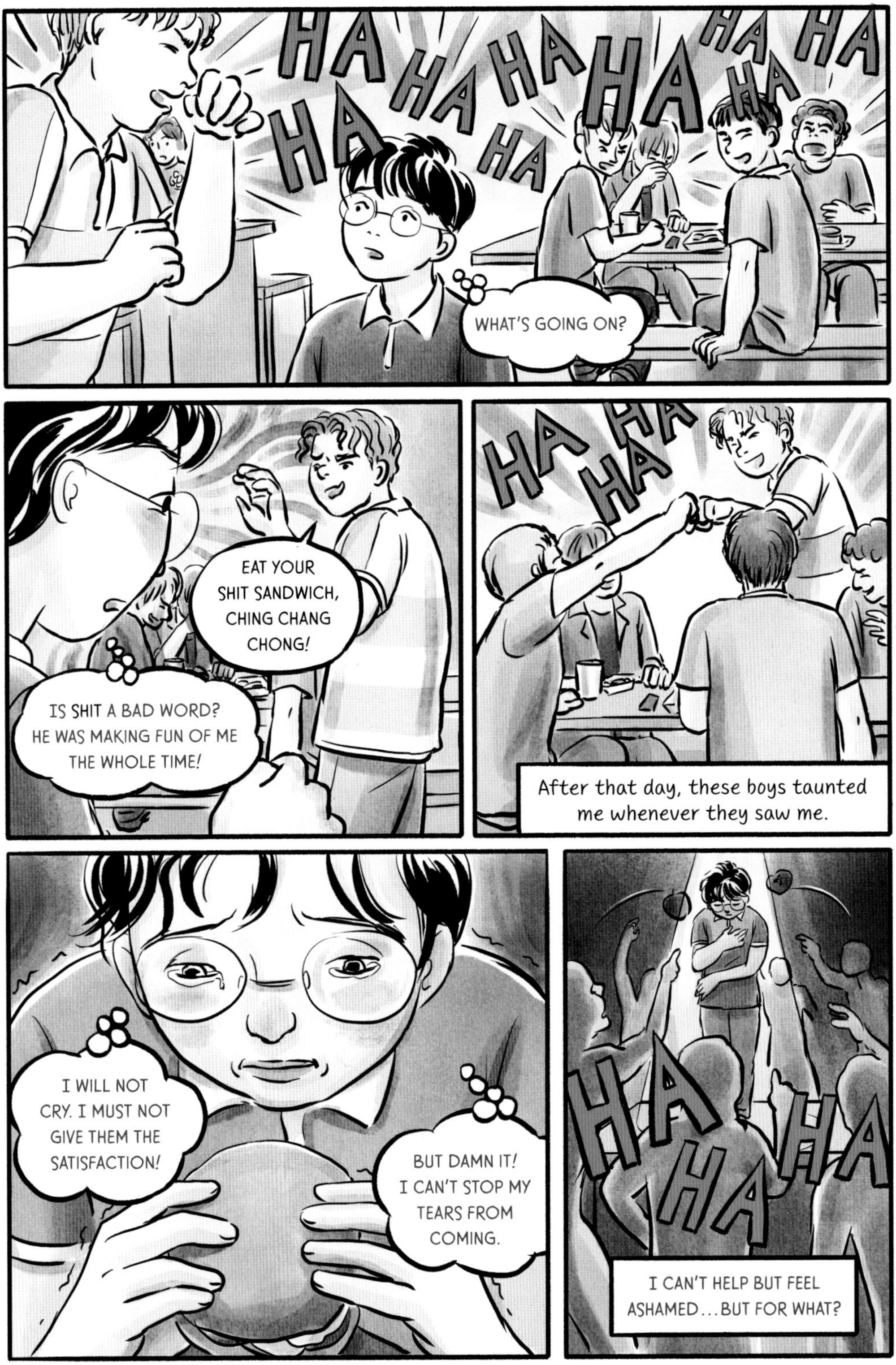
HA HA HA HA HA HA HA HA HA HA HA
WHAT'S GOING ON?
EAT YOUR SHIT SANDWICH, CHING CHANG CHONG!
IS SHIT A BAD WORD? HE WAS MAKING FUN OF ME THE WHOLE TIME!
HA HA HA HA
After that day, these boys taunted me whenever they saw me.
I WILL NOT CRY. I MUST NOT GIVE THEM THE SATISFACTION!
BUT DAMN IT! I CAN'T STOP MY TEARS FROM COMING.
HA HA HA HA
I CAN'T HELP BUT FEEL ASHAMED...BUT FOR WHAT?

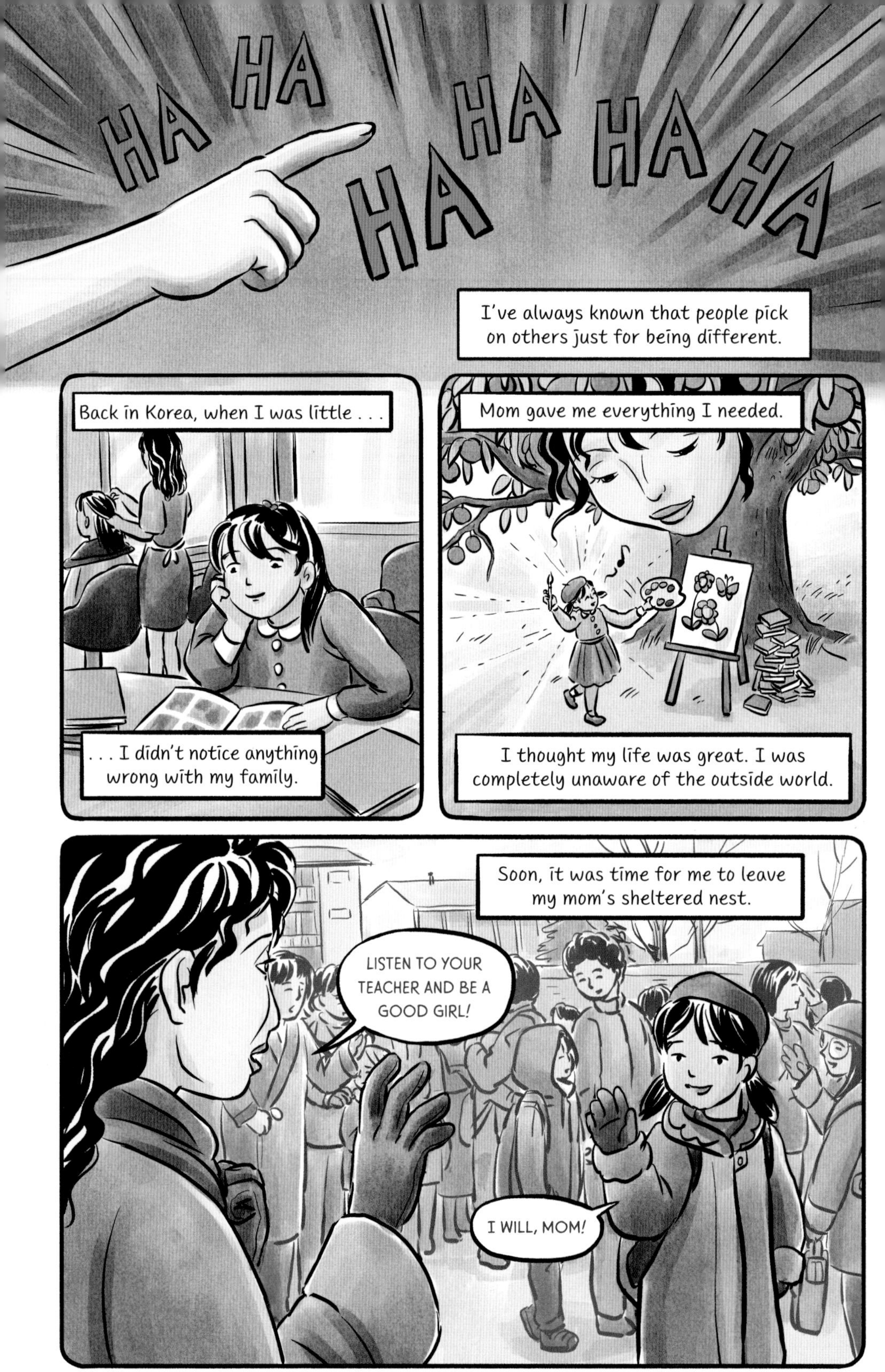
HA HA HA HA HA HA HA HA HA
I've always known that people pick on others just for being different.
Back in Korea, when I was little . . .
. . . I didn't notice anything wrong with my family.
Mom gave me everything I needed.
I thought my life was great. I was completely unaware of the outside world.
Soon, it was time for me to leave my mom's sheltered nest.
LISTEN TO YOUR TEACHER AND BE A GOOD GIRL!
I WILL, MOM!

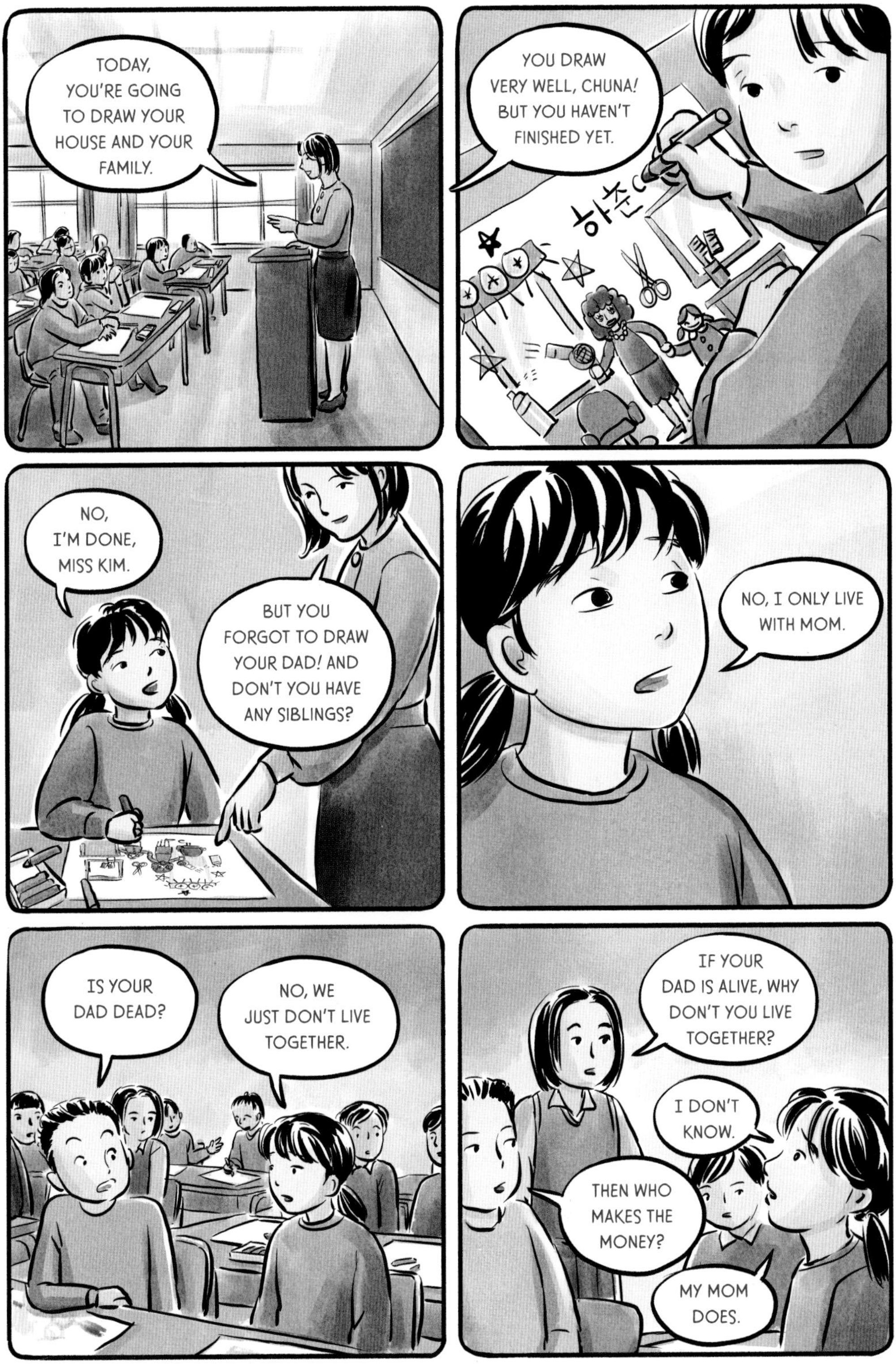
TODAY, YOU'RE GOING TO DRAW YOUR HOUSE AND YOUR FAMILY.
YOU DRAW VERY WELL, CHUNA! BUT YOU HAVEN'T FINISHED YET.
NO, I'M DONE, MISS KIM.
BUT YOU FORGOT TO DRAW YOUR DAD! AND DON'T YOU HAVE ANY SIBLINGS?
NO, I ONLY LIVE WITH MOM.
IS YOUR DAD DEAD?
NO, WE JUST DON'T LIVE TOGETHER.
IF YOUR DAD IS ALIVE, WHY DON'T YOU LIVE TOGETHER?
I DON'T KNOW.
THEN WHO MAKES THE MONEY?
MY MOM DOES.

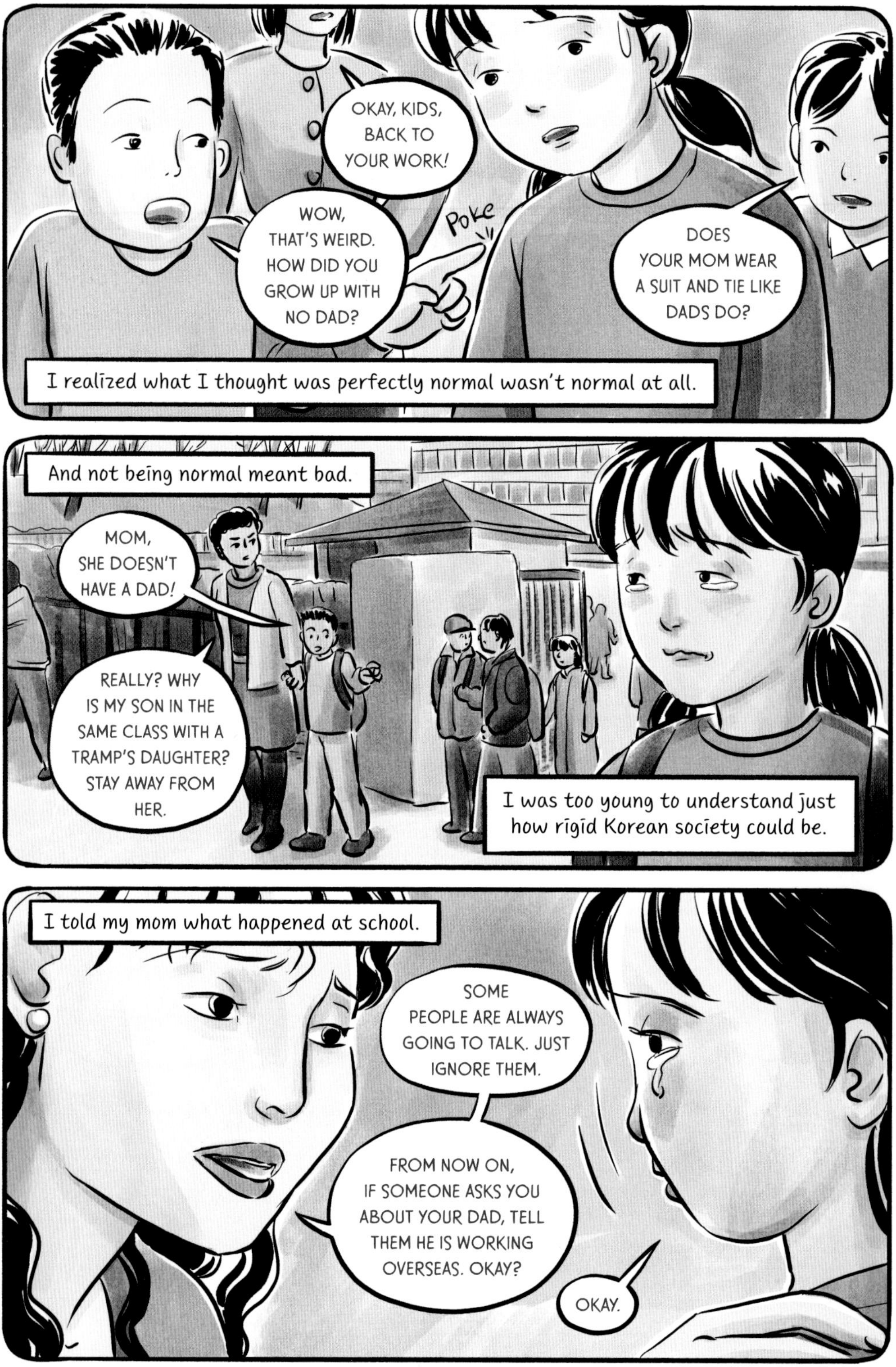

OKAY, KIDS, BACK TO YOUR WORK!
WOW, THAT'S WEIRD. HOW DID YOU GROW UP WITH NO DAD?
POKE
DOES YOUR MOM WEAR A SUIT AND TIE LIKE DADS DO?
I realized what I thought was perfectly normal wasn't normal at all.
And not being normal meant bad.
MOM, SHE DOESN'T HAVE A DAD!
REALLY? WHY IS MY SON IN THE SAME CLASS WITH A TRAMP'S DAUGHTER? STAY AWAY FROM HER.
I was too young to understand just how rigid Korean society could be.
I told my mom what happened at school.
SOME PEOPLE ARE ALWAYS GOING TO TALK. JUST IGNORE THEM.
FROM NOW ON, IF SOMEONE ASKS YOU ABOUT YOUR DAD, TELL THEM HE IS WORKING OVERSEAS. OKAY?
OKAY.

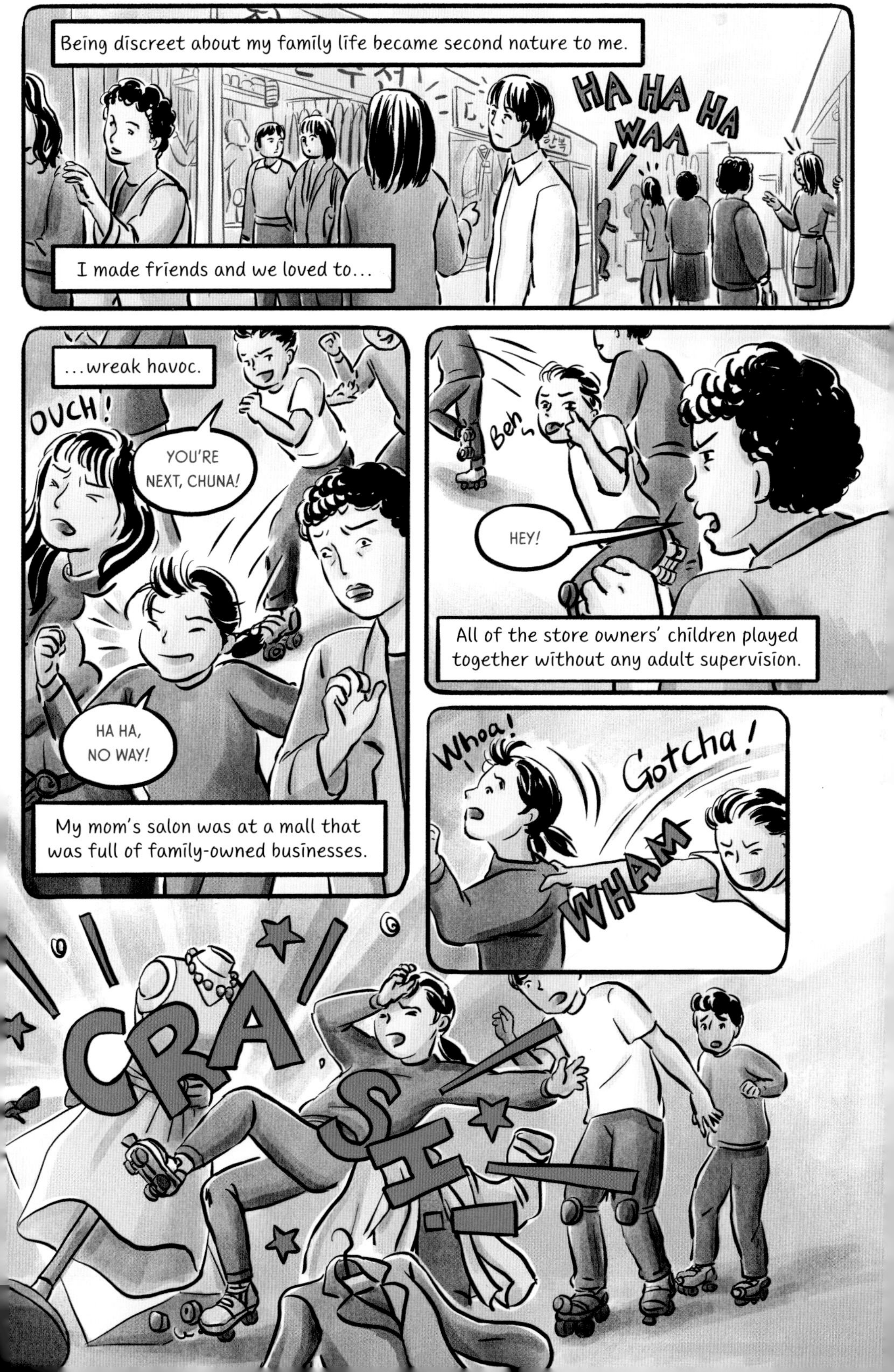
Being discreet about my family life became second nature to me.
한복
HA HA HA
WAA
I made friends and we loved to...
...wreak havoc.
OUCH!
YOU'RE NEXT, CHUNA!
HA HA, NO WAY!
My mom's salon was at a mall that was full of family-owned businesses.
Beh
HEY!
All of the store owners' children played together without any adult supervision.
Whoa!
Gotcha!
WHAM
CRASH

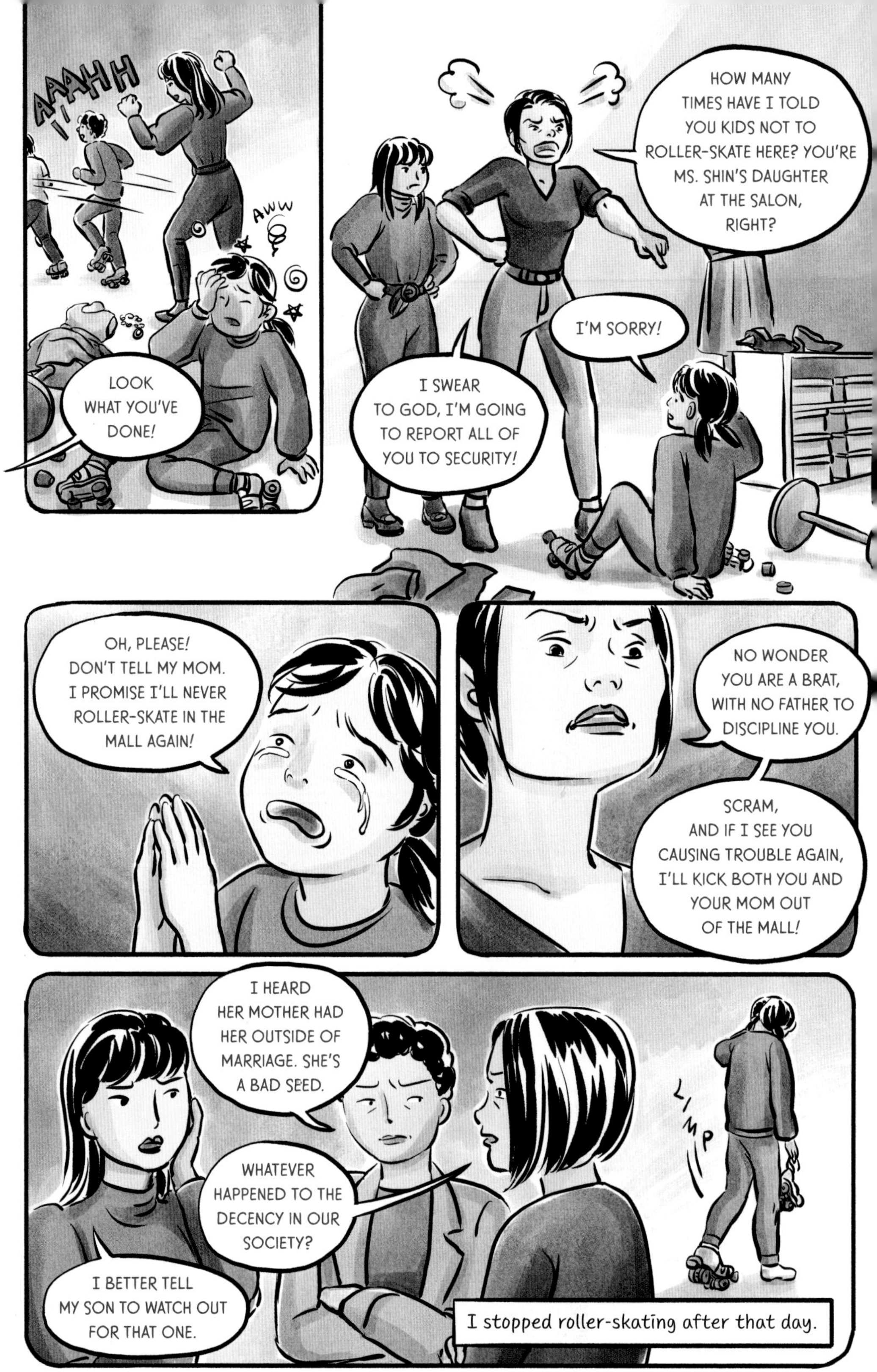
AAAHH
AWW
LOOK WHAT YOU'VE DONE!
HOW MANY TIMES HAVE I TOLD YOU KIDS NOT TO ROLLER-SKATE HERE? YOU'RE MS. SHIN'S DAUGHTER AT THE SALON, RIGHT?
I'M SORRY!
I SWEAR TO GOD, I'M GOING TO REPORT ALL OF YOU TO SECURITY!
OH, PLEASE! DON'T TELL MY MOM. I PROMISE I'LL NEVER ROLLER-SKATE IN THE MALL AGAIN!
NO WONDER YOU ARE A BRAT, WITH NO FATHER TO DISCIPLINE YOU.
SCRAM, AND IF I SEE YOU CAUSING TROUBLE AGAIN, I'LL KICK BOTH YOU AND YOUR MOM OUT OF THE MALL!
I HEARD HER MOTHER HAD HER OUTSIDE OF MARRIAGE. SHE'S A BAD SEED.
WHATEVER HAPPENED TO THE DECENCY IN OUR SOCIETY?
I BETTER TELL MY SON TO WATCH OUT FOR THAT ONE.
LIMP
I stopped roller-skating after that day.

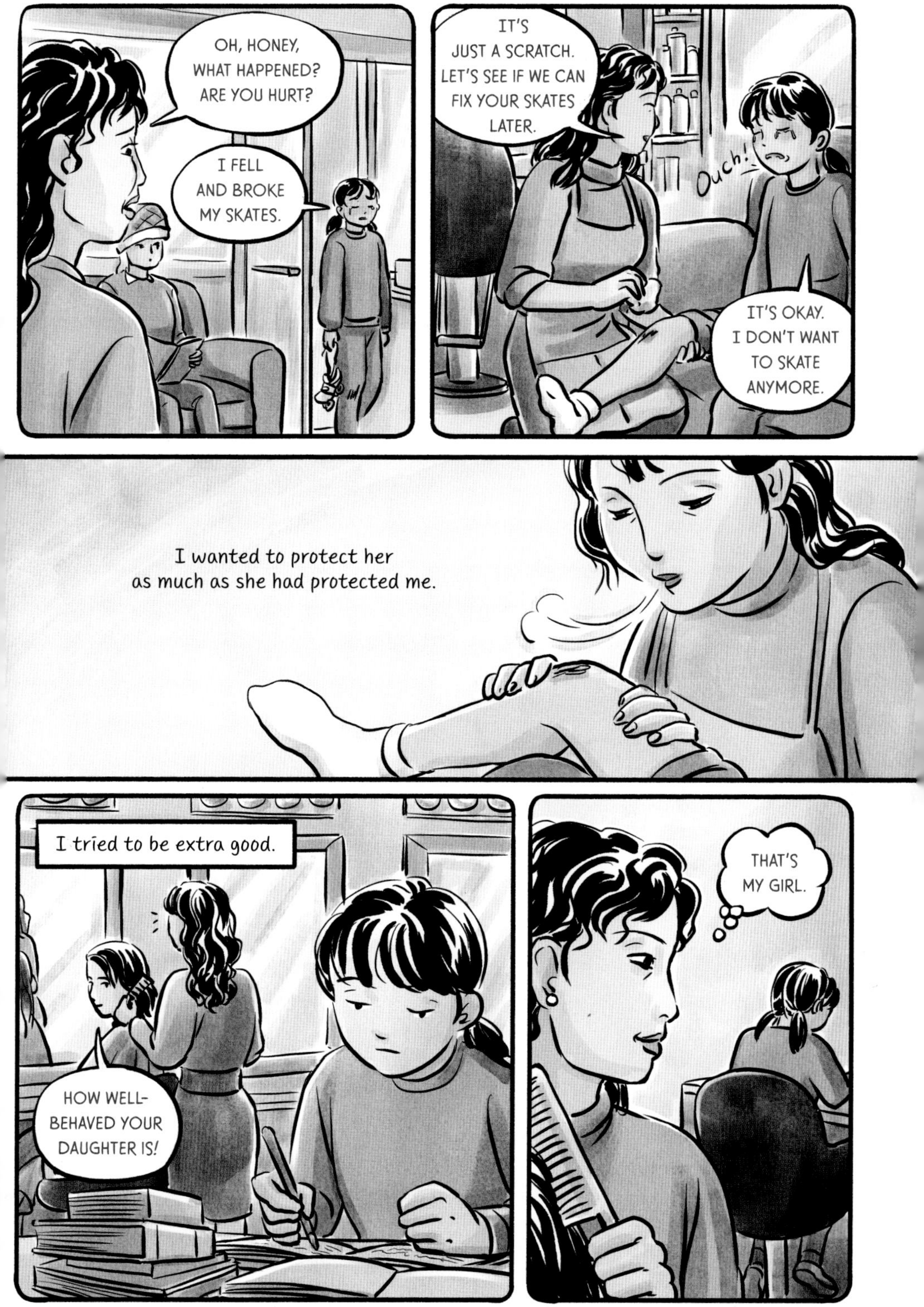
OH, HONEY, WHAT HAPPENED? ARE YOU HURT?
I FELL AND BROKE MY SKATES.
IT'S JUST A SCRATCH. LET'S SEE IF WE CAN FIX YOUR SKATES LATER.
Ouch!
IT'S OKAY. I DON'T WANT TO SKATE ANYMORE.
I wanted to protect her as much as she had protected me.
I tried to be extra good.
HOW WELL-BEHAVED YOUR DAUGHTER IS!
THAT'S MY GIRL.

Mom was a master at diverting gossip by working extra hard to be successful.
When I was a toddler we lived in a dingy room in the back of a tiny hair salon.
By the time I was in middle school, Mom became the owner of the biggest
hair salon in the neighborhood and bought us a large three-bedroom apartment.

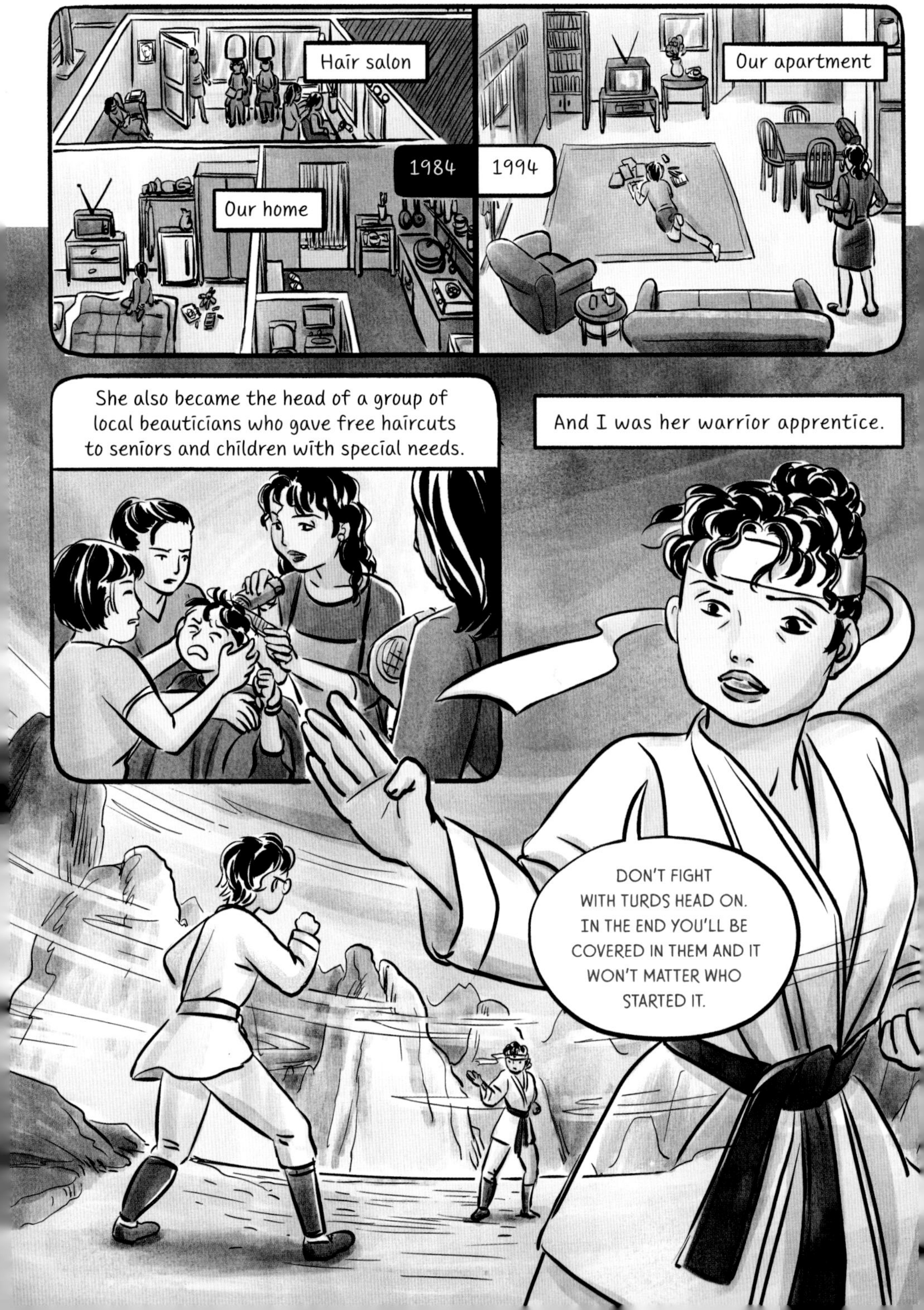
Hair salon
Our home
1984
1994
Our apartment
She also became the head of a group of local beauticians who gave free haircuts to seniors and children with special needs.
And I was her warrior apprentice.
DON'T FIGHT WITH TURDS HEAD ON. IN THE END YOU'LL BE COVERED IN THEM AND IT WON'T MATTER WHO STARTED IT.

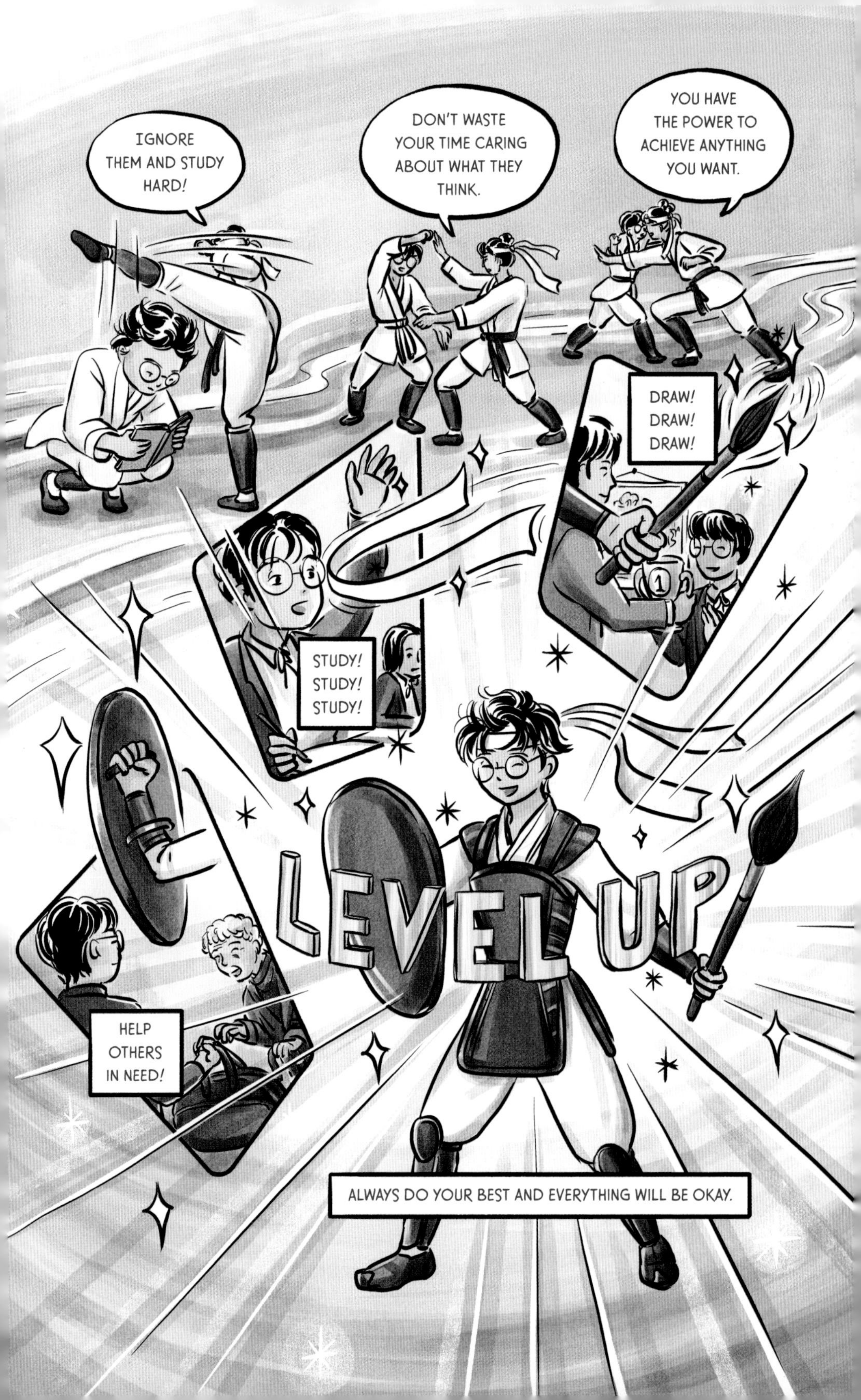
IGNORE THEM AND STUDY HARD!
DON'T WASTE YOUR TIME CARING ABOUT WHAT THEY THINK.
YOU HAVE THE POWER TO ACHIEVE ANYTHING YOU WANT.
DRAW! DRAW! DRAW!
STUDY! STUDY! STUDY!
LEVEL UP
HELP OTHERS IN NEED!
ALWAYS DO YOUR BEST AND EVERYTHING WILL BE OKAY.

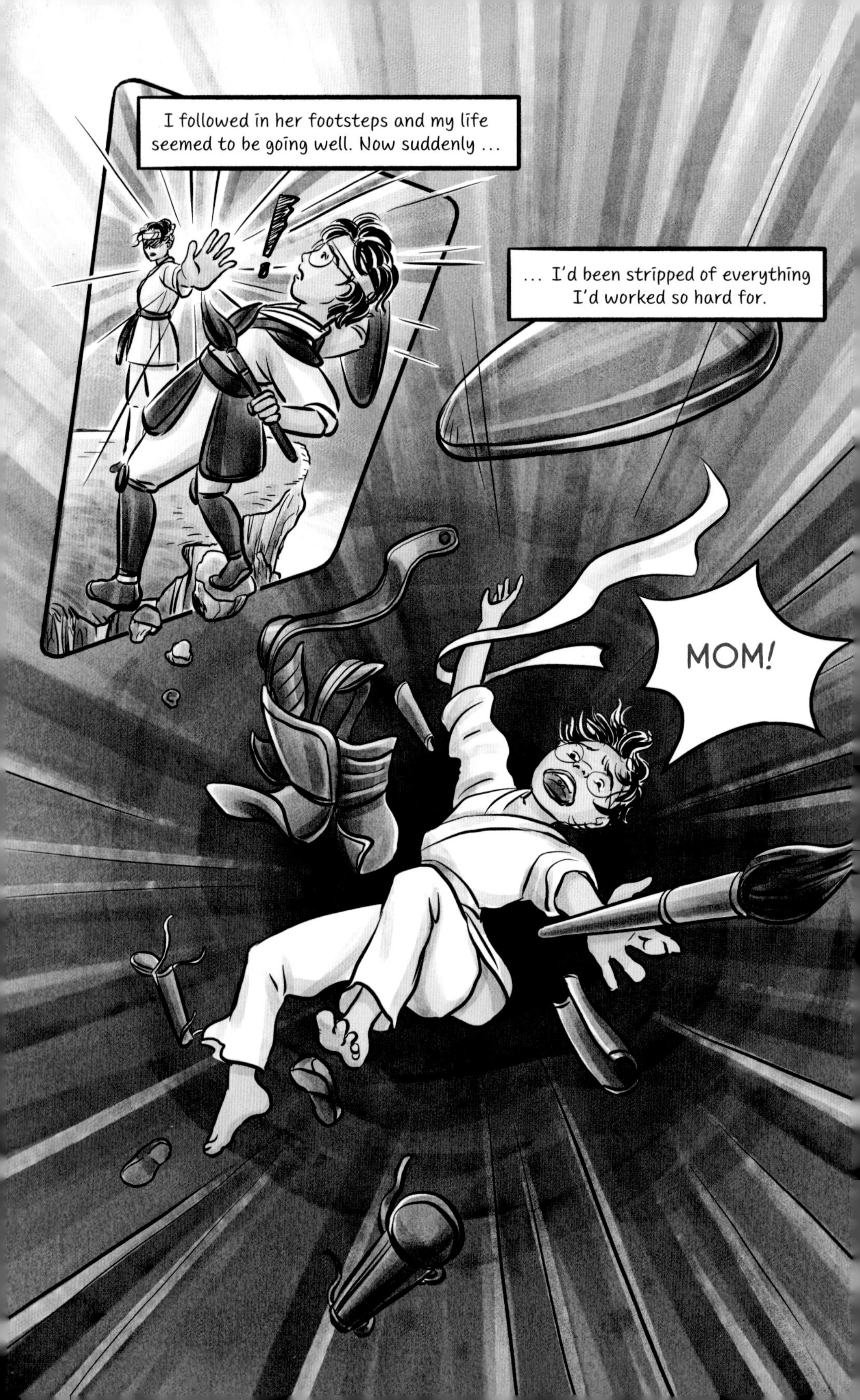
I followed in her footsteps and my life seemed to be going well. Now suddenly ...
... I'd been stripped of everything I'd worked so hard for.
MOM!

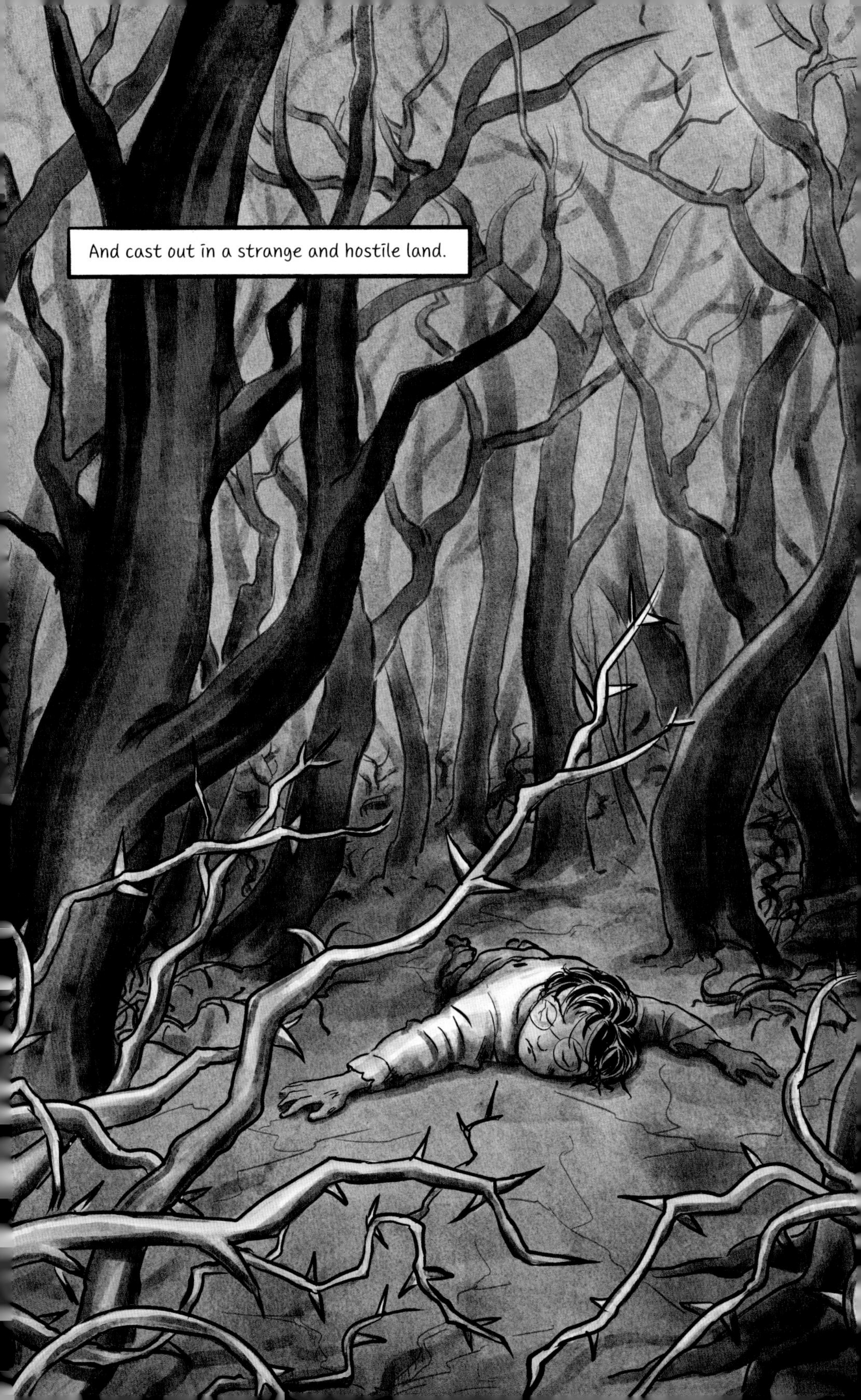
And cast out in a strange and hostile land.

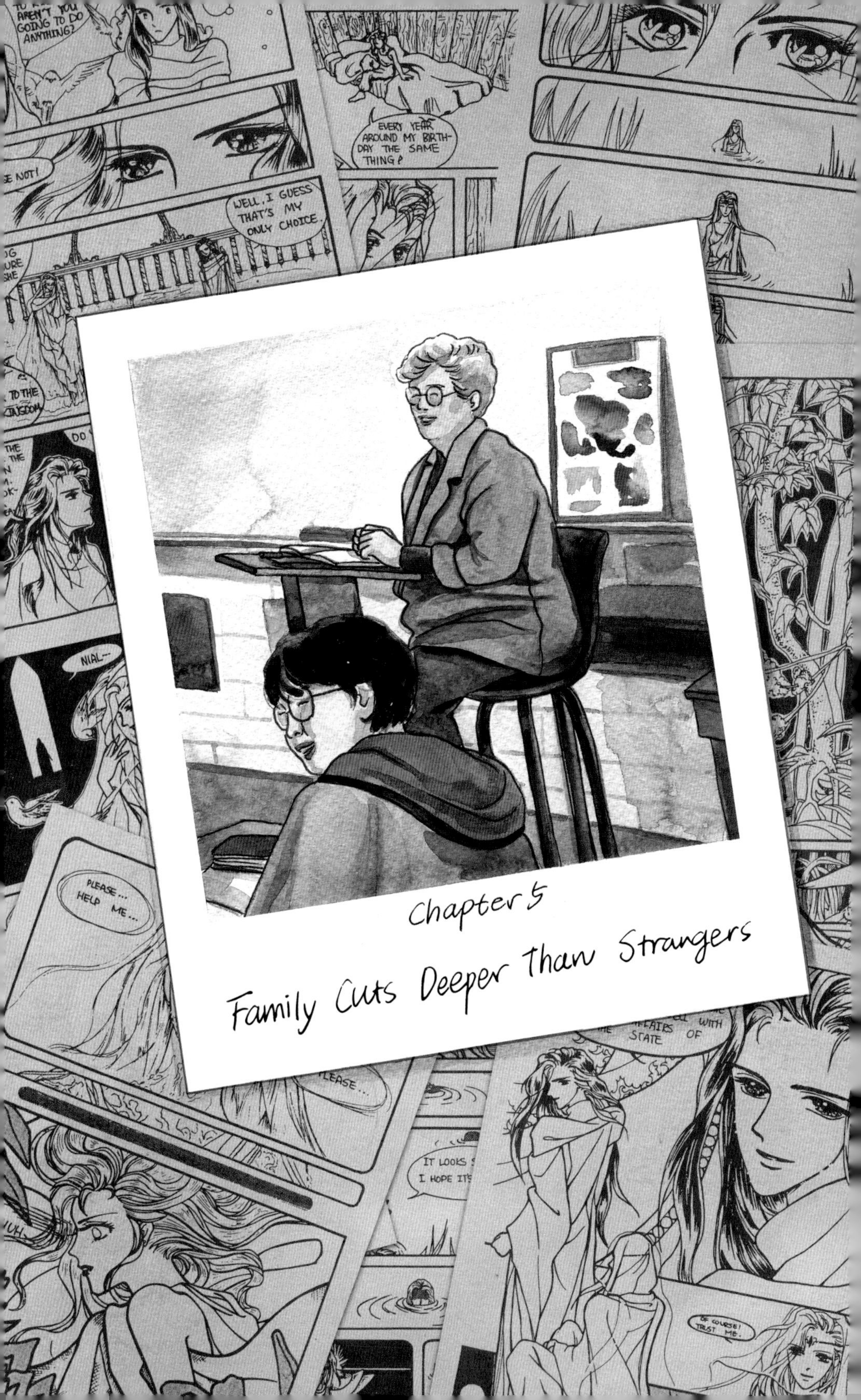
AREN'T YOU GOING TO DO ANYTHING?
EVERY YEAR AROUND MY BIRTHDAY THE SAME THING?
WELL, I GUESS THAT'S MY ONLY CHOICE.
NIAL--
PLEASE... HELP ME...
OF COURSE! TRUST ME.

Chapter 5

Family Cuts Deeper Than Strangers

The first month of school went by, and things had not changed much.

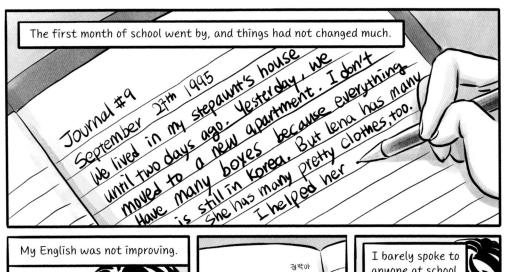

Journal #9
September 27th 1995
We lived in my stepaunt's house until two days ago. Yesterday, we moved to a new apartment. I don't Have many boxes because everything is still in Korea. But Lena has many She has many pretty clothes,too. I helped her

My English was not improving.

HMM...HOW DO AMERICANS SAY 정리하다 ?

정박아

portional taxation.
정리(廷吏) a court clerk.
정리(定理) a theorem.
정리(整理) (정돈) arrangement;(re.) adjustment; (해제·해소) liquida-tion; (계산(청산)) (강원) cur-tailment. ~하다 put (the room) in order; arrange; readjust; dis-pose (of one's ~) (처분); (배체·정산) liq settle (clear off) (one's liqu (the staff) (감원); (교통의). ‖~안(~

SO MANY DIFFERENT WAYS TO SAY THE SAME THING.... WHICH ONE OF THESE IS RIGHT?

I barely spoke to anyone at school.

I GUESS I'LL GO WITH THE FIRST ONE.

The only person I connected with at school was Mrs. Halls, my English teacher.

She knew that eighth-grade English would be too hard for me. So she told me that we could write to each other in a journal instead.

She also brought me children's books to read.

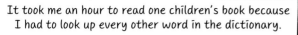

It took me an hour to read one children's book because I had to look up every other word in the dictionary.

ARGH, A FIVE-YEAR-OLD AMERICAN KID COULD READ THIS FASTER THAN ME.

GOOD JOB, ROBIN.

Getting Mrs. Hall's response back in my journal was the highlight of my day...

...even though it was hard for me to decipher what she wrote.

Robin, I am so proud of you. I am very glad that you write a lot in class.
Q: How was your day so far?

P...R...O...U...D... PROUD...THERE IT IS!

HOW... WAS...YOUR...DAY... SO...FAR? SO FAR? LIKE IN DISTANCE? OR LIKE SOFA, THE COUCH?

I KNOW WHAT ALL THESE WORDS MEAN, BUT I CAN'T FIGURE OUT WHAT THEY MEAN TOGETHER!

I WILL answer tomorrow

I'LL HAVE TO ASK LENA WHAT "SO FAR" MEANS WHEN I GET HOME.

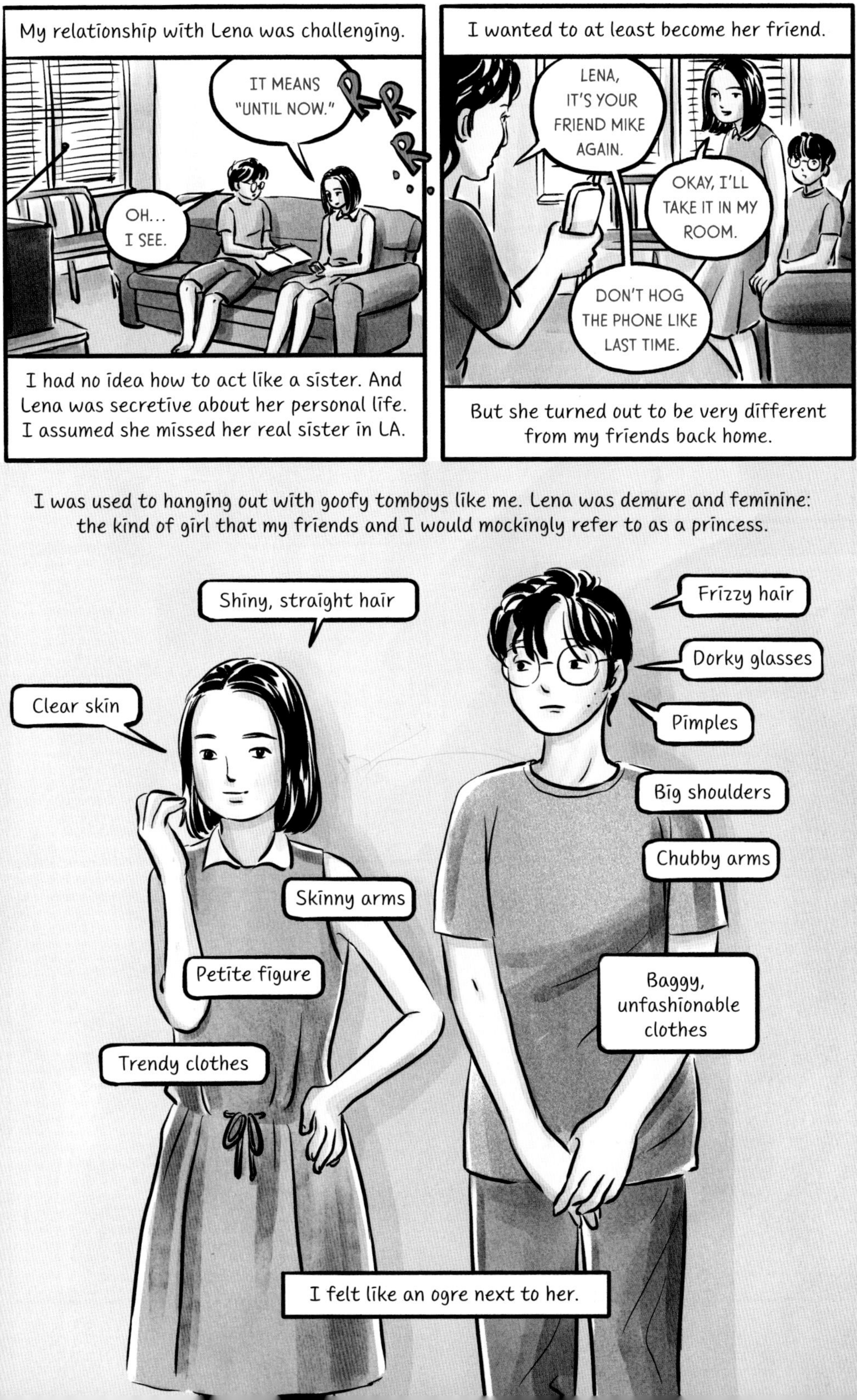
My relationship with Lena was challenging.
IT MEANS "UNTIL NOW."
RRR
OH... I SEE.
I had no idea how to act like a sister. And Lena was secretive about her personal life. I assumed she missed her real sister in LA.
I wanted to at least become her friend.
LENA, IT'S YOUR FRIEND MIKE AGAIN.
OKAY, I'LL TAKE IT IN MY ROOM.
DON'T HOG THE PHONE LIKE LAST TIME.
But she turned out to be very different from my friends back home.
I was used to hanging out with goofy tomboys like me. Lena was demure and feminine: the kind of girl that my friends and I would mockingly refer to as a princess.
Shiny, straight hair
Clear skin
Skinny arms
Petite figure
Trendy clothes
Frizzy hair
Dorky glasses
Pimples
Big shoulders
Chubby arms
Baggy, unfashionable clothes
I felt like an ogre next to her.

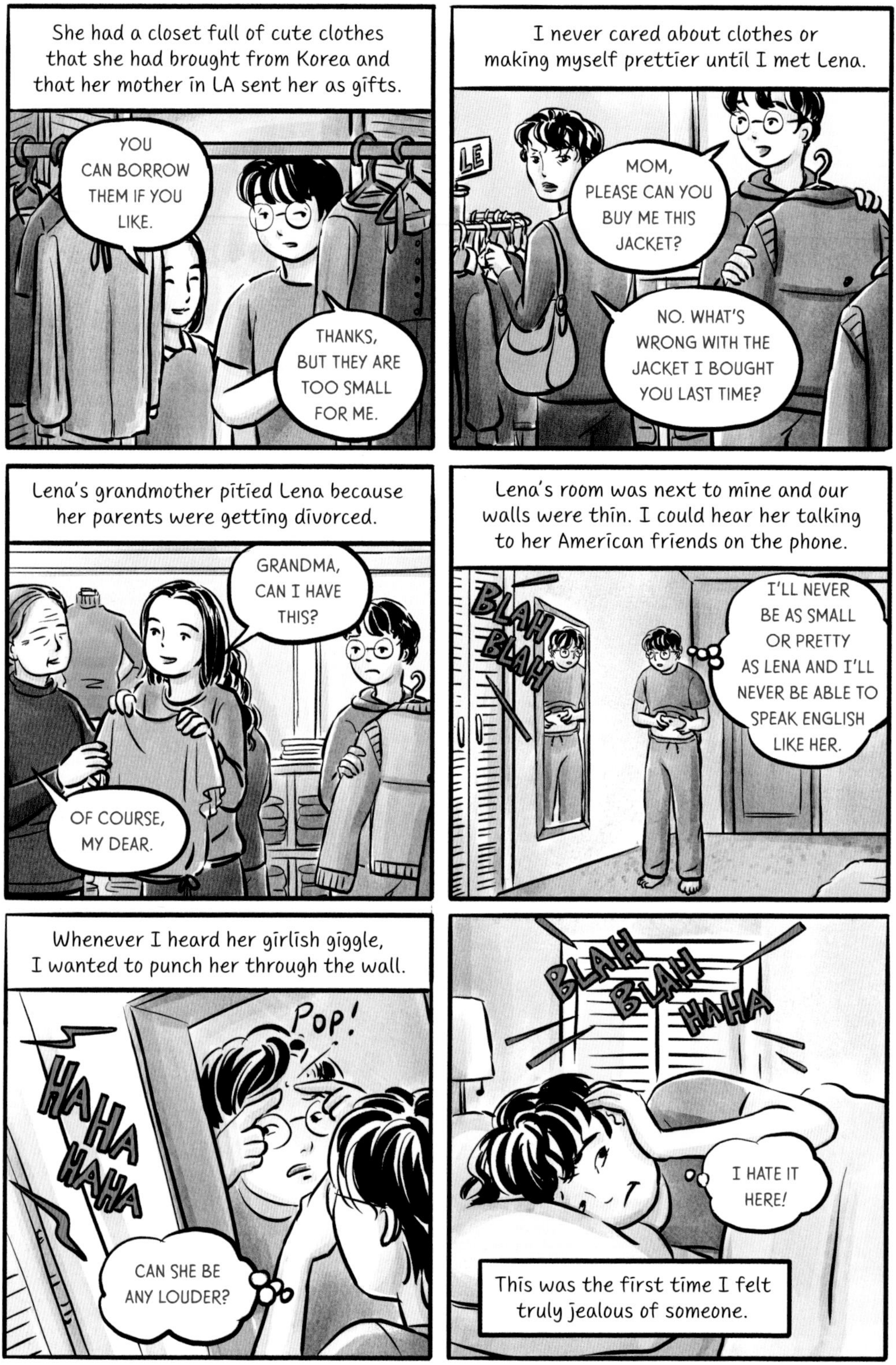
She had a closet full of cute clothes that she had brought from Korea and that her mother in LA sent her as gifts.
YOU CAN BORROW THEM IF YOU LIKE.
THANKS, BUT THEY ARE TOO SMALL FOR ME.
I never cared about clothes or making myself prettier until I met Lena.
LE
MOM, PLEASE CAN YOU BUY ME THIS JACKET?
NO. WHAT'S WRONG WITH THE JACKET I BOUGHT YOU LAST TIME?
Lena's grandmother pitied Lena because her parents were getting divorced.
GRANDMA, CAN I HAVE THIS?
OF COURSE, MY DEAR.
Lena's room was next to mine and our walls were thin. I could hear her talking to her American friends on the phone.
BLAH BLAH
I'LL NEVER BE AS SMALL OR PRETTY AS LENA AND I'LL NEVER BE ABLE TO SPEAK ENGLISH LIKE HER.
Whenever I heard her girlish giggle, I wanted to punch her through the wall.
POP!
HAHA HAHA
CAN SHE BE ANY LOUDER?
BLAH BLAH HAHA
I HATE IT HERE!
This was the first time I felt truly jealous of someone.

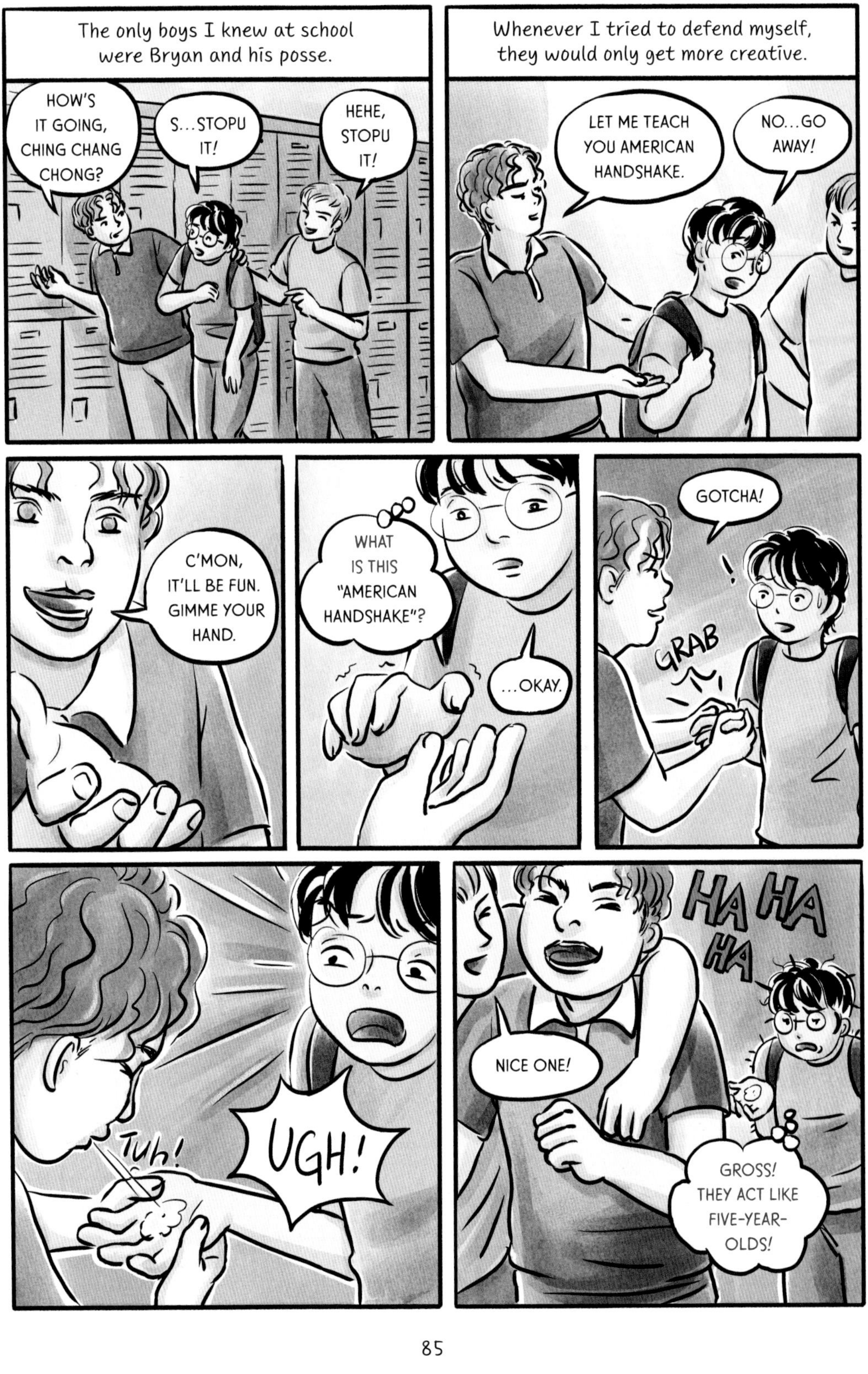
The only boys I knew at school were Bryan and his posse.
HOW'S IT GOING, CHING CHANG CHONG?
S...STOPU IT!
HEHE, STOPU IT!
Whenever I tried to defend myself, they would only get more creative.
LET ME TEACH YOU AMERICAN HANDSHAKE.
NO...GO AWAY!
C'MON, IT'LL BE FUN. GIMME YOUR HAND.
WHAT IS THIS "AMERICAN HANDSHAKE"?
...OKAY.
GOTCHA!
!
GRAB
Tuh!
UGH!
HA HA HA
NICE ONE!
GROSS! THEY ACT LIKE FIVE-YEAR-OLDS!

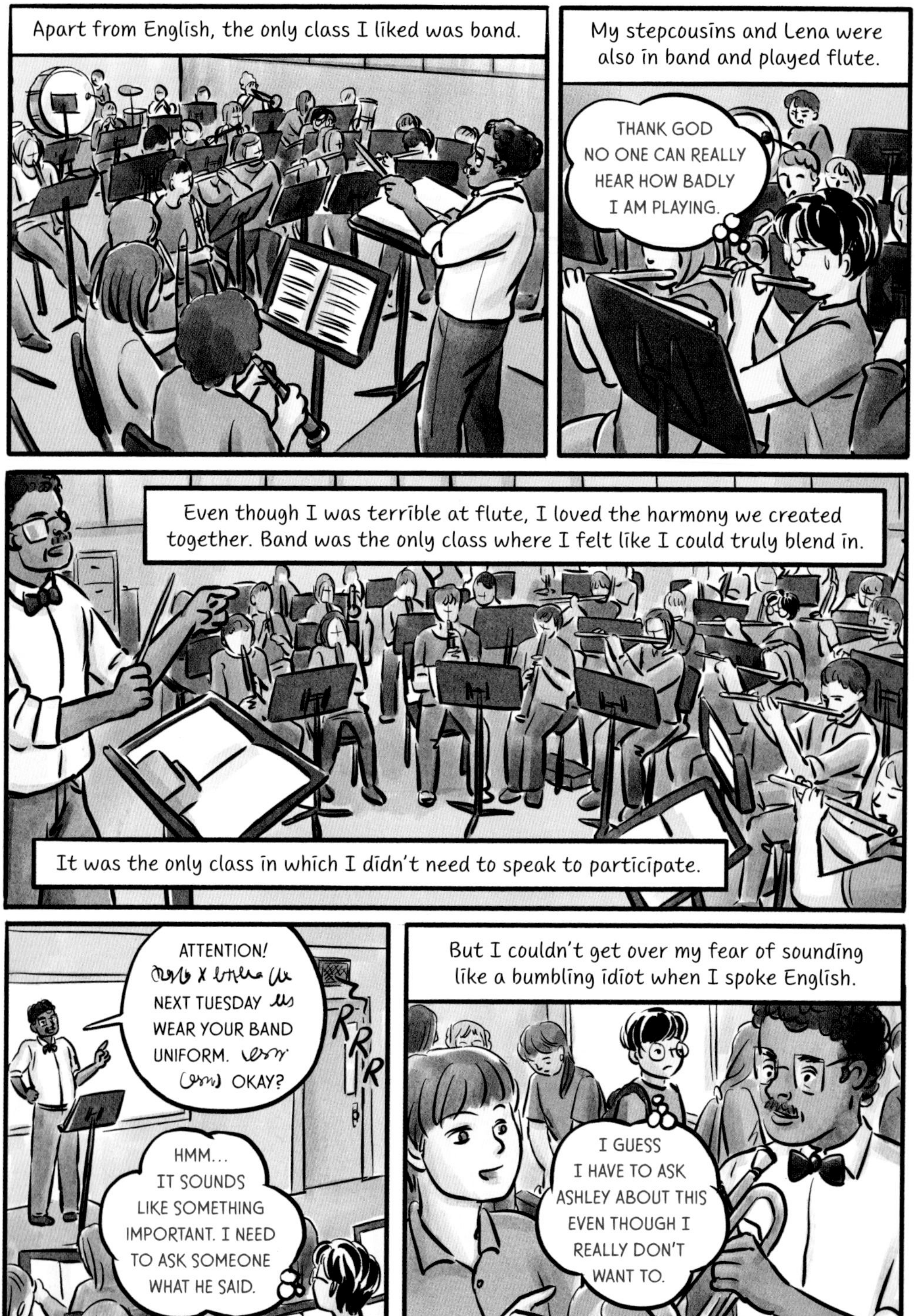
Apart from English, the only class I liked was band.
My stepcousins and Lena were also in band and played flute.
THANK GOD NO ONE CAN REALLY HEAR HOW BADLY I AM PLAYING.
Even though I was terrible at flute, I loved the harmony we created together. Band was the only class where I felt like I could truly blend in.
It was the only class in which I didn't need to speak to participate.
ATTENTION!
NEXT TUESDAY
WEAR YOUR BAND UNIFORM.
OKAY?
RRR
HMM... IT SOUNDS LIKE SOMETHING IMPORTANT. I NEED TO ASK SOMEONE WHAT HE SAID.
But I couldn't get over my fear of sounding like a bumbling idiot when I spoke English.
I GUESS I HAVE TO ASK ASHLEY ABOUT THIS EVEN THOUGH I REALLY DON'T WANT TO.

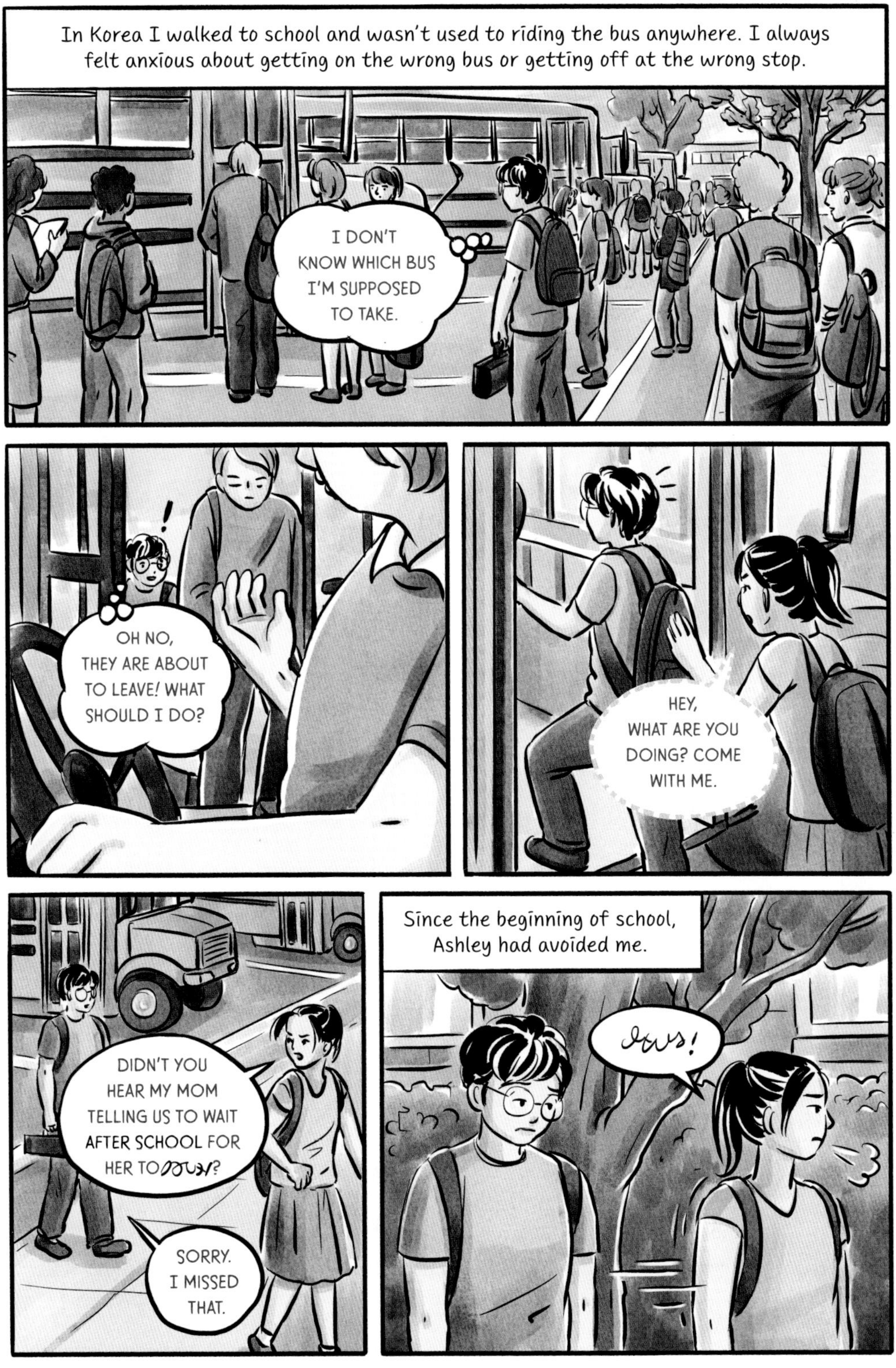
In Korea I walked to school and wasn't used to riding the bus anywhere. I always felt anxious about getting on the wrong bus or getting off at the wrong stop.
I DON'T KNOW WHICH BUS I'M SUPPOSED TO TAKE.
OH NO, THEY ARE ABOUT TO LEAVE! WHAT SHOULD I DO?
HEY, WHAT ARE YOU DOING? COME WITH ME.
DIDN'T YOU HEAR MY MOM TELLING US TO WAIT AFTER SCHOOL FOR HER TO
SORRY. I MISSED THAT.
Since the beginning of school, Ashley had avoided me.

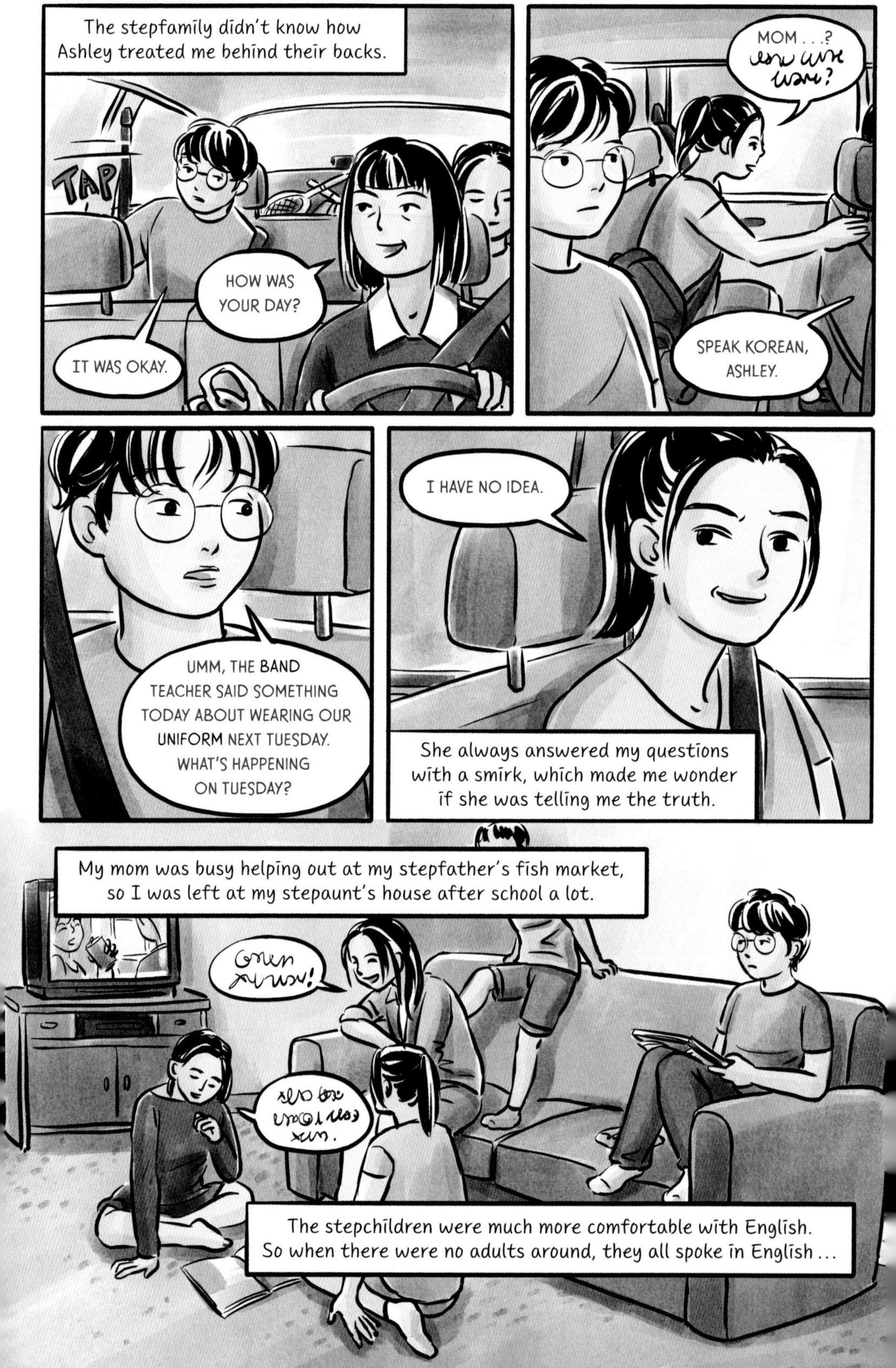
The stepfamily didn't know how Ashley treated me behind their backs.
TAP
HOW WAS YOUR DAY?
IT WAS OKAY.
MOM . . .?
SPEAK KOREAN, ASHLEY.
UMM, THE BAND TEACHER SAID SOMETHING TODAY ABOUT WEARING OUR UNIFORM NEXT TUESDAY. WHAT'S HAPPENING ON TUESDAY?
I HAVE NO IDEA.
She always answered my questions with a smirk, which made me wonder if she was telling me the truth.
My mom was busy helping out at my stepfather's fish market, so I was left at my stepaunt's house after school a lot.
The stepchildren were much more comfortable with English. So when there were no adults around, they all spoke in English . . .

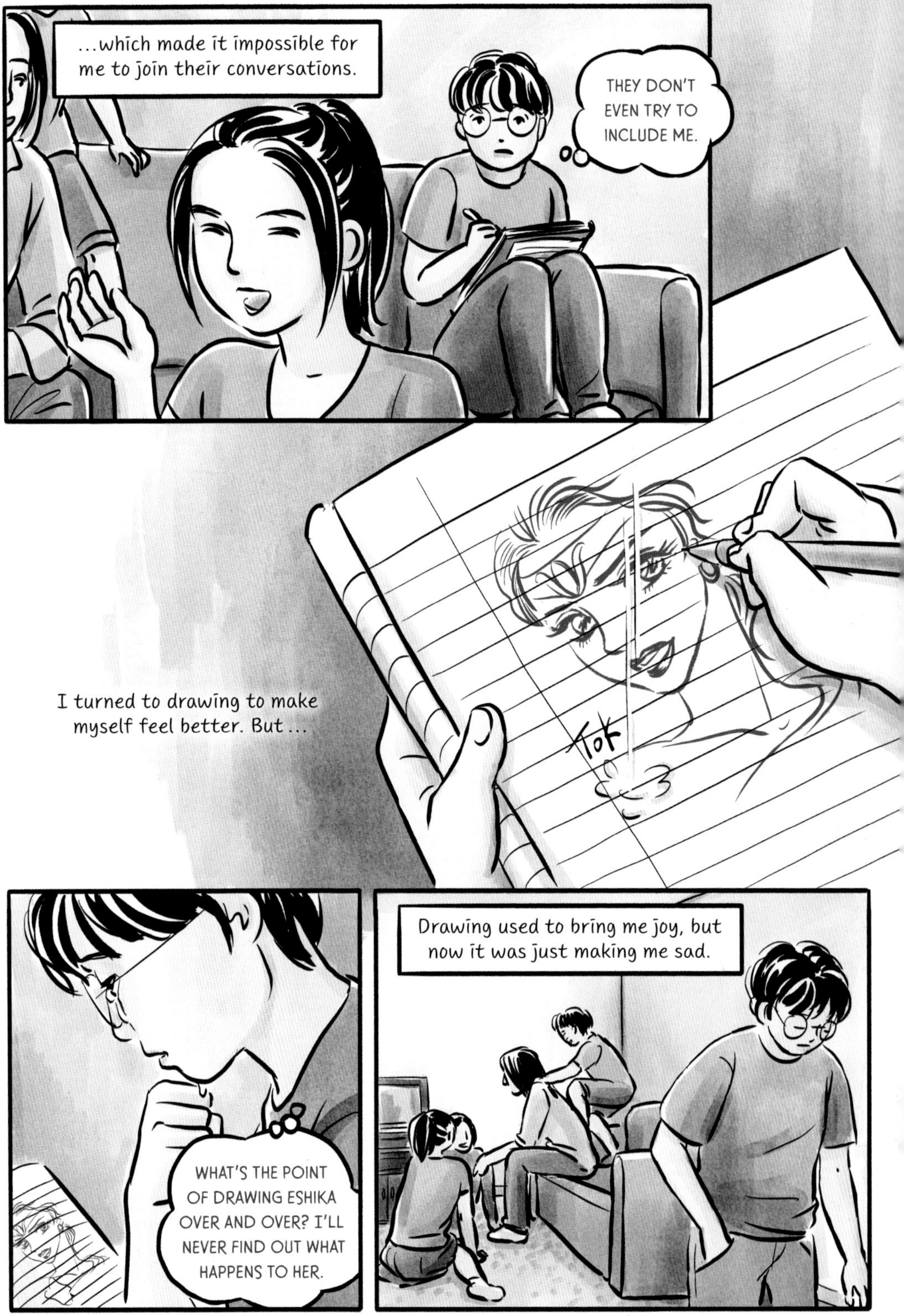
...which made it impossible for me to join their conversations.
THEY DON'T EVEN TRY TO INCLUDE ME.
I turned to drawing to make myself feel better. But...
WHAT'S THE POINT OF DRAWING ESHIKA OVER AND OVER? I'LL NEVER FIND OUT WHAT HAPPENS TO HER.
Drawing used to bring me joy, but now it was just making me sad.

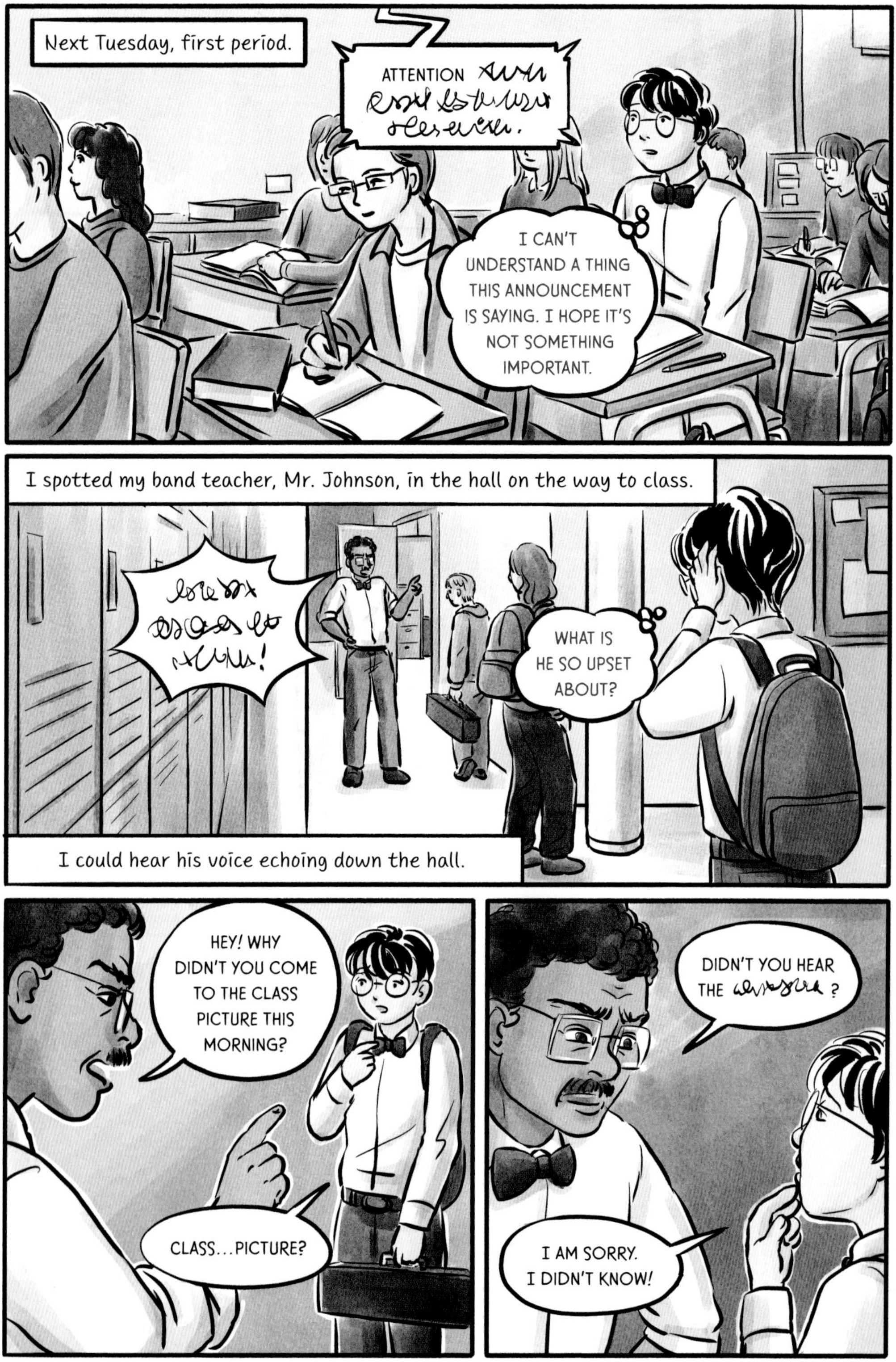
Next Tuesday, first period.
ATTENTION
I CAN'T UNDERSTAND A THING THIS ANNOUNCEMENT IS SAYING. I HOPE IT'S NOT SOMETHING IMPORTANT.
I spotted my band teacher, Mr. Johnson, in the hall on the way to class.
WHAT IS HE SO UPSET ABOUT?
I could hear his voice echoing down the hall.
HEY! WHY DIDN'T YOU COME TO THE CLASS PICTURE THIS MORNING?
CLASS...PICTURE?
DIDN'T YOU HEAR THE ?
I AM SORRY. I DIDN'T KNOW!

I wasn't the only one who missed the photo. More than half of my class had missed it, and that's why Mr. Johnson was so upset.

I DON'T KNOW WHY THE OTHER KIDS MISSED IT. IT'S UNFAIR FOR HIM TO BE MAD AT ME. I EVEN WORE MY UNIFORM.

I WISH I COULD EXPLAIN MYSELF, BUT I CAN'T FIND THE RIGHT WORDS IN ENGLISH!

When I saw Ashley in the hallway with her band uniform on, my heart filled with rage.

I BET SHE DIDN'T TELL ME ON PURPOSE!

CHITTER CHATTER

I had no friends to vent my frustration to.

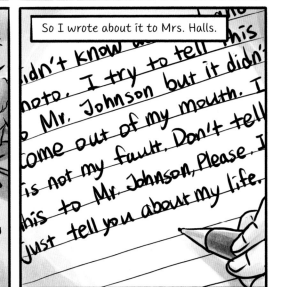

So I wrote about it to Mrs. Halls.

idn't know ... his noto. I try to tell this Mr. Johnson but it didn' come out of my mouth. I is not my fault. Don't tell his to Mr. Johnson, Please. I Just tell you about my life.

91

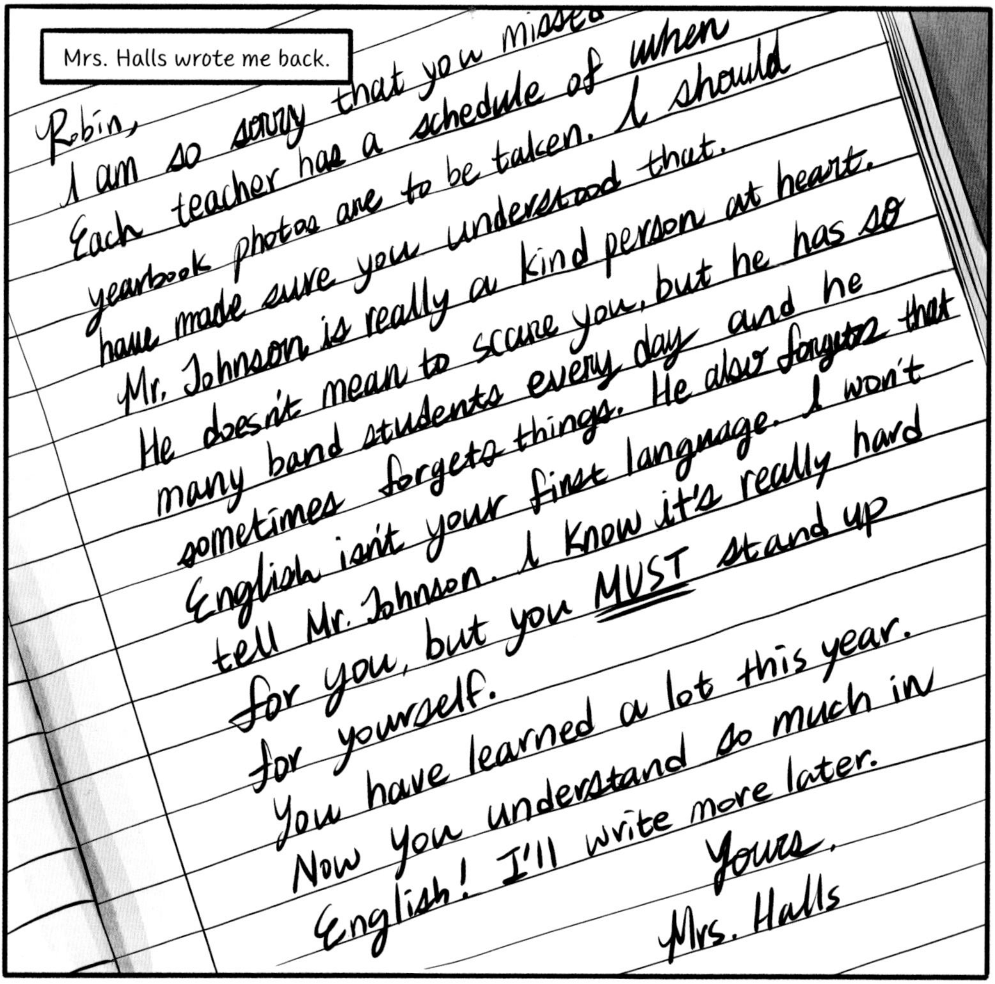
Mrs. Halls wrote me back.
Robin,
I am so sorry that you misse
Each teacher has a schedule of when
yearbook photos are to be taken. I should
have made sure you understood that.
Mr. Johnson is really a kind person at heart.
He doesn't mean to scare you, but he has so
many band students every day and he
sometimes forgets things. He also forgets that
English isn't your first language. I won't
tell Mr. Johnson. I know it's really hard
for you, but you MUST stand up
for yourself.
You have learned a lot this year.
Now you understand so much in
English! I'll write more later.
Yours,
Mrs. Halls

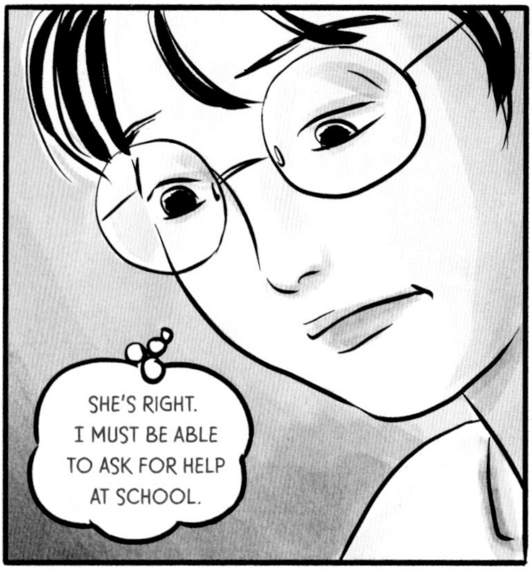
SHE'S RIGHT. I MUST BE ABLE TO ASK FOR HELP AT SCHOOL.

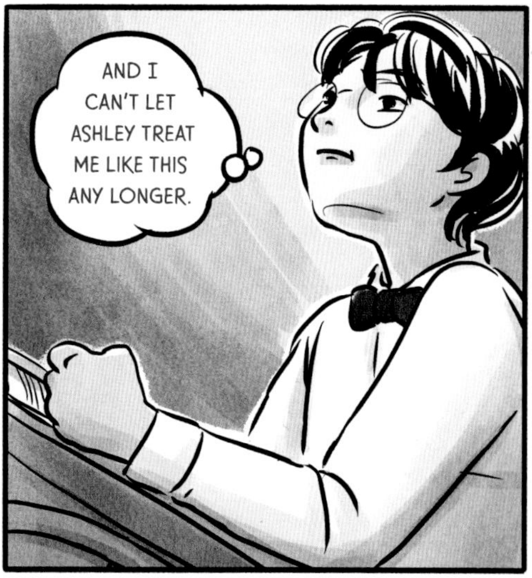
AND I CAN'T LET ASHLEY TREAT ME LIKE THIS ANY LONGER.

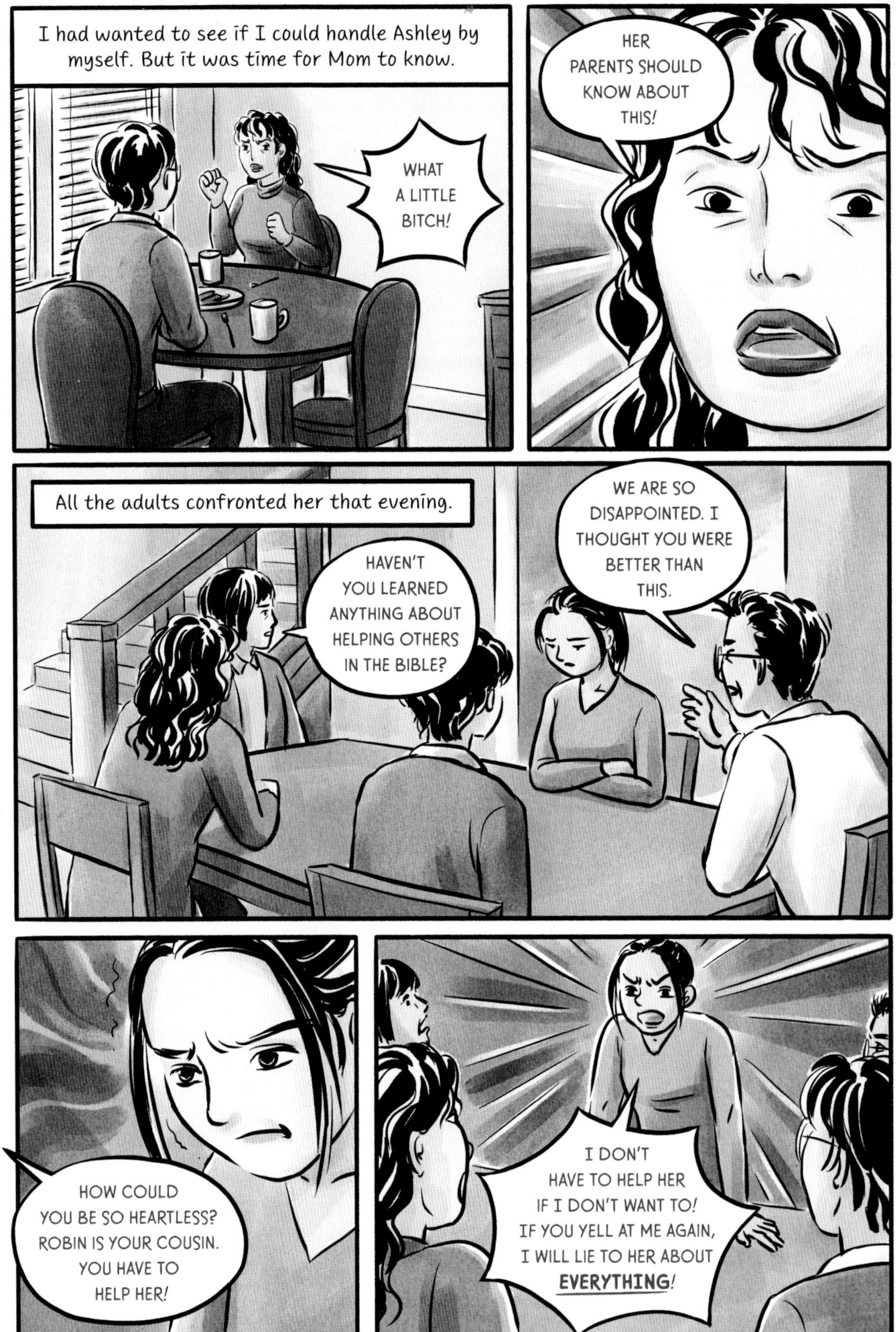
I had wanted to see if I could handle Ashley by myself. But it was time for Mom to know.
WHAT A LITTLE BITCH!
HER PARENTS SHOULD KNOW ABOUT THIS!
All the adults confronted her that evening.
HAVEN'T YOU LEARNED ANYTHING ABOUT HELPING OTHERS IN THE BIBLE?
WE ARE SO DISAPPOINTED. I THOUGHT YOU WERE BETTER THAN THIS.
HOW COULD YOU BE SO HEARTLESS? ROBIN IS YOUR COUSIN. YOU HAVE TO HELP HER!
I DON'T HAVE TO HELP HER IF I DON'T WANT TO! IF YOU YELL AT ME AGAIN, I WILL LIE TO HER ABOUT EVERYTHING!

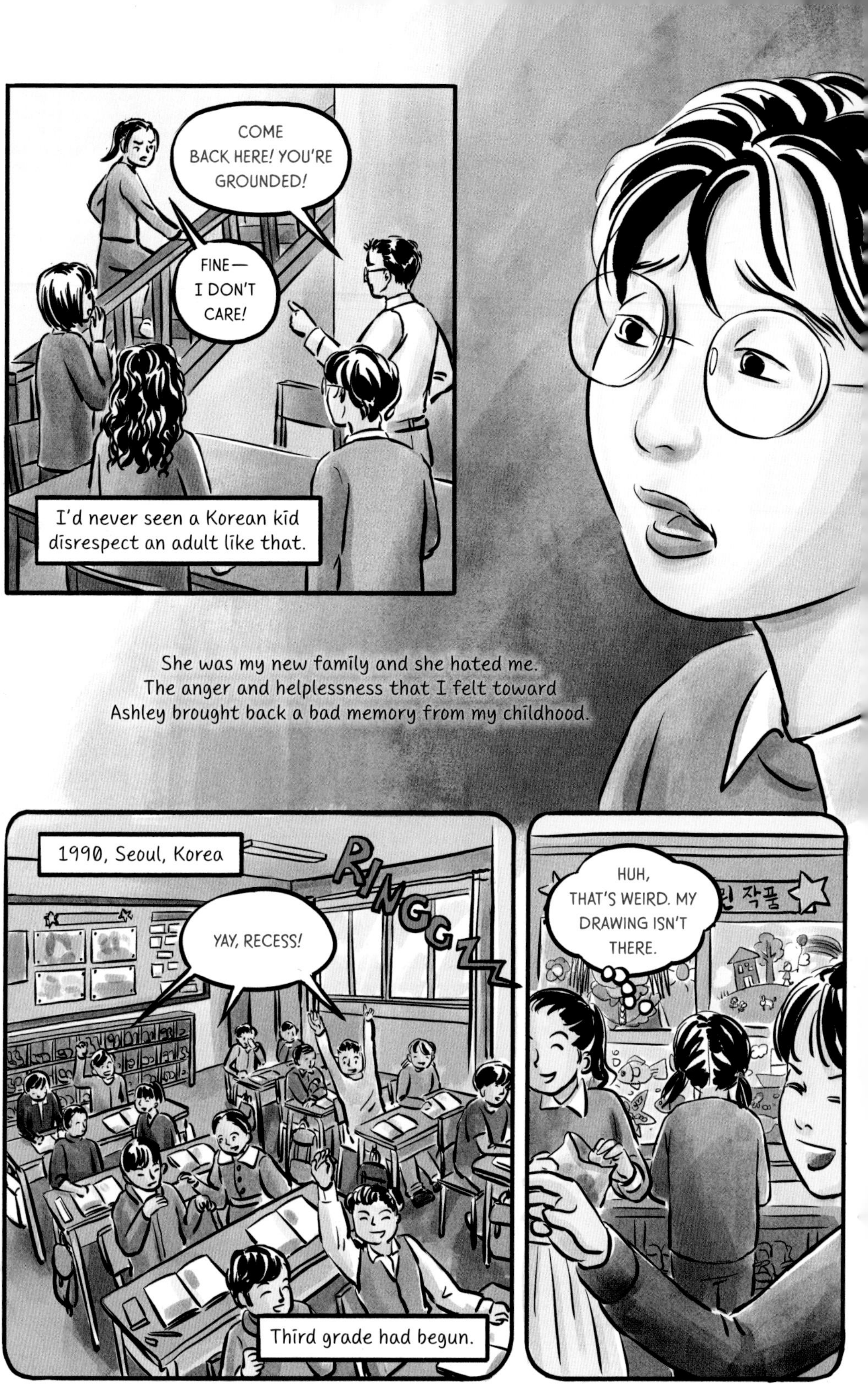
COME BACK HERE! YOU'RE GROUNDED!
FINE— I DON'T CARE!
I'd never seen a Korean kid disrespect an adult like that.
She was my new family and she hated me. The anger and helplessness that I felt toward Ashley brought back a bad memory from my childhood.
1990, Seoul, Korea
RINGGZZZ
YAY, RECESS!
Third grade had begun.
작품
HUH, THAT'S WEIRD. MY DRAWING ISN'T THERE.

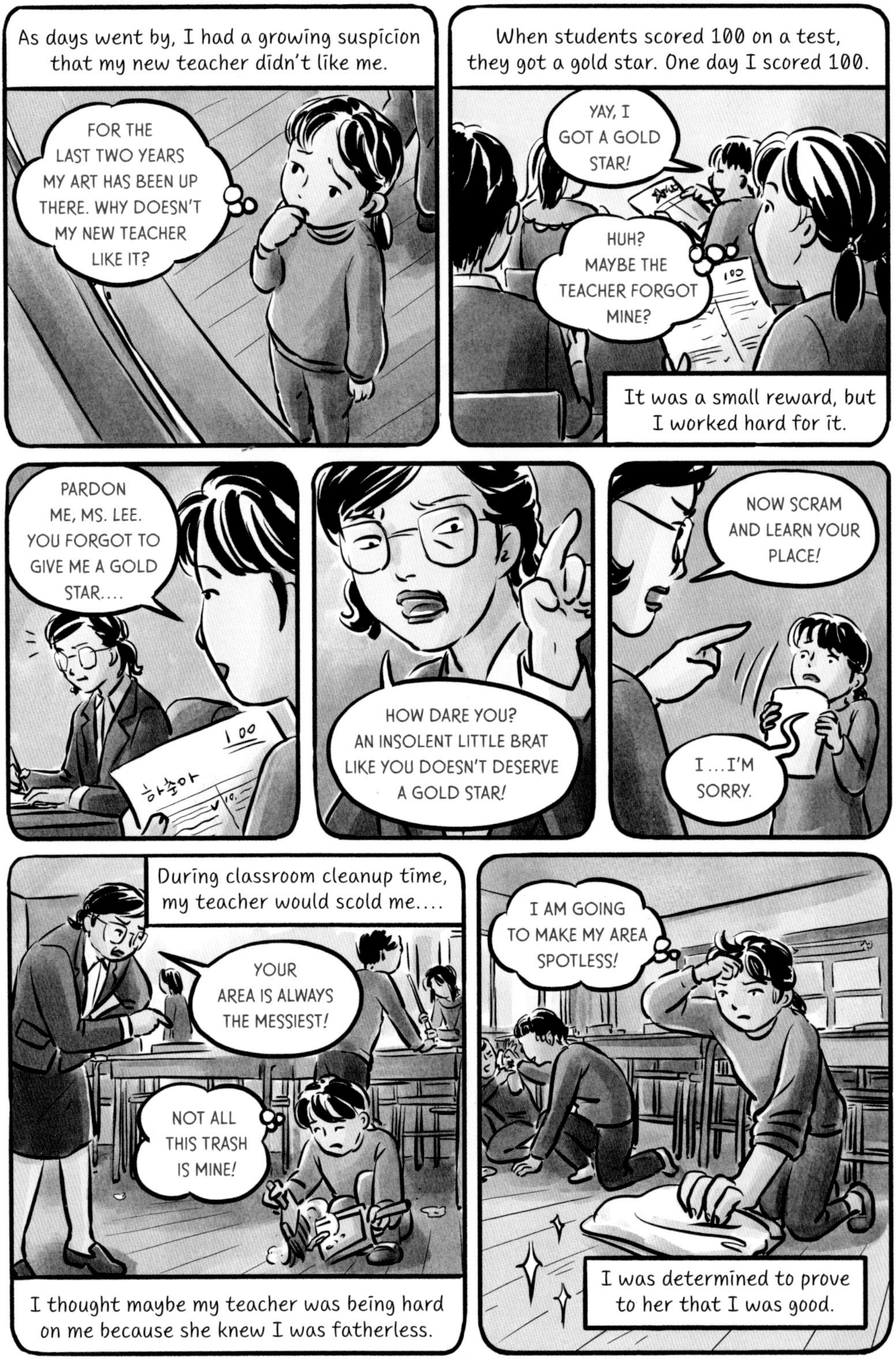
As days went by, I had a growing suspicion that my new teacher didn't like me.
FOR THE LAST TWO YEARS MY ART HAS BEEN UP THERE. WHY DOESN'T MY NEW TEACHER LIKE IT?
When students scored 100 on a test, they got a gold star. One day I scored 100.
YAY, I GOT A GOLD STAR!
HUH? MAYBE THE TEACHER FORGOT MINE?
It was a small reward, but I worked hard for it.
PARDON ME, MS. LEE. YOU FORGOT TO GIVE ME A GOLD STAR....
HOW DARE YOU? AN INSOLENT LITTLE BRAT LIKE YOU DOESN'T DESERVE A GOLD STAR!
NOW SCRAM AND LEARN YOUR PLACE!
I...I'M SORRY.
During classroom cleanup time, my teacher would scold me....
YOUR AREA IS ALWAYS THE MESSIEST!
NOT ALL THIS TRASH IS MINE!
I thought maybe my teacher was being hard on me because she knew I was fatherless.
I AM GOING TO MAKE MY AREA SPOTLESS!
I was determined to prove to her that I was good.

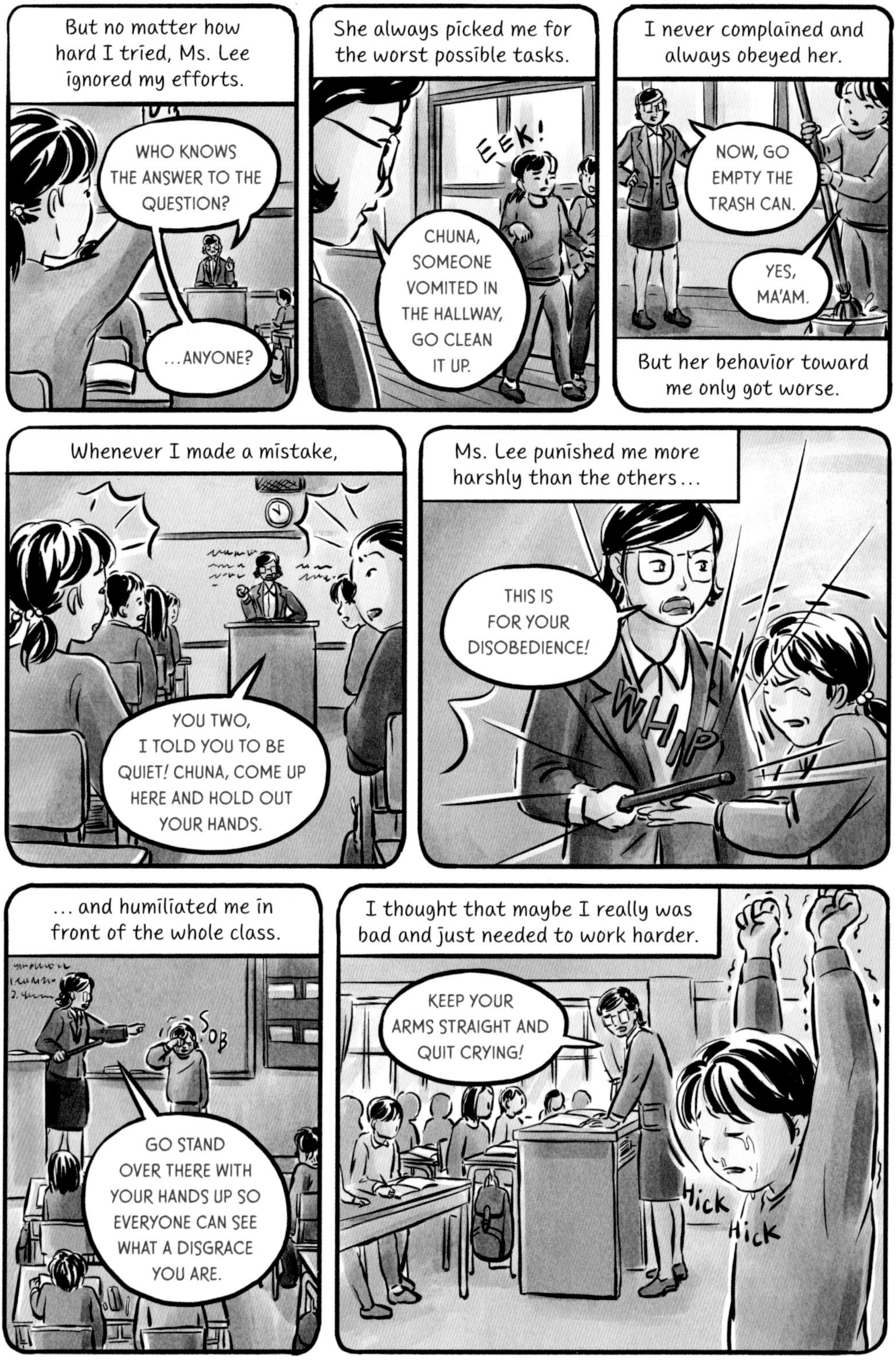
But no matter how hard I tried, Ms. Lee ignored my efforts.
WHO KNOWS THE ANSWER TO THE QUESTION?
...ANYONE?
She always picked me for the worst possible tasks.
EEK!
CHUNA, SOMEONE VOMITED IN THE HALLWAY, GO CLEAN IT UP.
I never complained and always obeyed her.
NOW, GO EMPTY THE TRASH CAN.
YES, MA'AM.
But her behavior toward me only got worse.
Whenever I made a mistake,
YOU TWO, I TOLD YOU TO BE QUIET! CHUNA, COME UP HERE AND HOLD OUT YOUR HANDS.
Ms. Lee punished me more harshly than the others...
THIS IS FOR YOUR DISOBEDIENCE!
WHIP
... and humiliated me in front of the whole class.
SOB
GO STAND OVER THERE WITH YOUR HANDS UP SO EVERYONE CAN SEE WHAT A DISGRACE YOU ARE.
I thought that maybe I really was bad and just needed to work harder.
KEEP YOUR ARMS STRAIGHT AND QUIT CRYING!
Hick
Hick

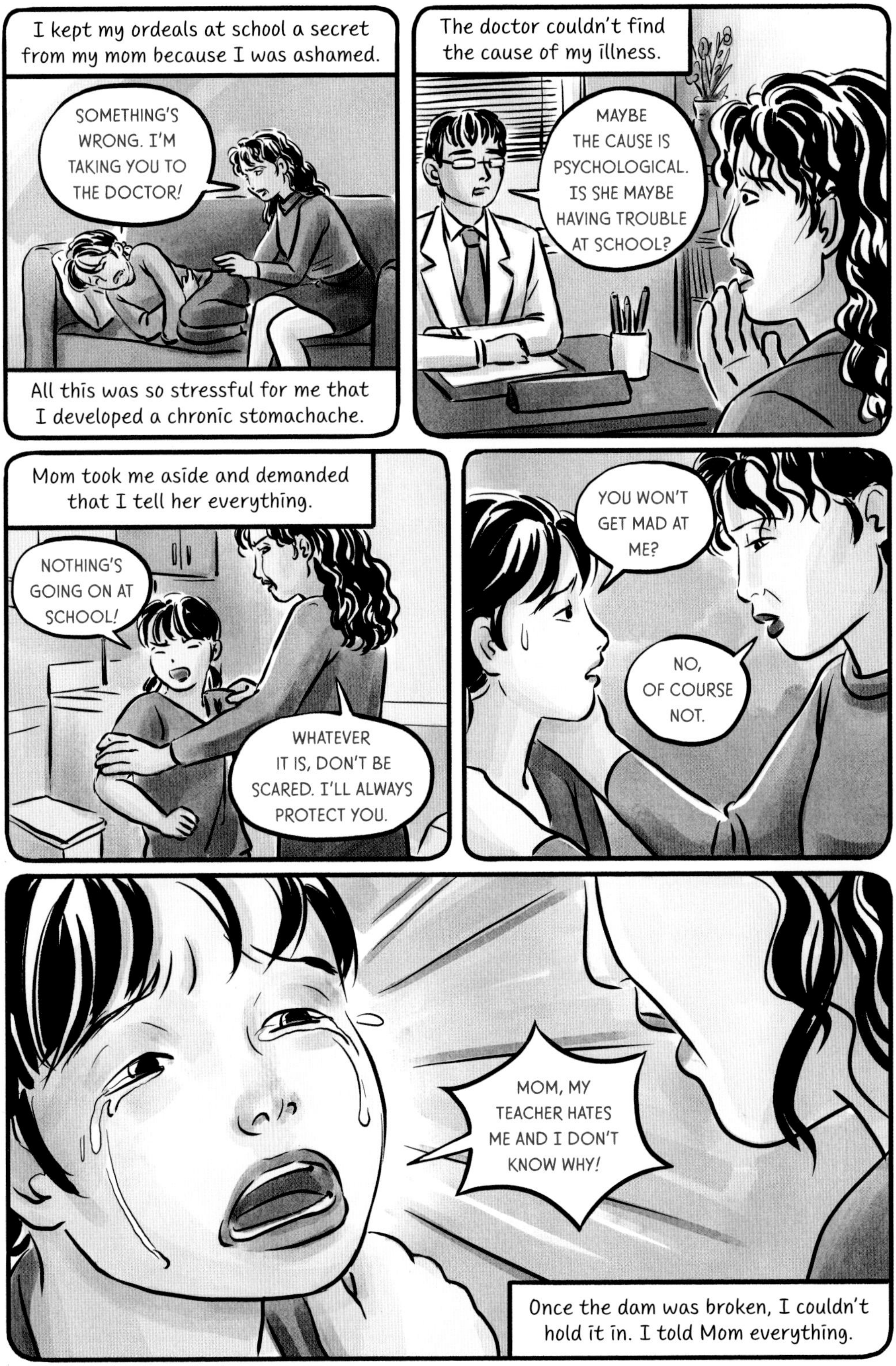
I kept my ordeals at school a secret from my mom because I was ashamed.
SOMETHING'S WRONG. I'M TAKING YOU TO THE DOCTOR!
All this was so stressful for me that I developed a chronic stomachache.
The doctor couldn't find the cause of my illness.
MAYBE THE CAUSE IS PSYCHOLOGICAL. IS SHE MAYBE HAVING TROUBLE AT SCHOOL?
Mom took me aside and demanded that I tell her everything.
NOTHING'S GOING ON AT SCHOOL!
WHATEVER IT IS, DON'T BE SCARED. I'LL ALWAYS PROTECT YOU.
YOU WON'T GET MAD AT ME?
NO, OF COURSE NOT.
MOM, MY TEACHER HATES ME AND I DON'T KNOW WHY!
Once the dam was broken, I couldn't hold it in. I told Mom everything.

I expected my mom to scold me for not being a better student.

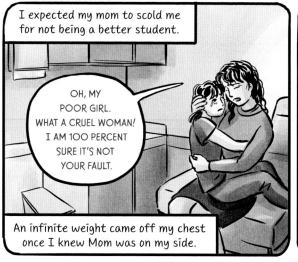

OH, MY POOR GIRL. WHAT A CRUEL WOMAN! I AM 100 PERCENT SURE IT'S NOT YOUR FAULT.

An infinite weight came off my chest once I knew Mom was on my side.

NO MATTER HOW BADLY SHE TREATS YOU, BE STRONG AND STUDY HARD.

Knowing that third grade would end in a few months helped me to get through it.

THIS YEAR WILL FLY BY AND YOU WILL GET A MUCH BETTER TEACHER NEXT YEAR.

I HOPE SO.

And my fourth-grade teacher turned out to be one of the best teachers I'd ever had.

Ashley's spitefulness seemed far more upsetting than that of my third-grade teacher, because she was my new family. This problem wasn't going to go away in a few months.

The only way to be free of her tyranny was to learn English.

Chapter 6

A Ghost of Me

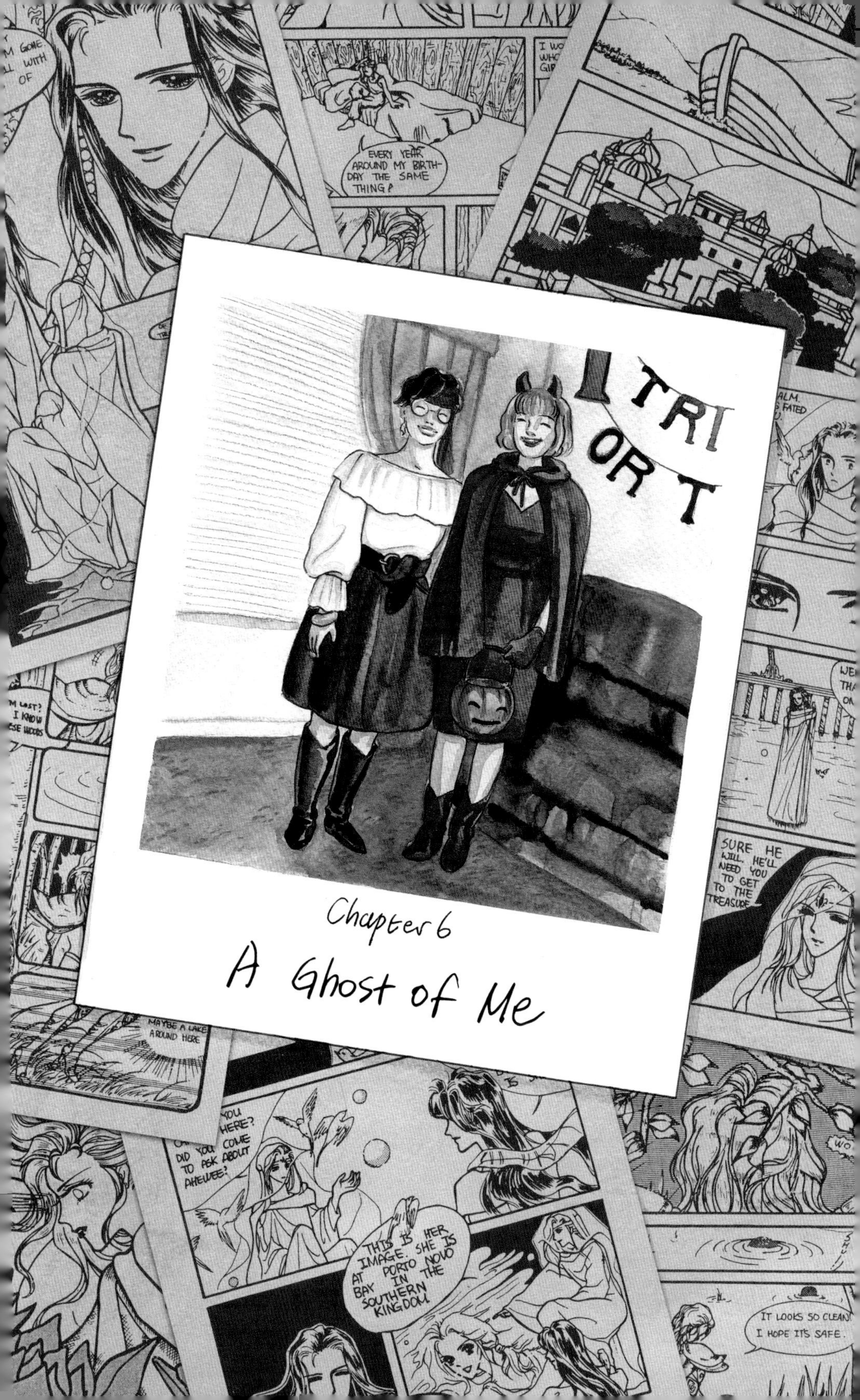
EVERY YEAR AROUND MY BIRTH-DAY THE SAME THING?
MAYBE A LAKE AROUND HERE
SURE HE WILL. HE'LL NEED YOU TO GET TO THE TREASURE
THIS IS HER IMAGE. SHE IS AT PORTO NOVO BAY IN THE SOUTHERN KINGDOM
IT LOOKS SO CLEAN! I HOPE IT'S SAFE.

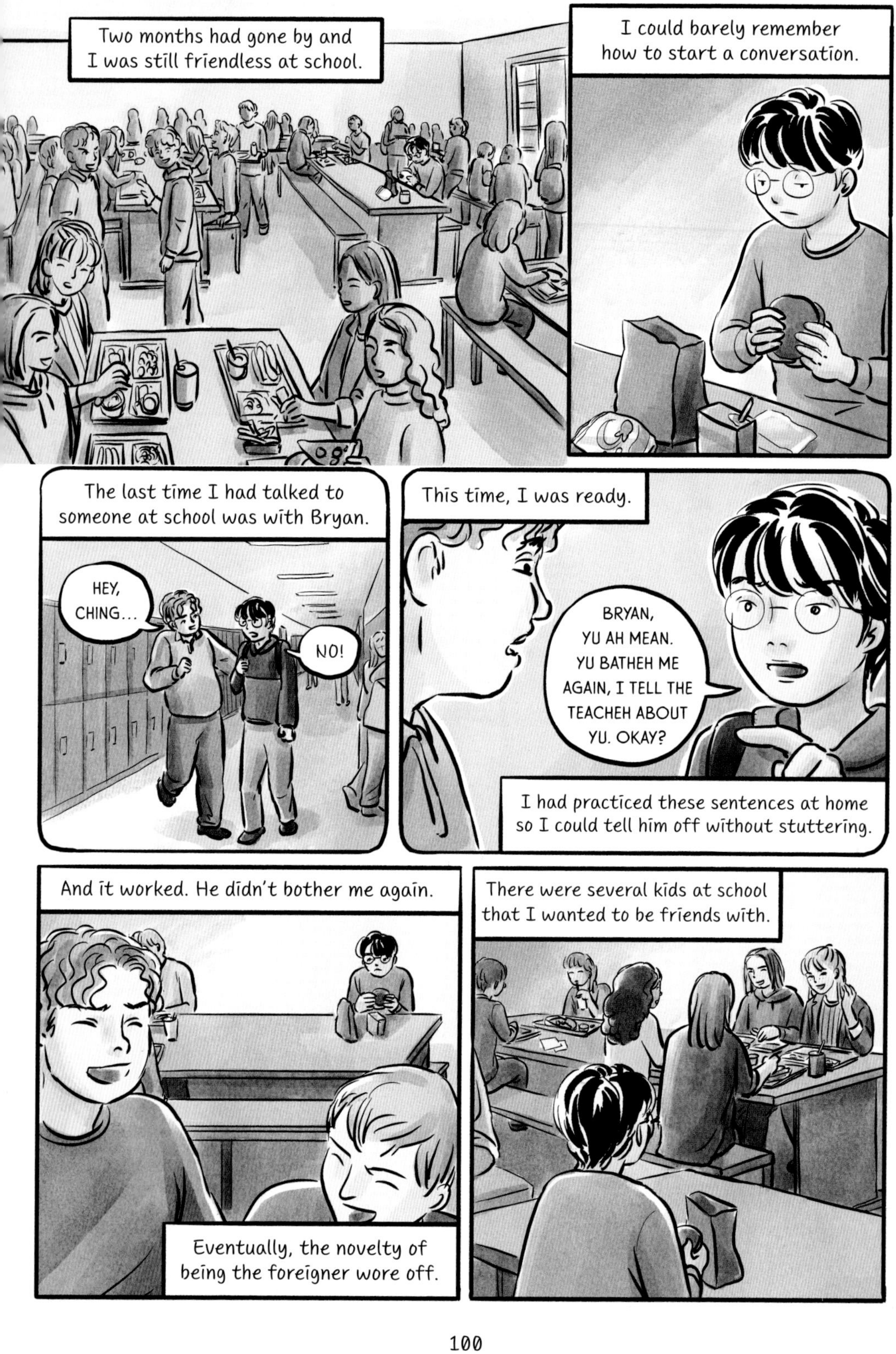
Two months had gone by and I was still friendless at school.
I could barely remember how to start a conversation.
The last time I had talked to someone at school was with Bryan.
HEY, CHING...
NO!
This time, I was ready.
BRYAN, YU AH MEAN. YU BATHEH ME AGAIN, I TELL THE TEACHEH ABOUT YU. OKAY?
I had practiced these sentences at home so I could tell him off without stuttering.
And it worked. He didn't bother me again.
Eventually, the novelty of being the foreigner wore off.
There were several kids at school that I wanted to be friends with.

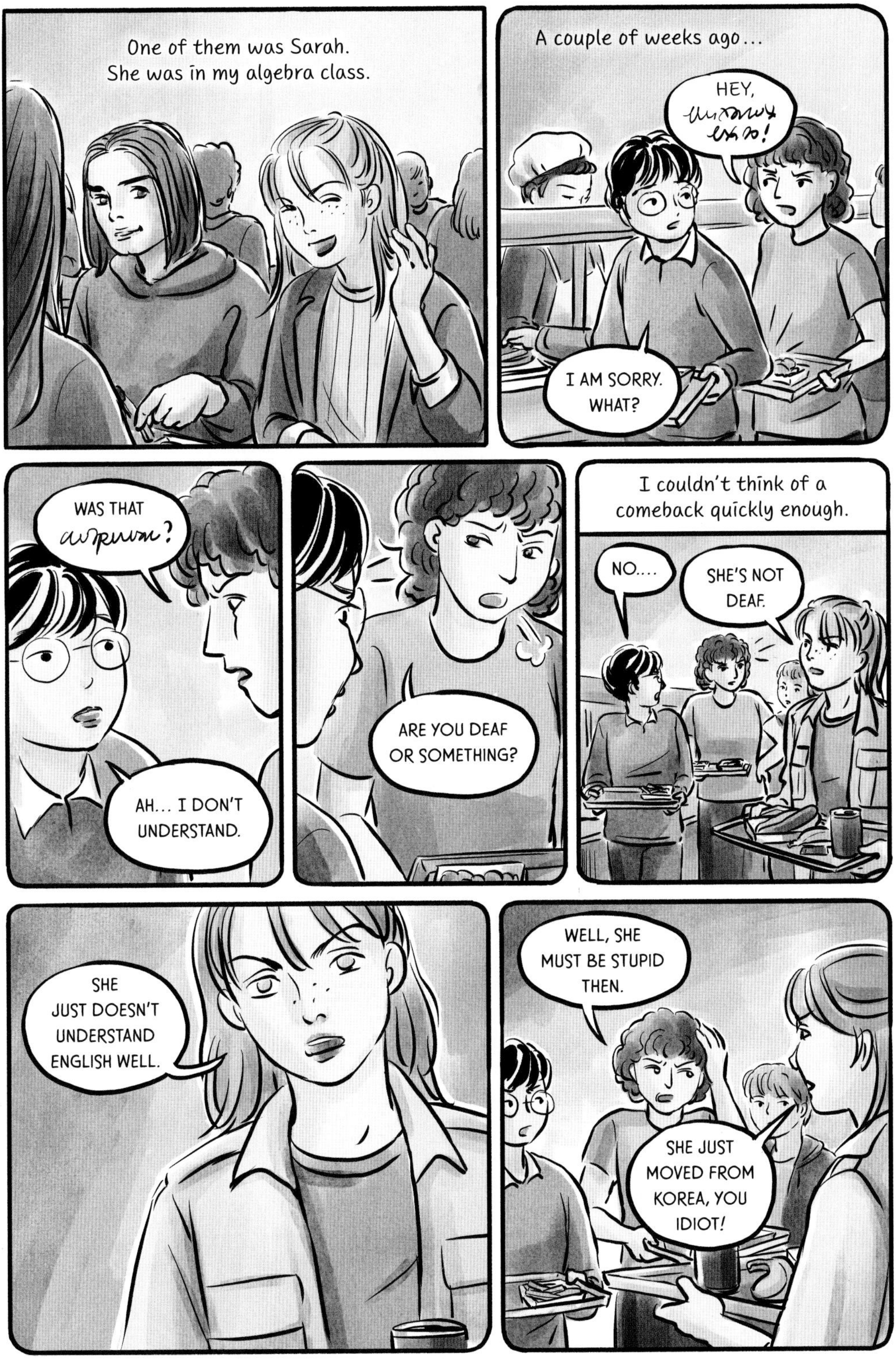
One of them was Sarah. She was in my algebra class.
A couple of weeks ago...
HEY,
I AM SORRY. WHAT?
WAS THAT
AH... I DON'T UNDERSTAND.
ARE YOU DEAF OR SOMETHING?
I couldn't think of a comeback quickly enough.
NO....
SHE'S NOT DEAF.
SHE JUST DOESN'T UNDERSTAND ENGLISH WELL.
WELL, SHE MUST BE STUPID THEN.
SHE JUST MOVED FROM KOREA, YOU IDIOT!

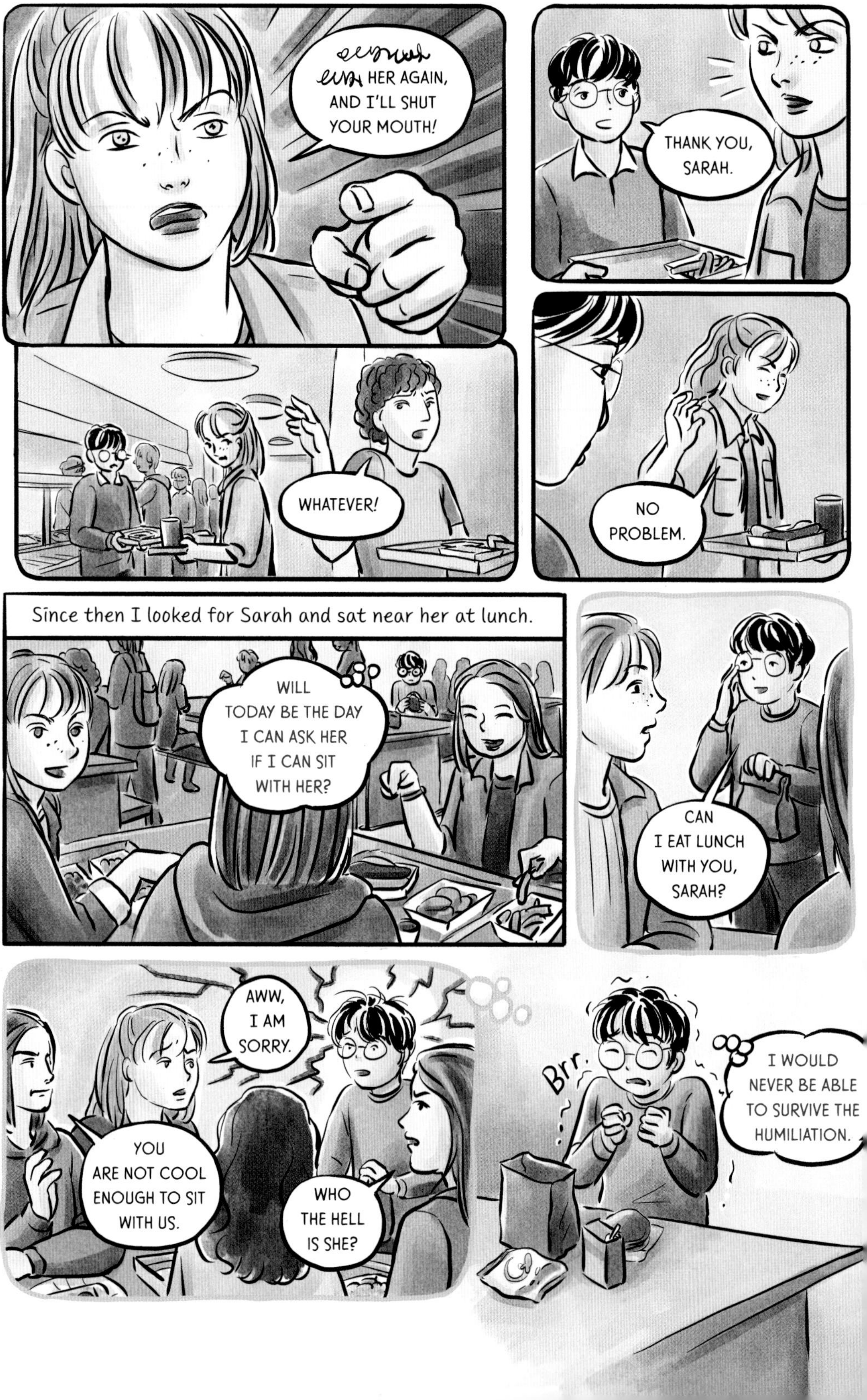
HER AGAIN, AND I'LL SHUT YOUR MOUTH!
THANK YOU, SARAH.
WHATEVER!
NO PROBLEM.
Since then I looked for Sarah and sat near her at lunch.
WILL TODAY BE THE DAY I CAN ASK HER IF I CAN SIT WITH HER?
CAN I EAT LUNCH WITH YOU, SARAH?
AWW, I AM SORRY.
YOU ARE NOT COOL ENOUGH TO SIT WITH US.
WHO THE HELL IS SHE?
Brr.
I WOULD NEVER BE ABLE TO SURVIVE THE HUMILIATION.

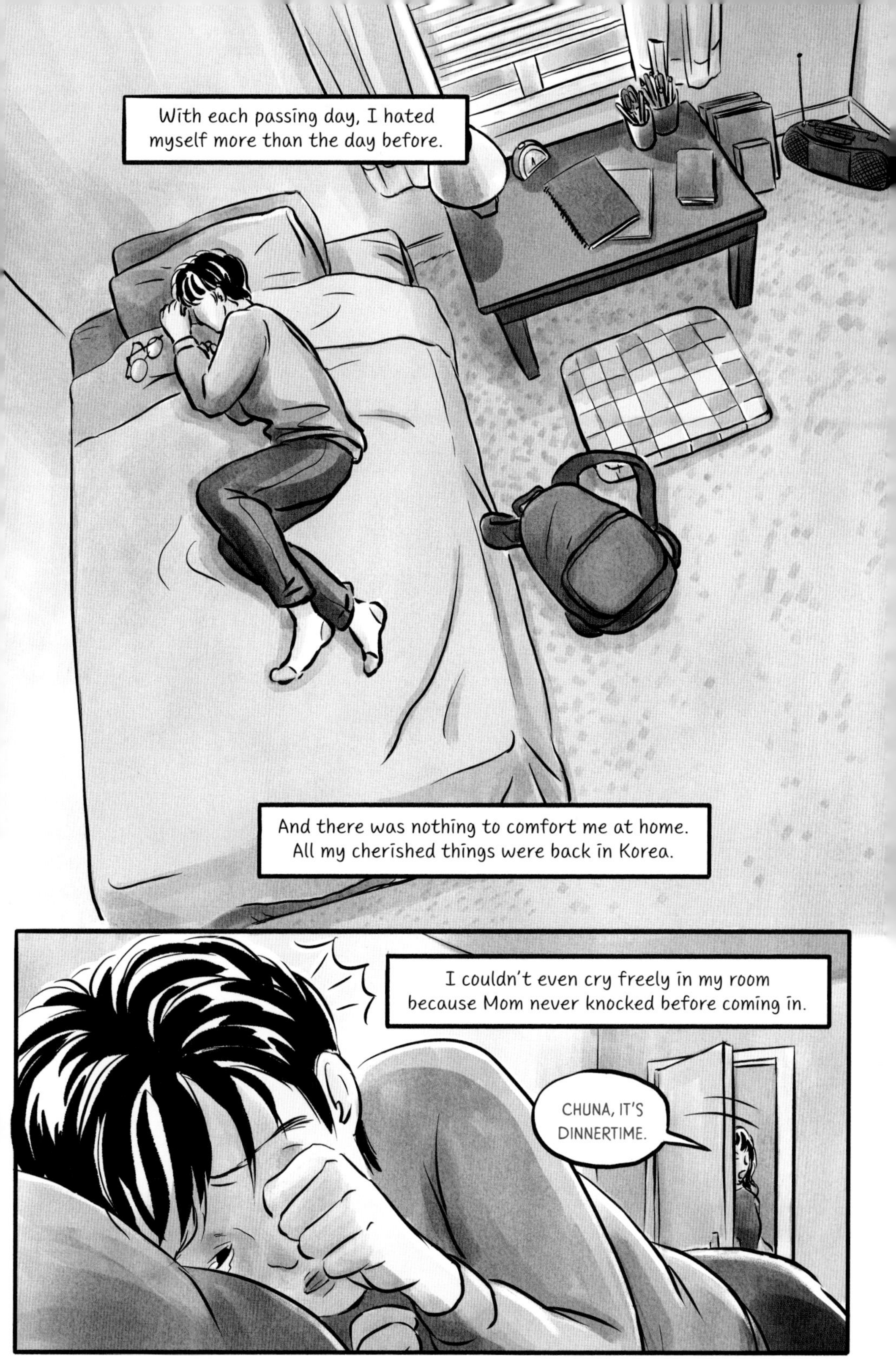
With each passing day, I hated myself more than the day before.
And there was nothing to comfort me at home. All my cherished things were back in Korea.
I couldn't even cry freely in my room because Mom never knocked before coming in.
CHUNA, IT'S DINNERTIME.

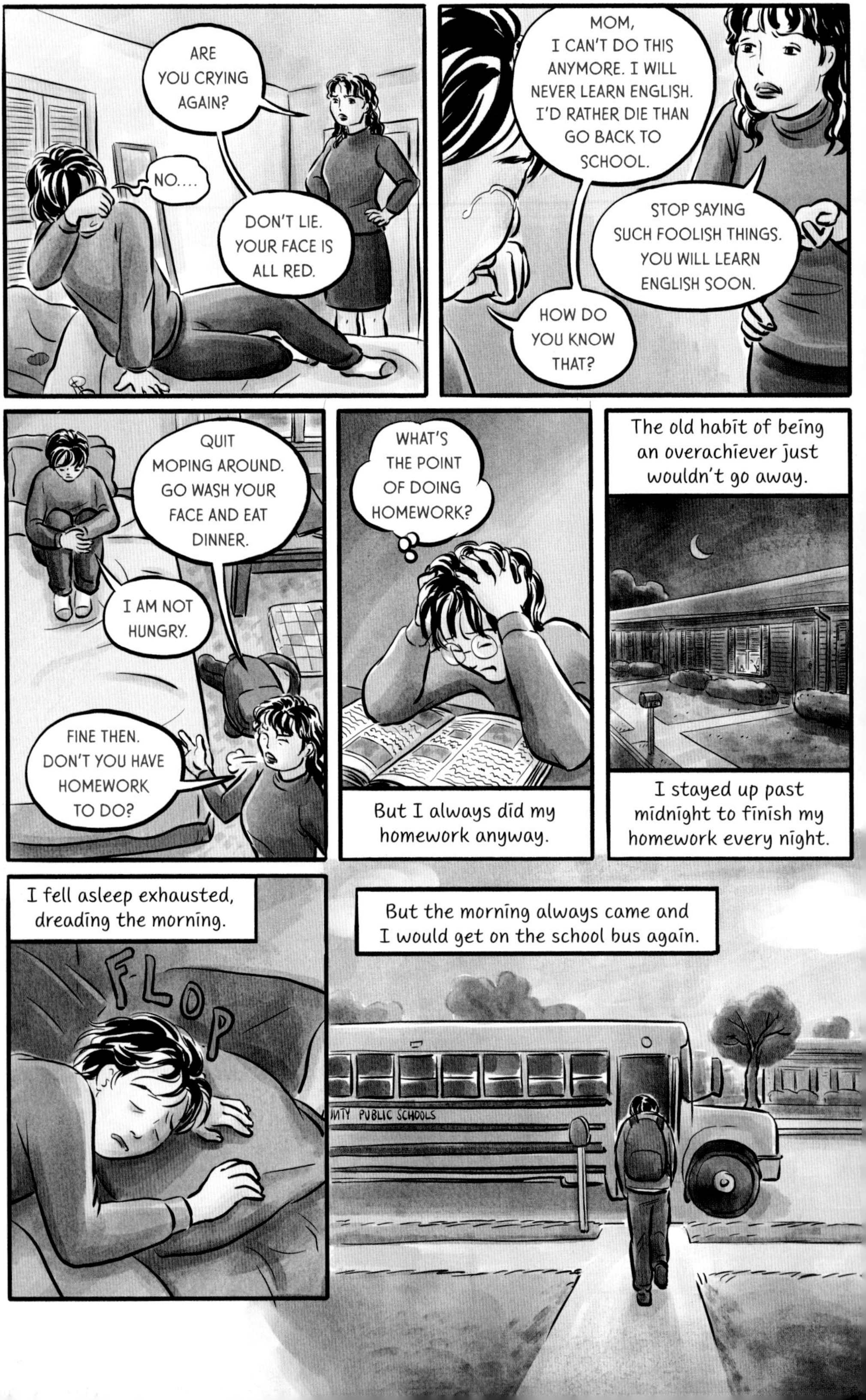
ARE YOU CRYING AGAIN?
NO....
DON'T LIE. YOUR FACE IS ALL RED.
MOM, I CAN'T DO THIS ANYMORE. I WILL NEVER LEARN ENGLISH. I'D RATHER DIE THAN GO BACK TO SCHOOL.
STOP SAYING SUCH FOOLISH THINGS. YOU WILL LEARN ENGLISH SOON.
HOW DO YOU KNOW THAT?
QUIT MOPING AROUND. GO WASH YOUR FACE AND EAT DINNER.
I AM NOT HUNGRY.
FINE THEN. DON'T YOU HAVE HOMEWORK TO DO?
WHAT'S THE POINT OF DOING HOMEWORK?
But I always did my homework anyway.
The old habit of being an overachiever just wouldn't go away.
I stayed up past midnight to finish my homework every night.
I fell asleep exhausted, dreading the morning.
FLOP
But the morning always came and I would get on the school bus again.
PUBLIC SCHOOLS

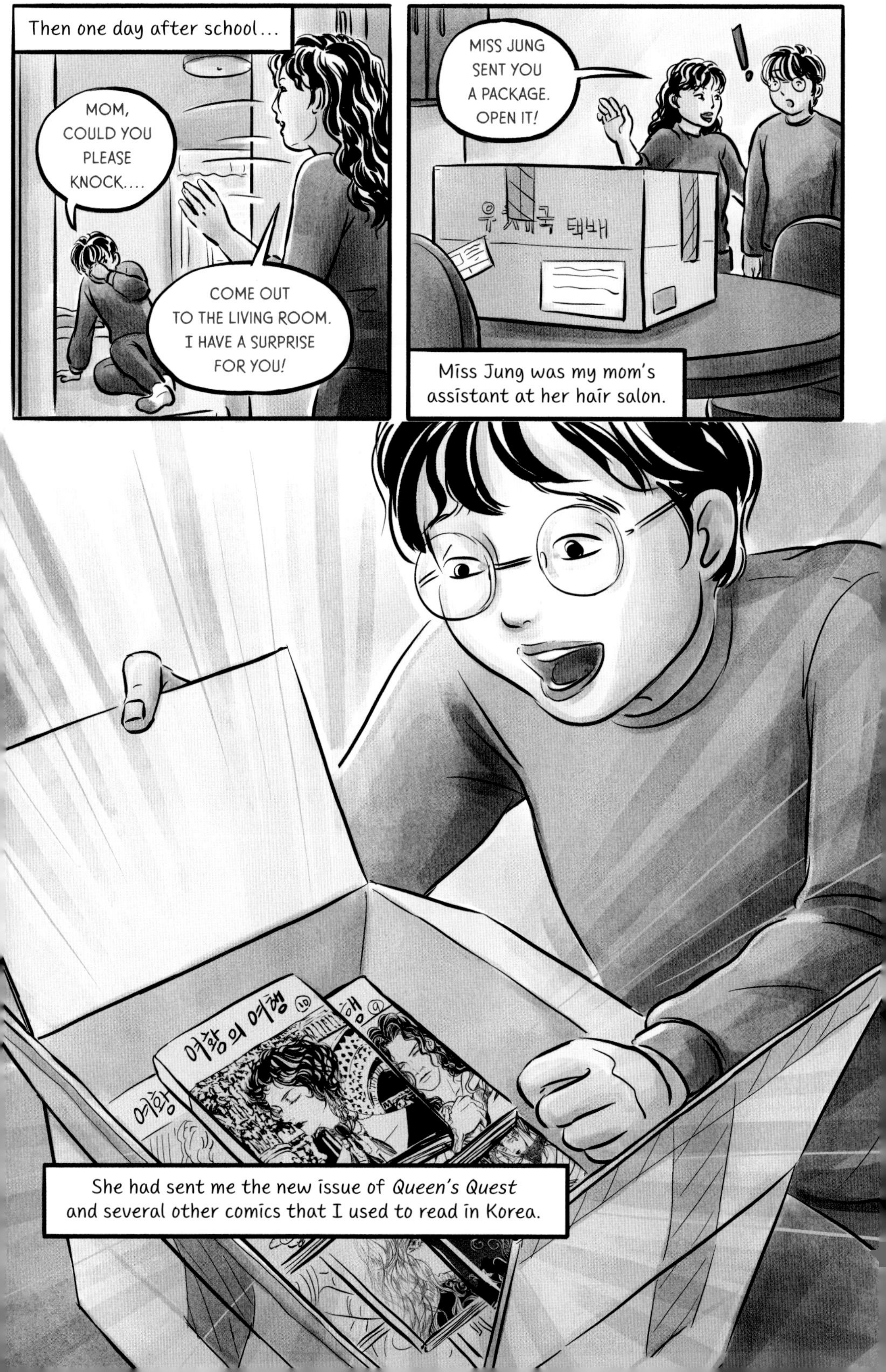
Then one day after school...
MOM, COULD YOU PLEASE KNOCK....
COME OUT TO THE LIVING ROOM. I HAVE A SURPRISE FOR YOU!
MISS JUNG SENT YOU A PACKAGE. OPEN IT!
!
Miss Jung was my mom's assistant at her hair salon.
여황의 여행
She had sent me the new issue of *Queen's Quest* and several other comics that I used to read in Korea.

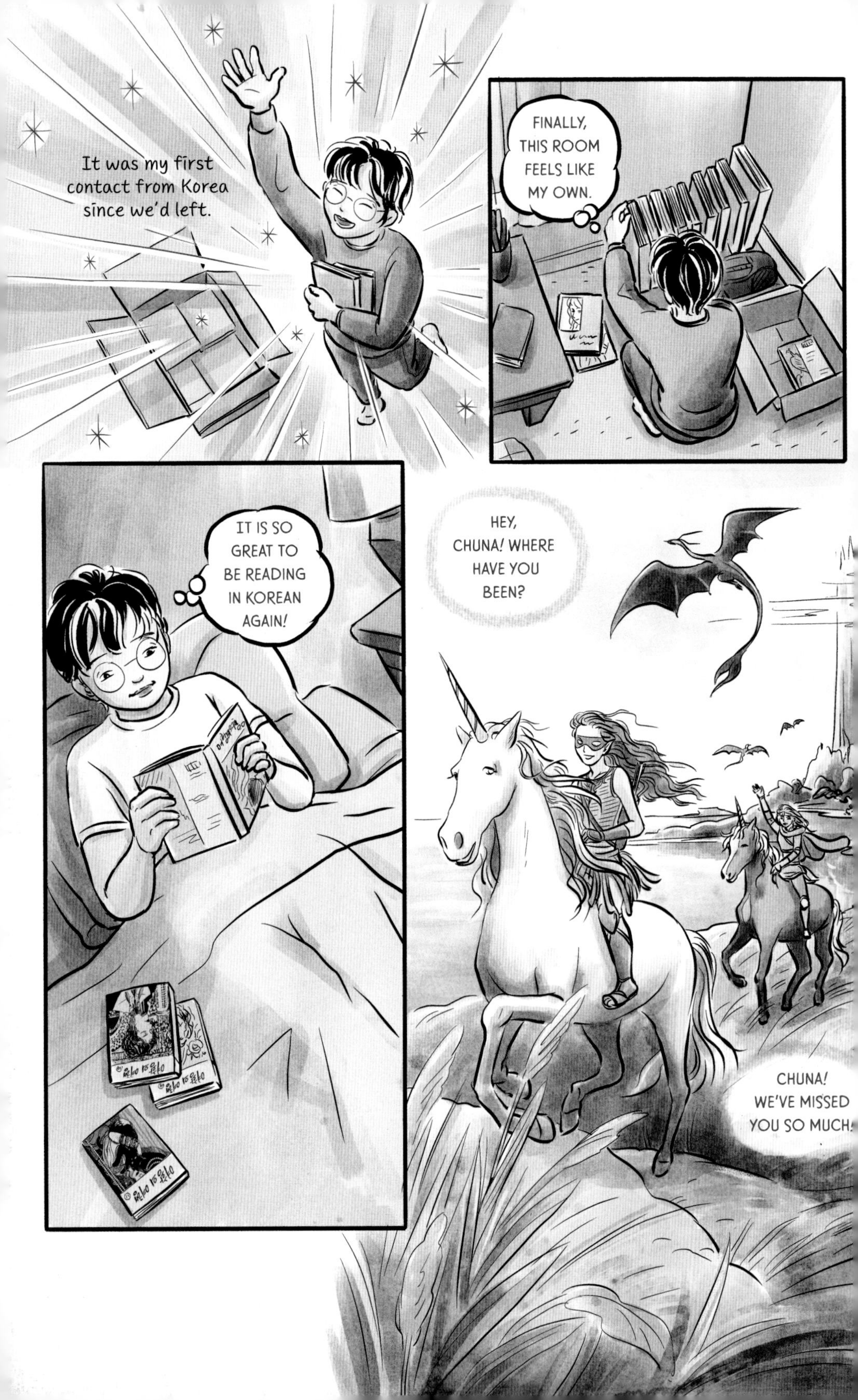
It was my first contact from Korea since we'd left.
FINALLY, THIS ROOM FEELS LIKE MY OWN.
IT IS SO GREAT TO BE READING IN KOREAN AGAIN!
HEY, CHUNA! WHERE HAVE YOU BEEN?
CHUNA! WE'VE MISSED YOU SO MUCH!

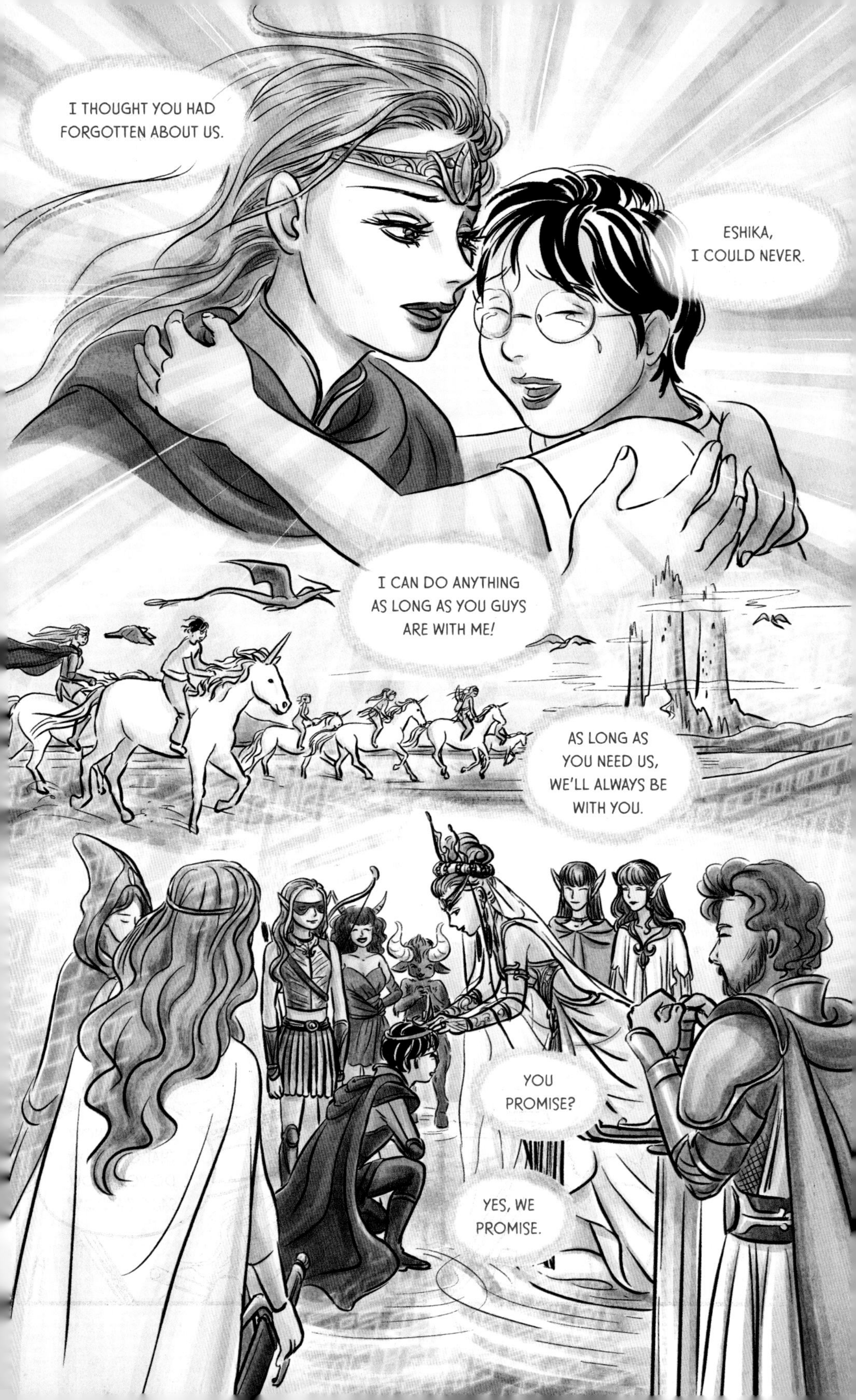
I THOUGHT YOU HAD FORGOTTEN ABOUT US.
ESHIKA, I COULD NEVER.
I CAN DO ANYTHING AS LONG AS YOU GUYS ARE WITH ME!
AS LONG AS YOU NEED US, WE'LL ALWAYS BE WITH YOU.
YOU PROMISE?
YES, WE PROMISE.

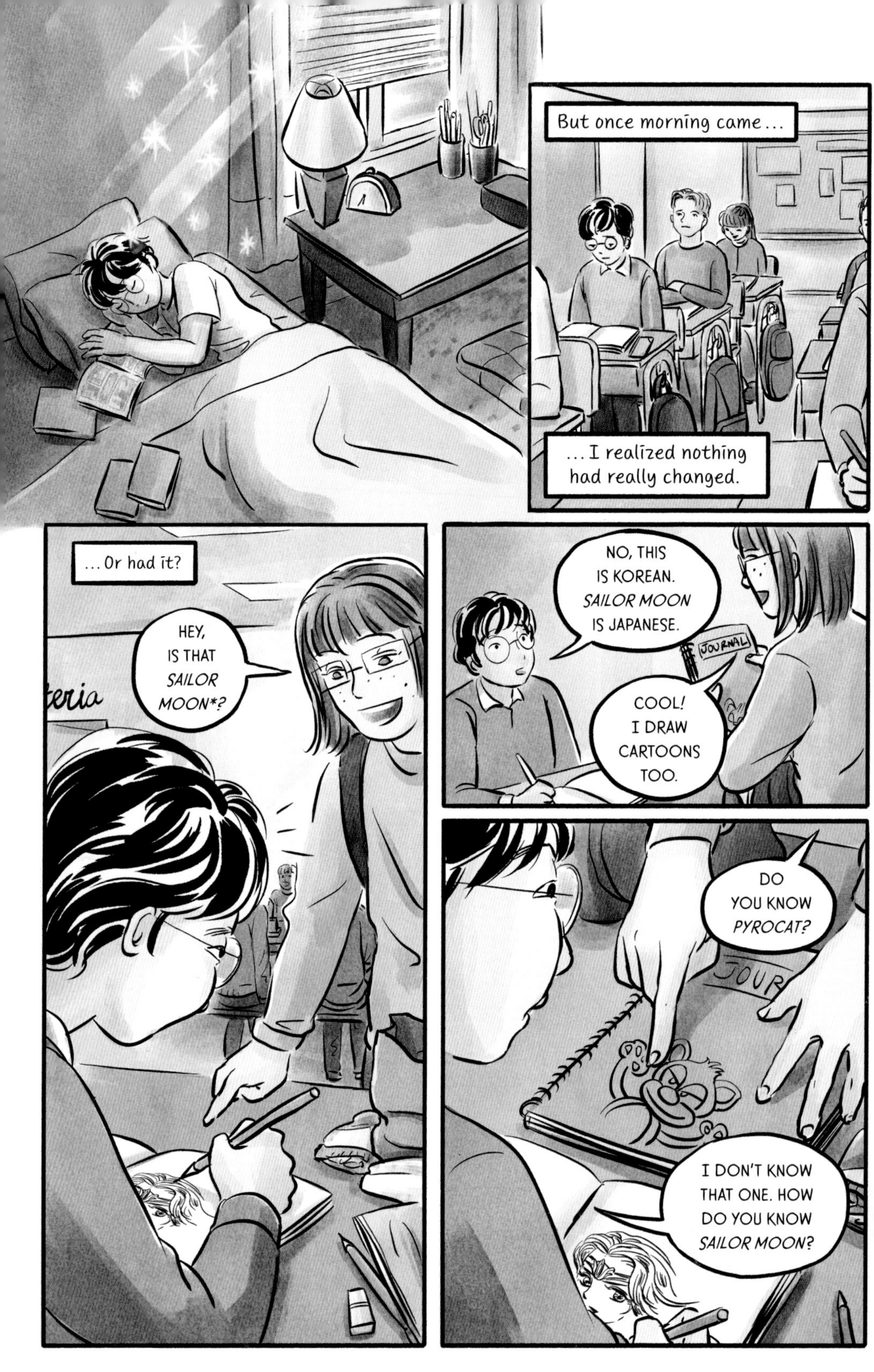
But once morning came...
...I realized nothing had really changed.
...Or had it?
HEY, IS THAT *SAILOR MOON**?
NO, THIS IS KOREAN. *SAILOR MOON* IS JAPANESE.
JOURNAL
COOL! I DRAW CARTOONS TOO.
DO YOU KNOW *PYROCAT?*
I DON'T KNOW THAT ONE. HOW DO YOU KNOW *SAILOR MOON?*

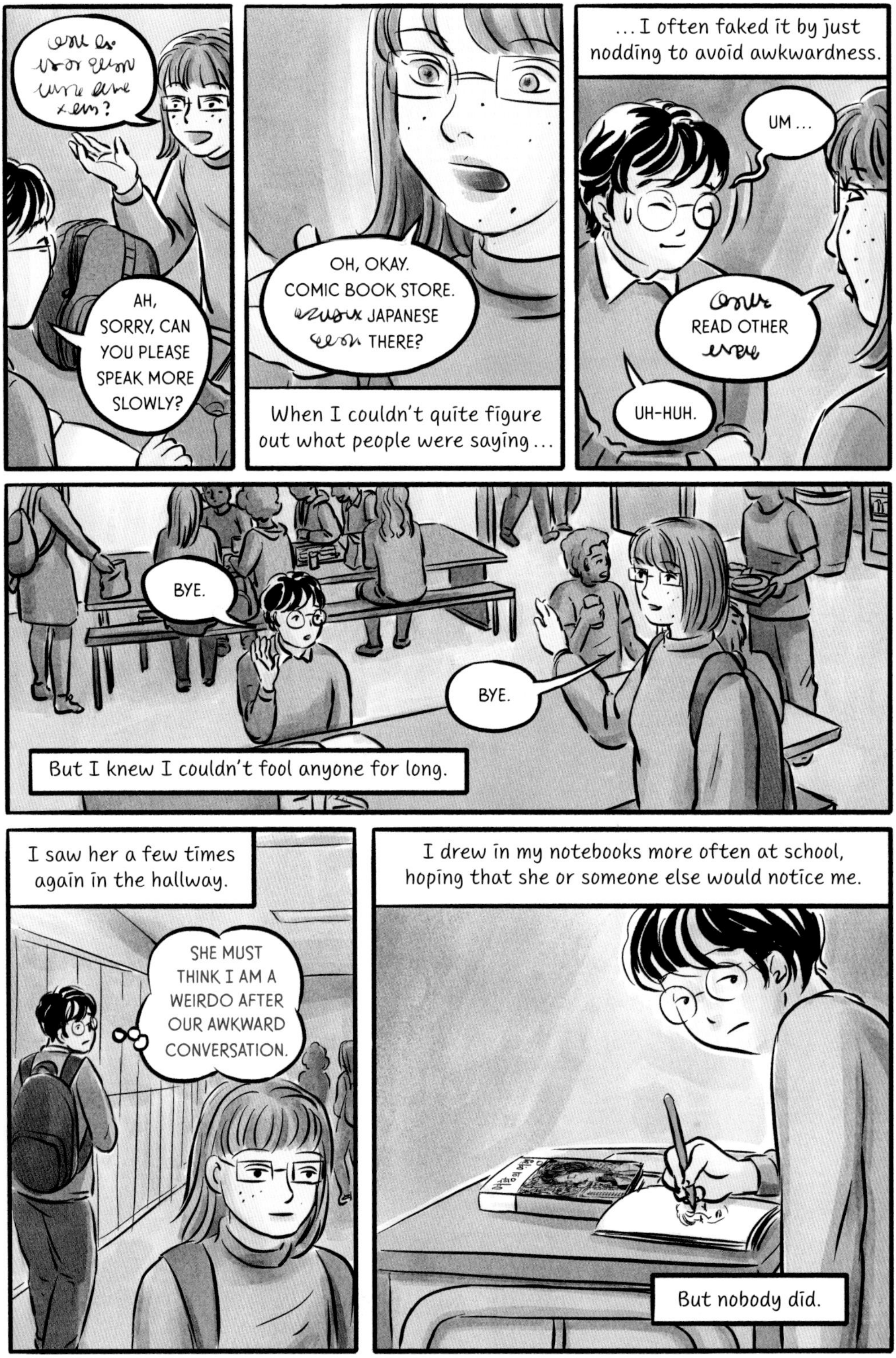
AH, SORRY, CAN YOU PLEASE SPEAK MORE SLOWLY?
OH, OKAY. COMIC BOOK STORE. JAPANESE THERE?
When I couldn't quite figure out what people were saying . . .
. . . I often faked it by just nodding to avoid awkwardness.
UM . . .
READ OTHER
UH-HUH.
BYE.
BYE.
But I knew I couldn't fool anyone for long.
I saw her a few times again in the hallway.
SHE MUST THINK I AM A WEIRDO AFTER OUR AWKWARD CONVERSATION.
I drew in my notebooks more often at school, hoping that she or someone else would notice me.
But nobody did.

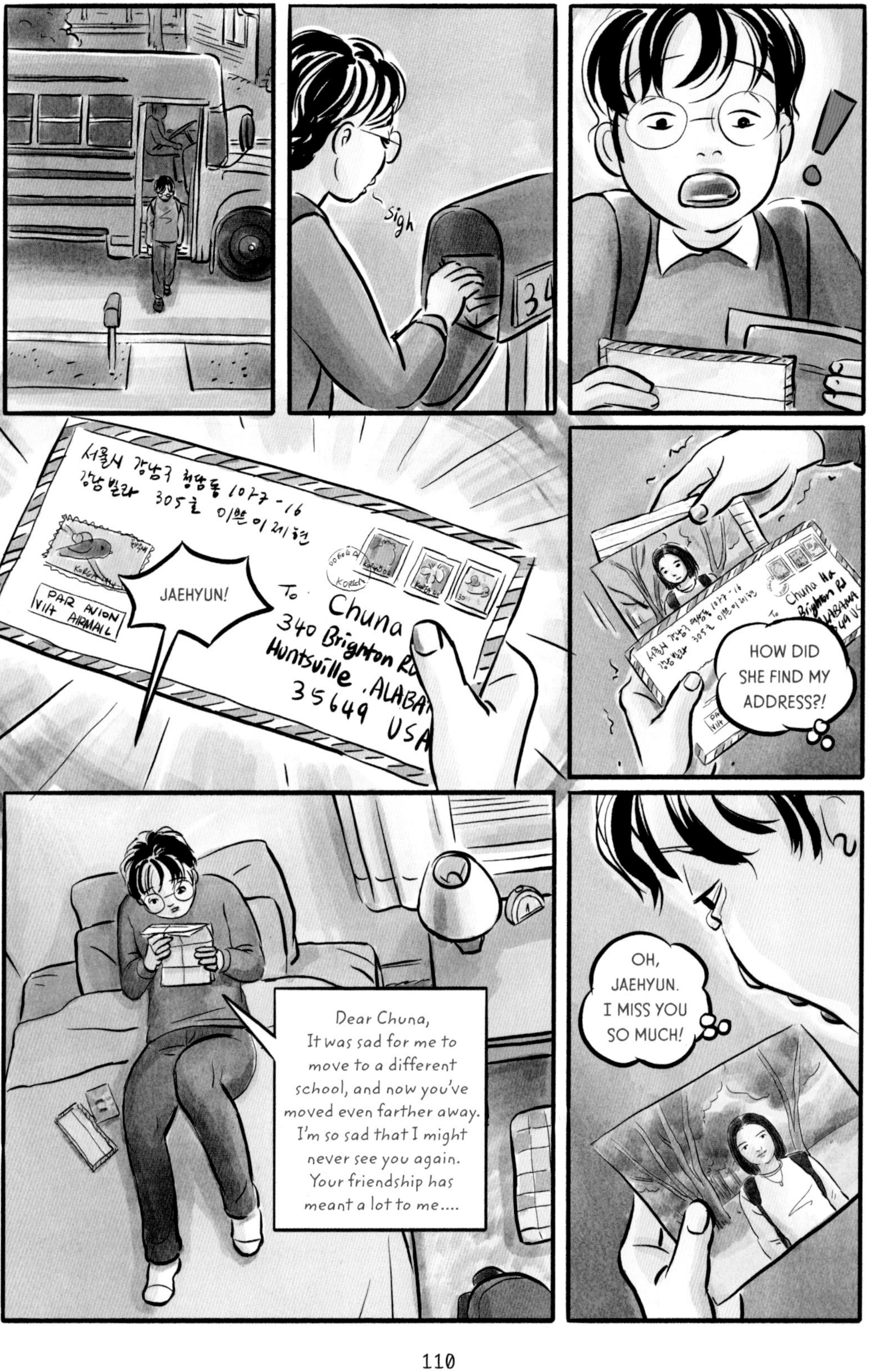
Sigh
서울시 강남구 청담동 1077-16
강남빌라 305호 이쁜 이재현
PAR AVION
VIA AIRMAIL
JAEHYUN!
To Chuna
340 Brighton RD
Huntsville, ALABA
35649 USA
HOW DID SHE FIND MY ADDRESS?!
Dear Chuna,
It was sad for me to move to a different school, and now you've moved even farther away. I'm so sad that I might never see you again. Your friendship has meant a lot to me....
OH, JAEHYUN. I MISS YOU SO MUCH!

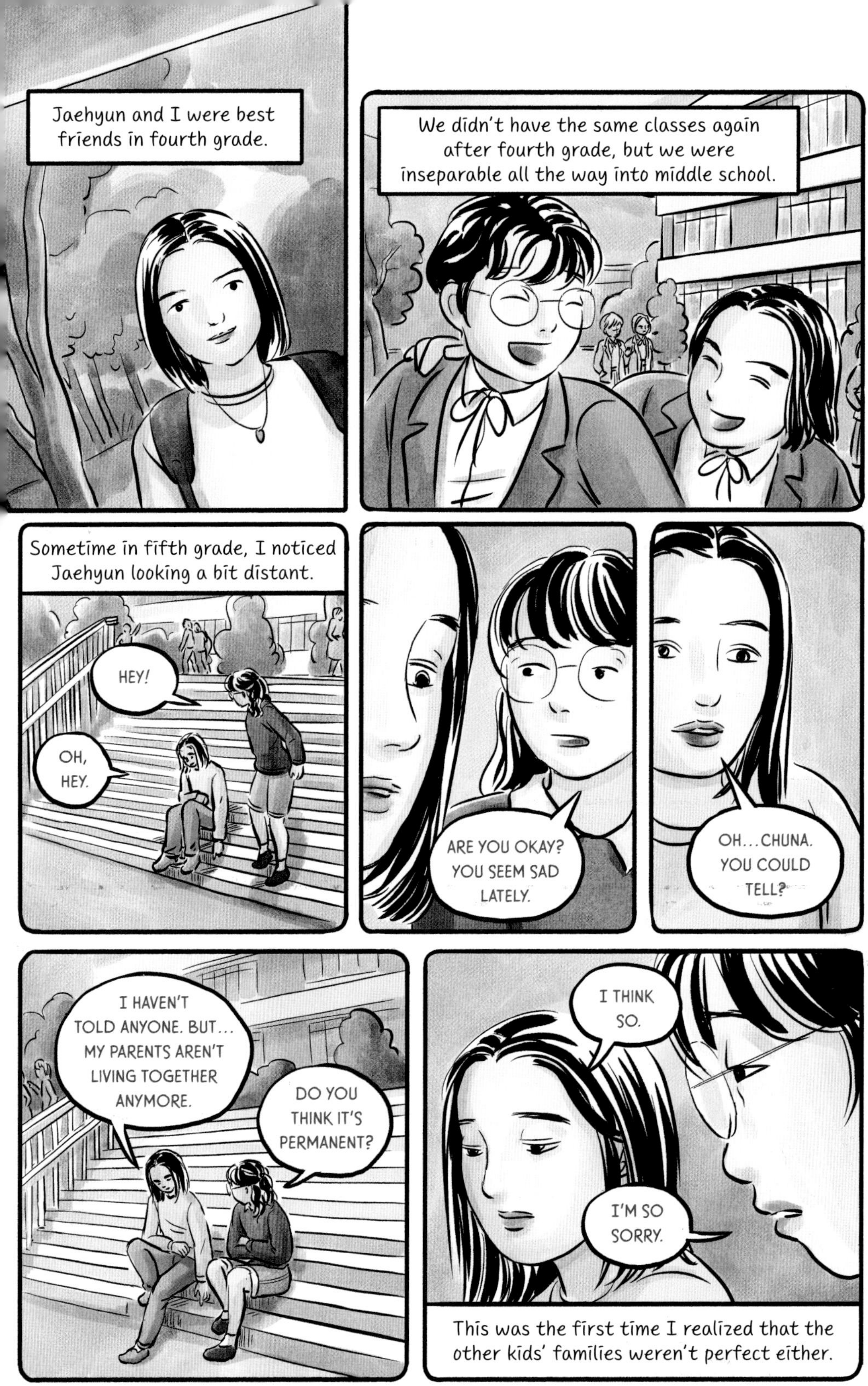
Jaehyun and I were best friends in fourth grade.
We didn't have the same classes again after fourth grade, but we were inseparable all the way into middle school.
Sometime in fifth grade, I noticed Jaehyun looking a bit distant.
HEY!
OH, HEY.
ARE YOU OKAY? YOU SEEM SAD LATELY.
OH... CHUNA. YOU COULD TELL?
I HAVEN'T TOLD ANYONE. BUT... MY PARENTS AREN'T LIVING TOGETHER ANYMORE.
DO YOU THINK IT'S PERMANENT?
I THINK SO.
I'M SO SORRY.
This was the first time I realized that the other kids' families weren't perfect either.

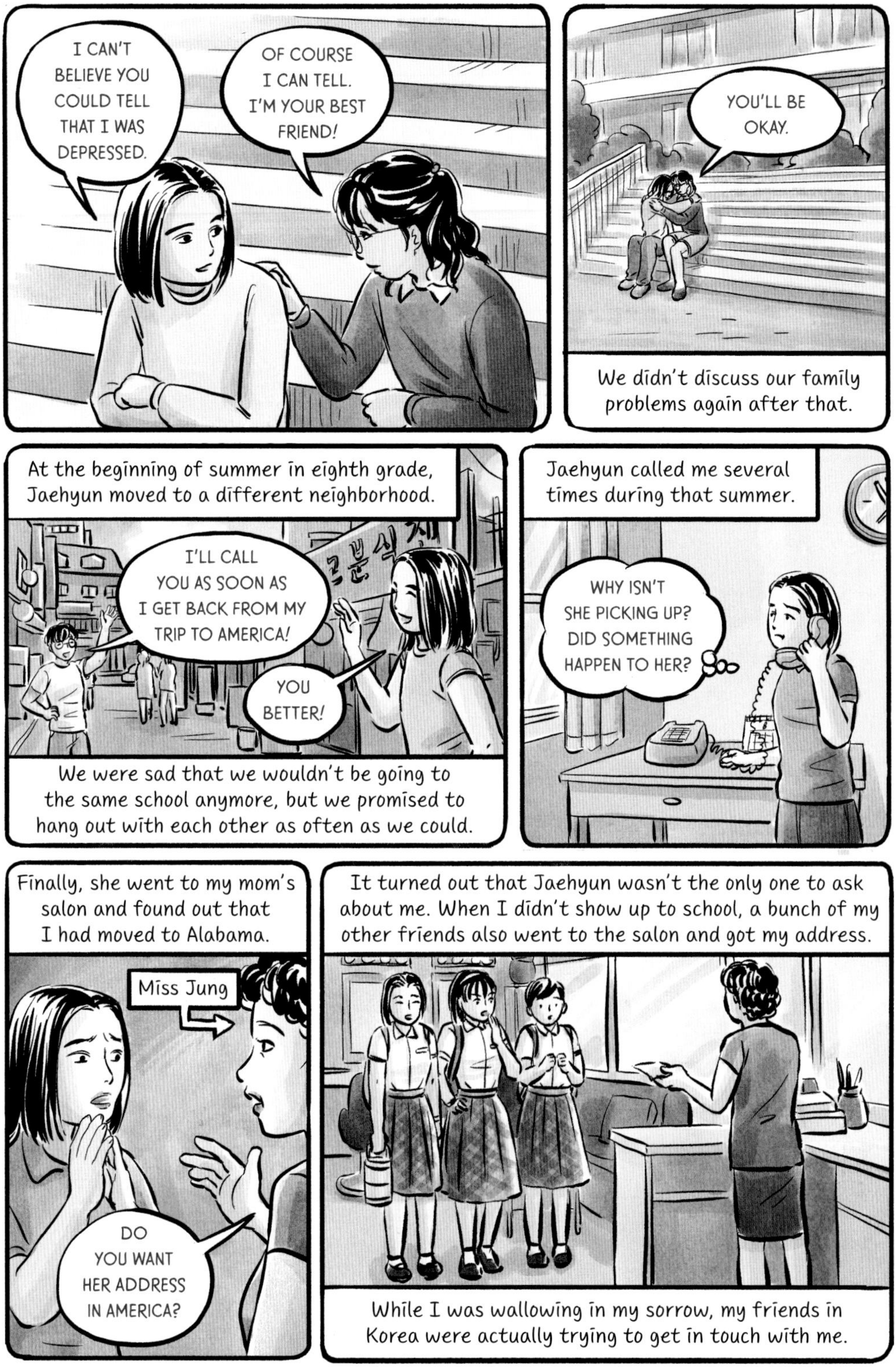
I CAN'T BELIEVE YOU COULD TELL THAT I WAS DEPRESSED.
OF COURSE I CAN TELL. I'M YOUR BEST FRIEND!
YOU'LL BE OKAY.
We didn't discuss our family problems again after that.
At the beginning of summer in eighth grade, Jaehyun moved to a different neighborhood.
I'LL CALL YOU AS SOON AS I GET BACK FROM MY TRIP TO AMERICA!
YOU BETTER!
We were sad that we wouldn't be going to the same school anymore, but we promised to hang out with each other as often as we could.
Jaehyun called me several times during that summer.
WHY ISN'T SHE PICKING UP? DID SOMETHING HAPPEN TO HER?
Finally, she went to my mom's salon and found out that I had moved to Alabama.
Miss Jung
DO YOU WANT HER ADDRESS IN AMERICA?
It turned out that Jaehyun wasn't the only one to ask about me. When I didn't show up to school, a bunch of my other friends also went to the salon and got my address.
While I was wallowing in my sorrow, my friends in Korea were actually trying to get in touch with me.

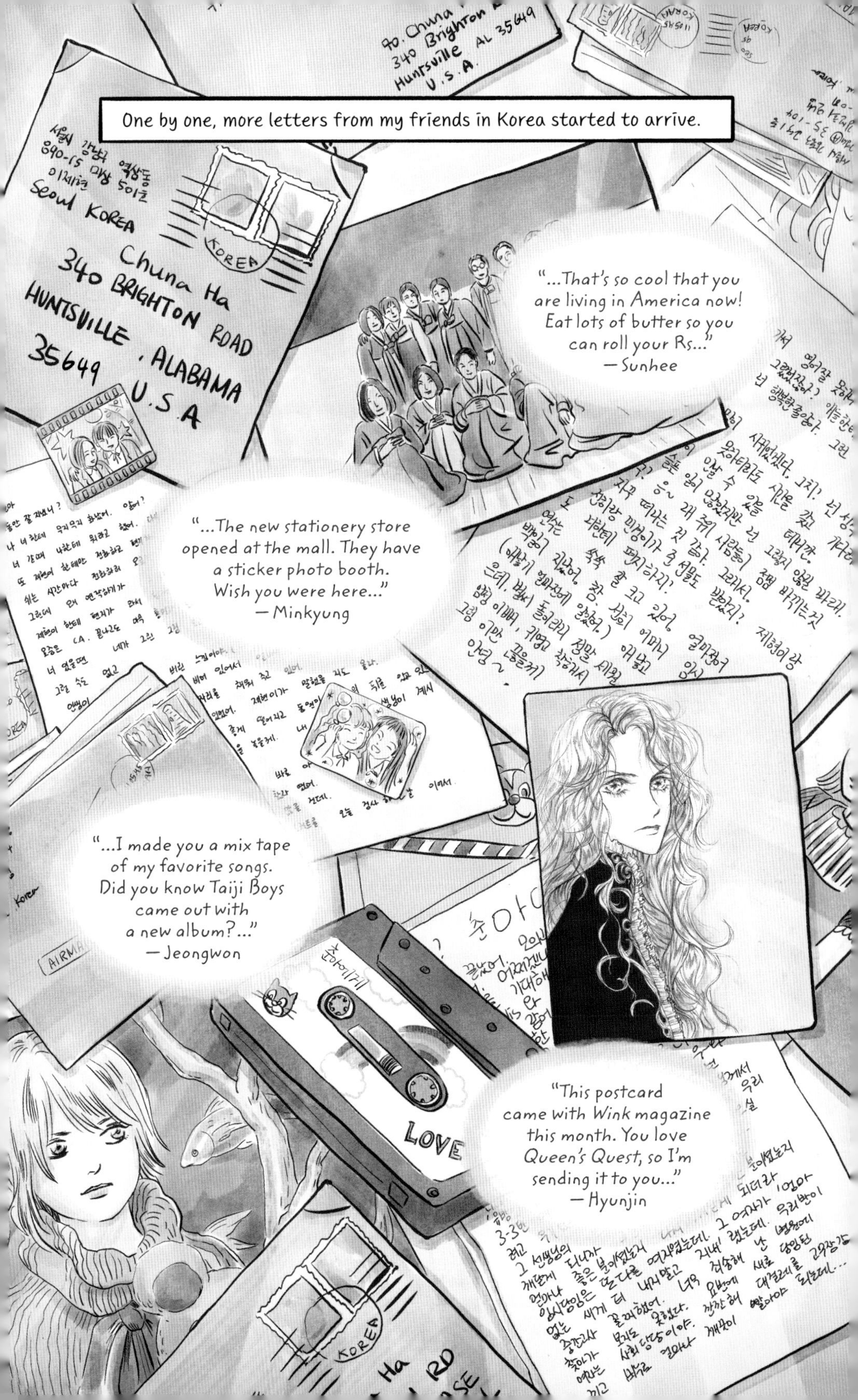
One by one, more letters from my friends in Korea started to arrive.
Chuna Ha 340 BRIGHTON ROAD HUNTSVILLE, ALABAMA 35649 U.S.A
"...That's so cool that you are living in America now! Eat lots of butter so you can roll your Rs..." —Sunhee
"...The new stationery store opened at the mall. They have a sticker photo booth. Wish you were here..." —Minkyung
"...I made you a mix tape of my favorite songs. Did you know Taiji Boys came out with a new album?..." —Jeongwon
LOVE
"This postcard came with Wink magazine this month. You love Queen's Quest, so I'm sending it to you..." —Hyunjin

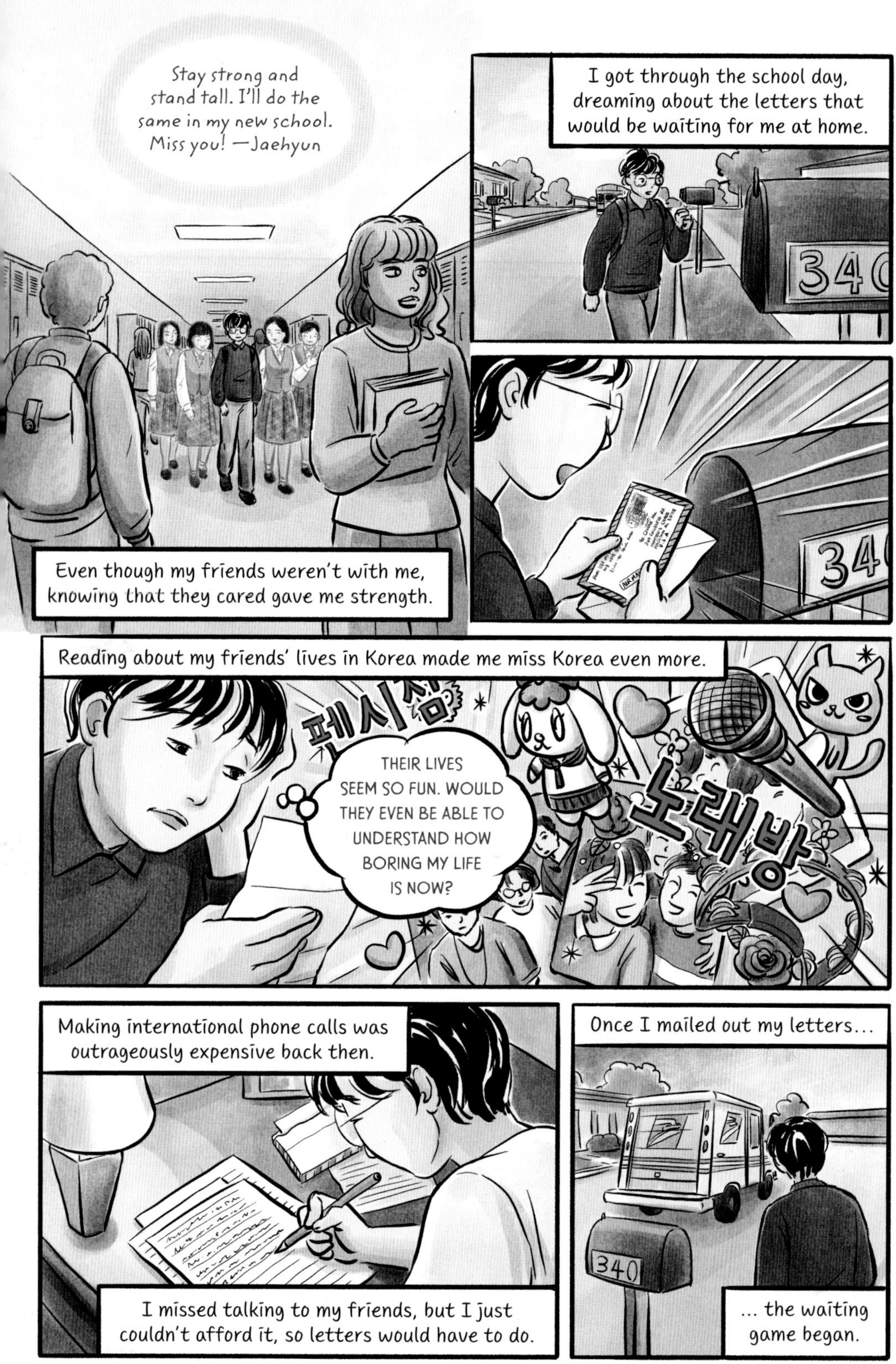
Stay strong and stand tall. I'll do the same in my new school. Miss you! —Jaehyun
Even though my friends weren't with me, knowing that they cared gave me strength.
I got through the school day, dreaming about the letters that would be waiting for me at home.
340
340
Reading about my friends' lives in Korea made me miss Korea even more.
펜시점
THEIR LIVES SEEM SO FUN. WOULD THEY EVEN BE ABLE TO UNDERSTAND HOW BORING MY LIFE IS NOW?
노래방
Making international phone calls was outrageously expensive back then.
I missed talking to my friends, but I just couldn't afford it, so letters would have to do.
Once I mailed out my letters...
340
... the waiting game began.

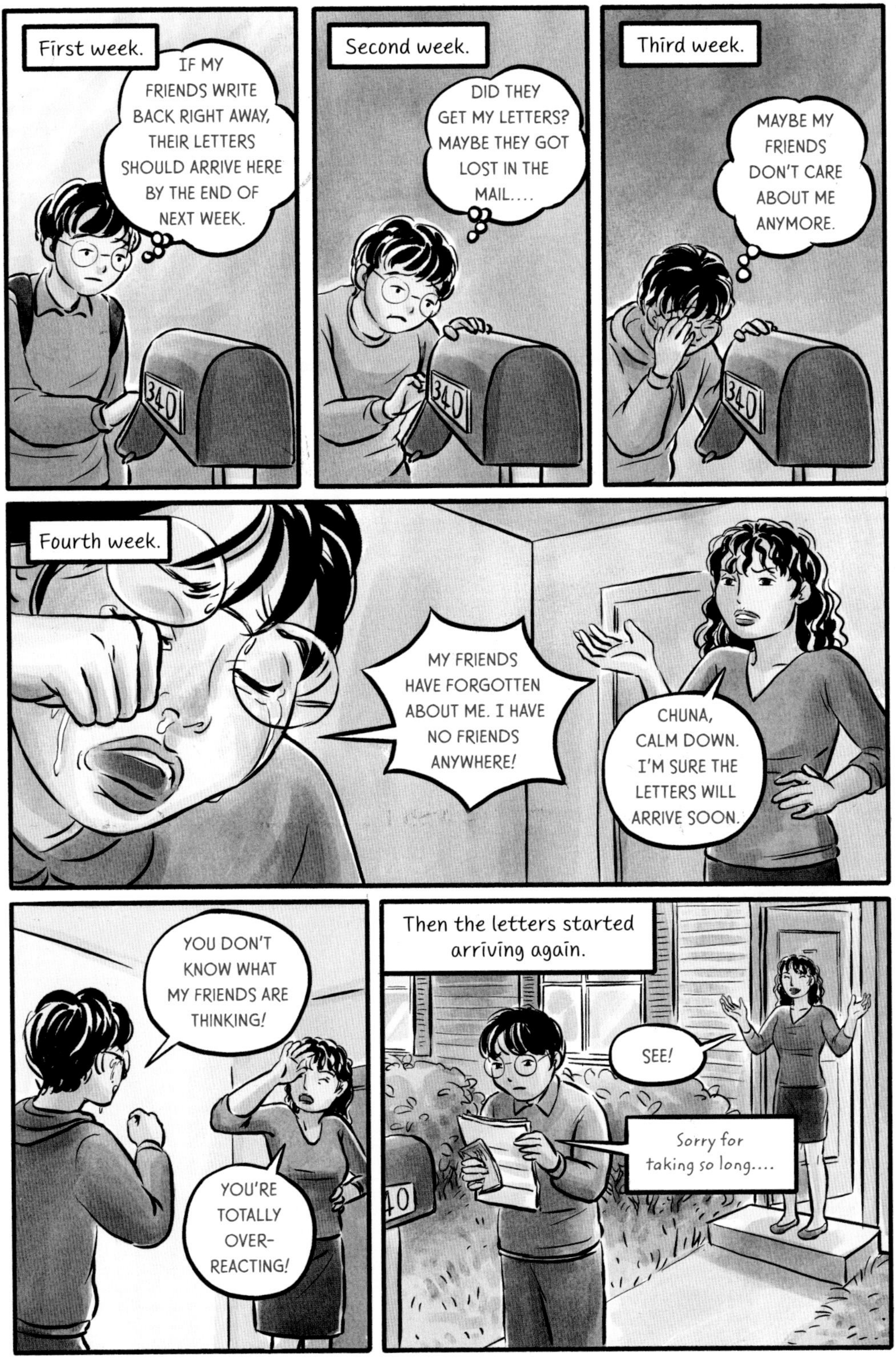

First week.
IF MY FRIENDS WRITE BACK RIGHT AWAY, THEIR LETTERS SHOULD ARRIVE HERE BY THE END OF NEXT WEEK.
340
Second week.
DID THEY GET MY LETTERS? MAYBE THEY GOT LOST IN THE MAIL....
340
Third week.
MAYBE MY FRIENDS DON'T CARE ABOUT ME ANYMORE.
340
Fourth week.
MY FRIENDS HAVE FORGOTTEN ABOUT ME. I HAVE NO FRIENDS ANYWHERE!
CHUNA, CALM DOWN. I'M SURE THE LETTERS WILL ARRIVE SOON.
YOU DON'T KNOW WHAT MY FRIENDS ARE THINKING!
YOU'RE TOTALLY OVER-REACTING!
Then the letters started arriving again.
SEE!
Sorry for taking so long....

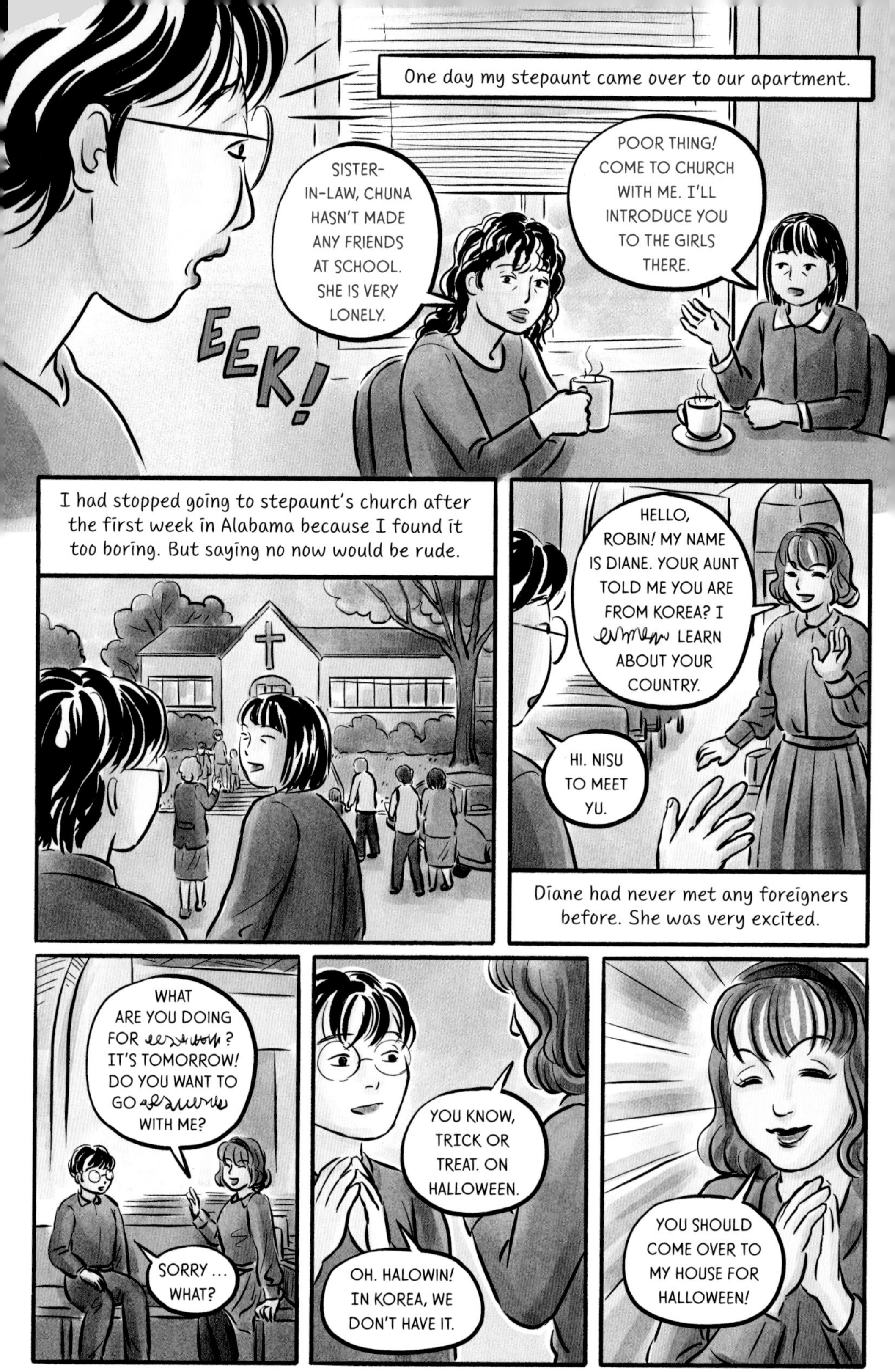
One day my stepaunt came over to our apartment.
SISTER-IN-LAW, CHUNA HASN'T MADE ANY FRIENDS AT SCHOOL. SHE IS VERY LONELY.
POOR THING! COME TO CHURCH WITH ME. I'LL INTRODUCE YOU TO THE GIRLS THERE.
EEK!
I had stopped going to stepaunt's church after the first week in Alabama because I found it too boring. But saying no now would be rude.
HELLO, ROBIN! MY NAME IS DIANE. YOUR AUNT TOLD ME YOU ARE FROM KOREA? I LEARN ABOUT YOUR COUNTRY.
HI. NISU TO MEET YU.
Diane had never met any foreigners before. She was very excited.
WHAT ARE YOU DOING FOR ? IT'S TOMORROW! DO YOU WANT TO GO WITH ME?
SORRY ... WHAT?
YOU KNOW, TRICK OR TREAT. ON HALLOWEEN.
OH. HALOWIN! IN KOREA, WE DON'T HAVE IT.
YOU SHOULD COME OVER TO MY HOUSE FOR HALLOWEEN!

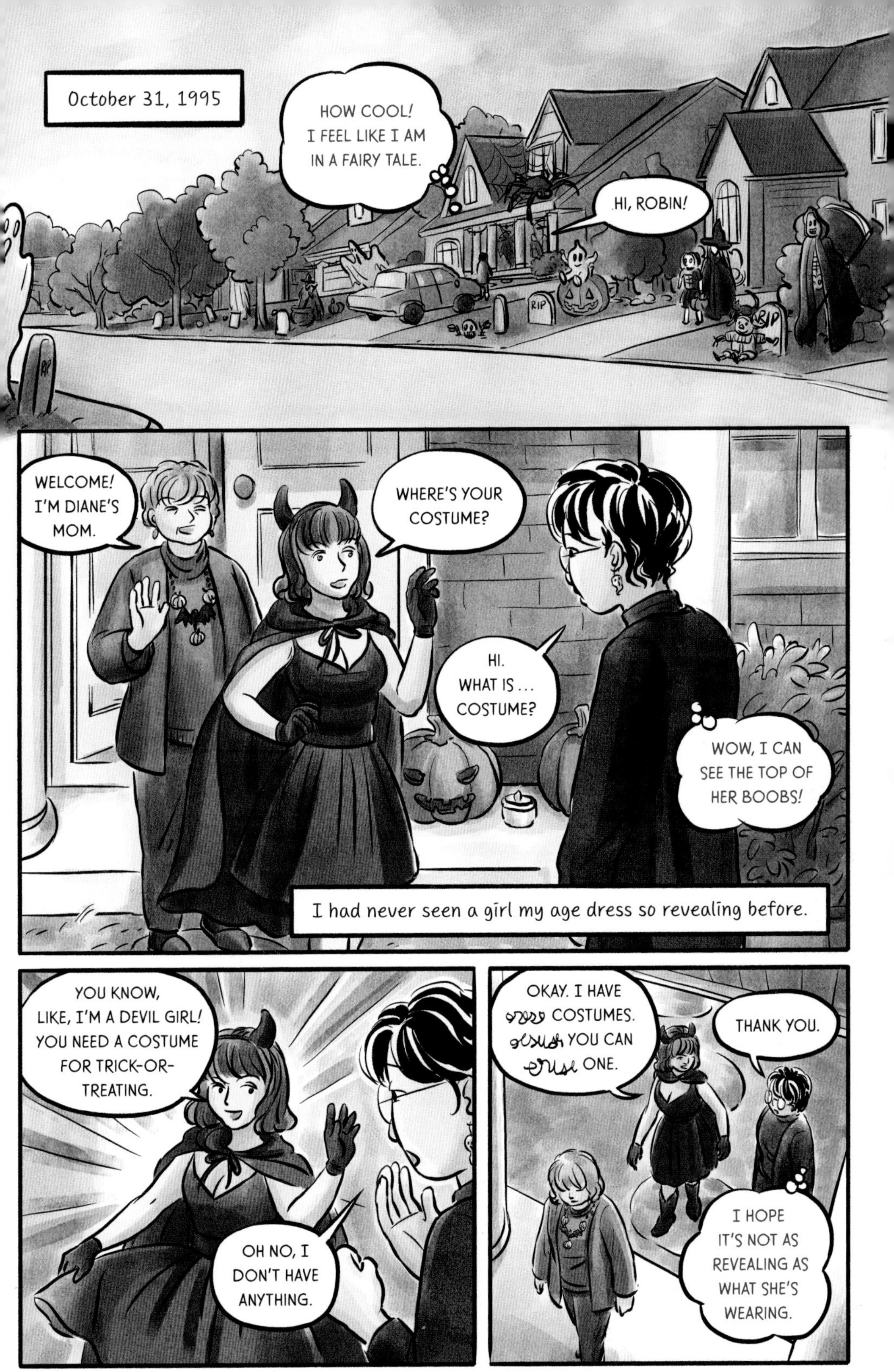
October 31, 1995
HOW COOL! I FEEL LIKE I AM IN A FAIRY TALE.
HI, ROBIN!
RIP
RIP
RIP
RIP
WELCOME! I'M DIANE'S MOM.
WHERE'S YOUR COSTUME?
HI. WHAT IS . . . COSTUME?
WOW, I CAN SEE THE TOP OF HER BOOBS!
I had never seen a girl my age dress so revealing before.
YOU KNOW, LIKE, I'M A DEVIL GIRL! YOU NEED A COSTUME FOR TRICK-OR-TREATING.
OH NO, I DON'T HAVE ANYTHING.
OKAY. I HAVE COSTUMES. YOU CAN ONE.
THANK YOU.
I HOPE IT'S NOT AS REVEALING AS WHAT SHE'S WEARING.

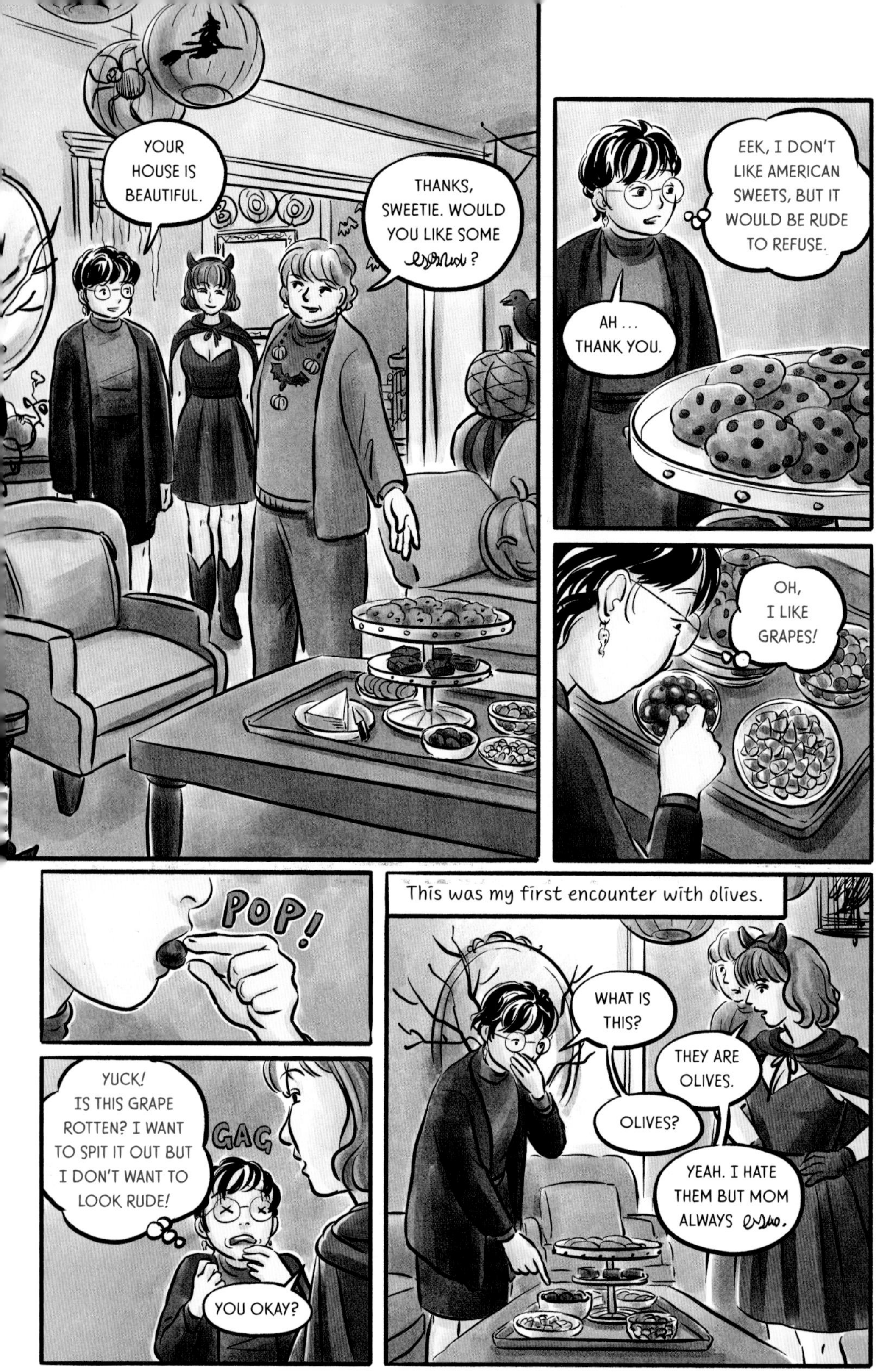

YOUR HOUSE IS BEAUTIFUL.
THANKS, SWEETIE. WOULD YOU LIKE SOME ?
EEK, I DON'T LIKE AMERICAN SWEETS, BUT IT WOULD BE RUDE TO REFUSE.
AH . . . THANK YOU.
OH, I LIKE GRAPES!
POP!
YUCK! IS THIS GRAPE ROTTEN? I WANT TO SPIT IT OUT BUT I DON'T WANT TO LOOK RUDE!
GAG
YOU OKAY?
This was my first encounter with olives.
WHAT IS THIS?
THEY ARE OLIVES.
OLIVES?
YEAH. I HATE THEM BUT MOM ALWAYS

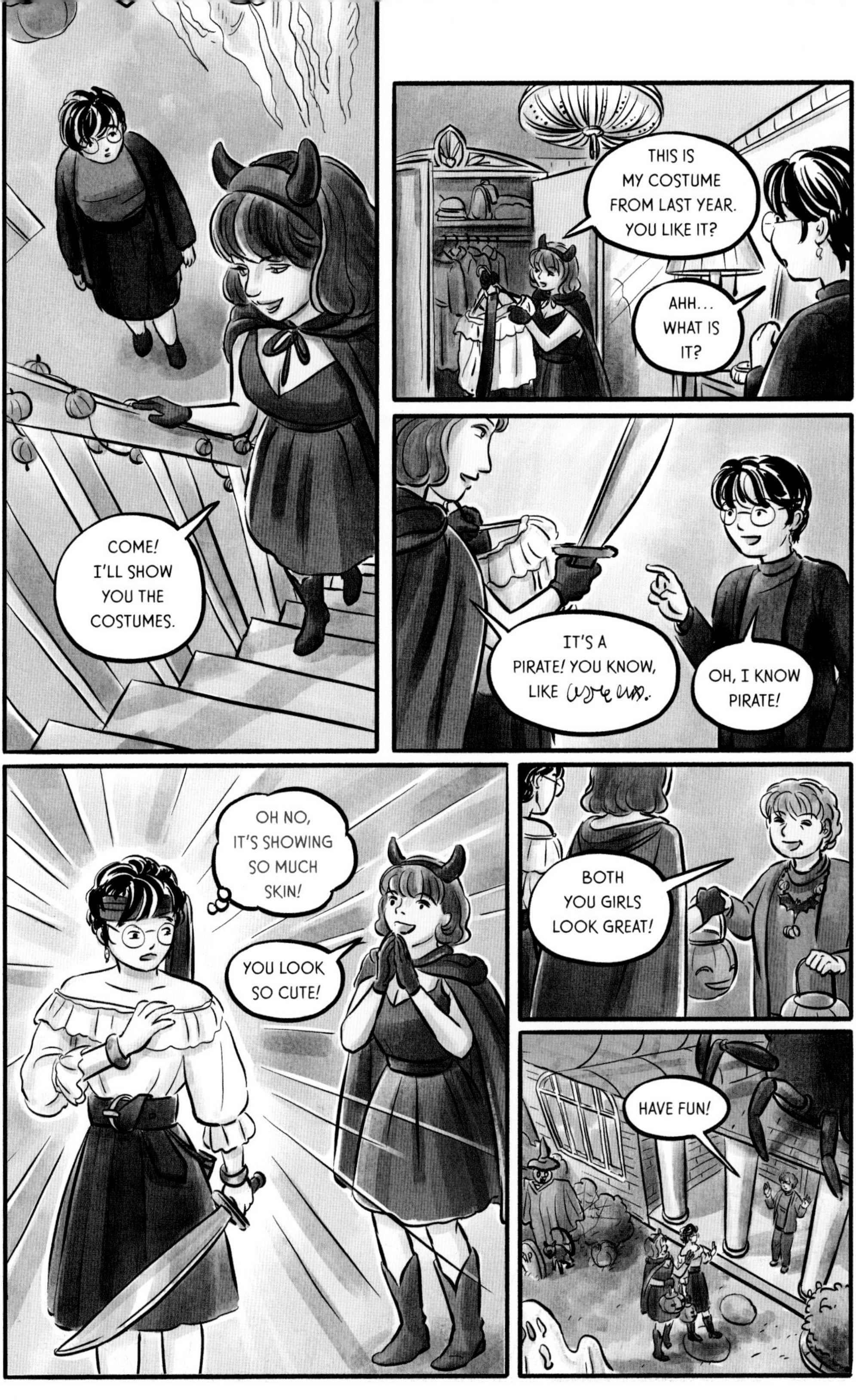
COME! I'LL SHOW YOU THE COSTUMES.
THIS IS MY COSTUME FROM LAST YEAR. YOU LIKE IT?
AHH... WHAT IS IT?
IT'S A PIRATE! YOU KNOW, LIKE
OH, I KNOW PIRATE!
OH NO, IT'S SHOWING SO MUCH SKIN!
YOU LOOK SO CUTE!
BOTH YOU GIRLS LOOK GREAT!
HAVE FUN!

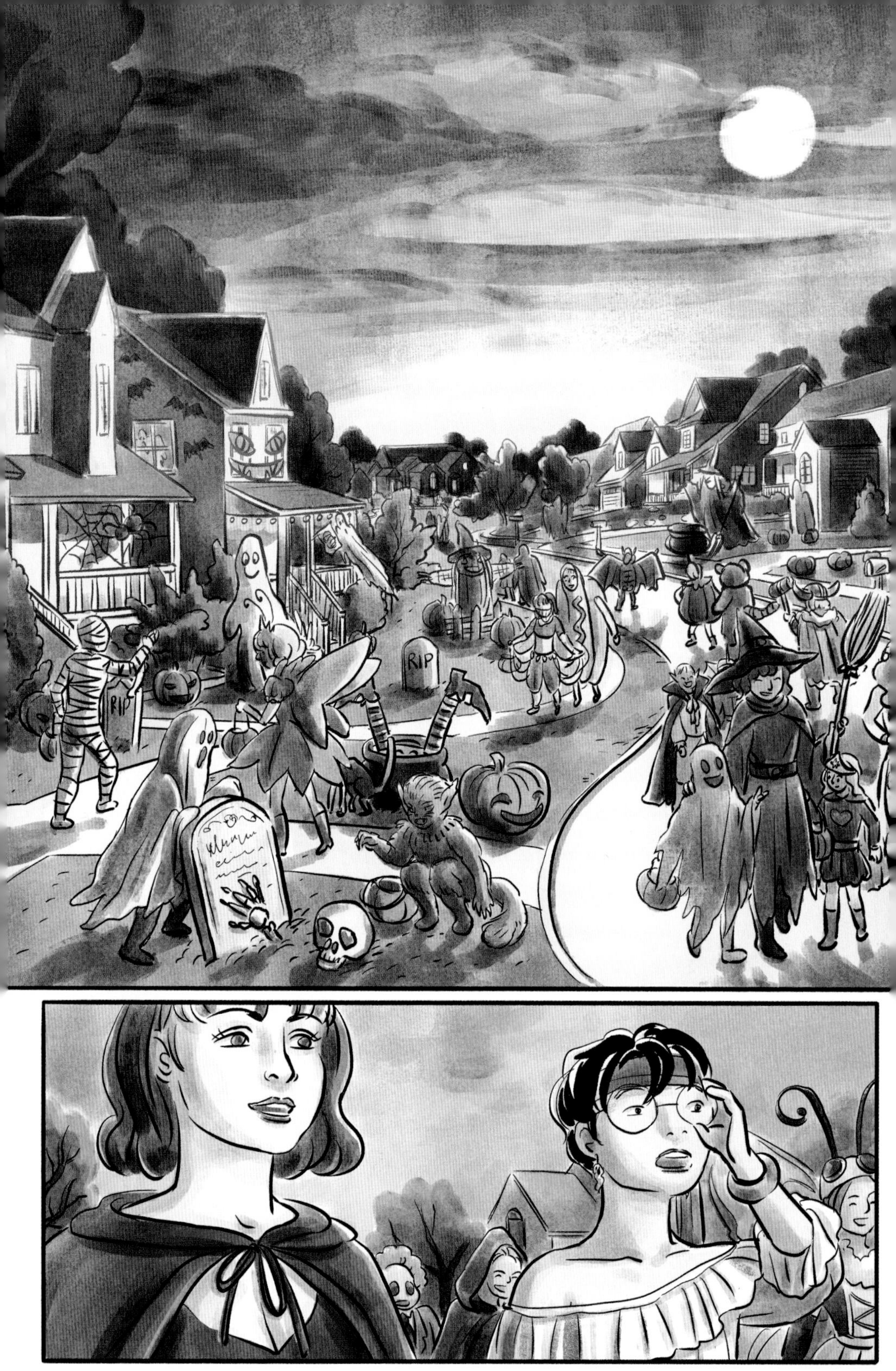
RIP
RIP

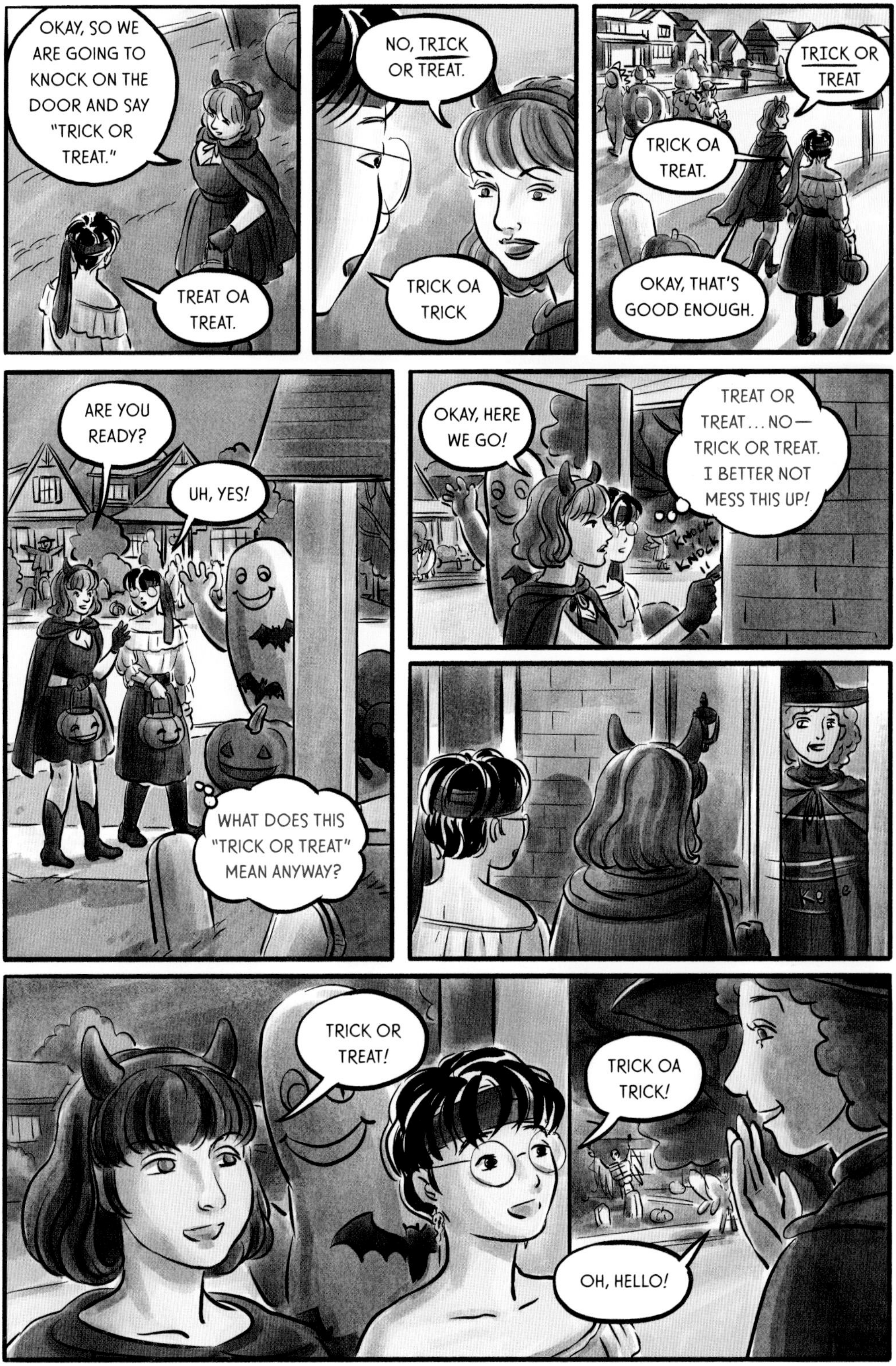
OKAY, SO WE ARE GOING TO KNOCK ON THE DOOR AND SAY "TRICK OR TREAT."
TREAT OA TREAT.
NO, TRICK OR TREAT.
TRICK OA TRICK
TRICK OR TREAT
TRICK OA TREAT.
OKAY, THAT'S GOOD ENOUGH.
ARE YOU READY?
UH, YES!
WHAT DOES THIS "TRICK OR TREAT" MEAN ANYWAY?
OKAY, HERE WE GO!
TREAT OR TREAT... NO— TRICK OR TREAT. I BETTER NOT MESS THIS UP!
KNOCK KNOCK
TRICK OR TREAT!
TRICK OA TRICK!
OH, HELLO!

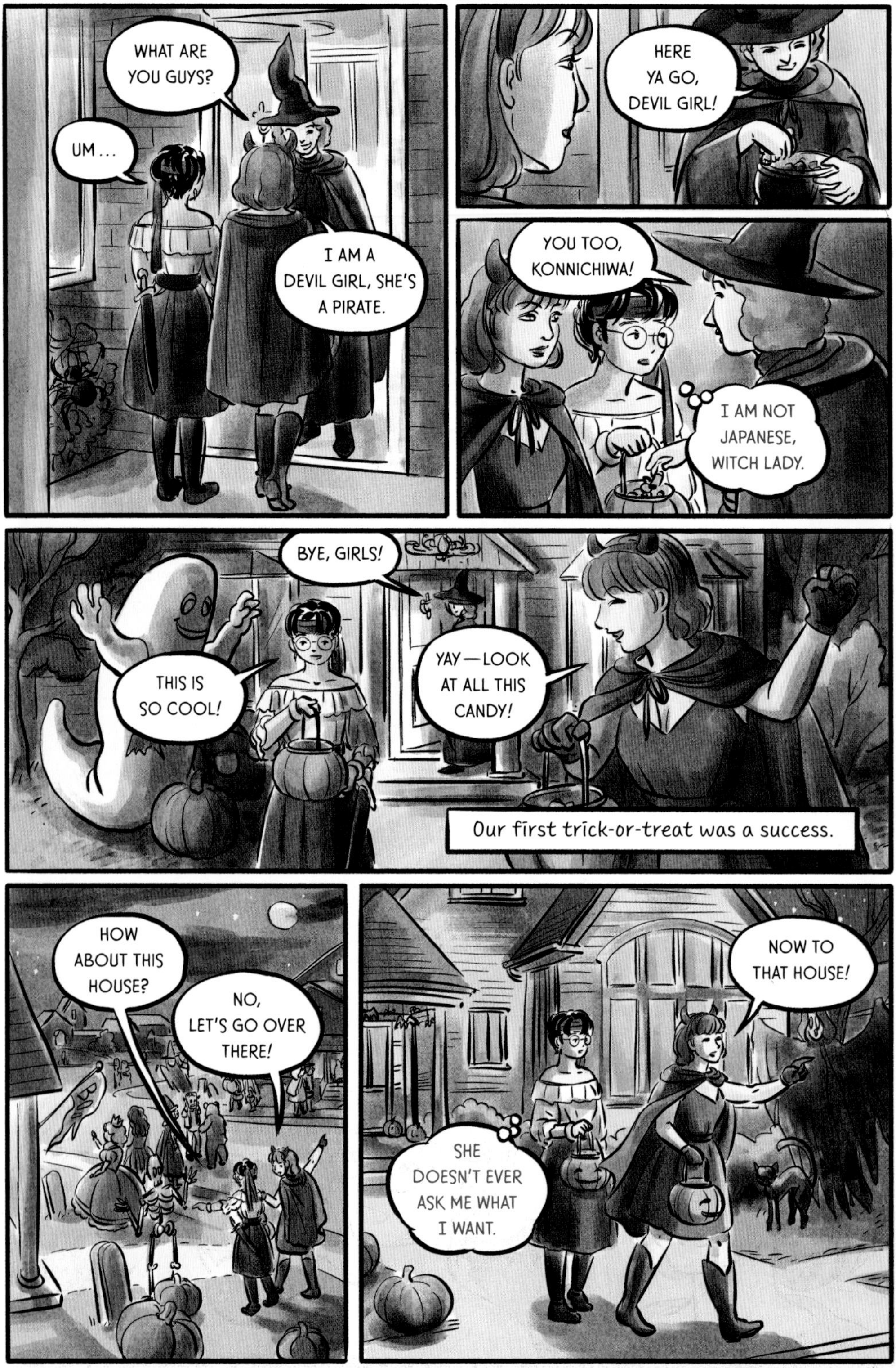
WHAT ARE YOU GUYS?
UM...
I AM A DEVIL GIRL, SHE'S A PIRATE.
HERE YA GO, DEVIL GIRL!
YOU TOO, KONNICHIWA!
I AM NOT JAPANESE, WITCH LADY.
BYE, GIRLS!
THIS IS SO COOL!
YAY—LOOK AT ALL THIS CANDY!
Our first trick-or-treat was a success.
HOW ABOUT THIS HOUSE?
NO, LET'S GO OVER THERE!
NOW TO THAT HOUSE!
SHE DOESN'T EVER ASK ME WHAT I WANT.

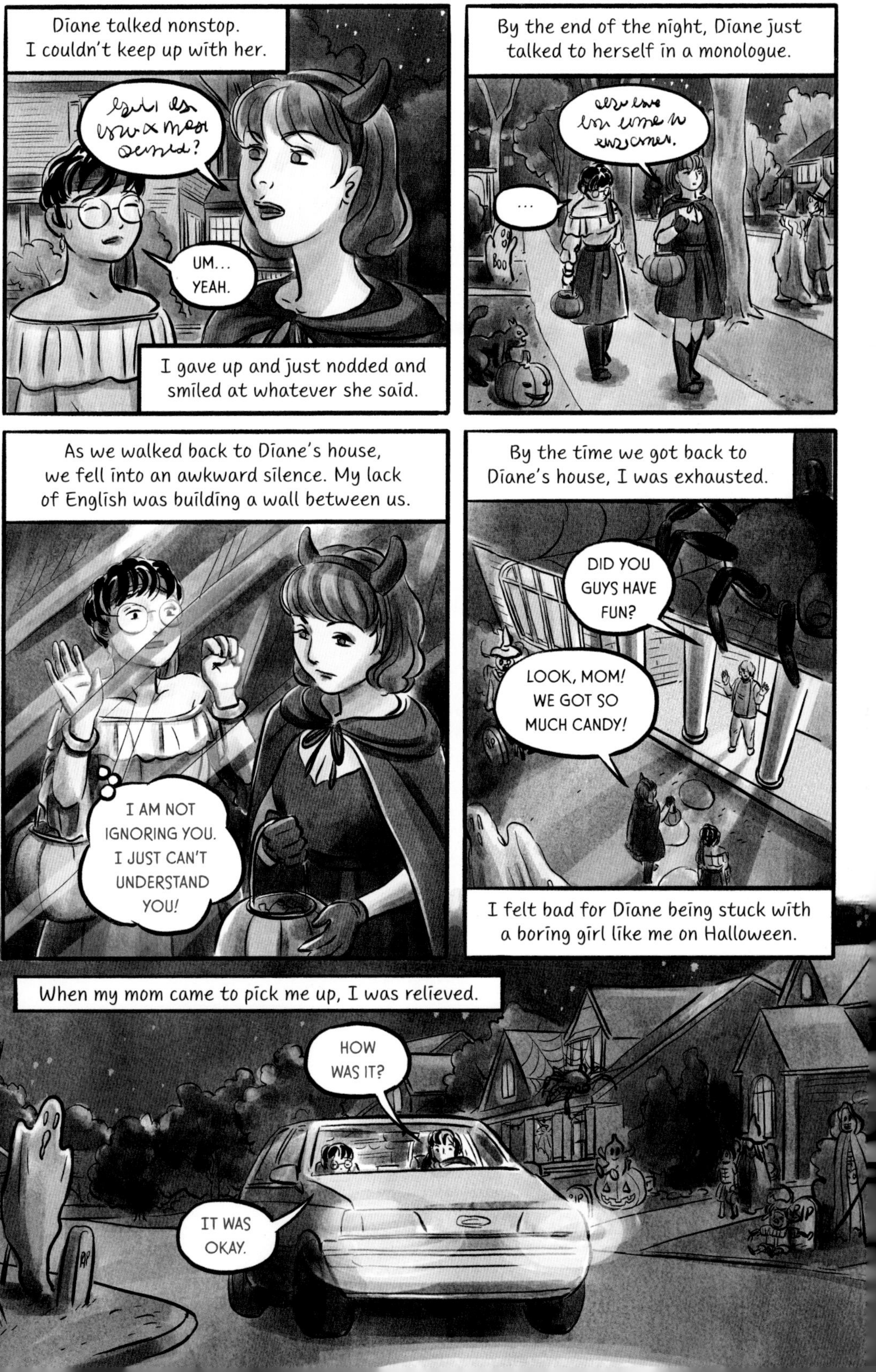
Diane talked nonstop.
I couldn't keep up with her.
UM... YEAH.
I gave up and just nodded and smiled at whatever she said.
By the end of the night, Diane just talked to herself in a monologue.
...
As we walked back to Diane's house, we fell into an awkward silence. My lack of English was building a wall between us.
I AM NOT IGNORING YOU. I JUST CAN'T UNDERSTAND YOU!
By the time we got back to Diane's house, I was exhausted.
DID YOU GUYS HAVE FUN?
LOOK, MOM! WE GOT SO MUCH CANDY!
I felt bad for Diane being stuck with a boring girl like me on Halloween.
When my mom came to pick me up, I was relieved.
HOW WAS IT?
IT WAS OKAY.

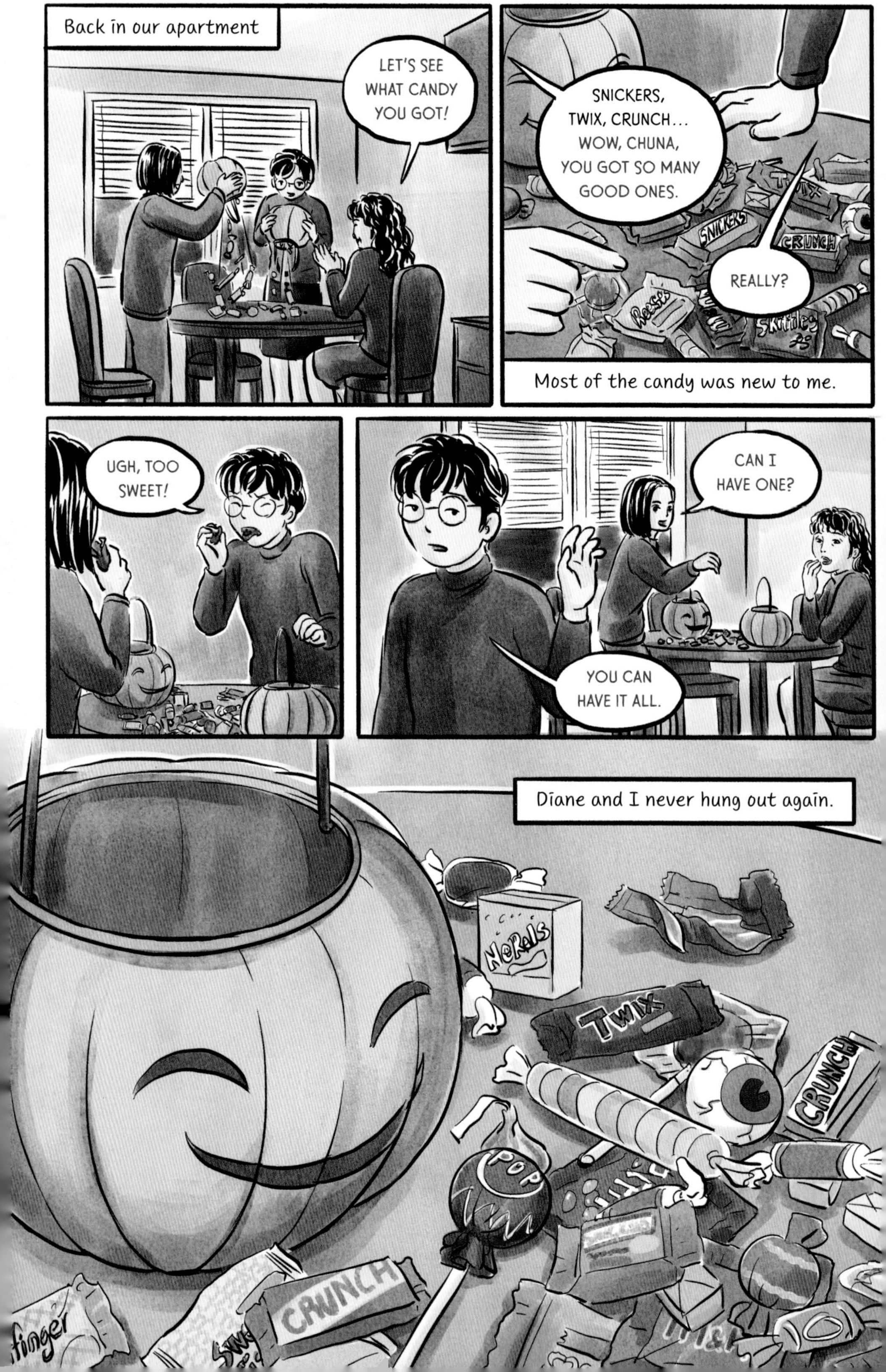
Back in our apartment
LET'S SEE WHAT CANDY YOU GOT!
SNICKERS, TWIX, CRUNCH... WOW, CHUNA, YOU GOT SO MANY GOOD ONES.
REALLY?
Most of the candy was new to me.
UGH, TOO SWEET!
CAN I HAVE ONE?
YOU CAN HAVE IT ALL.
Diane and I never hung out again.

Chapter 7

The Cage

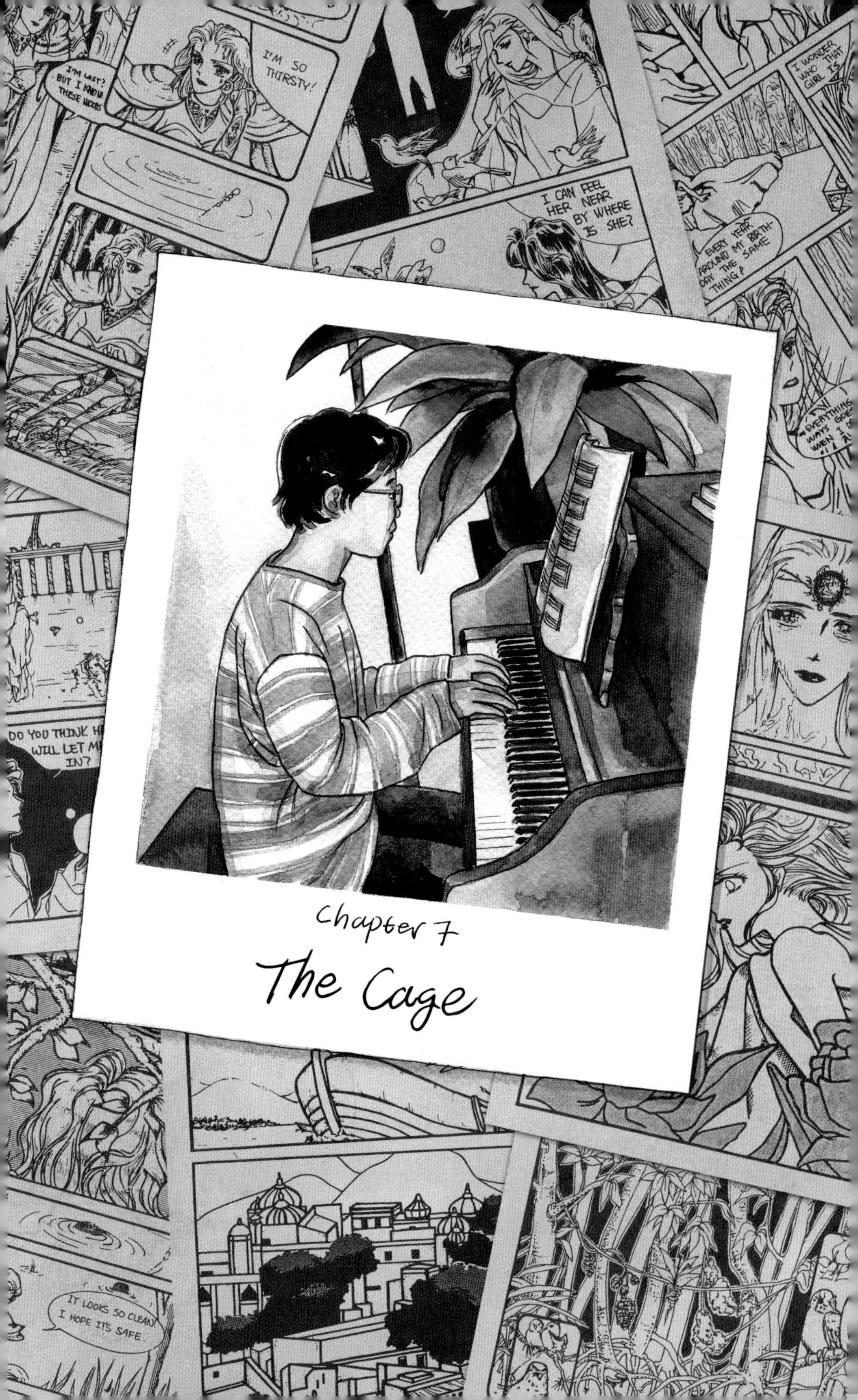
I'M LOST? BUT I KNOW THESE WOODS
I'M SO THIRSTY!
I CAN FEEL HER NEAR BY WHERE IS SHE?
I WONDER WHO THAT GIRL IS
EVERY YEAR AROUND MY BIRTHDAY THE SAME THING?
IT LOOKS SO CLEAN! I HOPE IT'S SAFE.

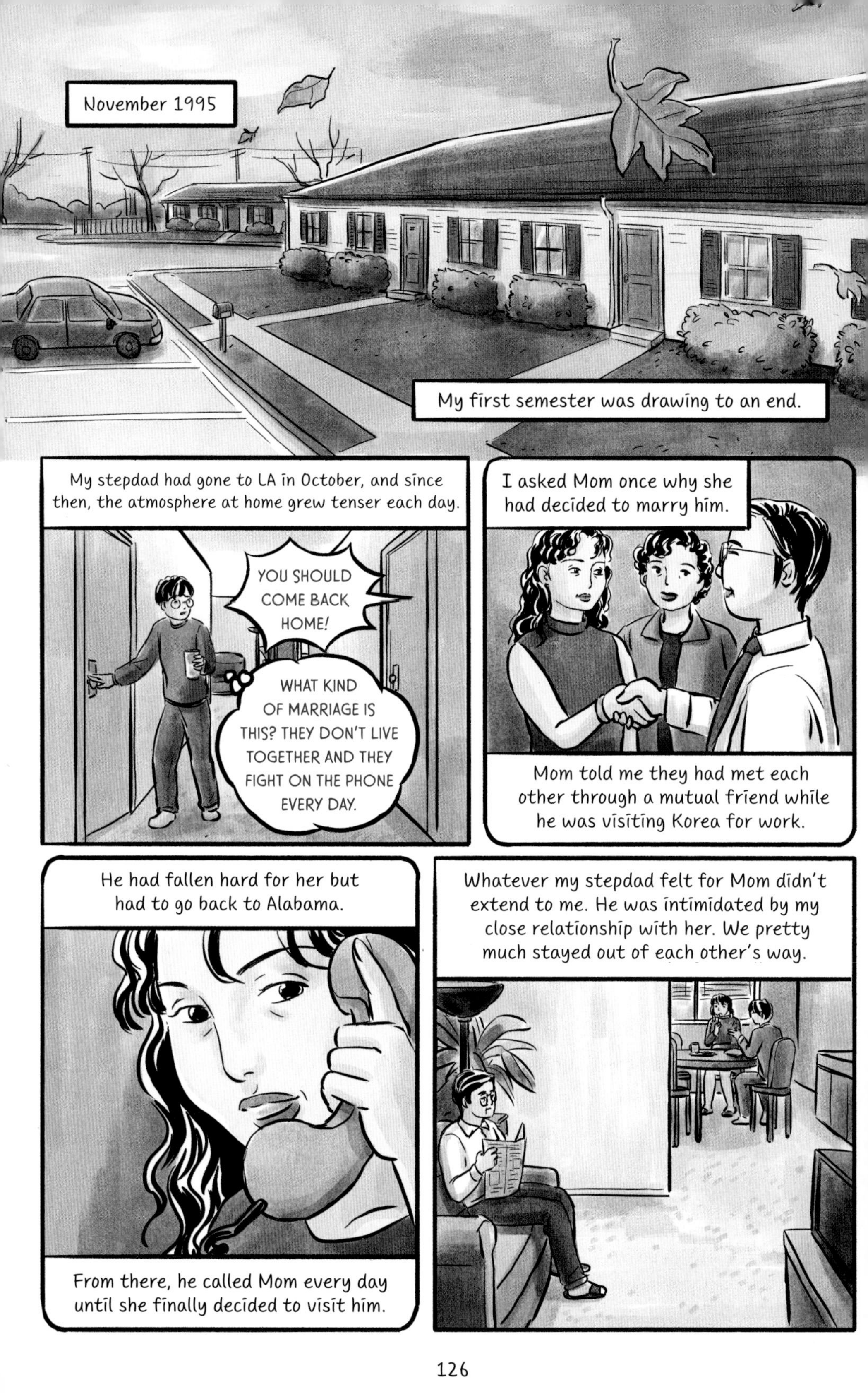
November 1995
My first semester was drawing to an end.
My stepdad had gone to LA in October, and since then, the atmosphere at home grew tenser each day.
YOU SHOULD COME BACK HOME!
WHAT KIND OF MARRIAGE IS THIS? THEY DON'T LIVE TOGETHER AND THEY FIGHT ON THE PHONE EVERY DAY.
I asked Mom once why she had decided to marry him.
Mom told me they had met each other through a mutual friend while he was visiting Korea for work.
He had fallen hard for her but had to go back to Alabama.
From there, he called Mom every day until she finally decided to visit him.
Whatever my stepdad felt for Mom didn't extend to me. He was intimidated by my close relationship with her. We pretty much stayed out of each other's way.

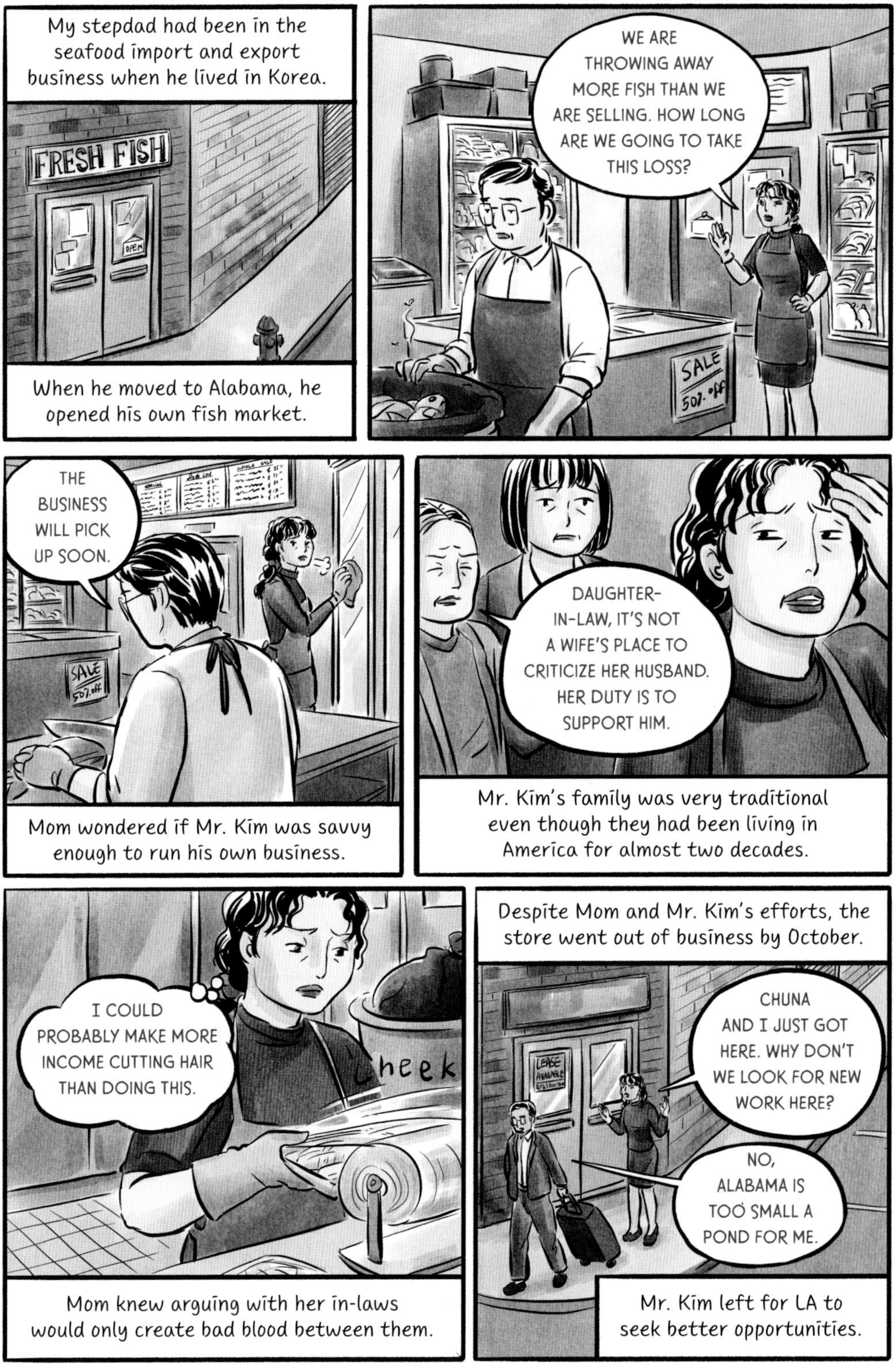
My stepdad had been in the seafood import and export business when he lived in Korea.
FRESH FISH
OPEN
When he moved to Alabama, he opened his own fish market.
WE ARE THROWING AWAY MORE FISH THAN WE ARE SELLING. HOW LONG ARE WE GOING TO TAKE THIS LOSS?
SALE 50% off
THE BUSINESS WILL PICK UP SOON.
SALE 50% off
Mom wondered if Mr. Kim was savvy enough to run his own business.
DAUGHTER-IN-LAW, IT'S NOT A WIFE'S PLACE TO CRITICIZE HER HUSBAND. HER DUTY IS TO SUPPORT HIM.
Mr. Kim's family was very traditional even though they had been living in America for almost two decades.
I COULD PROBABLY MAKE MORE INCOME CUTTING HAIR THAN DOING THIS.
Mom knew arguing with her in-laws would only create bad blood between them.
Despite Mom and Mr. Kim's efforts, the store went out of business by October.
LEASE AVAILABLE
CHUNA AND I JUST GOT HERE. WHY DON'T WE LOOK FOR NEW WORK HERE?
NO, ALABAMA IS TOO SMALL A POND FOR ME.
Mr. Kim left for LA to seek better opportunities.

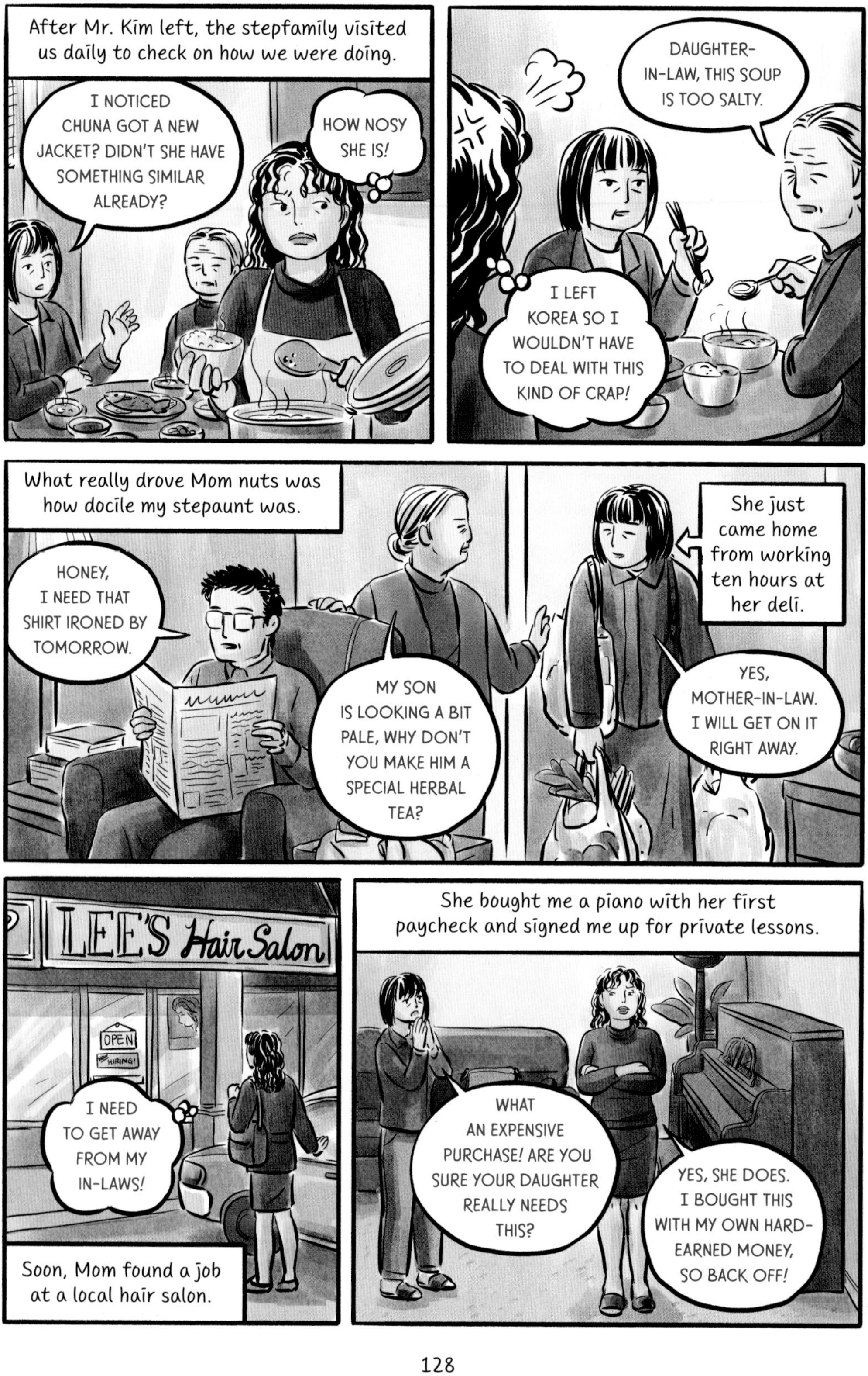
After Mr. Kim left, the stepfamily visited us daily to check on how we were doing.
I NOTICED CHUNA GOT A NEW JACKET? DIDN'T SHE HAVE SOMETHING SIMILAR ALREADY?
HOW NOSY SHE IS!
DAUGHTER-IN-LAW, THIS SOUP IS TOO SALTY.
I LEFT KOREA SO I WOULDN'T HAVE TO DEAL WITH THIS KIND OF CRAP!
What really drove Mom nuts was how docile my stepaunt was.
HONEY, I NEED THAT SHIRT IRONED BY TOMORROW.
MY SON IS LOOKING A BIT PALE, WHY DON'T YOU MAKE HIM A SPECIAL HERBAL TEA?
She just came home from working ten hours at her deli.
YES, MOTHER-IN-LAW. I WILL GET ON IT RIGHT AWAY.
LEE'S Hair Salon
OPEN
I NEED TO GET AWAY FROM MY IN-LAWS!
Soon, Mom found a job at a local hair salon.
She bought me a piano with her first paycheck and signed me up for private lessons.
WHAT AN EXPENSIVE PURCHASE! ARE YOU SURE YOUR DAUGHTER REALLY NEEDS THIS?
YES, SHE DOES. I BOUGHT THIS WITH MY OWN HARD-EARNED MONEY, SO BACK OFF!

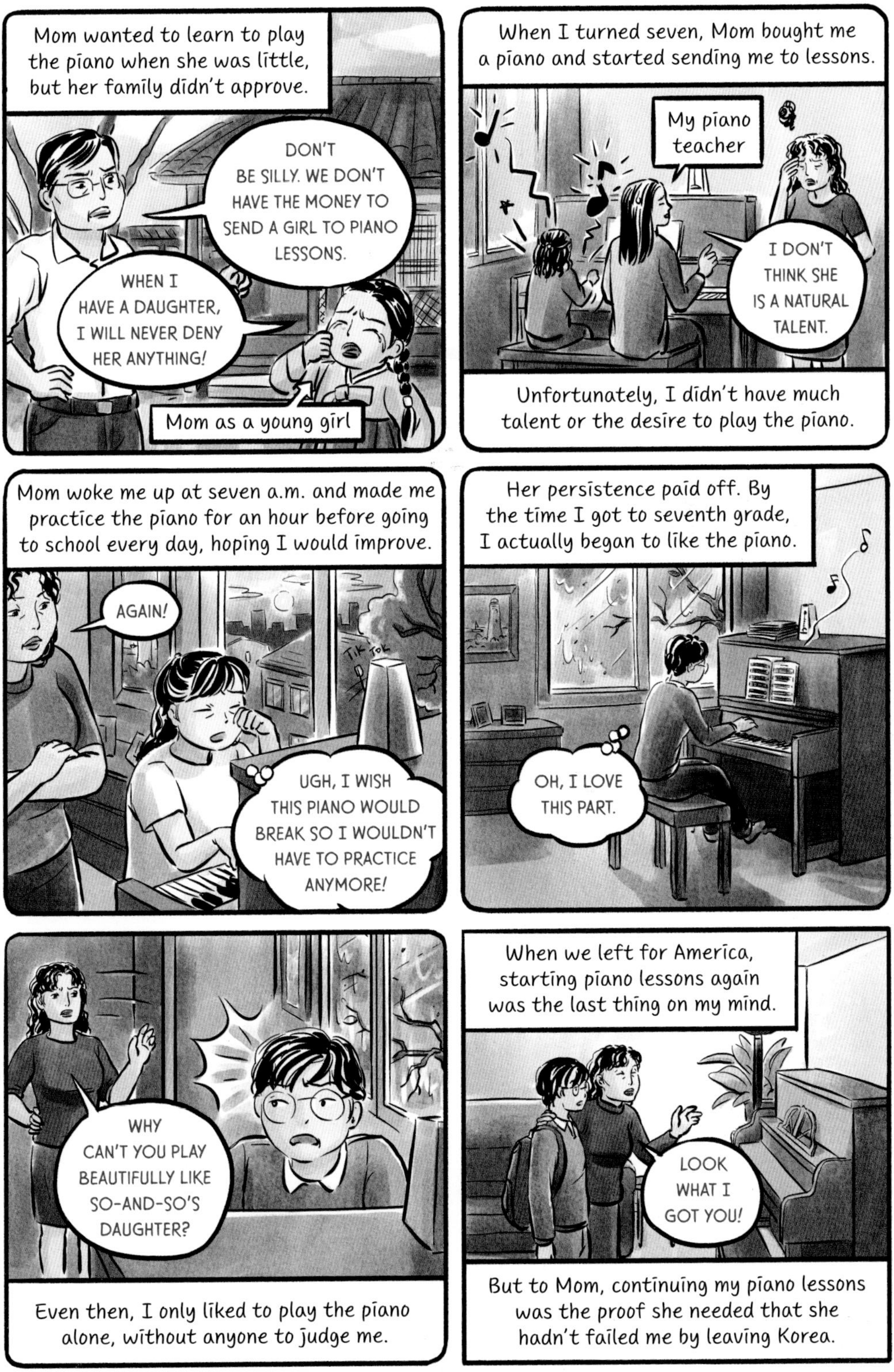
Mom wanted to learn to play the piano when she was little, but her family didn't approve.
DON'T BE SILLY. WE DON'T HAVE THE MONEY TO SEND A GIRL TO PIANO LESSONS.
WHEN I HAVE A DAUGHTER, I WILL NEVER DENY HER ANYTHING!
Mom as a young girl
When I turned seven, Mom bought me a piano and started sending me to lessons.
My piano teacher
I DON'T THINK SHE IS A NATURAL TALENT.
Unfortunately, I didn't have much talent or the desire to play the piano.
Mom woke me up at seven a.m. and made me practice the piano for an hour before going to school every day, hoping I would improve.
AGAIN!
TIK TOK
UGH, I WISH THIS PIANO WOULD BREAK SO I WOULDN'T HAVE TO PRACTICE ANYMORE!
Her persistence paid off. By the time I got to seventh grade, I actually began to like the piano.
OH, I LOVE THIS PART.
WHY CAN'T YOU PLAY BEAUTIFULLY LIKE SO-AND-SO'S DAUGHTER?
Even then, I only liked to play the piano alone, without anyone to judge me.
When we left for America, starting piano lessons again was the last thing on my mind.
LOOK WHAT I GOT YOU!
But to Mom, continuing my piano lessons was the proof she needed that she hadn't failed me by leaving Korea.

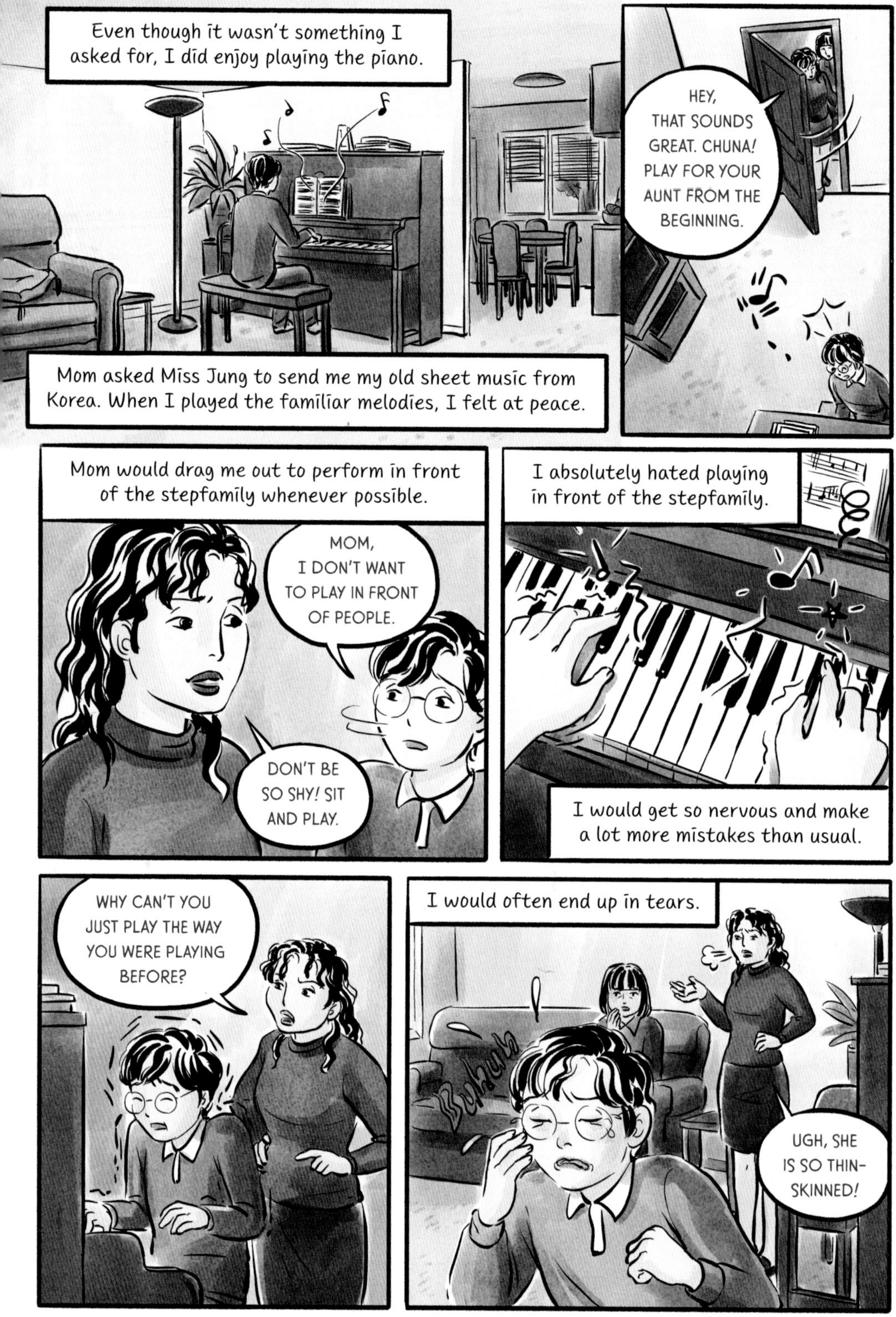
Even though it wasn't something I asked for, I did enjoy playing the piano.
Mom asked Miss Jung to send me my old sheet music from Korea. When I played the familiar melodies, I felt at peace.
HEY, THAT SOUNDS GREAT. CHUNA! PLAY FOR YOUR AUNT FROM THE BEGINNING.
Mom would drag me out to perform in front of the stepfamily whenever possible.
MOM, I DON'T WANT TO PLAY IN FRONT OF PEOPLE.
DON'T BE SO SHY! SIT AND PLAY.
I absolutely hated playing in front of the stepfamily.
I would get so nervous and make a lot more mistakes than usual.
WHY CAN'T YOU JUST PLAY THE WAY YOU WERE PLAYING BEFORE?
I would often end up in tears.
UGH, SHE IS SO THIN-SKINNED!

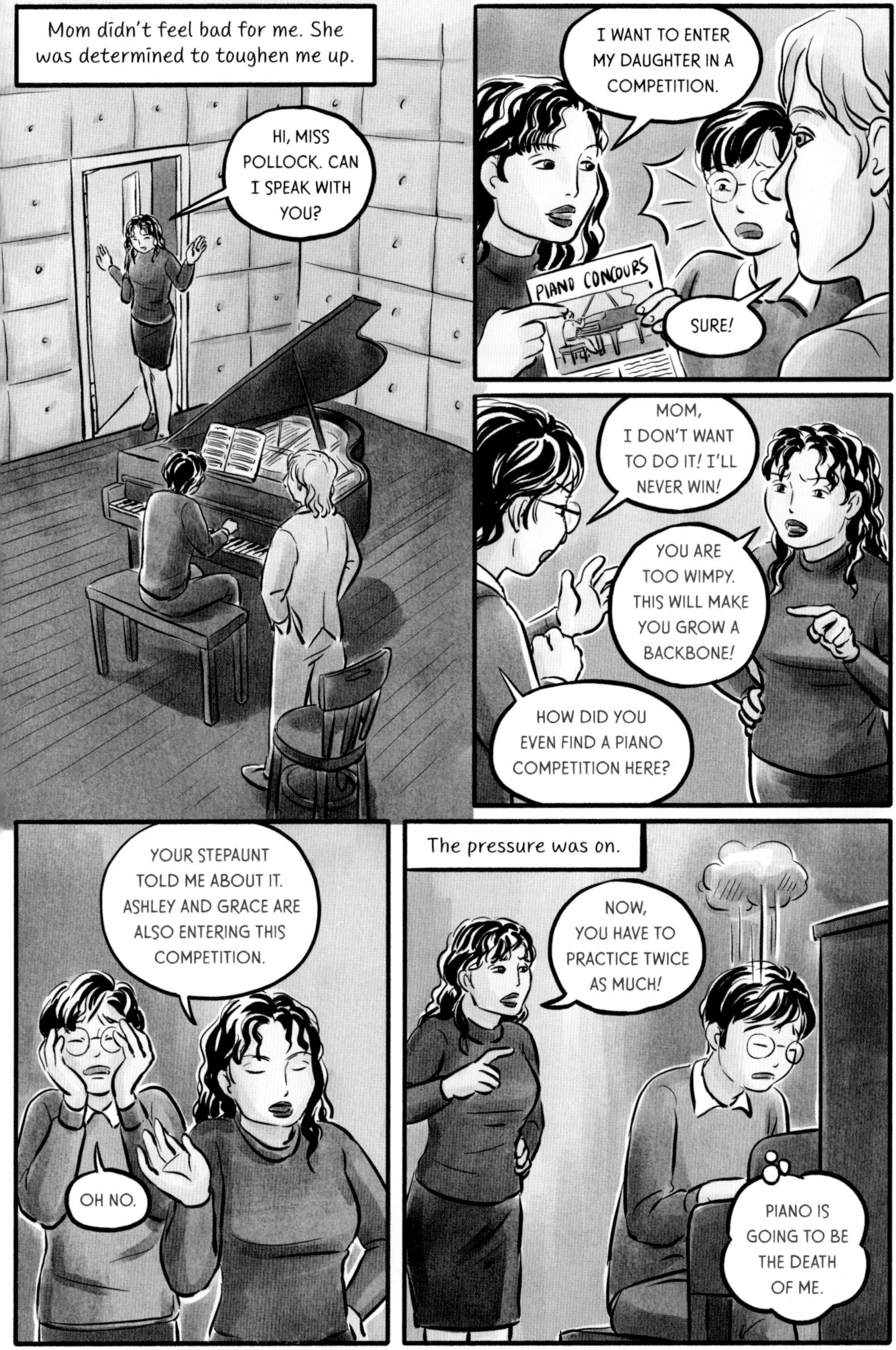
Mom didn't feel bad for me. She was determined to toughen me up.
HI, MISS POLLOCK. CAN I SPEAK WITH YOU?
I WANT TO ENTER MY DAUGHTER IN A COMPETITION.
PIANO CONCOURS
SURE!
MOM, I DON'T WANT TO DO IT! I'LL NEVER WIN!
YOU ARE TOO WIMPY. THIS WILL MAKE YOU GROW A BACKBONE!
HOW DID YOU EVEN FIND A PIANO COMPETITION HERE?
YOUR STEPAUNT TOLD ME ABOUT IT. ASHLEY AND GRACE ARE ALSO ENTERING THIS COMPETITION.
OH NO.
The pressure was on.
NOW, YOU HAVE TO PRACTICE TWICE AS MUCH!
PIANO IS GOING TO BE THE DEATH OF ME.

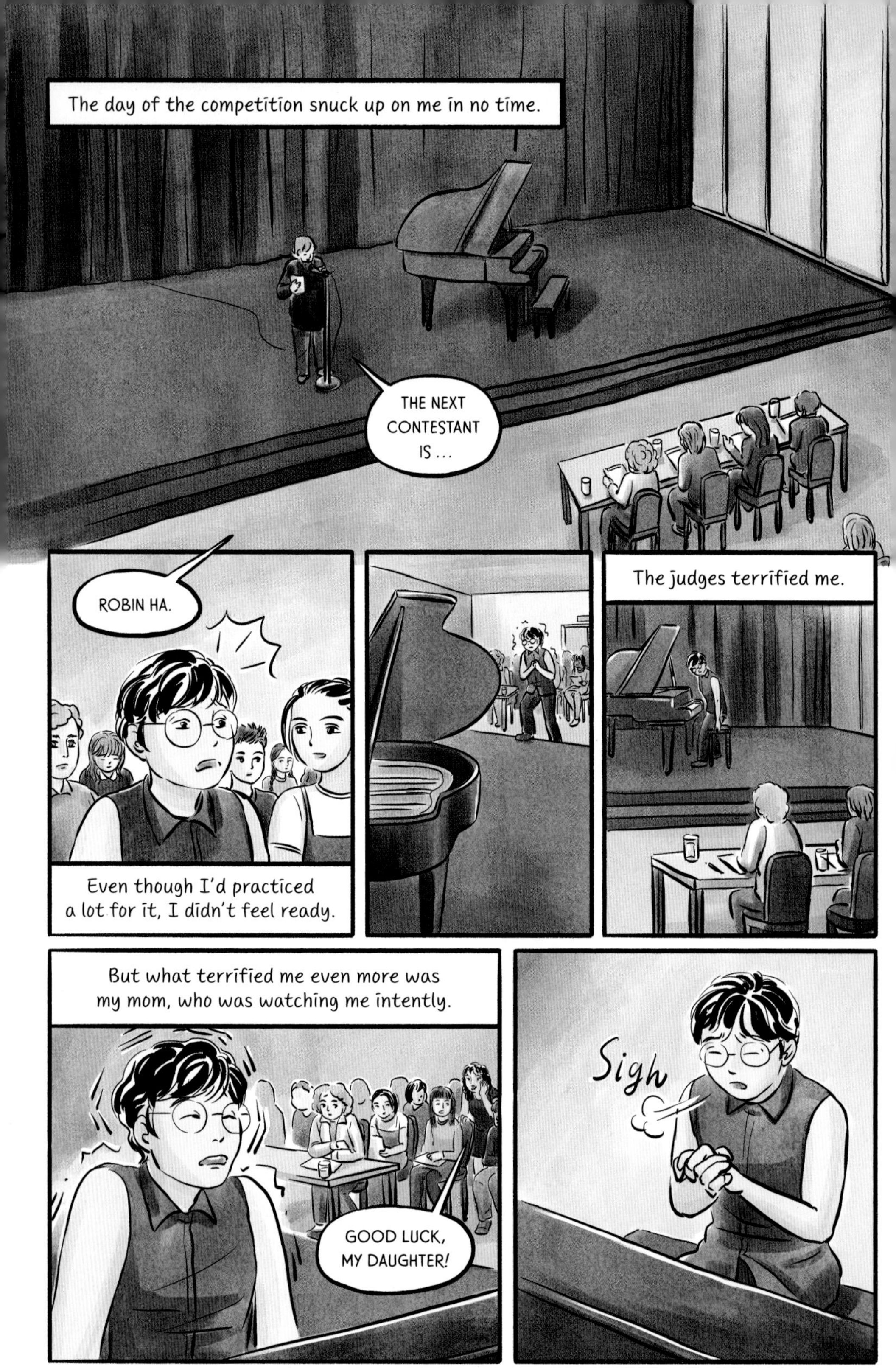
The day of the competition snuck up on me in no time.
THE NEXT CONTESTANT IS . . .
ROBIN HA.
Even though I'd practiced a lot for it, I didn't feel ready.
The judges terrified me.
But what terrified me even more was my mom, who was watching me intently.
GOOD LUCK, MY DAUGHTER!
Sigh

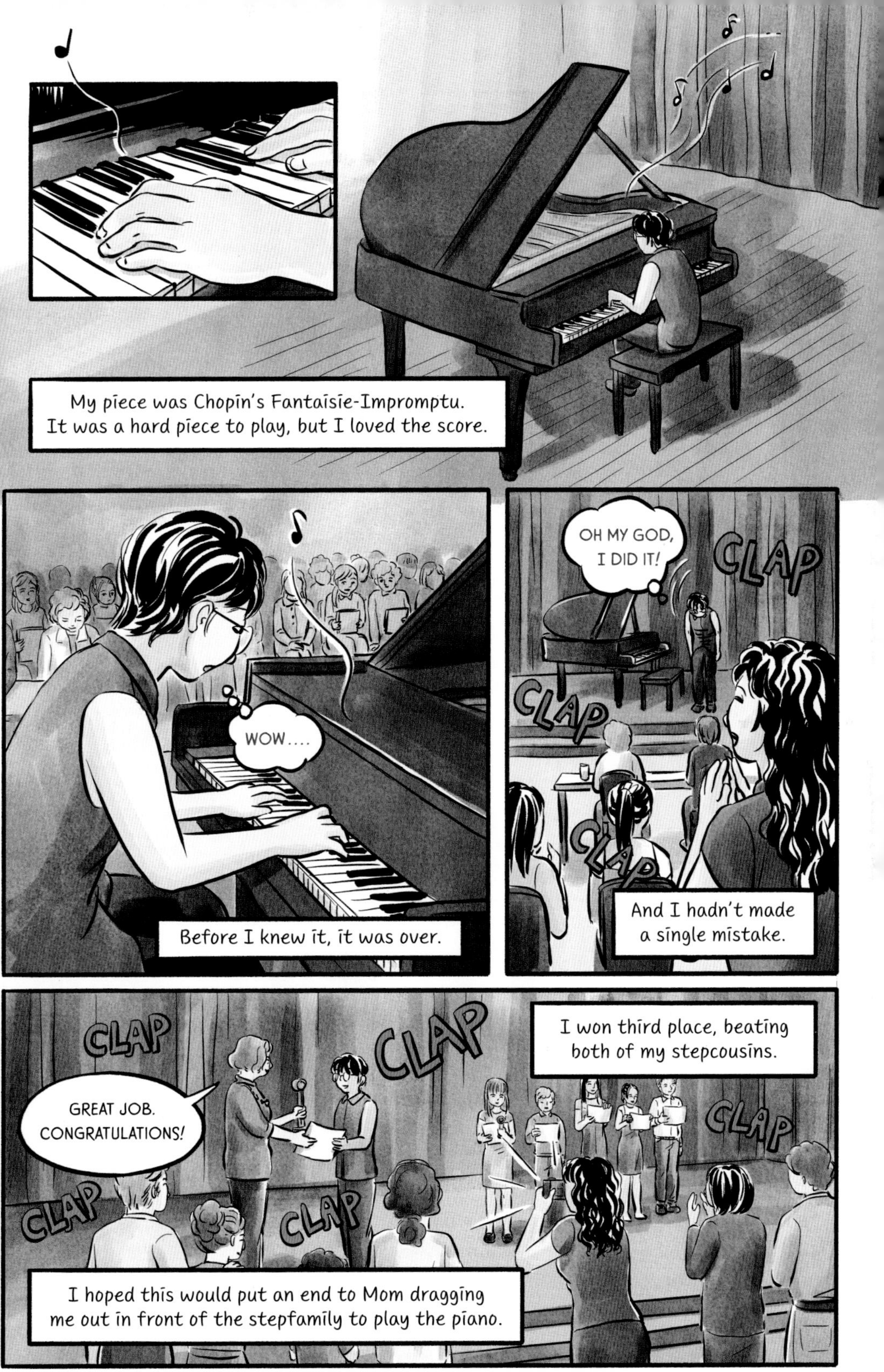
My piece was Chopin's Fantaisie-Impromptu.
It was a hard piece to play, but I loved the score.
WOW....
Before I knew it, it was over.
OH MY GOD, I DID IT!
CLAP
CLAP
CLAP
And I hadn't made a single mistake.
CLAP
GREAT JOB. CONGRATULATIONS!
CLAP
I won third place, beating both of my stepcousins.
CLAP
CLAP
CLAP
I hoped this would put an end to Mom dragging me out in front of the stepfamily to play the piano.

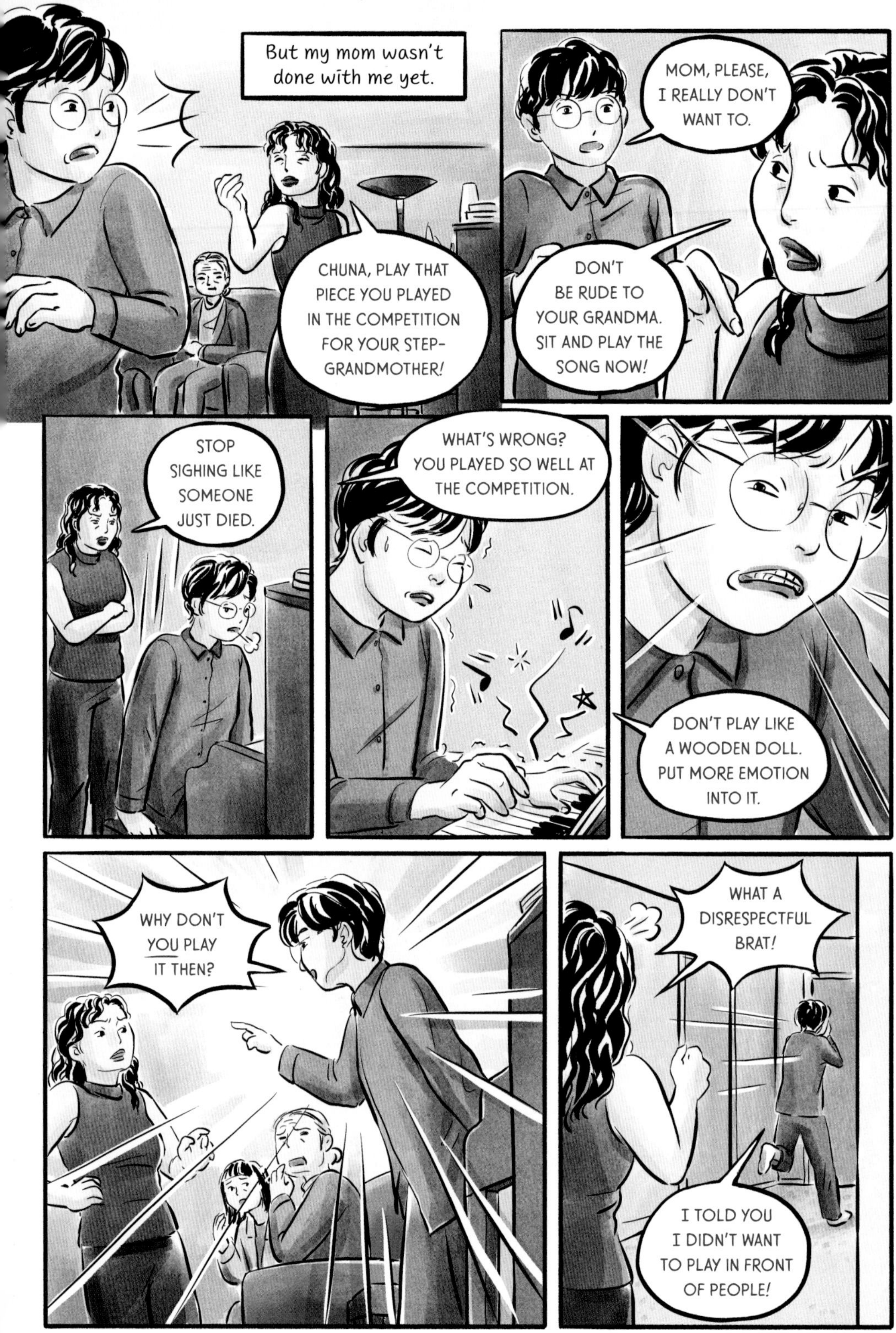
But my mom wasn't done with me yet.
CHUNA, PLAY THAT PIECE YOU PLAYED IN THE COMPETITION FOR YOUR STEP-GRANDMOTHER!
MOM, PLEASE, I REALLY DON'T WANT TO.
DON'T BE RUDE TO YOUR GRANDMA. SIT AND PLAY THE SONG NOW!
STOP SIGHING LIKE SOMEONE JUST DIED.
WHAT'S WRONG? YOU PLAYED SO WELL AT THE COMPETITION.
DON'T PLAY LIKE A WOODEN DOLL. PUT MORE EMOTION INTO IT.
WHY DON'T YOU PLAY IT THEN?
WHAT A DISRESPECTFUL BRAT!
I TOLD YOU I DIDN'T WANT TO PLAY IN FRONT OF PEOPLE!

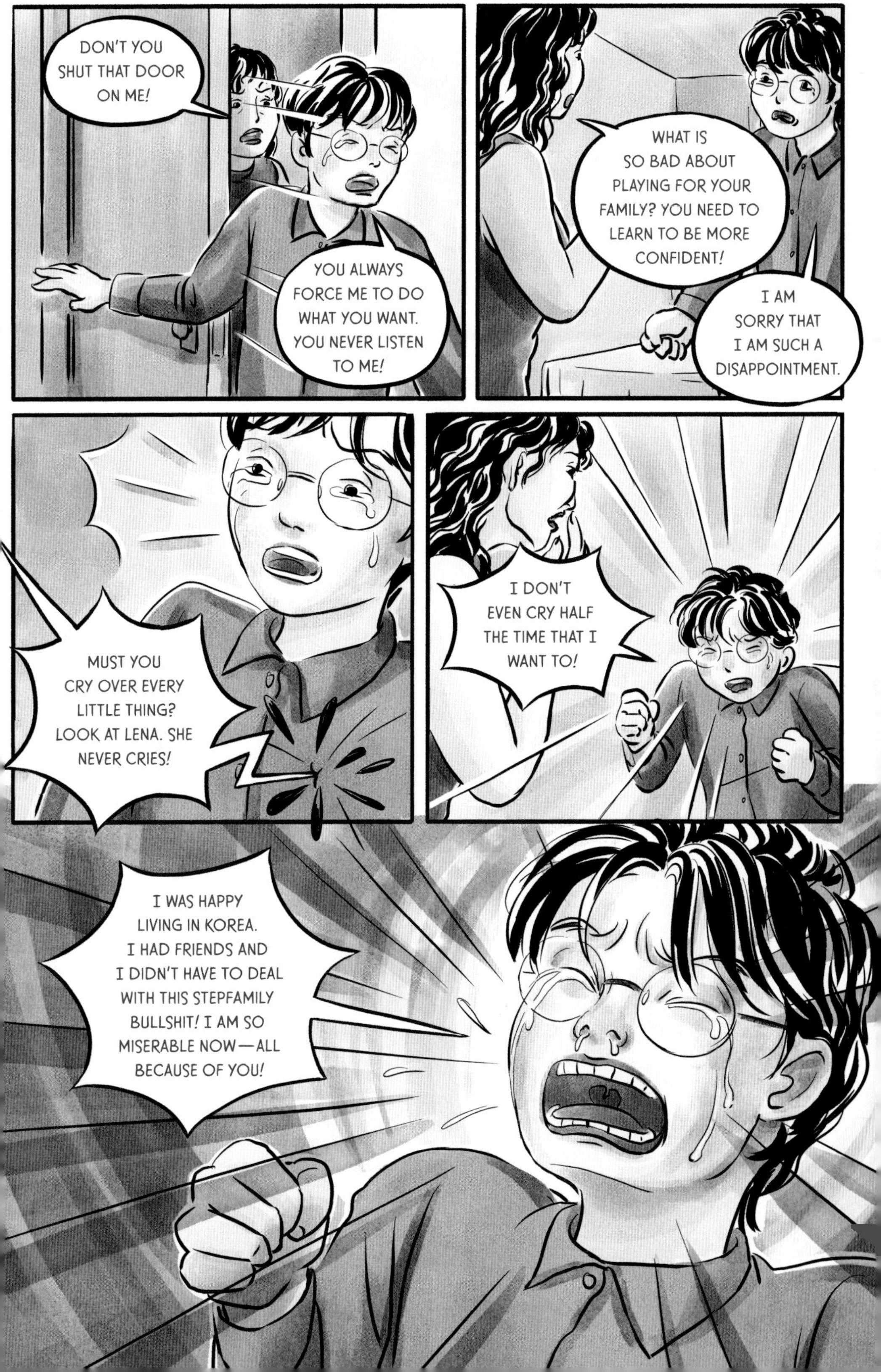
DON'T YOU SHUT THAT DOOR ON ME!
YOU ALWAYS FORCE ME TO DO WHAT YOU WANT. YOU NEVER LISTEN TO ME!
WHAT IS SO BAD ABOUT PLAYING FOR YOUR FAMILY? YOU NEED TO LEARN TO BE MORE CONFIDENT!
I AM SORRY THAT I AM SUCH A DISAPPOINTMENT.
MUST YOU CRY OVER EVERY LITTLE THING? LOOK AT LENA. SHE NEVER CRIES!
I DON'T EVEN CRY HALF THE TIME THAT I WANT TO!
I WAS HAPPY LIVING IN KOREA. I HAD FRIENDS AND I DIDN'T HAVE TO DEAL WITH THIS STEPFAMILY BULLSHIT! I AM SO MISERABLE NOW—ALL BECAUSE OF YOU!

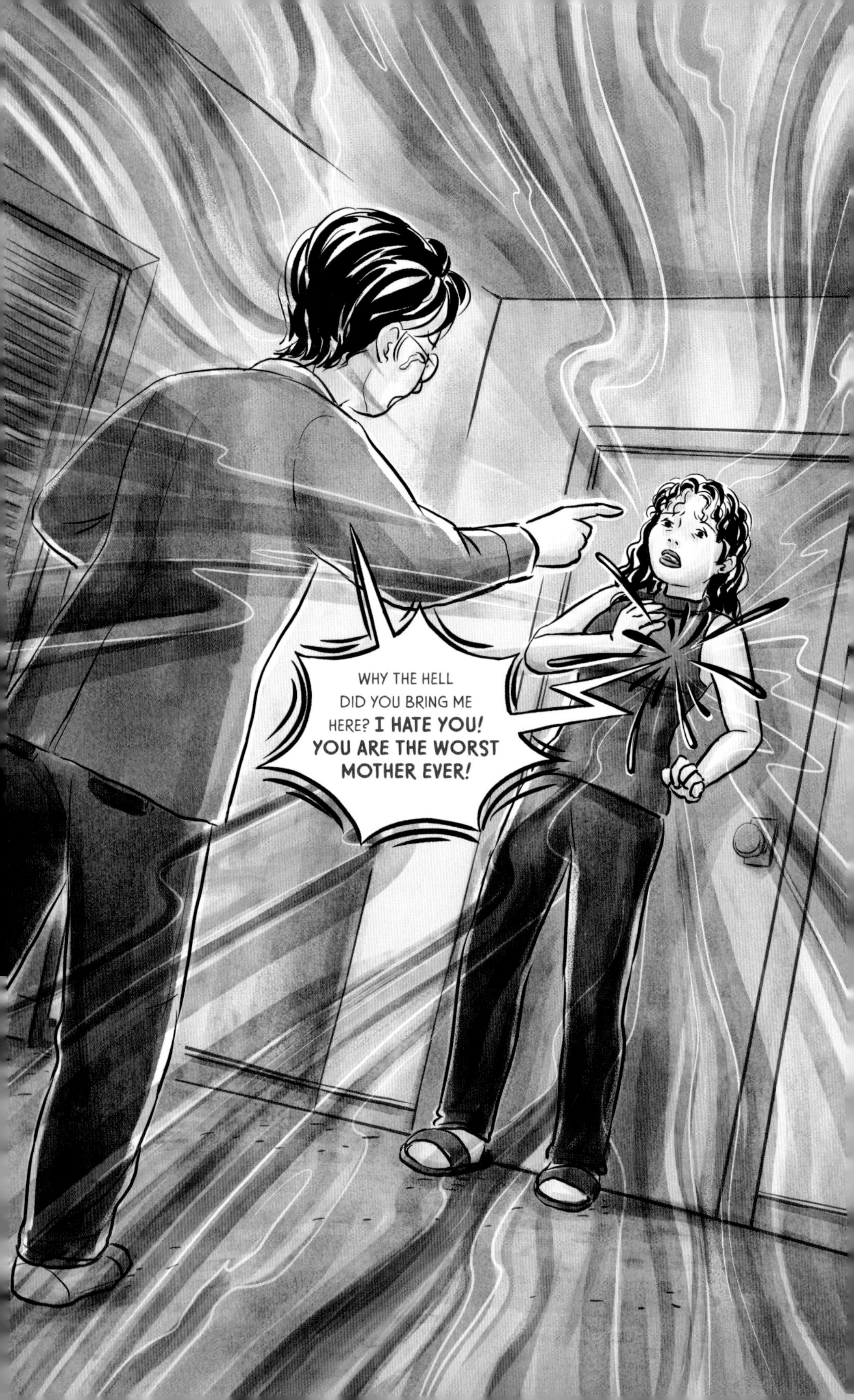
WHY THE HELL DID YOU BRING ME HERE? **I HATE YOU! YOU ARE THE WORST MOTHER EVER!**

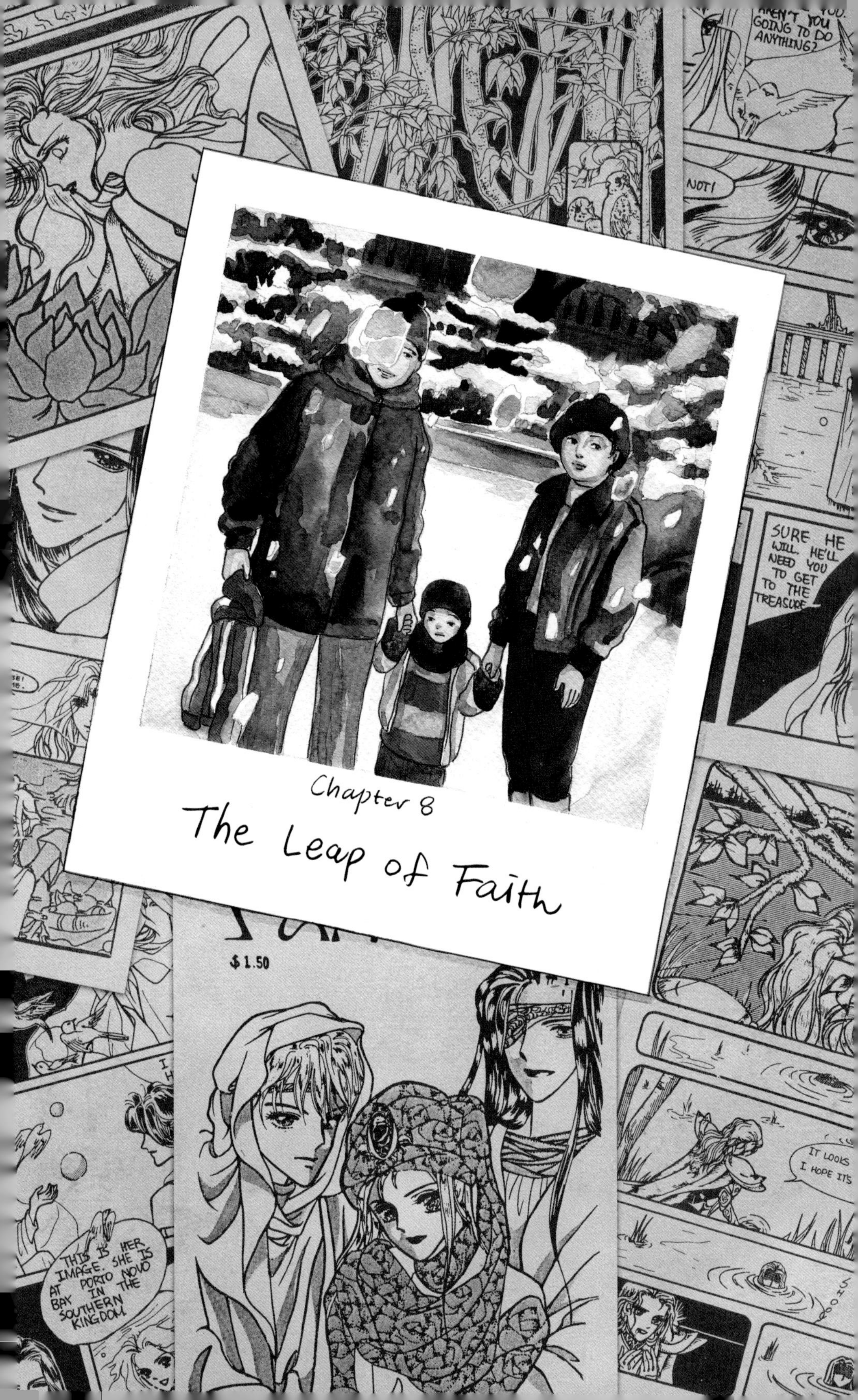
AREN'T YOU GOING TO DO ANYTHING?
NOT!
SURE HE WILL. HE'LL NEED YOU TO GET TO THE TREASURE
Chapter 8
The Leap of Faith
$ 1.50
IT LOOKS
I HOPE IT'S
THIS IS HER IMAGE. SHE IS AT PORTO NOVO BAY IN THE SOUTHERN KINGDOM

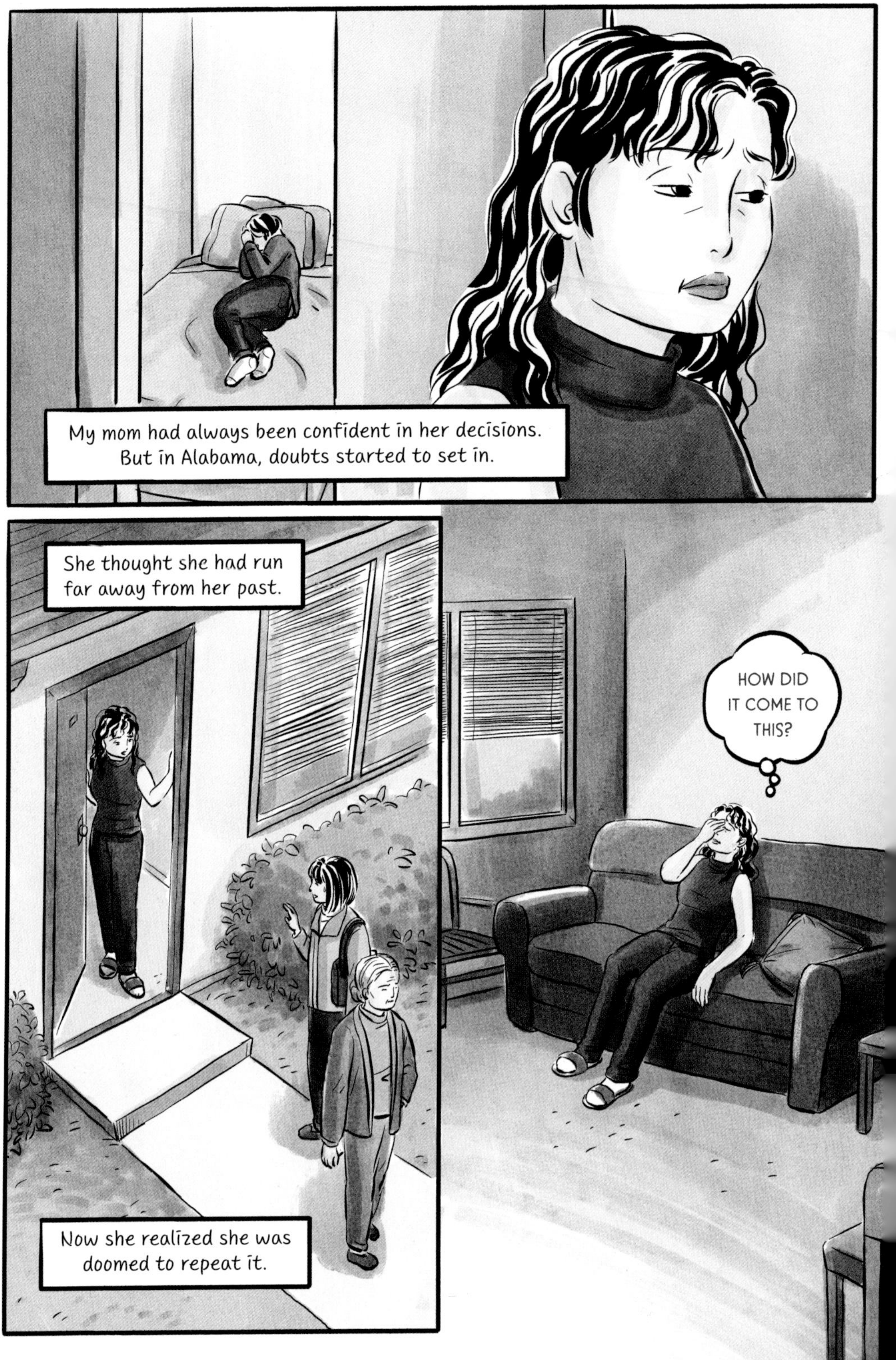
My mom had always been confident in her decisions. But in Alabama, doubts started to set in.
She thought she had run far away from her past.
Now she realized she was doomed to repeat it.
HOW DID IT COME TO THIS?

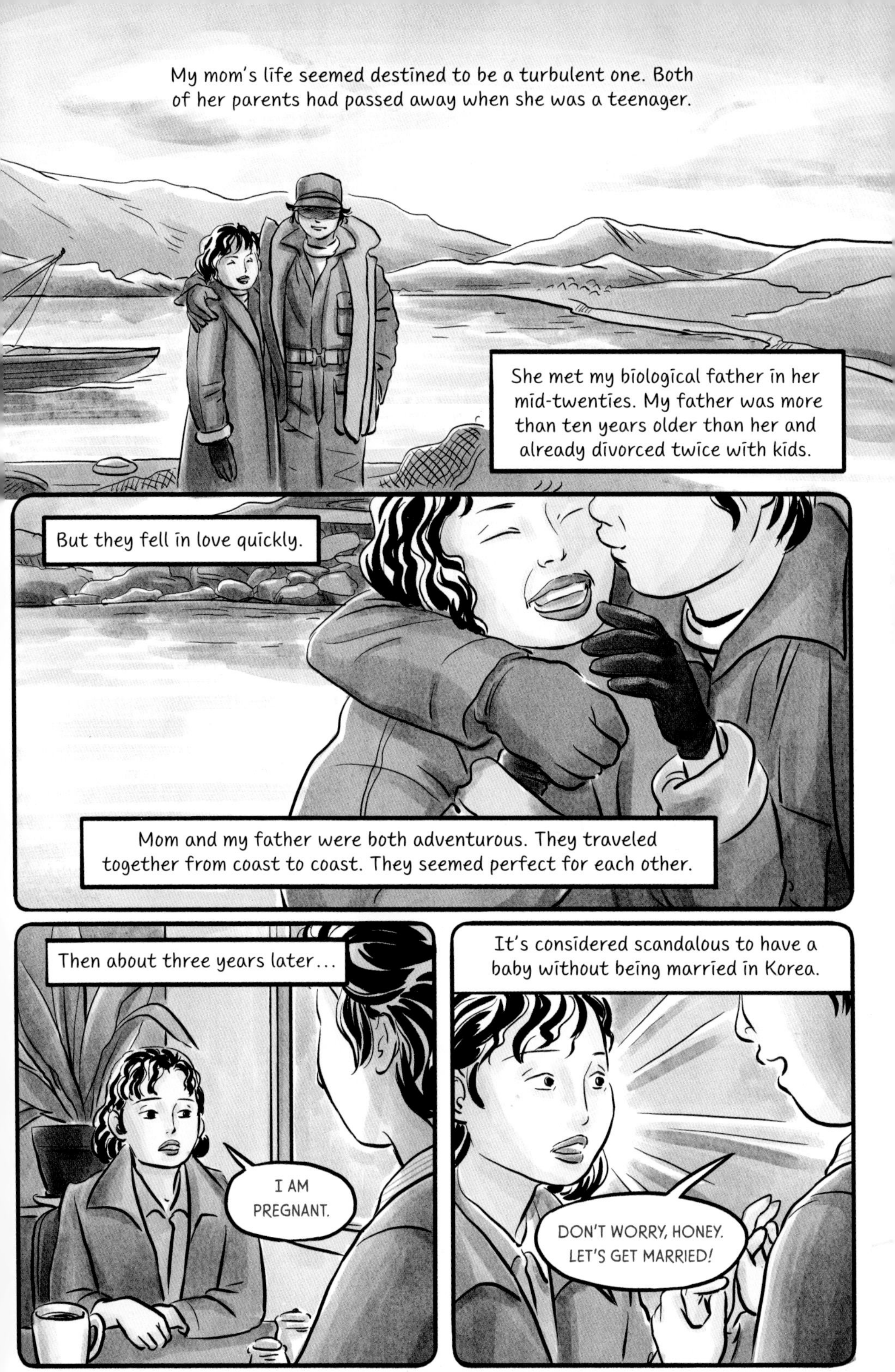
My mom's life seemed destined to be a turbulent one. Both of her parents had passed away when she was a teenager.
She met my biological father in her mid-twenties. My father was more than ten years older than her and already divorced twice with kids.
But they fell in love quickly.
Mom and my father were both adventurous. They traveled together from coast to coast. They seemed perfect for each other.
Then about three years later...
I AM PREGNANT.
It's considered scandalous to have a baby without being married in Korea.
DON'T WORRY, HONEY. LET'S GET MARRIED!

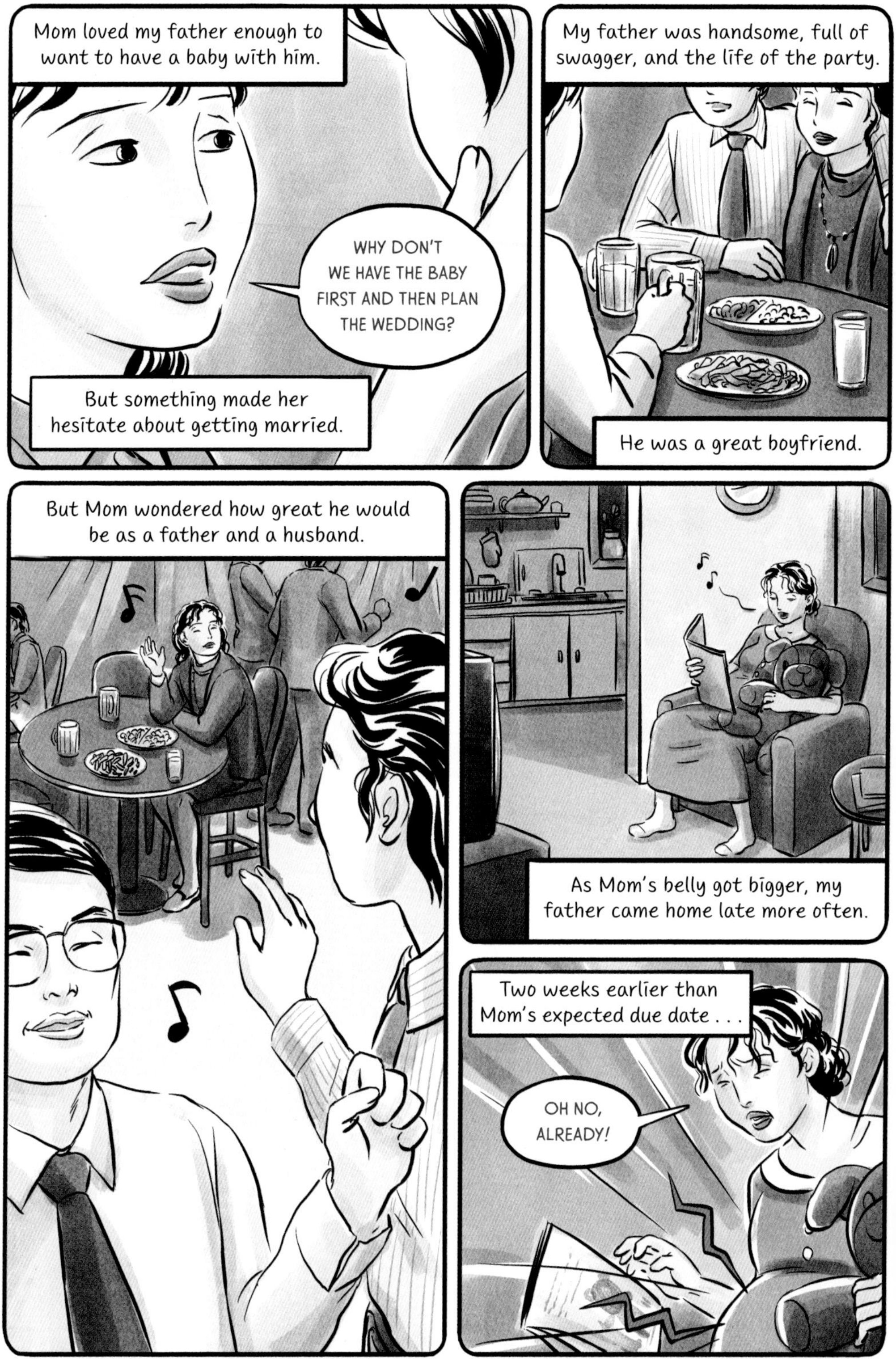
Mom loved my father enough to want to have a baby with him.
WHY DON'T WE HAVE THE BABY FIRST AND THEN PLAN THE WEDDING?
But something made her hesitate about getting married.
My father was handsome, full of swagger, and the life of the party.
He was a great boyfriend.
But Mom wondered how great he would be as a father and a husband.
As Mom's belly got bigger, my father came home late more often.
Two weeks earlier than Mom's expected due date . . .
OH NO, ALREADY!

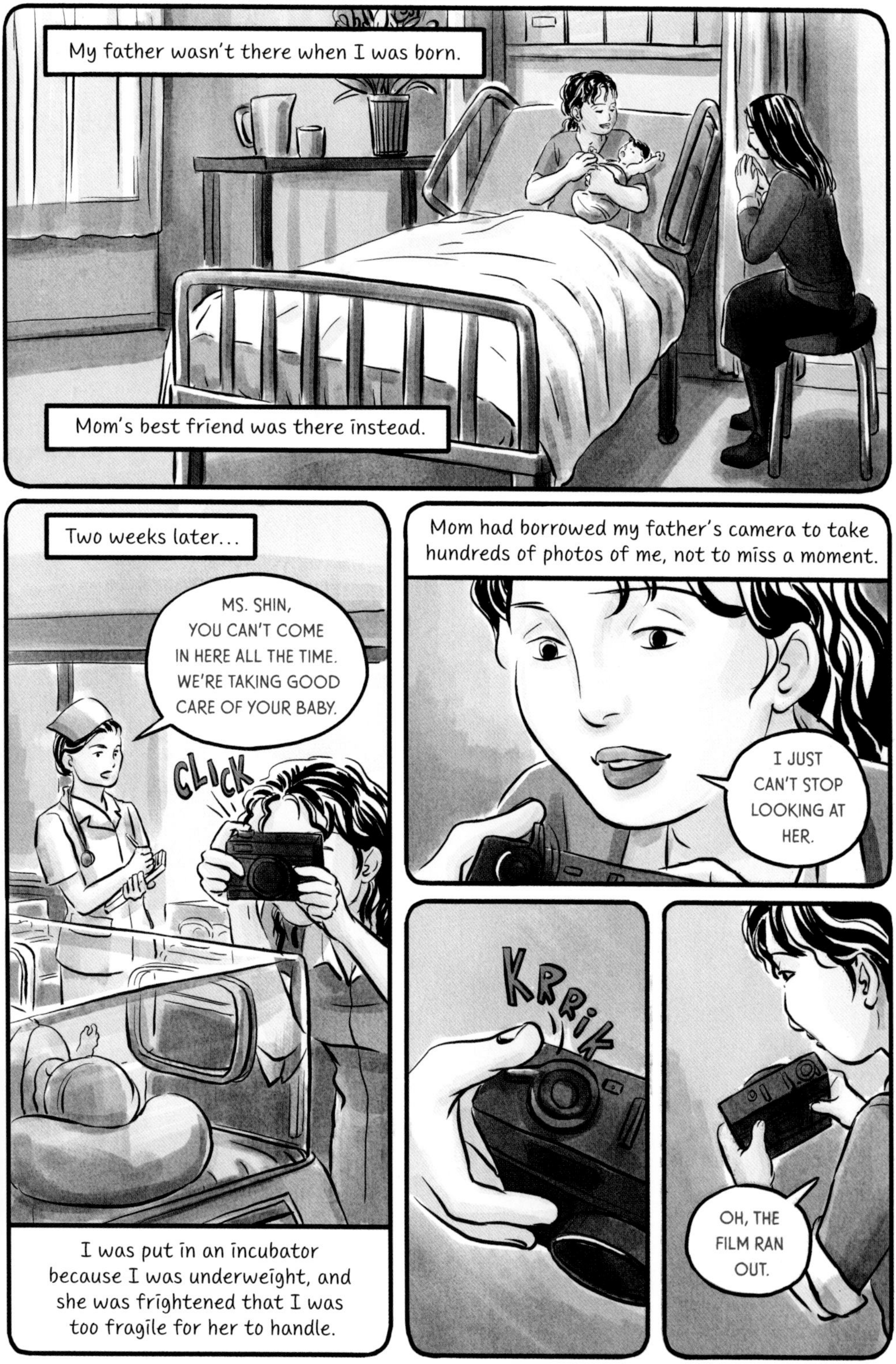
My father wasn't there when I was born.
Mom's best friend was there instead.
Two weeks later...
MS. SHIN, YOU CAN'T COME IN HERE ALL THE TIME. WE'RE TAKING GOOD CARE OF YOUR BABY.
CLICK
I was put in an incubator because I was underweight, and she was frightened that I was too fragile for her to handle.
Mom had borrowed my father's camera to take hundreds of photos of me, not to miss a moment.
I JUST CAN'T STOP LOOKING AT HER.
KRRIK
OH, THE FILM RAN OUT.

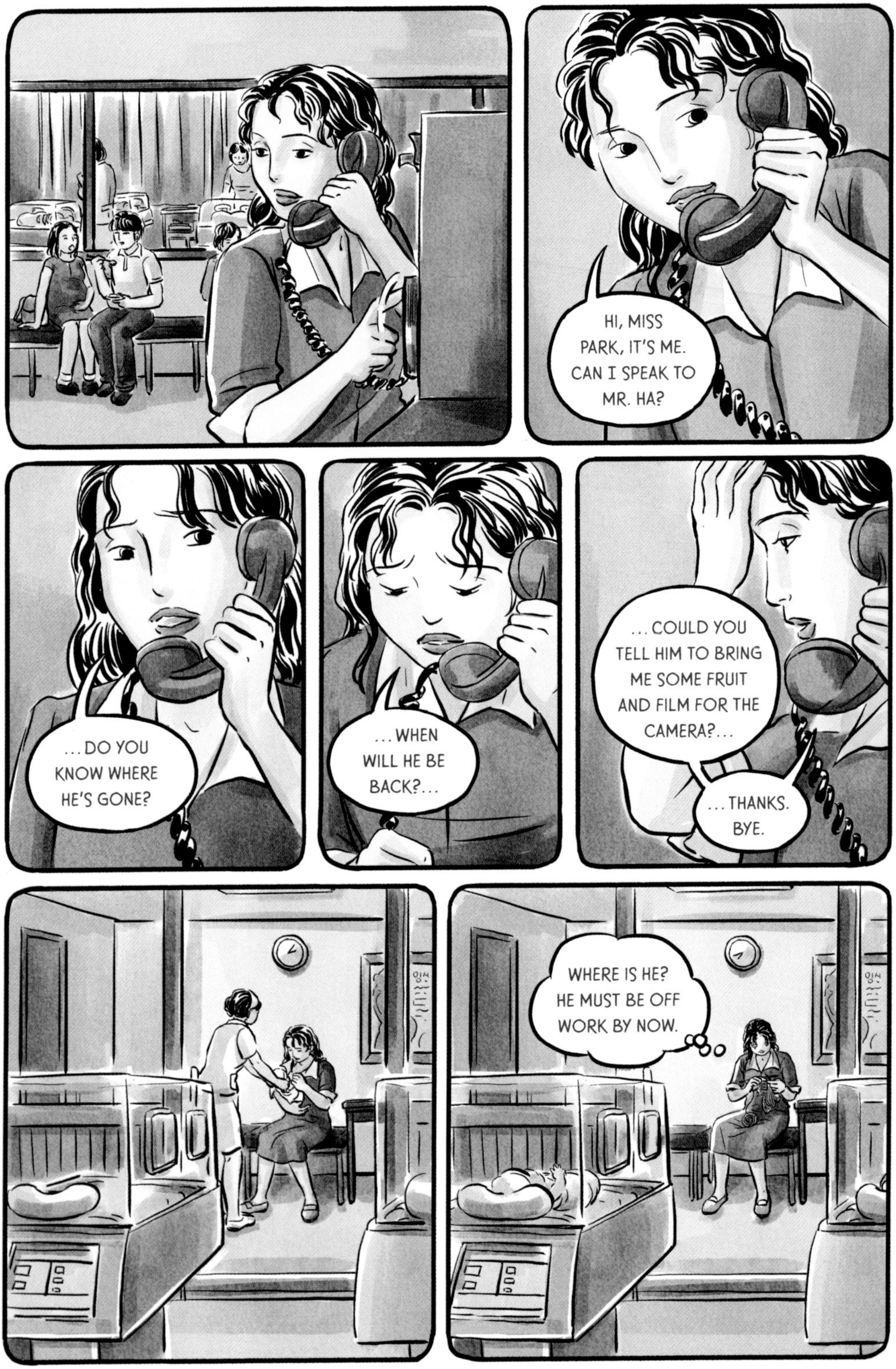
HI, MISS PARK, IT'S ME. CAN I SPEAK TO MR. HA?
...DO YOU KNOW WHERE HE'S GONE?
...WHEN WILL HE BE BACK?...
...COULD YOU TELL HIM TO BRING ME SOME FRUIT AND FILM FOR THE CAMERA?...
...THANKS. BYE.
WHERE IS HE? HE MUST BE OFF WORK BY NOW.

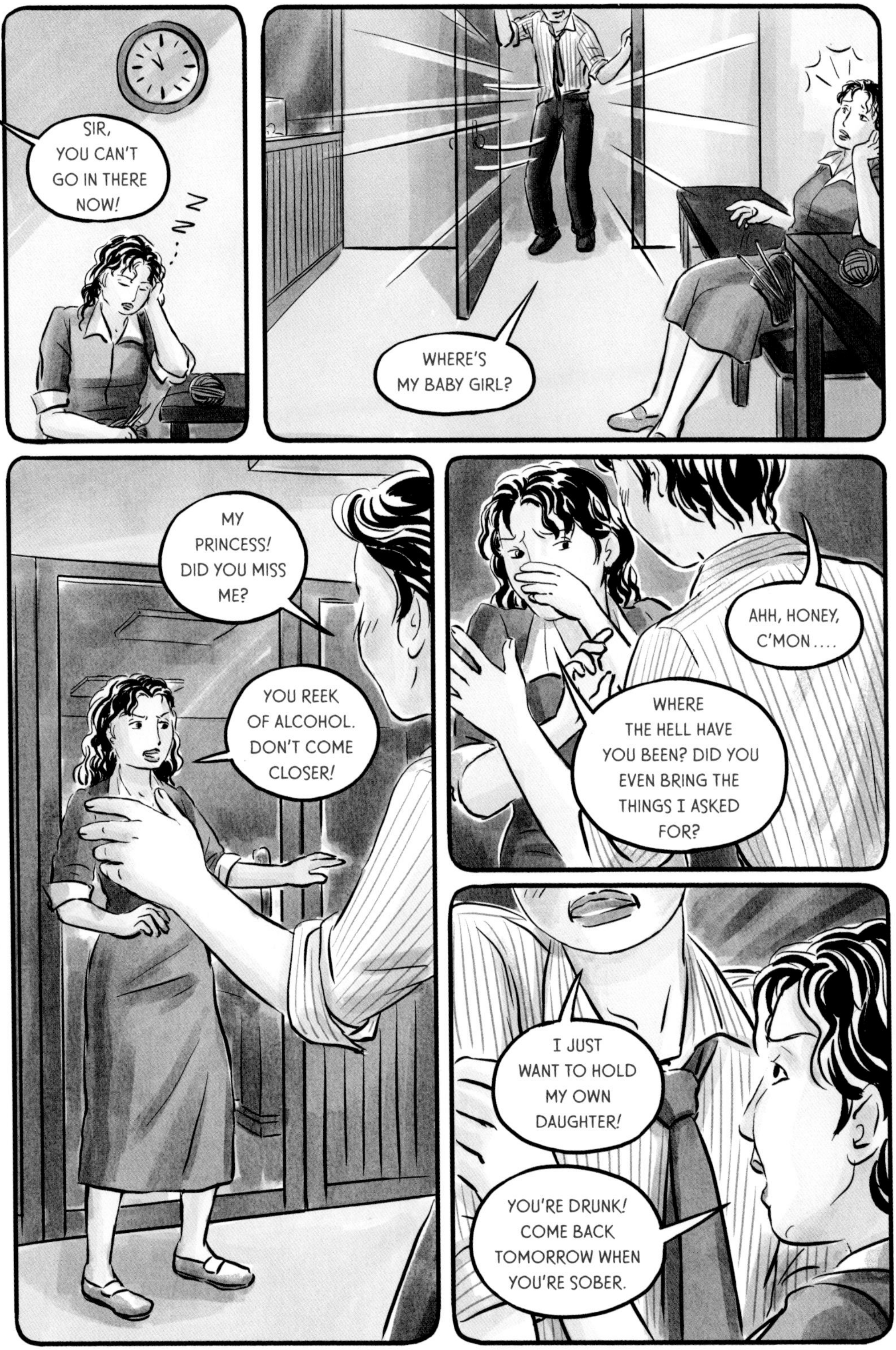
SIR, YOU CAN'T GO IN THERE NOW!
Z Z Z ...
WHERE'S MY BABY GIRL?
MY PRINCESS! DID YOU MISS ME?
YOU REEK OF ALCOHOL. DON'T COME CLOSER!
AHH, HONEY, C'MON....
WHERE THE HELL HAVE YOU BEEN? DID YOU EVEN BRING THE THINGS I ASKED FOR?
I JUST WANT TO HOLD MY OWN DAUGHTER!
YOU'RE DRUNK! COME BACK TOMORROW WHEN YOU'RE SOBER.

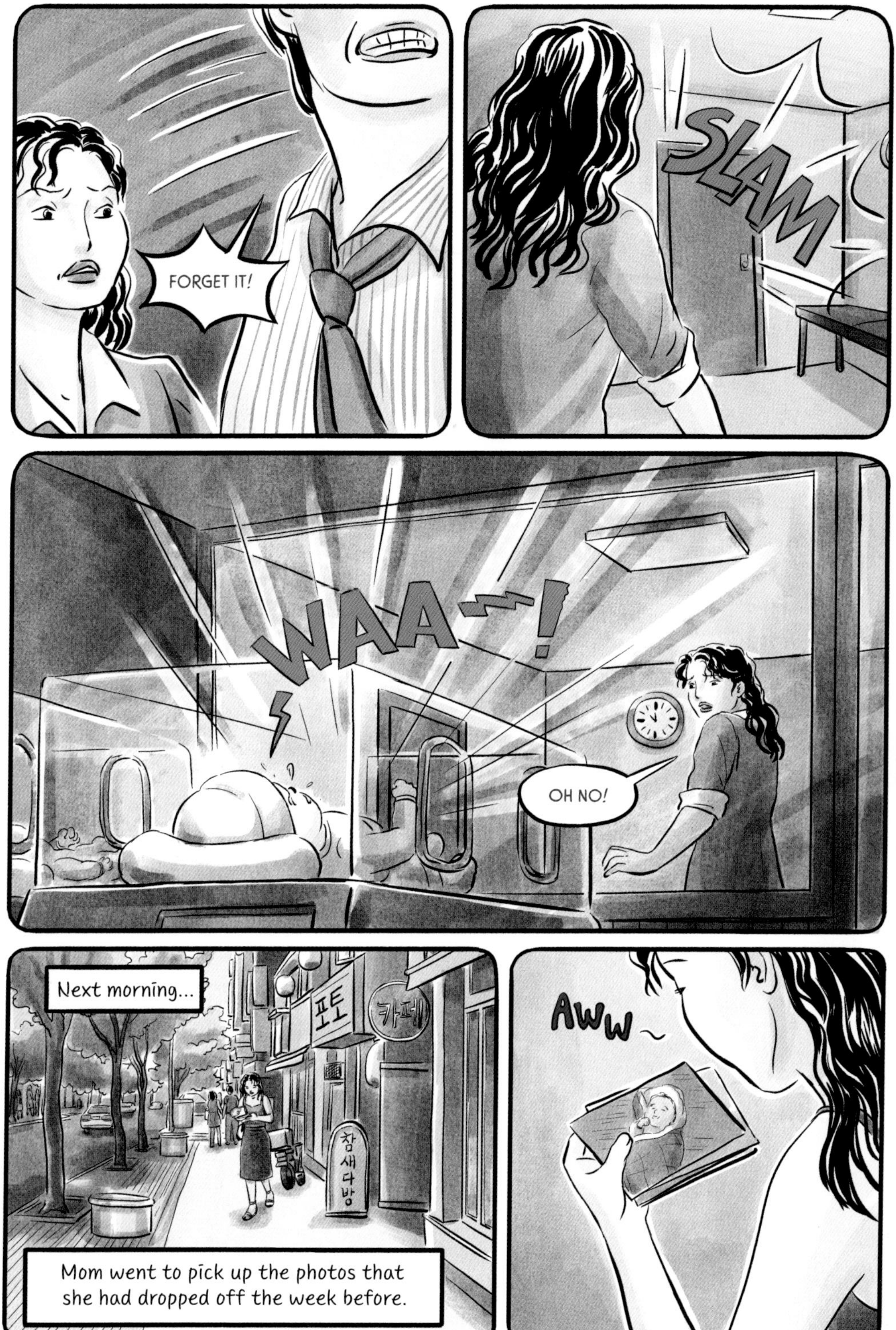
FORGET IT!
SLAM
WAA~~!
OH NO!
Next morning...
포토
카페
참새다방
Mom went to pick up the photos that she had dropped off the week before.
AWW~

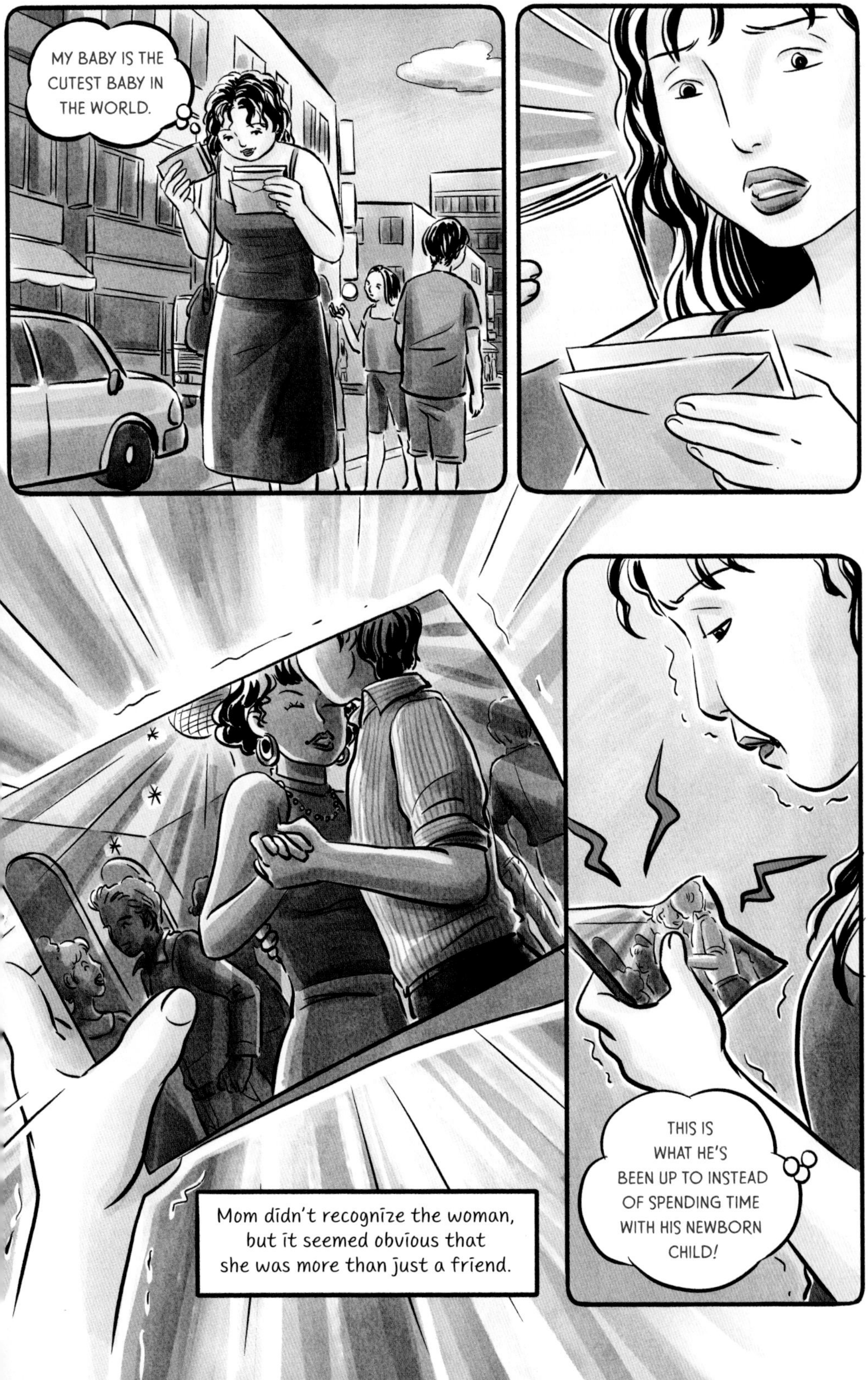
MY BABY IS THE CUTEST BABY IN THE WORLD.
Mom didn't recognize the woman, but it seemed obvious that she was more than just a friend.
THIS IS WHAT HE'S BEEN UP TO INSTEAD OF SPENDING TIME WITH HIS NEWBORN CHILD!

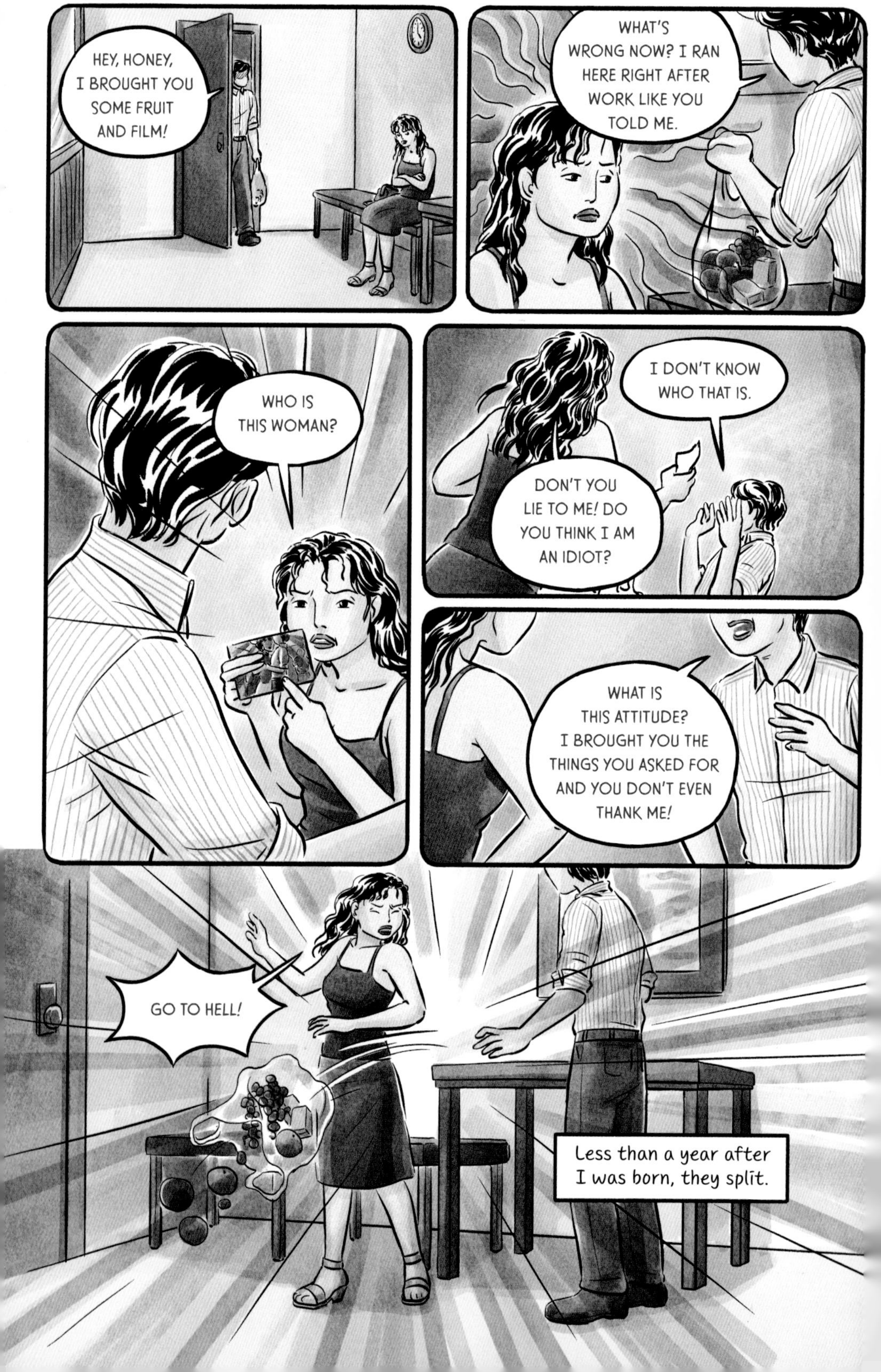
HEY, HONEY, I BROUGHT YOU SOME FRUIT AND FILM!
WHAT'S WRONG NOW? I RAN HERE RIGHT AFTER WORK LIKE YOU TOLD ME.
WHO IS THIS WOMAN?
I DON'T KNOW WHO THAT IS.
DON'T YOU LIE TO ME! DO YOU THINK I AM AN IDIOT?
WHAT IS THIS ATTITUDE? I BROUGHT YOU THE THINGS YOU ASKED FOR AND YOU DON'T EVEN THANK ME!
GO TO HELL!
Less than a year after I was born, they split.

HORSEY!

A few years after my parents split, Mom met Mr. An and they dated for about ten years. I have more memories of Mr. An than of my father.

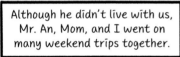

Although he didn't live with us, Mr. An, Mom, and I went on many weekend trips together.

CHUNA, BE CAREFUL.

He loved me like his own daughter. We seemed like a perfect family.

DO YOU WANT TO RIDE WITH YOUR DAD?

But I was my mom's daughter and no one else's.

HE'S NOT MY DAD. I'LL RIDE WITH MY MOM.

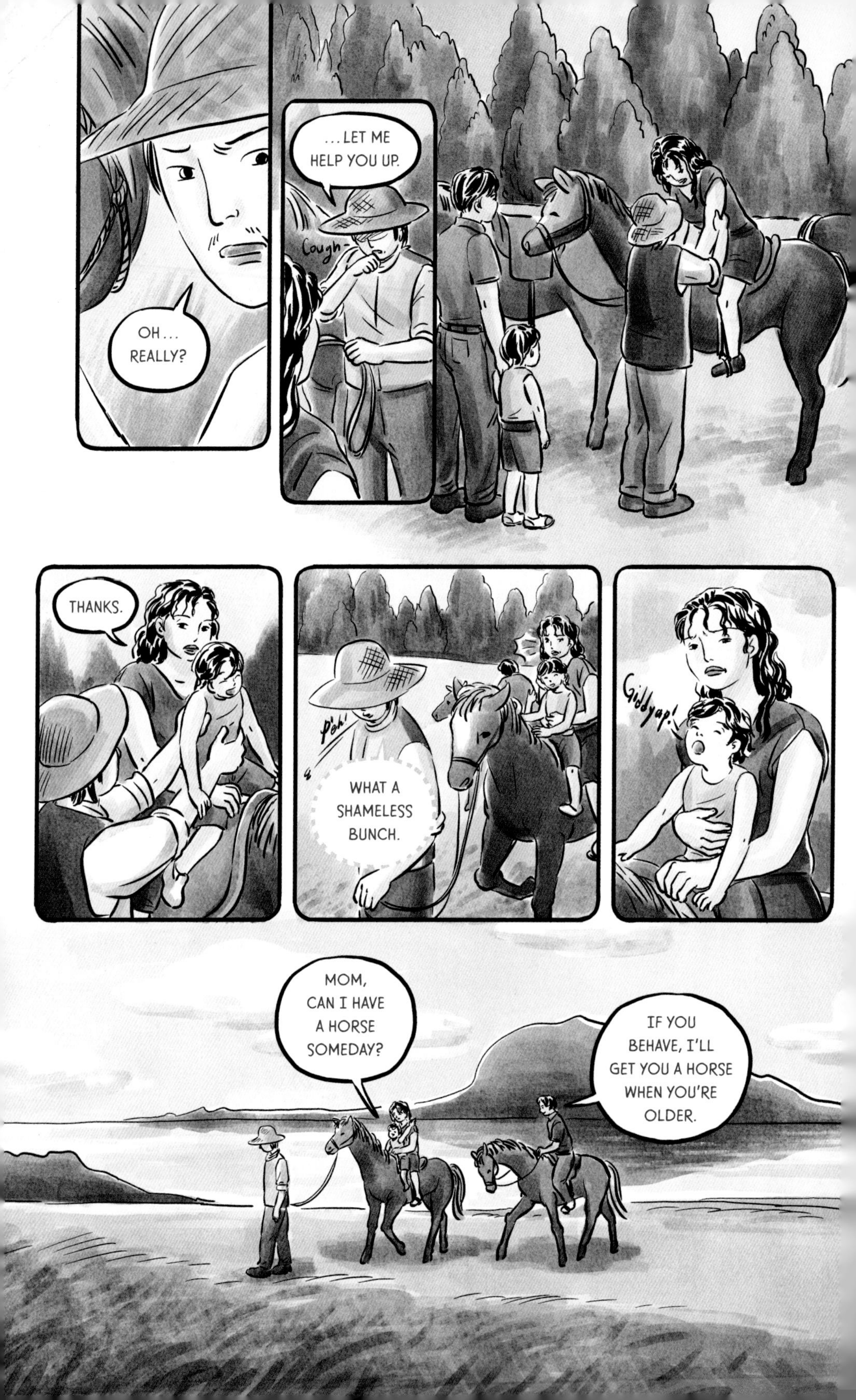
OH... REALLY?
...LET ME HELP YOU UP.
Cough-
THANKS.
Pah!
WHAT A SHAMELESS BUNCH.
Giddyap!
MOM, CAN I HAVE A HORSE SOMEDAY?
IF YOU BEHAVE, I'LL GET YOU A HORSE WHEN YOU'RE OLDER.

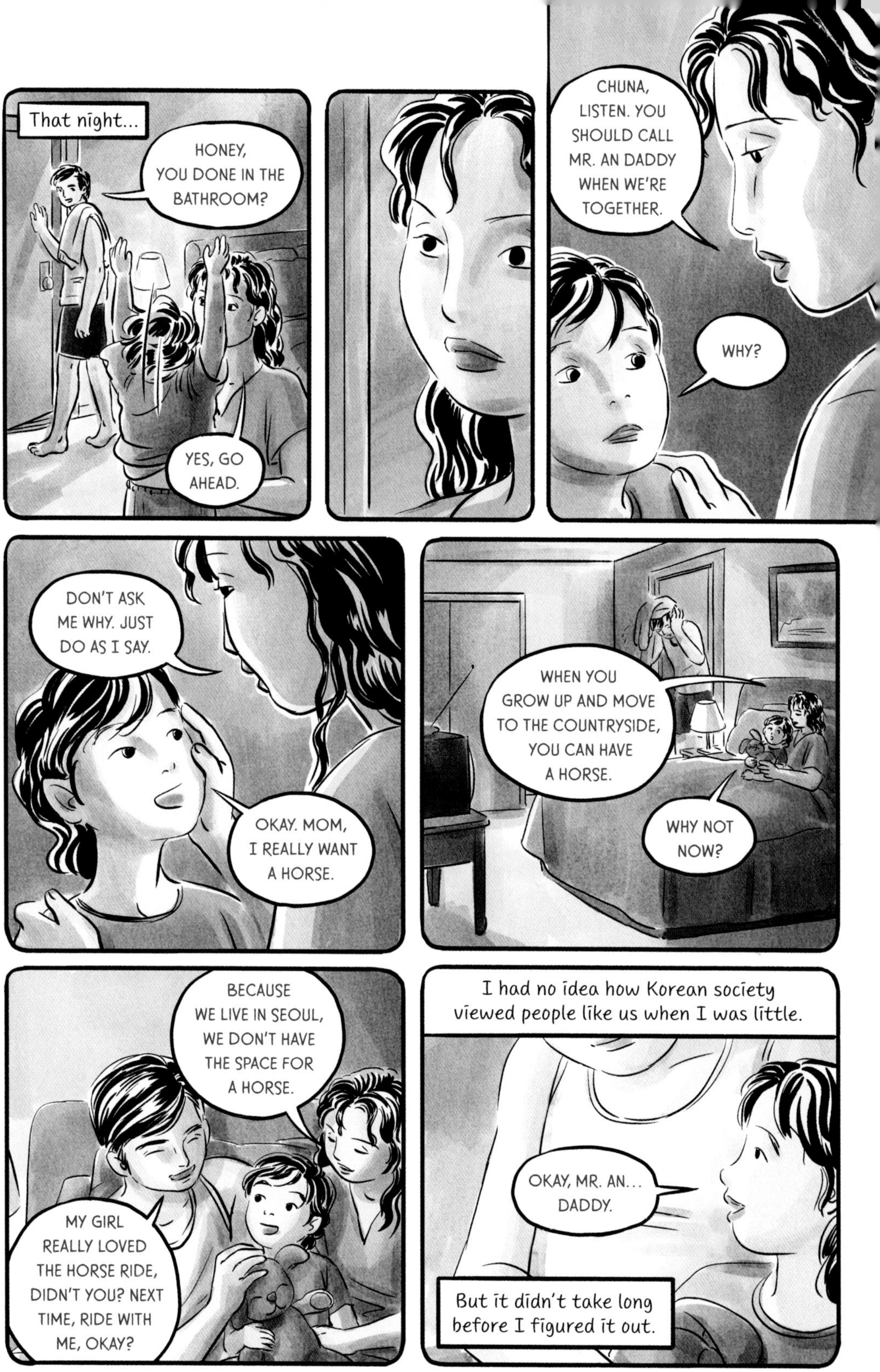
That night...
HONEY, YOU DONE IN THE BATHROOM?
YES, GO AHEAD.
CHUNA, LISTEN. YOU SHOULD CALL MR. AN DADDY WHEN WE'RE TOGETHER.
WHY?
DON'T ASK ME WHY. JUST DO AS I SAY.
OKAY. MOM, I REALLY WANT A HORSE.
WHEN YOU GROW UP AND MOVE TO THE COUNTRYSIDE, YOU CAN HAVE A HORSE.
WHY NOT NOW?
BECAUSE WE LIVE IN SEOUL, WE DON'T HAVE THE SPACE FOR A HORSE.
MY GIRL REALLY LOVED THE HORSE RIDE, DIDN'T YOU? NEXT TIME, RIDE WITH ME, OKAY?
I had no idea how Korean society viewed people like us when I was little.
OKAY, MR. AN... DADDY.
But it didn't take long before I figured it out.

Once I opened my eyes, I saw the judgment and prejudice everywhere.

YOU SHAMED US ALL BY HAVING AN ILLEGITIMATE CHILD. WHAT A DISGRACE!

HOW COULD YOU DO THIS TO OUR FAMILY?

HE SAID HE WAS GOING TO MARRY ME.

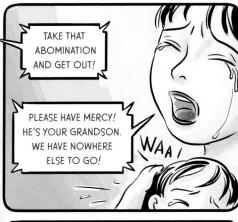

TAKE THAT ABOMINATION AND GET OUT!

PLEASE HAVE MERCY! HE'S YOUR GRANDSON. WE HAVE NOWHERE ELSE TO GO!

WAA!

I DIDN'T RAISE A SLUT! YOU ARE NO CHILD OF MINE....

BEEP!

I especially couldn't stand how single mothers were portrayed in the media.

They were always either evil mistresses or helpless victims—

nothing like my mom.

In Korea, it is common for single mothers to be disowned by their family.

YOU'RE A BAD EXAMPLE TO MY CHILDREN.

My mom didn't keep in touch with most of her relatives.

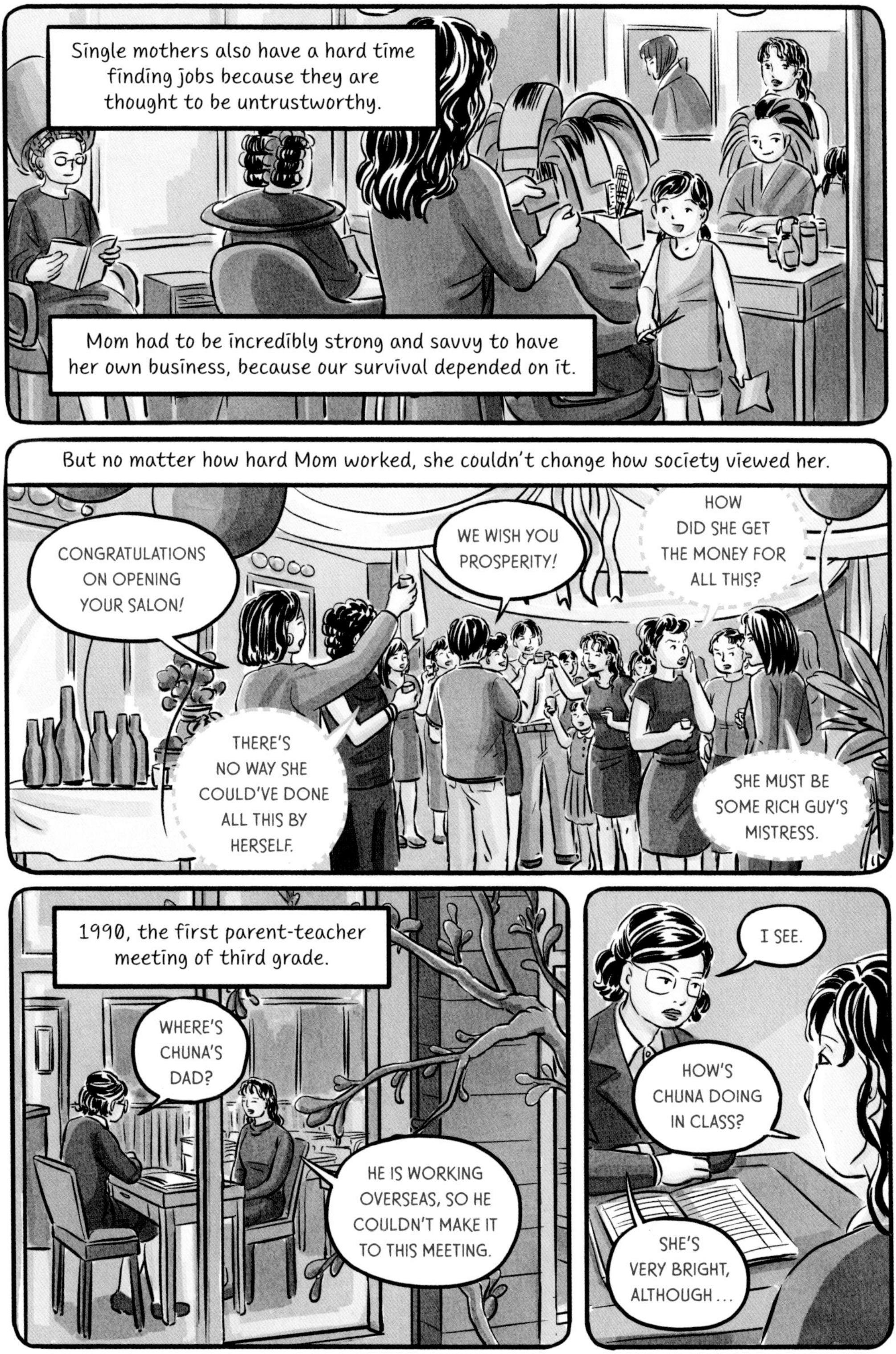
Single mothers also have a hard time finding jobs because they are thought to be untrustworthy.
Mom had to be incredibly strong and savvy to have her own business, because our survival depended on it.
But no matter how hard Mom worked, she couldn't change how society viewed her.
CONGRATULATIONS ON OPENING YOUR SALON!
THERE'S NO WAY SHE COULD'VE DONE ALL THIS BY HERSELF.
WE WISH YOU PROSPERITY!
HOW DID SHE GET THE MONEY FOR ALL THIS?
SHE MUST BE SOME RICH GUY'S MISTRESS.
1990, the first parent-teacher meeting of third grade.
WHERE'S CHUNA'S DAD?
HE IS WORKING OVERSEAS, SO HE COULDN'T MAKE IT TO THIS MEETING.
I SEE.
HOW'S CHUNA DOING IN CLASS?
SHE'S VERY BRIGHT, ALTHOUGH . . .

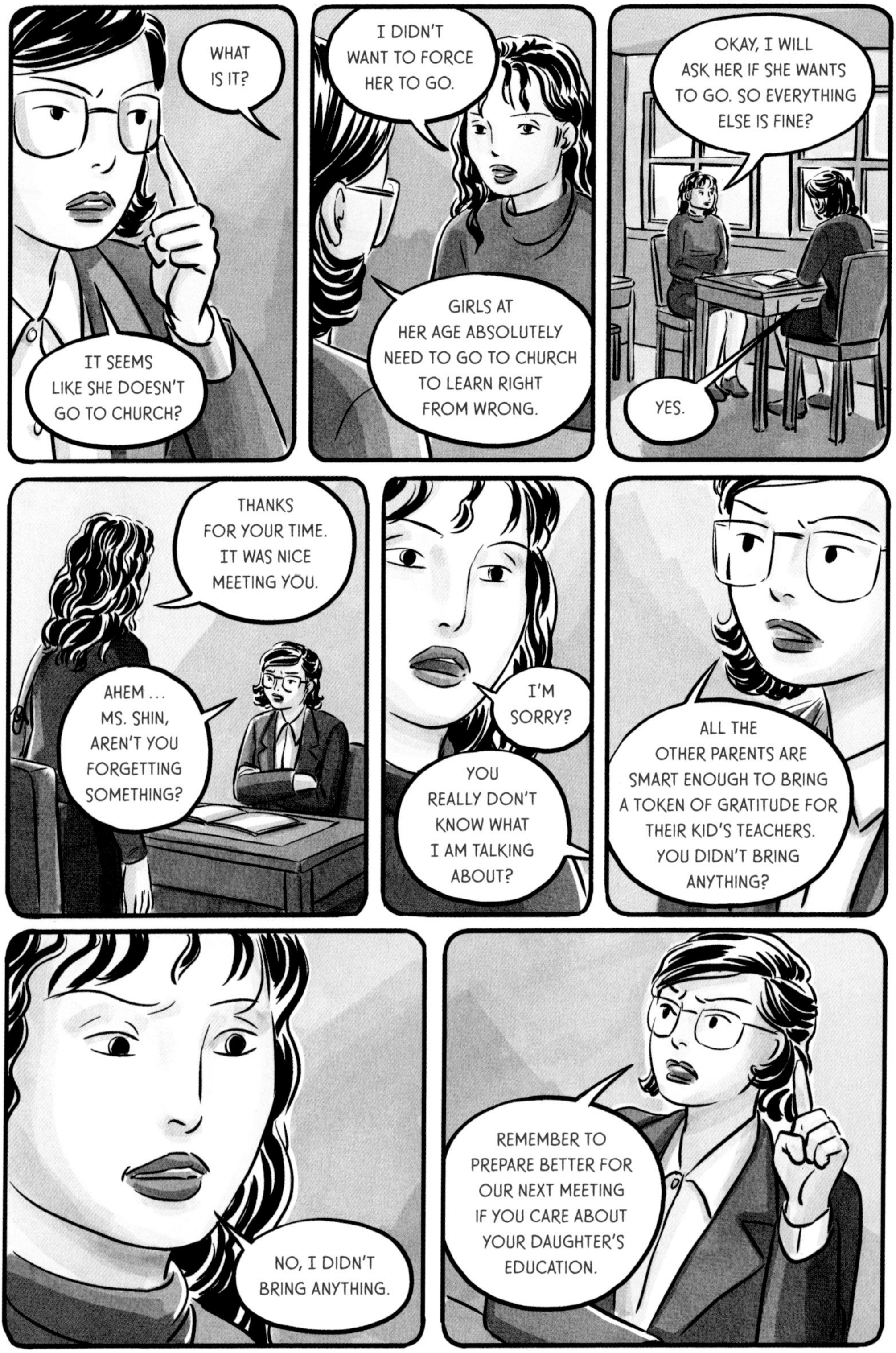
WHAT IS IT?
IT SEEMS LIKE SHE DOESN'T GO TO CHURCH?
I DIDN'T WANT TO FORCE HER TO GO.
GIRLS AT HER AGE ABSOLUTELY NEED TO GO TO CHURCH TO LEARN RIGHT FROM WRONG.
OKAY, I WILL ASK HER IF SHE WANTS TO GO. SO EVERYTHING ELSE IS FINE?
YES.
THANKS FOR YOUR TIME. IT WAS NICE MEETING YOU.
AHEM ... MS. SHIN, AREN'T YOU FORGETTING SOMETHING?
I'M SORRY?
YOU REALLY DON'T KNOW WHAT I AM TALKING ABOUT?
ALL THE OTHER PARENTS ARE SMART ENOUGH TO BRING A TOKEN OF GRATITUDE FOR THEIR KID'S TEACHERS. YOU DIDN'T BRING ANYTHING?
NO, I DIDN'T BRING ANYTHING.
REMEMBER TO PREPARE BETTER FOR OUR NEXT MEETING IF YOU CARE ABOUT YOUR DAUGHTER'S EDUCATION.

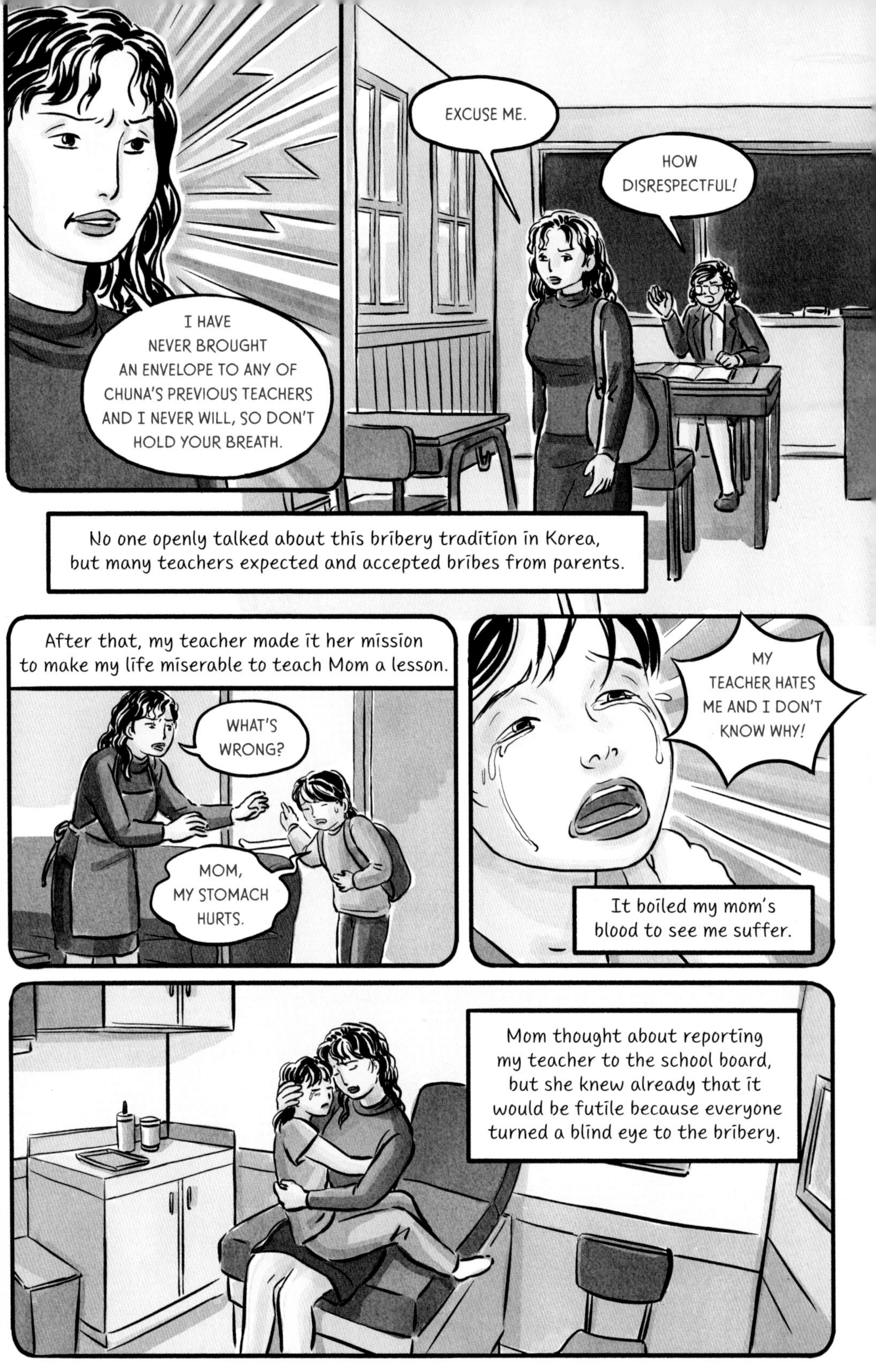
I HAVE NEVER BROUGHT AN ENVELOPE TO ANY OF CHUNA'S PREVIOUS TEACHERS AND I NEVER WILL, SO DON'T HOLD YOUR BREATH.
EXCUSE ME.
HOW DISRESPECTFUL!
No one openly talked about this bribery tradition in Korea, but many teachers expected and accepted bribes from parents.
After that, my teacher made it her mission to make my life miserable to teach Mom a lesson.
WHAT'S WRONG?
MOM, MY STOMACH HURTS.
MY TEACHER HATES ME AND I DON'T KNOW WHY!
It boiled my mom's blood to see me suffer.
Mom thought about reporting my teacher to the school board, but she knew already that it would be futile because everyone turned a blind eye to the bribery.

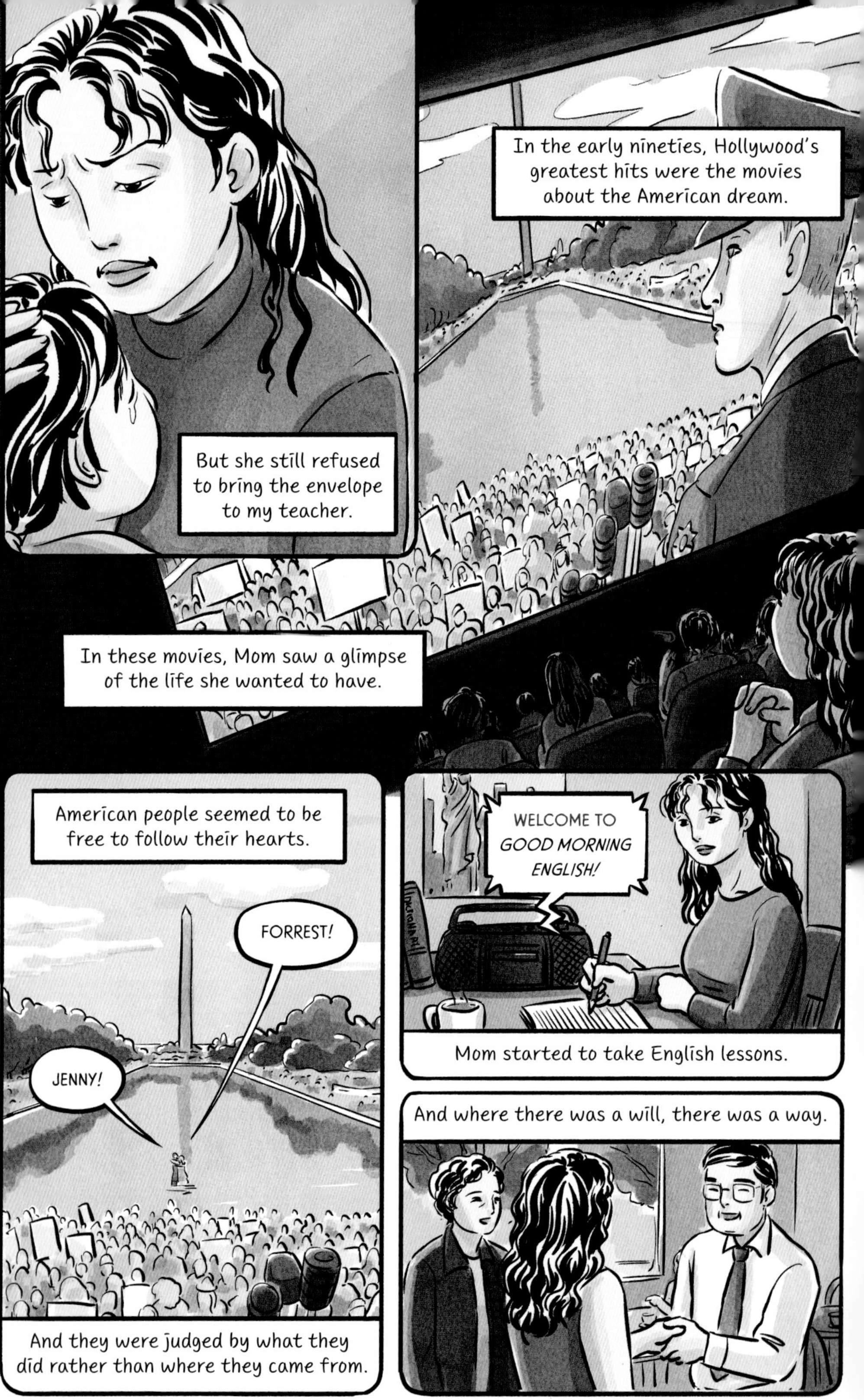
But she still refused to bring the envelope to my teacher.
In the early nineties, Hollywood's greatest hits were the movies about the American dream.
In these movies, Mom saw a glimpse of the life she wanted to have.
American people seemed to be free to follow their hearts.
FORREST!
JENNY!
And they were judged by what they did rather than where they came from.
WELCOME TO GOOD MORNING ENGLISH!
Mom started to take English lessons.
And where there was a will, there was a way.

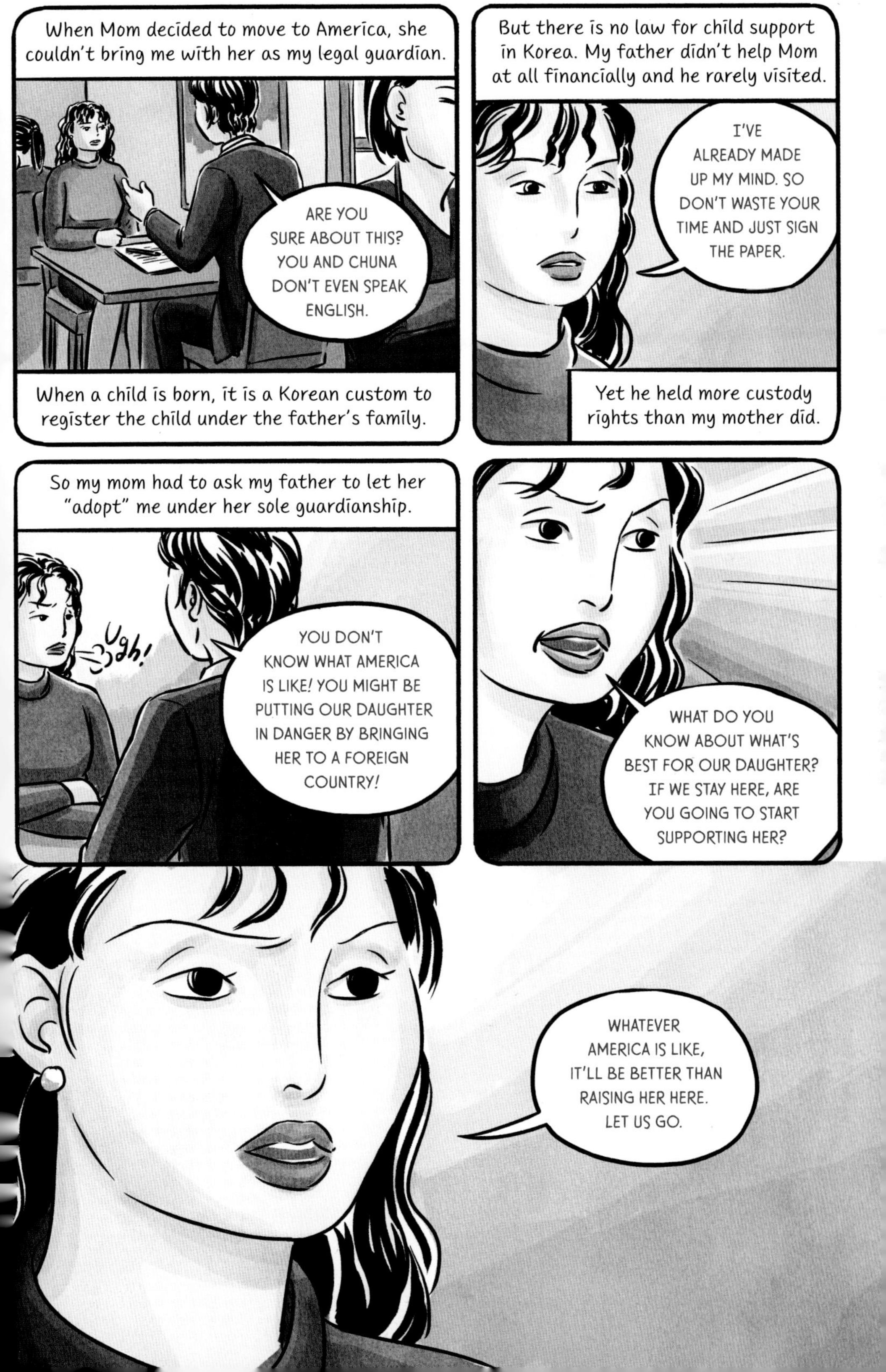
When Mom decided to move to America, she couldn't bring me with her as my legal guardian.
ARE YOU SURE ABOUT THIS? YOU AND CHUNA DON'T EVEN SPEAK ENGLISH.
When a child is born, it is a Korean custom to register the child under the father's family.
But there is no law for child support in Korea. My father didn't help Mom at all financially and he rarely visited.
I'VE ALREADY MADE UP MY MIND. SO DON'T WASTE YOUR TIME AND JUST SIGN THE PAPER.
Yet he held more custody rights than my mother did.
So my mom had to ask my father to let her "adopt" me under her sole guardianship.
Ugh!
YOU DON'T KNOW WHAT AMERICA IS LIKE! YOU MIGHT BE PUTTING OUR DAUGHTER IN DANGER BY BRINGING HER TO A FOREIGN COUNTRY!
WHAT DO YOU KNOW ABOUT WHAT'S BEST FOR OUR DAUGHTER? IF WE STAY HERE, ARE YOU GOING TO START SUPPORTING HER?
WHATEVER AMERICA IS LIKE, IT'LL BE BETTER THAN RAISING HER HERE. LET US GO.

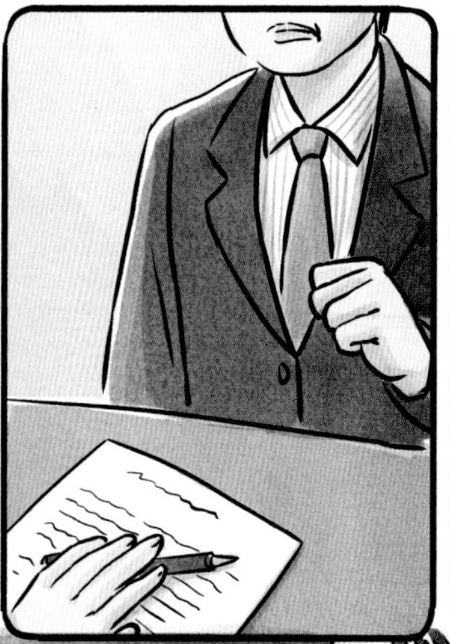

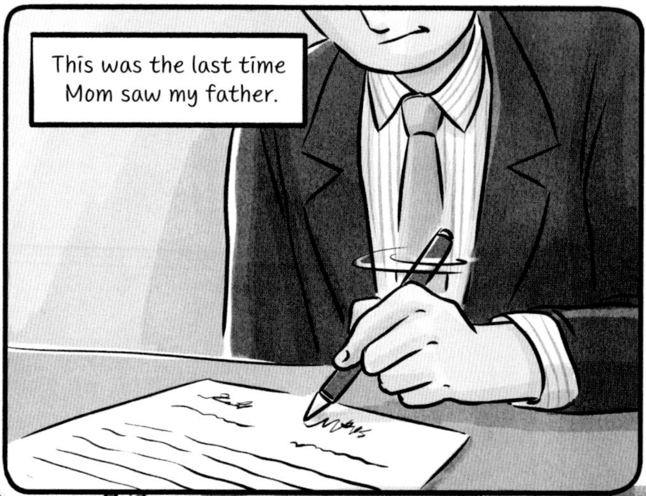
This was the last time
Mom saw my father.

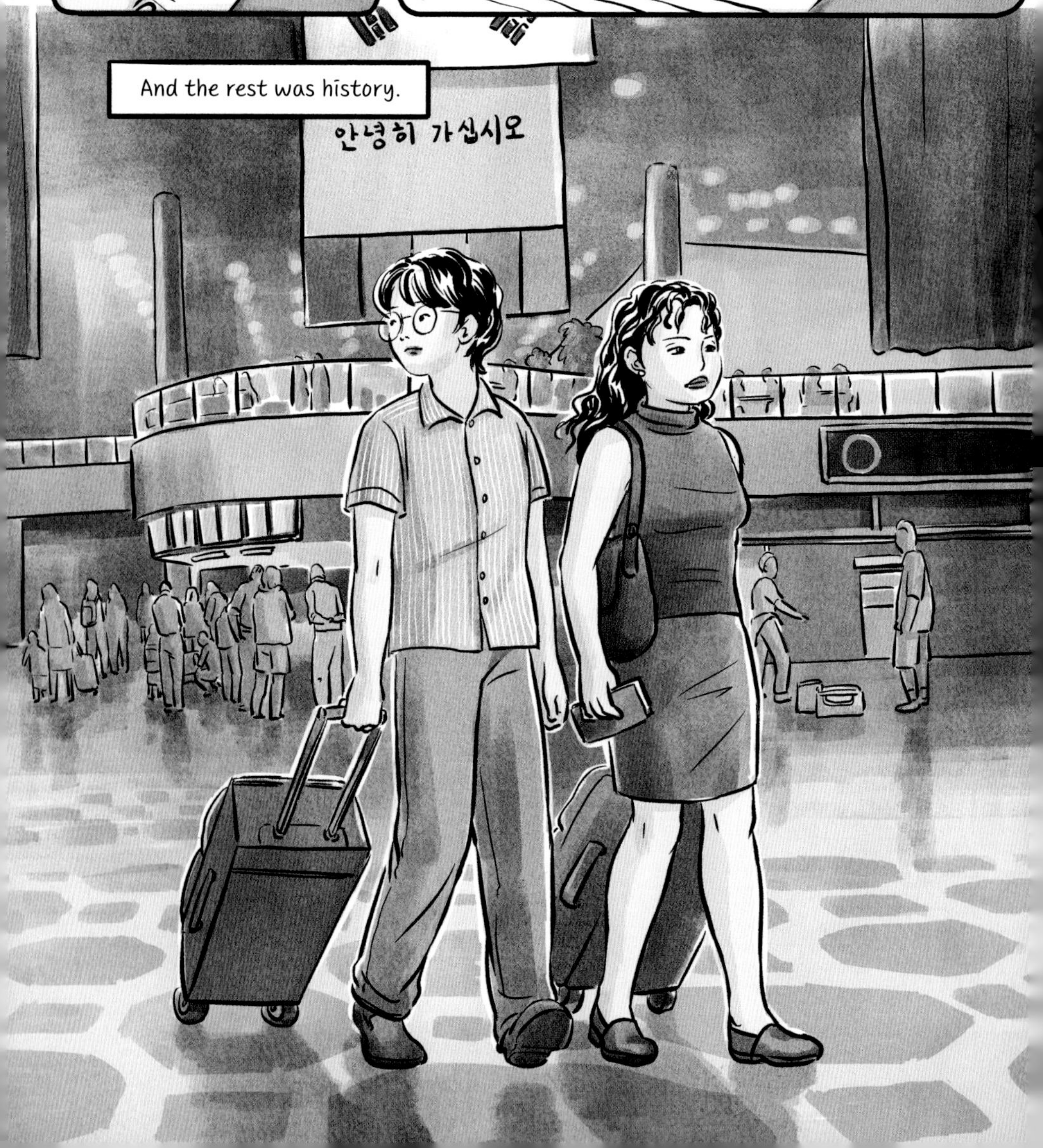
And the rest was history.
안녕히 가십시오

Chapter 9
Comics to the Rescue!

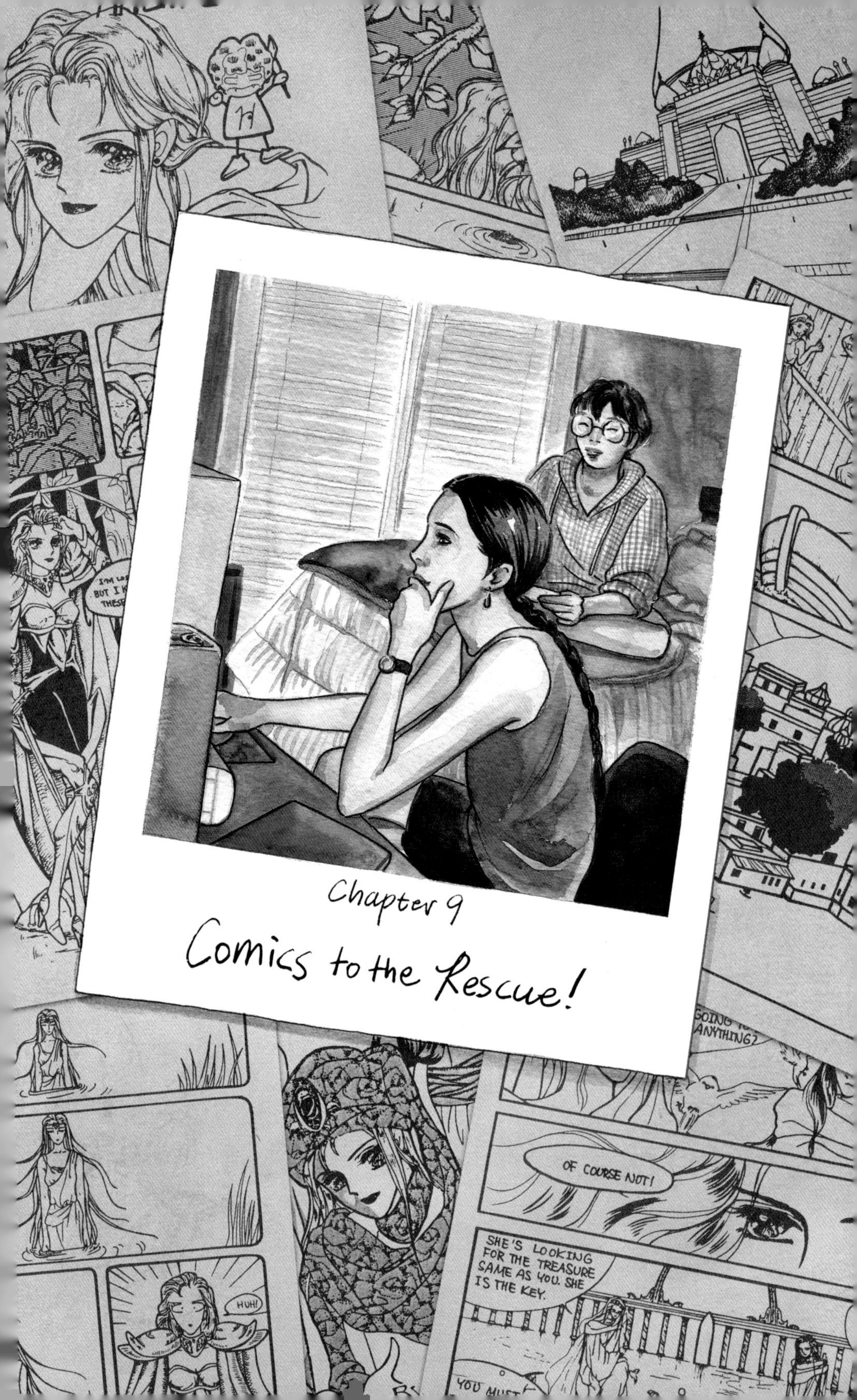

HUH!
ANYTHING?
OF COURSE NOT!
SHE'S LOOKING FOR THE TREASURE SAME AS YOU. SHE IS THE KEY.

After our fight, Mom and I hadn't spoken in over a week.

IT'S ALREADY 7:30?!

MOM DOESN'T EVEN WAKE ME UP ANYMORE.

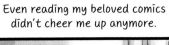
BuuNg-

I thought she'd given up on me.

Even reading my beloved comics didn't cheer me up anymore.

One of my favorite parts of *Queen's Quest* was when Eshika has been banished from her kingdom.

She is lost in the desert and almost at the brink of death.

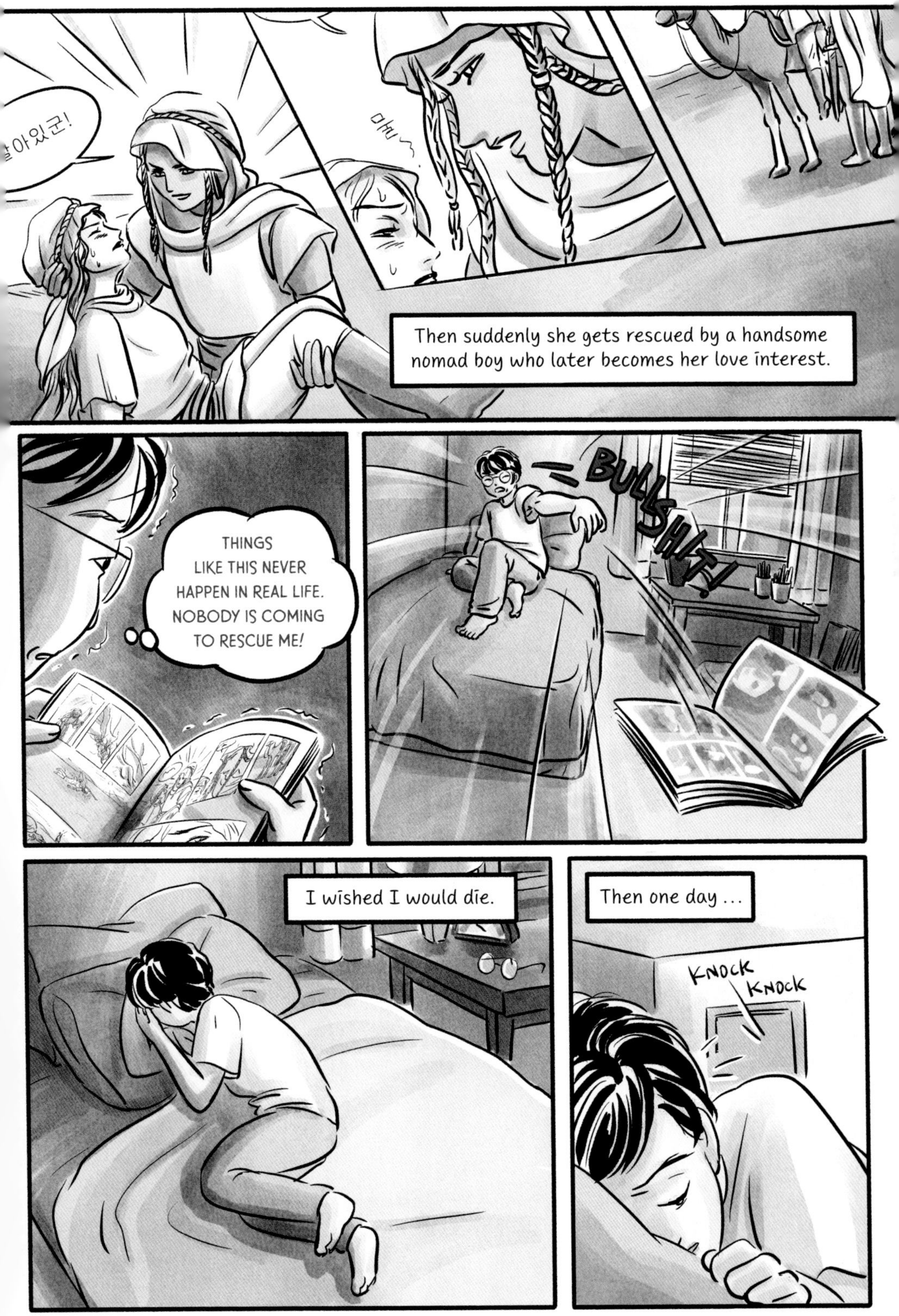
아있군!
Then suddenly she gets rescued by a handsome nomad boy who later becomes her love interest.
THINGS LIKE THIS NEVER HAPPEN IN REAL LIFE. NOBODY IS COMING TO RESCUE ME!
BULLSHIT!
I wished I would die.
Then one day . . .
KNOCK KNOCK

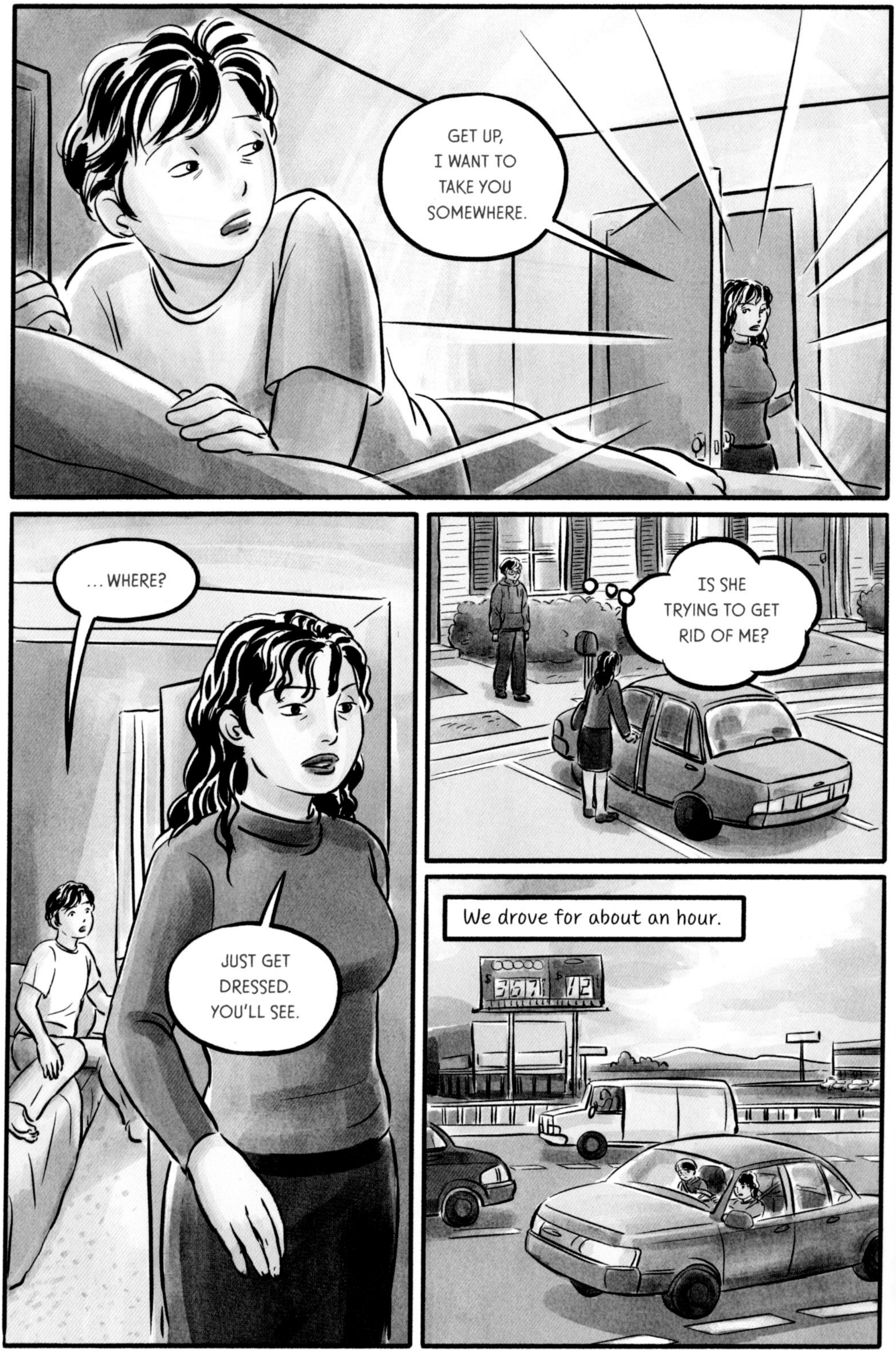
GET UP, I WANT TO TAKE YOU SOMEWHERE.
...WHERE?
JUST GET DRESSED. YOU'LL SEE.
IS SHE TRYING TO GET RID OF ME?
We drove for about an hour.

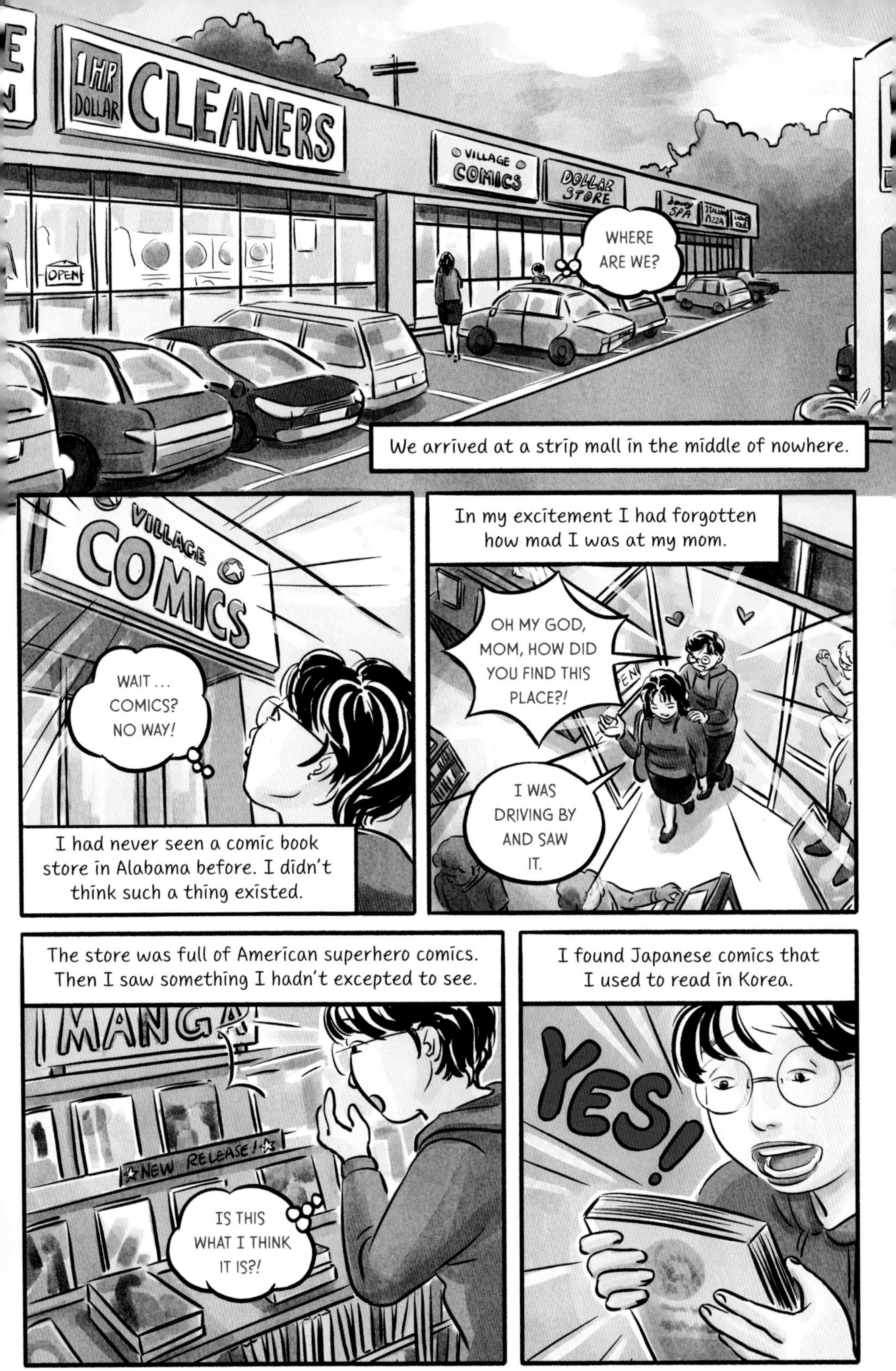
1 HR DOLLAR CLEANERS
VILLAGE COMICS
DOLLAR STORE
ITALIAN PIZZA
OPEN
WHERE ARE WE?
We arrived at a strip mall in the middle of nowhere.
VILLAGE COMICS
WAIT . . . COMICS? NO WAY!
I had never seen a comic book store in Alabama before. I didn't think such a thing existed.
In my excitement I had forgotten how mad I was at my mom.
OH MY GOD, MOM, HOW DID YOU FIND THIS PLACE?!
I WAS DRIVING BY AND SAW IT.
The store was full of American superhero comics. Then I saw something I hadn't excepted to see.
MANGA
NEW RELEASE!
IS THIS WHAT I THINK IT IS?!
I found Japanese comics that I used to read in Korea.
YES!

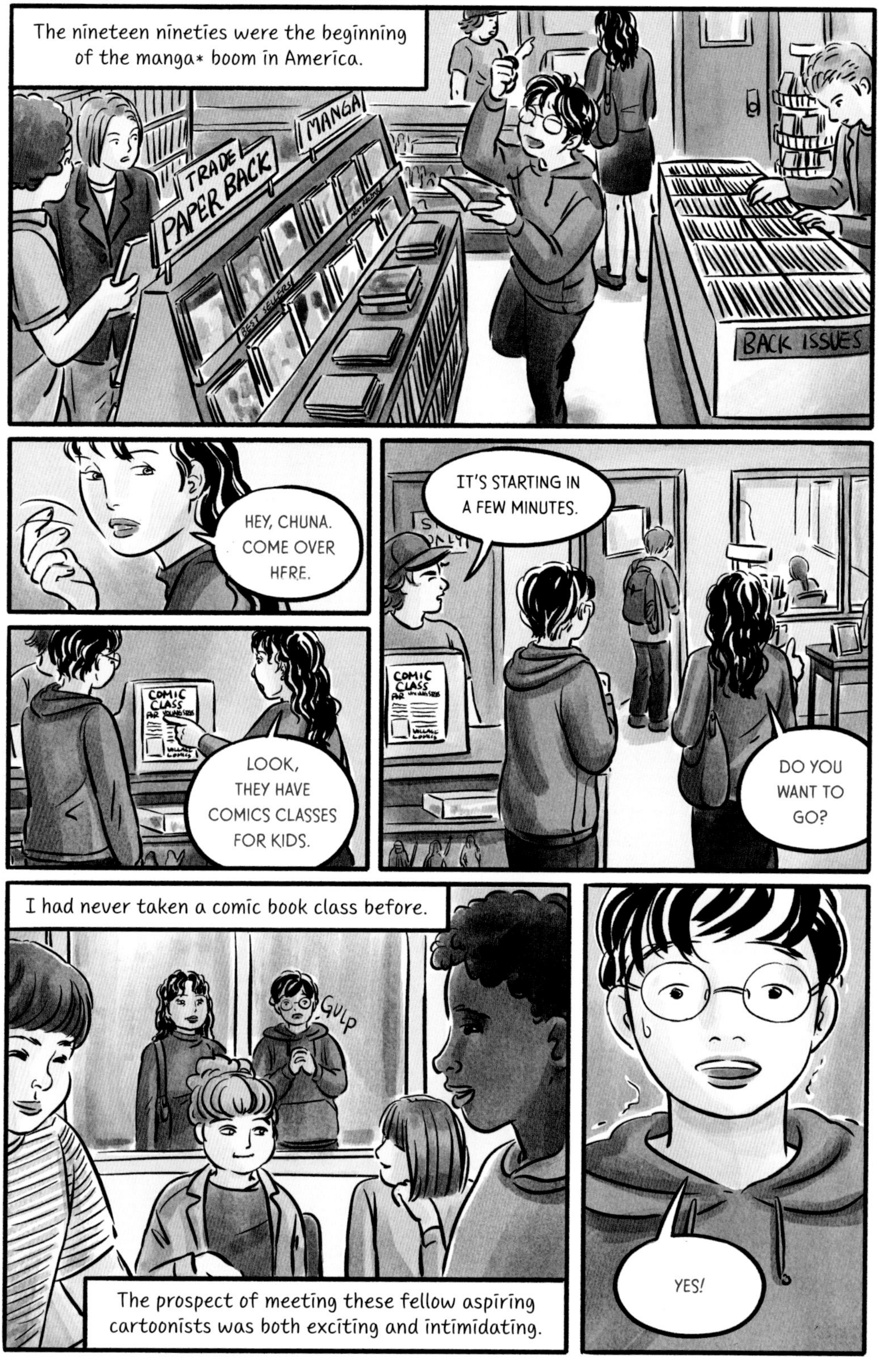
The nineteen nineties were the beginning of the manga* boom in America.
TRADE PAPER BACK
MANGA
BEST SELLERS
BACK ISSUES
HEY, CHUNA. COME OVER HERE.
COMIC CLASS
LOOK, THEY HAVE COMICS CLASSES FOR KIDS.
IT'S STARTING IN A FEW MINUTES.
COMIC CLASS
DO YOU WANT TO GO?
I had never taken a comic book class before.
GULP
The prospect of meeting these fellow aspiring cartoonists was both exciting and intimidating.
YES!

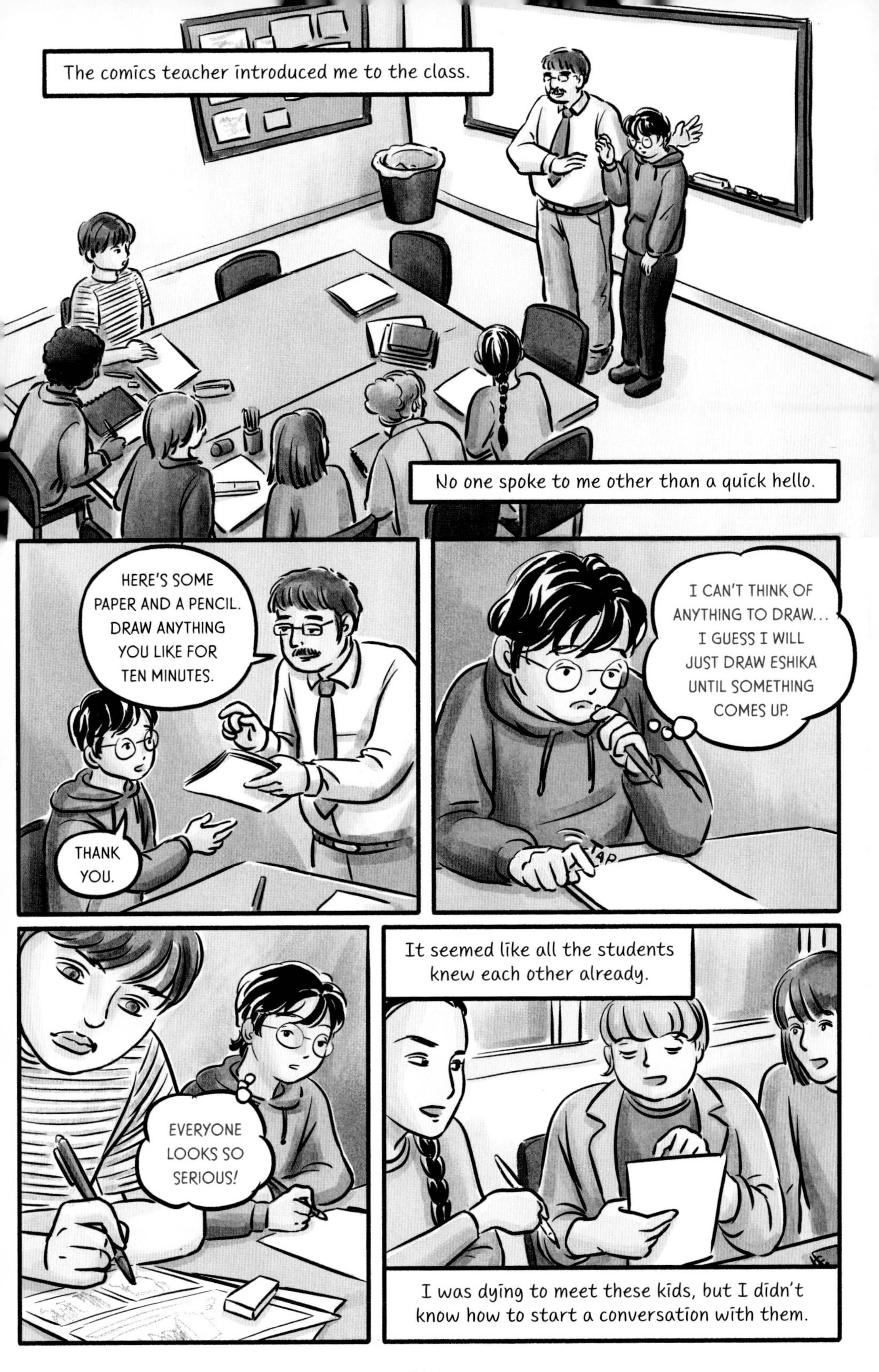
The comics teacher introduced me to the class.
No one spoke to me other than a quick hello.
HERE'S SOME PAPER AND A PENCIL. DRAW ANYTHING YOU LIKE FOR TEN MINUTES.
THANK YOU.
I CAN'T THINK OF ANYTHING TO DRAW... I GUESS I WILL JUST DRAW ESHIKA UNTIL SOMETHING COMES UP.
TAP
EVERYONE LOOKS SO SERIOUS!
It seemed like all the students knew each other already.
I was dying to meet these kids, but I didn't know how to start a conversation with them.

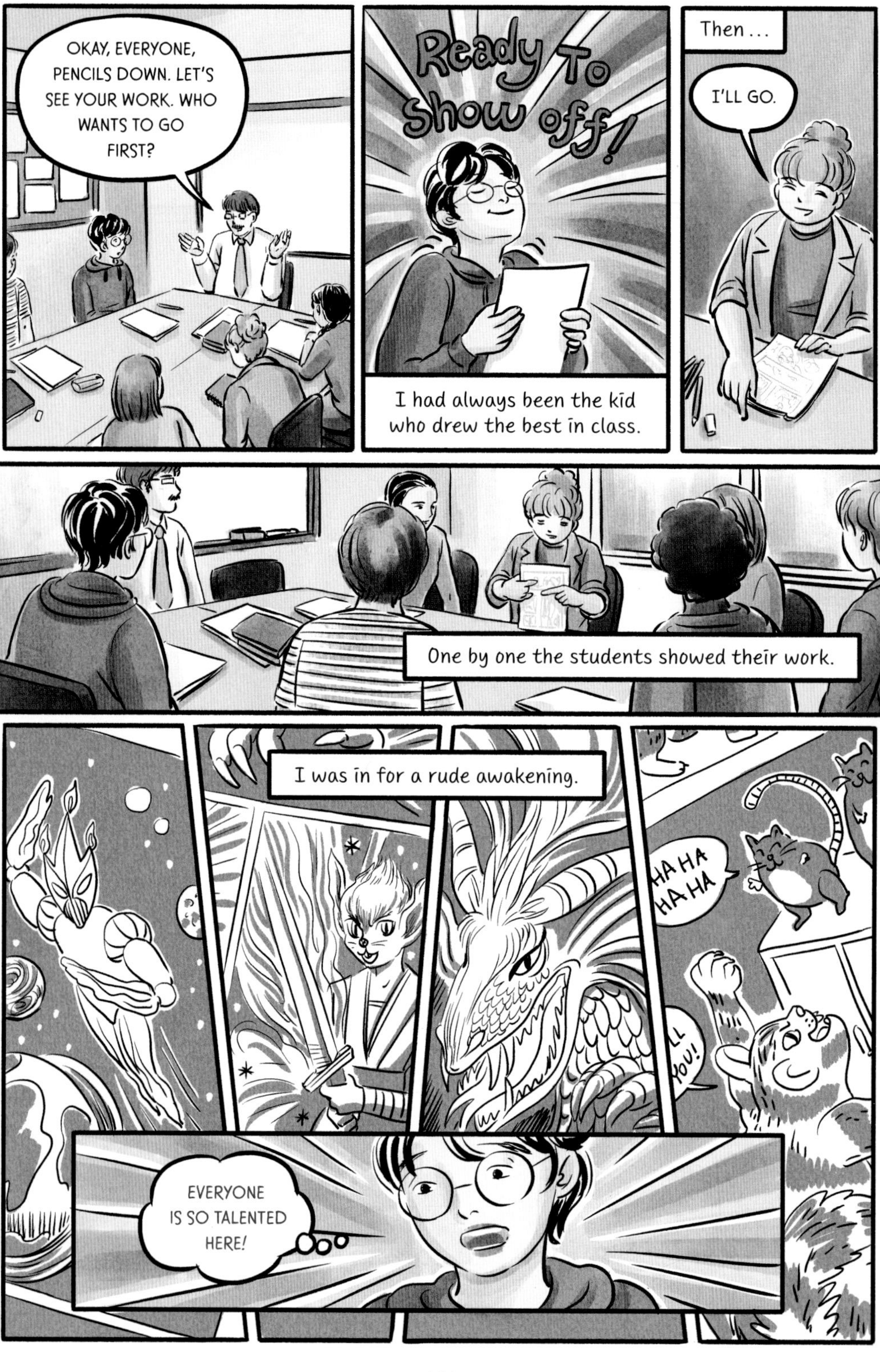
OKAY, EVERYONE, PENCILS DOWN. LET'S SEE YOUR WORK. WHO WANTS TO GO FIRST?
Ready To Show off!
I had always been the kid who drew the best in class.
Then ...
I'LL GO.
One by one the students showed their work.
I was in for a rude awakening.
HA HA HA HA
EVERYONE IS SO TALENTED HERE!

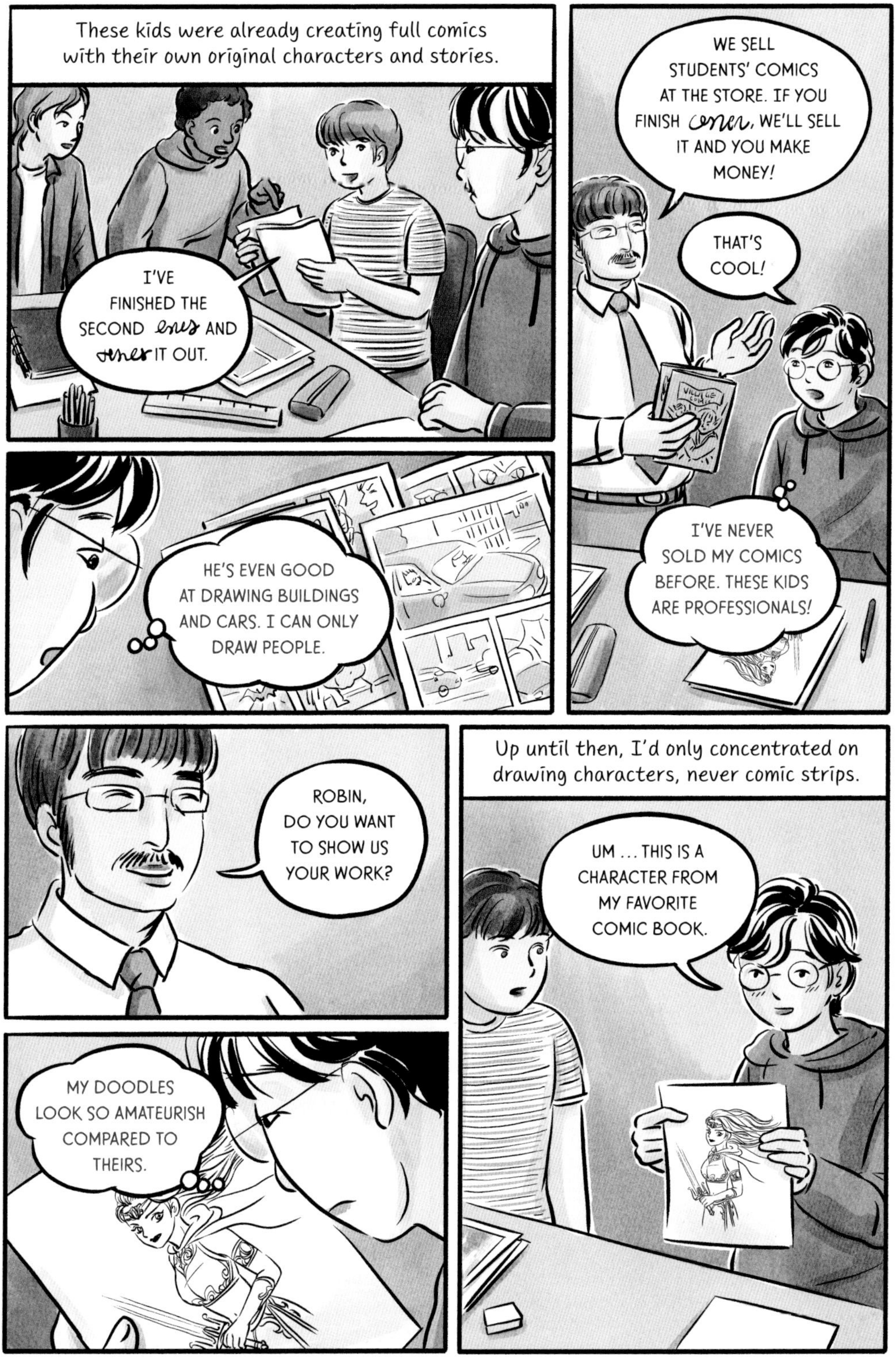
These kids were already creating full comics with their own original characters and stories.
I'VE FINISHED THE SECOND AND IT OUT.
HE'S EVEN GOOD AT DRAWING BUILDINGS AND CARS. I CAN ONLY DRAW PEOPLE.
WE SELL STUDENTS' COMICS AT THE STORE. IF YOU FINISH , WE'LL SELL IT AND YOU MAKE MONEY!
THAT'S COOL!
I'VE NEVER SOLD MY COMICS BEFORE. THESE KIDS ARE PROFESSIONALS!
ROBIN, DO YOU WANT TO SHOW US YOUR WORK?
MY DOODLES LOOK SO AMATEURISH COMPARED TO THEIRS.
Up until then, I'd only concentrated on drawing characters, never comic strips.
UM ... THIS IS A CHARACTER FROM MY FAVORITE COMIC BOOK.

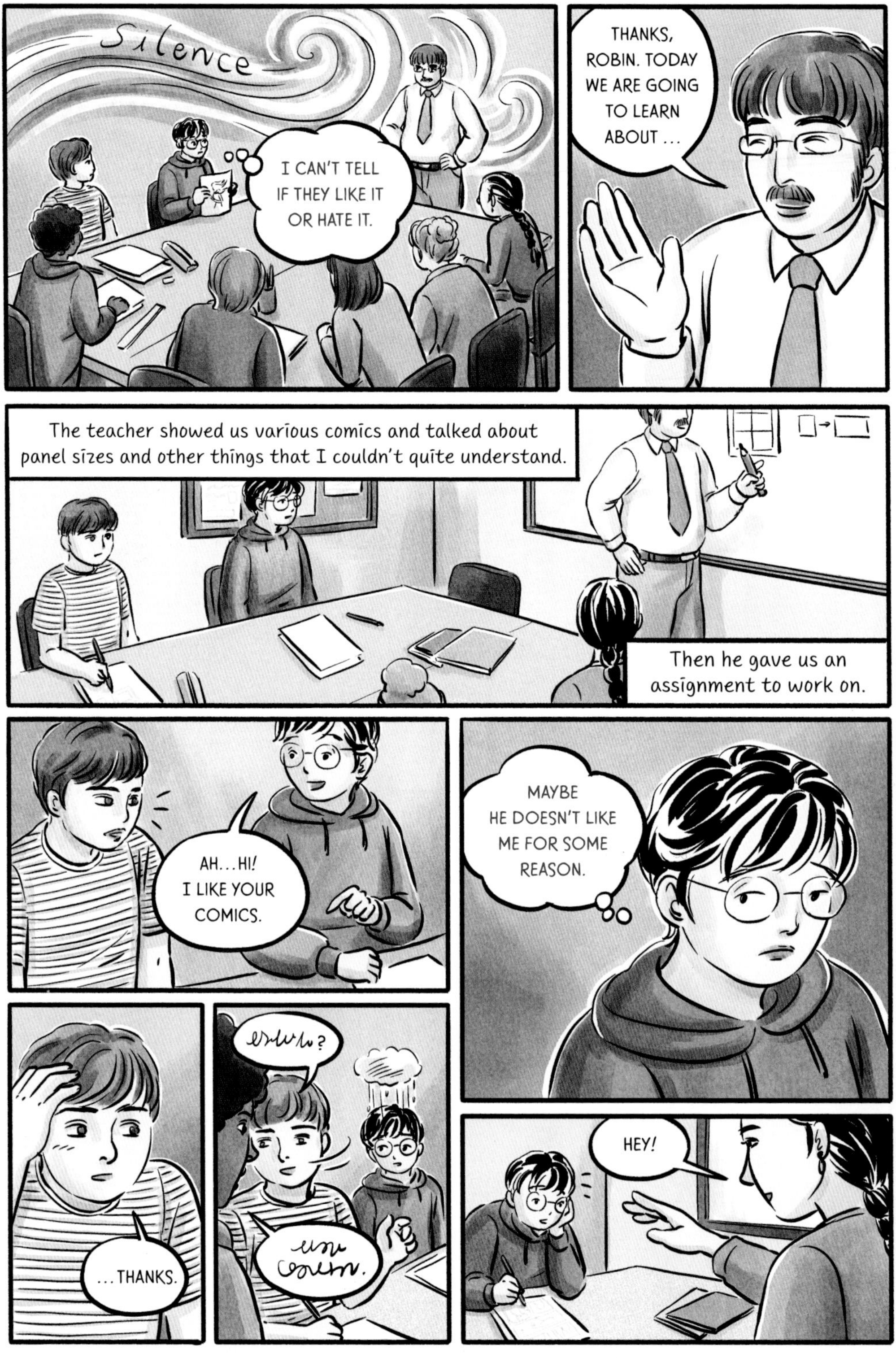
Silence
I CAN'T TELL IF THEY LIKE IT OR HATE IT.
THANKS, ROBIN. TODAY WE ARE GOING TO LEARN ABOUT ...
The teacher showed us various comics and talked about panel sizes and other things that I couldn't quite understand.
Then he gave us an assignment to work on.
AH...HI! I LIKE YOUR COMICS.
MAYBE HE DOESN'T LIKE ME FOR SOME REASON.
...THANKS.
HEY!

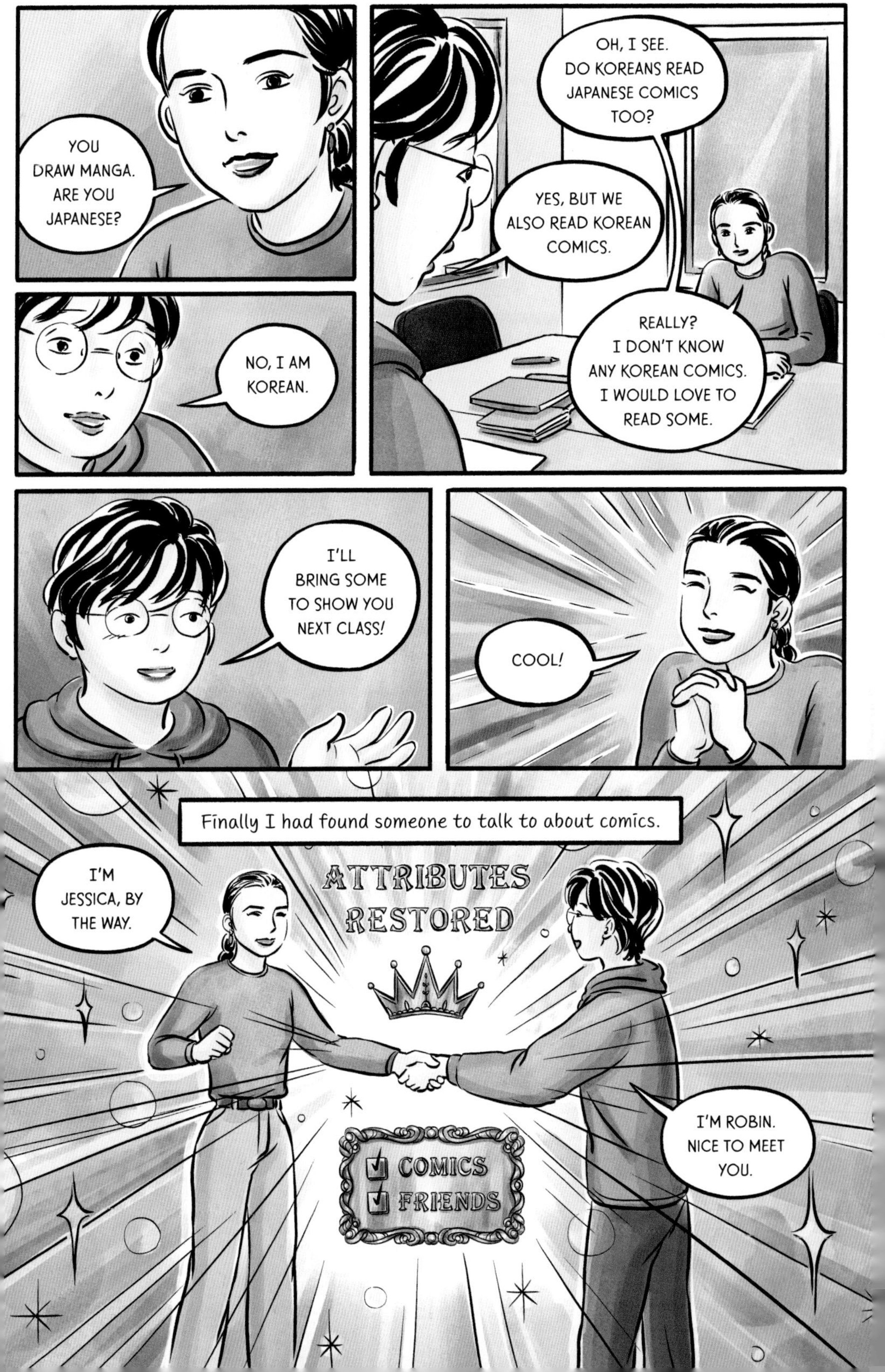
YOU DRAW MANGA. ARE YOU JAPANESE?
OH, I SEE. DO KOREANS READ JAPANESE COMICS TOO?
YES, BUT WE ALSO READ KOREAN COMICS.
NO, I AM KOREAN.
REALLY? I DON'T KNOW ANY KOREAN COMICS. I WOULD LOVE TO READ SOME.
I'LL BRING SOME TO SHOW YOU NEXT CLASS!
COOL!
Finally I had found someone to talk to about comics.
I'M JESSICA, BY THE WAY.
ATTRIBUTES RESTORED
COMICS
FRIENDS
I'M ROBIN. NICE TO MEET YOU.

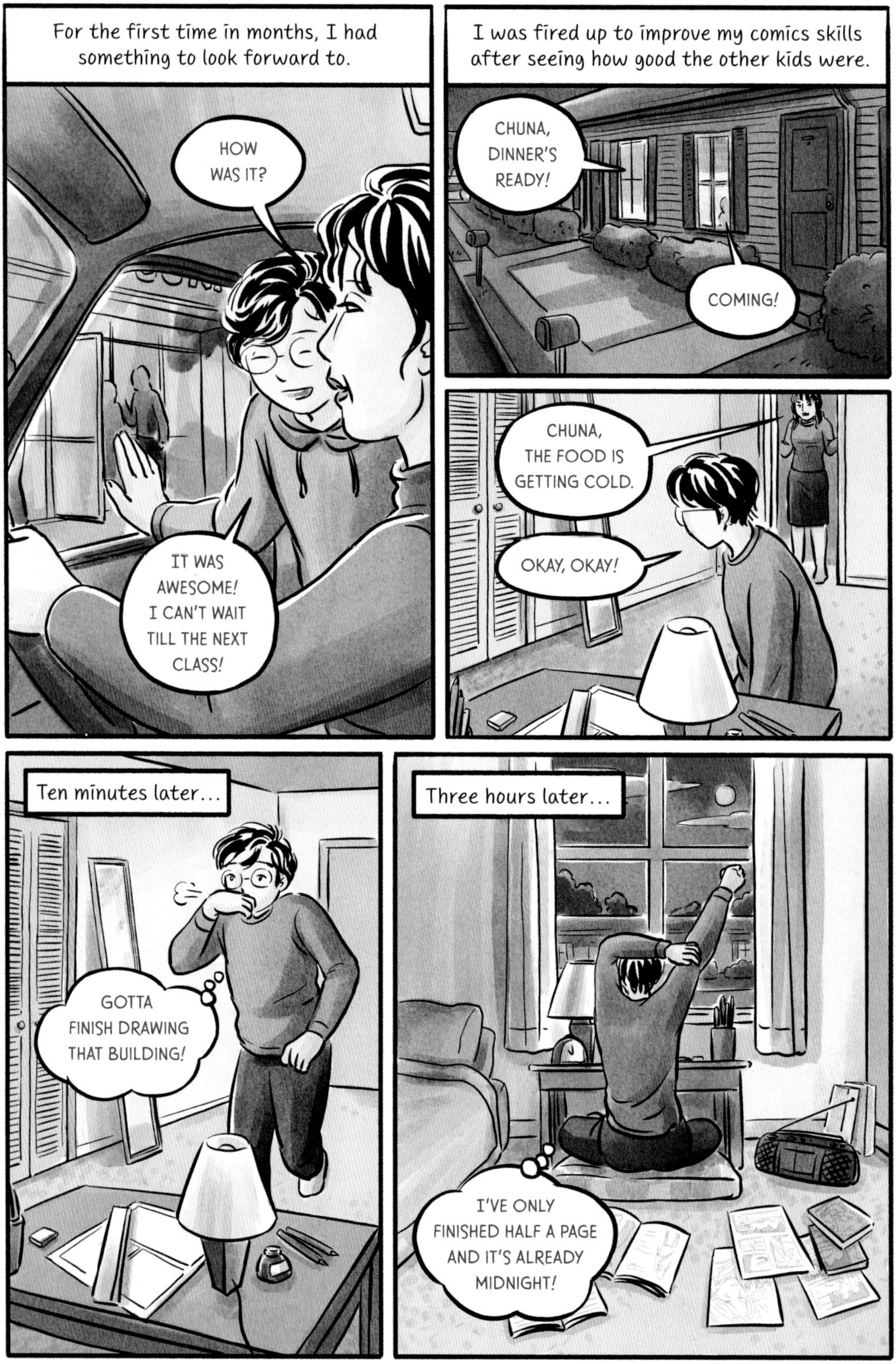
For the first time in months, I had something to look forward to.
HOW WAS IT?
IT WAS AWESOME! I CAN'T WAIT TILL THE NEXT CLASS!
I was fired up to improve my comics skills after seeing how good the other kids were.
CHUNA, DINNER'S READY!
COMING!
CHUNA, THE FOOD IS GETTING COLD.
OKAY, OKAY!
Ten minutes later...
GOTTA FINISH DRAWING THAT BUILDING!
Three hours later...
I'VE ONLY FINISHED HALF A PAGE AND IT'S ALREADY MIDNIGHT!

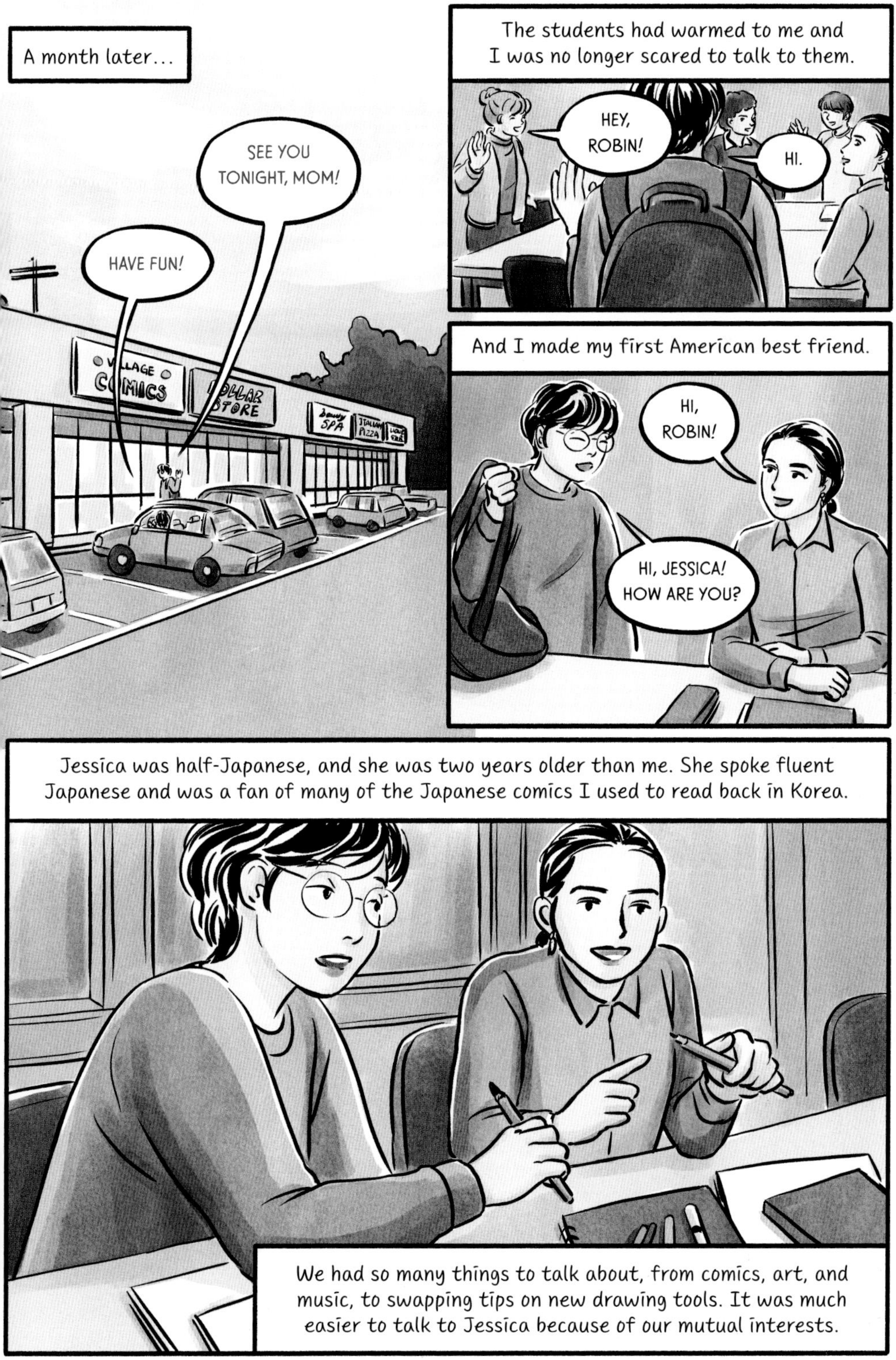
A month later...
SEE YOU TONIGHT, MOM!
HAVE FUN!
VILLAGE COMICS
DOLLAR STORE
The students had warmed to me and I was no longer scared to talk to them.
HEY, ROBIN!
HI.
And I made my first American best friend.
HI, ROBIN!
HI, JESSICA! HOW ARE YOU?
Jessica was half-Japanese, and she was two years older than me. She spoke fluent Japanese and was a fan of many of the Japanese comics I used to read back in Korea.
We had so many things to talk about, from comics, art, and music, to swapping tips on new drawing tools. It was much easier to talk to Jessica because of our mutual interests.

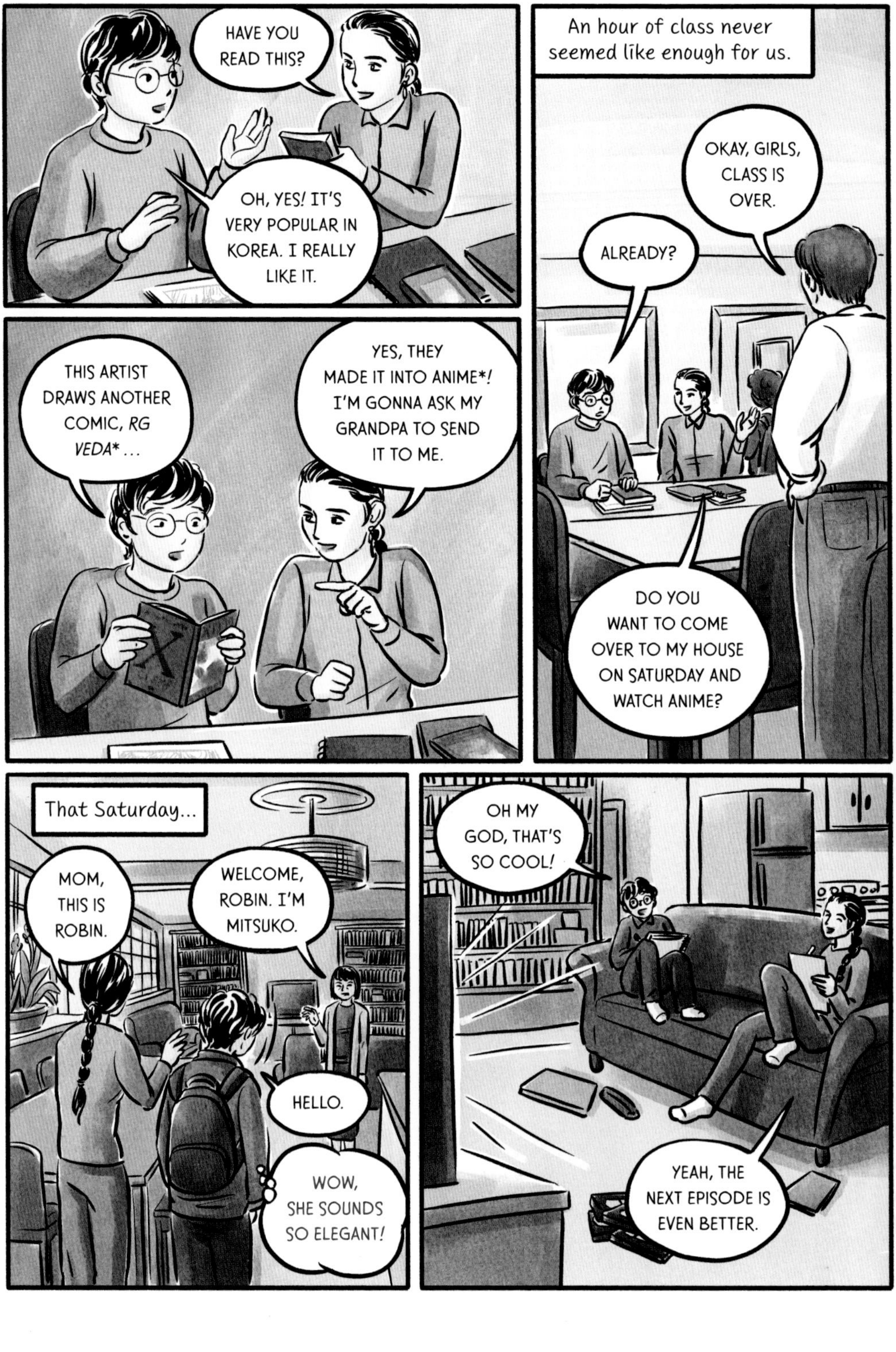
HAVE YOU READ THIS?
OH, YES! IT'S VERY POPULAR IN KOREA. I REALLY LIKE IT.
An hour of class never seemed like enough for us.
OKAY, GIRLS, CLASS IS OVER.
ALREADY?
THIS ARTIST DRAWS ANOTHER COMIC, *RG VEDA**...
YES, THEY MADE IT INTO ANIME*! I'M GONNA ASK MY GRANDPA TO SEND IT TO ME.
DO YOU WANT TO COME OVER TO MY HOUSE ON SATURDAY AND WATCH ANIME?
That Saturday...
MOM, THIS IS ROBIN.
WELCOME, ROBIN. I'M MITSUKO.
HELLO.
WOW, SHE SOUNDS SO ELEGANT!
OH MY GOD, THAT'S SO COOL!
YEAH, THE NEXT EPISODE IS EVEN BETTER.

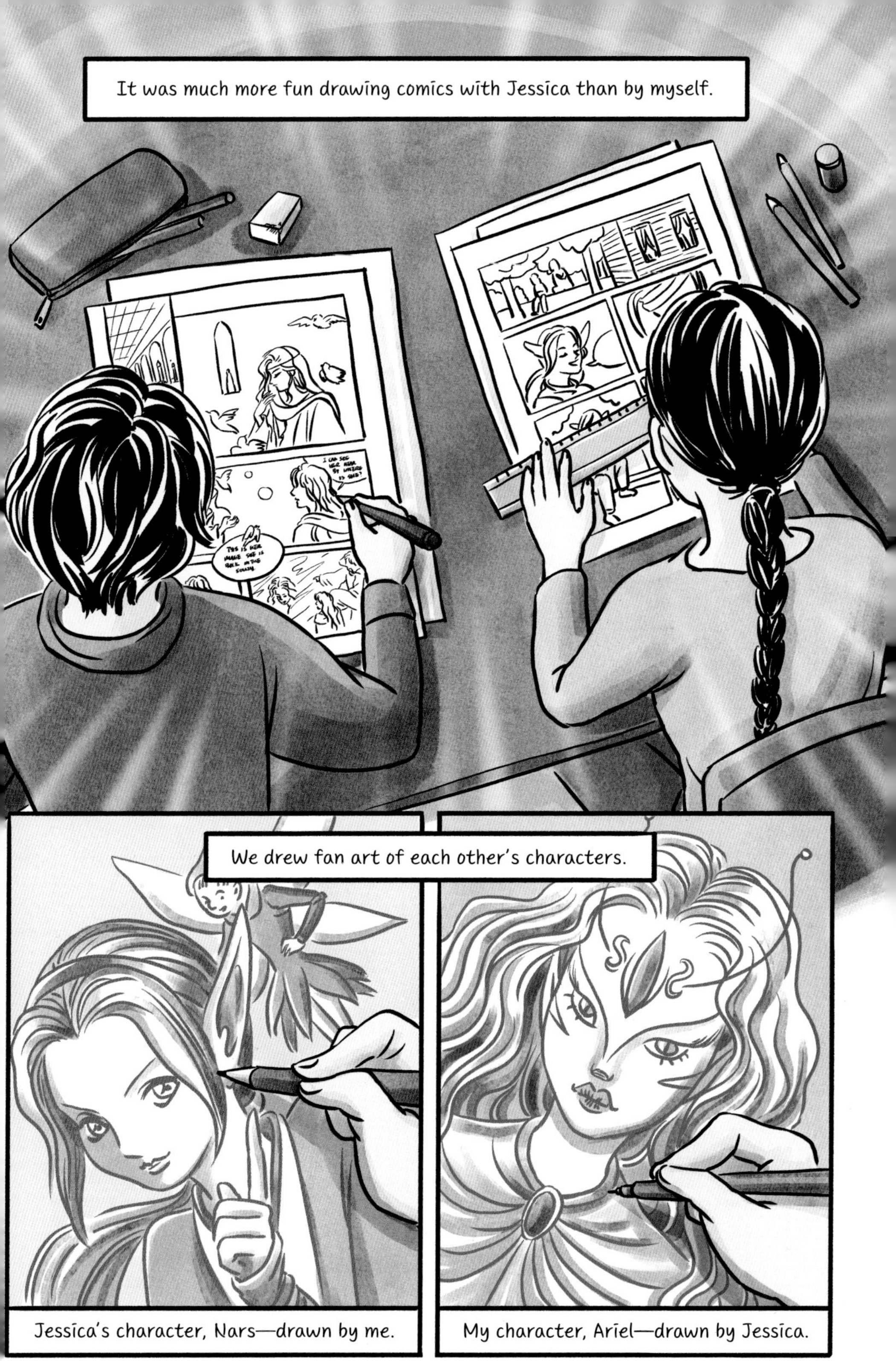
It was much more fun drawing comics with Jessica than by myself.
We drew fan art of each other's characters.
Jessica's character, Nars—drawn by me.
My character, Ariel—drawn by Jessica.

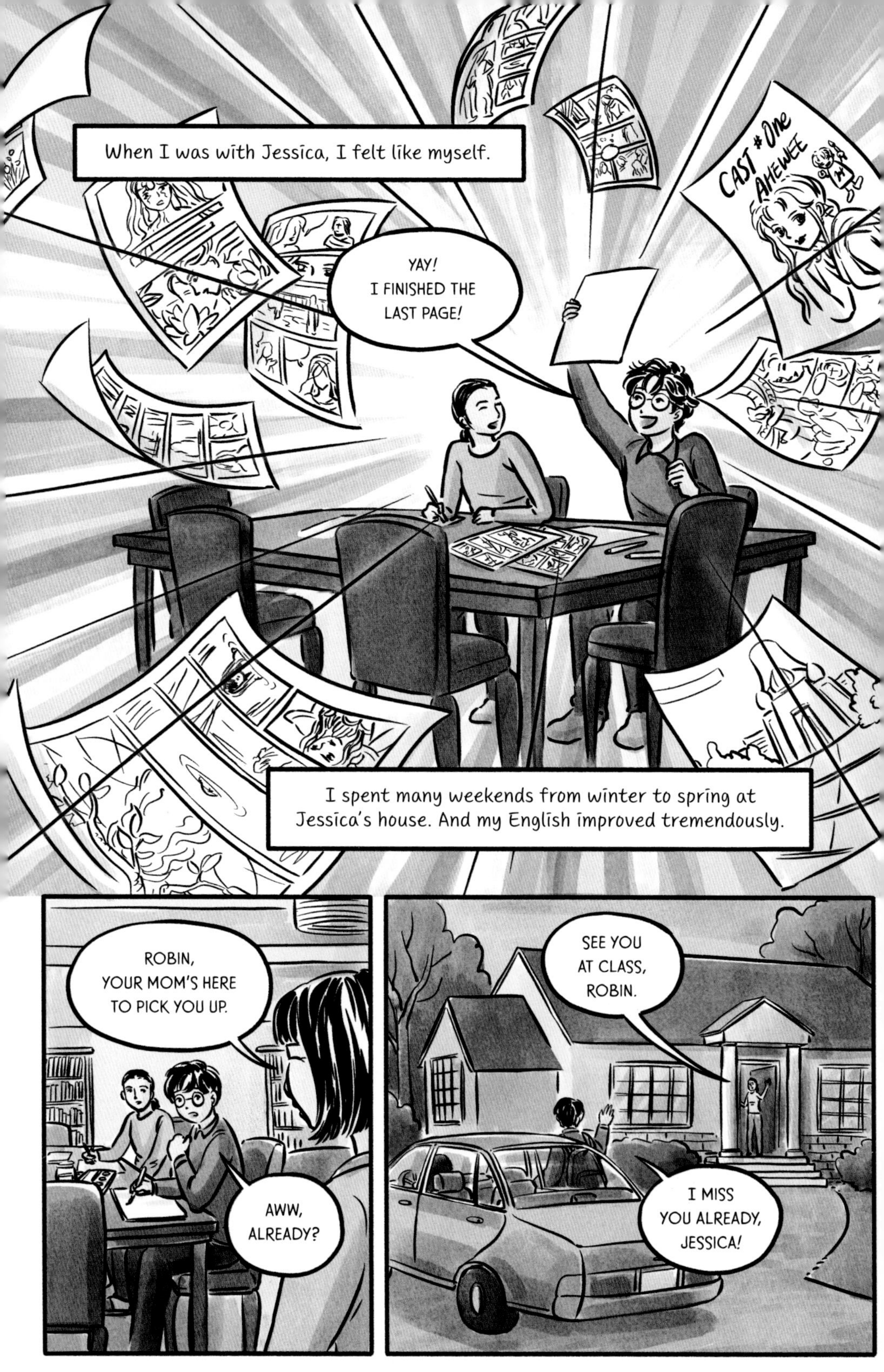
When I was with Jessica, I felt like myself.
CAST #One AHEWEE
YAY! I FINISHED THE LAST PAGE!
I spent many weekends from winter to spring at Jessica's house. And my English improved tremendously.
ROBIN, YOUR MOM'S HERE TO PICK YOU UP.
AWW, ALREADY?
SEE YOU AT CLASS, ROBIN.
I MISS YOU ALREADY, JESSICA!

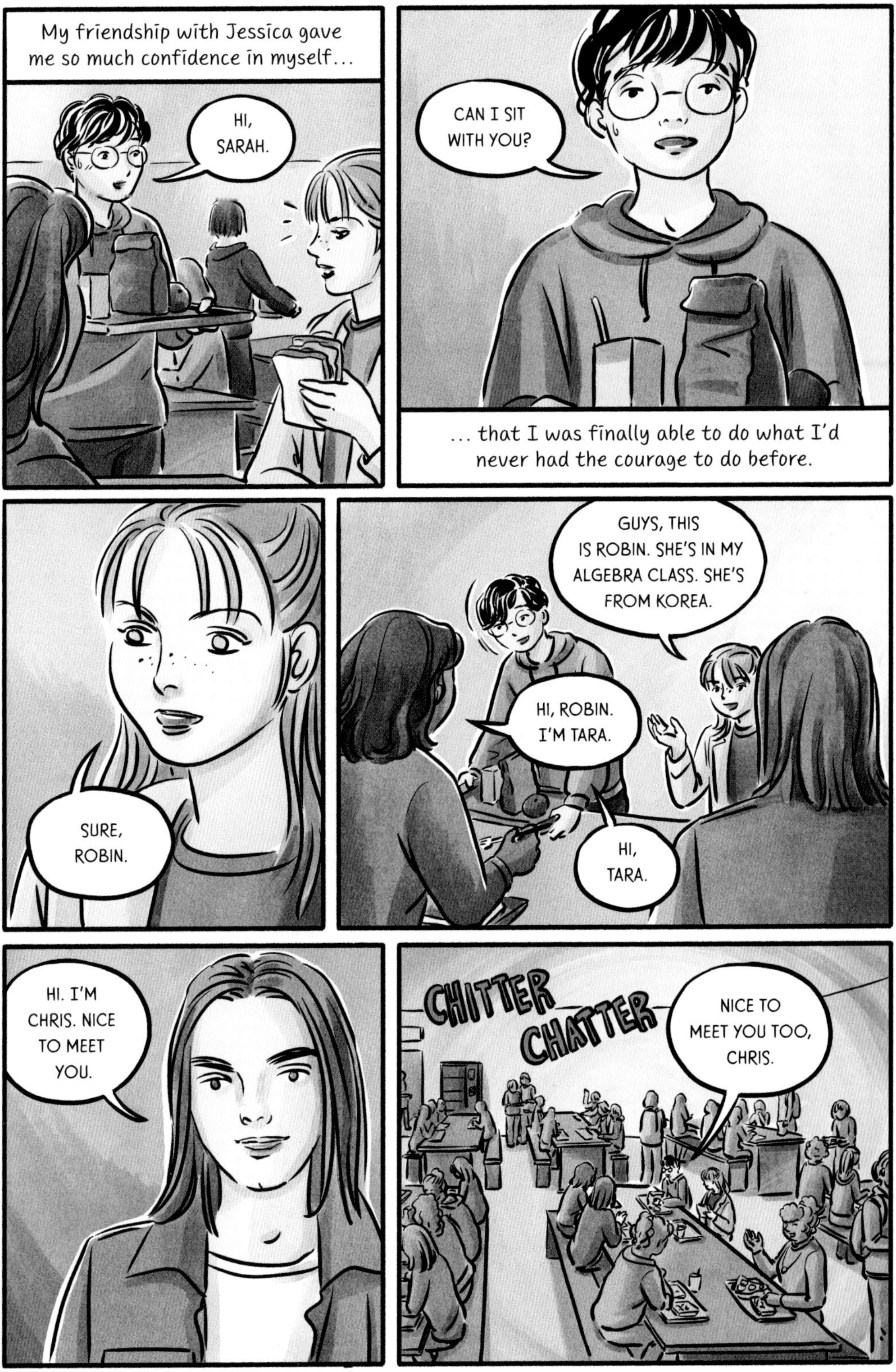
My friendship with Jessica gave me so much confidence in myself…
HI, SARAH.
CAN I SIT WITH YOU?
… that I was finally able to do what I'd never had the courage to do before.
SURE, ROBIN.
GUYS, THIS IS ROBIN. SHE'S IN MY ALGEBRA CLASS. SHE'S FROM KOREA.
HI, ROBIN. I'M TARA.
HI, TARA.
HI. I'M CHRIS. NICE TO MEET YOU.
CHITTER
CHATTER
NICE TO MEET YOU TOO, CHRIS.

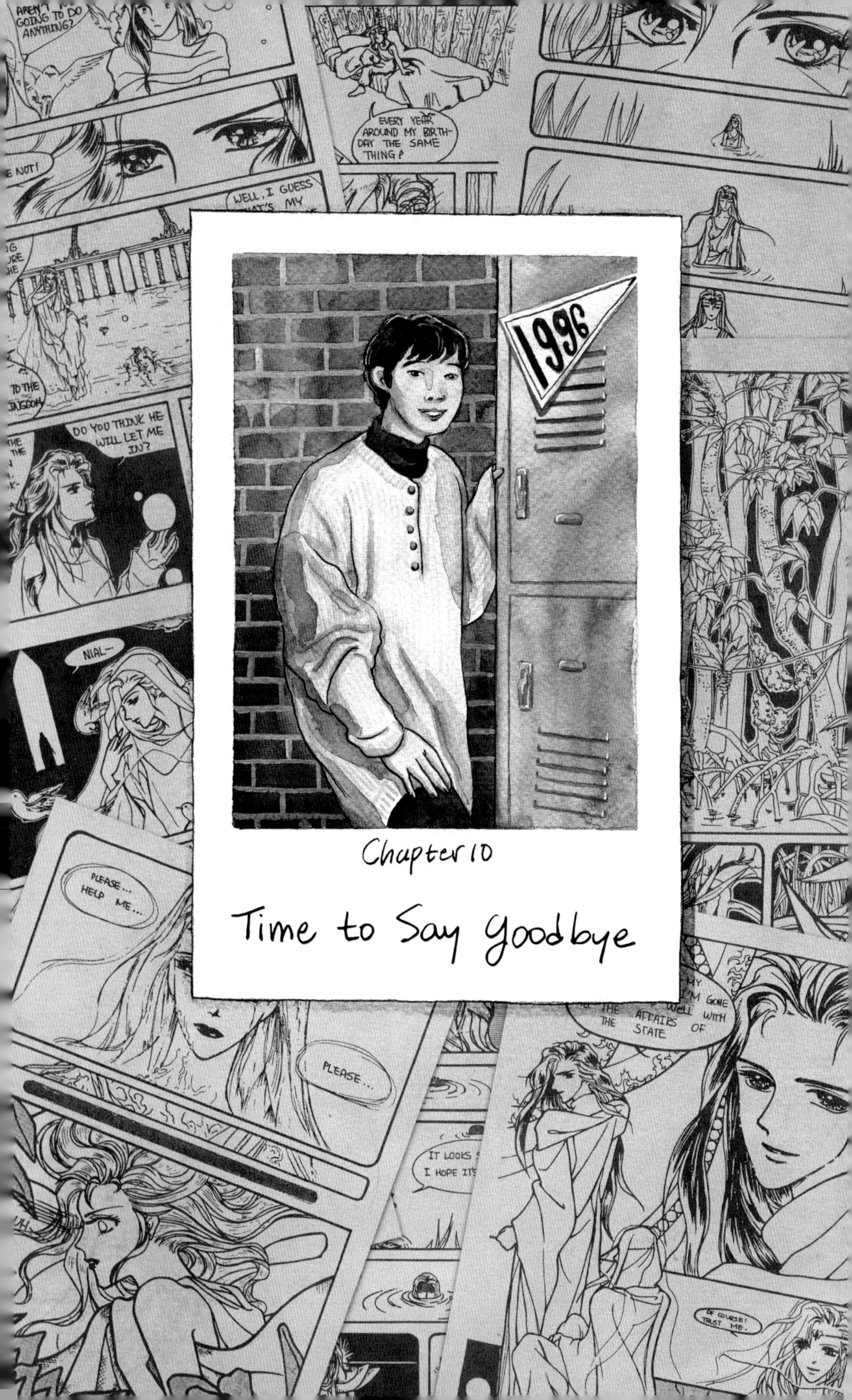
EVERY YEAR AROUND MY BIRTH-DAY THE SAME THING!
DO YOU THINK HE WILL LET ME IN?
NIAL--
1996
PLEASE... HELP ME...
PLEASE...
OF COURSE! TRUST ME.

Chapter 10

Time to Say Goodbye

While I was busy drawing comics and hanging out with Jessica...

I TOLD YOU I DON'T WANT TO MOVE TO LA!

...the rift between Mom and the stepfamily was getting deeper.

Stepdad called Mom every day.

CHUNA IS FINALLY GETTING USED TO LIVING HERE.

The pressure from the stepfamily grew unbearable.

HOW COULD YOU LEAVE YOUR HUSBAND ALL BY HIMSELF ACROSS THE COUNTRY?

YOU NEED TO GO HELP HIM NOW.

LEAVE CHUNA AND LENA TO ME. I'LL TAKE GOOD CARE OF THEM WHILE YOU'RE GONE.

... BUT LA IS TOO DANGEROUS A PLACE TO RAISE TWO TEENAGE GIRLS.

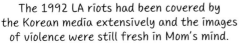

The 1992 LA riots had been covered by the Korean media extensively and the images of violence were still fresh in Mom's mind.

Mom was skeptical, but she couldn't continue to refuse.

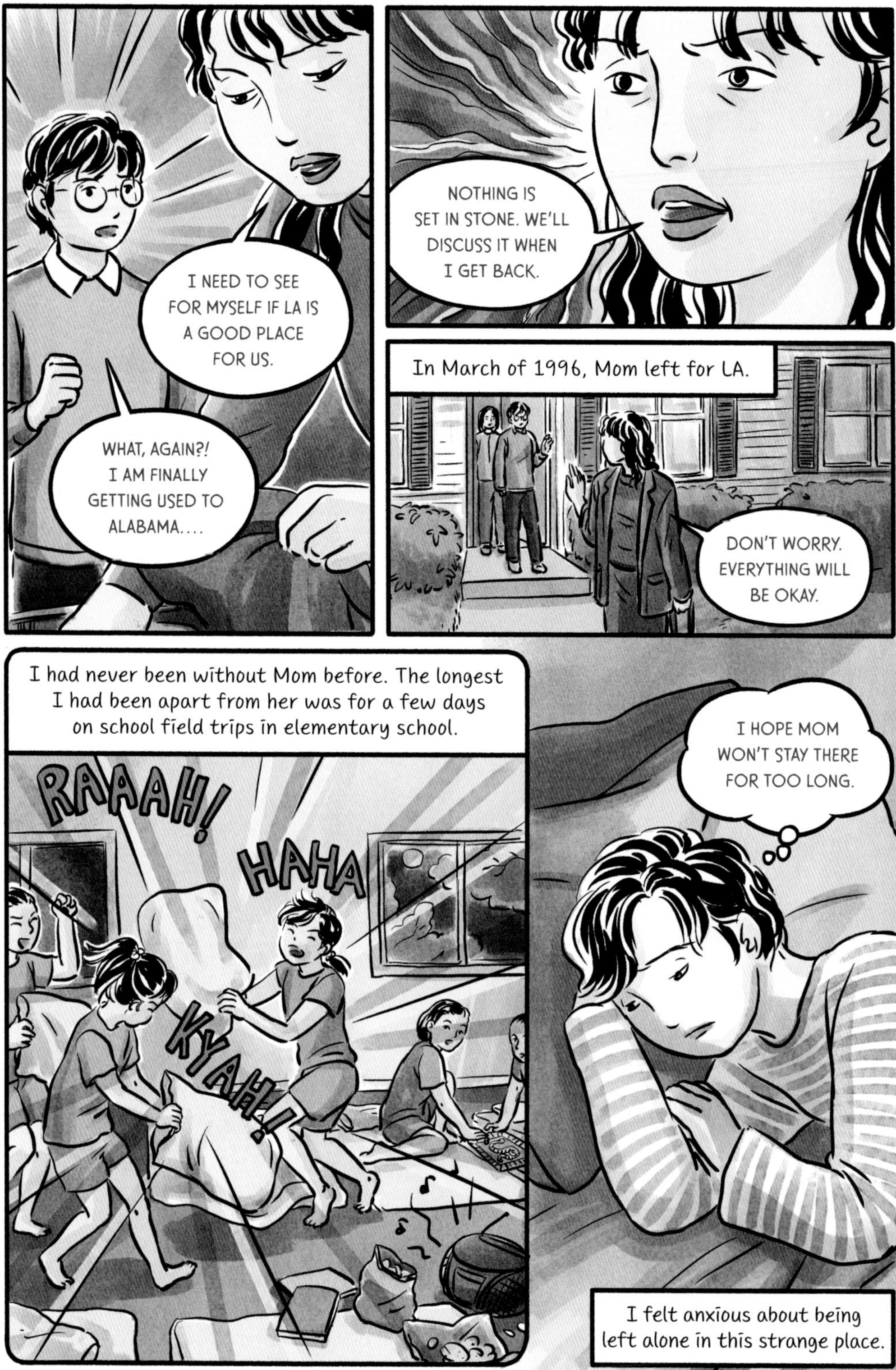
I NEED TO SEE FOR MYSELF IF LA IS A GOOD PLACE FOR US.
WHAT, AGAIN?! I AM FINALLY GETTING USED TO ALABAMA....
NOTHING IS SET IN STONE. WE'LL DISCUSS IT WHEN I GET BACK.
In March of 1996, Mom left for LA.
DON'T WORRY. EVERYTHING WILL BE OKAY.
I had never been without Mom before. The longest I had been apart from her was for a few days on school field trips in elementary school.
RAAAH!
HAHA
KYAAH!
I HOPE MOM WON'T STAY THERE FOR TOO LONG.
I felt anxious about being left alone in this strange place.

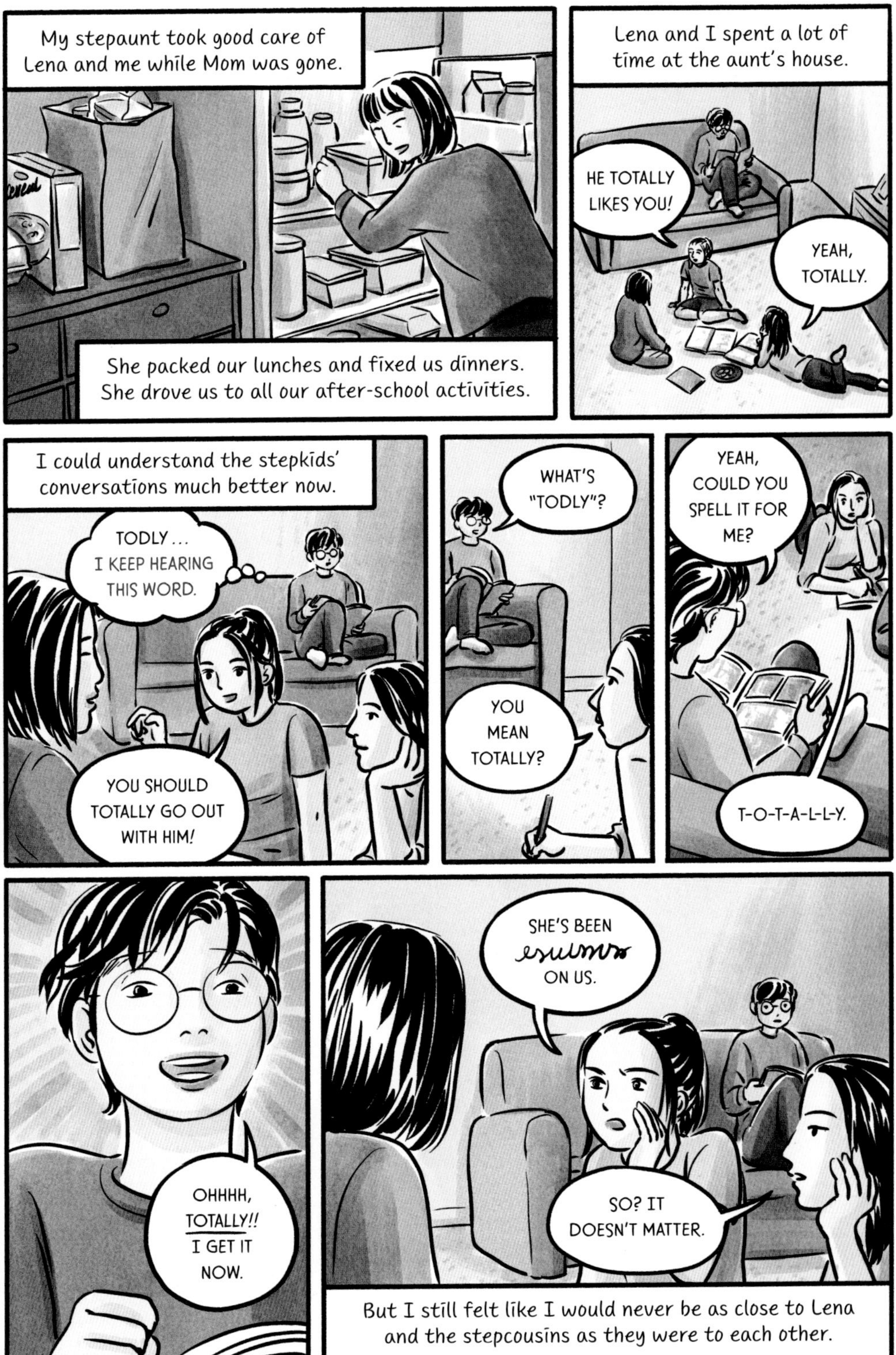
My stepaunt took good care of Lena and me while Mom was gone.
She packed our lunches and fixed us dinners. She drove us to all our after-school activities.
Lena and I spent a lot of time at the aunt's house.
HE TOTALLY LIKES YOU!
YEAH, TOTALLY.
I could understand the stepkids' conversations much better now.
TODLY... I KEEP HEARING THIS WORD.
YOU SHOULD TOTALLY GO OUT WITH HIM!
WHAT'S "TODLY"?
YOU MEAN TOTALLY?
YEAH, COULD YOU SPELL IT FOR ME?
T-O-T-A-L-L-Y.
OHHHH, TOTALLY!! I GET IT NOW.
SHE'S BEEN
ON US.
SO? IT DOESN'T MATTER.
But I still felt like I would never be as close to Lena and the stepcousins as they were to each other.

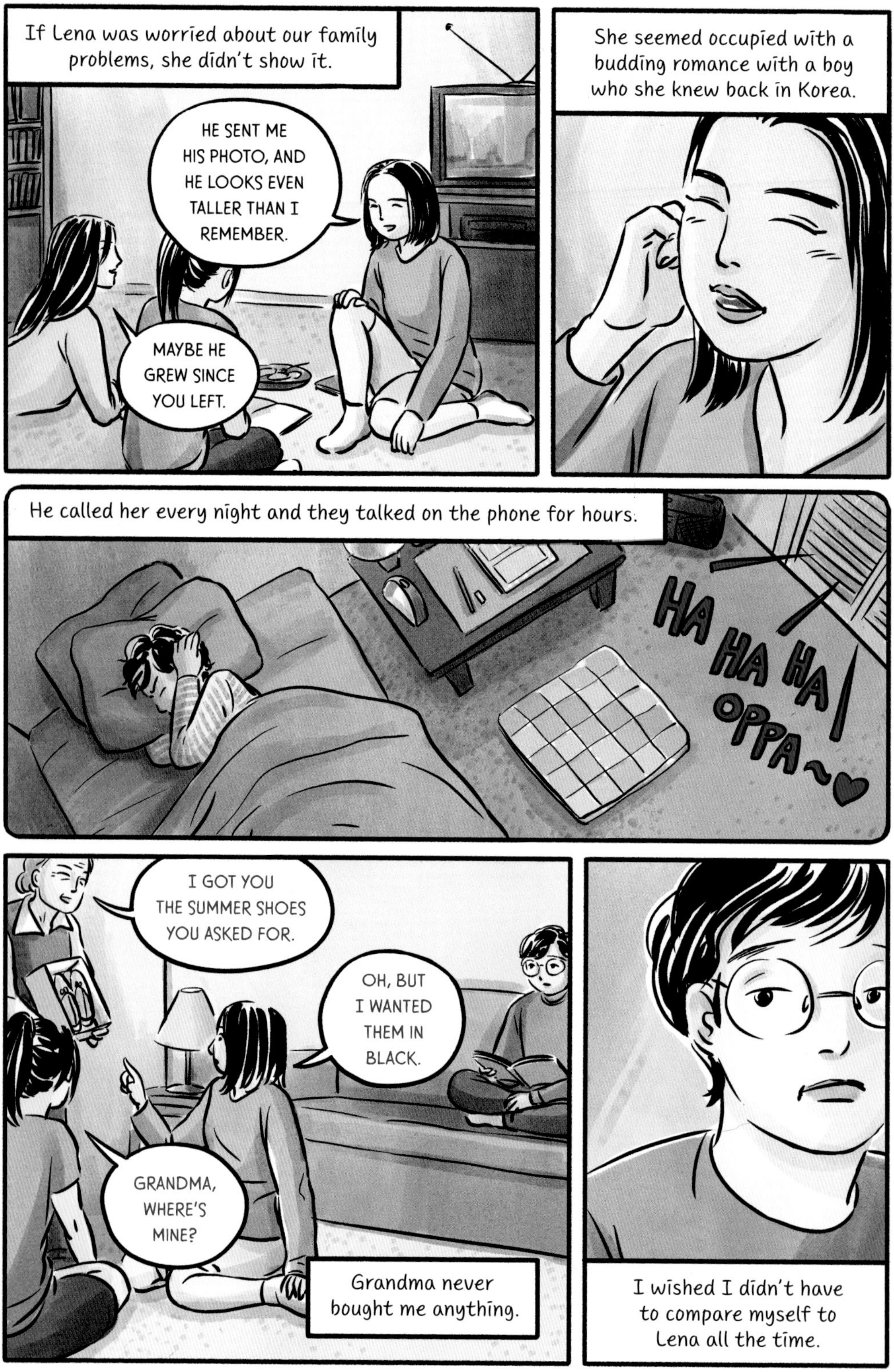
If Lena was worried about our family problems, she didn't show it.
HE SENT ME HIS PHOTO, AND HE LOOKS EVEN TALLER THAN I REMEMBER.
MAYBE HE GREW SINCE YOU LEFT.
She seemed occupied with a budding romance with a boy who she knew back in Korea.
He called her every night and they talked on the phone for hours.
HA HA HA
OPPA~♥
I GOT YOU THE SUMMER SHOES YOU ASKED FOR.
OH, BUT I WANTED THEM IN BLACK.
GRANDMA, WHERE'S MINE?
Grandma never bought me anything.
I wished I didn't have to compare myself to Lena all the time.

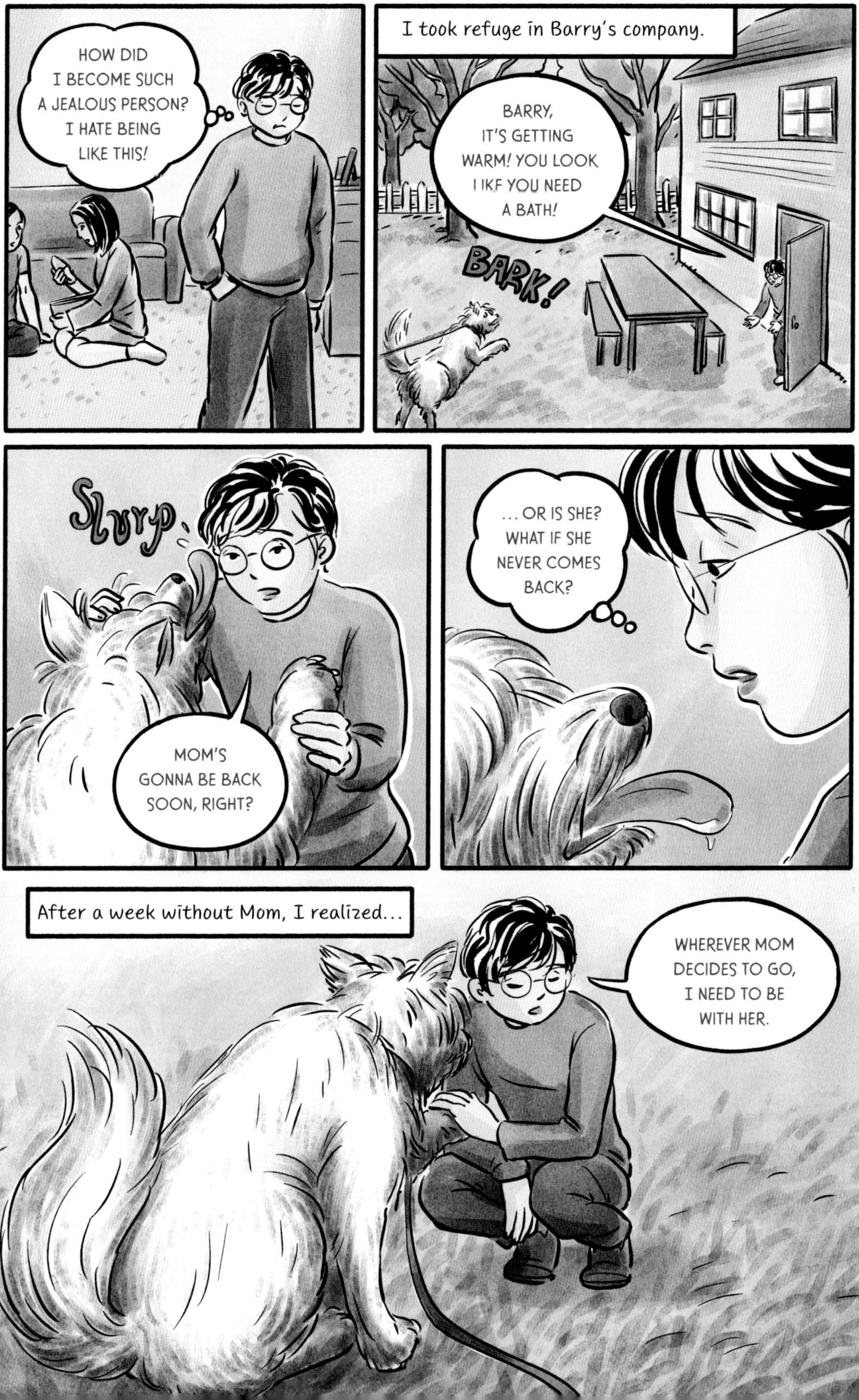

HOW DID I BECOME SUCH A JEALOUS PERSON? I HATE BEING LIKE THIS!
I took refuge in Barry's company.
BARRY, IT'S GETTING WARM! YOU LOOK LIKE YOU NEED A BATH!
BARK!
Slurp
MOM'S GONNA BE BACK SOON, RIGHT?
...OR IS SHE? WHAT IF SHE NEVER COMES BACK?
After a week without Mom, I realized...
WHEREVER MOM DECIDES TO GO, I NEED TO BE WITH HER.

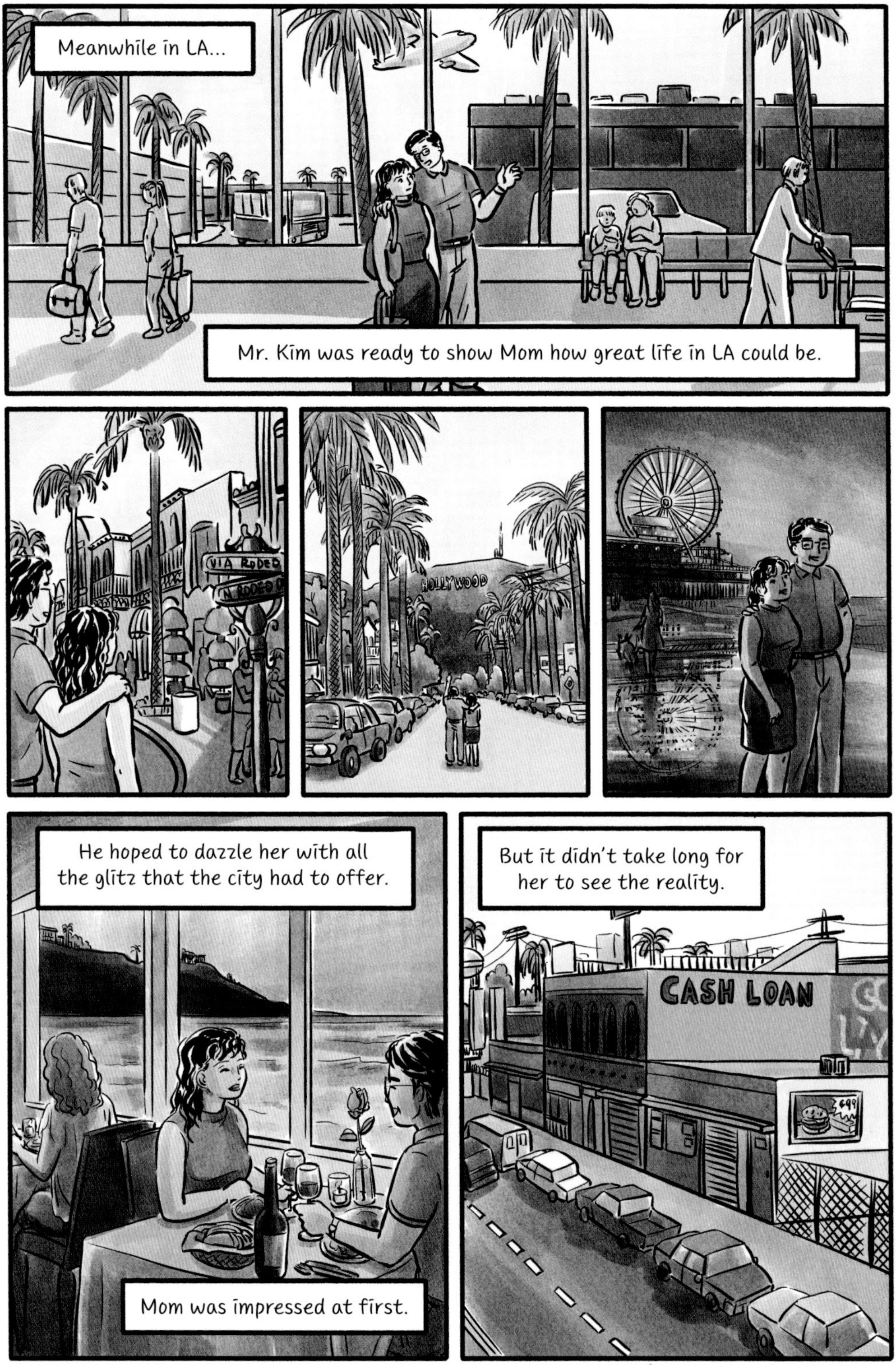
Meanwhile in LA...
Mr. Kim was ready to show Mom how great life in LA could be.
VIA RODEO
N RODEO D
HOLLYWOOD
He hoped to dazzle her with all the glitz that the city had to offer.
Mom was impressed at first.
But it didn't take long for her to see the reality.
CASH LOAN

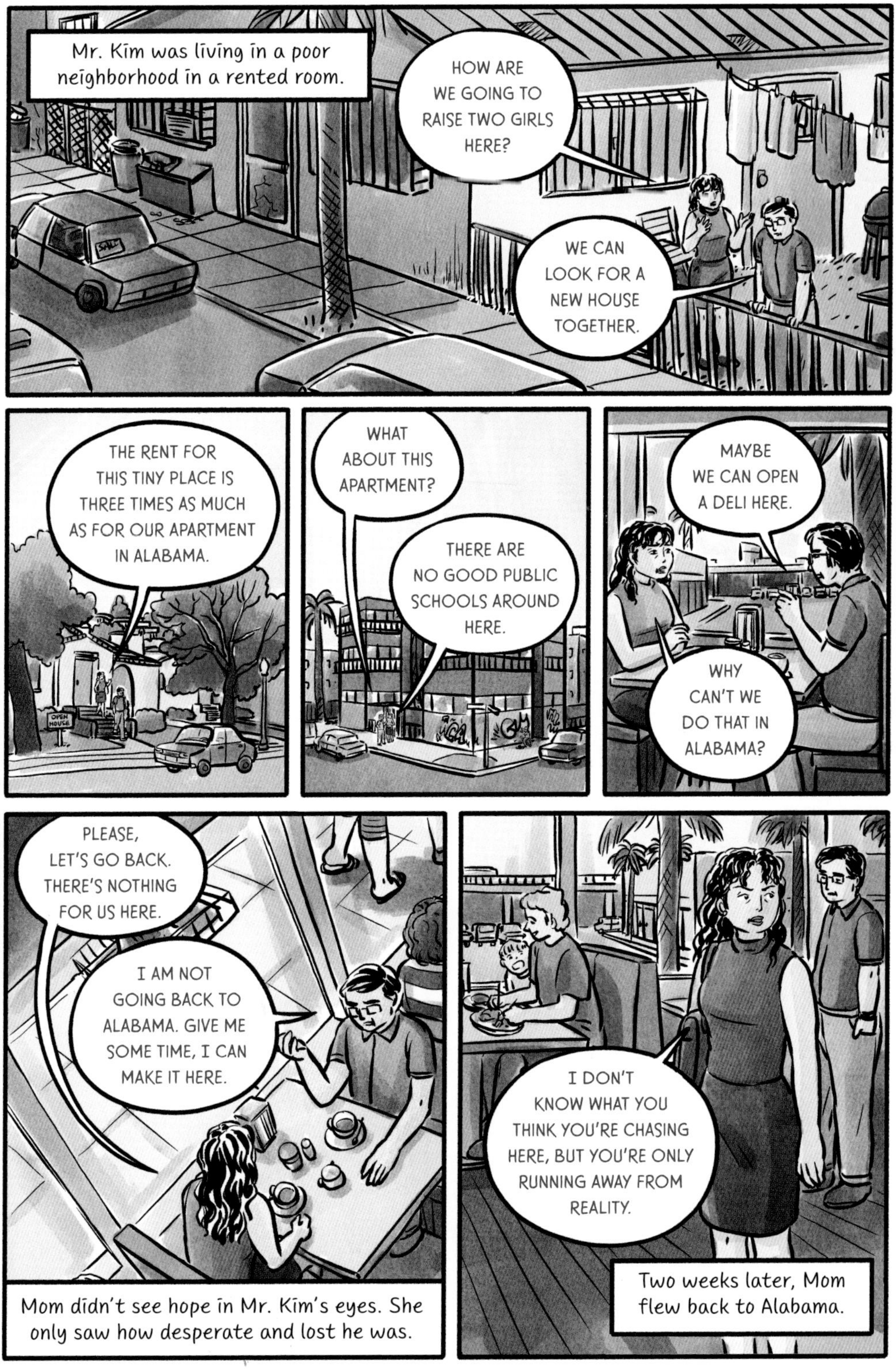
Mr. Kīm was līving īn a poor neīghborhood īn a rented room.
HOW ARE WE GOING TO RAISE TWO GIRLS HERE?
WE CAN LOOK FOR A NEW HOUSE TOGETHER.
THE RENT FOR THIS TINY PLACE IS THREE TIMES AS MUCH AS FOR OUR APARTMENT IN ALABAMA.
OPEN HOUSE
WHAT ABOUT THIS APARTMENT?
THERE ARE NO GOOD PUBLIC SCHOOLS AROUND HERE.
MAYBE WE CAN OPEN A DELI HERE.
WHY CAN'T WE DO THAT IN ALABAMA?
PLEASE, LET'S GO BACK. THERE'S NOTHING FOR US HERE.
I AM NOT GOING BACK TO ALABAMA. GIVE ME SOME TIME, I CAN MAKE IT HERE.
Mom dīdn't see hope īn Mr. Kīm's eyes. She only saw how desperate and lost he was.
I DON'T KNOW WHAT YOU THINK YOU'RE CHASING HERE, BUT YOU'RE ONLY RUNNING AWAY FROM REALITY.
Two weeks later, Mom flew back to Alabama.

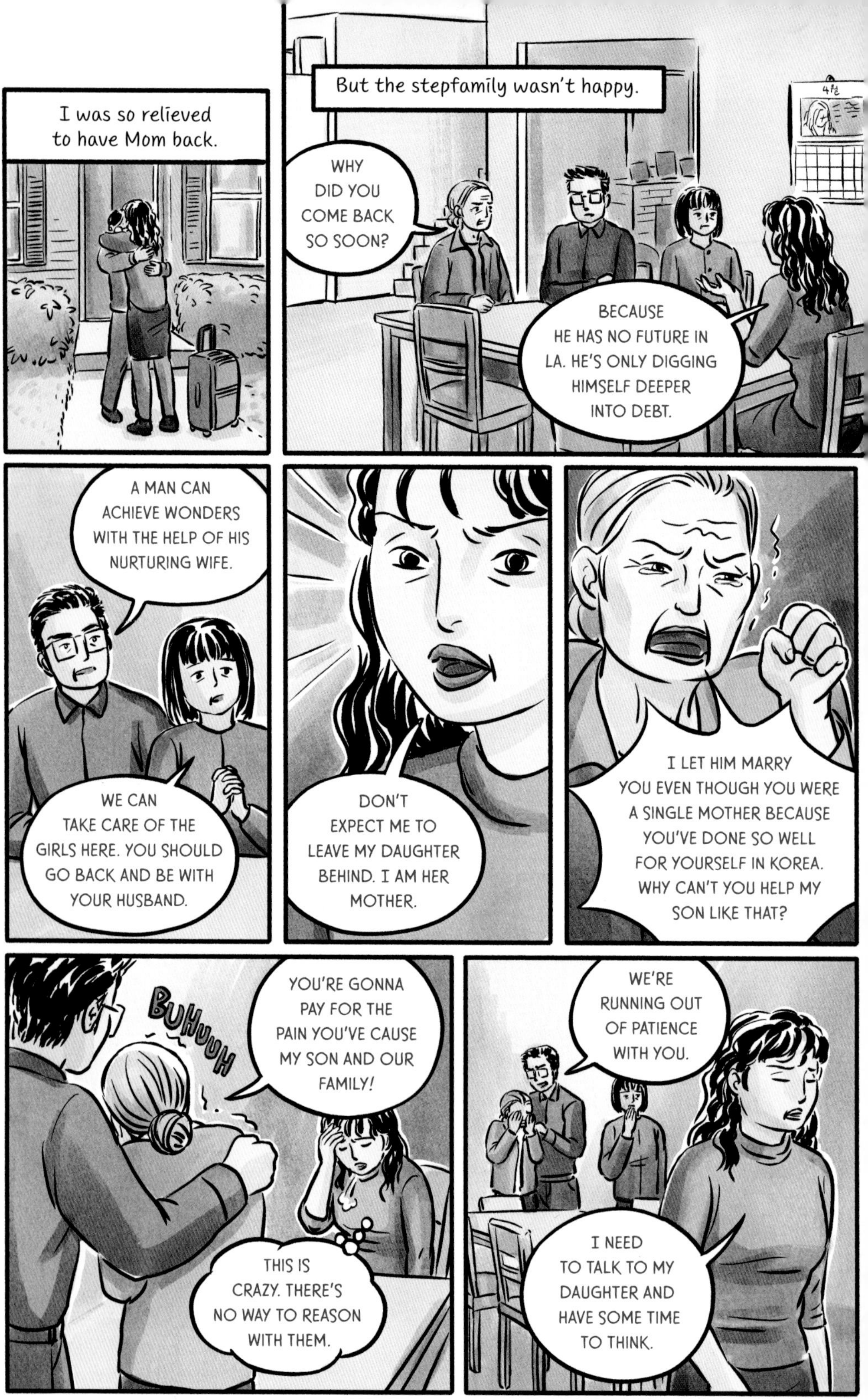
I was so relieved to have Mom back.
But the stepfamily wasn't happy.
WHY DID YOU COME BACK SO SOON?
BECAUSE HE HAS NO FUTURE IN LA. HE'S ONLY DIGGING HIMSELF DEEPER INTO DEBT.
A MAN CAN ACHIEVE WONDERS WITH THE HELP OF HIS NURTURING WIFE.
WE CAN TAKE CARE OF THE GIRLS HERE. YOU SHOULD GO BACK AND BE WITH YOUR HUSBAND.
DON'T EXPECT ME TO LEAVE MY DAUGHTER BEHIND. I AM HER MOTHER.
I LET HIM MARRY YOU EVEN THOUGH YOU WERE A SINGLE MOTHER BECAUSE YOU'VE DONE SO WELL FOR YOURSELF IN KOREA. WHY CAN'T YOU HELP MY SON LIKE THAT?
BUHUUH
YOU'RE GONNA PAY FOR THE PAIN YOU'VE CAUSE MY SON AND OUR FAMILY!
THIS IS CRAZY. THERE'S NO WAY TO REASON WITH THEM.
WE'RE RUNNING OUT OF PATIENCE WITH YOU.
I NEED TO TALK TO MY DAUGHTER AND HAVE SOME TIME TO THINK.

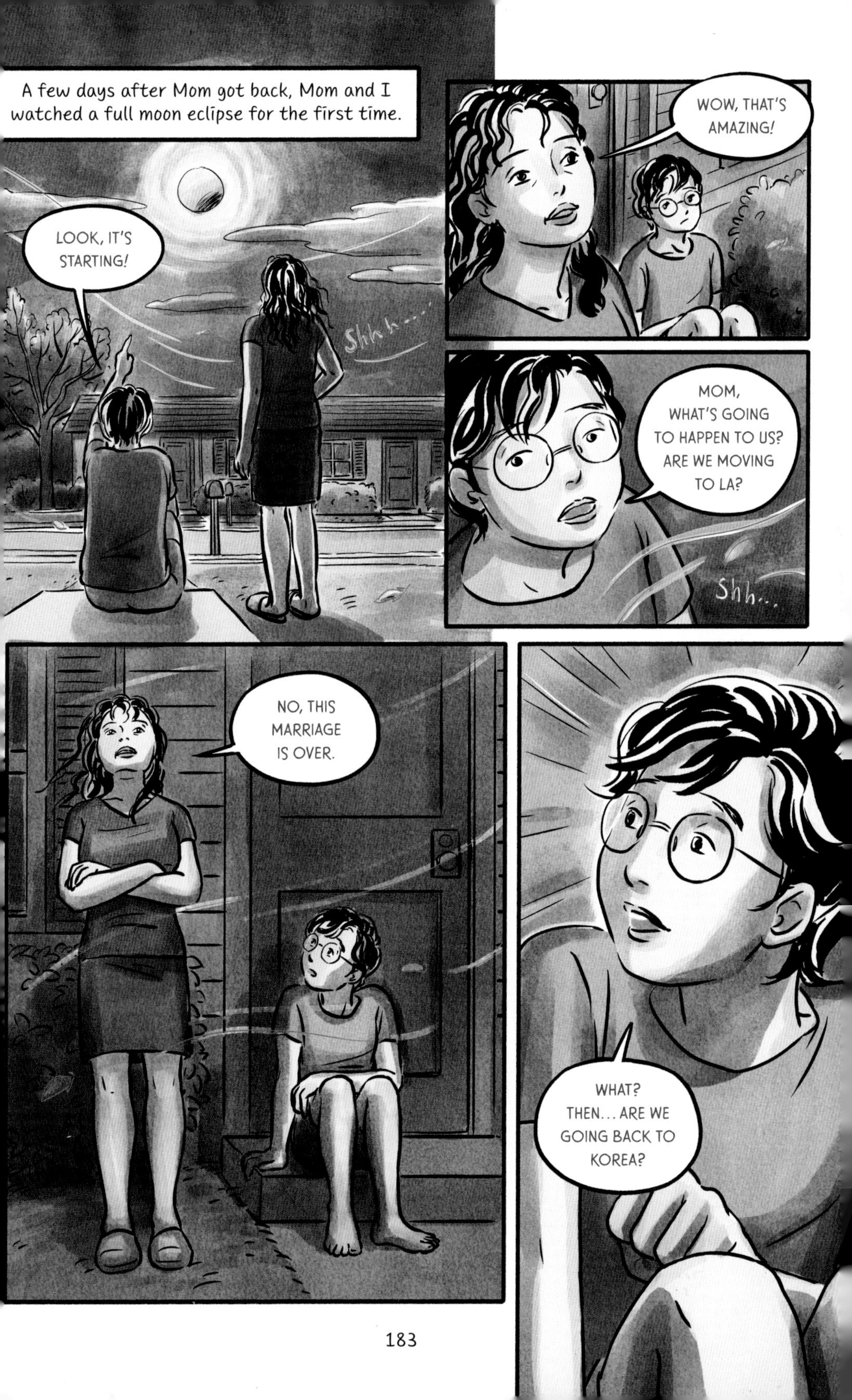
A few days after Mom got back, Mom and I watched a full moon eclipse for the first time.
LOOK, IT'S STARTING!
Shhh...
WOW, THAT'S AMAZING!
MOM, WHAT'S GOING TO HAPPEN TO US? ARE WE MOVING TO LA?
Shh...
NO, THIS MARRIAGE IS OVER.
WHAT? THEN... ARE WE GOING BACK TO KOREA?

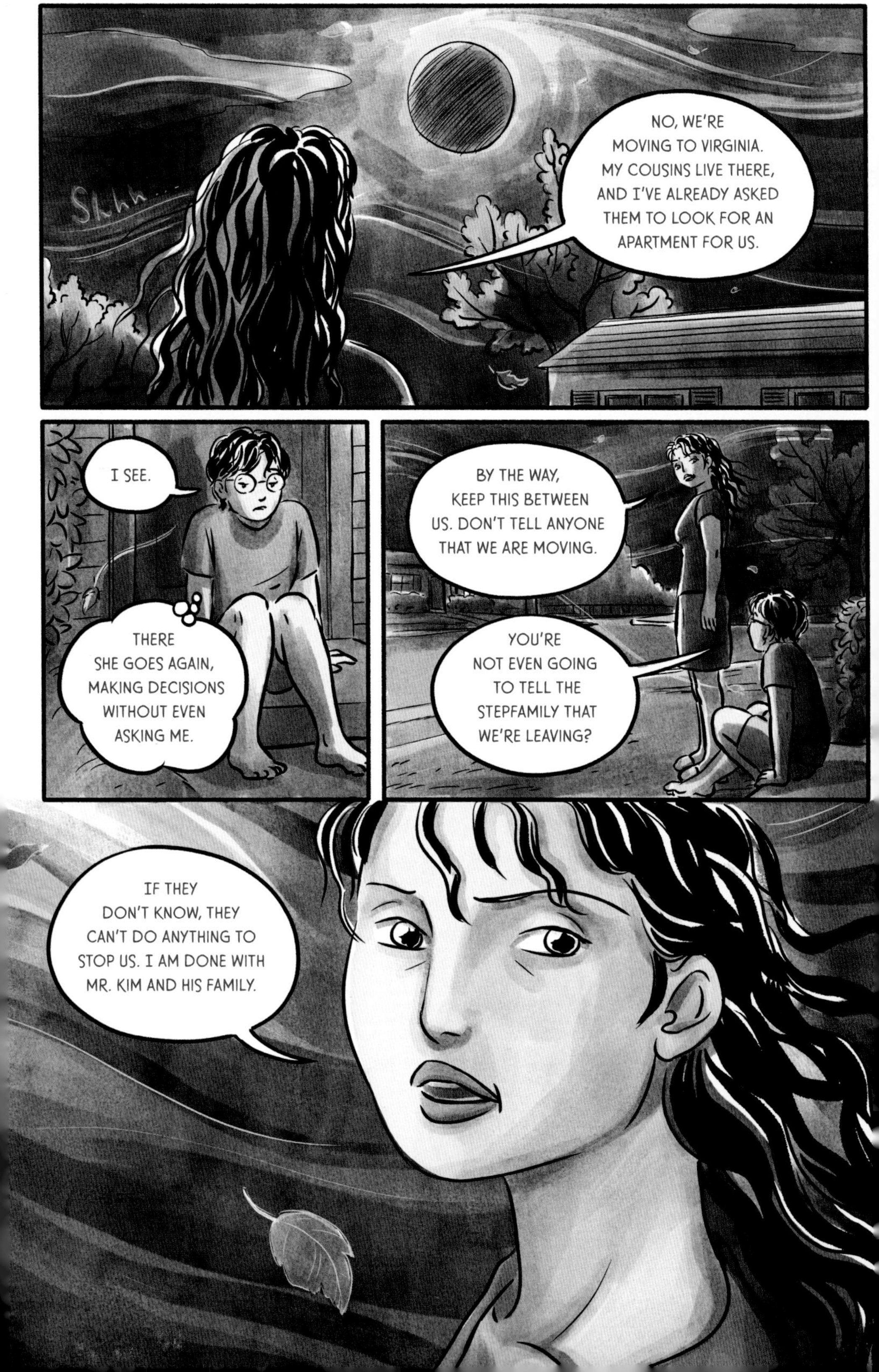
Shhh...
NO, WE'RE MOVING TO VIRGINIA. MY COUSINS LIVE THERE, AND I'VE ALREADY ASKED THEM TO LOOK FOR AN APARTMENT FOR US.
I SEE.
THERE SHE GOES AGAIN, MAKING DECISIONS WITHOUT EVEN ASKING ME.
BY THE WAY, KEEP THIS BETWEEN US. DON'T TELL ANYONE THAT WE ARE MOVING.
YOU'RE NOT EVEN GOING TO TELL THE STEPFAMILY THAT WE'RE LEAVING?
IF THEY DON'T KNOW, THEY CAN'T DO ANYTHING TO STOP US. I AM DONE WITH MR. KIM AND HIS FAMILY.

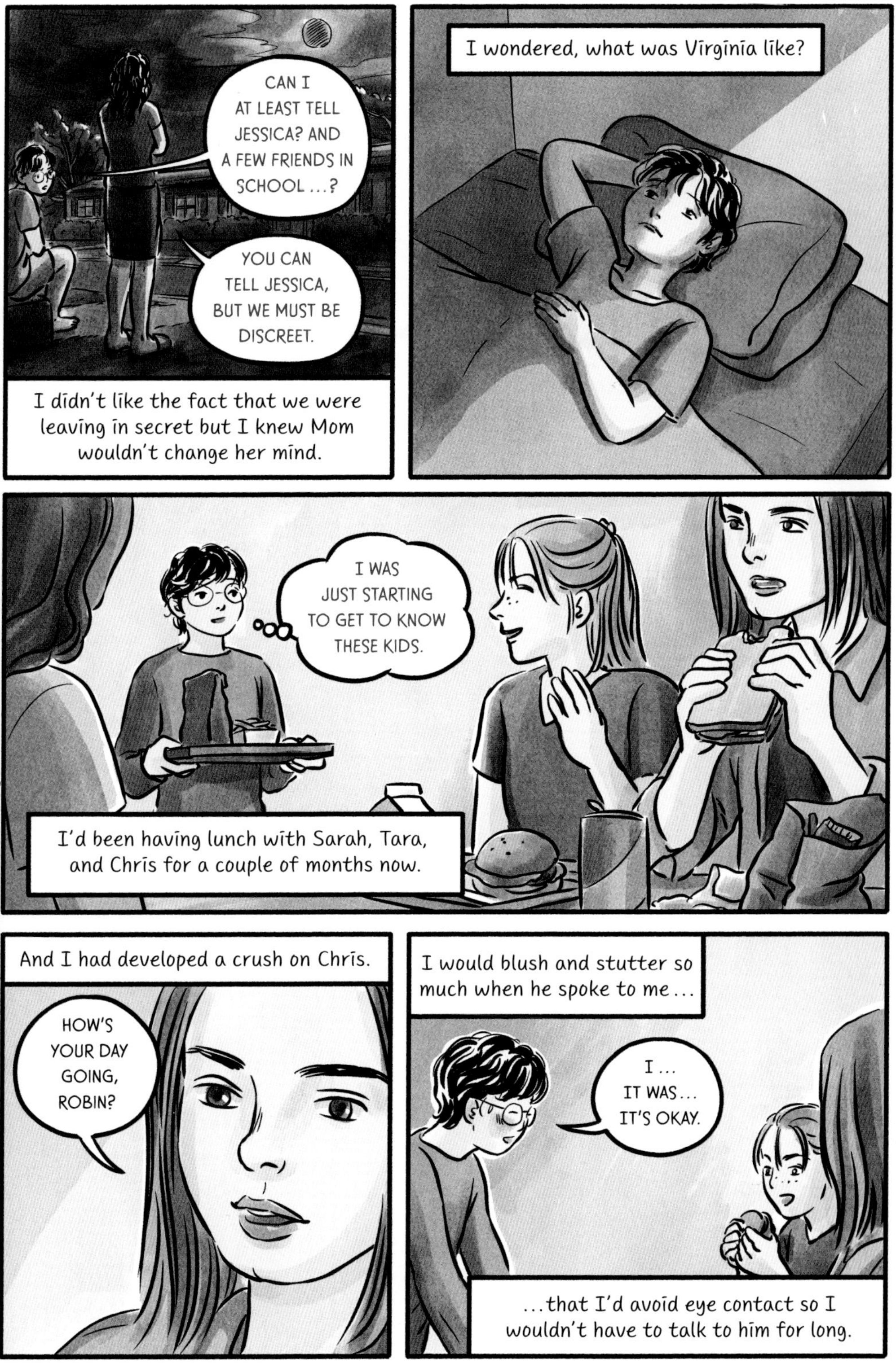
CAN I AT LEAST TELL JESSICA? AND A FEW FRIENDS IN SCHOOL . . . ?
YOU CAN TELL JESSICA, BUT WE MUST BE DISCREET.
I didn't like the fact that we were leaving in secret but I knew Mom wouldn't change her mind.
I wondered, what was Virginia like?
I WAS JUST STARTING TO GET TO KNOW THESE KIDS.
I'd been having lunch with Sarah, Tara, and Chris for a couple of months now.
And I had developed a crush on Chris.
HOW'S YOUR DAY GOING, ROBIN?
I would blush and stutter so much when he spoke to me . . .
I . . . IT WAS . . . IT'S OKAY.
. . . that I'd avoid eye contact so I wouldn't have to talk to him for long.

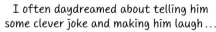
I often daydreamed about telling him some clever joke and making him laugh...

... the way Sarah made him laugh with her jokes.

It was clear that Chris and Sarah were more than just friends. I knew there would've been no chance for me even if I spoke perfect English.

Still, I would miss my new friends.

I wished I had more time with them.

UM... I HAVE SOMETHING TO TELL YOU GUYS.

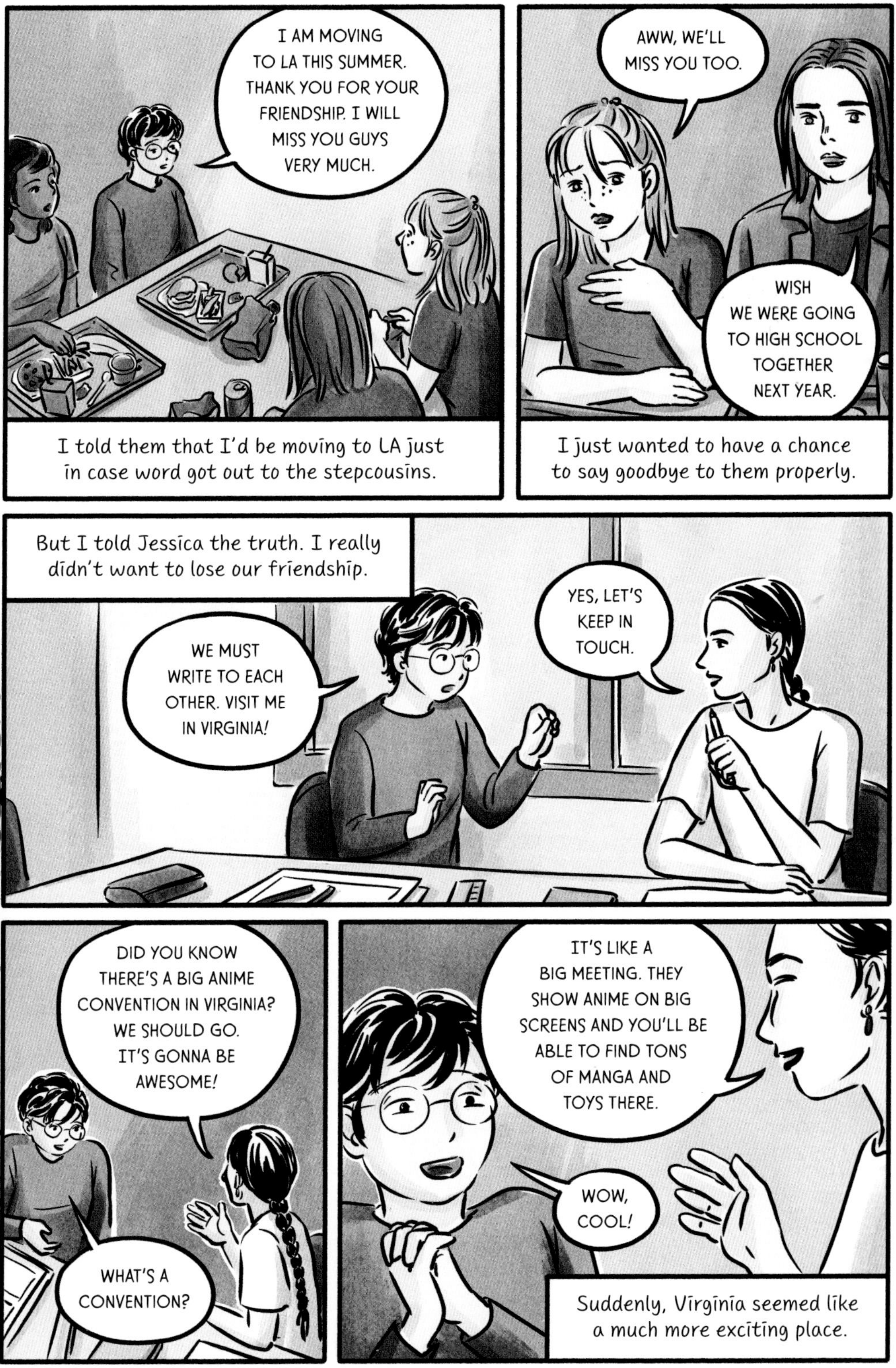
I AM MOVING TO LA THIS SUMMER. THANK YOU FOR YOUR FRIENDSHIP. I WILL MISS YOU GUYS VERY MUCH.
I told them that I'd be moving to LA just in case word got out to the stepcousins.
AWW, WE'LL MISS YOU TOO.
WISH WE WERE GOING TO HIGH SCHOOL TOGETHER NEXT YEAR.
I just wanted to have a chance to say goodbye to them properly.
But I told Jessica the truth. I really didn't want to lose our friendship.
WE MUST WRITE TO EACH OTHER. VISIT ME IN VIRGINIA!
YES, LET'S KEEP IN TOUCH.
DID YOU KNOW THERE'S A BIG ANIME CONVENTION IN VIRGINIA? WE SHOULD GO. IT'S GONNA BE AWESOME!
WHAT'S A CONVENTION?
IT'S LIKE A BIG MEETING. THEY SHOW ANIME ON BIG SCREENS AND YOU'LL BE ABLE TO FIND TONS OF MANGA AND TOYS THERE.
WOW, COOL!
Suddenly, Virginia seemed like a much more exciting place.

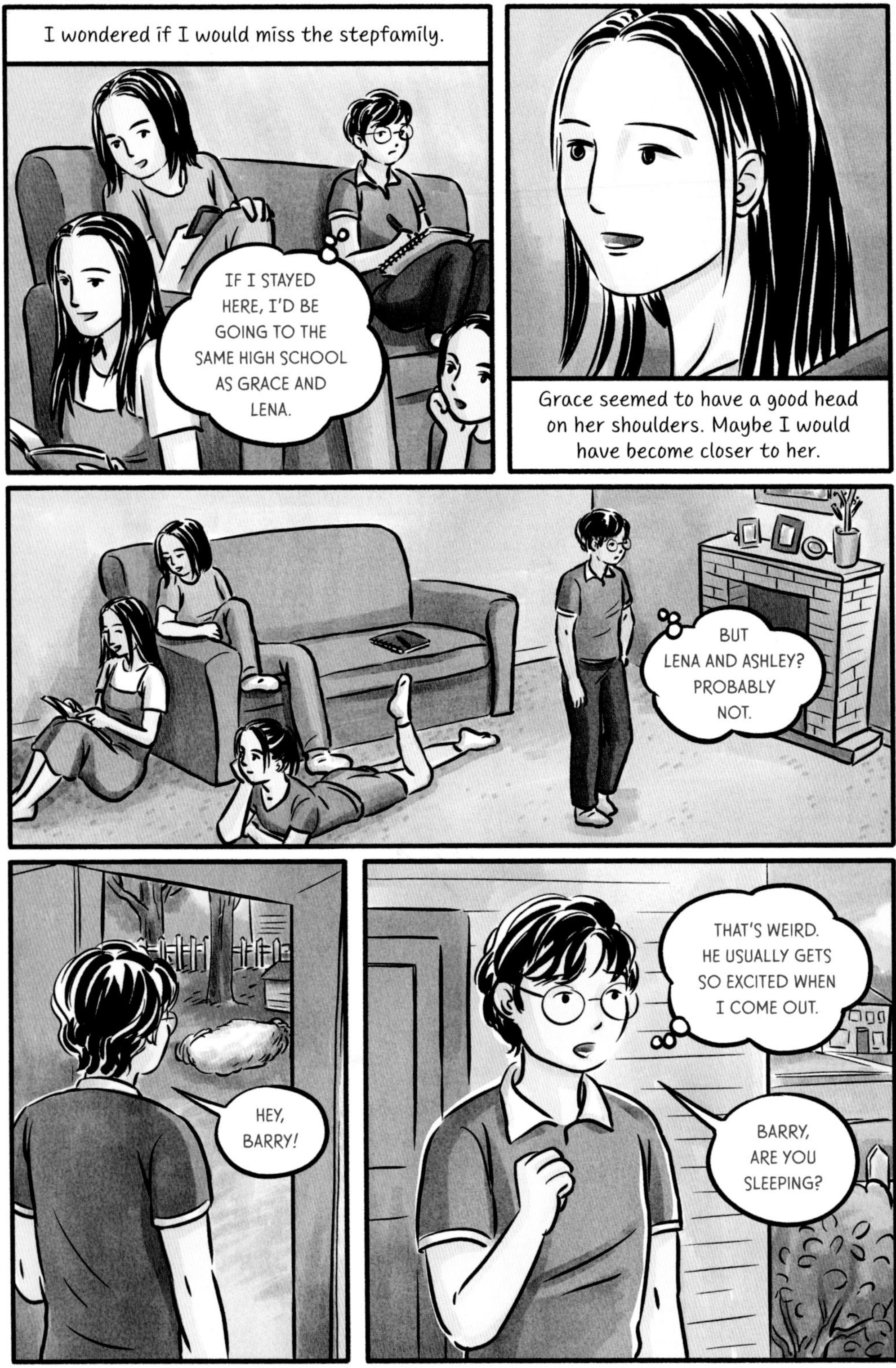
I wondered if I would miss the stepfamily.
IF I STAYED HERE, I'D BE GOING TO THE SAME HIGH SCHOOL AS GRACE AND LENA.
Grace seemed to have a good head on her shoulders. Maybe I would have become closer to her.
BUT LENA AND ASHLEY? PROBABLY NOT.
HEY, BARRY!
THAT'S WEIRD. HE USUALLY GETS SO EXCITED WHEN I COME OUT.
BARRY, ARE YOU SLEEPING?

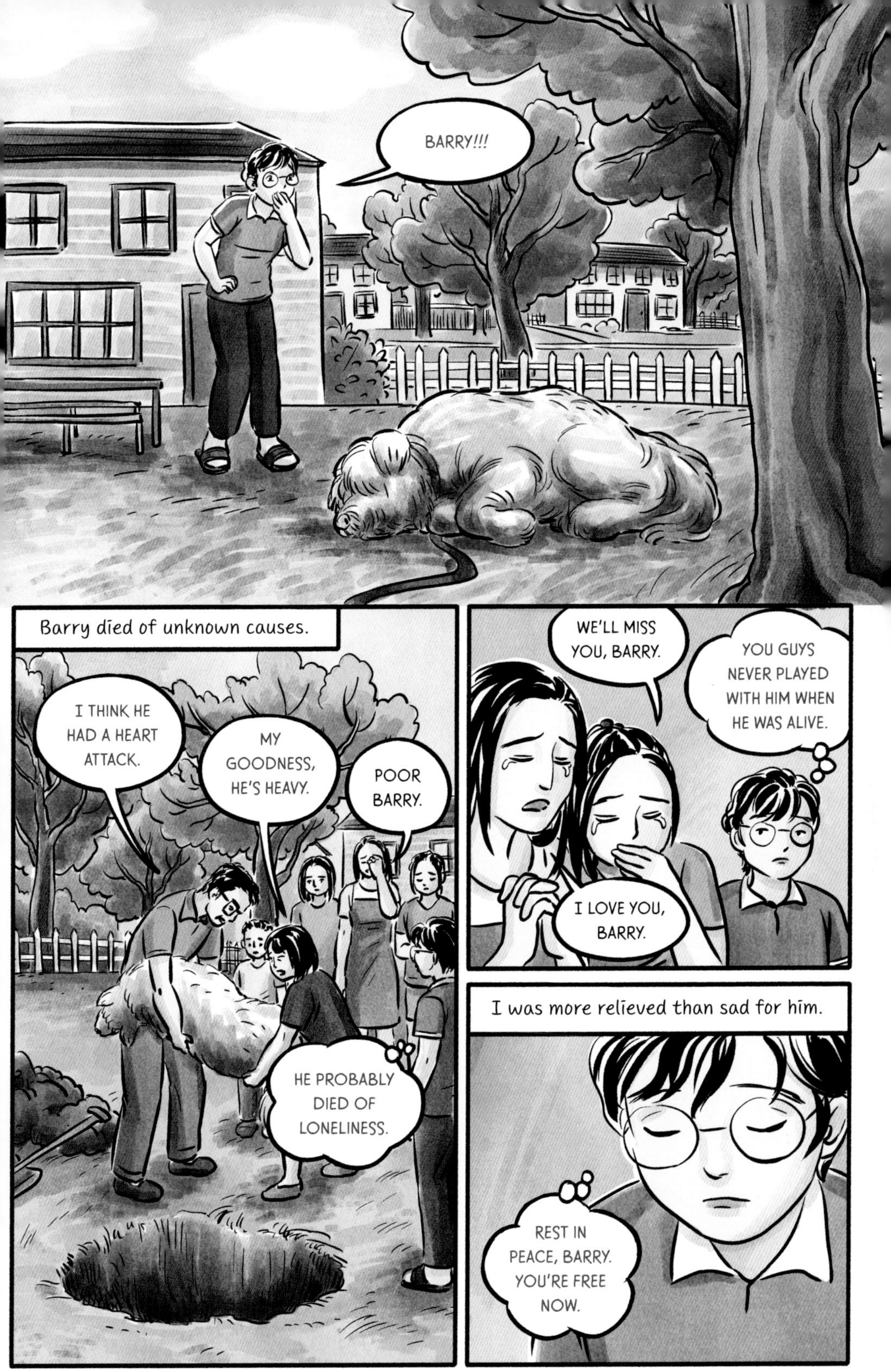
BARRY!!!
Barry died of unknown causes.
I THINK HE HAD A HEART ATTACK.
MY GOODNESS, HE'S HEAVY.
POOR BARRY.
HE PROBABLY DIED OF LONELINESS.
WE'LL MISS YOU, BARRY.
YOU GUYS NEVER PLAYED WITH HIM WHEN HE WAS ALIVE.
I LOVE YOU, BARRY.
I was more relieved than sad for him.
REST IN PEACE, BARRY. YOU'RE FREE NOW.

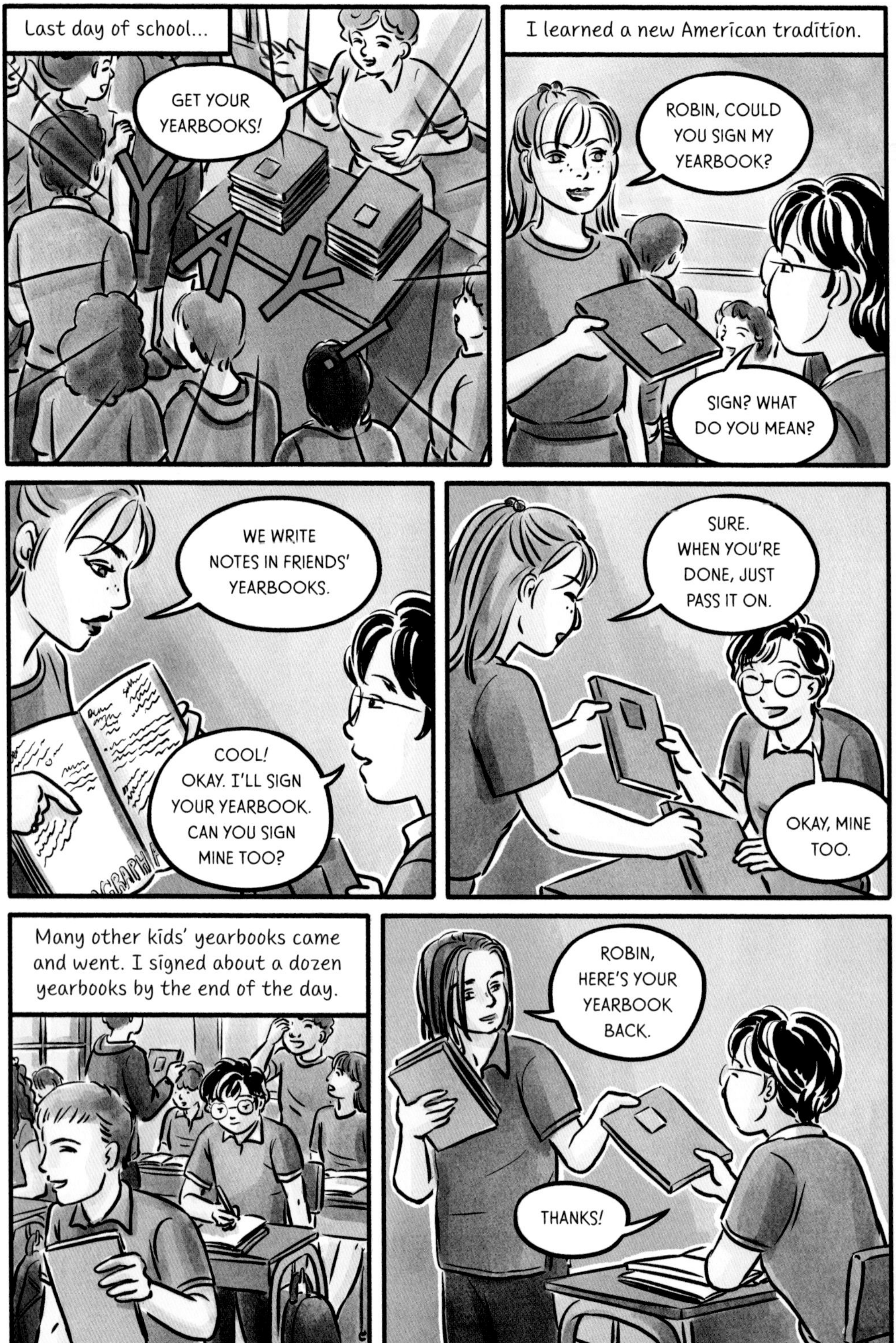
Last day of school...
GET YOUR YEARBOOKS!
YAY!
I learned a new American tradition.
ROBIN, COULD YOU SIGN MY YEARBOOK?
SIGN? WHAT DO YOU MEAN?
WE WRITE NOTES IN FRIENDS' YEARBOOKS.
COOL! OKAY. I'LL SIGN YOUR YEARBOOK. CAN YOU SIGN MINE TOO?
SURE. WHEN YOU'RE DONE, JUST PASS IT ON.
OKAY, MINE TOO.
Many other kids' yearbooks came and went. I signed about a dozen yearbooks by the end of the day.
ROBIN, HERE'S YOUR YEARBOOK BACK.
THANKS!

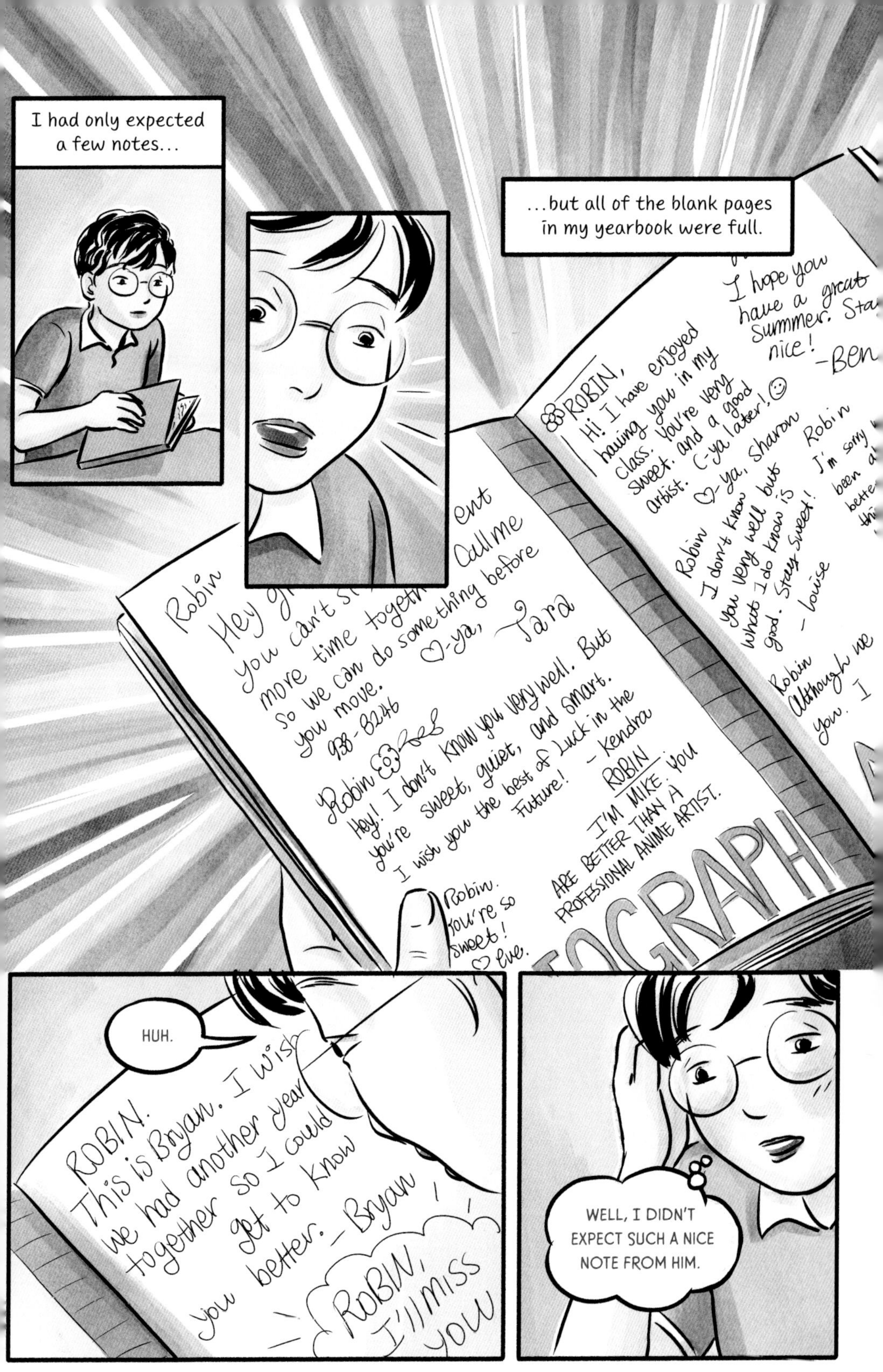
I had only expected a few notes...
...but all of the blank pages in my yearbook were full.
I hope you have a great Summer. Stay nice! -Ben
ROBIN, Hi! I have enjoyed having you in my class. You're very sweet. and a good artist. C-ya later! ♡-ya, Sharon
Robin I don't know you very well but what I do know is good. Stay sweet! -Louise
Robin I'm sorry I've been a better this
Robin Although we you. I you.
Robin Hey gi you can't st more time togeth so we can do something before you move. Call me ♡-ya, Tara 938-8246
Robin Hey! I don't know you very well. But you're sweet, quiet, and smart. I wish you the best of luck in the Future! -Kendra
ROBIN I'M MIKE. YOU ARE BETTER THAN A PROFESSIONAL ANIME ARTIST.
Robin. You're so sweet! ♡ Eve.
TOGRAPH
HUH.
ROBIN. This is Bryan. I wish we had another year together so I could get to know you better. _Bryan
ROBIN, I'll MISS YOU
WELL, I DIDN'T EXPECT SUCH A NICE NOTE FROM HIM.

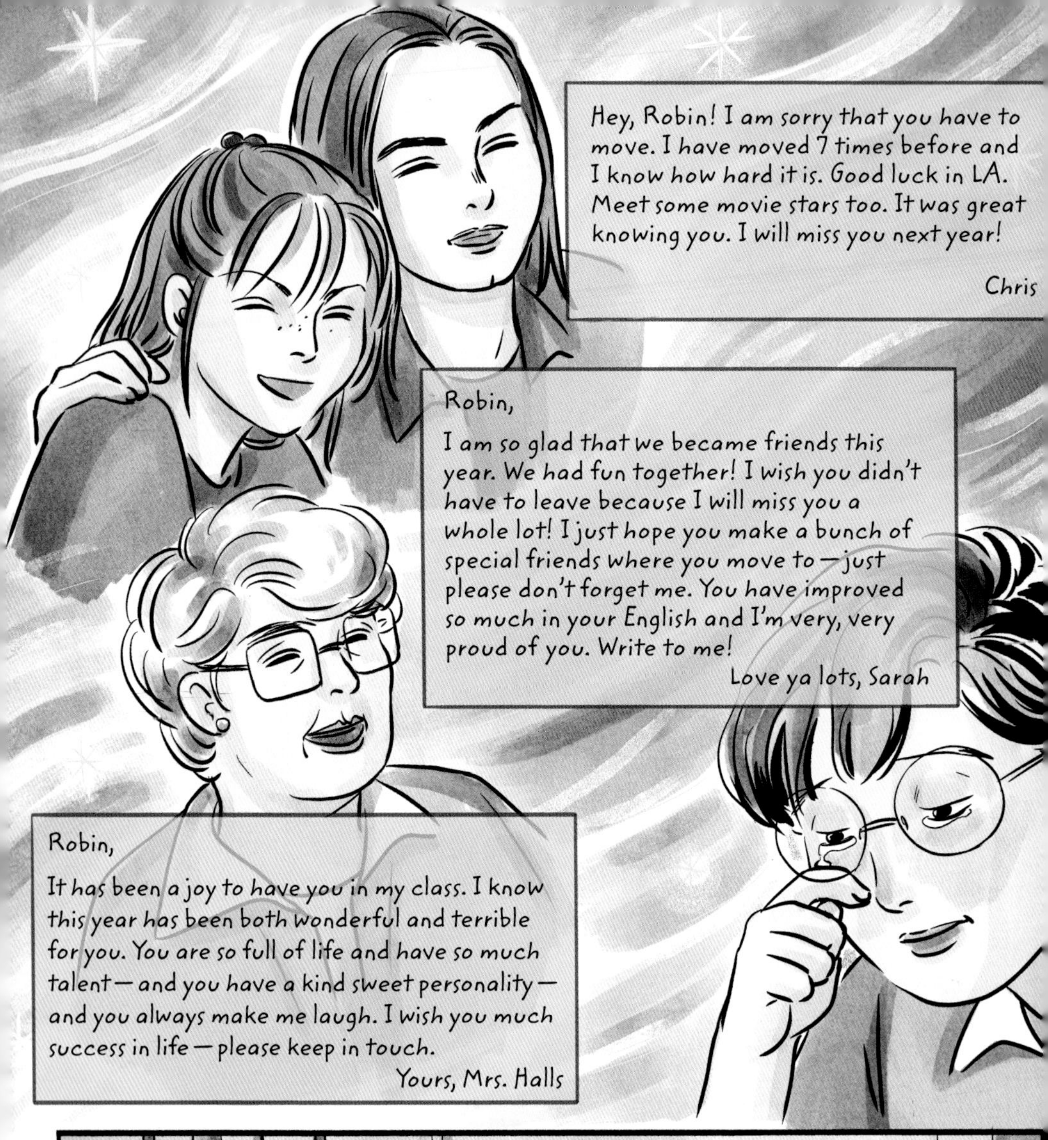
Hey, Robin! I am sorry that you have to move. I have moved 7 times before and I know how hard it is. Good luck in LA. Meet some movie stars too. It was great knowing you. I will miss you next year!
Chris
Robin,
I am so glad that we became friends this year. We had fun together! I wish you didn't have to leave because I will miss you a whole lot! I just hope you make a bunch of special friends where you move to — just please don't forget me. You have improved so much in your English and I'm very, very proud of you. Write to me!
Love ya lots, Sarah
Robin,
It has been a joy to have you in my class. I know this year has been both wonderful and terrible for you. You are so full of life and have so much talent — and you have a kind sweet personality — and you always make me laugh. I wish you much success in life — please keep in touch.
Yours, Mrs. Halls

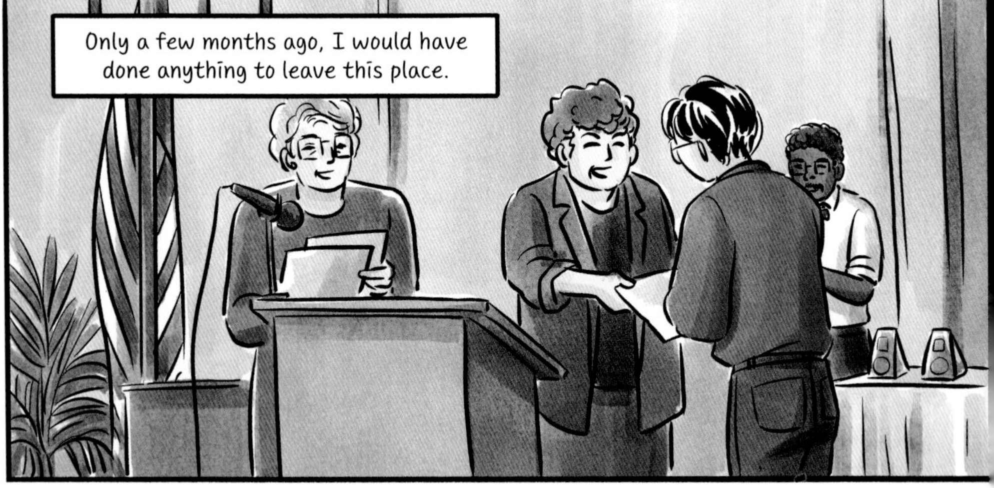
Only a few months ago, I would have done anything to leave this place.

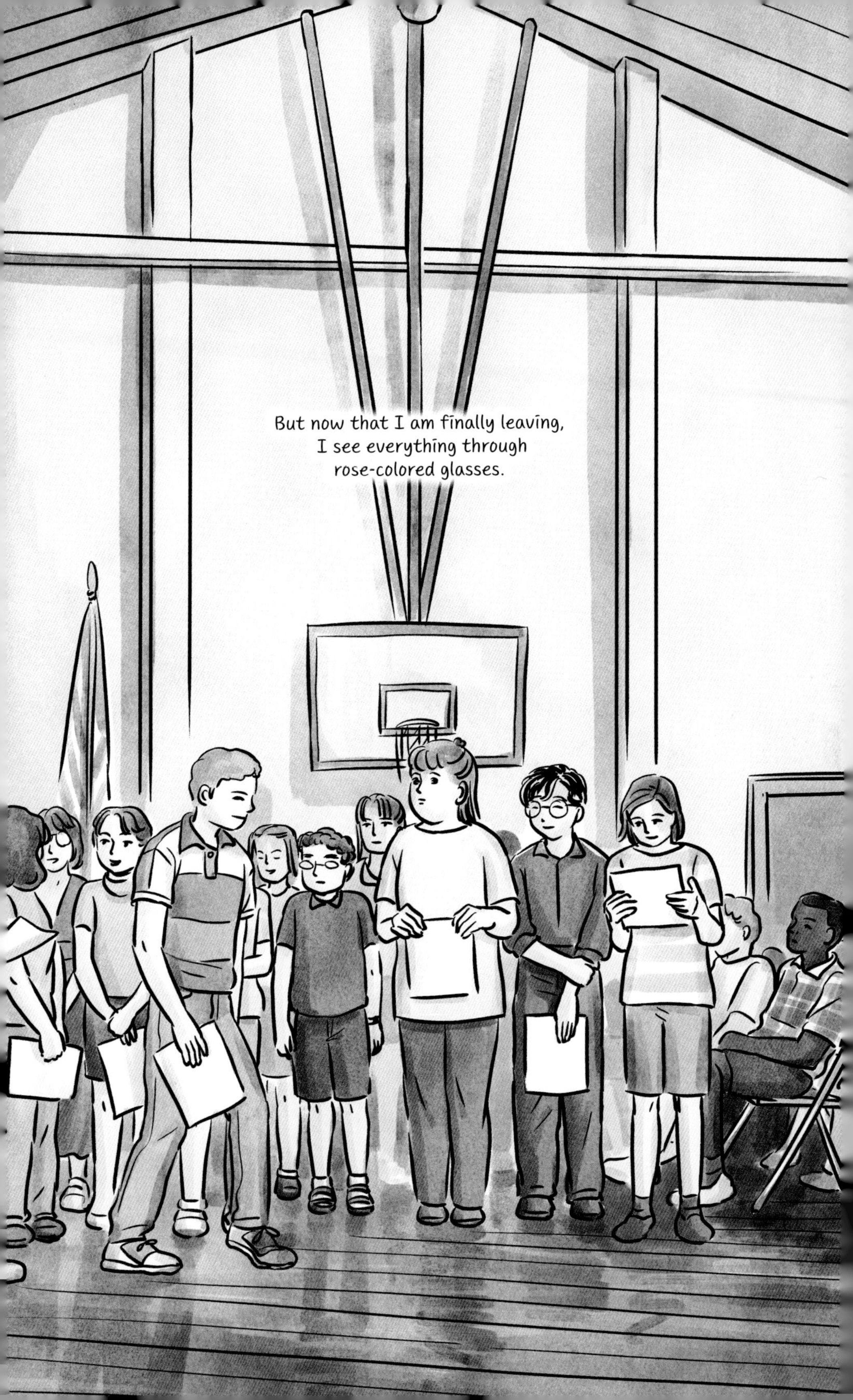
But now that I am finally leaving, I see everything through rose-colored glasses.

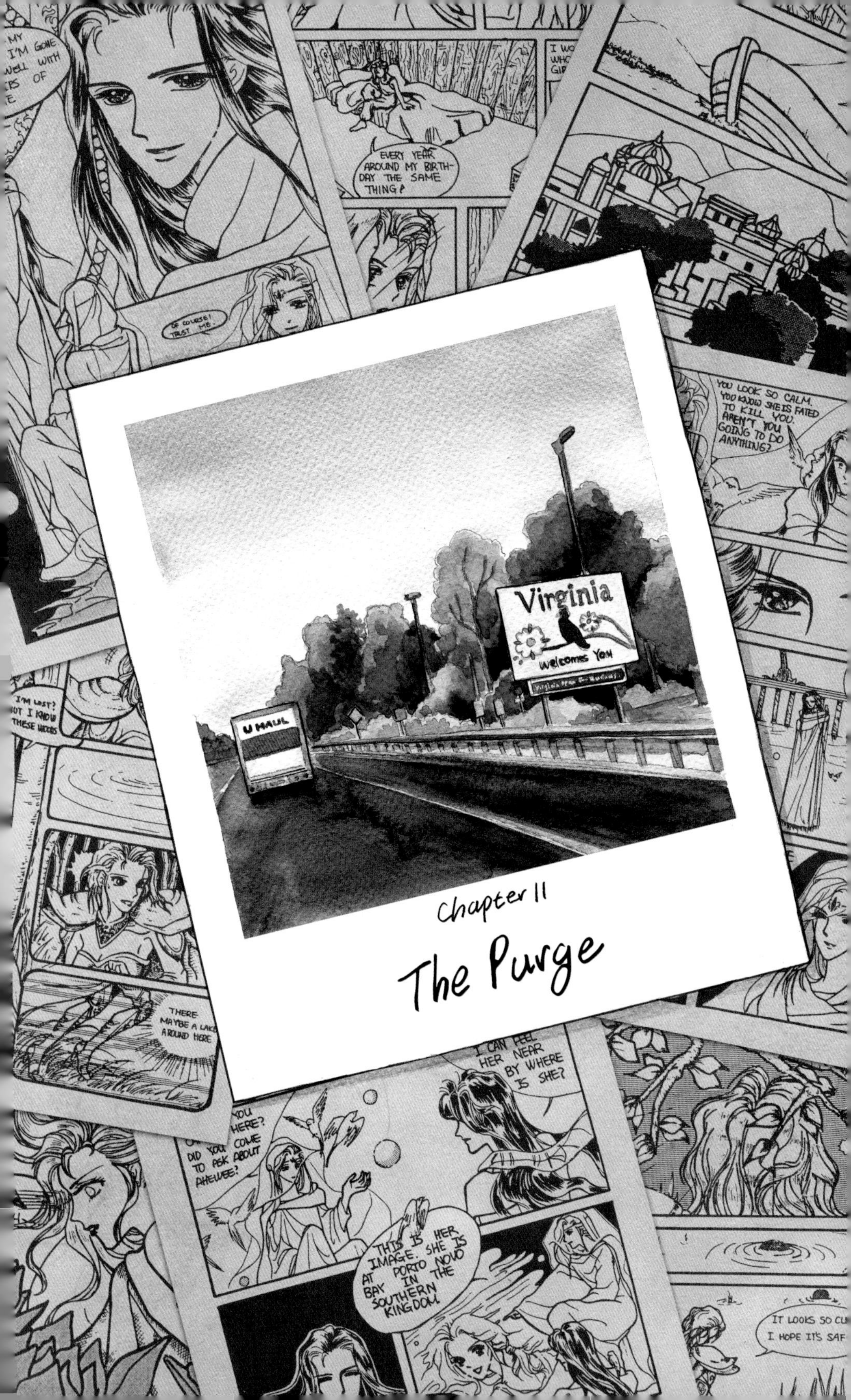
EVERY YEAR AROUND MY BIRTH-DAY THE SAME THING?
OF COURSE! TRUST ME.
YOU LOOK SO CALM. YOU KNOW SHE IS FATED TO KILL YOU. AREN'T YOU GOING TO DO ANYTHING?
U HAUL
Virginia
Welcomes You
THERE MAYBE A LAKE AROUND HERE
I CAN FEEL HER NEAR BY WHERE IS SHE?
DID YOU COME TO ASK ABOUT AHEWEE?
THIS IS HER IMAGE. SHE IS AT PORTO NOVO BAY IN THE SOUTHERN KINGDOM

Chapter 11

The Purge

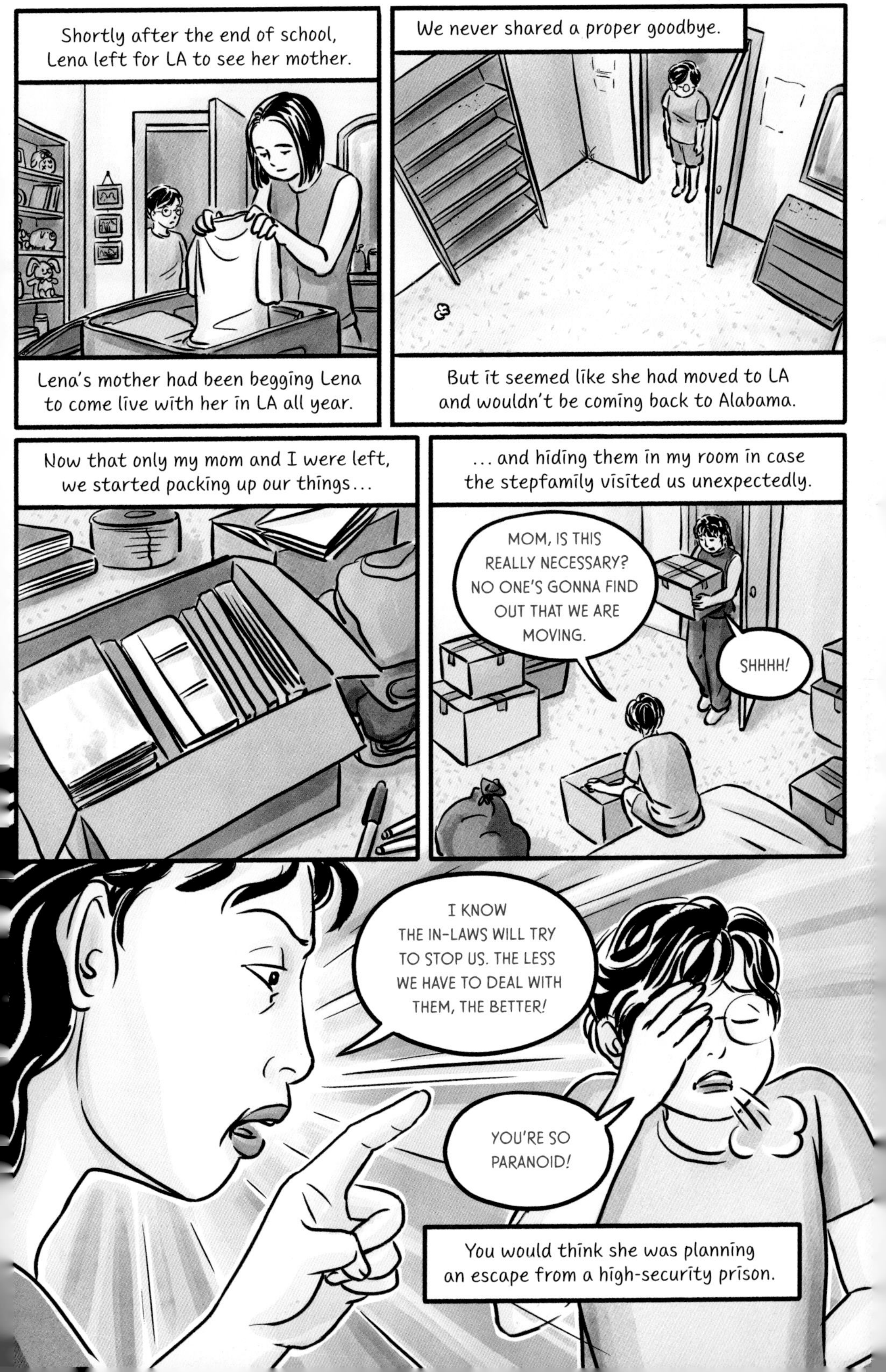
Shortly after the end of school, Lena left for LA to see her mother.
Lena's mother had been begging Lena to come live with her in LA all year.
We never shared a proper goodbye.
But it seemed like she had moved to LA and wouldn't be coming back to Alabama.
Now that only my mom and I were left, we started packing up our things...
...and hiding them in my room in case the stepfamily visited us unexpectedly.
MOM, IS THIS REALLY NECESSARY? NO ONE'S GONNA FIND OUT THAT WE ARE MOVING.
SHHHH!
I KNOW THE IN-LAWS WILL TRY TO STOP US. THE LESS WE HAVE TO DEAL WITH THEM, THE BETTER!
YOU'RE SO PARANOID!
You would think she was planning an escape from a high-security prison.

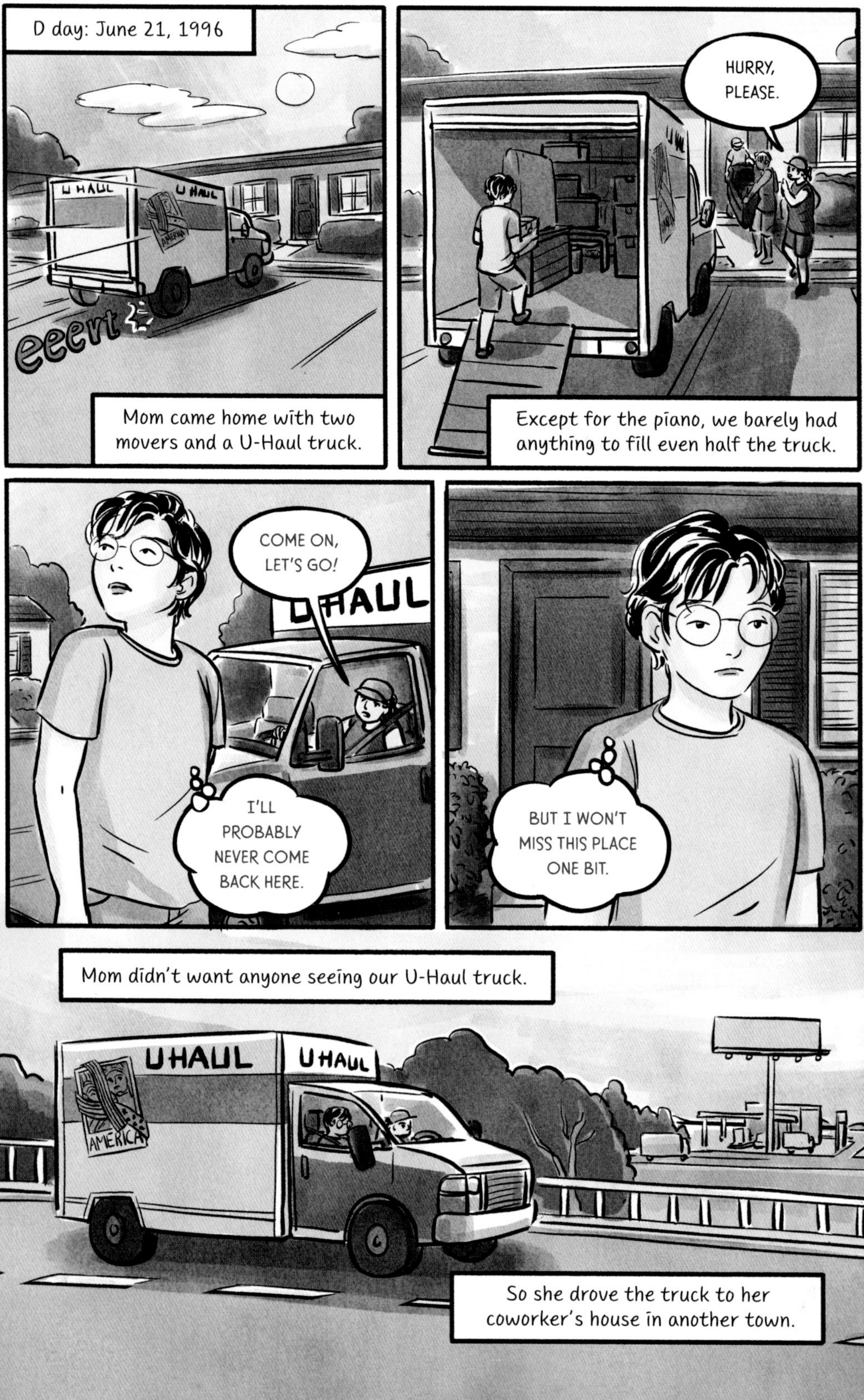
D day: June 21, 1996
eeert
Mom came home with two movers and a U-Haul truck.
HURRY, PLEASE.
Except for the piano, we barely had anything to fill even half the truck.
COME ON, LET'S GO!
I'LL PROBABLY NEVER COME BACK HERE.
BUT I WON'T MISS THIS PLACE ONE BIT.
Mom didn't want anyone seeing our U-Haul truck.
UHAUL
UHAUL
AMERICA
So she drove the truck to her coworker's house in another town.

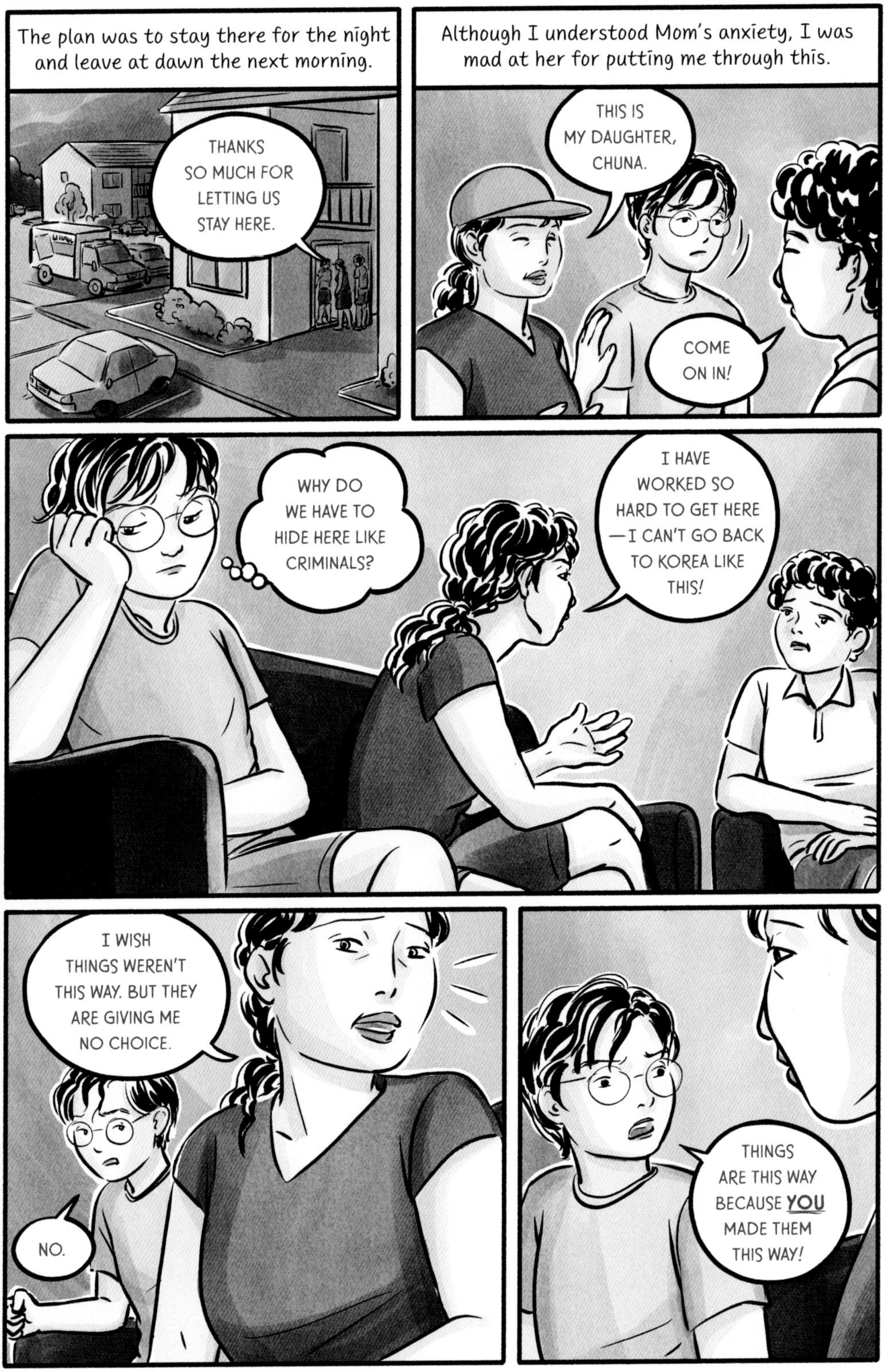
The plan was to stay there for the night and leave at dawn the next morning.
THANKS SO MUCH FOR LETTING US STAY HERE.
Although I understood Mom's anxiety, I was mad at her for putting me through this.
THIS IS MY DAUGHTER, CHUNA.
COME ON IN!
WHY DO WE HAVE TO HIDE HERE LIKE CRIMINALS?
I HAVE WORKED SO HARD TO GET HERE —I CAN'T GO BACK TO KOREA LIKE THIS!
I WISH THINGS WEREN'T THIS WAY. BUT THEY ARE GIVING ME NO CHOICE.
NO.
THINGS ARE THIS WAY BECAUSE YOU MADE THEM THIS WAY!

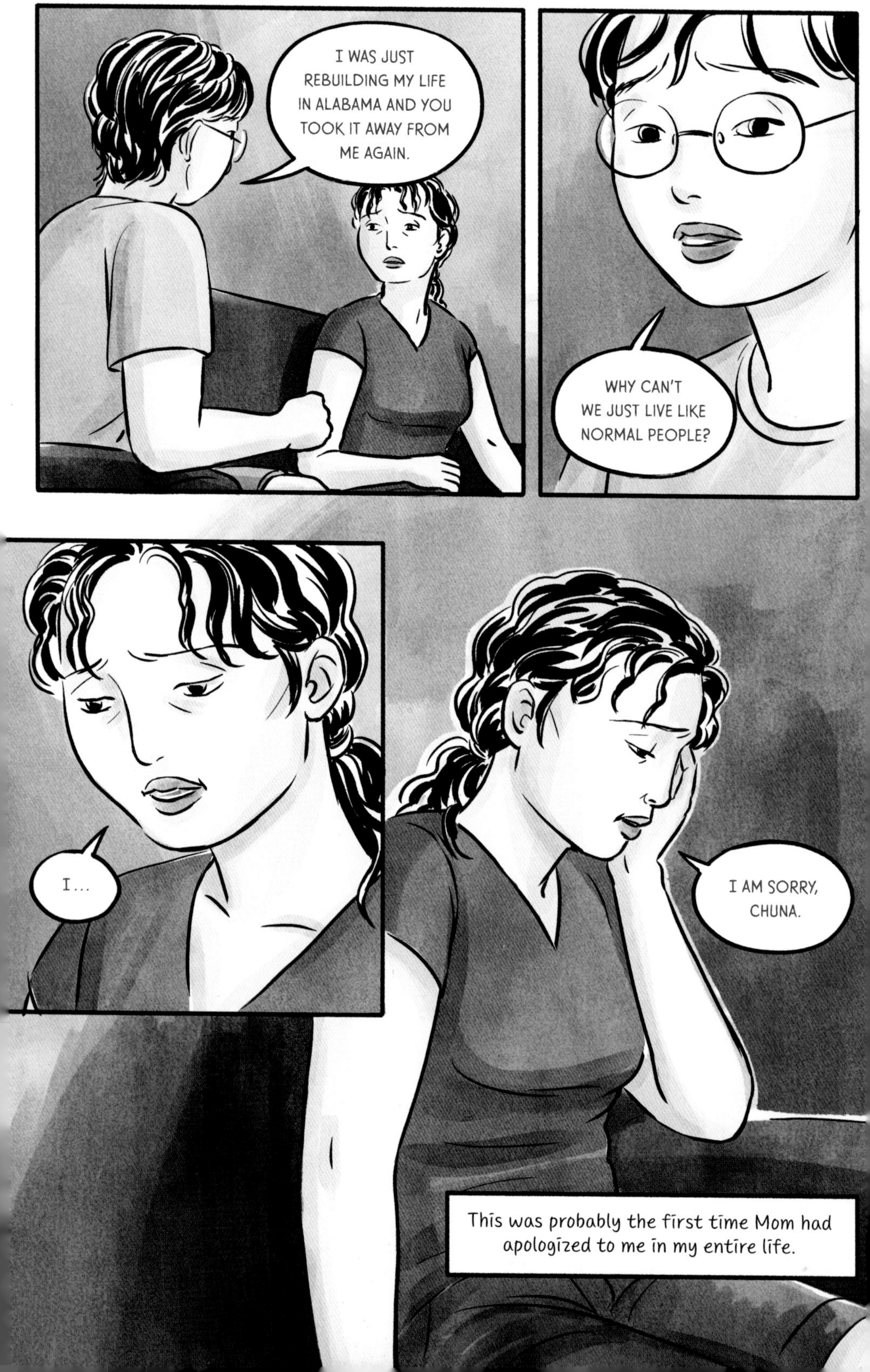
I WAS JUST REBUILDING MY LIFE IN ALABAMA AND YOU TOOK IT AWAY FROM ME AGAIN.
WHY CAN'T WE JUST LIVE LIKE NORMAL PEOPLE?
I...
I AM SORRY, CHUNA.
This was probably the first time Mom had apologized to me in my entire life.

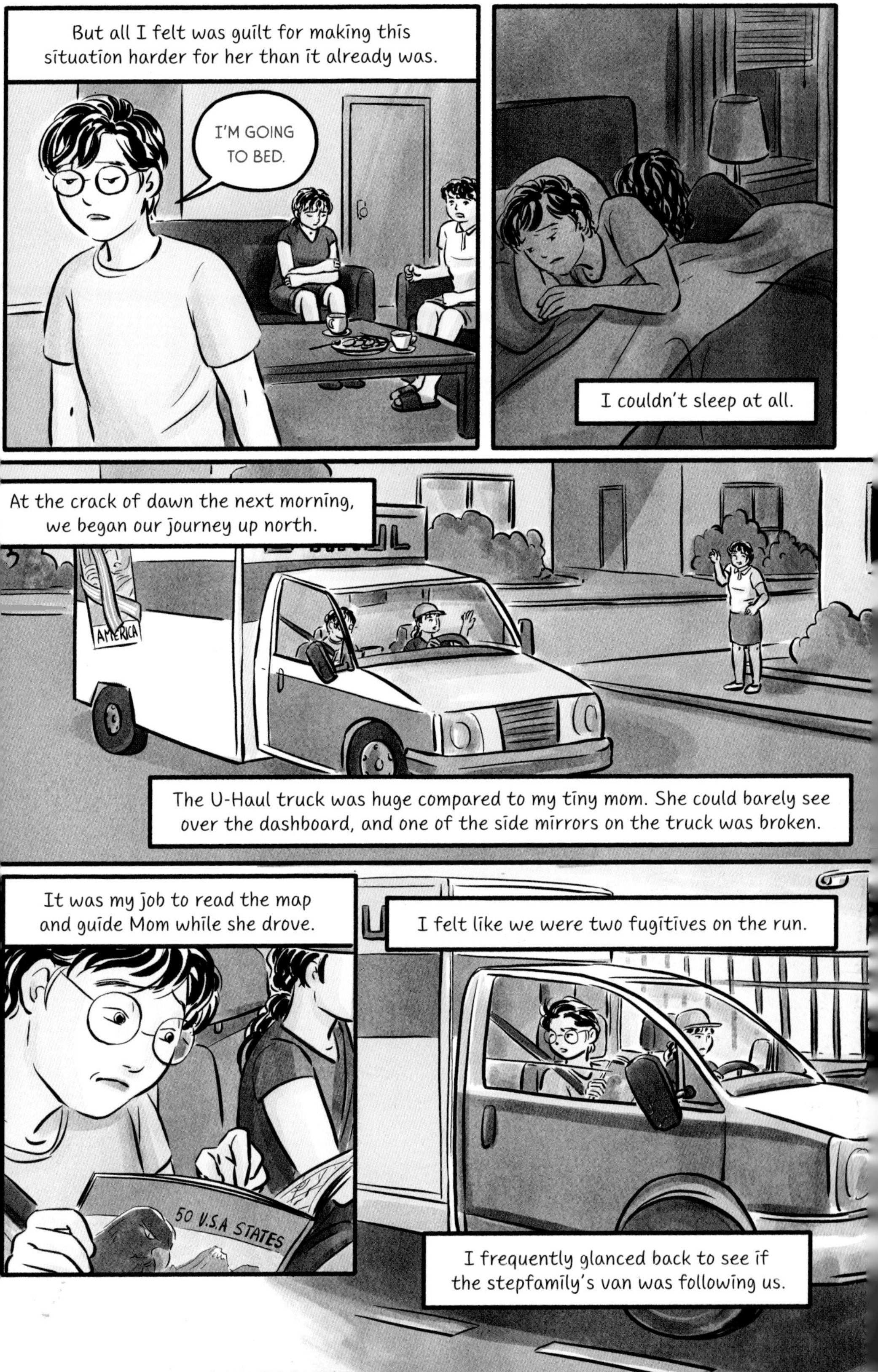
But all I felt was guilt for making this situation harder for her than it already was.
I'M GOING TO BED.
I couldn't sleep at all.
At the crack of dawn the next morning, we began our journey up north.
AMERICA
The U-Haul truck was huge compared to my tiny mom. She could barely see over the dashboard, and one of the side mirrors on the truck was broken.
It was my job to read the map and guide Mom while she drove.
50 U.S.A STATES
I felt like we were two fugitives on the run.
I frequently glanced back to see if the stepfamily's van was following us.

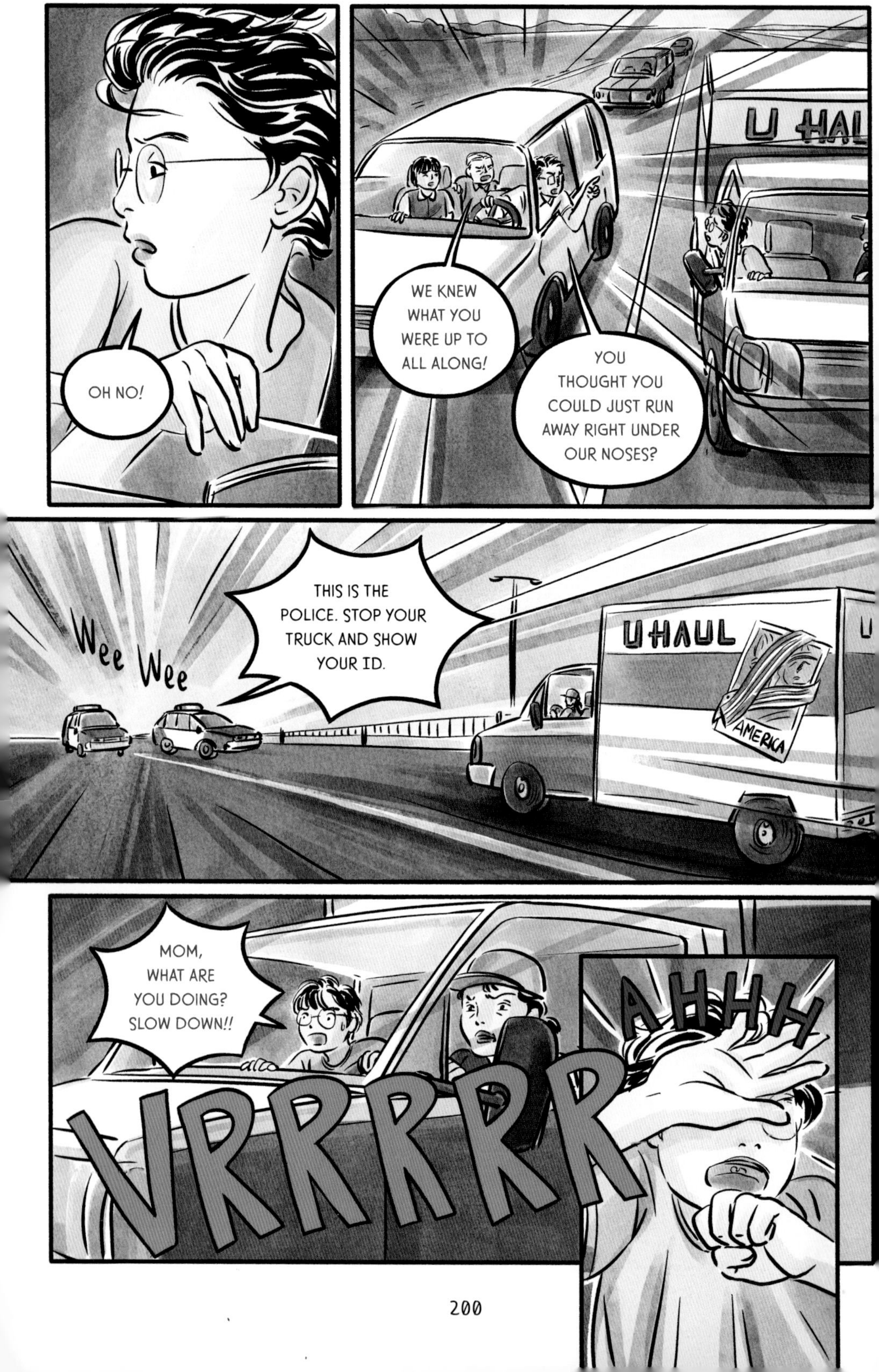
OH NO!
U HAL
WE KNEW WHAT YOU WERE UP TO ALL ALONG!
YOU THOUGHT YOU COULD JUST RUN AWAY RIGHT UNDER OUR NOSES?
Wee Wee
THIS IS THE POLICE. STOP YOUR TRUCK AND SHOW YOUR ID.
UHAUL
AMERICA
MOM, WHAT ARE YOU DOING? SLOW DOWN!!
VRRRRR
AHHH

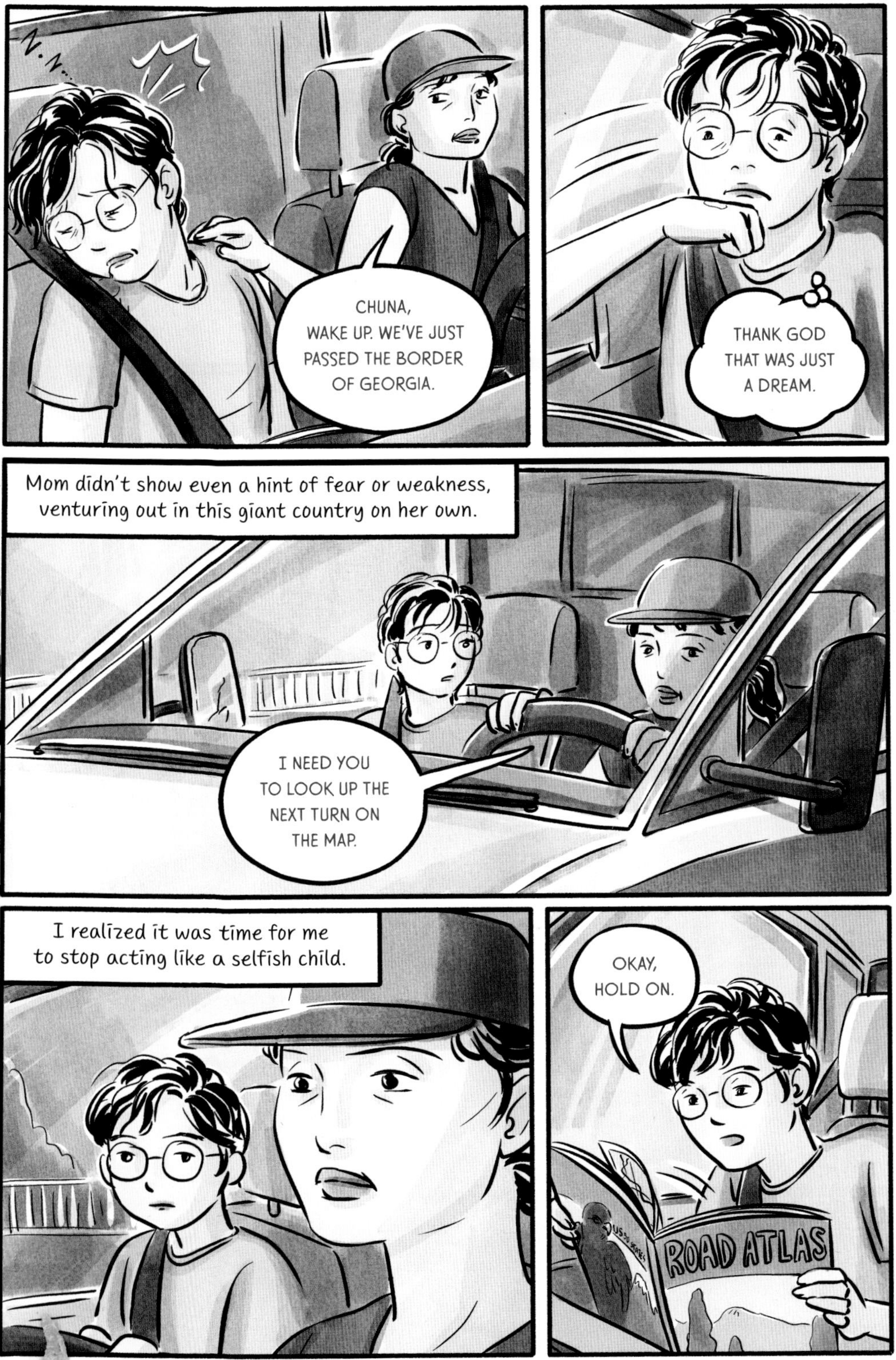
Z..Z...
CHUNA, WAKE UP. WE'VE JUST PASSED THE BORDER OF GEORGIA.
THANK GOD THAT WAS JUST A DREAM.
Mom didn't show even a hint of fear or weakness, venturing out in this giant country on her own.
I NEED YOU TO LOOK UP THE NEXT TURN ON THE MAP.
I realized it was time for me to stop acting like a selfish child.
OKAY, HOLD ON.
ROAD ATLAS

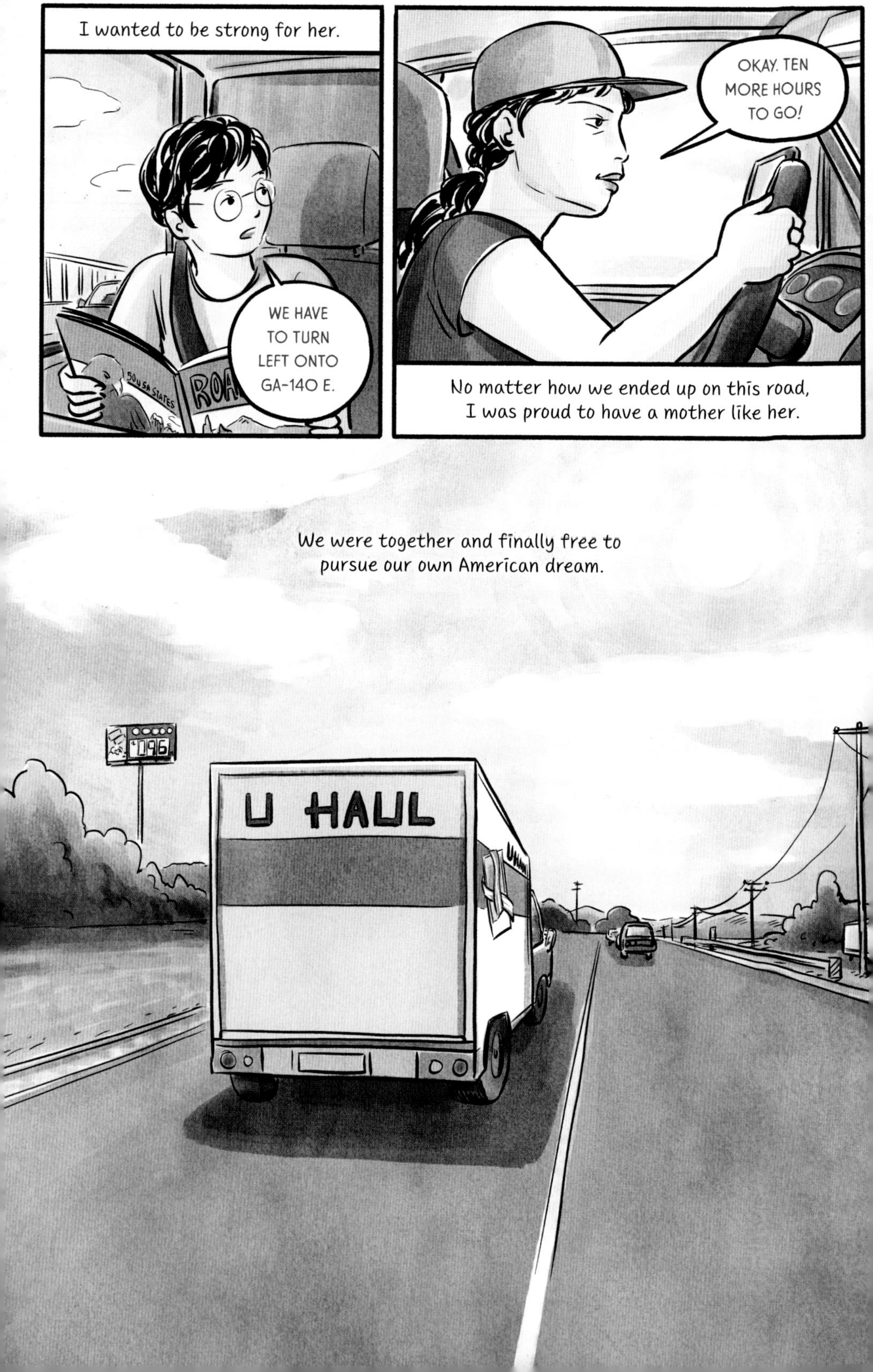
I wanted to be strong for her.
WE HAVE TO TURN LEFT ONTO GA-140 E.
OKAY. TEN MORE HOURS TO GO!
No matter how we ended up on this road, I was proud to have a mother like her.
We were together and finally free to pursue our own American dream.
U HAUL

Chapter 12
Sweet Home Virginia

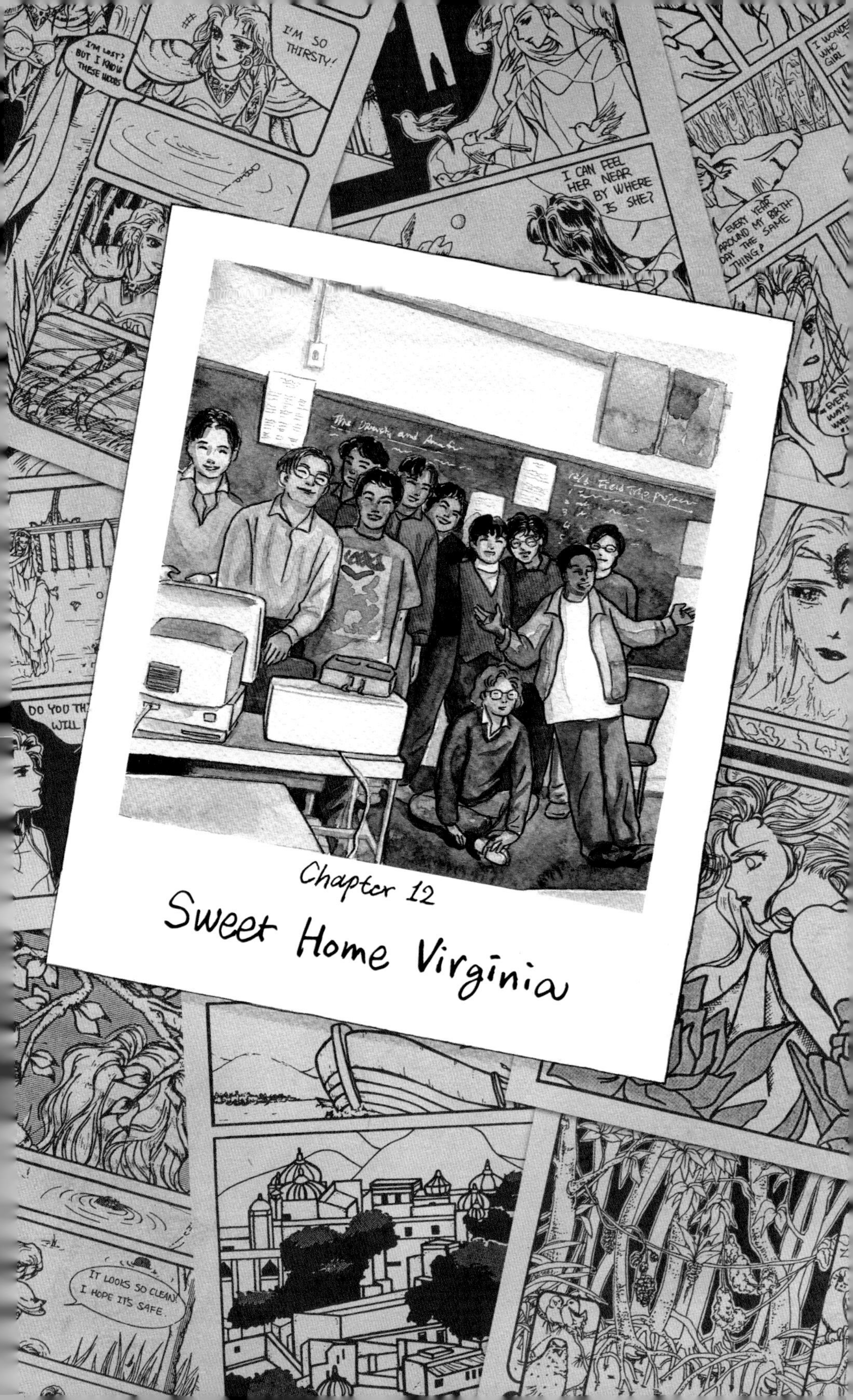

I'M LOST? BUT I KNOW THESE WOODS
I'M SO THIRSTY!
I CAN FEEL HER NEAR BY WHERE IS SHE?
EVERY YEAR AROUND MY BIRTH-DAY THE SAME THING?
IT LOOKS SO CLEAN! I HOPE IT'S SAFE.

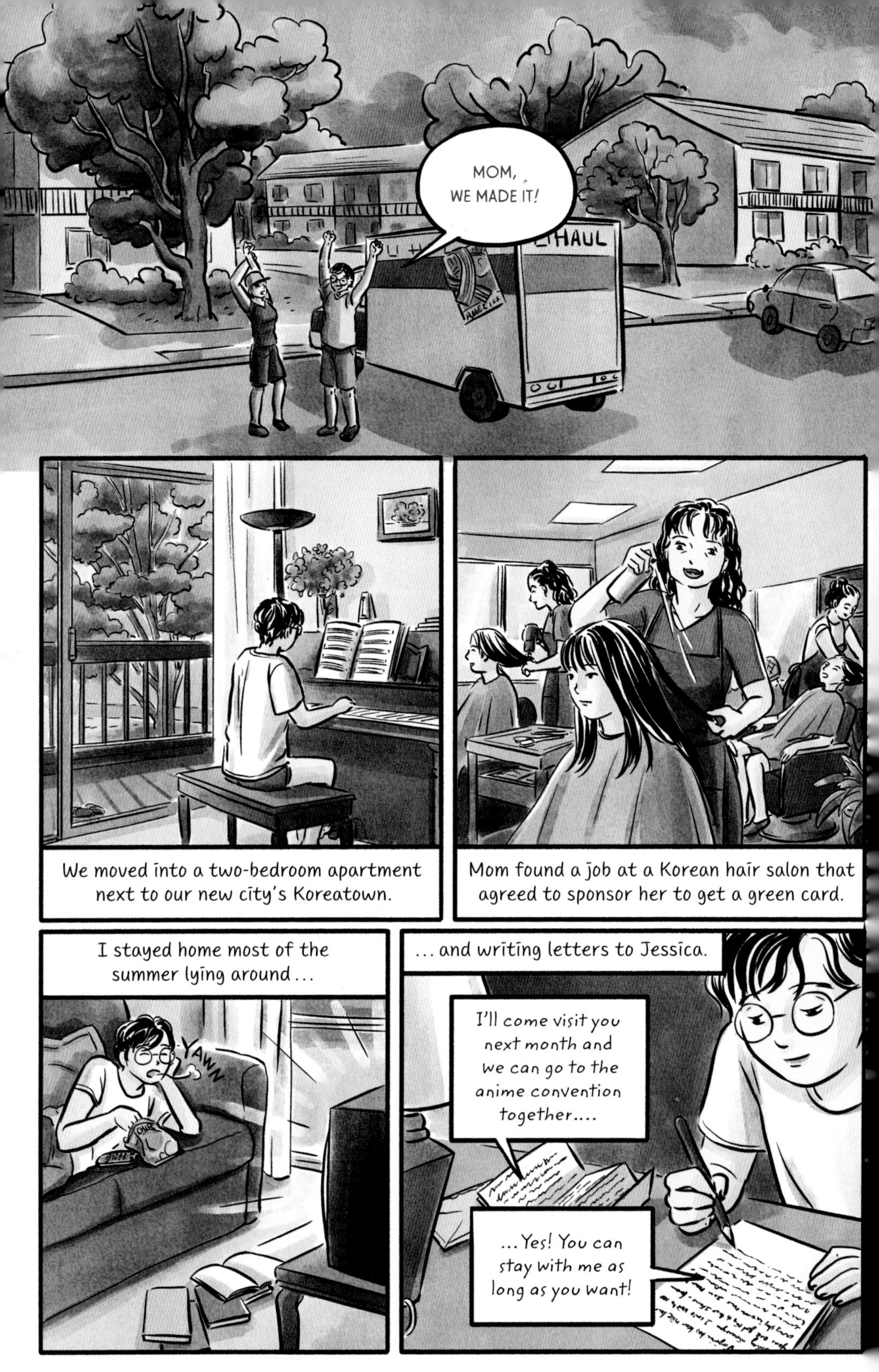
MOM, WE MADE IT!
We moved into a two-bedroom apartment next to our new city's Koreatown.
Mom found a job at a Korean hair salon that agreed to sponsor her to get a green card.
I stayed home most of the summer lying around...
YAWN
...and writing letters to Jessica.
I'll come visit you next month and we can go to the anime convention together....
...Yes! You can stay with me as long as you want!

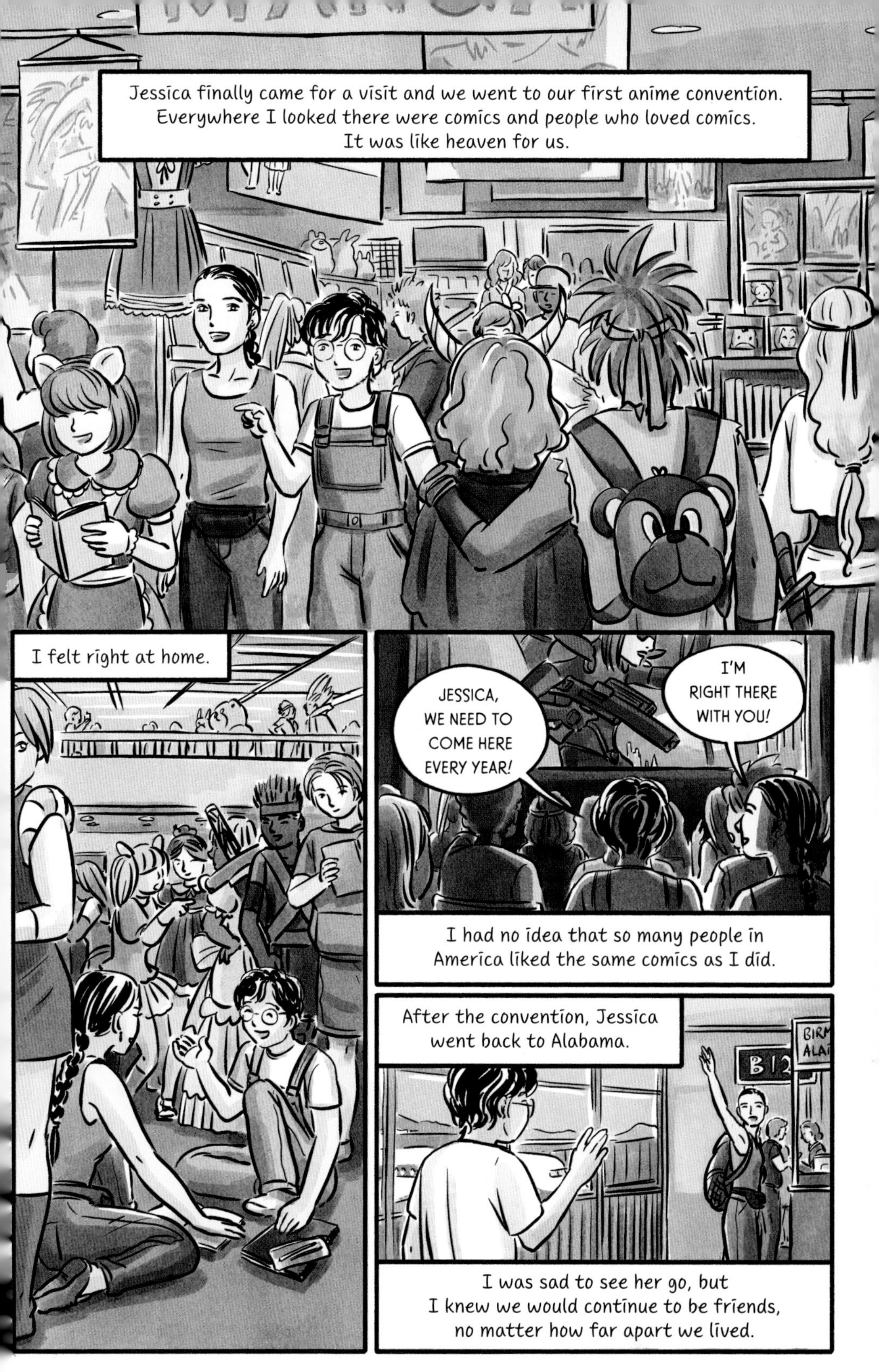
Jessica finally came for a visit and we went to our first anime convention.
Everywhere I looked there were comics and people who loved comics.
It was like heaven for us.
I felt right at home.
JESSICA, WE NEED TO COME HERE EVERY YEAR!
I'M RIGHT THERE WITH YOU!
I had no idea that so many people in America liked the same comics as I did.
After the convention, Jessica went back to Alabama.
B12
I was sad to see her go, but
I knew we would continue to be friends,
no matter how far apart we lived.

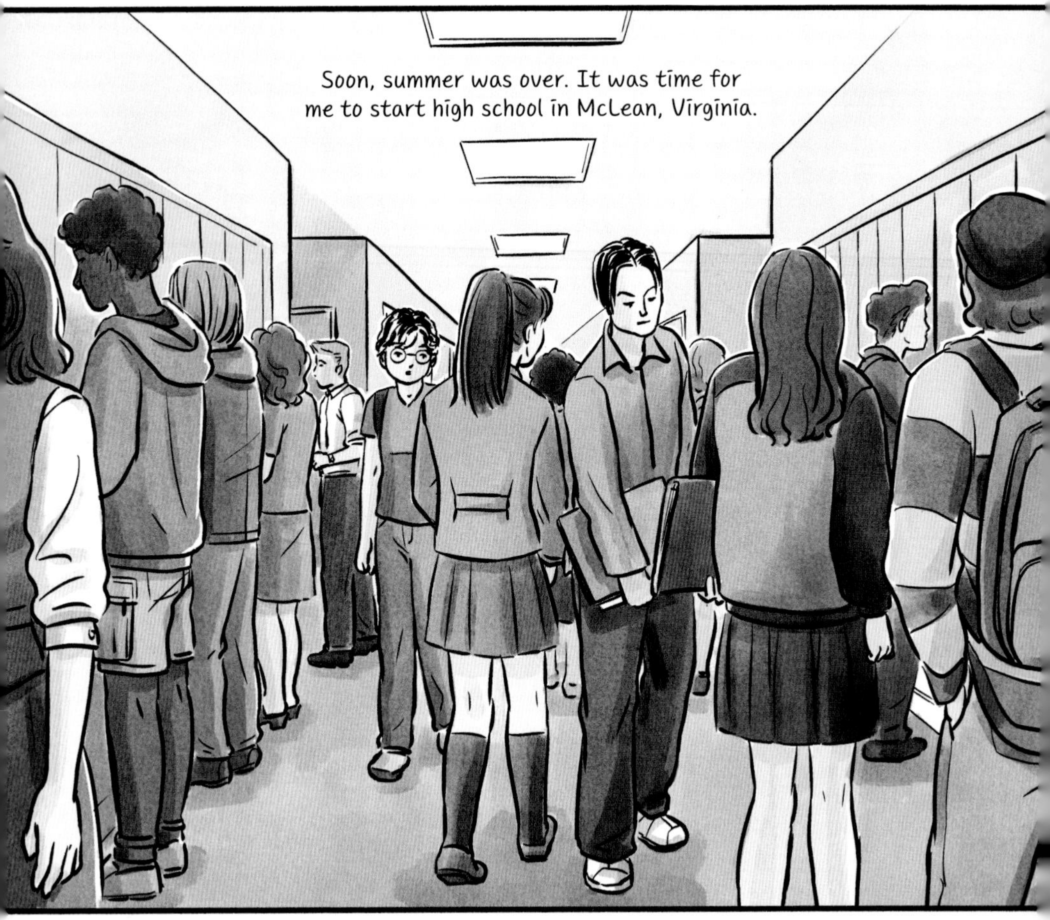
Soon, summer was over. It was time for me to start high school in McLean, Virginia.

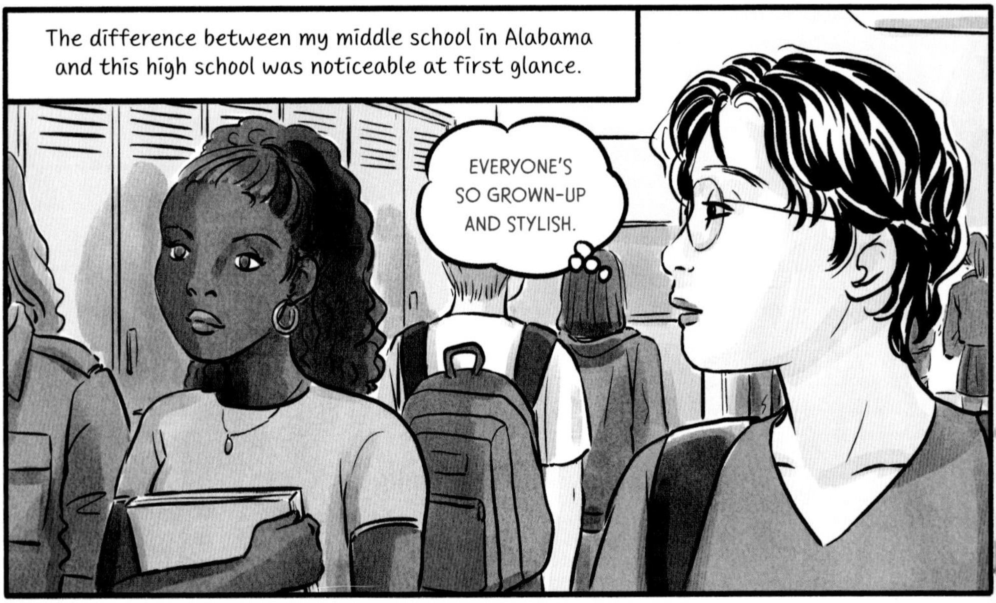
The difference between my middle school in Alabama and this high school was noticeable at first glance.
EVERYONE'S SO GROWN-UP AND STYLISH.

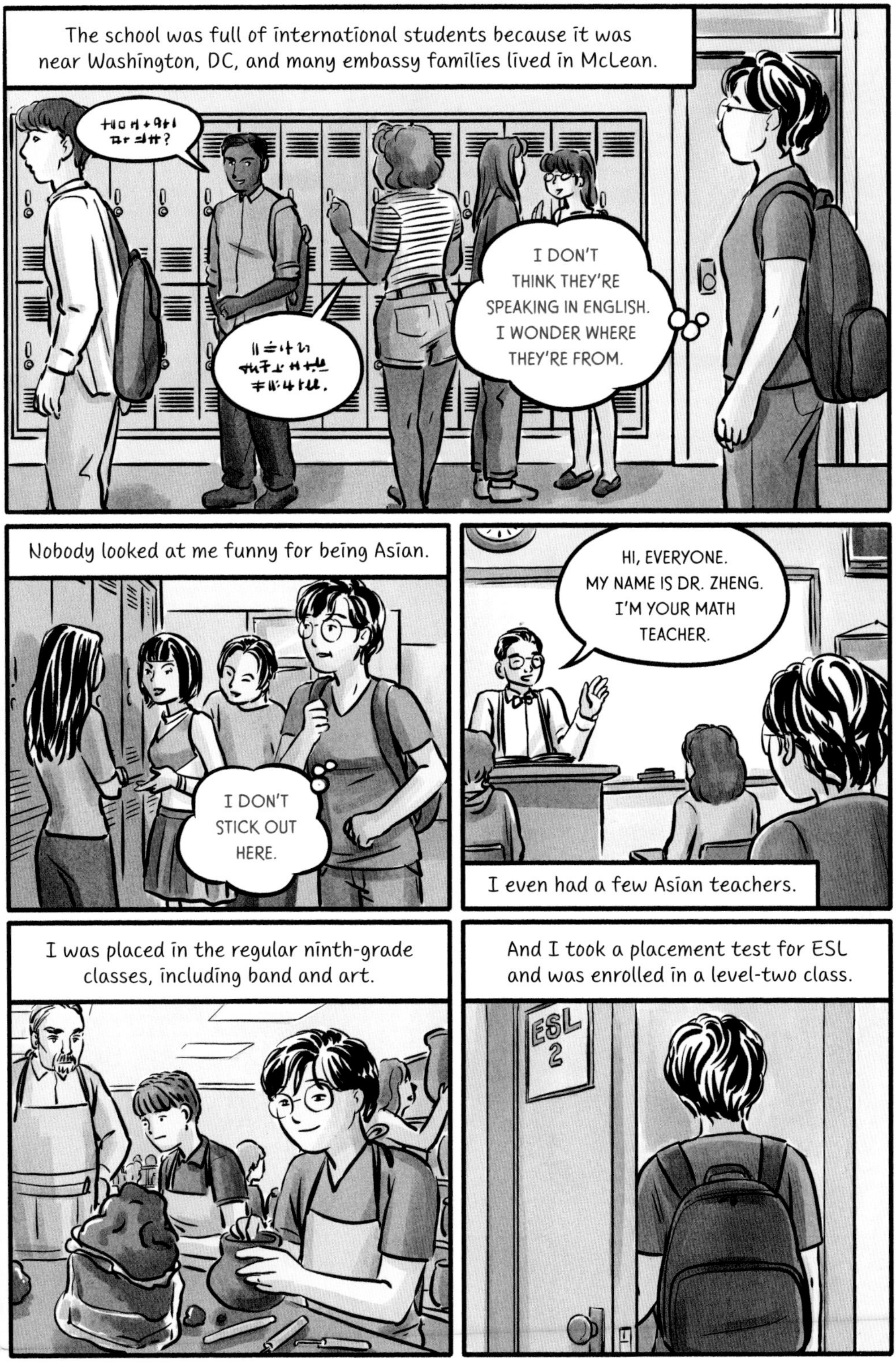
The school was full of international students because it was near Washington, DC, and many embassy families lived in McLean.
I DON'T THINK THEY'RE SPEAKING IN ENGLISH. I WONDER WHERE THEY'RE FROM.
Nobody looked at me funny for being Asian.
I DON'T STICK OUT HERE.
HI, EVERYONE. MY NAME IS DR. ZHENG. I'M YOUR MATH TEACHER.
I even had a few Asian teachers.
I was placed in the regular ninth-grade classes, including band and art.
And I took a placement test for ESL and was enrolled in a level-two class.
ESL 2

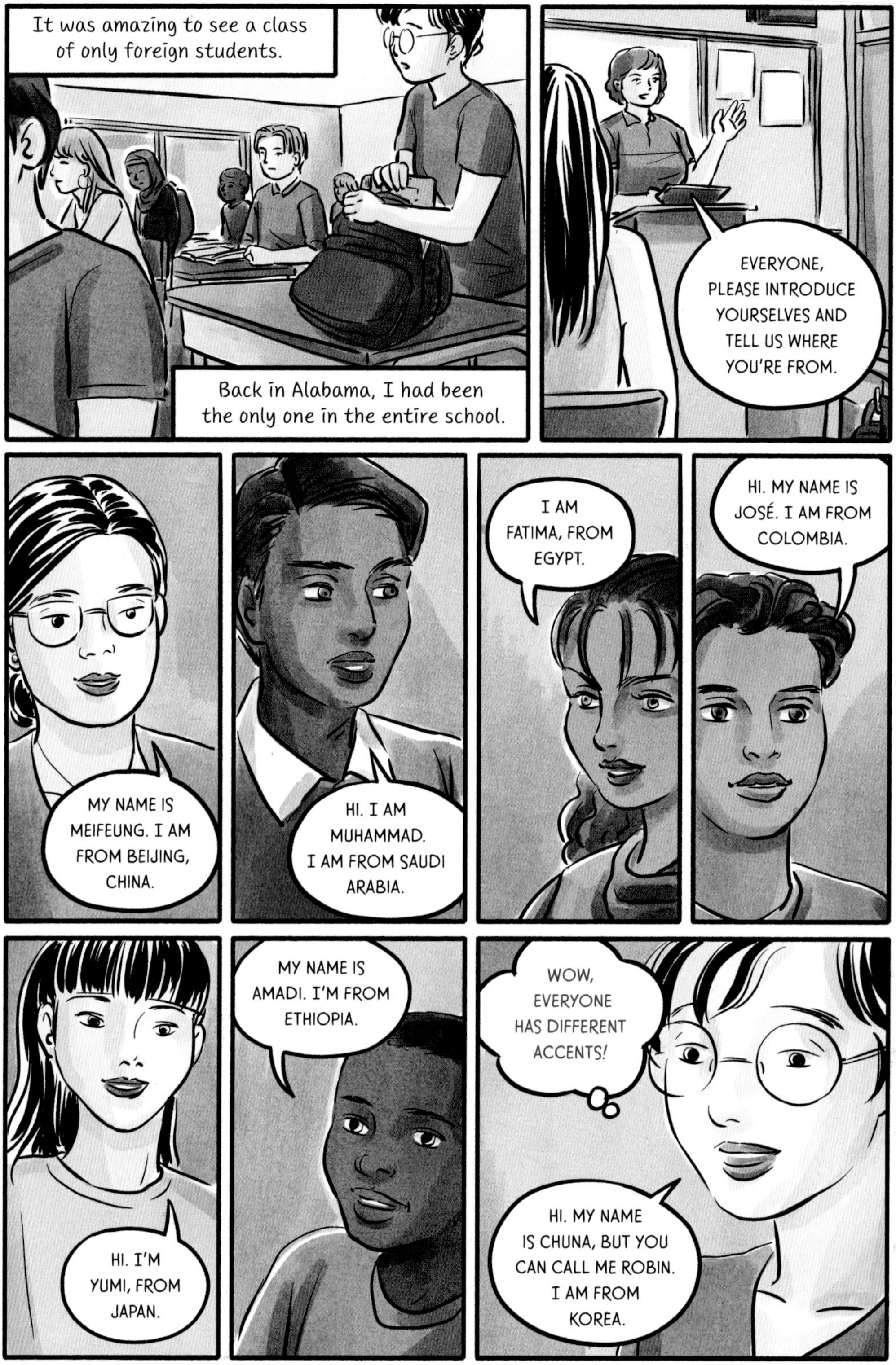

It was amazing to see a class of only foreign students.
Back in Alabama, I had been the only one in the entire school.
EVERYONE, PLEASE INTRODUCE YOURSELVES AND TELL US WHERE YOU'RE FROM.
MY NAME IS MEIFEUNG. I AM FROM BEIJING, CHINA.
HI. I AM MUHAMMAD. I AM FROM SAUDI ARABIA.
I AM FATIMA, FROM EGYPT.
HI. MY NAME IS JOSÉ. I AM FROM COLOMBIA.
HI. I'M YUMI, FROM JAPAN.
MY NAME IS AMADI. I'M FROM ETHIOPIA.
WOW, EVERYONE HAS DIFFERENT ACCENTS!
HI. MY NAME IS CHUNA, BUT YOU CAN CALL ME ROBIN. I AM FROM KOREA.

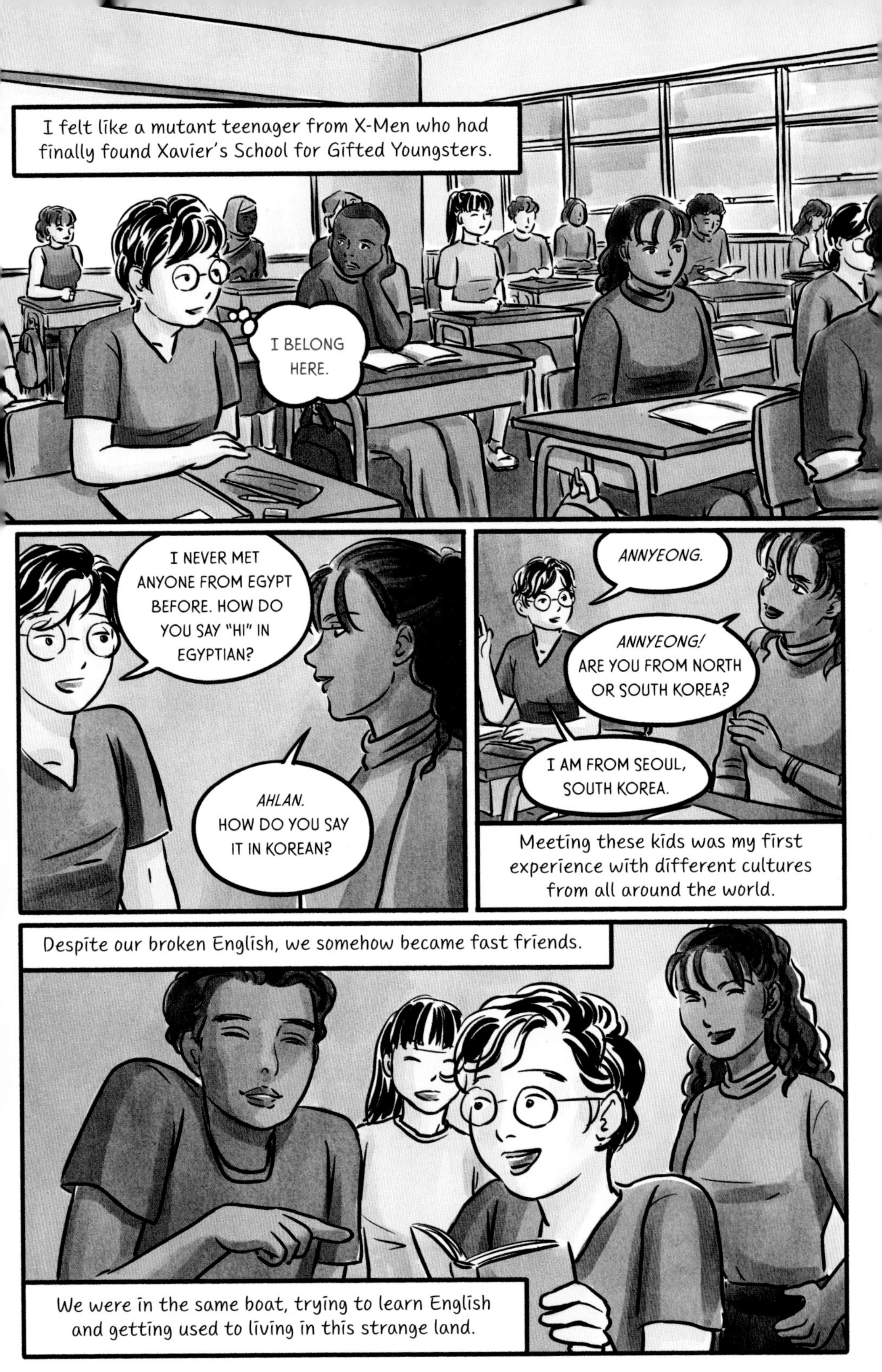
I felt like a mutant teenager from X-Men who had finally found Xavier's School for Gifted Youngsters.
I BELONG HERE.
I NEVER MET ANYONE FROM EGYPT BEFORE. HOW DO YOU SAY "HI" IN EGYPTIAN?
AHLAN. HOW DO YOU SAY IT IN KOREAN?
ANNYEONG.
ANNYEONG! ARE YOU FROM NORTH OR SOUTH KOREA?
I AM FROM SEOUL, SOUTH KOREA.
Meeting these kids was my first experience with different cultures from all around the world.
Despite our broken English, we somehow became fast friends.
We were in the same boat, trying to learn English and getting used to living in this strange land.

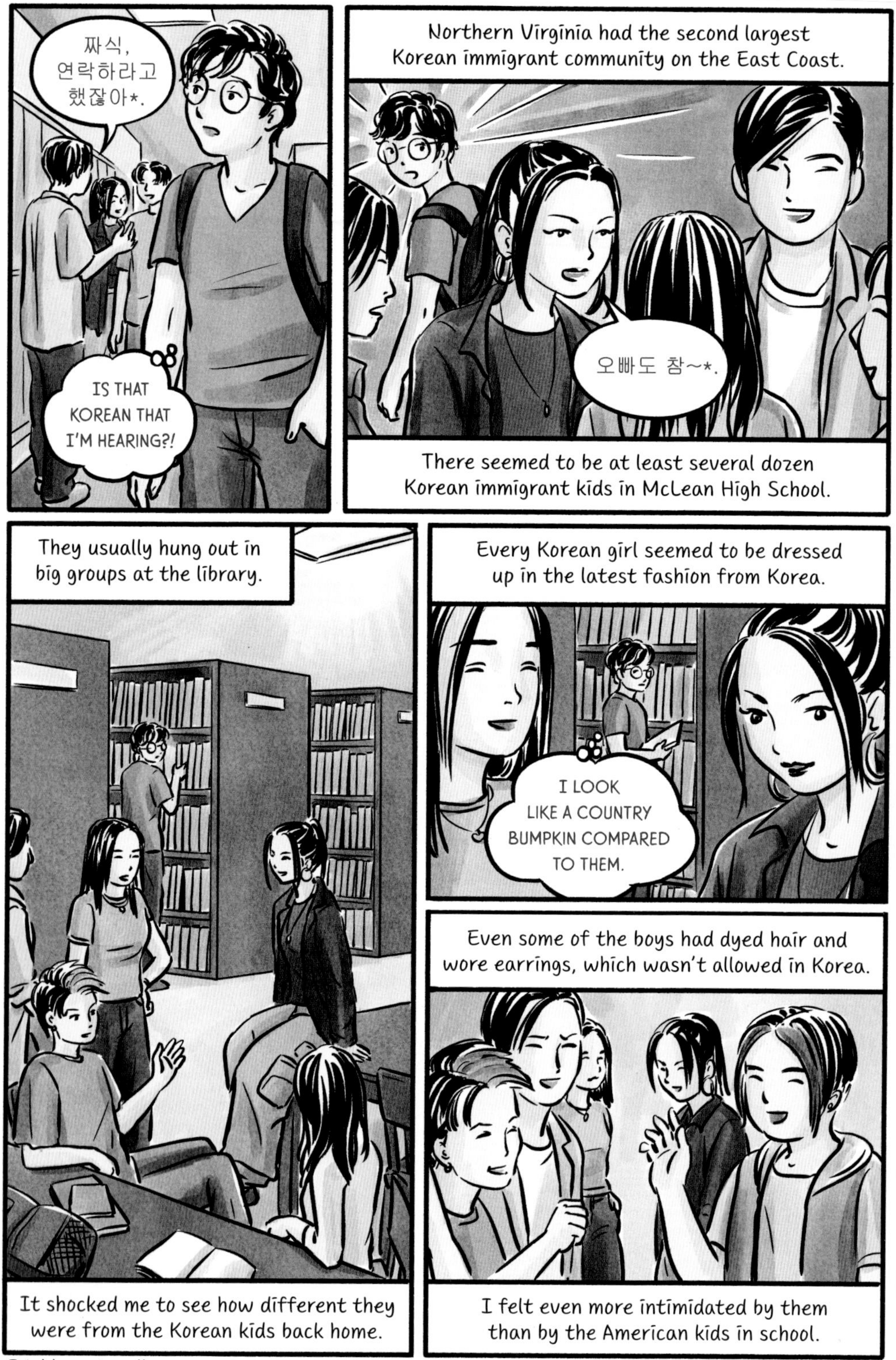
짜식,
연락하라고
했잖아*.
IS THAT KOREAN THAT I'M HEARING?!
Northern Virginia had the second largest Korean immigrant community on the East Coast.
오빠도 참~*.
There seemed to be at least several dozen Korean immigrant kids in McLean High School.
They usually hung out in big groups at the library.
It shocked me to see how different they were from the Korean kids back home.
Every Korean girl seemed to be dressed up in the latest fashion from Korea.
I LOOK LIKE A COUNTRY BUMPKIN COMPARED TO THEM.
Even some of the boys had dyed hair and wore earrings, which wasn't allowed in Korea.
I felt even more intimidated by them than by the American kids in school.

*I told you to call me.
*Oh Brother—

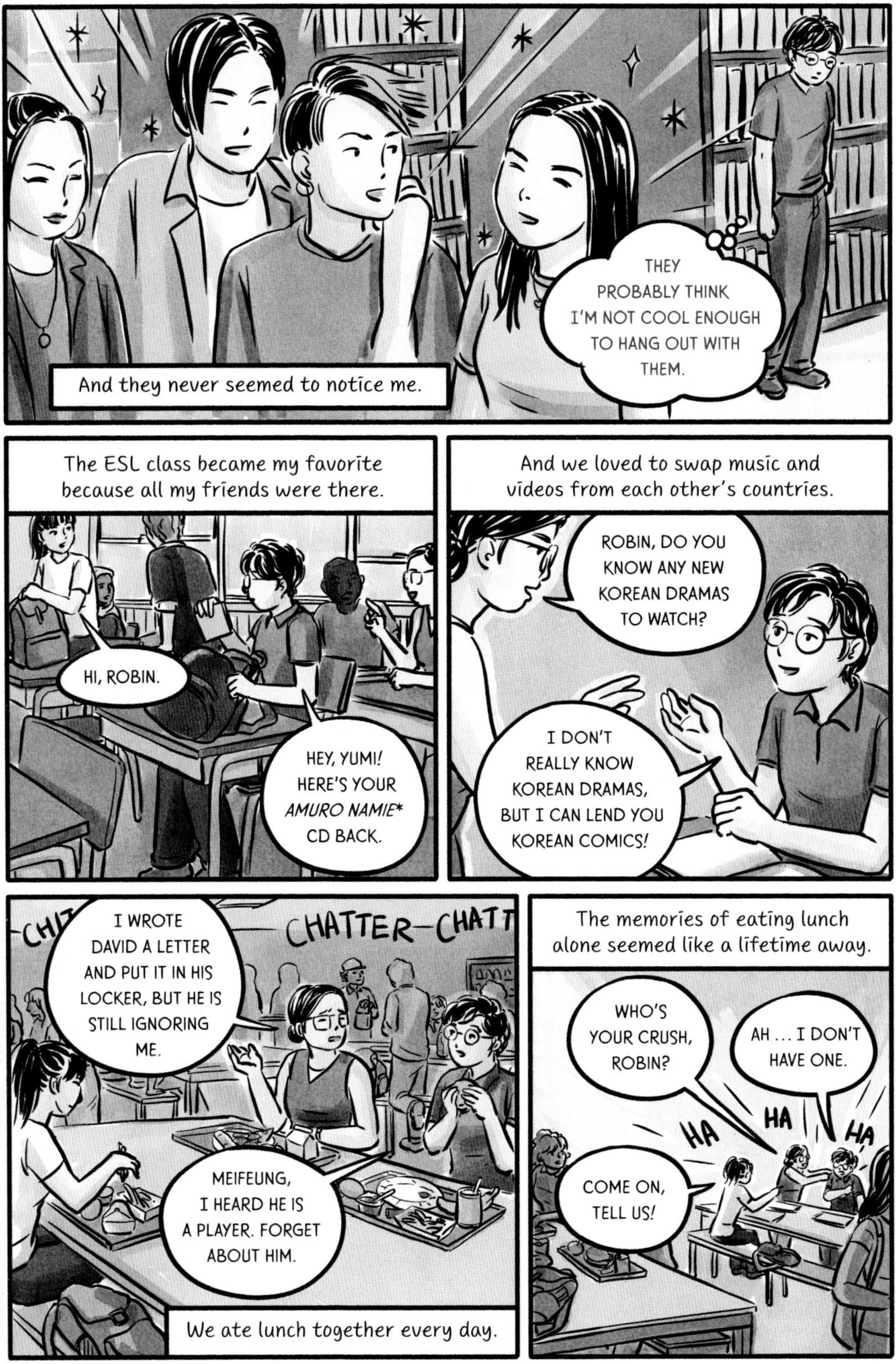
THEY PROBABLY THINK I'M NOT COOL ENOUGH TO HANG OUT WITH THEM.
And they never seemed to notice me.
The ESL class became my favorite because all my friends were there.
HI, ROBIN.
HEY, YUMI! HERE'S YOUR *AMURO NAMIE** CD BACK.
And we loved to swap music and videos from each other's countries.
ROBIN, DO YOU KNOW ANY NEW KOREAN DRAMAS TO WATCH?
I DON'T REALLY KNOW KOREAN DRAMAS, BUT I CAN LEND YOU KOREAN COMICS!
CHATTER—CHATT
I WROTE DAVID A LETTER AND PUT IT IN HIS LOCKER, BUT HE IS STILL IGNORING ME.
MEIFEUNG, I HEARD HE IS A PLAYER. FORGET ABOUT HIM.
We ate lunch together every day.
The memories of eating lunch alone seemed like a lifetime away.
WHO'S YOUR CRUSH, ROBIN?
AH ... I DON'T HAVE ONE.
HA
HA
HA
COME ON, TELL US!

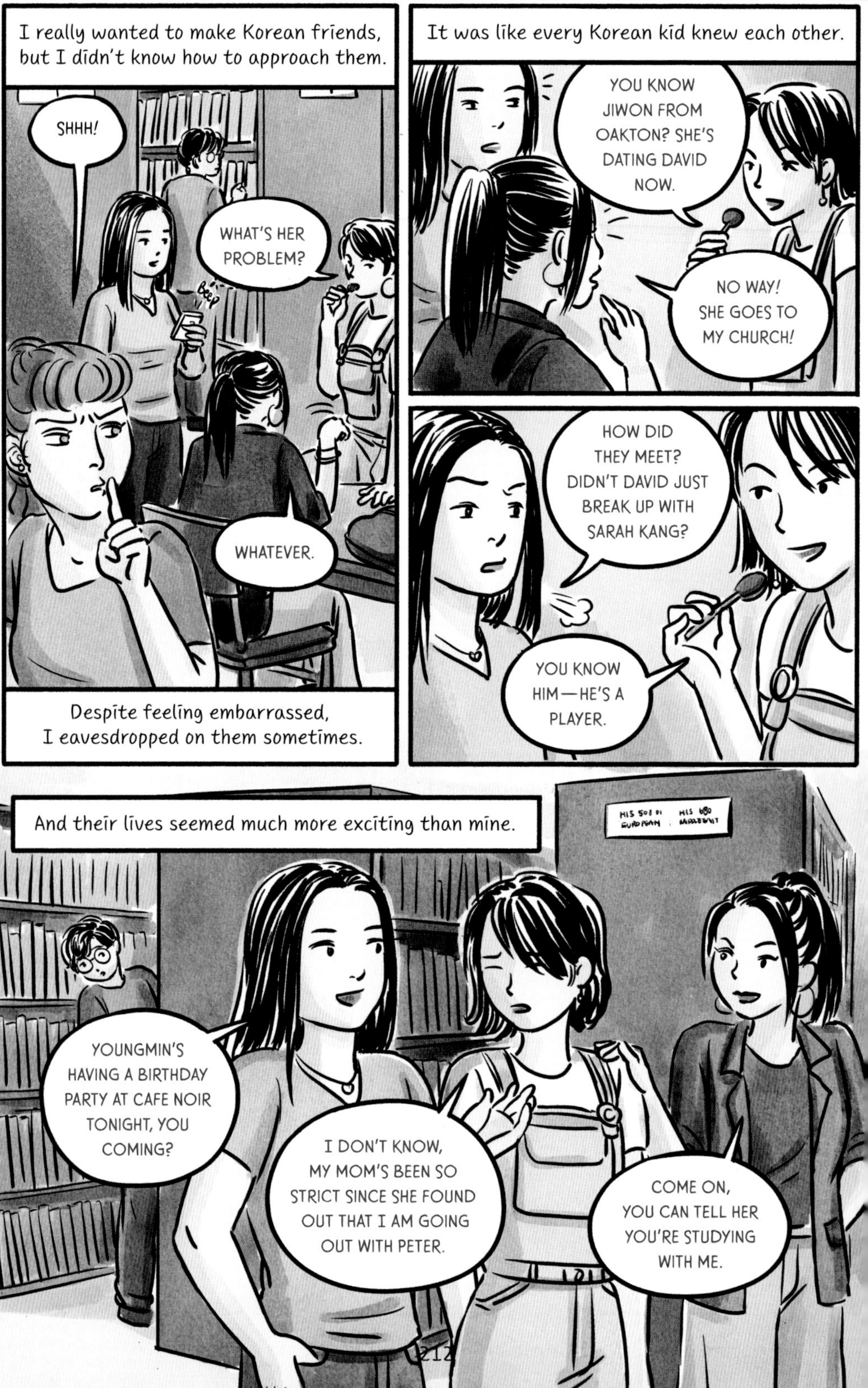
I really wanted to make Korean friends, but I didn't know how to approach them.
SHHH!
WHAT'S HER PROBLEM?
Beep
WHATEVER.
Despite feeling embarrassed, I eavesdropped on them sometimes.
It was like every Korean kid knew each other.
YOU KNOW JIWON FROM OAKTON? SHE'S DATING DAVID NOW.
NO WAY! SHE GOES TO MY CHURCH!
HOW DID THEY MEET? DIDN'T DAVID JUST BREAK UP WITH SARAH KANG?
YOU KNOW HIM—HE'S A PLAYER.
And their lives seemed much more exciting than mine.
YOUNGMIN'S HAVING A BIRTHDAY PARTY AT CAFE NOIR TONIGHT, YOU COMING?
I DON'T KNOW, MY MOM'S BEEN SO STRICT SINCE SHE FOUND OUT THAT I AM GOING OUT WITH PETER.
COME ON, YOU CAN TELL HER YOU'RE STUDYING WITH ME.

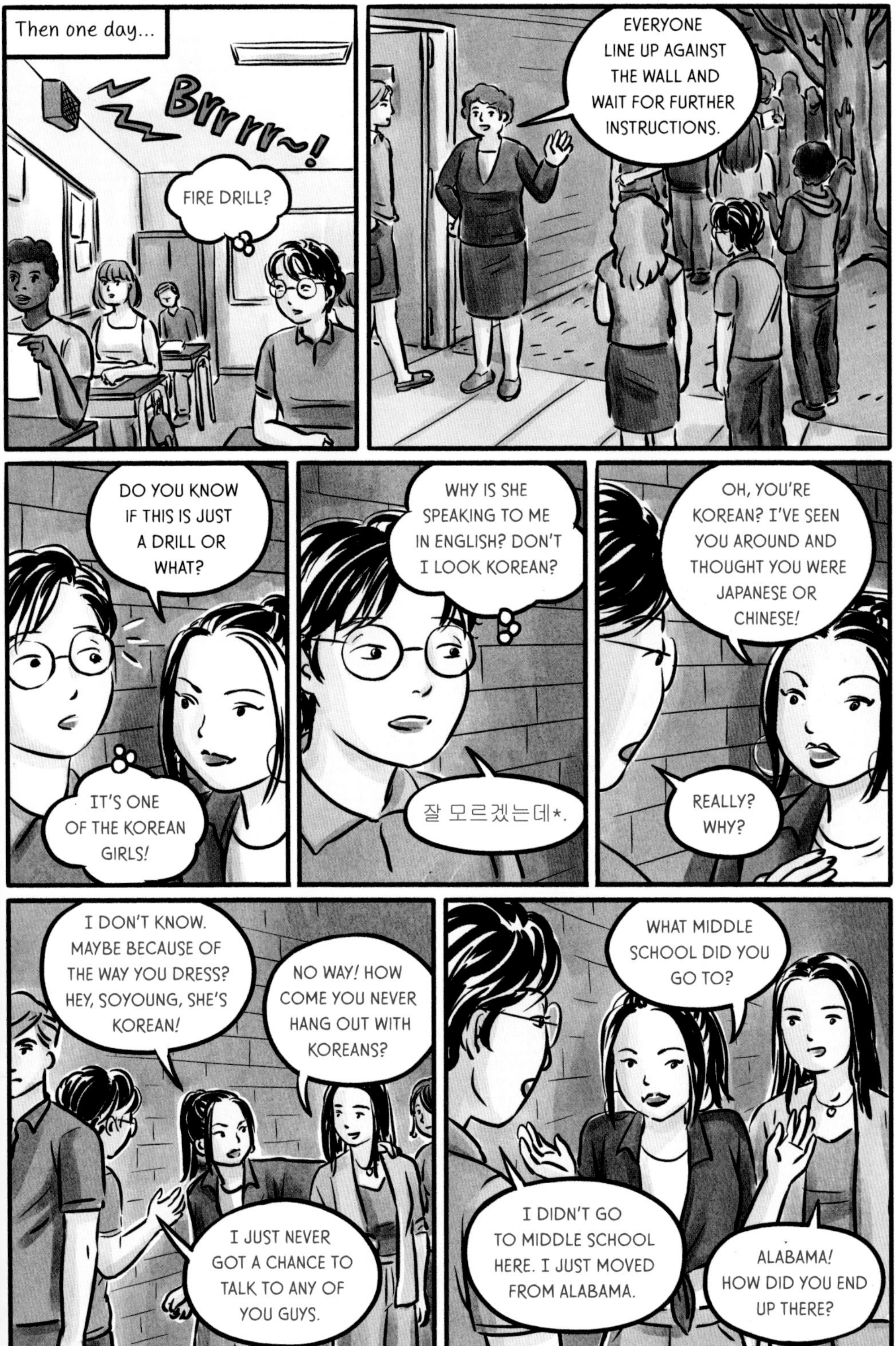
Then one day...
Brrrr~!
FIRE DRILL?
EVERYONE LINE UP AGAINST THE WALL AND WAIT FOR FURTHER INSTRUCTIONS.
DO YOU KNOW IF THIS IS JUST A DRILL OR WHAT?
IT'S ONE OF THE KOREAN GIRLS!
WHY IS SHE SPEAKING TO ME IN ENGLISH? DON'T I LOOK KOREAN?
잘 모르겠는데*.
OH, YOU'RE KOREAN? I'VE SEEN YOU AROUND AND THOUGHT YOU WERE JAPANESE OR CHINESE!
REALLY? WHY?
I DON'T KNOW. MAYBE BECAUSE OF THE WAY YOU DRESS? HEY, SOYOUNG, SHE'S KOREAN!
NO WAY! HOW COME YOU NEVER HANG OUT WITH KOREANS?
I JUST NEVER GOT A CHANCE TO TALK TO ANY OF YOU GUYS.
WHAT MIDDLE SCHOOL DID YOU GO TO?
I DIDN'T GO TO MIDDLE SCHOOL HERE. I JUST MOVED FROM ALABAMA.
ALABAMA! HOW DID YOU END UP THERE?

*I don't know.

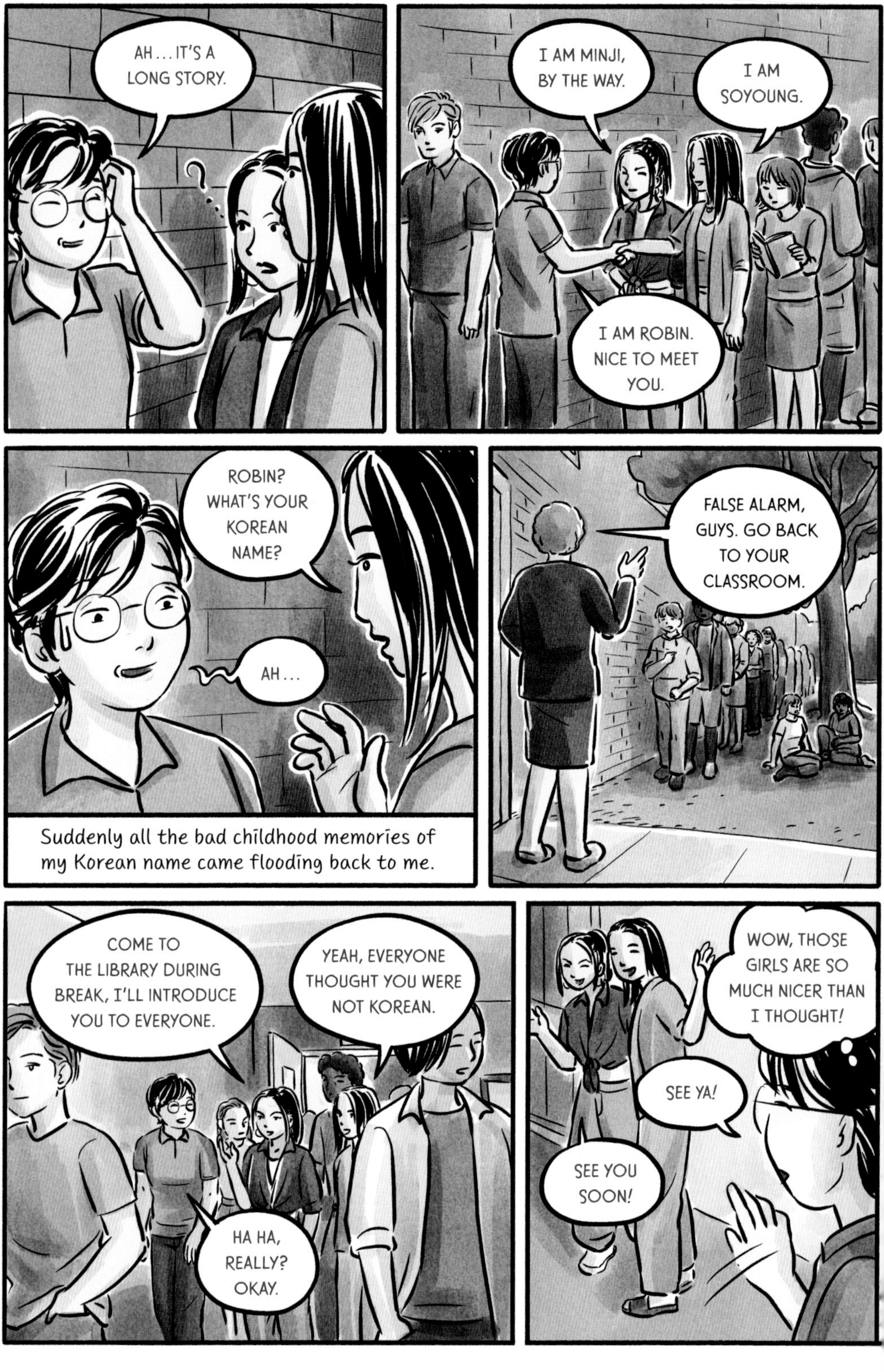
AH... IT'S A LONG STORY.
I AM MINJI, BY THE WAY.
I AM SOYOUNG.
I AM ROBIN. NICE TO MEET YOU.
ROBIN? WHAT'S YOUR KOREAN NAME?
AH...
Suddenly all the bad childhood memories of my Korean name came flooding back to me.
FALSE ALARM, GUYS. GO BACK TO YOUR CLASSROOM.
COME TO THE LIBRARY DURING BREAK, I'LL INTRODUCE YOU TO EVERYONE.
YEAH, EVERYONE THOUGHT YOU WERE NOT KOREAN.
HA HA, REALLY? OKAY.
WOW, THOSE GIRLS ARE SO MUCH NICER THAN I THOUGHT!
SEE YA!
SEE YOU SOON!

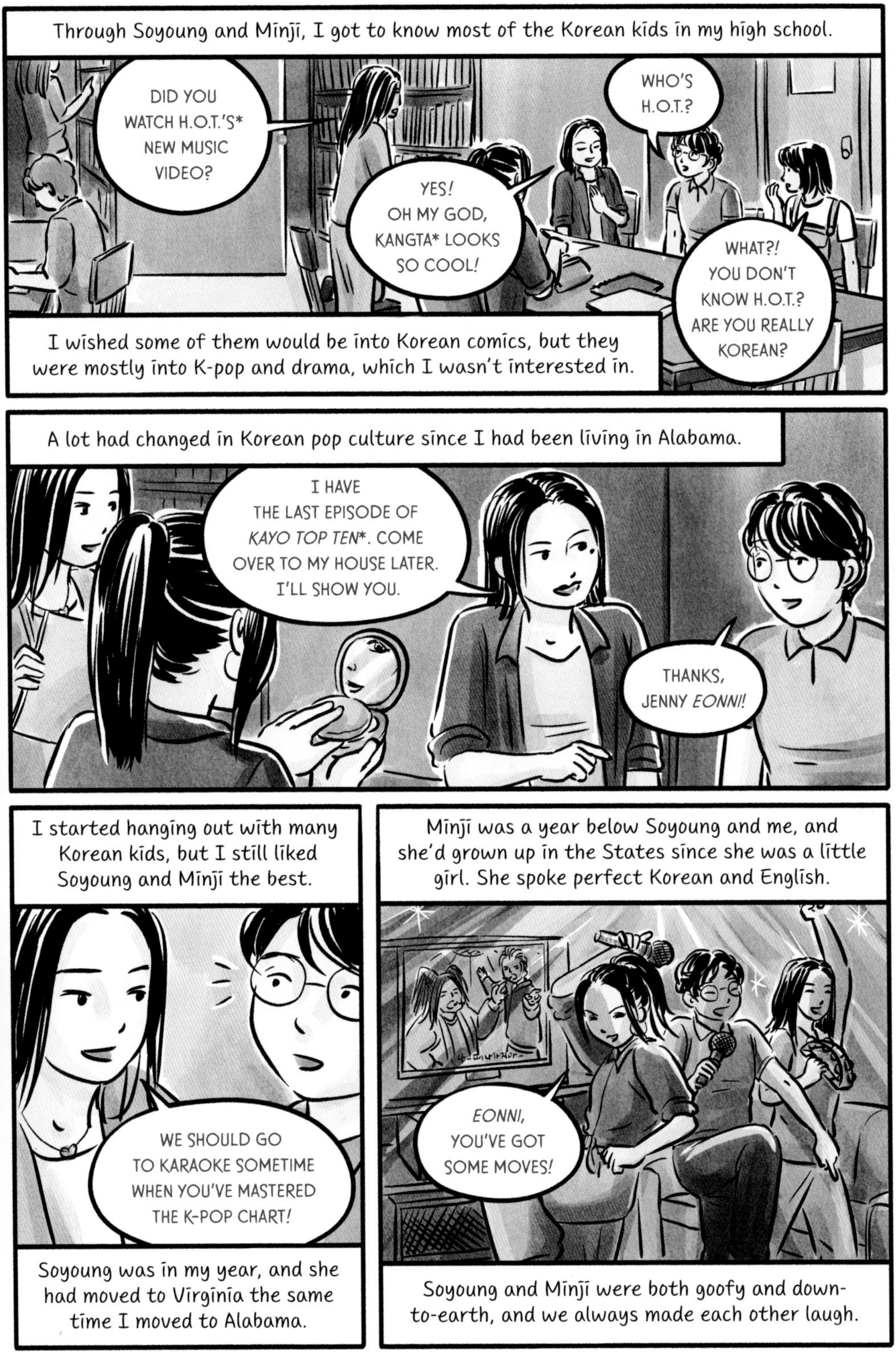
Through Soyoung and Minji, I got to know most of the Korean kids in my high school.
DID YOU WATCH H.O.T.'S* NEW MUSIC VIDEO?
YES! OH MY GOD, KANGTA* LOOKS SO COOL!
WHO'S H.O.T.?
WHAT?! YOU DON'T KNOW H.O.T.? ARE YOU REALLY KOREAN?
I wished some of them would be into Korean comics, but they were mostly into K-pop and drama, which I wasn't interested in.
A lot had changed in Korean pop culture since I had been living in Alabama.
I HAVE THE LAST EPISODE OF *KAYO TOP TEN**. COME OVER TO MY HOUSE LATER. I'LL SHOW YOU.
THANKS, JENNY *EONNI*!
I started hanging out with many Korean kids, but I still liked Soyoung and Minji the best.
WE SHOULD GO TO KARAOKE SOMETIME WHEN YOU'VE MASTERED THE K-POP CHART!
Soyoung was in my year, and she had moved to Virginia the same time I moved to Alabama.
Minji was a year below Soyoung and me, and she'd grown up in the States since she was a little girl. She spoke perfect Korean and English.
EONNI, YOU'VE GOT SOME MOVES!
Soyoung and Minji were both goofy and down-to-earth, and we always made each other laugh.

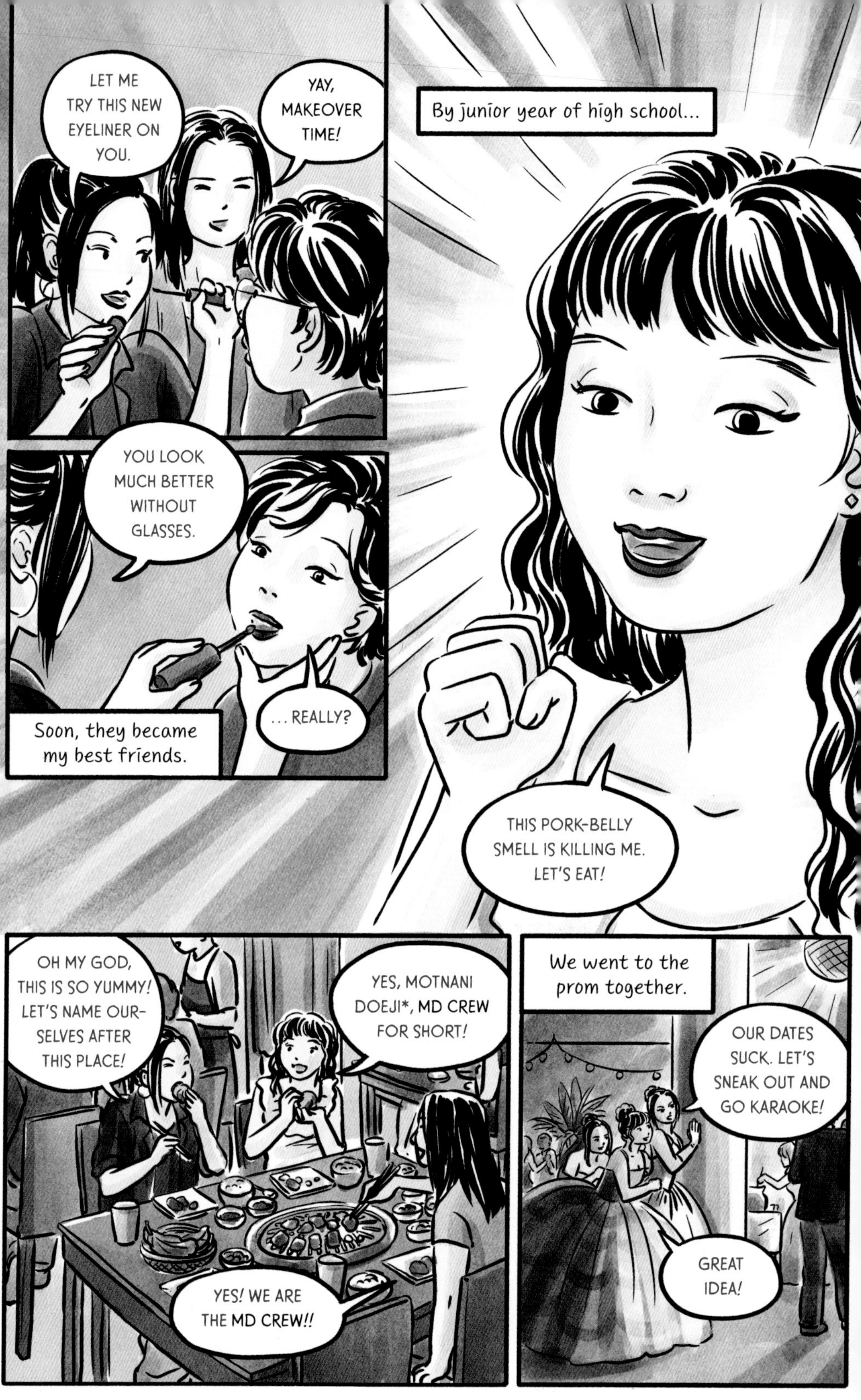
LET ME TRY THIS NEW EYELINER ON YOU.
YAY, MAKEOVER TIME!
By junior year of high school...
THIS PORK-BELLY SMELL IS KILLING ME. LET'S EAT!
YOU LOOK MUCH BETTER WITHOUT GLASSES.
...REALLY?
Soon, they became my best friends.
OH MY GOD, THIS IS SO YUMMY! LET'S NAME OURSELVES AFTER THIS PLACE!
YES, MOTNANI DOEJI*, MD CREW FOR SHORT!
YES! WE ARE THE MD CREW!!
We went to the prom together.
OUR DATES SUCK. LET'S SNEAK OUT AND GO KARAOKE!
GREAT IDEA!

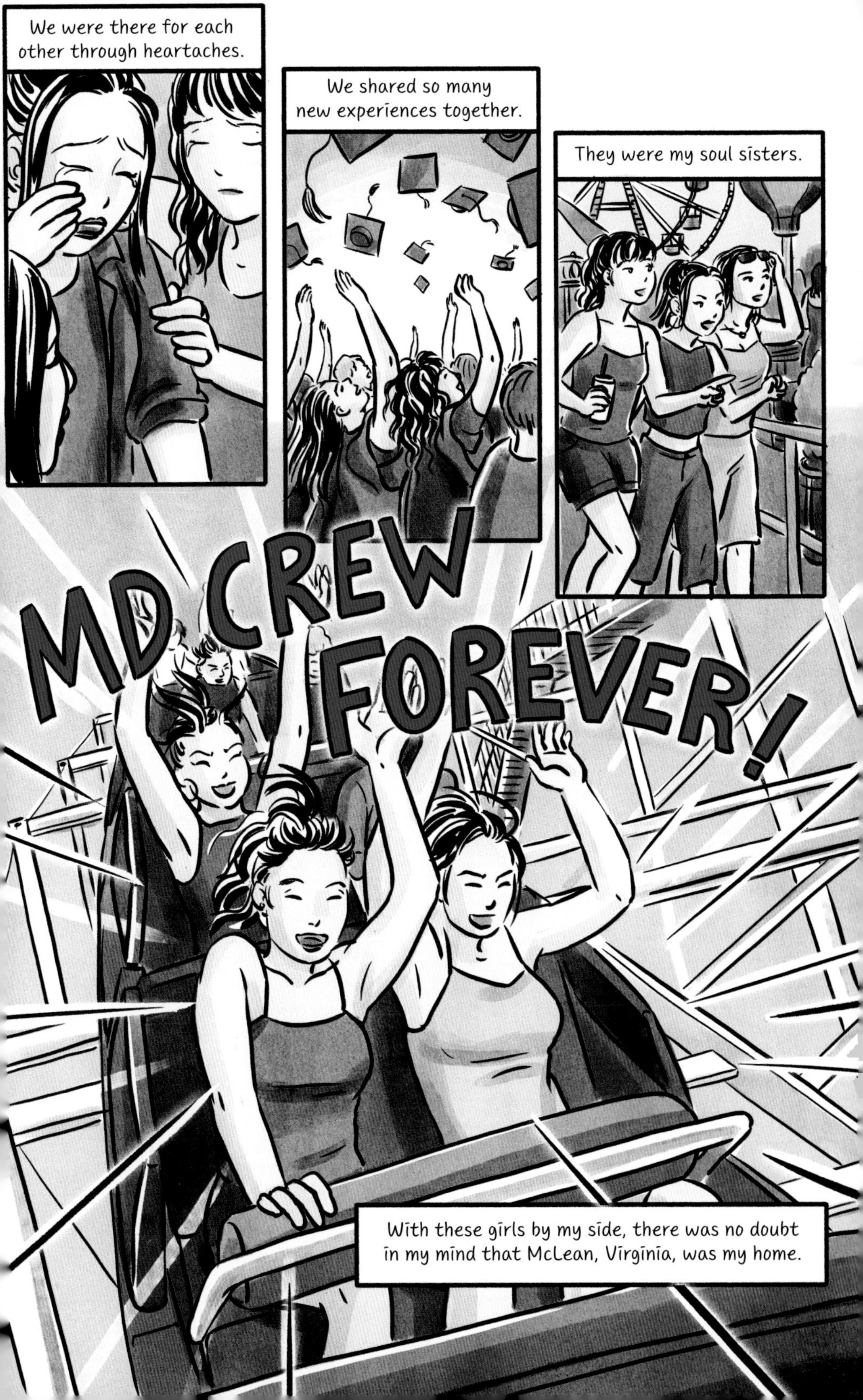

We were there for each other through heartaches.
We shared so many new experiences together.
They were my soul sisters.
MD CREW FOREVER!
With these girls by my side, there was no doubt in my mind that McLean, Virginia, was my home.

Epilogue: Motherland Vs. Homeland

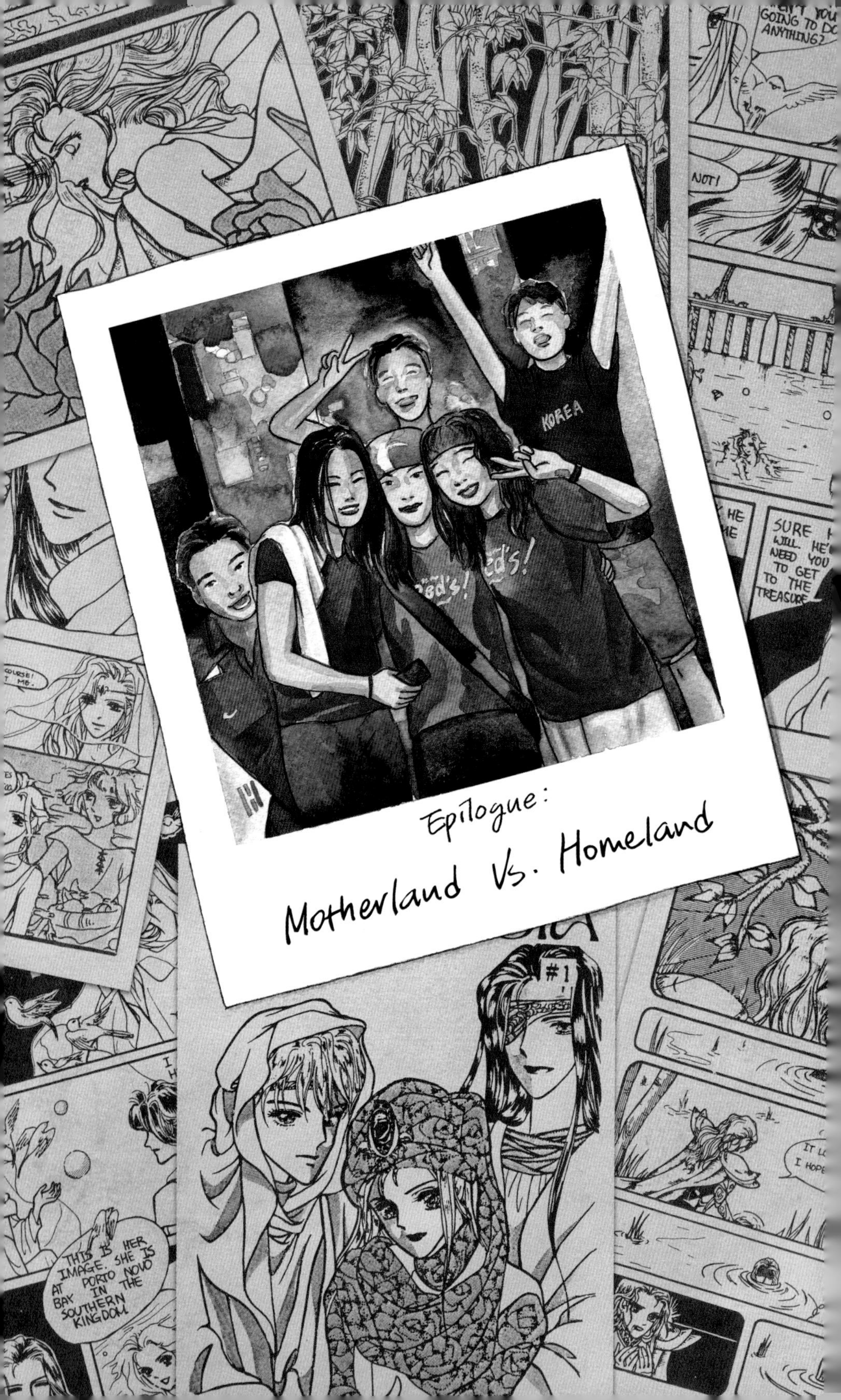
NOT!
KOREA
#1
THIS IS HER IMAGE. SHE IS AT PORTO NOVO BAY IN THE SOUTHERN KINGDOM.

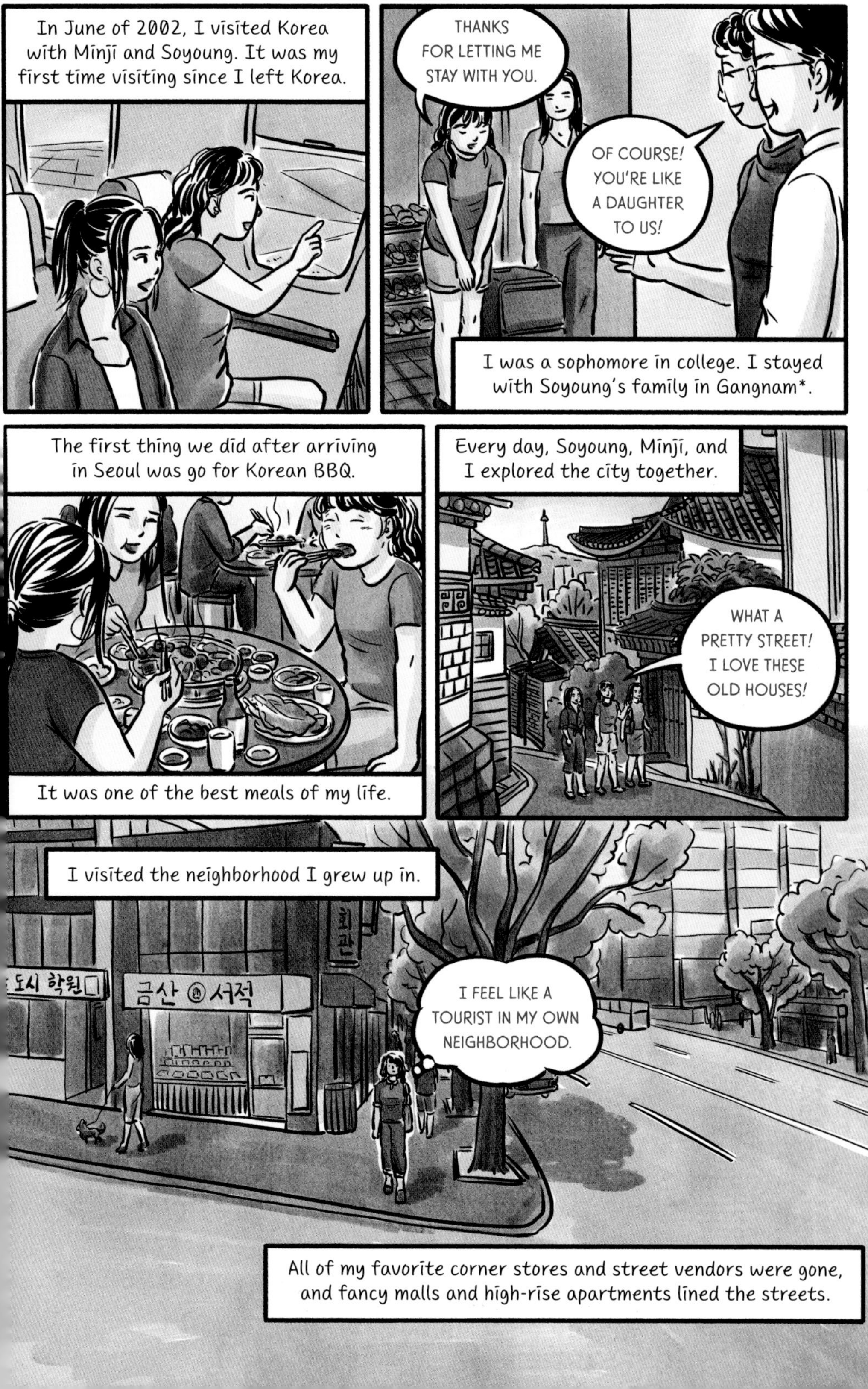
In June of 2002, I visited Korea with Minji and Soyoung. It was my first time visiting since I left Korea.
THANKS FOR LETTING ME STAY WITH YOU.
OF COURSE! YOU'RE LIKE A DAUGHTER TO US!
I was a sophomore in college. I stayed with Soyoung's family in Gangnam*.
The first thing we did after arriving in Seoul was go for Korean BBQ.
It was one of the best meals of my life.
Every day, Soyoung, Minji, and I explored the city together.
WHAT A PRETTY STREET! I LOVE THESE OLD HOUSES!
I visited the neighborhood I grew up in.
회관
도시 학원
금산 서적
I FEEL LIKE A TOURIST IN MY OWN NEIGHBORHOOD.
All of my favorite corner stores and street vendors were gone, and fancy malls and high-rise apartments lined the streets.

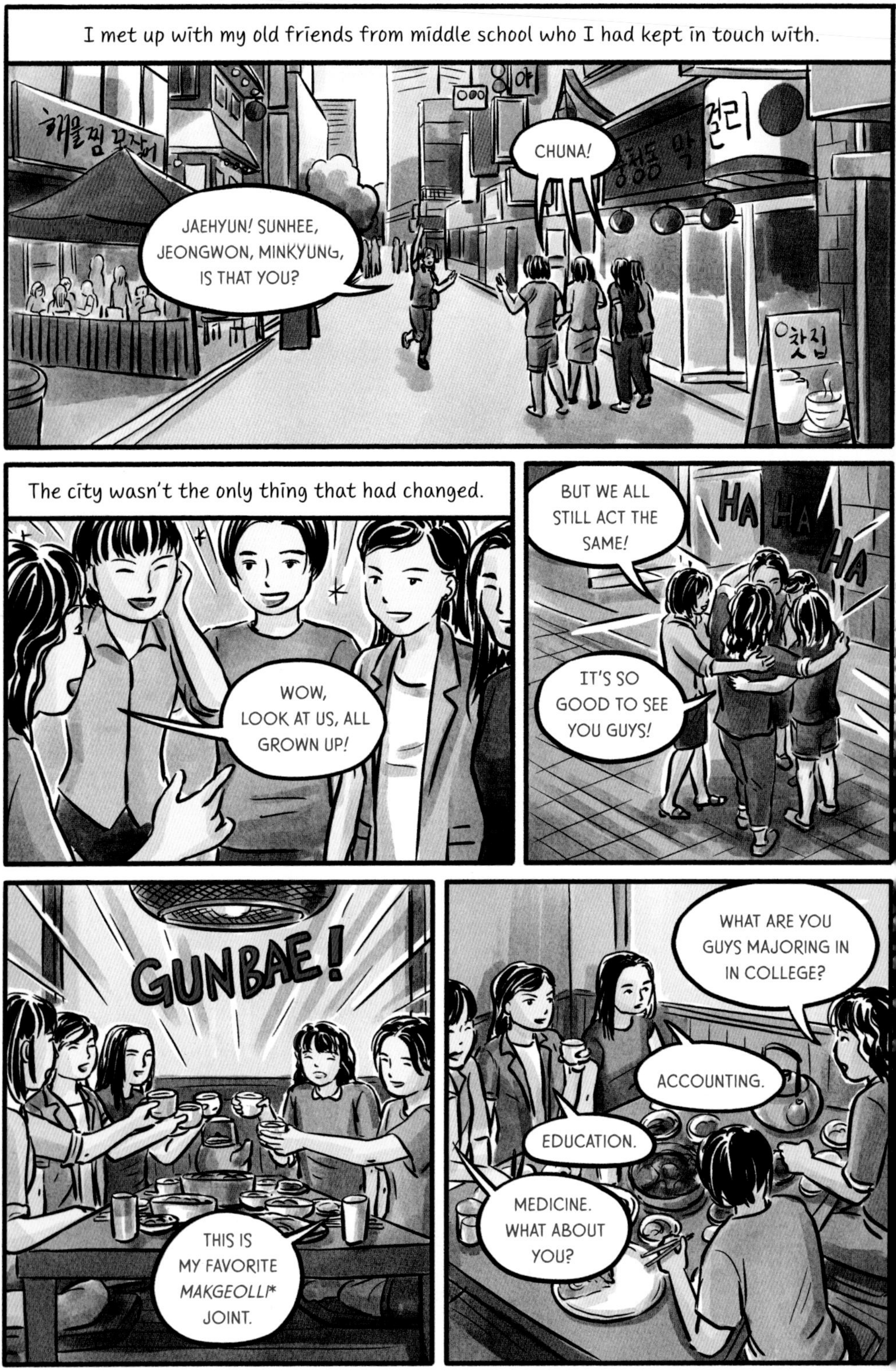
I met up with my old friends from middle school who I had kept in touch with.
JAEHYUN! SUNHEE, JEONGWON, MINKYUNG, IS THAT YOU?
CHUNA!
The city wasn't the only thing that had changed.
WOW, LOOK AT US, ALL GROWN UP!
BUT WE ALL STILL ACT THE SAME!
HA HA HA
IT'S SO GOOD TO SEE YOU GUYS!
GUNBAE!
THIS IS MY FAVORITE *MAKGEOLLI** JOINT.
WHAT ARE YOU GUYS MAJORING IN IN COLLEGE?
ACCOUNTING.
EDUCATION.
MEDICINE. WHAT ABOUT YOU?

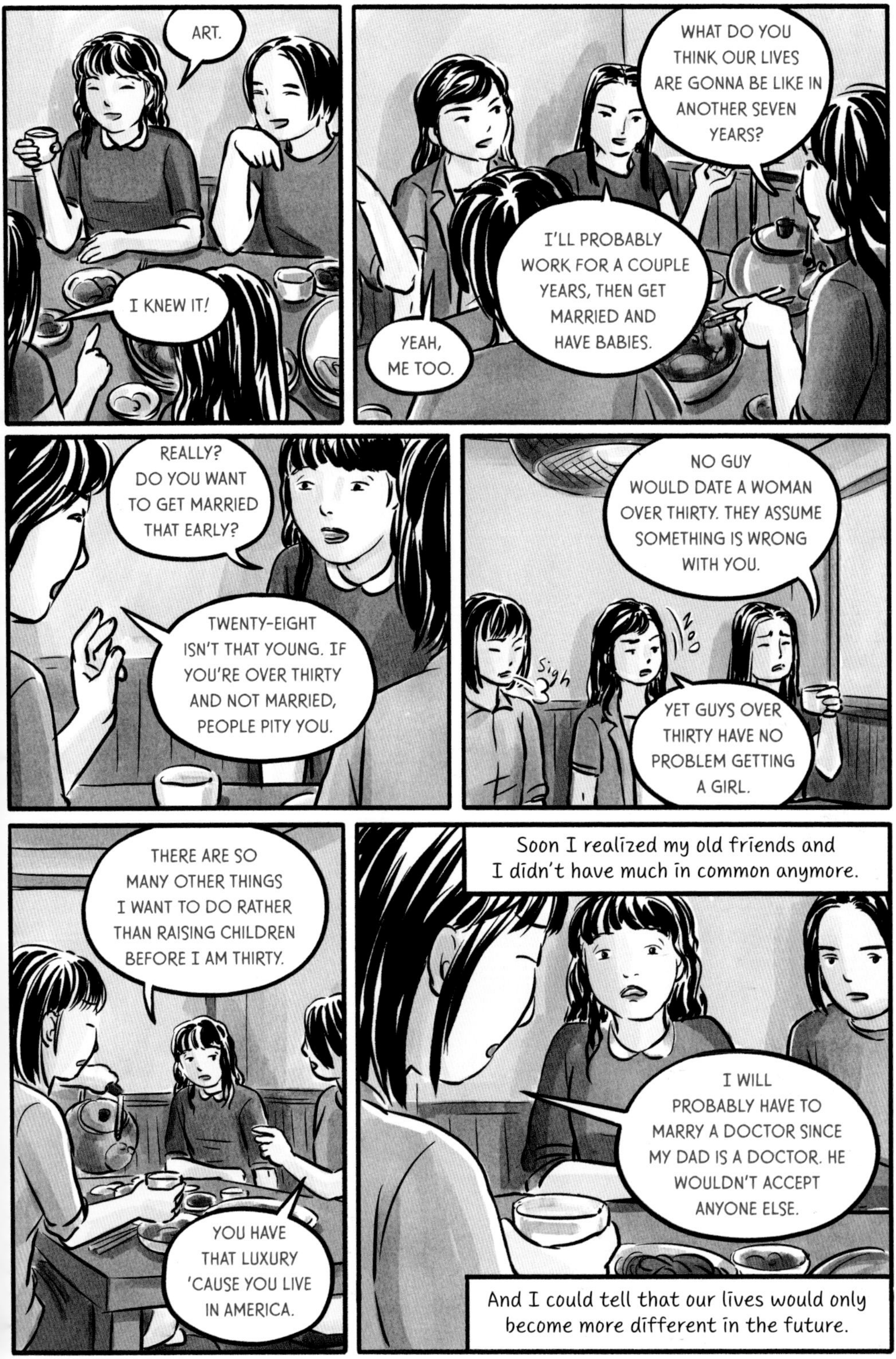
ART.
I KNEW IT!
WHAT DO YOU THINK OUR LIVES ARE GONNA BE LIKE IN ANOTHER SEVEN YEARS?
I'LL PROBABLY WORK FOR A COUPLE YEARS, THEN GET MARRIED AND HAVE BABIES.
YEAH, ME TOO.
REALLY? DO YOU WANT TO GET MARRIED THAT EARLY?
TWENTY-EIGHT ISN'T THAT YOUNG. IF YOU'RE OVER THIRTY AND NOT MARRIED, PEOPLE PITY YOU.
NO GUY WOULD DATE A WOMAN OVER THIRTY. THEY ASSUME SOMETHING IS WRONG WITH YOU.
Sigh
Noo
YET GUYS OVER THIRTY HAVE NO PROBLEM GETTING A GIRL.
THERE ARE SO MANY OTHER THINGS I WANT TO DO RATHER THAN RAISING CHILDREN BEFORE I AM THIRTY.
YOU HAVE THAT LUXURY 'CAUSE YOU LIVE IN AMERICA.
Soon I realized my old friends and I didn't have much in common anymore.
I WILL PROBABLY HAVE TO MARRY A DOCTOR SINCE MY DAD IS A DOCTOR. HE WOULDN'T ACCEPT ANYONE ELSE.
And I could tell that our lives would only become more different in the future.

Korea was hosting the 2002 World Cup, and the entire country was in a festive mood.

ROBIN, MINJI, SOYOUNG! THIS IS LIKE A HIGH SCHOOL REUNION!

JENNY *EONNI!*

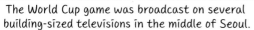

Many of our other high school Korean friends from Virginia were also visiting Korea. We all met up to watch the soccer game together.

The World Cup game was broadcast on several building-sized televisions in the middle of Seoul.

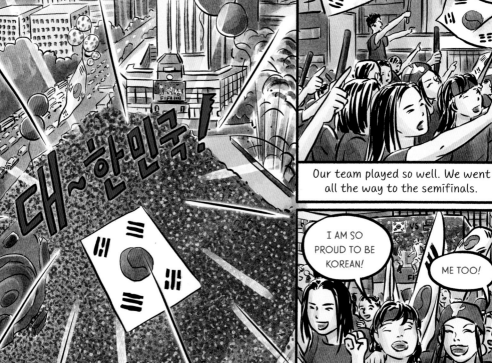

Our team played so well. We went all the way to the semifinals.

The entire country wore our team color, red, and cheered together. It was the biggest celebration of Korean patriotic spirit I'd ever seen.

I AM SO PROUD TO BE KOREAN!

ME TOO!

I had never been a sports fan, but the passion everyone felt for our team and country was infectious.

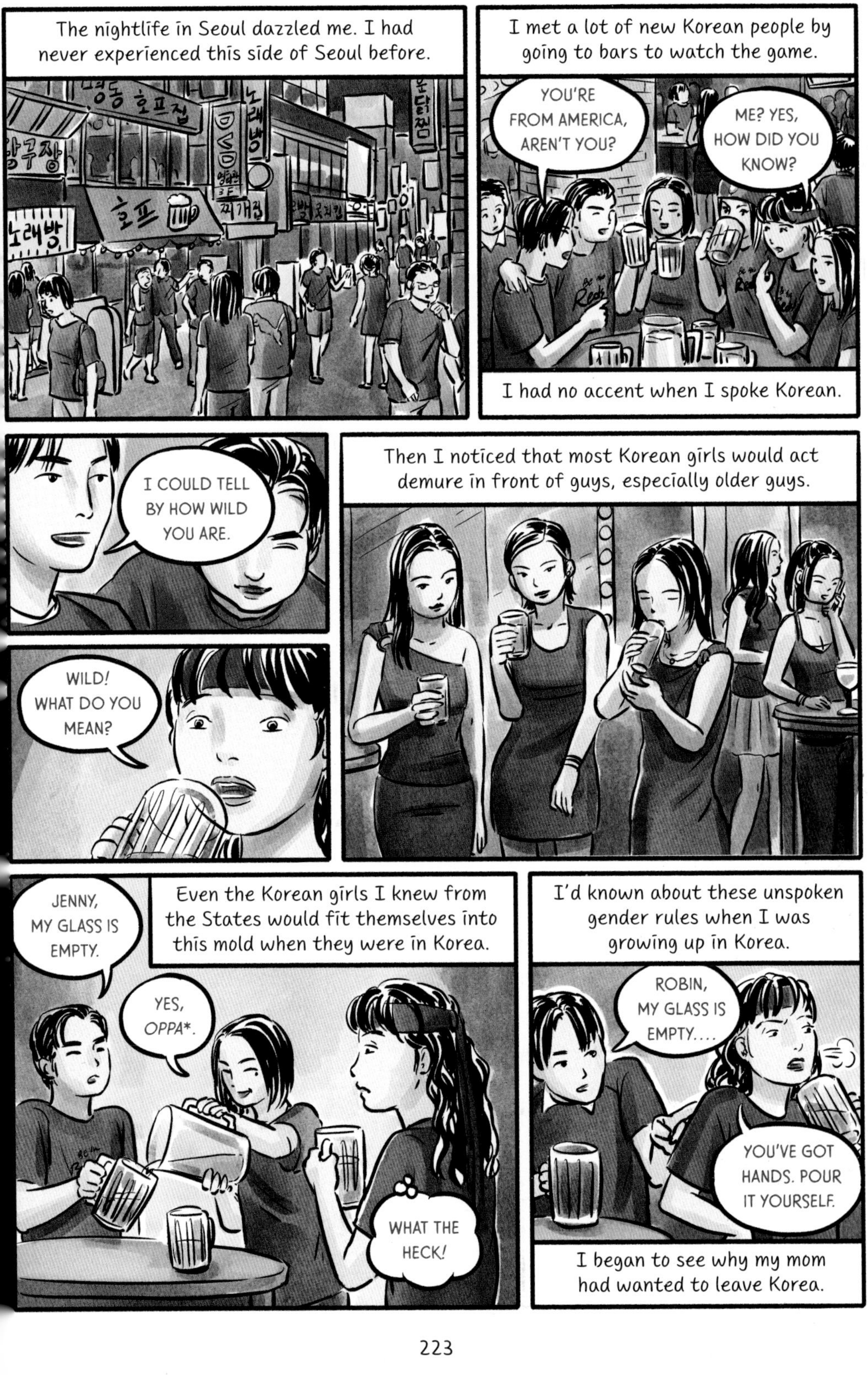
The nightlife in Seoul dazzled me. I had never experienced this side of Seoul before.
호프
노래방
DVD
찌개집
I met a lot of new Korean people by going to bars to watch the game.
YOU'RE FROM AMERICA, AREN'T YOU?
ME? YES, HOW DID YOU KNOW?
I had no accent when I spoke Korean.
I COULD TELL BY HOW WILD YOU ARE.
WILD! WHAT DO YOU MEAN?
Then I noticed that most Korean girls would act demure in front of guys, especially older guys.
JENNY, MY GLASS IS EMPTY.
Even the Korean girls I knew from the States would fit themselves into this mold when they were in Korea.
YES, OPPA*.
WHAT THE HECK!
I'd known about these unspoken gender rules when I was growing up in Korea.
ROBIN, MY GLASS IS EMPTY....
YOU'VE GOT HANDS. POUR IT YOURSELF.
I began to see why my mom had wanted to leave Korea.

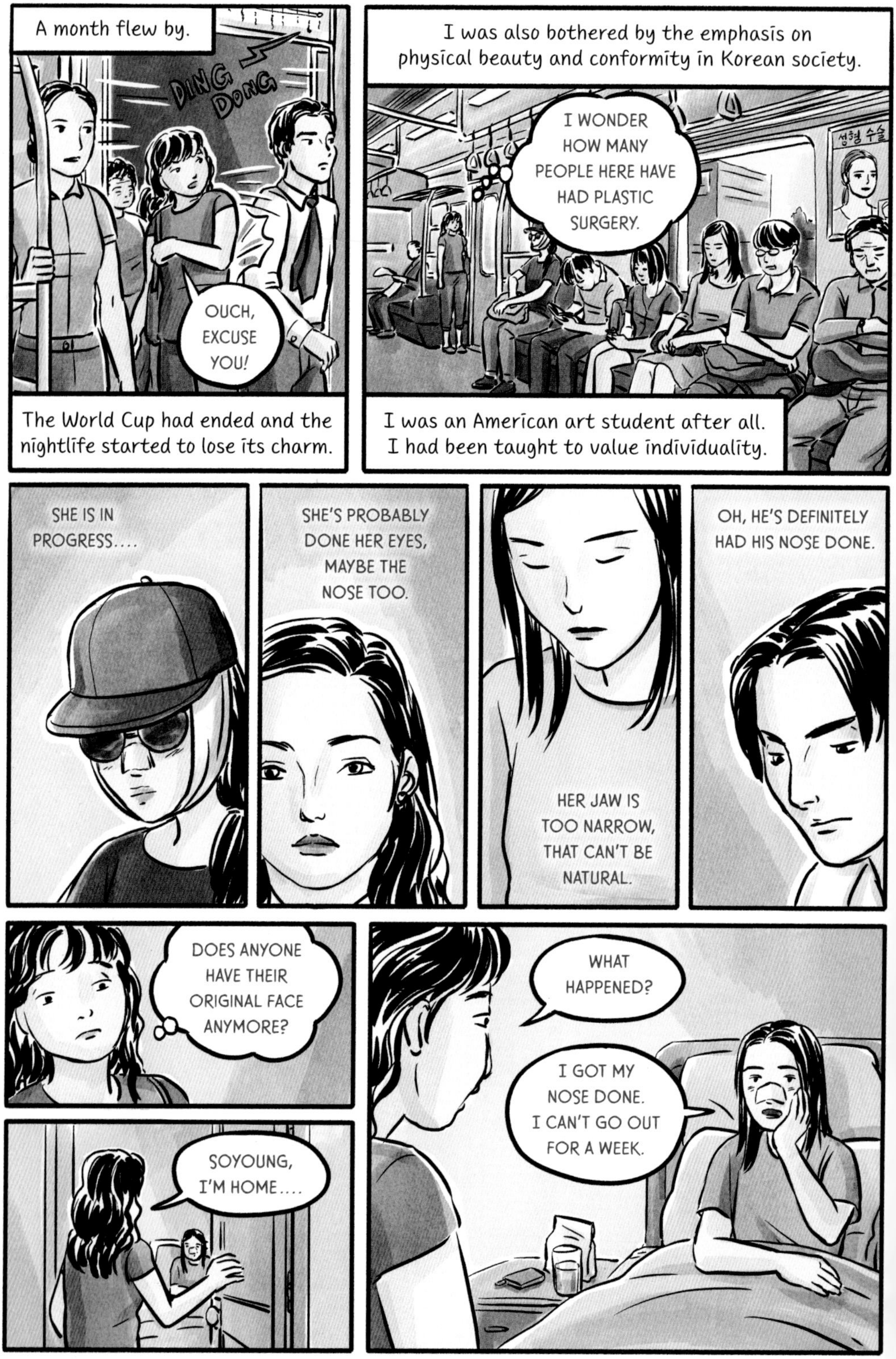
A month flew by.
DING DONG
OUCH, EXCUSE YOU!
The World Cup had ended and the nightlife started to lose its charm.
I was also bothered by the emphasis on physical beauty and conformity in Korean society.
I WONDER HOW MANY PEOPLE HERE HAVE HAD PLASTIC SURGERY.
성형 수술
I was an American art student after all. I had been taught to value individuality.
SHE IS IN PROGRESS....
SHE'S PROBABLY DONE HER EYES, MAYBE THE NOSE TOO.
HER JAW IS TOO NARROW, THAT CAN'T BE NATURAL.
OH, HE'S DEFINITELY HAD HIS NOSE DONE.
DOES ANYONE HAVE THEIR ORIGINAL FACE ANYMORE?
SOYOUNG, I'M HOME....
WHAT HAPPENED?
I GOT MY NOSE DONE. I CAN'T GO OUT FOR A WEEK.

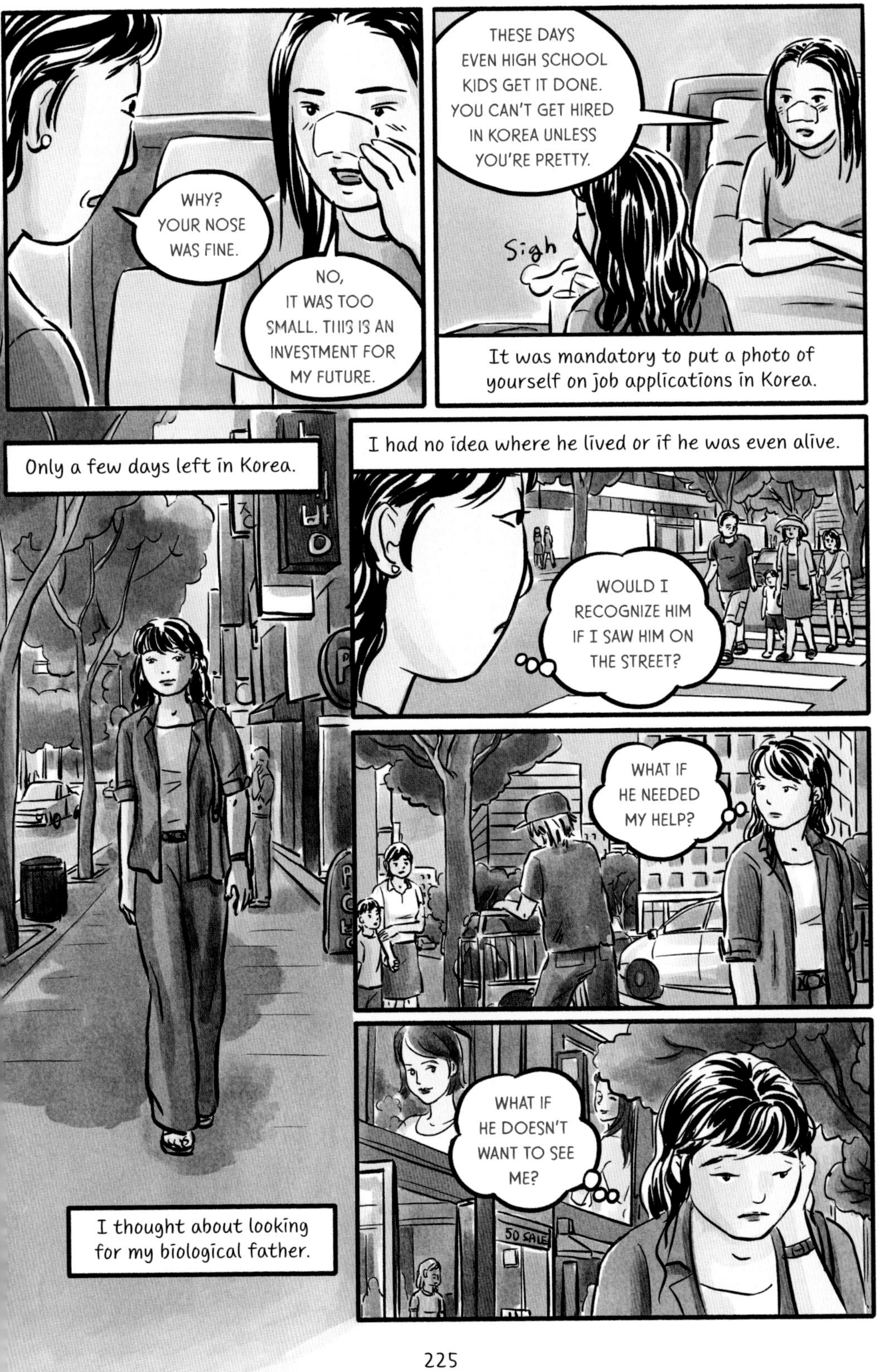
WHY? YOUR NOSE WAS FINE.
NO, IT WAS TOO SMALL. THIS IS AN INVESTMENT FOR MY FUTURE.
THESE DAYS EVEN HIGH SCHOOL KIDS GET IT DONE. YOU CAN'T GET HIRED IN KOREA UNLESS YOU'RE PRETTY.
Sigh
It was mandatory to put a photo of yourself on job applications in Korea.
Only a few days left in Korea.
I thought about looking for my biological father.
I had no idea where he lived or if he was even alive.
WOULD I RECOGNIZE HIM IF I SAW HIM ON THE STREET?
WHAT IF HE NEEDED MY HELP?
WHAT IF HE DOESN'T WANT TO SEE ME?

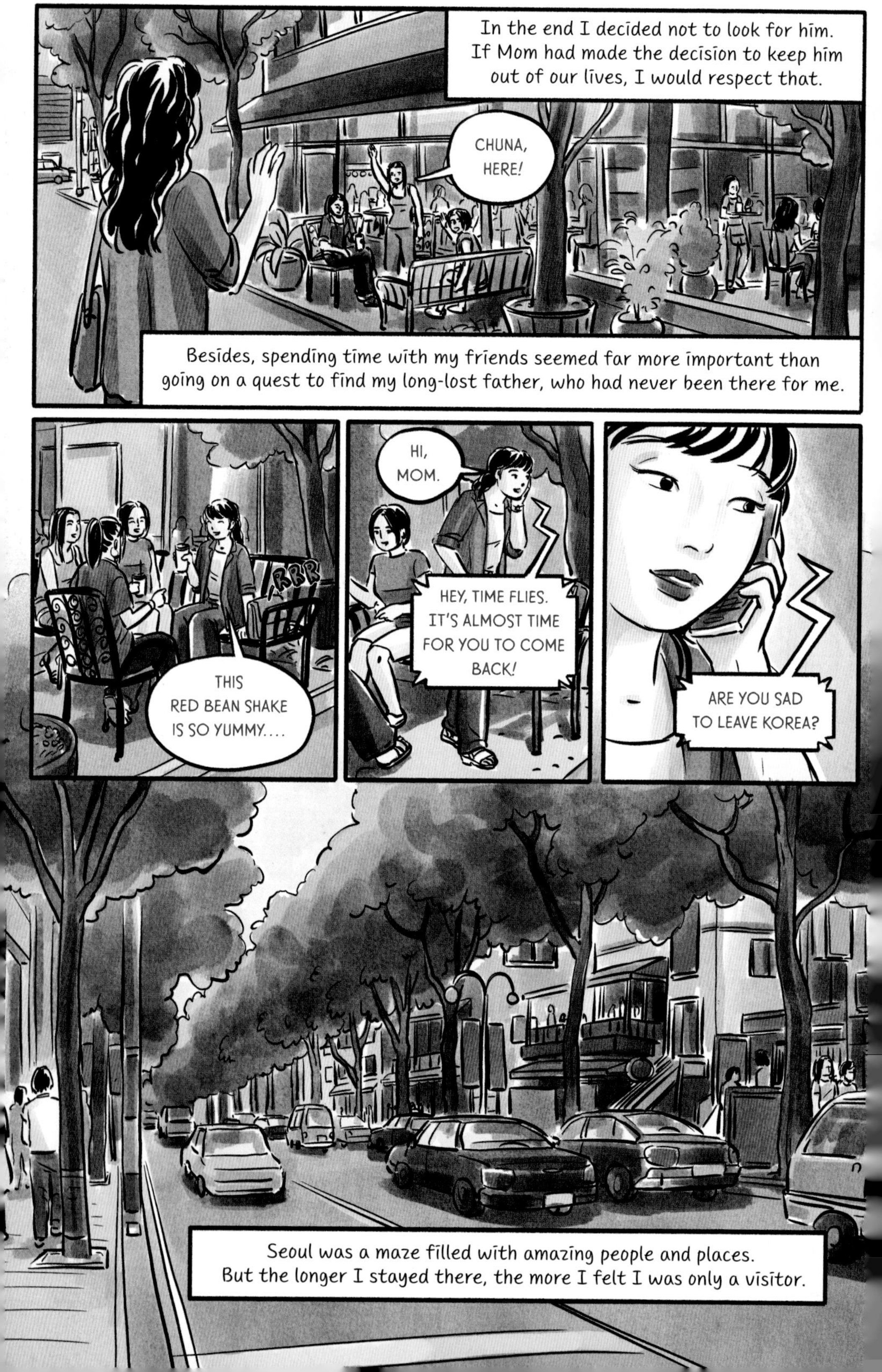
In the end I decided not to look for him. If Mom had made the decision to keep him out of our lives, I would respect that.
CHUNA, HERE!
Besides, spending time with my friends seemed far more important than going on a quest to find my long-lost father, who had never been there for me.
RBR
THIS RED BEAN SHAKE IS SO YUMMY....
HI, MOM.
HEY, TIME FLIES. IT'S ALMOST TIME FOR YOU TO COME BACK!
ARE YOU SAD TO LEAVE KOREA?
Seoul was a maze filled with amazing people and places. But the longer I stayed there, the more I felt I was only a visitor.

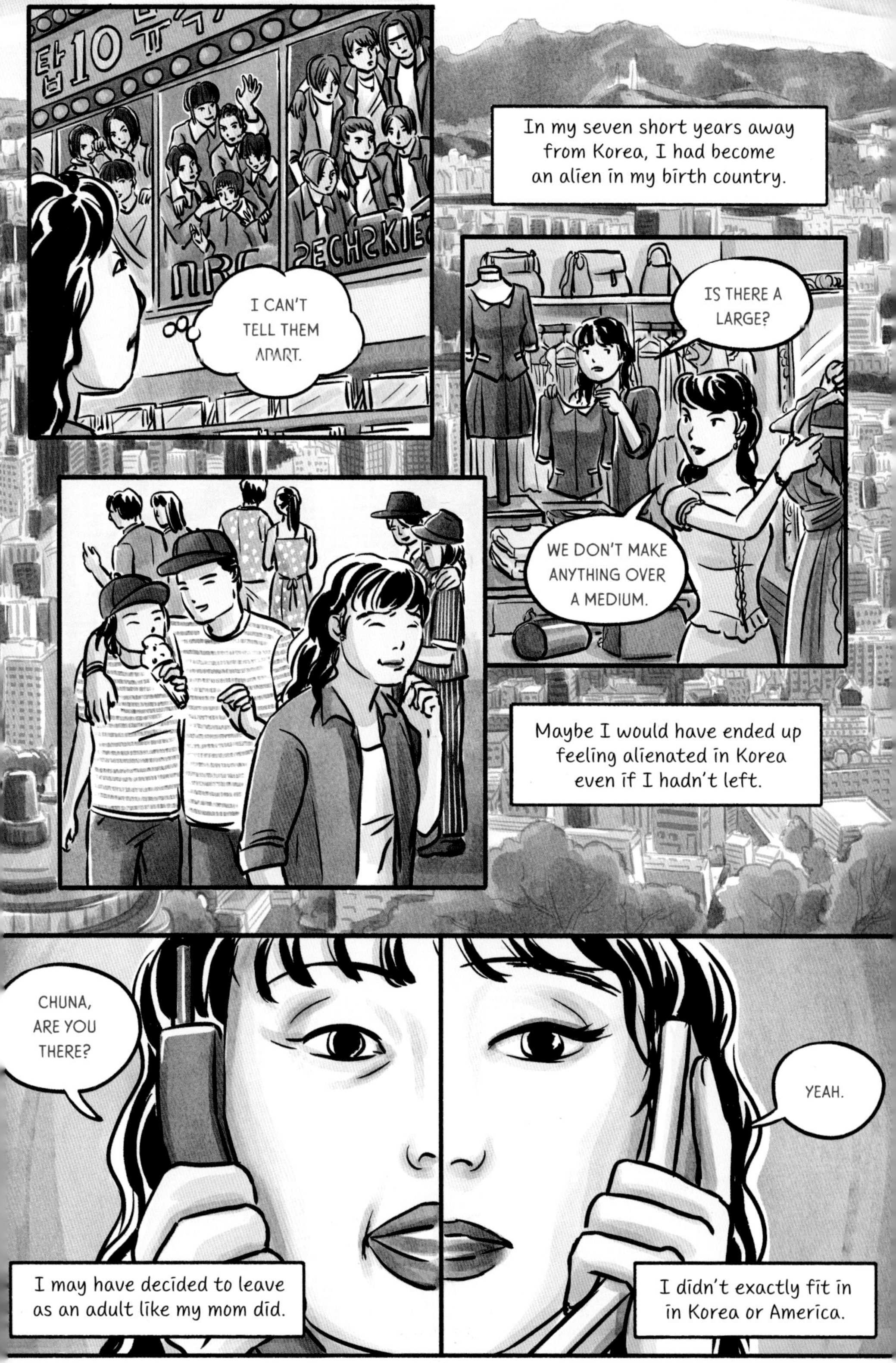
I CAN'T TELL THEM APART.
In my seven short years away from Korea, I had become an alien in my birth country.
IS THERE A LARGE?
WE DON'T MAKE ANYTHING OVER A MEDIUM.
Maybe I would have ended up feeling alienated in Korea even if I hadn't left.
CHUNA, ARE YOU THERE?
I may have decided to leave as an adult like my mom did.
YEAH.
I didn't exactly fit in in Korea or America.

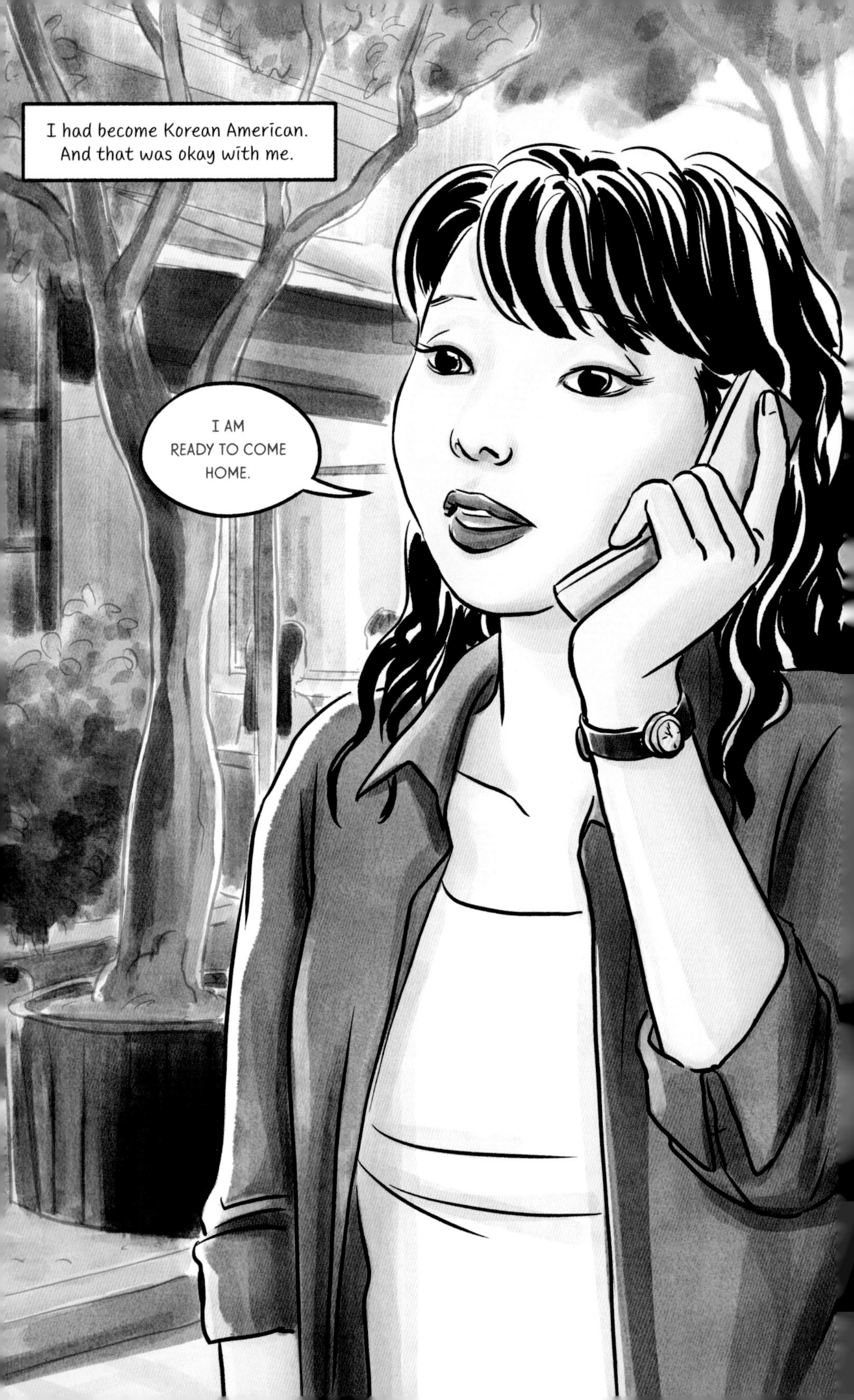

I had become Korean American.
And that was okay with me.
I AM READY TO COME HOME.

Glossary

Amuro Namie: Japanese pop star from the 1990s. Think the Britney Spears of Japan.

Anime: Japanese animated TV series and films

Bungeoppang (붕어빵): Korean street snack of waffles filled with sweet red-bean paste. It is shaped like a fish, which is where its name comes from: Bungeo (fish) ppang (bread).

Eonni (언니): Term for a female to call her older female relatives or older female friends

Gangnam (강남): A district in Seoul. Yes, the same one from popular K-pop song "Gangnam Style," by Psy.

Gomujul (고무줄): Korean version of jumping rope

Hagwon (학원): Cram school in South Korea. These for-profit institutes can provide supplementary education outside of regular school education. They can also specialize in sports, music, and art for extracurricular activities.

H.O.T.: A Korean boy band from the mid 1990s. Think NSYNC of Korea.

Hotteok (호떡): Korean street food of fried yeasty bread with various fillings. Most common fillings are brown sugar with crushed nuts or sweet potato noodles.

Kangta (강타): The most popular member of H.O.T.

Kayo Top Ten (가요톱10): The most influential K-pop chart-ranking show from the 1980s through the '90s

Kimchi (김치): Korean fermented vegetable side dish. Most common vegetables used are napa cabbage and daikon radish.

Makgeolli (막걸리): Traditional Korean rice wine

Manga: Japanese comics

Motnani Doeji (못난이돼지): Means "ugly pig." It was the name of our favorite restaurant, which specialized in grilled pork belly.

Oppa (오빠): A term for a female to call her older male relatives or older male friends

Patbingsu (팥빙수): Korean summer treat of shaved ice topped with sweet red beans, rice cake, fruits, and condensed milk

RG Veda: A fantasy comic series by CLAMP, an all-female Japanese cartoonists' group. It was first published in Japan in 1989 as CLAMP's debut. The plot is based on Vedic mythology contained in the Rigveda.

Sailor Moon: A popular Japanese comic series by Naoko Takeuchi. It was later adapted into an animated TV series and became one of the first Japanese comics to break into the American market, in the mid-1990s.

Tteokbokki (떡볶이): Korean street food made with rice cake, fish cake, and boiled egg, cooked in Korean red pepper sauce

Tteokkochi (떡꼬치): Fried rice cake skewers

Twigim (튀김): Korean street food that is battered and fried. Most commonly made with squid legs, assorted vegetables, or potato.

Acknowledgments

For most of my life, I never truly understood why Mom had uprooted our lives in Korea and caused us so much pain by moving to America. Our lives in Korea didn't seem that bad at all. Mom was a successful business owner and I was doing well in school. Whenever I asked Mom why, she would give me the most nonchalant answers like: "America is a better country than Korea." Or, "There are so many golf courses in America that I want to play on." Mom is an avid golfer, to the point that she wants her ashes to be spread on her favorite golf courses all over the world. But still, these answers just didn't cut it for me. If I pressed her further, she'd clam up and say, "We are doing well in America now, so what's the matter? You're making me tired. Leave me alone!"

So, you can only imagine how thrilled Mom was when I finally told her I had been working on this memoir for over a year and found a publisher for it. After realizing there was no turning back on this project, Mom insisted that I at least leave her out of my story completely. I told her that would be impossible. She was the driving force behind it. If she hadn't wanted me to write this story, she shouldn't have brought me to America in the first place. Mom was so upset with me that she avoided me for months.

My desire to make this book overpowered my guilt about causing Mom anxiety. I pushed on, chasing her down to talk to me. Exasperated, Mom asked, "Why this story? Couldn't you just make up some story to draw comics?"

I told her this was my way of understanding why things happened the way they did. What happened when I was fourteen changed my life forever, and I wanted to write about it. I wanted people to read it and feel understood if they were experiencing the depression and isolation I did when I moved to Alabama. And if Mom wanted to have a say in how she was portrayed in it, she'd better start answering my questions seriously. (These weren't really fighting words. Only the truth.)

Mom stopped insisting I take her out of my story, but she still would give me only glib answers when I asked her about the past. Through numerous painful conversations, I convinced her that I was not going to portray her in any kind of demonizing, hurtful ways. And I promised to show her the manuscript before it was published.

Finally, Mom started telling me great stories about her past—things I didn't know about or didn't remember much about. The more I talked to her, the clearer it became to me that Mom is a much more interesting character than I am. To borrow from Mary Karr, one of my favorite memoirists, why would I make up a story when my own family is already so interesting?

To write a truthful memoir, I knew I had to write about things that Mom would be uncomfortable with. I feared it might damage my relationship with her and wondered if my effort in writing this memoir was even worth it. But whenever I tried to retreat from it, this project would come back to haunt me. I just had to see it through. When I finished inking and lettering all the pages, I gave a copy of the manuscript to Mom. A few days later, she gave it back to me with a note that began with "Great Job!" followed by a couple of minor factual edits. Like the stoic Korean mother she is, she didn't say much else, but I knew she was proud of it.

I am so grateful that she loves me enough to overcome her fear of being exposed. Writing a memoir is like wearing your heart on your sleeve for the whole world to see. And in my case, I was dangling my mom's heart along with my own. Writing this memoir was the hardest thing I've done in my life, apart from moving to America when I was fourteen. I can't say I'd do it again, but it healed me and made me understand and respect my mother a lot more. And I hope Mom finds more peace with her past by reading it, too. For that, I am glad to have done it.

This book wouldn't have been possible without the help of three great women: I thank Cassie, my mom; Samantha, my agent; and Alessandra, my editor, for giving me the chance to deliver this book to the real world.

I would also like to thank my comics community—including the members of DrawBridge and Hypothetical Island in Gowanus, Brooklyn, and the artists at Atlantic Center for the Arts residency #155 and #163—for encouraging me to continue on this project whenever I faltered.